THE DEVELOPMENT
OF INTERSENSORY PERCEPTION:
Comparative Perspectives

THE DEVELOPMENT
OF INTERSENSORY PERCEPTION:
Comparative Perspectives

Edited by

David J. Lewkowicz
*New York State Institute for Basic Research
in Developmental Disabilities*

Robert Lickliter
Virginia Polytechnic Institute and State University

LEA LAWRENCE ERLBAUM ASSOCIATES, PUBLISHERS
1994 Hillsdale, New Jersey   Hove, UK

Lawrence Erlbaum Associates, Inc., Publishers
365 Broadway
Hillsdale, New Jersey 07642

Cover design by Debra Karrel

Library of Congress Cataloging-in-Publication Data

The development of intersensory perception : comparative perspectives / [edited by] David J. Lewkowicz, Robert Lickliter.
p. cm.
Includes bibliographical references and index.
ISBN 0-8058-1217-2
1. Perception in infants. 2. Sensorimotor integration. 3.
Perceptual-motor processes. 4. Intersensory effects. 5. Psychology, Comparative. I. Lewkowicz, David J. II. Lickliter,
Robert.
BF720.P47D48 1994
152.1—dc20   94-1382
                                                              CIP

Books published by Lawrence Erlbaum Associates are printed on
acid-free paper, and their bindings are chosen for strength and dura-
bility.

Printed in the United States of America
10 9 8 7 6 5 4 3 2 1

Contents

Part III Intersensory Interactions
in Human Development

Part IV Future Directions

Foreword

Linda B. Smith
Indiana University

The 16 chapters that comprise this book show how far knowledge has advanced since the 1960s. Indeed, the very question that motivated the research enterprise in the first place has been answered. But with this answer comes the opportunity to answer an even more fundamental question. Accordingly, in this foreword, I attempt to place this book in context by considering where research on intersensory functioning has come from, where it is today, and where it may be going.

THE PAST

The central question behind research in intersensory functioning derives from the classic view of the mammalian brain as a highly modular device in which sensory information is transmitted along parallel modality-specific "labeled" lines (Bullock & Horridge, 1965). At least since Johanne Muller's Law of Specific Energies (1838/1842), it has seemed patently clear that the brain specifically and separately organizes each modality. This modular view of the brain, however, contradicts psychological reality. Our perceptions are unitary. Sights, sounds, and the haptic feel of things are coordinated. Thus, we have the central theoretical problem, the *binding problem*: How are the separate and qualitatively distinct modalities coordinated and put together? The traditional solution to the binding problem has been to assume that the distinct sensory streams are merged and integrated in the association areas of the cortex—at the top of the hierarchy of brain functioning. This classic view is summarized by Fig. 1: There are separate tracks of sensory experience, and these separate tracks are mapped to each other late in processing. Given this classic view, the central *developmental* question has been whether such a mapping is innate or learned.

Piaget (1952) presented the traditional developmental answer: Like the neuroscientists of his day, he placed intersensory coordination in the higher processes and proposed that infants slowly developed mappings from one modality to another as a consequence of their activity in the world. As in so many other areas of development, Piaget's formulation set the research agenda, with developmental psychologists seeking either to support his description or, more recently, to reject it. Through all this, the empirical question in developmental studies boiled down to, "Do they or don't they? Do infants perceive cross-modal correspondences?"

THE PRESENT

We now have the answer to this question and it is unambiguously that human infants are sensitive to intersensory correspondences from the first hours of life. Much of the evidence is reviewed in the chapters of this book—for example, in the chapters of Lewkowicz, Bushnell, Morrongiello, Streri and Molina, and Meltzoff and Kuhl, among others. We also now know that the original formulation of the binding problem is itself wrong. If Fig. 1 is the old view of intersensory interactions in the brain, Fig. 2 is the new view. Although there is a primary organization of separate modalities, there is also rich interconnectivity in phylogenetically old and early maturing systems and in phylogenetically new and late maturing systems (for reviews and discussions see Damasio, 1989; Smith & Katz, 1994; Thelen & Smith, 1993).

In their chapter, Stein, Meredith, and Wallace present one example of the fundamentally multimodal and interactive nature of brain processing.

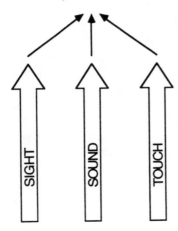

FIG. 1. The traditional view of separate noninteracting modalities.

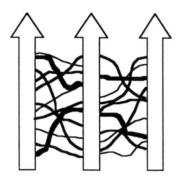

FIG. 2. The current view of separate and interacting modalities.

Their research concerns the cat superior colliculus, a structure that textbooks describe as exhibiting three topographically organized and connected maps of space—a visual map, an auditory map, and a somatosensory map. Thus, the superior colliculus is one site at which modality-specific experiences might be said to be "bound" together. The results of Stein et al., however, suggest that this "binding" is not truly a mapping of one modality-specific representation to another. Instead, it is more like a real binding—a continuous intermeshing of the senses. Specifically, they found that the topographic map of visual space in the cat superior colliculus is composed primarily of *multisensory neurons*—neurons that fire in response to auditory and somatic stimulation as well as visual stimulation. Put most boldly, the results suggest that the brain activity that corresponds to seeing does not involve vision alone; rather, seeing depends on auditory and somatic events as well as visual ones. The multisensory neurons in the cat's superior colliculus project to the brain centers that control the orientation of the cat's head, ears, and eyes. Thus, the cat "knows" to look toward sounds, not because perceived visual location is mapped to a perceived auditory one, but because auditory events directly alter what one sees and where one looks. In the cat's multimodal superior colliculus, intersensory coordination is created in the simultaneous influences of the modalities on each other.

Thus, we have the answers to the classic questions: The modalities are bound together at no one site, intersensory interactions are the rule up and down the brain, and as many of the chapters in this volume attest, these intersensory interactions are behaviorally evident in very young infants. Despite the clear answers to the classic questions, it is doubtful that readers will finish this book with a sense of a job completed. Particularly troubling are the data on intersensory sensitivity in human infants. As more and more data have been collected, it has become clear that the fact of early intersensory interactions has brought with it little insight into intersensory functioning beyond the fact that it is there early. In some ways, this is not surprising. As researchers, we only get answers to the empirical questions we ask, and the question "Do they?" allows only two limited kinds of answers.

Across the many studies that addressed this question, there are ample demonstrations that "infants do." But there are also many examples of "don't." All the chapters on the human infant's sensitivity to cross-modal correspondences—and particularly those by Walker-Andrews, Lewkowicz, Bushnell, Streri and Molina, and Rose—make clear that intersensory interactions in infancy are not a singular phenomenon, not one kind of thing. Rather, the correspondences that infants are sensitive to depend on the kind of correspondence, the task, the modalities involved, and the development of the infant.

In many ways, the chapters in this book may be viewed as searching for the right new empirical question—one that goes beyond the mere demonstration of intersensory sensitivities. Across the chapters, three kinds of reformulations of the old developmental question are offered. I consider each of these in turn.

Kinds of Intersensory Correspondences

The finding that infants (and other developing organisms) are sensitive to some cross-modal correspondences but not to others suggests that there are different kinds of cross-modal correspondences. Thus, Turkewitz, Tees, Bushnell, and Walker-Andrews suggest that a better empirical question than "do they?" might be: What kinds of cross-modal correspondences are infants sensitive to early and what kinds are they sensitive to later?

One distinction that is talked about in many of the chapters (e.g., Tees, Bahrick & Pickens, Walker-Andrews, Bushnell) is the distinction between amodal and intermodal correspondences. The distinction between these two kinds of correspondences is illustrated in Fig. 3. Amodal correspondences are presumed to reflect common dimensions of sensory experience that transcend specific modalities—for example, bright is like loud because both are intense on the amodal dimension of intensity. In this view, then, the reason that brighter lights are perceived to be like louder sounds is because they share a common property, intensity. Intermodal correspondences, in contrast, are presumed to reflect mappings (that could be innate or learned) between the distinct sensory experiences. Thus, objects that are visually large are expected to make low-pitched sounds.

It is clearly useful, as Walker-Andrews and Bushnell show, to think about these different kinds of correspondences and what they might mean for development—to try to sort some order into these data by sorting them into conceptually coherent bins. However, in these initial attempts at a taxonomy, it is important to worry about the distinctions themselves. Do they have unambiguous empirical support, and what would that support look like if we could find it? For example, there are no unambiguous data that I know of to support the hypothesized correspondences in Fig. 3 over those in Fig.

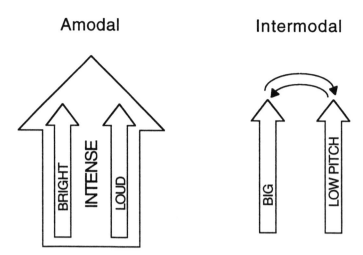

FIG. 3.   Amodal versus intermodal correspondences.

4: For all we know, bright and loud might be an intermodal correspondence and big and low-pitch an amodal one. And, then, for all we know, intermodal correspondences might be developmentally earlier than amodal ones. Or, for all we presently know, there may be no such distinction realized in the processes of intersensory interactions at all.

There are two reasons, however, that researchers have generally posited certain dimensions to be amodal and others to be intermodal. The first is our adult introspections. Some correspondences *seem* to us as we reflect on them to be analytically true; with the certainty of naive realism, bright and loud are conceptually understood as being *about* some amount of physical energy. Other correspondences *seem* to us to be "merely" and probabilistically true; big things usually but not invariably make low-pitched sounds.

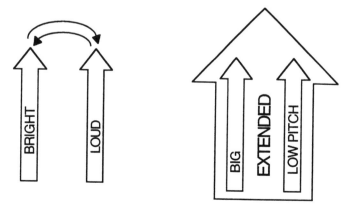

FIG. 4.   An alternative view of amodal versus intermodal correspondences.

These intuitions may be reasonably accurate reflections of underlying processes, but then again, they may not be. We as scientists are the products of developmental process and the structure of our end-state beliefs need not in any direct way reflect the processes that give rise to them. Caution on this point is strongly suggested by recent evidence showing that language learning plays a strong role in the developmental emergence and organization of dimensions and in qualitative shifts in how one perceptual dimension is mapped to another (see Smith, 1993; Smith & Sera, 1992). What is needed to make these introspections about amodal and intermodal correspondences scientifically useful is clear evidence about the implied differences in the psychological processes, in the mechanisms, through which amodal versus intermodal correspondences are made in real time.

The second reason developmental researchers posit distinctions between amodal and intermodal correspondences is the developmental evidence. Infants are sensitive to some correspondences earlier than others. But, of course, we cannot use the developmental data both to test the hypothesis that some forms of correspondences are earlier than others and to confirm the validity of such a distinction between kinds of correspondences. If we do, we are in grave danger of circular definitions. Again, what is needed is independent evidence for the hypothesized distinctions—evidence that is not merely logical argument from adult introspections nor the simple connection of amodal with developmentally early. Rather, we need evidence showing that qualitatively different processes underlie the hypothesized qualitatively different kinds of correspondences. Given this, one could then ask whether certain kinds of mechanisms are in place before others.

In the chapters of this book, there are a number of signposts to phenomena worthy of greater study in the interest of understanding process and mechanism. One example is Lewkowicz and Turkewitz's (1980) findings on the joint arousing effects of brightness and loudness in early infancy. Other examples are the inverse effectiveness rule in the cat superior colliculus (Stein et al.), the role of movement (Bloch), models of integration in lip reading (Massaro), and Lewkowicz and Lickliter's more comprehensive consideration of possible mechanisms in the final chapter. Looking across these various examples, it seems unlikely that the mechanisms of multimodal correspondence will fall neatly into the bins "amodal" and "intermodal."

The Direction of Developmental Change

Intermodal perception has a chimeric quality. We perceive the feel and sight of a rigid object to be unitary aspects of the same singular thing, yet we also experience the feel of things and the sight of them to be qualitatively distinct experiences. Thus one potential developmental question is which of these aspects of experience is primary: Is the direction of development from wholistic unity to differentiated modalities, or from separated senses to coordinated multimodal experience?

The dominant view in the present volume appears to be that development goes from wholistic to more differentiated multimodal experiences. Spear and McKinzie suggest that immature animals may be more likely to show intersensory interactions than older ones. Also consistent with this view are the findings of Lewkowicz and Turkewitz of the arousing synergy of sights and sounds that is characteristic only of early development, as is the synergy between seen facial gestures and the motor behaviors corresponding to them (Meltzoff & Kuhl).

Bushnell suggests, in contrast, that both directions of development are apt. According to her analysis, sensitivity to "amodal" correspondences often require selective attention; the infant must find the amodal dimension amid other dimensions. Bushnell also considers the possibility that some dimensions, such as haptic sensitivity to shape, may have to be learned. Thus although evident early, children's performances using "amodal" dimensions will be limited by their emerging ability to selectively attend and by the development of the modality-specific sensitivities that provide access to the "amodal" information. Bushnell argues further that although "inter-modal" correspondences derive from learned associations, they involve a simpler matching mechanism. Thus, these kinds of correspondences are not evident early but develop rapidly—often outpacing amodal development.

Bushnell's chapter, and also those of Streri and Molina and of Rose, represent an advance in the study of cross-modal correspondences by systematically asking how sensory interactions change with development and how those developments are related to other developing abilities. Thus, we see in Bushnell's, Streri and Molina's, and Rose's chapters how the dimensions of tactual and haptic experience may develop from changes in the hand movements used to explore objects and how visual–haptic connections may grow out of and depend on these experiences of actively exploring objects.

As the field takes this broader developmental outlook, it seems likely that even richer and more complicated developmental dependencies will be found. For example, the onset of reaching occurs developmentally close to developmental advances in binocular depth perception, and it seems likely that reaching (and hand–eye coordination) may depend on that visual achievement (see Thelen & Smith, 1993). There is also considerable evidence to suggest that visual development (including stereopsis) is facilitated and/or calibrated by self-produced movement (e.g., Held & Hein, 1963). Consistent with these findings, it seems likely that the visual effects of moving one's hands and picking up and rotating objects will play a role in visual percep-tion. Indeed, given the work of Kellman and Spelke (1983; see also Spelke, 1990) on the importance of perceived motion in early object segregation, watching oneself rotate objects may be critical to the development of visual sensitivity to the "amodal" dimension of shape (see Thelen & Smith, 1993) as well as haptic sensitivity to shape (see Bushnell's chapter). Thus, we might view Fig. 2 not just as a model of real-time processes in the brain but also as a model of developmental time—showing continuing and continually changing influences of one modality on the development of others.

Questions about Developmental Process

The chapters of this book illustrate how researchers are beginning to replace simple questions about developmental origins, "do they or don't they" questions, with questions about the course of development—about the kinds of sensory interactions that are early and late and questions about the direction of development. These kinds of empirical questions seem likely to lead to the most fundamental developmental question of all: What makes change happen?

Lickliter and Banker's chapter offers a glimpse of developmental process. They suggest that change derives from a "complex coaction of organic, organismic, and environmental factors." Such an activity-dependent process in which heterogeneous subsystems (including the distinct modalities) interact means that experiences in one modality can have cascading influences on the development of others. Building on Turkewitz's earlier proposal, Lickliter and Banker show how sensory limitations during early development may mediate the timing of development by reducing the information available. Thus, in some instances, in a bobwhite's learning to recognize its mother's call, auditory development is slowed by early visual stimulation. On the other hand, the visual recognition of conspecifics is enhanced by early auditory input. These results show the diffuse control and reciprocal determination that appear to be characteristic across developing sensory systems. This result brings us to the future.

THE FUTURE

Much of the research reviewed and discussed in this book began with the research question depicted in Fig. 1: How and when are the separate modalities conjoined together? The answer is that the picture in Fig. 1 is all wrong; interactions look like Fig. 2 from the start of development. This answer suggests a new developmental question—a question that reverses the question with which this research began. Instead of asking how interactions between the sensory systems are made in development, the new question is how interactions between the sensory systems make development.

Edelman (1987, 1992; see also Thelen & Smith, 1993) offered a theory of development in which change is caused by interacting heterogeneous systems. The key idea is that qualitatively different sensory systems provide unique but coupled takes on experience; what we see and what we feel provide different information, but those two kinds of information are time locked to each other and thus the two can educate each other and create something new.

Consider Bushnell's example of an infant touching and looking at a potato. The infant's visual and haptic experiences will each be unique: Each provides *different* information about the physical world. But as the infant explores the object, visually and haptically, there will be time-locked correspondences between what is seen and what is felt. Edelman's theory would explain the situation in terms of the four mappings illustrated in Fig. 5. One map is between the physical properties of the potato and neuronal activity in the visual system. One map is between the physical properties of the potato and neuronal activity in the haptic system. The third and fourth mappings are what Edelman calls the reentrant maps: Activity in the visual system is mapped to the haptic system and activity in the haptic system is mapped to the visual system. Thus, two independent mappings of the stimulus to internal activity take qualitatively different glosses on the world, and by being correlated in real time, they educate each other. Edelman specifically proposes a self-organizing selectionist process in which active connections between the heterogeneous systems are maintained and strengthened.

The developmental power of this theory is in the coupling of two independent, unique processes in real time. At the same time the visual system is

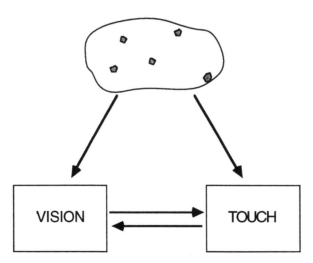

FIG. 5. An example of the mappings between physical events and coupled sensory systems during haptic and visual exploration of a potato.

activated by time-varying changes in shading and texture and collinear move-ments of points on the potato, the haptic system is activated by time-locked changes in pressures and textures. According to the theory, at every step in real time, the activities in each of these two heterogeneous processes are mapped to each other, enabling the system in its own activity to discover complex time-varying relations. In computer simulations and in the develop-ment of perceiving and acting robots, Edelman (1992) showed that this time-locked coupling yields self-organizing developmental change—change powered by the activity of the system itself.

The system proposed by Edelman is multimodal in the same way the cat superior colliculus is. It is not simply that touch and vision are being mapped to each other; rather, they are in their very processes mutually dependent on each other. Thus in the example in Fig. 5, neuronal activity in the visual system at each moment in time will depend on the visual input at that moment in time and the haptic input at the just preceding moment in time. The relations that emerge in the time-locked interactions and mutual education of the two sensory systems seem neither properly "amodal" nor "intermodal" in the senses depicted in Figs. 3 and 4. Theoretical ideas such as Edelman's offer a new agenda for research on intersensory functioning, one that goes beyond demonstration, description, and labeling to insights about the causes of change.

In sum, this book offers a selection of findings in an area of research that is crossing an exciting threshold. On the other side of that threshold are new discoveries about developmental process—the opportunity to answer the question of what causes change. The evidence reported in this book shows intersensory interactions to be developmentally primitive and pervasive. Intersensory interactions thus may not be the product of development but a cause that propels development forward.

REFERENCES

Bullock, T. H., & Horridge, G. A. (1965). *Structure and function in the nervous systems of invertebrates* (Vol. 1). San Francisco: Freeman.

Damasio, A. R. (1989). Time-locked multiregional retroactivation: A systems-level proposal for the neural substrates of recall and recognition. *Cognition, 33*, 25–62.

Edelman, G. M. (1987). *Neural Darwinism.* New York: Basic Books.

Edelman, G. M. (1992). *Bright air, brilliant fire: On the matter of mind.* New York: Basic Books.

Held, R., & Hein, A. (1963). Movement produced stimulation in the development of visually guided behavior. *Journal of Comparative and Physiological Psychology, 56*, 872–876.

Kellman, P. J., & Spelke, E. S. (1983). Perception of partly occluded objects in infancy. *Cognitive Psychology, 15*, 483–524.

Lewkowicz, D. J., & Turkewitz, G. (1980). Cross-modal equivalence in early infancy: Auditory-visual intensity matching. *Developmental Psychology, 16*, 597–607.

Muller, J. (1842). *Elements of physiology* (W. Baly, Trans.). London. (Original work published as *Handbuch der physiologie des menschen*, Coblenz, 1838)

Piaget, J. (1952). *The origins of intelligence in children.* New York: International Universities Press.

Smith, L. B. (1993). The concept of same. *Advances in Child Development and Behavior, 24*, 215–252.

Smith, L. B., & Katz, D. B. (in press). Activity-dependent processes in perceptual and cognitive development. In R. Gelman & T. Au (Eds.), *Handbook of perception and cognition* (Vol. 13).

Smith, L. B., & Sera, M. (1992). A developmental analysis of the polar structure of dimensions. *Cognitive Psychology, 24*, 99–142.

Spelke, E. S. (1990). Origins of visual knowledge. In D. N. Osherson, S. M. Kosslyn, & J. M. Hollerbach (Eds.), *An invitation to cognitive science: Visual cognition and action* (pp. 99–128). Cambridge, MA: MIT Press.

Thelen, E., & Smith, L. B. (1994). *A dynamic systems approach to the development of cognition and action.* Cambridge, MA: MIT Press.

PART ONE

CONCEPTUAL ISSUES

CHAPTER ONE

Sources of Order for Intersensory Functioning

Gerald Turkewitz
Hunter College,
Graduate Center of the City University of New York
Albert Einstein College of Medicine

Intersensory functioning has frequently been referred to as if it were a process, when in fact it is an outcome. That is, intersensory functioning is involved whenever there are joint influences of stimulation in more than one modality. However, different instances of intersensory functioning need not have any mechanisms in common. It can therefore be likened to other functional classes of behavior such as feeding or social behavior, where similarity of outcome has no implications with regard to the mechanisms whereby the outcome is accomplished. For example, although both amoebas and humans feed and the amoeba's extension of a pseudopod and Oliver Twist's extension of his porridge bowl can both be seen as related to feeding, any similarity in the mechanisms underlying the two "feeding responses" is at best trivial. The task is to determine how a similar outcome (e.g., feeding or intersensory function) is accomplished by different organisms in different contexts.

This analytic task is particularly meaningful with regard to developmental processes as mechanisms utilized, developed, or sharpened within one domain or phase of development are available for incorporation into new organizations in new domains at later periods in development. In addition, because intersensory functioning enhances adaptive responding, it is likely to be involved at most stages of development. The mechanisms involved in such functions may, however, change during ontogeny. The transitions in the mechanisms underlying a particular phenomenon are likely to have important implications for the overall functions of an organism. Consequently, it is important to delineate the mechanisms involved in intersensory functions at different stages of development. In this chapter I discuss three aspects of intersensory development:

1. The different types of intersensory functioning and the mechanisms underlying them.
2. Some of the determinants of these mechanisms.
3. Aspects of development that lead to changes in the configuration in which these mechanisms operate.

I pay particular attention to the way in which heterochronaxial development (i.e., different times of onset and rates of development) of the sense systems can influence the relationships between the sensory modalities. In particular, I examine how the nature of intersensory relationships can contribute to shaping functional organization in fundamental ways.

TYPES OF INTERSENSORY FUNCTION

A number of different types of intersensory functioning have been previously identified (Botuck & Turkewitz, 1990; Mendelson & Haith, 1976; Turkewitz & McGuire, 1978). These include:

1. Independent functioning, in which stimulation in one modality has no effect on responsiveness to stimuli in other modalities.
2. Intersensory facilitation or inhibition, in which stimulation in one modality either enhances or reduces responsiveness to stimuli in other modalities.
3. Association of polymodal characteristics.
4. Abstraction of common information. Abstraction of common information involves equivalence between modalities with regard to what have been termed amodal properties such as location, extent, texture, movement, duration, number and form.

In this chapter I am primarily concerned with the way in which independent functioning and developmental changes in the separation between the senses influence the other modes of intersensory functioning, particularly the abstraction of common information.

Independent Functioning

In their listing of possible types of auditory–visual relationships, Mendelson and Haith (1976) included no relation, although they believed the possibility "was dispelled by existing data." Although that is undoubtedly true with regard to auditory–visual relationships following birth, it is not at all the case that no relationship between particular sense systems represents a null set when a more extended perspective on development is assumed. Thus, given the sequential onset of functioning of the various sense systems, which has been documented by Alberts (1984) and Gottlieb (1971), it is a virtual certainty that at some time in embryogenesis there is independence of functioning between functional and nonfunctional systems. Although this particular mechanism (i.e., the nonfunctional state of one or more sense systems) for achieving independence between systems seems so obvious as to not bear mentioning, it should be noted that such independence is not a design requirement for the development of a multimodally responsive organism. It is easy to conceive of organisms in which all sense systems began to develop simultaneously and continue to develop at equivalent rates so that there is never any effective isolation of developing systems. Despite the relative simplicity of differential time of onset as a mechanism, consequences deriving from its operation are far from trivial. As has been previously suggested (Turkewitz & Kenny, 1982), the absence of input from an as yet nonfunctional modality could reduce competition between sense systems and could reduce the amount of information to be dealt with. This would simplify processing requirements and make it easier for developing organisms to create a structure for dealing with the available input. The information and structure gained from the operation of the earlier developing system would be available for utilization in the organization of later developing systems. In reviewing the literature on compensatory function in relation to time of onset of impairment, Burnstine, Greenough, and Tees (1984) concluded that overall the findings fit well with Turkewitz and Kenny's view that information in one modality is used in the organization of another.

According to Turkewitz and Kenny (1982), the timing of the onset of relationships between systems plays a crucial role not only in determining the nature of the relationships between the systems but also in shaping the nature of functioning within a modality. By far, the greatest number of studies examining factors contributing to the development of sensory and perceptual development have focused on the influence of experience, or lack of it, on functioning within the exposed or deprived modality. A few studies, however, have examined the effects of deprivation in one modality on functioning in another modality. Finally, several recent studies have examined the effects of unusually early stimulation in one modality on functioning in other modalities. The latter two types of studies are obviously relevant to issues concerning the timing of shifts from conditions when two systems are unrelated to a condition when they are related.

Though obvious, it should be noted that the absence of functioning within a modality is not the only possible basis for independence of functioning between modalities. Birch and Lefford (1963) used as an example of independence Abbott's demonstration:

. . . that the frog was incapable of modifying a visually determined response on the basis of information obtained through pain sensation. Thus, a frog who was permitted to strike at a live fly impaled on a central post which was surrounded by a sharp palisade of stakes continued to strike at the moving fly despite the fact that every outthrust of its tongue resulted in its being impaled upon the sharp points of the palisade. . . . In contrast, in the same organism, the visually determined striking response is capable of being modified by information received through gustatory avenues of stimulation. Thus, as Schaeffer (28) has pointed out, a frog in very few trials will learn to inhibit its visually determined striking response to a bitter hairy caterpillar. (Birch & Lefford, 1963, p. 3)

The frog's failure to relate the visual and tactile stimulation represents a clear instance of independence of functioning between two functioning systems where the independence is determined by the absence of any common final pathway between the two modalities. Another form of independent functioning between functional systems is exhibited in the prey-finding behavior of pit vipers, which exhibit a serial use of different sense systems in different phases of the hunting sequence, with chemical cues guiding tracking and thermal cues guiding striking. Similar examples of the sequential use of different sense systems in the guidance of complex sequences of behavior are not rare in the study of animal behavior but have not been suggested nor looked for in humans. Although such serial switching of control by different modalities is unlikely in adults, it may well exist during early stages of development. Thus, it is possible that the sequential nature of children's exploratory behavior of the type documented by Ruff (1976; Ruff, Saltarelli, Capozzoli, & Dubiner, 1992) is governed by a hierarchical set of relationships between sense systems with successive habituation of different modalities. So, for example, reported transitions from looking at to mouthing of an object could stem from an initially dominant response to the visual aspects of an object becoming habituated so that the infant then responds to the tactile properties of the object. It should be noted that this proposition entails a functional isolation between systems, based on sensory dominance. This idea of dominance is somewhat different from the usual one. Discussions of dominance have usually implied an age or stagelike character to dominance, with a particular system being dominant at one age or stage of development (Birch & Lefford, 1963; Lewkowicz, 1988a, 1988b). The current proposition, although not precluding such age or stagelike dominance, would make it a somewhat more dynamic phenomenon with the dominant sense system changing during the course of a sequence of behavior. This processing-dependent dominance is consistent with Lewkowicz's (1992) recent finding of differences in dominance in response to moving as opposed to static figures in infants during the first year of life. In addition to the kind of dominance thus far discussed, which is essentially a process resulting in independence between systems, there is another sense that does not involve independence of systems nor even reduced attention to one or more systems. Therefore, it should be differentiated from the other. This second type of dominance is one in which input in one modality is assimilated to that in another modality. A particularly striking example is the phenomenon of visual capture when, for instance, the sounds from speakers located at the sides of a movie theater are localized as coming from the front of the theater where the visual image from which the sound is putatively emanating is located. Although this type of dominance is clearly relevant to intersensory functioning, it is not relevant to independent functioning between modalities and therefore is not further pursued in this chapter.

Some of the developmental implications and consequences of initial independence between sense systems are captured in an analysis of the homing behavior of kittens (Rosenblatt, Turkewitz, & Schneirla, 1969). When reared in the laboratory, kittens spend almost all of the time during their first 3 weeks of life together with littermates and mother in one corner of their living cage. There is clear evidence that the kittens become attached to this area of their living space and develop a pattern of returning to it when displaced from the "home corner." When the mother and other kittens are removed from the cage and kittens are tested one at a time by being placed in various areas of the cage, they show an increasing tendency to return to the home corner during a 3-min test period. This pattern is first evidenced at 5–7 days of age, when almost 75% of tests begun by placing a kitten in a corner adjacent to the home corner are concluded with the kitten in the home corner. It is not until they are almost 2 weeks old that kittens exhibit homing reliably when started in the corner diagonally opposite the home corner. It should be noted that homing from the adjacent corner begins at a time when the kittens' eyes, which open between the seventh and ninth day of age, are still closed. There is evidence that the earliest phase of homing is under olfactory and thermal control (Freeman & Rosenblatt, 1978), with a gradual transition to joint visual and olfactory control, ending with primarily visual control (Rosenblatt, Turkewitz, & Schneirla, 1969). Turkewitz and Kenny (1982, 1985) suggested that this pattern was in part shaped by the initial absence of intersensory competition followed by its gradual development. Thus, they suggested that the development of homing from the adjacent corner, which took place in the absence of patterned visual input, was facilitated by the absence of competition from vision. It should be noted that this suggestion received some indirect support from a study with rats in which it was found that rat pups that had their eyes surgically opened at an earlier than normal age, thereby providing abnormally early intersensory competition, failed to discriminate home cage shavings from fresh shavings at an age when littermate controls clearly preferred the home cage shavings (Celenza, Kenny, & Turkewitz, 1984).

The transition to joint olfactory and visual control does not occur at the time of eye opening but several days later. In this connection it is important to note that eye opening in the kitten is generally a gradual process occurring over a 2- to 3-day period, with separation between the lids gradually increasing over this period. From my perspective, the gradual increase in visual input is important because it does not produce the kind of disruption in functioning that would be expected from a sudden increase in input in a modality. In fact, in the rat pup, in which eye opening occurs considerably later (usually during the third week of life; Altman & Dittmer, 1972) and somewhat less gradually than in the kitten, there is evidence that eye opening is associated with a disruption in homing (Johanson, Turkewitz, & Hamburgh, 1980; Kenny & Turkewitz, 1986). It is possible that it is the gradual increase in visual input in the kitten that is responsible for the failure to find any evidence of the use of vision for several days after the eyes have opened, despite the fact that there is evidence that elements of the visual system are functional well before the age of eye opening (Hubel & Wiesel, 1963). In other words, when patterned visual information first becomes available, the kitten may not utilize it in directing its behavior and may merely continue to behave in accordance with the pattern it had developed in the absence of vision. This, however, provides an opportunity for visual information to be mapped onto the already organized olfactory based pattern and might be the basis for the development of joint, multimodal control. Once vision begins to be used for guiding behavior, the increased information can result in a reorganization of the entire pattern so that the earlier types of behaviors such as homing disappear.

I have explored this example at some length because it illustrates some of the complexities that result from the heterochronic development of sense systems. The heterochronic development normally enables one modality to function unperturbed by stimulation from another, and ontogenetic relaxation of that separation can shape and modify behavior. Thus, the onset of later developing systems can have different consequences for the organization of behavior depending on the state of organization of the earlier developing systems, as well as on the manner of onset of the latter system. For example, the onset of functioning of a newly developed system can result in no immediate change in ongoing behavior, as appears to be the case when the kitten's eyes open, or can result in disruption of an ongoing pattern, as appears to be the case for the rat. The disruption seen in the rat may have a somewhat unanticipated source. Unlike the cat, the rat does not appear to be a highly visual animal, as is apparent when its behavior on a visual cliff is examined. When placed on a visual cliff apparatus, cats routinely descend on the shallow side (Turkewitz, Gilbert, & Birch, 1974). In contrast, rats are as likely to descend on the deep as on the shallow side unless their whiskers are clipped prior to testing (Schiffman, Lore, Passafiume, & Neeb, 1970). These data indicate that when tested under comparable circumstances in which tactile and visual cues are in conflict, cats respond to visual cues whereas rats essentially ignore the visual differences on the two sides of the cliff and respond instead to their tactile similarity. When examined developmentally, further differences, which may in part be due to differences in the manner of eye opening, are exhibited by kittens and rats. As has previously been noted, adult cats respond differently to the two sides of the visual cliff even with their vibrissae intact. The response to the visual characteristics of the cliff does not appear, however, until day 29 (approximately 3 weeks after eye opening), at which time kittens begin to systematically descend on the shallow side. However, the early failure to respond systematically on the two sides is not due to inadequate development of the visual apparatus, because kittens with clipped whiskers respond differentially by day 24 (Turkewitz et al., 1974). Somewhat surprisingly, two studies have found that shortly after eye opening rat pups respond to the visual rather than the tactile aspects of the visual cliff. On day 16 (2–3 days after the age of eye opening) rat pups preferentially descend on the shallow side (Bauer, 1973; Kenny, 1984), although they exhibit no such preference before or after that age unless their whiskers are clipped. These findings suggest that at this time vision is salient for the rat and that this transient visual salience is responsible for the disruption in homing previously noted. There is evidence to suggest that the visual salience is a consequence of the relatively abrupt eye opening, whereas the transience of this visual dominance may be the result of the relatively late time of eye opening in the rat. When pups' eyes were surgically opened on day 7, approximately 1 week prior to the typical age of eye opening, the disruption in homing characteristically noted following normal eye opening failed to occur, and pups so treated improved in their homing at an age when their littermate controls were showing a decline (Kenny & Turkewitz, 1986). There is evidence that this difference between early eye-opened pups and littermate controls was based on a difference in the use of visual input. When visual differences between cage regions were reduced, experimental animals behaved like controls and exhibited the same decline in homing typically seen toward the end of the second week of life (Kenny & Turkewitz, 1986). These results suggest that the time at which a later developing system (e.g., vision) begins to function can influence the nature of relationships between systems, resulting in a variety of functional relationships.

The literature provides some hints about the specific types of effects that timing of onset of visual functioning has on intersensory functioning. It should be noted that timing is not synonymous with age or even time but rather "relates to the temporal relationships between the components of an integrated system" (Turkewitz & Devenny, 1993, p. 1). Although scanty information concerning dominance makes it difficult to be secure in any generalization, it appears that early availability of visual input accompanies greater visual dominance, with later onset being associated with absent or reduced visual dominance. As Turkewitz and Mellon (1989) pointed out, empirical observations of the relationship between age of eye opening and nature of intersensory function would be a valuable adjunct to studies in which earlier than normal visual experience was provided. There are, however, enough data currently available to justify the hypothesis that prematurely born infants that have visual input available earlier than is usually the case would not exhibit the sequence of initial auditory dominance followed by visual dominance obtained by Lewkowicz (1988a, 1988b). Instead, it would be predicted that the early exposure to patterned light during a period when auditory responsiveness was not yet fully established would result in either an attenuated auditory dominance, no dominance at all, or even an initial visual dominance. It would further be anticipated that the earlier the premature birth, the more marked the shift toward visual dominance.

There is a growing body of evidence suggesting that the earlier than normal introduction of visual input can result in the failure to process information from other modalities that would normally be processed. Thus, as previously noted, Celenza et al. (1984) found that rat pups that had their eyes prematurely opened failed to discriminate between shavings from their home cage and shavings with other odors at an age when their littermate controls were clearly making such discriminations. Gottlieb, Tomlinson, and Radell (1989) found that ducklings that were given premature exposure to patterned visual input by having their heads extended from the egg so that they could see other ducklings and their surround failed to learn the characteristics of a mallard call. In contrast, dark-reared ducklings did learn the mallard call and preferred it to a novel one. Similarly, Lickliter and Hellewell (1992) showed that bobwhite quail exposed to unusually early visual stimulation by having their heads exposed as embryos failed to learn the species-specific maternal call whereas control chicks did. Lickliter's research is of particular importance in this connection because he has provided evidence that it is not just that peculiar things happen when peculiar things are done but that sensory limitations are probably an important contributor to normal development as well (Lickliter, 1993). Thus, Lickliter and Hellewell (1992) found that communally incubated embryos were able to learn and remember an individual maternal call if they were exposed to it before hatching but were unable to learn it when they were exposed to the call after hatching. This difference appeared to be due to the more complex posthatch environment, because when quail hatchlings were reared under conditions of attenuated visual and social experience they learned the individual call.

The findings from the early exposure studies reviewed have one clear-cut set of implications and are suggestive of others. The clearest generalization thus far indicated is that unusually early exposure to input from a later developing system interferes with the utilization of input from an earlier developing system. The interference may not be permanent and may not generalize to use of the sensory modality generally but may be restricted to effects occurring during concurrent stimulation or other situations that are more demanding for the organism. The failure to process concurrently presented information, which is processed when presented in the absence of competition, has been attributed to attentional difficulties. For example, Gottlieb et al. (1989) found that early exposure to visual input resulted in the failure to learn the maternal call when auditory and visual stimulation were concurrently applied only during the prenatal period (i.e., birds given early visual experience learned the maternal call after hatching even when it was presented concurrently with visual stimulation). They concluded that the effects of early exposure were transient and that it was unlikely that the early exposure resulted in neural changes where the neural space normally dedicated to audition was now allocated to vision. This was contrary to the hypothesis initially suggested by Turkewitz and Kenny (1982).

These findings and this interpretation begin to specify ways in which ontogenetic changes in the nature of sensory input ultimately contribute to intersensory functional organization. They also provide an important first step in the elaboration of a dynamic approach to investigating intersensory relationships. Such an approach must, however, take into account the facts that:

1. Exposure to similar circumstances at different stages of development can have radically different consequences.
2. Circumstances systematically and unsystematically change during the life course of the individual.
3. There are reciprocal relationships between structure and function.
4. Intersensory function represents a variety of different types of relationships that are governed by a variety of mechanisms.

Therefore, it is obvious that any overarching generalizations will be, to say the least, difficult to come by. Instead, it is possible that the best strategy for the developmental analysis of intersensory functioning first may involve the identification of possible mechanisms underlying transition in various aspects of intersensory functioning and then a search for the conditions under which particular mechanisms may be operating. In a sense, this represents an abandonment of Popper's paradigm for scientific investigation according to which science advances by stating falsifiable hypotheses and then seeking to reject them.

It is my contention that this approach is not likely to be of great value in the case of the development of intersensory functioning because so many factors may be involved that any falsifiable hypothesis is likely to be so broad as to be vacuous, or highly improbable to start with, or so narrow that its rejection would hardly reduce the available population of equally narrow hypotheses. Therefore, I suggest that our understanding, at least at this stage of our knowledge, would be better advanced by descriptive studies than by those aimed at hypothesis testing.

The Gottlieb et al. (1989) study is a case in point. Although it was designed as a hypothesis-testing study and, in fact, has some value as such, the study is more valuable as a descriptive one. Thus, Gottlieb and his co-workers tested the hypothesis that early exposure of a later developing system would result in the allocation of an atypically large amount of neural space to that system, producing a relatively permanent deficiency in the functioning of the earlier developing system. The finding that the failure to learn an auditory signal was transient served as the basis for rejecting the hypothesis under scrutiny. This is clearly good science. However, the research hypothesis that a relatively limited period of early exposure to visual stimulation would permanently impair the organism's ability to learn a complex auditory discrimination is a very narrow and qualified one. Thus, it is possible that the learning of the maternal call that occurred during the posthatch phase entailed the use of alternative or compensatory mechanisms such as these suggested by Burnstine et al. (1984) and Neville (1988, 1990) to account for apparently enhanced compensatory function in intact modalities following damage to another modality. This makes it difficult to rule out the hypothesis of changes in the allocation of neural space. Furthermore, although the study provides evidence that premature visual exposure can lead to auditory attentional deficits during conjoint visual and auditory exposure, the deficits may be mediated by a sensory threshold mechanism rather than or in addition to an attentional one. In addition, there is no reason to believe that the effects of input in one modality on functioning in another modality will be independent of the state of organization of the other modality or modalities. Finally, the disappearance of an effect that prevents learning under conditions that could be considered intermodal distraction or competition does not imply the absence or disappearance of other cross-modal effects such as those that might influence polysensory facilitation or inhibition. Therefore, the Gottlieb et al. (1989) study has only limited utility for hypothesis testing, but it does provide valuable descriptive data concerning conditions under which changes in the timing of intersensory relationships will influence certain aspects of functioning. Furthermore, it calls attention to the fact that different types of intersensory demands and effects must be considered. I believe that more frankly descriptive studies, which focus on exploring rather than testing hypotheses, will provide a better guide to developing more meaningful hypothesis-testing studies and that they will suggest fruitful areas in which to concentrate further research.

One potentially important mechanism that could mediate the effects of the development of an organized response to stimulation in an earlier developing modality on the development of functional organization by a later developing modality has been provided by Schneirla (1959, 1965). According to Schneirla, young organisms respond to the intensity of a stimulus rather than to its organizational features, including its modality of presentation. My associates and I have explored this suggestion and found that young infants do in fact seem to ignore the modality in which a stimulus is presented and respond instead to the amount of stimulation (for reviews see Karmel, Gardner, & Magnano, 1991; Lewkowicz, 1991; Turkewitz, Gardner, & Lewkowicz, 1984; Turkewitz, Lewkowicz, & Gardner, 1983). Thus, the effects of stimulation in different modalities can be added to one another or substituted for one another. To the extent that stimuli from different modalities are equivalent with regard to the amount of stimulation that they provide, it would be possible for stimulation in a previously naive modality to evoke responses that had been organized around an earlier developing modality. According to this view, early limitations on functioning in one or more modalities would facilitate (by reducing input and competition) the development of organized responses to earlier developing systems. Organized responses to even the initial stimulation of later developing systems could then result from intensity-based equivalence between the earlier and later developing systems. The introduction of attributes of stimulation unique to the later developing system (e.g., color in the case of vision) could then result in a change in the organization of behavior.

The initial intensity-based responsiveness of the young organism, together with the orderly sequence of emergence of the various senses, provides a mechanism for first establishing intensity-based equivalence between stimuli in different modalities. This can, in turn, lead to the development of mechanisms that enable the organism to abstract equivalent information from stimuli in different modalities. It is possible for stimulation in an early developing modality to come to be defined for the organism in terms of weak or strong by virtue of its physiologic effects. Schneirla proposed that A type responses (which loosely correspond to approach responses) involve, among other things, parasympathetic innervation, whereas W type (or withdrawal responses) involve sympathetic responses. In that weak stimuli engender A responses and strong stimuli W responses, the organism's physiology could provide a yardstick for grading stimuli. The advent of new sources of stimulation, with the onset of functioning of relatively late developing systems, at a time when stimulation from earlier developing systems already had been assessed a value, could provide a basis for equating stimulation from different modalities. For example, if a previously experienced auditory stimulus was within the approach range, then a concomitant visual stimulus might also come to elicit an approach response. Visual stimuli of an intensity characteristic of that during presentation of the particular auditory stimulus might come to be responded to as approach-eliciting stimuli, resulting in a general alignment of the scales in different modalities. This would be dependent on the stimulus in the earlier developing modality already having achieved some degree of familiarity so that it was no longer responded to with a form of generalized activation.

The proposal that I am making departs from previous suggestions in that it is based on the view that the intensity-based responding of young organisms is at least in part a consequence of the exuberant connections that characterize early neurogenesis (Greenough, Black, & Wallace, 1987). I am postulating that one of the consequences of large numbers of neural connections would be that stimulation would promote generalized excitation or activation in addition to whatever specific effects it might have. It is these generalized effects that would result in intensity-based equivalence of both intra- and intermodal stimuli. Neural connections would become more tightly specified by virtue of neuronal pruning based on disuse and increased efficiency based on use. When this occurred, the additivity and substitutability of stimuli characteristic of earlier stages of development would no longer operate. Instead, what might be expected to occur is that stimulation of a relatively novel sort, which co-occurred with a stimulus that had a history of prior exposure, might come to be equivalent to the earlier experienced stimulus by virtue of the existence of an already privileged pathway. Further experience with the newly available input could serve to accentuate the modality-specific properties of the input and result in the loss of the contiguity-based intermodal equivalence.

To recapitulate, the model suggests three stages of intersensory effects: first, a stage of additivity or substitutability based on generalized excitatory effects of relatively unfamiliar stimulus sources; second, a stage in which a stimulus in a later developing modality achieves a specific valence (in terms of approach or withdrawal) by virtue of temporal contiguity with a stimulus in an earlier developing modality that had already lost its general excitatory effects because of experience-based pruning; and finally, when both inputs were familiar, temporal contiguity would allow for the abstraction of common information based on the unique characteristics of each stimulus.

This model has several rather direct implications. First, it suggests that during the period when a young organism responds to unfamiliar stimuli additively it would not respond additively to an unfamiliar and a familiar stimulus nor to two familiar stimuli. Therefore, it suggests that transitions from intensity-based to organizationally based responding are not age dependent nor characteristic of a stage of development but are rather stimulus specific in relation to the experiential history of the individual involved. It should be noted, however, that because of the sequential onset of functioning of sense systems there will be a degree of communality to the exposure history of stimuli within a modality, so that at a certain point in development all visual input will be novel. Although these implications have yet to be examined empirically, they are readily open to investigation.

I believe that our understanding of intersensory functioning is truly in its infancy. However, the recent increase in our recognition of its importance together with the development of increasingly refined techniques for its investigation holds promise for a healthy development. If the study of the development of intersensory functioning is to fulfill this promise, I believe it is necessary to do the descriptive studies that will provide a realistically complex taxonomy of intersensory function. In addition, the models that we develop for aiding our understanding of the ontogenesis of intersensory functioning will probably need to be broadly conceived integrations of multiple aspects and levels of functioning. Although they may be open to empirical scrutiny, they are not likely to lend themselves to formal hypothesis testing. Therefore, it is likely that examination of the problem with the method of converging operations will be the method of choice, at least in the immediate future.

REFERENCES

Alberts, J. R. (1984). Sensory-perceptual development in the Norway rat: A view toward comparative studies. In R. Kail & N. E. Spear (Eds.), *Comparative perspectives on the development of memory* (pp. 65–101). Hillsdale, NJ: Lawrence Erlbaum Associates.

Altman, P. L., & Dittmer, D. S. (Eds.). (1972). *Biology data book* (Vol. 1). Bethesda, MD: Federation of Societies for Experimental Biology.

Bauer, J. H. (1973). Development of visual cliff discrimination by infant hooded rats. *Journal of Comparative and Physiological Psychology, 84,* 380–385.

Birch, H. G., & Lefford, A. (1963). Intersensory development in children. *Monographs of the Society for Research in Child Development, 28* (5, Serial No. 89).

Botuck, S., & Turkewitz, G. (1990). Intersensory functioning: Auditory-visual pattern equivalence in younger and older children. *Developmental Psychology, 26,* 115–120.

Burnstine, T. H., Greenough, W. T., & Tees, R. C. (1984). Intermodal compensation following damage or deprivation. In C.R. Almli & S. Finger (Eds.), *The behavioral biopsychology of early brain damage* (pp. 3–34). New York: Plenum.

Celenza, M. A., Kenny, P. A., & Turkewitz, G. (1984, November). *The effects of premature eye-opening on olfactory discrimination in the infant rat.* Paper presented at the annual meeting of the International Society For Developmental Psychobiology, Baltimore.

Freeman, N. C. G., & Rosenblatt, J. S. (1978). The interrelationship between thermal and olfactory stimulation in the development of home orientation in newborn kittens. *Developmental Psychobiology, 11,* 437–457.

Gottlieb, G. (1971). Ontogenesis of sensory functioning in birds and mammals. In E. Tobach, L. R. Aronson, & E. Shaw (Eds.), *The biopsychology of development* (pp. 67–128). San Diego: Academic Press.

Gottlieb, G., Tomlinson, W. T., & Radell, P. L. (1989). Developmental intersensory interference: Premature visual experience suppresses auditory learning in ducklings. *Infant Behavior and Development, 12,* 1–12.

Greenough, W. T., Black, J. E., & Wallace, C. S. (1987). Experience and brain development. *Child Development, 58,* 539–559.

Hubel, D. H., & Wiesel, T. N. (1963). Receptive fields of cells in striate cortex of very young, visually inexperienced kittens. *Journal of Neurophysiology, 26,* 994–1002.

Johanson, I. B., Turkewitz, G., & Hamburgh, M. (1980). Development of home orientation in hypothyroid and hyperthyroid rat pups. *Developmental Psychobiology, 13,* 331–342.

Karmel, B. Z., Gardner, J. M., & Magnano, C. L. (1991). Attention and arousal in early infancy. In M. J. S. Weiss & P. R. Zelazo (Eds.), *Newborn attention: Biological constraints and the influence of experience* (pp. 339–376). Norwood, NJ: Ablex.

Kenny, P. A. (1984). *The effects of early eyelid opening on the development of intersensory relationships in the rat.* Unpublished doctoral dissertation, City University of New York.

Kenny, P. A., & Turkewitz, G. (1986). Effects of unusually early visual stimulation on the development of homing behavior in the rat pup. *Developmental Psychobiology, 19,* 57–66.

Lewkowicz, D. J. (1988a). Sensory dominance in infants: I. 6-Month-old infants response to auditory-visual compounds. *Developmental Psychology, 24,* 155–171.

Lewkowicz, D. J. (1988b). Sensory dominance in infants: II. 10-Month-old infants' response to auditory-visual compounds. *Developmental Psychology, 24,* 172–182.

Lewkowicz, D. J. (1991). Development of intersensory functions in human infancy: Auditory/visual interactions. In M. J. S. Weiss & P. R. Zelazo (Eds.), *Newborn attention. Biological constraints and the influence of experience* (pp. 308–338). Norwood, NJ: Ablex.

Lewkowicz, D. J. (1992). Infants' responsiveness to the auditory and visual attributes of a sounding/moving stimulus. *Perception and Psychophysics, 52,* 519–528.

Lickliter, R. (1993). Timing and the development of perinatal perceptual organization. In G. Turkewitz & D. A. Devenny (Eds.), *Developmental time and timing* (pp. 105–123). Hillsdale, NJ: Lawrence Erlbaum Associates.

Lickliter, R., & Hellewell, T. B. (1992). Contextual determinants of auditory learning in bobwhite quail embryos and hatchlings. *Developmental Psychobiology, 25,* 17–24.

Mendelson, M. J., & Haith, M. M. (1976). The relation between audition and vision in the human newborn. *Monographs of the Society for Research in Child Development, 41* (4, Serial No. 167).

Neville, H. J. (1988). Cerebral organization for spatial attention: Effects of early sensory and language experience. In J. Stiles-Davis, U. Bellugi, & M. Kritchevsky (Eds.), *The development of spatial cognition* (pp. 327–341). Hillsdale, NJ: Lawrence Erlbaum Associates.

Neville, H. J. (1990). Intermodal competition and compensation in development. In *The development and neural bases of higher cognitive functions. Annals of the New York Academy of Sciences, 608,* 71–91.

Rosenblatt, J. R., Turkewitz, G., & Schneirla, T. C. (1969). Development of home orientation in newborn kittens. *Transactions of the New York Academy of Sciences, 31,* 231–250.

Ruff, H. A. (1976). The coordination of manipulation and visual fixation; A response to Schaffer (1975). *Child Development, 47,* 868–871.

Ruff, H. A., Saltarelli, L. M., Capozzoli, M., & Dubiner, K. (1992). The differentiation of activity in infants' exploration of objects. *Developmental Psychology, 28,* 851–861.

Schiffman, H. R., Lore, R., Passafiume, J., & Neeb, R. (1970). Role of vibrissae for depth perception in the rat. *Animal Behaviour, 18,* 290–292.

Schneirla, T. C. (1959). An evolutionary and developmental theory of biphasic processes underlying approach and withdrawal. In M. R. Jones (Ed.), *Current theory and research on motivation* (Vol. 7, pp. 1–42). Omaha: University of Nebraska Press.

Schneirla, T. C. (1965). Aspects of stimulation and organization in approach/withdrawal processes underlying vertebrate behavioral development. In D. S. Lehrman, R. A. Hinde, & E. Shaw (Eds.), *Advances in the study of behavior* (Vol. 1, pp. 1–74). New York: Academic Press.

Turkewitz, G., & Devenny, D. A. (1993). Timing and the Shape of development. In G. Turkewitz & D. A. Devenny (Eds.), *Developmental time and timing* (pp. 1–11). Hillsdale, NJ: Lawrence Erlbaum Associates.

Turkewitz, G., Gardner, J. M., & Lewkowicz, D. J. (1984). Sensory/perceptual functioning during early infancy: The implications of a quantitative basis for responding. In G. Greenberg & E. Tobach (Eds.), *Behavioral evolution and integrative levels* (pp. 167–195). Hillsdale, NJ: Lawrence Erlbaum Associates.

Turkewitz, G., Gilbert, M., & Birch, H. G. (1974). Early restriction of tactile stimulation and visual functioning in the kitten. *Developmental Psychobiology, 7,* 243–248.

Turkewitz, G., & Kenny, P. A. (1982). Limitations on input as a basis for neural organization and perceptual development: A preliminary theoretical statement. *Developmental Psychobiology, 15,* 357–368.

Turkewitz, G., & Kenny, P. A. (1985). The role of developmental limitations of sensory input on sensory/perceptual organization. *Journal of Developmental and Behavioral Pediatrics, 6,* 302–306.

Turkewitz, G., Lewkowicz, D. J., & Gardner, J. M. (1983). Determinants of infants perception. In J. S. Rosenblatt, R. A. Hinde, C. Beer, & M. C. Busnel (Eds.), *Advances in the Study of Behavior* (Vol. 13, pp. 39–62). New York: Academic Press.

Turkewitz, G., & McGuire, I. (1978). Intersensory functioning during early development. *International Journal of Mental Health, 7,* 165–182.

Turkewitz, G., & Mellon, R. C. (1989). Dynamic organization of intersensory function. *Canadian Journal of Psychology, 43,* 286–301.

CHAPTER TWO

A Dual-Processing Approach to Cross-Modal Matching: Implications for Development

Emily W. Bushnell
Tufts University

Mature human perceivers typically know from just handling an object what it will look like when brought into view. Conversely, they know from just looking at an object what it will feel like when eventually grasped. This ability is referred to as cross-modal transfer or cross-modal matching, and it has attracted the attention of psychologists from the earliest days of the discipline (cf. Berkeley, 1709/1948; Locke, 1690/1959). Current researchers have worked to establish the limits of performance for this ability, to compare it with within-mode discrimination and identification, and to demonstrate it on the part of infrahuman species (e.g., Davenport, Rogers, & Russell, 1973; Frampton, Milner, & Ettlinger, 1973; Friedes, 1974; Jones, 1981). Recently, developmental psychologists have documented that surprisingly young human infants are capable of cross-modal matching, at least under some circumstances (see, e.g., Bushnell, 1982; Meltzoff & Borton, 1979; Rose, Gottfried, & Bridger, 1981; also see the review by Rose & Ruff, 1987).

Despite all the attention cross-modal matching has received, however, the underlying processes that account for this ability and the factors that influence its development are not fully understood. Predictably, explanations for cross-modal matching divide along the lines of the Kantian/Empiricist or nature/nurture debate. The former position is strongly advocated by James and Eleanor Gibson and their students, who argue that amodal invariants in the stimulus situation provide information sufficient for cross-modal matching (see Bower, 1974, 1977; E. J. Gibson, 1969; J. J. Gibson, 1966, 1979; Marks, 1978), whereas the latter position is most recently represented in the writings of Piaget, which characterize the infant as having to "reciprocally assimilate" the separate modalities through activity with objects (see Piaget, 1952, 1954). In this chapter, I support neither of these accounts to the exclusion of the other, but instead I accept that they make reference to two distinct processes that are both available to the mature perceiver for matching objects across vision and touch. Each of these processes has its own special advantages and limitations; likewise, each follows its own separate course of development. Careful consideration of these matters suggests some resolutions to several ambiguities in the literature on early cross-modal matching and points to avenues for further research.

TWO TYPES OF CROSS-MODAL PERCEPTION

The two processes to be discussed can perhaps best be distinguished by an illustrative Gedank (thought) experiment. Imagine an individual performing in a speeded, cross-modal matching task. The subject is presented with an object of a given size, shape, texture, color, and temperature to examine only with the hands (e.g., under an opaque cloth). At the same time, the subject is visually presented with another object, also of a given size, shape, etc. The subject's task is to judge as rapidly and accurately as possible whether the two objects are the "same" or "different."

One plausible approach to this task would be to cross-check object properties that can be perceived with both the hands and the eyes for a possible mismatch. Thus one could proceed to determine whether the size of the haptic stimulus was the same as the size of the visual stimulus, whether the shape of the haptic stimulus was the same as the shape of the visual stimulus, and so on. Though the process is surely more rapid and unconscious, the perceiver might be portrayed as thinking, "I feel something thus-and-so big; is what I see also that big? I feel something of such-and-such a shape; is what I see likewise that shape?" and so on. If any instance of mismatch is discovered, the objects are judged to be "different"; otherwise, they are the "same."

The solution process just described, which I call *matching-by-analysis,* clearly requires that the dimensional values determined haptically be comparable to those determined visually. That is, the perceiver must have a single idea or "scale" of size (and analogously, of shape, texture, etc.) to which both haptic apprehension and visual apprehension make reference. "Large" for the hands must also be "large" for the eyes. This kind of unity of the senses is the central tenet of the Gibsonian explanation for cross-modal matching alluded to earlier, and it is important to note that the matching-by-analysis process relies on it.

An alternative approach to the cross-modal matching task we have imagined becomes possible if we further suppose that the stimuli are familiar, common objects. In this event, the subject could simply recognize the haptic stimulus as some known object and then, knowing what such an object looks like, check whether the visual stimulus was also recognizable as the same thing. Here the perceiver might be portrayed as thinking, "I feel something that feels like a potato (for example); I know what a potato looks like; does what I see look like that?" If identifying the haptic stimulus evokes an image with which the visual stimulus is congruent, the objects are judged to be the "same"; otherwise, they are "different."

This second approach, which I call *matching-by-recognition*, obviously requires that the haptic stimulus be recognizable to the perceiver and able to conjure up its visual appearance. That is, the perceiver must have encountered the object before and must have formed some linkage in memory between how the object feels and how it looks. The matching process in this case is supposed to be something akin to word recognition, in which a perceived auditory pattern activates the corresponding meaning linked to it during lexical acquisition; here, a perceived haptic pattern activates the corresponding visual image linked to it during some prior experience. Of course, the existence in memory of linkages between specific haptic experiences and specific visual ones is central to the empiricist account for cross-modal matching cited earlier. Thus, the matching-by-recognition solution to our cross-modal task instantiates the empiricist position regarding cross-modal matching, just as the matching-by-analysis solution instantiates the Kantian or Gibsonian position.

My working hypothesis, as stated at the outset, is that matching-by-analysis and matching-by-recognition are both viable and both available ways to accomplish cross-modal matching; they are not mutually exclusive answers to the issue of how humans are able to do so. The existence of such dual processes in perception is not unprecedented. Bamber (1969), Cooper (1976, 1980), Smith (1981), and others have provided evidence for an "analytic" mode and a "holistic" mode of processing in visual pattern perception, whereas Lederman and Klatzky (1987) similarly contrasted "apprehension" with "recognition" in haptic perception. In more general terms, Logan (1988) compared "performance by algorithm" to "performance by memory re-trieval." A final example is commonplace; for reading printed text, moderately skillful readers employ both the "phonetic method," as they sound out new words letter by letter, and the "whole word method," as they recognize familiar words at a glance. In each of these dichotomies, the application of one process rather than the other in any given context is dictated by preference, task parameters, or considerations of computational load, not by availability per se. I presume the case is the same with respect to cross-modal matching-by-analysis and matching-by-recognition.

Given this presumption, it is then appropriate to outline some potentially important differences between the two supposed processes for matching across vision and touch. One of these has already been introduced in the characterizations of the two processes, and that is that matching-by-recognition can only proceed with objects for which the perceiver has an established haptic–visual linkage in memory, that is, with familiar objects. Matching-by-analysis is not similarly constrained. One can attempt to compare haptically perceived size and visually perceived size even with utterly novel objects, and the same for shape, texture, and any other amodal dimension.

Another difference, which may serve to offset the limited range of matching-by-recognition, is that it is probably a faster process than matching-by-analysis. For one thing, only one decision component is involved in matching-by-recognition, namely, whether or not the visual stimulus corresponds to the visual image conjured up by recognizing the haptic stimulus. In matching-by-analysis, there is potentially a decision component for each and every relevant dimension. Thus, except when the first dimension considered yields a mismatch, more than one decision component would pertain in this process. Furthermore, except in cases of gross mismatch, these dimensional comparisons in matching-by-analysis seem to be deliberate and effortful, whereas the activation of the corresponding visual image that takes place in matching-by-recognition is thought to be automatic and obligatory, following the analogy with word recognition.

Also favoring matching-by-recognition is the fact that it is more "comprehensive" than matching-by-analysis, meaning that matching-by-recognition can make use of a greater portion of the assorted information available than can matching-by-analysis. This is because some of the object qualities that may contribute to the recognition of an object are modality specific, that is, they are not amodal or accessible to both vision and touch. For example, temperature can be apprehended haptically but not visually, and color can be apprehended visually but not haptically. Thus, neither assessments of temperature nor of color can figure into cross-modal matching-by-analysis. With this process, the subject's judgment in our hypothetical same/different task must rest solely on comparisons of size, shape, texture, and other amodal properties. However, with matching-by-recognition, an object's temperature may be entailed in the haptic experience that is recognized, and likewise color may be entailed in the visual image that is activated by the haptic experience. The same sort of argument would apply for all other object properties perceivable exclusively by touch or exclusively by vision.

The difference in comprehensiveness for the two processes means that for certain special objects, matching-by-recognition can proceed toward a solution whereas matching-by-analysis cannot. For example, Taylor, Lederman, and Gibson (1973) noted that metal is haptically distinguishable from plastic mainly on the basis of a temperature cue, metal being a poorer retainer of heat. It is also true that metal is always opaque, whereas plastic can be transparent. Thus a perceiver shown a piece of metal and a piece of Plexiglas identical in size, shape, and texture could nevertheless accurately determine which of these was the duplicate of a piece held in the hand, via matching-by-recognition. The person could recognize the haptic stimulus as either metal or plastic, according to its temperature, and could then recognize which of the two visible pieces was likewise metal or plastic, according to their opacity/transparency. However, this matching problem could not be definitively solved via matching-by-analysis. After feeling the temperature of the haptic stimulus to be either warm or cold, the person could not then check to see which of the visual stimuli *looked* warm or cold. Neither could the person assess the opacity/transparency of the haptic stimulus, in order to check it against this obvious aspect of the visual stimuli.

A related matter, probably more generally important, has to do with the different effects of saliency hierarchies on the two sorts of cross-modal perception. Within touch and also within vision, some object properties are apprehended more quickly and more precisely than others. Furthermore, the rankings of various properties are not likely to be the same in the two modalities. For example, configurational shape is perceived relatively slowly and inaccurately with the hands (see Millar, 1978; Lederman & Klatzky, 1987). Instead, an object's texture and hardness are the most readily perceived properties in haptic perception (Klatzky, Lederman, & Reed, 1987; Lederman & Klatzky, 1987; see also Krantz, 1972). In contrast, configurational shape is apprehended extremely rapidly and accurately in vision, with other properties merely ancillary to it (see Biederman & Ju, 1988).

Such reversals in the speed and accuracy with which certain properties are apprehended in the two senses may interfere with matching-by-analysis, because each dimension must be assessed within each modality. If shape is apprehended relatively poorly by touch and texture relatively poorly by vision, then first one sensory system and then the other must operate at a less-than-optimal level in matching-by-analysis, as the decisions regarding the dimensions of shape and texture are attempted. Differential hierarchies for the two modalities do not similarly interfere with matching-by-recognition. Certainly the characteristic "feel" of an object might be most dependent on its texture, whereas the typical image of the object might be most dependent on its shape, in the sense that alterations in texture would disrupt haptic recognition more than other changes would, whereas alterations in shape would similarly disrupt visual recognition the most. However, given intact objects in a visual–tactual matching task, as long as the haptic and visual stimuli each can be recognized, no matter whether on the same or different bases, matching-by-recognition can proceed with full effectiveness. The perceiver might recognize the haptic stimulus primarily on the basis of its texture, thereby activating its corresponding visual image, which might then be judged against the actual visual stimulus primarily on the basis of shape.

The differences just outlined suggest that in circumstances where both processes can proceed (i.e., in cross-modal tasks involving commonplace objects *qua* objects), matching-by-recognition is most likely to determine the response, on account of its automaticity and greater speed, its comprehensiveness, and its invulnerability to differential saliencies. Matching-by-analysis must determine the response, however, whenever the task involves unfamiliar objects, and also when it demands a focus on one or more individual properties (e.g., when matching different familiar objects for size, irrespective of shape, texture, etc.). Research designed to confirm these predictions and indeed to empirically establish matching-by-analysis and matching-by-recognition as dual processes for accomplishing cross-modal matching is currently being developed. For the purposes of further discussion here, I simply assume that these two sorts of cross-modal perception operate as described in the mature perceiver, and I go on to consider certain developmental issues and implications that derive from this dual-processing approach.

THE DEVELOPMENT OF MATCHING-BY-RECOGNITION

Because matching-by-analysis and matching-by-recognition are distinct processes, it is possible and even likely that they follow different developmental courses. The development of cross-modal perception in general is then a reflection of the interplay between these separate developments. Hence, our understanding of cross-modal perception in infants and young children may be advanced by examining the development of each process in turn. The development of matching-by-recognition is discussed first, as one outcome of this discussion bears on the development of the remaining process, matching-by-analysis.

For charting the development of matching-by-recognition, there are at least three important matters to consider. Two of these relate to the fact that in order for matching-by-recognition to be viable over any range of objects, the perceiver must be able to visually and haptically recognize a good many objects. If these within-mode recognition abilities are limited, then matching-by-recognition will be compromised accordingly, and there is reason to believe that both visual and haptic object recognition are constrained during the first 6 months of life.

Regarding the visual recognition of objects, the literature suggests that young infants perceive and remember visual stimuli predominantly in terms of their separable attributes, disembodied from one another, rather than as unique gestalts or combinations of these attributes. As Aslin and Smith (1988) summarized, "younger infants seem sensitive to parts (features and attributes), and only with maturation or experience do they seem to represent the separate parts as conjoined wholes (correlations among attributes)" (p. 455). For example, following habituation to particular combinations of attributes, 4-month-olds dishabituate only to stimuli containing novel attributes, whereas 10-month-olds also dishabituate to new combinations of the familiar attributes (Younger & Cohen, 1983, 1986). The implication is that young infants may not visually recognize individual objects per se; instead they recognize an object's largeness as similar to the largeness of many other objects, its roundness as similar to the roundness of many other objects, etc. This kind of memory in terms of constituent attributes does not serve to single out individual objects, as is required for effective matching-by-recognition. That is, a young infant who might appropriately conjure up the image of a large round object upon feeling it might then construe any visually large object or any visually round object as a match, instead of accepting only an object that is both visually large and visually round.

Regarding infants' haptic recognition of objects, analogous research focused on the perception of parts versus wholes during infancy has yet to be conducted. However, a consideration here is that young infants cannot be deemed to haptically recognize very many objects at all, never mind the terms in which they might perceive and remember them. Until they are able to obtain objects for themselves, infants haptically experience only those things that adults place in their hands (or mouths) and those that are routinely so nearby that they are encountered fortuitously. These would include parts of their own bodies, certain parts of other persons' bodies such as breasts and fingers, infant accoutrements such as pacifiers and rattles, and parts of their clothing, car seats, cribs, etc. But many, many objects, even entire classes of common objects, would remain haptically unfamiliar to the prereaching infant. Thus, in the earliest stages of development, only a small glossary of linkages between specific haptic and visual experiences could possibly exist in memory and be available for matching-by-recognition. The number of haptically familiar objects would increase somewhat after visually guided reaching emerges at about 4 months of age, and it would increase dramatically once the infant becomes independently mobile at 8 or 9 months of age.

A third consideration important for charting the development of matching-by-recognition involves the formation of memory linkages between haptic and visual experiences, even accepting that numerous experiences of each sort have been encoded and furthermore encoded as conjoined wholes. The haptic–visual linkages in memory that are integral to matching-by-recognition have been likened to the sound–meaning pairings that enable word recognition. Like sound–meaning pairings, these haptic–visual linkages must be viewed as arbitrary; that is, in theory, any one haptic experience could potentially become linked with any one visual experience. This point then raises the question of why the haptic–visual linkages in the memories of mature perceivers are in fact not arbitrary, but instead are systematic and appropriate so as to enable accurate cross-modal perception. Just as students of language acquisition must explain how a child comes to use precisely those sound–meaning pairings that everyone else in the language community uses, we must explain how a child forms precisely those haptic–visual linkages that are correct. Following the example introduced earlier, in order to account for accurate matching-by-recognition, we must explain how the haptic experience deriving from a potato comes to be linked with and therefore conjure up the visual experience also deriving from a potato, rather than some other one of the myriad of visual experiences it might theoretically be linked with and conjure up.

At first this issue seems a trivial one. Because a potato is a potato, its haptic experience will necessarily accompany its visual experience in bimodal encounters, and this co-occurrence will lead to their linkage in memory. Simultaneous visual–haptic experience with objects need only be invoked to account for the proper pairings required for matching-by-recognition. (Indeed, the role of such simultaneous experience was stressed by the Empiricists in their accounting for cross-modal perception.) However, the matter is actually more complicated than it first seems. Consider an infant handling an object such that it can be looked at as well. Typically, while handling the one object, the infant is likely to look at it some of the time and likely to look away from it, toward other things, some of the time, too. Paralleling one of the complications of lexical acquisition, there exists what amounts to a correspondence problem with respect to forming linkages between haptic experiences and visual experiences. During any one haptic experience, several visual experiences may occur and therefore any or all of them might become linked with the haptic experience.

For the process of matching-by-recognition to be at all credible, some solution to this correspondence problem must be identified. Some constraint must be presumed to operate on the formation of haptic–visual linkages, in order to preclude or correct the equivalent of "mismatches" in lexical acquisition, that is, in order to ensure that linkages only form between haptic experiences and visual experiences that actually derive from the same object. One possible candidate that might serve this constraining function is location in space. It could be supposed that linkages between haptic experiences and visual ones form only if the two experiences are perceived as originating from the same place. Thus an infant holding an object might localize (proprioceptively) its "feel" as coming from wherever the right hand was positioned, from a point some specified distance and direction relative to dead ahead, for example. The baby would then link only the object's appearance with that "feel" because, of all the visual experiences that might occur while the infant is holding the object, only its appearance is likewise localized (visually now) at that same distance and direction relative to dead ahead. Of course, this solution presupposes that proprioceptive space and visual space are isomorphic or even unified for the infant. Conveniently, there is evidence for hand–eye coordination of at least a rudimentary sort very early in life (see pp. 139–143 of Bushnell, 1985), and in any event, this prerequisite is certainly met by the time visually guided reaching emerges at about 4 months of age.

Another possible candidate for the constraint that must operate on the formation of haptic–visual linkages involves temporal patterning. It could be supposed that such linkages form only if a haptic experience and a visual one are perceived to modulate according to the same temporal structure. Thus, extending an example cited by Rose and Ruff (1987), an infant kneading a blanket with the hands and simultaneously looking at a mobile would not link the "feel" of the blanket with the visual experience of the mobile because these two experiences do not share a common fate, temporally speaking. The mobile's movements are not in any way synchronous with the kneading activity and the haptic experience it entails. However, on the occasions when the infant looks away from the mobile and down at the blanket while kneading it, the visual experience of the blanket will be seen deforming according to the same rhythm with which the haptic experience of the blanket modulates. This common rhythm may serve as the "instruction" to link together these two experiences in particular in memory.

The temporal patterning solution to the correspondence problem is especially compelling for several reasons. First, there is substantial evidence that young infants are sensitive to temporal patterning (see the review by Rose & Ruff, 1987), as this solution would require. Second, the results of several studies (e.g., Spelke, 1979, 1981; Spelke, Born, & Chu, 1983) indicate that common rhythms compel infants to link together particular auditory and visual experiences, in much the same way as I am suggesting they may direct haptic–visual linkages. It would not be surprising if the same constraint were involved in intersensory linkages of all sorts. Finally, infants frequently engage in play activities with objects that involve temporal modulations of haptic and visual experiences. Researchers have observed that from about 6 months of age to about 10 months, the predominant style of interacting with objects is "examining behavior" (Fenson, Kagan, Kearsley, & Zelazo, 1976; Ruff, 1984, 1986; Schofield & Uzgiris, 1969), in which the infant devotes intense, multisensory attention to a single object. Similarly, in her work on motor development, Thelen (1981) observed that manual "rhythmical stereotypies" emerge at about 4 months and peak at about 7 months of age. Thus, while looking at an object, a baby in this age range is apt to poke it, pat it, rotate it, rub it, pass it from hand to hand, and so on. All of these activities produce rich and synchronous rhythmic information for both touch and vision. Thus, accepting temporal patterning as the constraint that operates on the formation of haptic–visual linkages means that the naturally behaving infant would have ample opportunity to develop a full repertoire of such linkages to figure in matching-by-recognition.

The several considerations just discussed suggest that the process of matching-by-recognition would be relatively ineffective during the first 5 or 6 months of life, and then its effectiveness would grow explosively during the latter part of infancy. The very young infant does not perceive visual stimuli as embodied wholes, does not have haptic access to very many objects, and does not interact with objects in the rhythmical ways that might promote haptic–visual linkages. However, each of these limitations is surpassed soon after the midpoint of the first year; the infant begins to recognize objects *qua* objects (i.e., as correlations of attributes), becomes skillful at reaching and crawling and hence comes into haptic contact with hundreds of objects, and routinely engages in repetitive manipulations of objects that produce rich temporal information. Thus by the end of the first year, the infant would have an extensive and rapidly growing glossary of haptic–visual linkages in memory, and therefore matching-by-recognition could be effective over a wide range of stimuli. This predicted developmental function for matching-by-recognition is portrayed by the dotted line in Fig. 2.1. The solid line portrays the developmental course predicted for matching-by-analysis, which I address next.

THE DEVELOPMENT OF MATCHING-BY-ANALYSIS

A first consideration regarding the development of matching-by-analysis is that, at least in some limited way, matching-by-analysis must be effective earlier in development than is matching-by-recognition. This is so because of the point made earlier, that the haptic–visual linkages integral to matching-by-recognition can only be accounted for by admitting a constraint involving sensitivity to spatial location and/or to temporal patterning. This requisite sensitivity to the shared location or to the common rhythm of a haptic experience and a visual one is itself an instance of matching-by-analysis or amodal perception, and thus ipso facto, matching-by-analysis precedes matching-by-recognition in development. Furthermore, even if one takes the extreme empiricist position that the amodal perception of most dimensions is ultimately based on some associative or calibrative mechanism, a correspondence problem similar to the one discussed earlier would always exist in the end, and some inherent cross-modal isomorphism would have to be admitted to resolve the correspondence problem. Thus, it seems logically imperative to grant the infant amodal or unified perception of at

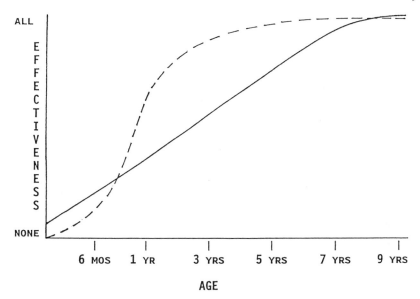

FIG. 2.1. A graphic summary of the developmental course of cross-modal perception. The dotted line traces the developmental function for matching-by-recognition; the solid line traces that for matching-by-analysis. The continuum represented on the *y* axis, effectiveness, refers to the proportion of object pairs, out of all possible object pairs, for which a particular process can yield correct responding in a cross-modal matching task.

least some one dimension at birth. This in turn means that matching-by-analysis must be rudimentarily effective at birth, at least for stimuli varying along this one dimension.

But which one dimension shall it be, and how many other dimensions are amodally perceivable at birth as well? Many dimensions or properties of objects can be thought of as derived from other more basic ones. For example, Triesman (1986) considered that the dimension of shape "emerges" as a composite of simpler aspects such as symmetry, curved/angular, open/closed, amount of contour, etc. The point here, so far as the development of matching-by-analysis is concerned, is that infants could conceivably begin life with amodal perception for only a few very basic dimensions or features, with all other amodal sensitivities emerging from these during the course of development. As a case in point, Lewkowicz and his colleagues (see e.g., Lewkowicz, 1991; Lewkowicz & Turkewitz, 1980; Turkewicz, Gardner, & Lewkowicz, 1984) have collected evidence suggesting that very young infants are primarily responsive to the quantitative attributes or "arousingness" (my term) of stimuli. Thus, neonates may successfully perform cross-modal matches based on the intensity of stimuli (e.g., brightness and loudness), but they may be unable to accomplish matching based on more qualitative or configurational properties such as rhythm, shape, or texture, except as these may somehow translate into intensity or level of arousal.

To the extent that some relevant dimensions require maturation or experience to emerge from others, the range of objects over which matching-by-analysis could be effective for young infants would be compromised. An important dimension that may be subject to this problem is the aforementioned one of shape. There is evidence that very young infants are visually sensitive to several aspects that figure in shape, such as edge orientation, curved edge versus straight edge, straight edge versus angle, contour density, and symmetry (see the review by Banks & Salapatek, 1983). However, when these "lower order variables" are held constant and only the arrangement of certain edges, angles, and curves is varied across the stimuli, young infants often fail to evidence shape discrimination (see Fisher, Ferdinandsen, & Bornstein, 1981; Ruff, 1978). It seems that infants may visually encode shape only according to the amount of contour and according to whether or not the stimulus is symmetrical, whether or not it contains curves, and whether or not it contains angles. Thus they may see two stimuli as identical as long as they match in these basic respects.

Whether this incomplete analysis of shape also occurs in the haptic modality has not been empirically determined. However, in their account of the development of haptic perception based on the kinds of hand movements infants are capable of making at different ages, Bushnell and Boudreau (1991) concluded that infants might have difficulty haptically perceiving configurational shape before 10 or 12 months of age. Regardless of whether it occurs in both modalities or just in vision, either way, infants' incomplete analysis of shape would interfere with matching-by-analysis for certain kinds of stimuli, and the literature on cross-modal perception during infancy bears this out. In several studies, 6- to 15-month-old infants have evidenced cross-modal matching with pairs of stimuli differing with regard to the amount of contour or the presence versus absense of curves (see Rose & Ruff, 1987, for a review of studies that have yielded positive results). However, the reported failures of infants in this age range to evidence cross-modal matching have consistently involved stimulus pairs undifferentiated in these ways but differing only with regard to the configuration of edges and angles (cf. Bryant, Jones, Claxton, & Perkins, 1972; Bushnell, 1978; Bushnell & Weinberger, 1987).

A related issue that would affect the development of matching-by-analysis involves the "acuity" for perceiving various amodal dimensions. One might be responsive to a particular dimension as a distinct property of objects, and yet able to assess values along that dimension only rather crudely, within a large margin of error. Such a lack of acuity for any given dimension would interfere with matching-by-analysis, because relatively subtle differences between a visual and a haptic stimulus could not be detected. For example, there is evidence that preschoolers' haptic perception of shape and also that of length are relatively poor in comparison with their own visual abilities and in comparison with adults' haptic abilities (see the review by Warren, 1982). As one would expect, the imprecise haptic apprehension of these dimensions imposes limits on young children's cross-modal matching with regard to shape and length. Indeed, the haptic imprecision may be the only limiting factor here—comparisons of intramodal and cross-modal performance in tasks of shape and length matching generally show that children's visual–haptic and haptic–visual matching is much worse than their visual–visual matching, but neither worse nor better than their haptic–haptic matching (see Jones, 1981; Warren, 1982).

A final consideration for the development of matching-by-analysis relates to the matter of differential saliency hierarchies discussed earlier. The conclusion of that discussion was that reversals in the saliency hierarchies within vision as compared to within touch will interfere with matching-by-analysis. This kind of interference may be particularly serious early in development, when perception is relatively inflexible and subject to "capture" effects. That is, for infants and young children, it is especially difficult to shift attention away from the most salient aspect of a stimulus in order to focus on a less salient dimension (see, e.g., Bushnell, Shaw, & Strauss, 1985; Lane, 1979; Pick, Frankel, & Hess, 1975).

This tendency toward engrossment indeed may account for several observed cases of young infants failing to exhibit haptic–visual matching of shape (Brown & Gottfried, 1986; Rose et al., 1981 [Experiment 1]; Streri, Pecheux, & Vurpillot, 1984). Perhaps the infants in these studies attended to only the texture or hardness of the stimulus during the initial haptic exploration period, on account of the high salience of these properties in haptics (see Klatzky et al., 1987; Lederman & Klatzky, 1987). However, the novel and familiar objects offered on the pursuant visual test trial were different from one another only in shape. If the infants had not encoded the object's shape during familiarization, then for them the test shapes were equally novel (and the test textures or hardnesses were equally familiar); therefore they exhibited no preferential responding.

The same saliency consideration may explain certain asymmetries that have been observed in infants' cross-modal matching, too. For example, Streri et al. (1984) found that 5-month-olds did not exhibit matching when familiarized haptically and tested visually (T-V condition), but they did exhibit matching with the very same stimuli when familiarized visually and tested haptically (V-T condition). A focus on texture or hardness during haptic familiarization could account for the failure in the T-V condition, as described earlier. In the V-T condition, though, infants may have attended to shape during familiarization, in accord with its high salience in vision, and consequently they had a basis for distinguishing the test stimuli later presented haptically. Although ordinarily they would not focus on the shape of haptic stimuli, in the V-T condition attention to shape may have been "primed" by the preceding visual experience, in which attention to shape is only natural. Following this line of reasoning, we might speculate that if the Streri et al. test stimuli had differed in texture or hardness rather than in shape, perhaps the opposite asymmetry in results would have been observed.

These considerations raised with regard to the development of matching-by-analysis suggest that its effectiveness would be quite limited at first and then would increase gradually over a lengthy period of time. Although the completely inexperienced newborn infant must be able to engage in matching-by-analysis to some extent (e.g., perhaps where intensity is involved; see Lewkowicz & Turkewitz, 1980), the range of stimuli over which the neonate's matching-by-analysis could proceed effectively would be quite restricted. The young infant does not construe stimuli according to the full set of features or dimensions necessary to distinguish real-world objects, does not perceive with great acuity along the dimensions that are analyzed, and does not easily shift attention away from highly salient aspects of stimuli to less salient but potentially relevant ones. Each of these impediments to matching-by-analysis is overcome during the course of infancy and early childhood. We may guess that an essentially full set of perceptual dimensions for encoding objects has emerged by 12 or 18 months of age, but perceptual acuity and attentional flexibility are known to continue improving through the preschool years and perhaps into middle childhood. Accordingly, the prediction is that the effectiveness of matching-by-analysis would increase more or less steadily over a protracted period of development, as is portrayed by the solid line in Fig. 2.1.

DEVELOPMENTAL CONSIDERATIONS— CROSS-MODAL PERCEPTION GENERALLY

If the distinct courses of development predicted for matching-by-recognition and matching-by-analysis are examined together (see Fig. 2.1), three phases of development for cross-modal perception in general may be identified. In the first phase, from birth to about 8 or 9 months of age, the effectiveness of both processes for cross-modal perception is restricted, albeit by different factors in the two cases. Thus each process could mediate matching over a particular small range of objects, but there would be many object pairs that neither matching-by-recognition nor matching-by-analysis could effectively discriminate. Cross-modal perception in general would be "spotty" early in development; this characterization is consistent with Rose and Ruff's (1987) conclusion that "cross-modal transfer is a weaker phenomenon in 6-month-olds" (in comparison with in older infants; p. 329). Note that young infants' performance on various within-mode tasks would similarly be compromised. That is, the sources of difficulty for cross-modal perception during early infancy—the small number of haptically familiar objects, poor acuity for apprehending certain dimensions, capture effects, etc.—are not specific nor unique to cross-modal perception.

A converse point to emphasize regarding early cross-modal perception is that the occasional instances of successful matching might be mediated by either matching-by-recognition or matching-by-analysis. As the functions in Fig. 2.1 indicate, both processes are viable early on, although the effectiveness of each is highly constrained. Acknowledging that two distinct mechanisms are available for cross-modal perception, even for young infants, could help to clarify some inconsistencies in the literature. For example, both Meltzoff and Borton (1979) and Gibson and Walker (1984) have reported evidence for cross-modal (oral–visual) matching by 1-month-old infants. However, matching was manifested by a familiarity preference in the former study and by a novelty preference in the latter one. This contrast is all the more puzzling because the familiarization period was longer in the Meltzoff and Borton procedure; hence, the infants in that study should have been relatively more familiar with the initial stimulus and therefore more disposed to exhibit a novelty response (given that a novelty response indicates complete encoding; see Roder & Bushnell, 1987; Rose, Gottfried, Carminar-Melloy, & Bridger, 1982). This paradox can be understood if we surmise that the slower, more deliberate matching-by-analysis process was involved in the Meltzoff and Borton study, permitting only partial encoding despite the longer familiarization period, whereas the faster, more automatic matching-by-recognition process was involved in the Gibson and Walker study, allowing for complete encoding even with the briefer familiarization period. This speculation in turn is plausible because the stimuli in the Meltzoff and Borton study, a smooth sphere and a sphere with nubs, were presumably unlike anything a very young infant had orally experienced before, whereas the stimuli in the Gibson and Walker study, a flexible and a rigid cylinder, were not unlike nipples and fingers, respectively.

Referring again to Fig. 2.1, it can be seen that a second phase in the development of cross-modal perception commences with the exponential growth in the effectiveness of matching-by-recognition that takes place during the latter part of infancy. During this phase, which runs up to about 7 or 8 years of age, matching-by-recognition is more fully effective than matching-by-analysis is. An implication here is that young children would perform better on tasks demanding that they judge whether or not a haptically presented familiar object matches a visually presented familiar object than they would on analogous tasks with novel objects or on tasks requiring that they judge stimuli on isolated dimensions. The findings discussed by Abravenel (1981) and Warren (1982) indeed indicate that young children are rather poor at cross-modal matching with novel objects differing only in shape or length, presumably because of their relatively crude haptic apprehension of these properties.

In contrast, Bushnell (1991) recently observed that 5-year-olds' cross-modal matching with familiar objects was near perfect. In this research, children were presented eight commonplace objects to examine just visually or just haptically. These objects were then mixed with an equal number of distractor items and all of the objects were presented for recognition in the alternative modality. In their judgments of whether or not each item was one they had examined earlier in a different modality, children were on average 94% correct. However, on the same task with unusual objects, which like the commonplace objects varied along multiple dimensions, cross-modal recognition was significantly less accurate, on average 84% correct (despite the fact that within-mode recognition for the unusual objects averaged over 95% correct). These findings thus provide a direct confirmation of the advantage of matching-by-recognition over matching-by-analysis portrayed in Fig. 2.1 for this phase of development.

The third phase in the development of cross-modal perception evident from Fig. 2.1 has its onset at about 8 years of age, when matching-by-analysis finally reaches full effectiveness, as matching-by-recognition had done some years earlier. From this point on, both processes for accomplishing cross-modal matching are essentially as effective as they will ever be. With older children as with adults, one process or the other will come into play according to the task at hand, and performance mediated by matching-by-recognition should be no more nor less accurate than performance mediated by matching-by-analysis.

The only "developmental" point to emphasize regarding this final phase concerns the relative predominance of one process as compared to the other. Recall that matching-by-analysis is the "primary" process, in the sense that it is functional at birth and is even prerequisite to the formation of the haptic–visual linkages involved in matching-by-recognition. However, once appropriate haptic–visual linkages have been formed and exist in memory, matching-by-recognition stands on its own; in a given cross-modal task with objects for which linkages already exist, matching-by-recognition can proceed without recourse to matching-by-analysis. Furthermore, recall that in circumstances where both processes can proceed, matching-by-recognition will ordinarily take precedence (on account of its greater speed, automaticity, comprehensiveness, etc.). This means that upon haptically encountering a familiar object, a perceiver's "first" response will be to recognize the object for what it is and therefore know what it will look like, rather than to apprehend its size, its shape, its texture, and so forth individually and therefore know how big it will look, what shape it will look, and so on. The case here is analogous to that of words formed from visual patterns (letters); if these are commonplace words and one is a reader, it is virtually impossible to inhibit the activation of word meaning, even when word meaning is irrelevant and the situation calls for a response to the letters *qua* visual stimuli (cf. the Stroop effect). Hence, although matching-by-analysis is primary in the ontogenetic sense, matching-by-recognition ultimately becomes primary in the sense of being most frequently and spontaneously used in the context of everyday life. Development, like the automobile industry, often works according to the doctrine of planned obsolescence.

ACKNOWLEDGMENTS

Some of the ideas discussed in this chapter developed from research funded by NIH Research Grant RO1 HD18093. An earlier version of the chapter was written while I was a Visiting Fellow with the Department of Psychology at LaTrobe University. I thank the members of the Department for the support and intellectual stimulation they provided and for the use of their facilities. I also thank Holly A. Ruff for her helpful comments on the earlier draft.

REFERENCES

Abravanel, E. (1981). Integrating the information from eyes and hands: A developmental account. In R. D. Walk & H. L. Pick, Jr. (Eds.), *Intersensory perception and sensory integration* (pp. 71–108). New York: Plenum.

Aslin, R. N., & Smith, L. B. (1988). Perceptual development. *Annual Review of Psychology, 39*, 435–473.

Bamber, D. (1969). Reaction times and error rates for "same-different" judgments of multidimensional stimuli. *Perception and Psychophysics, 6*, 169–174.

Banks, M. S., & Salapatek, P. (1983). Infant visual perception. In P. H. Mussen (Ed.), *Handbook of child psychology: Vol. 2. Infancy and developmental psychobiology* (pp. 435–571). New York: Wiley.

Berkeley, G. (1709/1948). An essay towards a new theory of vision. In A. A. Luce & T. E. Jessup (Eds.), *The works of George Berkeley Bishop of Cloyne*. New York: Nelson.

Biederman, I. (1988). Surface versus edge-based determinants of visual recognition. *Cognitive Psychology, 20*, 38–64.

Bower, T. G. R. (1974). *Development in infancy*. San Francisco: Freeman.

Bower, T. G. R. (1977). *A primer of infant development*. San Francisco: Freeman.

Brown, K. W., & Gottfried, A. W. (1986). Cross-modal transfer of shape in early infancy: Is there reliable evidence? In L. P. Lipsitt & C. Rovee-Collier (Eds.), *Advances in infancy research* (Vol. 4, pp. 163–170). Norwood, NJ: Ablex.

Bryant, P. E., Jones, P., Claxton, V., & Perkins, G. M. (1972). Recognition of shapes across modalities by infants. *Nature, 240*, 303–304.

Bushnell, E. W. (1978, August). *Cross-modal object recognition in infancy*. Paper presented at the annual meeting of the American Psychological Association, Toronto.

Bushnell, E. W. (1982). Visual-tactual knowledge in 8-, 9½-, and 11-month-old infants. *Infant Behavior and Development, 5*, 63–75.

Bushnell, E. W. (1985). The decline of visually guided reaching during infancy. *Infant Behavior and Development, 8*, 139–155.

Bushnell, E. W. (1991, November). *Haptic and cross-modal recognition in children.* Paper presented at the meetings of the Psychonomics Society, San Francisco.

Bushnell, E. W., & Boudreau, J. P. (1991). The development of haptic perception during infancy. In M. A. Heller & W. Schiff (Eds.), *The psychology of touch* (pp. 139–161). Hillsdale, NJ: Lawrence Erlbaum Associates.

Bushnell, E. W., Shaw, L., & Strauss, D. (1985). The relationship between visual and tactual exploration by 6-month-olds. *Developmental Psychology, 21*, 591–600.

Bushnell, E. W., & Weinberger, N. (1987). Infants' detection of visual-tactual discrepancies: Asymmetries that indicate a directive role of visual information. *Journal of Experimental Psychology: Human Perception and Performance, 13*, 601–608.

Cooper, L. A. (1976). Individual differences in visual comparison processes. *Perception and Psychophysics, 19*, 433–444.

Cooper, L. A. (1980). Recent themes in visual information processing: A selected overview. In R. Nickerson (Ed.), *Attention and performance, VIII.* Hillsdale, NJ: Lawrence Erlbaum Associates.

Davenport, R. K., Rogers, C. M., & Russell, I. S. (1973). Cross-modal perception in apes. *Neuropsychologica, 11*, 21–28.

Fenson, L., Kagan, J., Kearsley, R. B., & Zelazo, P. R. (1976). The developmental progression of manipulative play in the first two years. *Child Development, 47*, 232–236.

Fisher, C. B., Ferdinandsen, K., & Bornstein, M. H. (1981). The role of symmetry in infant form discrimination. *Child Development, 52*, 457–462.

Frampton, G. G., Milner, A. D., & Ettlinger, G. (1973). Cross-modal transfer between vision and touch of go, no-go discrimination learning in the monkey. *Neuropsychologica, 11*, 231–233.

Friedes, D. (1974). Human information processing and sensory modality: Cross-modal functions, information complexity, and deficit. *Psychological Bulletin, 81*, 284–310.

Gibson, E. J. (1969). *Principles of perceptual learning and development.* New York: Appleton-Century-Crofts.

Gibson, E. J., & Walker, A. S. (1984). Development of knowledge of visual-tactual affordances of substance. *Child Development, 55*, 453–460.

Gibson, J. J. (1966). *The senses considered as perceptual systems.* London: George Allen & Unwin.

Gibson, J. J. (1979). *The ecological approach to visual perception.* Boston: Houghton Mifflin.

Jones, B. (1981). The developmental significance of cross-modal matching. In R. D. Walk & H. L. Pick, Jr. (Eds.), *Intersensory perception and sensory integration* (pp. 109–136). New York: Plenum.

Klatzky, R. L., Lederman, S. J., & Reed, C. (1987). There's more to touch than meets the eye: The salience of object attributes for haptics with and without vision. *Journal of Experimental Psychology: General, 116*, 356–369.

Krantz, M. (1972). Haptic recognition of objects in children. *Journal of Genetic Psychology, 120*, 121–133.

Lane, D. M. (1979). Developmental changes in attention-deployment skills. *Journal of Experimental Child Psychology, 28*, 16–29.

Lederman, S. J., & Klatzky, R. L. (1987). Hand movements: A window into haptic object recognition. *Cognitive Psychology, 19*, 342–368.

Lewkowicz, D. J. (1991). Development of intersensory functions in human infancy: Auditory/visual interactions. In M. J. Weiss & P. R. Zelazo (Eds.), *Newborn attention: Biological constraints and the influence of experience.* Norwood, NJ: Ablex.

Lewkowicz, D. J., & Turkewitz, G. (1980). Cross-modal equivalence in early infancy: Auditory-visual intensity matching. *Developmental Psychology, 16*, 597–607.

Locke, J. (1690/1959). *An essay concerning human understanding.* New York: Dover.

Logan, G. D. (1988). Toward an instance theory of automatization. *Psychological Review, 95*, 492–527.

Marks, L. E. (1978). *The unity of the senses.* New York: Academic Press.

Meltzoff, A. N., & Borton, R. W. (1979). Intermodal matching by human neonates. *Nature, 282*, 403–404.

Millar, S. (1978). Aspects of memory for information from touch and movement. In G. Gordon (Ed.), *Active touch: The mechanism of recognition of objects by manipulation.* Oxford: Pergamon.

Piaget, J. (1952). *The origins of intelligence in children.* New York: Norton.

Piaget, J. (1954). *The construction of reality in the child.* New York: Ballantine.

Pick, A. D., Frankel, D. G., & Hess, V. L. (1975). Children's attention: The development of selectivity. In E. M. Hetherington (Ed.), *Review of child development research* (Vol. 5). Chicago: University of Chicago Press.

Roder, B., & Bushnell, E. W. (1987, April). *The time-course of constructing a schema for a visual stimulus during infancy.* Poster presented at the biennial meeting of the Society for Research in Child Development, Baltimore.

Rose, S. A., Gottfried, A. W., & Bridger, W. H. (1981). Cross-modal transfer in 6-month-old infants. *Developmental Psychology, 17*, 661–669.

Rose, S. A., Gottfried, A. W., Carminar-Melloy, P. M., & Bridger, W. H. (1982). Familiarity and novelty preferences in infant recognition memory: Implications for information processing. *Developmental Psychology, 18*, 704–713.

Rose, S. A., & Ruff, H. A. (1987). Cross-modal abilities in human infants. In J. Osofsky (Ed.), *Handbook of infant development* (2nd ed., pp. 318–362). New York: Wiley.

Ruff, H. A. (1978). Infant recognition of the invariant form of objects. *Child Development, 49*, 293–306.

Ruff, H. A. (1984). Infants' manipulative exploration of objects: The effects of age and object characterisitics. *Developmental Psychology, 20*, 9–20.

Ruff, H. A. (1986). Components of attention during infants' manipulative exploration. *Child Development, 57*, 105–114.

Schofield, L., & Uzgiris, I. C. (1969, March). *Examining behavior and the development of the concept of object.* Paper presented at the biennial meetings of the Society for Research in Child Development, Santa Monica, CA.

Smith, L. B. (1981). Importance of the overall similarity of objects for adults' and children's classifications. *Journal of Experimental Psychology: Human Perception and Performance, 7*, 811–824.

Spelke, E. S. (1979). Perceiving bimodally specified events in infancy. *Developmental Psychology, 15*, 626–636.

Spelke, E. S. (1981). The infant's acquisition of knowledge of bimodally specified events. *Journal of Experimental Child Psychology, 31*, 279–299.

Spelke, E. S., Born, W. S., & Chu, F. (1983). Perception of moving, sounding objects by four-month-old infants. *Perception, 12*, 719–732.

Streri, A., Pecheux, M., & Vurpillot, E. (1984, April). *Cross-modal transfer of form in 5-month-old infants.* Paper presented at the International Conference on Infant Studies, New York.

Taylor, M. M., Lederman, S. J., & Gibson, R. H. (1973). Tactual perception of texture. In E. C. Carterette & M. P. Friedman (Eds.), *Handbook of perception, Vol. 3, Biology of perceptual systems.* New York: Academic Press.

Thelen, E. (1981). Rhythmical behavior in infancy: An ethological perspective. *Developmental Psychology, 17*, 237–257.

Triesman, A. (1986). Properties, parts, and objects. In K. R. Boff, L. Kaufman, & J. P. Thomas (Eds.), *Handbook of perception and human performance, Vol. II, Cognitive process and performance.* New York: Wiley.

Turkewitz, G., Gardner, J., & Lewkowicz, D. J. (1984). Sensory/perceptual functioning during early infancy: The implications of a quantitative basis for responding. In G. Greenberg & E. Tobach (Eds.), *Behavioral evolution and integrative levels.* Hillsdale, NJ: Lawrence Erlbaum Associates.

Warren, D. H. (1982). The development of haptic perception. In W. Schiff & E. Foulke (Eds.), *Tactual perception: A sourcebook* (pp. 82–129). Cambridge: Cambridge University Press.

Younger, B. A., & Cohen, L. B. (1983). Infant perception of correlations among attributes. *Child Development, 54,* 858–867.

Younger, B. A., & Cohen, L. B. (1986). Developmental change in infants' perception of correlations among attributes. *Child Development, 57,* 803–815.

CHAPTER THREE

Taxonomy for Intermodal Relations

Arlene Walker-Andrews
Rutgers University

A persistent and unresolved question concerning the development of inter-modal perception concerns whether infants' sense modalities are integrated or differentiated at birth. Even in the present volume, the contributors represent different views on this question. In brief, from an integration-asso-ciation account, sensations from different receptors are separate at birth. The developmental task is to coordinate these sensations to achieve a single percept (e.g., Birch & Lefford, 1963; Bryant, 1974; Piaget, 1954). Mechanisms proposed for coordinating sensations include learning principles such as association in some accounts and various mediating processes in others.

An entirely different view maintains that the infant possesses undifferenti-ated perceptual systems at birth. With development, differentiation occurs. For example, according to Bower's account (Bower, 1974), there is a *primitive unity* at birth. The infant is uninformed even of whether an object is seen, heard, or felt. My own view, which incorporates the theories of E. J. Gibson (1969) and J. J. Gibson (1979/1986), is that detection of invariant relations underlies the development of perception in general, and intermodal percep-tion in particular. That is, objects and events are multimodal, specified by redundant information abstracted by coordinated sensory systems. With experience, infants become sensitive to new invariant relationships and come to detect additional properties of objects and events. Learning itself results from changes in perceptual selection, leading to progressive differentiation of the environment. Infants appear to experience a world of perceptual unity based on the detection of amodal information or intermodal correspondences that specify properties of objects and events and their affordances (J. J. Gibson,

1979/1986). If one takes this view, it is essential to determine to what information infants are sensitive, describe the limits and mechanisms underlying such sensitivity, and discover how these mechanisms develop.

Most recent evidence indicates that infants are quite sensitive to intermodal information that is available in multimodal events. Infants detect temporal synchrony, tempo of action, rhythm, changes in distance, and affective information uniting visual and acoustic presentations (e.g., Bahrick, 1983, 1988; Dodd, 1979; Mendelson & Ferland, 1982; Spelke & Owsley, 1979; Walker, 1982; Walker-Andrews & Lennon, 1985). Such sensitivity to intermodal relations allows for the experience of organized wholes (objects, not colors and shapes and textures; persons, not disembodied voices and faces) and what objects and events afford.

There are some limitations to infants' intermodal abilities as well. In some instances infants appear to "overgeneralize"; they fail to observe constraints that an adult's perceptual system would recognize. For example, Spelke, Born, and Chu (1983) found that infants treated the sight of an object hitting against a surface and a simple change in trajectory of motion without a visual impact as equivalent. The infants looked preferentially to each of these types of display in the presence of a thumping sound that was synchronized to one of two filmed events. In addition, some investigators have reported asymmetries in the development of intermodal functioning. In a habituation study looking at infants' detection of changes in the temporal rate of the auditory and visual components of an audiovisual event, Lewkowicz (1988) discovered that 6-month-old infants did not respond to changes in visually presented rates, although they responded to changes presented either aurally or in both visual and auditory presentations.

In the present chapter, I introduce a classification scheme for intermodal relations with the hope that such a taxonomy will contribute to our understanding of the development of intermodal perception and point to significant avenues for research. Specifically, I introduce broad categories for classifying relations and then fit the evidence into the various categories I propose. The basic premise is that properties of objects or events may be specified to several sense modalities concurrently. Skilled perceivers detect invariant relationships that characterize the information about an object or event that reaches their senses. Likewise, the human infant possesses coordinated perceptual systems that allow for detection of many of these invariant relations. Whether or not an invariant relationship is actually detected, however, may be determined by several factors. These include (a) the level of maturity of an infant's sense modalities, (b) the task at hand, and (c) of special importance to us here, the type of relationship available to perception. A more adequate description of these types of invariant relations should permit us to gain better understanding of the infants' developing abilities to detect and act on the basis of these relations.

Two points need to be made before proceeding. First, the data we have on infants' intermodal abilities are rich in some areas, meager in others. The 4-month-old infant's auditory–visual capabilities have been studied extensively. On the other hand, there is almost no data on the auditory–visual abilities of younger infants or on the relationship between modalities other than auditory–visual and visual–tactual at any age. Second, a large number of obvious caveats must be acknowledged in any discussion of the development of intermodal perception. That is, there are bound to be some asymmetries in development owing to variations in the maturation rates and trajectories of the different modalities. In addition, there are likely to be differences in infants' demonstrated abilities when they are faced with objects and events that vary in complexity, familiarity, animacy, and other attributes, or with experimental paradigms that demand different responses and sensitivities. One aspect of complexity—level of event—is discussed initially because of its importance to any classification of events or relations.

Before going further, I must thank Lorraine Bahrick, with whom I have collaborated often, most recently in a study of infants' bimodal perception of gender in which the beginnings of this classification scheme were first introduced (Walker-Andrews, Bahrick, Raglioni, & Diaz, 1991).

NESTED EVENTS—THE EFFECTS OF COMPLEXITY

Most objects and events in the world are multimodal. We typically see, hear, touch, and perhaps smell and taste those things occupying space or unfolding in time. Because our sensory systems have overlapping functions, we perceive a unified world, rather than bits and pieces with modality-specific consequences. It is by considering the intersections between the sensory modalities that I hope to propose a classification for intermodal relations, but it is difficult to determine at what "level" to define events and relations. A description of two common events should suffice to illustrate the problem.

First, knowledge that a particular person's face goes with the unique sound of his or her voice is something that can only be learned through extended experience. Even so, infants by $3\frac{1}{2}$ months have already learned the idiosyncratic relation between the sight of their own mother's face and the sound of her voice (Burnham, Earnshaw, & Olymbios, 1986; Spelke & Owsley, 1979). Although one cannot predict precisely what a particular individual's voice will sound like, nevertheless there are biological constraints on characteristics of that voice. A given female's voice must be within a typical pitch range owing to properties of her particular vocal tract. When she speaks, the voice is coincident with the sight of her face: It occurs or emanates from the same location, and it shares a synchrony relation with the movements of her mouth. A closer look at these characteristics reveals, however, that (a) these constraints apply to different levels of the event "female person speaking" and (b) the intermodal relationships are variably available.

With respect to level of event, there are smaller events nested within larger events. As illustrated elegantly by Kuhl and Meltzoff (1982), by 4 months infants are sensitive to the relation between mouth shape and spectral characteristics of vowels. The ongoing changes in mouth shape and sound during the production of /i/ (as in "peep") comprise small events embedded in the larger event of speaking. Moreover, the relationships between the audible and visible information in this example are more or less available to our senses. The voice must emanate from the same location as the face; usually we can see the face at the place where the source of the vocal sound is also located. Temporal synchrony between face and voice is required and we can see lip movements co-occurring with many of the sounds we are hearing. The pitch of voice, however, is not absolutely specified by visible characteristics of the face, although it is determined by aspects of the vocal tract and related to gender. Further, a face may be present without a voice, a voice may occur without a face in view, and it is even possible through technical means to displace the face and voice in time and space. Both of these points need to be considered in any classification scheme.

Another example I borrow from Handel (1988). In a discussion of conceptions of space and time, Handel pointed out that events may have "spatial auditory characteristics of extension or movement. For example, a sound source with multiple surfaces generating similar but not identical sounds (like the rustling leaves of a tall tree) may be experienced as an extended source" (p. 316). Here is another instance of nested events. One may detect each moving, sounding leaf, perceiving a multiplicity of events, or may perceive the multiple surfaces generating sounds as a single event, or may detect both events simultaneously.

CLASSIFICATION OF RELATIONS IN OBJECTS AND EVENTS

Most researchers examining the development of intermodal perception make a distinction between the detection of amodal properties (size, texture, flexibility, duration, and intensity) that may be picked up by any modality (E. J. Gibson, 1969), and the ability to match two modality-specific properties of the same object or event (e.g., Reardon & Bushnell, 1988). For example, in one attempt at classifying intermodal relations, Harris (1983) made a distinction between nonarbitrary correlations and arbitrary links. A similar but more expanded set of categories is proposed here. The four major categories to be proposed include amodal information, artificial/arbitrary relations, arbitrary/natural relations, and typical relations. A fifth category, common affordances, is introduced at the end of this chapter.

Two separate but related bases are used to make the distinctions between the types of intermodal relations proposed. The first might be called *degree of constraint*. Physical laws require that objects behave in specific ways. The observer need not have knowledge of or understand the lawful relationships between the physical reality and the structure of stimulus arrays, however. The relations only must be perceptible (i.e., detectable) by the observer's sensory systems. Second, it is likely that the detection of intermodal correspondences is different depending on the type of relation. Some may be harder to differentiate, requiring more experience or different kinds of experience or different mechanisms to acquire. As hinted, the relationships could be "invisible" for various reasons (for example, we humans cannot discern ultraviolet light), but should they be perceptible, eventually an observer would be expected to detect them.

Amodal Specification

Amodal information is not specific to a particular sensory modality; rather, the same information can be detected by several modalities. Examples include temporal relations such as rhythm or tempo, and properties of an object such as size, shape, texture, and substance. Infants are sensitive to this type of information very early. Based on existing data, I conclude that infants are sensitive to this type of information earliest. I present a few examples drawn from work completed on infants' visual–tactual and auditory–visual perception.

Examples from Visual–Tactual Experiments. A small number of studies have examined the development of cross-modal matching across visual and tactual exploration. Meltzoff and Borton (1979) and E. J. Gibson and Walker (1984) reported that infants as young as 1 month demonstrated oral to visual transfer for objects. This should be possible because properties such as texture are specified both to vision and to touch. Meltzoff and Borton tested visual recognition of a smooth or nubbly sphere that previously had been explored orally for 90 sec. The infants looked preferentially at the novel sphere during the visual test, indicating recognition of either shape or texture. In the Gibson and Walker study, 1-month-old infants looked preferentially at an object constructed from a novel substance after 60 sec of oral familiarization with a rigid or pliable cylinder. Two groups of older infants, 12-month-olds, looked preferentially to a filmed object constructed of a familiar substance after either tactual familiarization only or a combination of visual and tactual exploration. Results from both age groups indicated that intermodal information about substance, carried by differentiating motions, is detected by infants.

Others have tested infants' visual–tactual (oral and manual) sensitivities to amodal information at later ages, meeting with inconsistent results. Many of these reported inconsistencies, however, are likely the result of variations in procedures (familiarization time, for example), stimulus objects (size, shapes selected, number of exemplars presented), context (presentation at test; e.g., Rolfe & Day, 1981), and, more importantly, changes in the modalities themselves. As to the latter, both Meltzoff and Borton and Gibson and Walker reported visual recognition of objects that had been explored orally. In contrast, Streri, Pecheux, and Vurpillot (1984) found cross-modal transfer in 5-month-old infants from vision to touch with objects of different shapes, but they reported less robust effects for tactual to visual transfer. Similarly, Gottfried and Rose and their colleagues concluded in a series of studies that 6-month-old infants often fail to demonstrate oral to visual transfer (Rose, Gottfried, & Bridger, 1981). On the other hand, Streri and her colleagues (Streri, Molina, & Millet, 1990) reported tactual to visual and visual to tactual transfer by 2-month-olds in studies that followed the initial tests with 5-month-olds.

Data presented by Rochat (1983, 1987) and Willats (1985) on the development of infants' tactual exploration may be relevant for understanding these contradictory reports. Rochat (1983) reported that newborn infants showed a greater frequency of oral compared to manual responses to objects, whereas at 2 and 3 months of age, the oral and manual responses were comparable in frequency rate. The newborns also showed the strongest differential responses to hard and soft objects in this study. Willats (1985) found that 6-month-olds recognized a familiar object through either vision or tactual exploration, although at 12 months they showed more fixation and manipulation of tactually novel stimuli. It seems that changes in the efficacy of oral and manual exploration with age may account for many of the discrepancies reported in the literature.

Examples from Auditory–Visual Experiments. There have been many more studies of infants' auditory–visual sensitivities than of their visual–tactual ones. Infants are clearly sensitive to amodal information presented aurally and visually, but most studies have examined the abilities of infants who are at least 4 months of age. These studies document that infants can detect synchrony and rate of movement (e.g., Spelke, 1979; but see Lewkowicz, 1985, 1992), intensity changes (Walker-Andrews & Lennon, 1985), duration (Lewkowicz, 1986), substance (Bahrick, 1983), spatial colocation (Lyons-Ruth, 1977), and other amodal relations. In addition, habituation by 7-month-olds to an aurally presented temporal pattern (rhythm) generalizes to the same pattern presented visually (Allen, Walker, Symonds, & Marcell, 1977).

In one of the few auditory–visual studies conducted with infants younger than 4 months, Lewkowicz and Turkewitz (1981) found that infants appeared to respond to sounds and sights of varying intensities (perceived loudness and perceived brightness) on the basis of quantitative differences rather than with cross-modal matching. Even so, the evidence in favor of infants detecting amodal information in auditory–visual events is bolstered by the numerous examples of auditory–visual coordination reported for neonates (e.g., Mendelson & Haith, 1976; Wertheimer, 1961), which would allow for rapid learning of amodal information presented both aurally and visually.

Results reported by Spelke et al. (1983) concerning infants' matching of a change in trajectory with an impact sound compared to the performance of adults on a similar test are relevant here as well. Normally a sound co-occurs with an object striking a surface. When there are two visible events, only one accompanied by a sound, ample intermodal correspondences specify which event is in sound—synchrony between visible impact and the incidence of sound, rate of movement and onset of sound, and rhythm. Spelke's subjects, however, looked preferentially at objects that merely changed direction, specifically pausing at the top of a bounce and then moving downward at the onset of sound. The infants appeared to rely on discontinuities in auditory and visual information. The developmental pattern seems to be toward increasing specificity, because adults in the study required that a sound co-occur with an actual impact on a surface.

Intermodal Correspondences

Some multimodal events or properties of objects are not amodal in nature. Therefore, detection of some intermodal correspondences may require intermodal learning from the start. I propose that there are at least three ways to describe the relations characterizing such multimodal events. Infants appear to detect these correspondences to varying degrees.

Arbitrary and Artificial. Some intermodal relations can be characterized as both arbitrary and artificial. We can draw numerous examples of these events from manmade objects. A telephone can ring, buzz, or play a melody, as can a doorbell. Why include this category if it applies primarily to manmade objects? First, infants are exposed often to these types of objects and events, and second, by examining infants' responses to carefully contrived arbitrary/artificial relations, we can investigate further what role associative and other types of learning may take in an infant's intermodal perception. Arbitrary/artificial relations are not so constrained by properties of objects such as size and substance or by relations such as synchrony. Studies of infants' perception of events characterized by arbitrary/artificial relations can be seen as similar to studies of adults' perception of illusions. The results allow us to examine perception in the face of inadequate or contrived information.

Several experimenters have manipulated modality-specific attributes of objects to provide these sorts of relationships to infants. They create a "multimodal compound" that does not normally occur. For example, Bushnell and her associates (Reardon & Bushnell, 1988) presented infants with combinations of taste and color, and temperature and color, in several experiments. Seven-month-olds were able to learn the relation between the color of a cup and the taste of the applesauce it contained (Reardon & Bushnell, 1988). They did not respond to the relation between color and temperature of vials (Bushnell, 1986). In an earlier study, however, Bushnell, Shaw, and Strauss (1985) reported that 6-month-olds responded to changes solely in temperature and looked longer to an object that had changed temperature as if, in the author's words, "an object is likely to also look different" (p. 598).

More recently, Bahrick (1992) found that 7- but not 3- or 5-month-old infants can detect the correspondence between the pitch of an impact sound and the color and shape of an object striking a surface. Infants were habituated to videotapes of two moving objects paired with distinctive (high or low pitch) sounds. On the posttests the sound/object pairings were reversed. In a companion study, however, infants as young as 3 months were able to detect differences in the modality-specific attributes when these were presented singly. In summary, infants younger than 7 months of age did not detect the relationships between these attributes across modalities. This latter result is important because it indicates that the detection of amodal information or intermodal correspondences is not always in parallel with the detection of modality-specific information, a point I return to.

Arbitrary but Natural. Other intermodal relations may be characterized as "arbitrary but natural" or perhaps "idiosyncratic but natural." For example, as stated earlier, the relation between the sight of a particular person's face and the unique sound of his or her voice is a relation that can only be learned through prolonged experience. Data from experiments by Cohen (1974) and Spelke and Owsley (1979) indicate that infants can match specific faces and voices. Cohen demonstrated that infants of 8 months would look longer to their own mother when her voice was played from her direction, than when a female stranger's was played. Spelke and Owsley tested infants' responses to their mother's or father's voice and showed that infants of $3\frac{1}{2}$ to $7\frac{1}{2}$ months looked preferentially to the parent whose voice was heard.

I am drawing a distinction here between "arbitrary and natural" relations and other arbitrary relations for a number of reasons. First, there are some inherent constraints on the character of naturally occurring sounds produced by any object or event: A falling feather cannot make a loud impact sound when it strikes a surface. Properties of a feather specified to the visual system during its descent allow one to predict the type of sound (or not) made by the floating, not plummeting, feather. In addition, because these events are "natural," and because they occur with regularity in the environment, infants are more likely to be exposed to them.

What are some examples of events that may be called arbitrary/natural? Most auditory–visual examples come from the realm of animate objects, both human and animal. The sounds that animals make—a barking dog, a purring cat, a speaking human—belong to this category, as opposed to the example of a falling feather given earlier. The sounds made by inanimate objects are usually determined by their shape, substance, type of move-ment—all properties available to touch and vision. In contrast, vocalizations result from a combination of structural properties that are not always visible to the observer. Other examples can be drawn from correspondences between sights and smells. These relations always occur together in the environment, but there is little or no redundancy between information available to the sense modalities. The smell and consistency of a banana originate in its molecular structure, which cannot be observed by the human observer unaided by technology. Only through repeated exposures to a banana can one determine that the two go together. The relation between the odor of a particular nursing mother and the sight of her face, as distinct from that of an unfamiliar nursing woman, is another instance, although recognition of the mother's odor has been shown by infants as young as 2 weeks (Cernoch & Porter, 1985). This may well be an example of "preparedness" to learn particular associations because of their potential importance (Lickliter, 1991; Reardon & Bushnell, 1988).

There is experimental evidence that infants can learn arbitrary/natural relations from a number of studies, particularly those examining perception of auditory–visual events. In one of the first studies purporting to examine whether infants can learn to associate arbitrary pairings of sights and sounds, Lyons-Ruth (1977) familiarized 4-month-old infants to an object that moved in synchrony with a sound coming from the same location. On a subsequent test, the sound emanated from a new location where either the familiarized or a novel object was placed. Infants looked away from the object more often when it was a novel combination of object and sound. On the other hand, it is not clear whether this event should have been characterized as arbitrary at all. The sound was spatially coincident and it was temporally synchronized with movements of the object. When Lawson (1980) looked more systematically at these variables, she found that infants learned the relation of object and sound when the two were spatially coincident and synchronized, but not when they were separated in space.

In some cases infants may learn about multimodal events purely on the basis of association—a sight and sound and smell may occur together repeatedly. In other cases, a specific face and a specific voice may go together and learning may be facilitated by the natural constraints built into the relation. Along these lines, repeated pairing of events is not always sufficient for intermodal learning to occur. Bahrick (1988) demonstrated that only the 3-month-old infants exposed to appropriate and synchronous film and soundtrack pairs in her experiment showed intermodal learning. Those provided with irrelevant or incorrect pairings did not. Similar results have been reported by Legerstee (1990). She presented infants, 3–4 months of age, vowel sounds (/a/ or /u/) accompanied by a visible adult speaker who silently articulated the appropriate vowel sound or the other, nonmatching vowel. Infants exposed to concordant presentations imitated the vowels; those exposed to the inappropriate pairings did not. Finally, Kuhl, Williams, and Meltzoff (1991) reported that infants do not match nonspeech sounds to visually presented vowels, although infants clearly match specific vowel sounds and shapes (Kuhl & Meltzoff, 1982).

Typical Relations. A third classification of intermodal relations is one describing those that are typically in the environment but are only partially specified by amodal invariants. These may be characterized as "typical" relations. For example, heavy objects often produce deeper and louder sounds on impact than do lighter objects, but there is some overlap depending on the composition of the impacting object and the substance of the surface. A second example may be found in the approach of an object. A looming object should get larger in the field of view as its sound becomes louder; on the other hand, persons may deliberately modulate their voices as they approach. Infants may easily detect the relations in the first, object, event (Walker-Andrews & Lennon, 1985), but find the second situation, involving a person, more difficult (Schiff, Benasich, & Bornstein, 1989). Detection of these relations may require more complex perceptual learning of arbitrary and/or amodal relations.

A recent experiment by Walker-Andrews et al. (1991) examined $3\frac{1}{2}$-, 4-, 6-, and 7-month-old infants' perception of intermodal information specifying gender across dynamic displays of faces and voices. Six- and 7-month-old infants looked preferentially at a female face when a female voice was heard and a male face when a male voice was heard. Infants at $3\frac{1}{2}$ months provided no evidence for intermodal matching. Four-month-old infants looked preferentially at the faces and voices based on gender information only after the second trial of the experiment. How did the infants accomplish the experimental task? They may have learned the intermodal correspond-ences over time, treating same-gender faces and voices as if the relations were entirely arbitrary. Conversely, they could have detected any number of invariant intermodal relations that typically define gender categories in the environment. Further research into how infants make these matches is needed in order to decide whether gender face/voice information is marked by typical or artificial/natural relations.

QUALIFYING FACTORS

A number of factors, some intrinsic to stimulus information and some characterizing the infant, will affect the perception of intermodal relations. Some of these are discussed briefly before presenting one additional type of intermodal relation.

Asymmetries

Throughout the literature on infants' intermodal perception there are indications that because the sense modalities do not mature at the same rate, intermodal abilities do not develop apace. Some investigators argue that infants are more sensitive to visual than tactual information (Rose & Ruff, 1987), that oral exploration leads to different results at test than manual exploration, and/or that auditory information dominates visual information in young infants (Lewkowicz, 1988). Further, it is typically accepted that intermodal perception cannot be "better than" intramodal perception (Bahrick, 1992).

Certainly it is the case that the auditory system is more mature than the visual system at birth. Lewkowicz (1988) concludes, in fact, that it is only between 6 and 10 months of age that the "visual modality begins to assert itself functionally when in competition with the auditory modality" (p. 182). It may be true also that, although the tactual modality develops earlier than vision, the latter may dominate in shape perception. Bushnell and Weinberger (1987) asserted that information detected visually serves a directive, goal-setting role for infants' manual exploration, for example. It is crucial, however, to point out that it is the interaction between intermodal abilities and the properties of objects and events that is important. Bushnell and Weinberger (1987) acknowledged this point, stating that if a tactually presented feature of an object is a particularly salient one, its absence might well be noted on a discrepancy trial. I would argue that the type of relation (amodal, arbitrary/natural, arbitrary/artificial, typical) is critical as well. Discrepancies in objects and events marked by typical relations should be less obvious than ones created for events usually marked by amodal relations.

Whether the development of intermodal perception is limited by the development of perception within modalities is another question. Granted, if the infants' visual acuity is not fine enough to allow for detection of details such as the movement of an isolated part of an object in synchrony with a sound, the infant is unlikely to perceive the intermodal relation. In other cases infants' intermodal perception seems more advanced than their intramodal perception. In the situation most familiar to me, infants appear to differentiate bimodally presented expressions of affect earlier than either auditory or visual ones. Walker-Andrews and Lennon (1991) found that

5-month-old infants habituated to a face and voice dishabituated to a change in voice (from happy to angry, angry to happy, or angry to sad), but those infants habituated to a checkerboard accompanied by a vocal expression did not. Other work by Caron and his colleagues (Caron, Caron, & MacLean, 1988) showed that 7-month-old infants cannot make discriminations of some dynamic facial expressions without an accompanying vocal expression. We cannot predict infants' performance on intermodal tasks simply by gauging the development of each sensory modality, although should infants of a particular age fail to show cross-modal matching we must determine whether infants of this age can make the appropriate intramodal distinctions. Finally, we need to be aware of the constant recalibration that may be occurring within and between each modality during development that may lead to inconsistent results from experiment to experiment (see Handel, 1988, for a brief discussion of this point).

Characteristics of Events

As stated earlier, events are nested within events within still larger events. In intermodal perception, in particular, the "grain" or the level of the event being attended to is critical. Simply being further away from an event will change one's ability to detect events at finer and finer levels. In an extreme example, it can even change the intermodal relations themselves. Lightning seen from a distance is accompanied by thunder, which is heard seconds later. Texture is not as discernible at a distance when one's acuity has become less sharp. Less obvious, perhaps, are the effects of familiarity, complexity, naturalness, and animacy on intermodal perception. All of these factors are important, and each of them can be implicated in differences found in infants' intermodal abilities from experiment to experiment. One or two comparisons should illustrate how these factors play a role.

In a recent article Lewkowicz (1992) contrasted results from a set of studies by Spelke et al. (1983) and by Bahrick (1987) with results from other investigators (e.g., Lewkowicz, 1985; Moore & Gibbons, 1988). The first set of studies indicated that infants are sensitive to synchrony, an amodal relation, by 4 months of age; the latter set failed to find auditory/visual matching of synchrony or rate until much later, if at all. Lewkowicz suggested that several differences between the stimulus objects/events used in the studies might have affected the results. I reiterate these and point out some others.

One difference between the stimulus events used in the studies Lewkowicz reviews is that Spelke and Bahrick used objects that moved in space, whereas spatially static objects were presented in most studies that reported no evidence for intermodal matching. In addition, the selection of sounds to accompany the visually presented events has been quite different.

More specifically, in Lewkowicz (1985) the sound that occurred in synchrony with a flashing checkerboard was a 1000-Hz tone. In contrast, Spelke recorded the sounds made by an object striking another object and Bahrick recorded the sounds made by the objects (single marble or 43 marbles colliding in a Plexiglas cylinder) as they were moved. Finally, in the studies in which intermodal matching has not been found, the rates of movement have typically been more rapid that those used by Bahrick, Spelke, and others who reported intermodal matching by infants at 4 months.

Each of these differences may be important to infants' intermodal perception, in some cases because of limits on infants' intramodal abilities and in others because the events are characterized by different types of relations. I would argue that infants have often failed to detect intermodal relations that have been presented to them, simply because the relations were arbitrary or typical rather than amodal ones. Infants have been less successful in matching sights and sounds when the two are paired arbitrarily rather than recorded live or carefully contrived to closely resemble the "real thing" (Bahrick, 1992; Kuhl et al., 1991). Such failures are, of course, interesting in themselves because they should allow us to bracket or determine the extent of infants' intermodal abilities. Dickson (1994) addressed this particular issue more fully. Infants of 4 months were tested for the detection of rate and synchrony presented either by videotaped recordings of an actual event (a bouncing ball) or a computer-generated display mimicking the event. Infants looked primarily at the nonspecified event, demonstrating intermodal perception, although not in the usual fashion. Others (e.g., Spelke, 1985) have reported similar preferences for nonspecified events using the intermodal preference procedure, especially when relatively simple events are used. Of particular interest to us here is that infants showed looking preferences for the slower moving event in a pair only when presented the computer-generated displays. Such displays seem particularly susceptible to the influence of intrinsic, stimulus-specific preferences.

SPECULATION: COMMON AFFORDANCES

The types of intermodal relations presented throughout this chapter primarily have captured quantifiable aspects of stimulus information. We can measure the tempo of a visual event and an auditory event and determine whether the two are equivalent. The shape of an object can be outlined either by hand or by eye. In some cases, as I have indicated, it is more difficult to do this, especially when the basis of a relation is not easily discernible, but usually the relation can be described. Consequently, it is relatively easy to investigate infants' perception of these types of invariant relations.

Not yet considered, however, is another type of intermodal relation, one that is more abstract and may subsume all of the others presented so far. Specifically, *common affordances* also provide a basis for unity. E. J. Gibson (1983) illustrated this possibility with several examples, one of which follows:

> My last example of an intermodal invariant is for a *place*. A cliff is a horizontal surface ending in a drop-off. One can walk or crawl to the edge and feel manually or by putting out a foot that the surface of support affords locomotion only so far. It is a ground only to the edge, and terrestrial animals fall if they proceed over the edge. But adults, if they are looking, do not do so, and neither do precocial animals of many species, such as newborn kids (Walk & Gibson, 1961). They do not have to poke with a hand, foot, or cane to know where the surface of support stops because there is visual information for a surface of support provided by characteristic texture, reflectance, and layout. The transition at the edge is optically well-defined by differential texture gradients, motion parallax, and progressive occlusion of texture elements of the surface below as the animal's head is moved. The affordance of haptic and visual information for the drop-off is so identical that a creature at a cliff edge is quite unaware of modality-specific experiences; the experience is perfectly unified, and the cliff is avoided. (p. 36)

Facial and vocal expressions share a common affordance as well. Although I have discussed experiments conducted on infants' intermodal perception of emotions in terms of specific invariant relations such as synchrony and rate, infants look preferentially to a facial expression accompanied by its characteristic vocal expression even when many of the relations are distorted or eliminated (Walker, 1982; Walker-Andrews, 1986, 1988). Both face and voice can specify the affordance for a friendly interaction versus some other, less benevolent one. Harris (1989), in particular, emphasized that it may be more "appropriate to interpret the results [of intermodal matching reported by Walker, 1982; Walker-Andrews, 1986] as showing that infants can treat quite disparate types of information as belonging together" (p. 27), although he proposed that the basis for intermodal matching is either concurrent experience of particular facial expressions and tones of voices or innate sensitivity to such information. In my view, the meaning that is expressed vocally is also expressed in behavior that can be seen. If infants detect this invariant information, they may be perceiving something abstract and amodal that is equivalent to the affordance of the entire expressive behavior.

A number of abilities demonstrated by infants in studies of intermodal perception may exemplify this type of intermodal relation. Examples include intermodal perception of affective expressions, cross-modal matching of number (Starkey, Spelke, & Gelman, 1982), metaphorical matching (Phillips, Wagner, Fells, & Lynch, 1990; Wagner, Winner, Cicchetti, & Gardner, 1981), and perhaps some instances of imitation (Meltzoff & Moore, 1977). As infants become progressively more skilled at detecting invariants that specify significant properties or events in the world, *meaning* or common affordance may become the most important of the intermodal relations to perception.

SUMMARY

One of the major ideas underlying the categories of intermodal relations proposed here is that the "learning of new meaning is an education of attention rather than an accrual of associations" (J. J. Gibson, 1966, p. 320). The developing perceiver, faced with a world consisting of multimodal objects and events, becomes increasingly sensitive to invariant relationships that specify properties of that world. We should continue to study the development of intermodal perception as it may well be a model for the process of differentiation in all of perception. One step is to describe in better detail the types of intermodal relations available to the infant and then to determine whether infants respond in specific and adaptive ways to that information.

REFERENCES

Allen, T. W., Walker, K., Symonds, L., & Marcell, M. (1977). Intrasensory and intersensory perception of temporal sequences during infancy. *Developmental Psychology, 13*, 225–229.

Bahrick, L. E. (1983). Infants' perception of substance and temporal synchrony. *Infant Behavior and Development, 6*, 429–450.

Bahrick, L. E. (1987). Infants' intermodal perception of two levels of temporal structure in natural events. *Infant Behavior and Development, 10*, 387–416.

Bahrick, L. E. (1988). Intermodal learning in infancy: Learning on the basis of two kinds of invariant relations in audible and visible events. *Child Development, 59*, 197–209.

Bahrick, L. E. (1992, May). *The development of infants' detection of arbitrary audiovisual relations.* Paper presented at the International Conference on Infant Studies, Miami.

Birch, H. G., & Lefford, A. (1963). Intersensory development in children. *Monographs of the Society for Research in Child Development, 28*(5, Serial No. 89).

Bower, T. G. R. (1974). *Development in infancy.* San Francisco: Freeman.

Bryant, P. (1974). *Perception and understanding in young children: An experimental approach.* London: Methuen.

Burnham, D., Earnshaw, L. J., & Olymbios, P. (1986, April). *Facilitation of mother/stranger face discrimination by voices.* International Conference on Infant Studies, Los Angeles.

Bushnell, E. W. (1986). The basis of infant visual-tactual functioning—Amodal dimensions or multimodal compounds? In L. P. Lipsitt & C. K. Rovee-Collier (Eds.), *Advances in infancy research* (pp. 182–194). Norwood, NJ: Ablex.

Bushnell, E. W., Shaw, L., & Strauss, D. (1985). Relationship between visual and tactual exploration by 6-month-olds. *Developmental Psychology, 21*, 591–600.

Bushnell, E. W., & Weinberger, N. (1987). Infant's detection of visual-tactual discrepancies: Asymmetries that indicate a directive role of visual information. *Journal of Experimental Psychology: Human Perception and Performance, 13*, 601–608.

Caron, A. J., Caron, R. F., & MacLean, D. J. (1988). Infant discrimination of naturalistic emotional expressions: The role of face and voice. *Child Development, 59*, 604–616.

Cernoch, J. M., & Porter, R. H. (1985). Recognition of maternal axillary odors by infants. *Child Development, 56*, 1593–1598.

Cohen, S. E. (1974). Developmental differences in infants' attentional responses to face-voice incongruity of mother and stranger. *Child Development, 45*, 1155–1158.

Dickson, L. R. (1994, April). *Intermodal perception of rate and synchrony in 4-month-olds: Computer-generated versus naturalistic displays.* Paper presented at the Human Development Conference, Pittsburgh.

Dodd, B. (1979). Lip reading in infants: Attention to speech presented in- and out-of-synchrony. *Cognitive Psychology, 11*, 478–484.

Gibson, E. J. (1969). *Principles of perceptual learning and development.* Englewood Cliffs, NJ: Prentice-Hall.

Gibson, E. J. (1983). Development of knowledge about intermodal unity: Two views. In L. S. Liben (Ed.), *Piaget and the foundations of knowledge* (pp. 19–41). Hillsdale, NJ: Lawrence Erlbaum Associates.

Gibson, E. J., & Walker, A. S. (1984). Development of knowledge of visual-tactual affordances of substance. *Child Development, 55*, 453–460.

Gibson, J. J. (1966). *The senses considered as perceptual systems.* Boston: Houghton Mifflin.

Gibson, J. J. (1979/1986). *The ecological approach to visual perception.* Hillsdale, NJ: Lawrence Erlbaum Associates.

Handel, S. (1988). Space is to time as vision is to audition: Seductive but misleading. *Journal of Experimental Psychology: Human Perception and Performance, 14*, 315–317.

Harris, P. L. (1983). Infant cognition. In M. M. Haith & J. J. Campos (Eds.), *Infancy and developmental psychobiology* (pp. 689–782). New York: Wiley.

Harris, P. L. (1989). *Children and emotion.* Oxford: Basil Blackwell.

Kuhl, P. K., & Meltzoff, A. N. (1982). The bimodal perception of speech in infancy. *Science, 218*, 1138–1141.

Kuhl, P. K., Williams, K. A., & Meltzoff, A. N. (1991). Cross-modal speech perception in adults and infants using nonspeech auditory stimuli. *Journal of Experimental Psychology: Human Perception and Performance, 17*, 829–840.

Lawson, K. R. (1980). Spatial and temporal congruity and auditory-visual integration in infants. *Developmental Psychology, 16*, 185–192.

Legerstee, M. (1990). Infants use multimodal information to imitate speech sounds. *Infant Behavior and Development, 13*, 343–354.

Lewkowicz, D. J. (1985). Bisensory response to temporal frequency in 4-month-old infants. *Developmental Psychology, 21*, 306–317.

Lewkowicz, D. J. (1986). Developmental changes in infants' bisensory response to synchronous durations. *Infant Behavior and Development, 9*, 335–353.

Lewkowicz, D. J. (1988). Sensory dominance in infants: 2. Ten-month-old infants' response to auditory-visual compounds. *Developmental Psychology, 24*, 172–182.

Lewkowicz, D. J. (1992). Infants' response to temporally based intersensory equivalence: The effect of synchronous sounds on visual preferences for moving stimuli. *Infant Behavior and Development, 15*, 297–324.

Lewkowicz, D. J., & Turkewitz, G. (1981). Intersensory interaction in newborns: Modification of visual preferences following exposure to sound. *Child Development, 52*, 827–832.

Lickliter, R. (1991). Context and animal behavior II: The role of conspecifics in species-typical perceptual development. *Ecological Psychology, 3*, 11–24.

Lyons-Ruth, K. (1977). Bimodal perception in infancy: Response to auditory-visual incongruity. *Child Development, 48,* 820–827.

Meltzoff, A. N., & Borton, R. W. (1979). Intermodal matching by human neonates. *Nature, 282,* 403–404.

Meltzoff, A. N., & Moore, M. K. (1977). Imitation of facial and manual gestures by human neonates. *Science, 198,* 75–78.

Mendelson, M. J., & Haith, M. M. (1976). The relation between audition and vision in the human newborn. *Monographs of the Society for Research in Child Development, 41*(4, Serial No. 167).

Mendelson, M. J., & Ferland, M. B. (1982). Auditory-visual transfer in four-mouth-old infants. *Child Development, 53,* 1022–1027.

Moore, D. S. G., & Gibbons, J. L. (1988, April). *Early auditory and visual integration in 4-month-old infants.* Paper presented at the International Conference on Infant Studies, Washington, DC.

Phillips, R. D., Wagner, S. H., Fells, C. A., & Lynch, M. (1990). Do infants recognize emotion in facial expressions?: Categorical and "metaphorical" evidence. *Infant Behavior and Development, 13,* 71–84.

Piaget, J. (1954). *The construction of reality in the child.* New York: Basic Books.

Reardon, P., & Bushnell, E. W. (1988). Infants' sensitivity to arbitrary pairings of color and taste. *Infant Behavior and Development, 11,* 245–250.

Rochat, P. (1983). Oral touch in young infants: Responses to variations of nipple characteristics in the first months of life. *International Journal of Behavioral Development, 6,* 123–133.

Rochat, P. (1987). Mouthing and grasping in neonates: Evidence for the early detection of what hard or soft substances afford for action. *Infant Behavior and Development, 10,* 435–449.

Rolfe, S. A., & Day, R. H. (1981). Effects of the similarity and dissimilarity between familiarization and test objects on recognition memory in infants following uni- and bi-modal familiarization. *Child Development, 52,* 1308–1312.

Rose, S. A., Gottfried, A. W., & Bridger, W. H. (1981). Cross-modal transfer in 6-month-old infants. *Developmental Psychology, 17,* 661–669.

Rose, S. A., & Ruff, H. A. (1987). Cross-modal abilities in human infants. In J. D. Osofsky (Ed.), *Handbook of infant development* (pp. 318–362). New York: Wiley.

Schiff, W., Benasich, A. A., & Bornstein, M. H. (1989). Infant sensitivity to audiovisually coherent events. *Psychological Research, 51,* 102–106.

Spelke, E. S. (1979). Perceiving bimodally specified events in infancy. *Developmental Psychology, 15,* 626–636.

Spelke, E. S. (1985). Preferential-looking methods as tools for the study of cognition in infancy. In G. Gottlieb & N. Krasnegor (Eds.), *Measurement of audition and vision in the first year of postnatal life* (pp. 323–363). Norwood, NJ: Ablex.

Spelke, E. S., Born, W. S., & Chu, F. (1983). Perception of moving, sounding objects by four-month-old infants. *Perception, 12,* 719–732.

Spelke, E. S., & Owsley, C. J. (1979). Intermodal exploration and knowledge in infancy. *Infant Behavior and Development, 2,* 13–27.

Starkey, P., Spelke, E. S., & Gelman, R. (1982, March). *Detection of intermodal numerical correspondence by human infants.* Paper presented at the International Conference on Infant Studies, Austin, TX.

Streri, A., Molina, M., & Millet, G. (1990, April). *Tactual representation in 2-month-old infants.* Paper presented at the International Conference on Infant Studies, Montreal.

Streri, A., Pecheux, M., & Vurpillot, E. (1984, April). *Crossmodal transfer of form in 5-month-old infants.* Paper presented at the International Conference on Infant Studies, New York.

Wagner, S., Winner, E., Cicchetti, D., & Gardner, H. (1981). "Metaphorical" mapping in human infants. *Child Development, 52,* 728–731.

Walker, A. S. (1982). Intermodal perception of expressive behaviors by human infants. *Journal of Experimental Child Psychology, 33,* 514–535.

Walker-Andrews, A. S. (1986). Intermodal perception of expressive behaviors: Relation of eye and voice? *Developmental Psychology, 22,* 373–377.

Walker-Andrews, A. S. (1988). Infants' perception of the affordances of expressive behaviors. In C. K. Rovee-Collier (Ed.), *Advances in infancy research* (pp. 173–221). Norwood, NJ: Ablex.

Walker-Andrews, A. S., Bahrick, L. E., Raglioni, S. S., & Diaz, I. (1991). Infants' bimodal perception of gender. *Ecological Psychology, 3,* 55–75.

Walker-Andrews, A. S., & Lennon, E. M. (1985). Auditory-visual perception of changing distance by human infants. *Child Development, 56,* 544–548.

Walker-Andrews, A. S., & Lennon, E. (1991). Infants' discrimination of vocal expressions: Contributions of auditory and visual information. *Infant Behavior and Development, 14,* 131–142.

Wertheimer, M. (1961). Psychomotor coordination of auditory and visual space at birth. *Science, 134,* 1692.

Willats, P. (1985, April). *Relations between visual and tactual processing in 6- and 12-month-old infants.* Presented at the Society for Research in Child Development, Toronto.

PART TWO

EFFECTS OF EARLY EXPERIENCE
AND NEURAL MECHANISMS
IN ANIMALS

CHAPTER FOUR

Prenatal Components of Intersensory Development in Precocial Birds

Robert Lickliter
Heather Banker
Virginia Polytechnic Institute and State University

The sequence in which the sensory systems become functional is important for comparative and evolutionary purposes, and it also provides a testing ground for our most basic conceptions of the epigenesis of behavior.

(Gottlieb, 1971b, p. 67)

Although scientific interest in the prenatal development of behavior has to some extent languished since its formative beginning early in this century (see Anokhin, 1964; Carmichael, 1933; Coghill, 1929; Gottlieb, 1973a; Hamburger, 1963; Herrick & Coghill, 1915; Hooker, 1952; Kuo, 1976; Oppenheim, 1982; Preyer, 1885; Windle, 1944), the last decade has seen a resurgence of interest in the role of prenatal experience on subsequent postnatal behavior (DeCasper & Spence, 1986; Fifer, 1987; Gottlieb, 1985, 1988; Gottlieb, Tomlinson, & Radell, 1989; Hepper, 1988; Lickliter, in press; Lickliter & Stoumbos, 1992; Radell & Gottlieb, 1992; Smotherman & Robinson, 1985, 1987, 1992). In a general sense, these studies of avian and mammalian neonates have all served to demonstrate the important role of prenatal sensory experience in the development of postnatal perceptual preferences. In particular, these studies have made clear that normally occurring embryonic sensory stimulation can play an active role in the construction of species-specific perceptual preferences evident after birth or hatching.

An appreciation of the constructive role of experiential factors in the achievement of behavioral traits or characteristics is a core feature of a *developmental systems perspective* on developmental issues (see Gottlieb,

1991; Lickliter & Berry, 1990; Oyama, 1985, 1989). In its most general sense, a developmental systems perspective holds that phenotypic traits or characters are not transmitted in the genes nor are they contained in features of the organism's environment. Rather, traits, characters, and capacities are always constructed by the complex coaction of organic, organismic, and environmental factors operating during individual development. As a result, the function of the genes, the physical surround, or any other influence on development can be understood only in relation to the developmental system of which they are a part. In other words, control for developmental outcomes resides in the structure and nature of relationships between factors or variables, not in individual variables themselves. Each factor or variable may appear to control some aspect of the system, but what it controls and how it affects the system are always dependent on features of other components of the system.

This pattern of diffuse control and reciprocal determination (for more detailed discussions of these ideas see Gottlieb, 1991; Lewontin & Levins, 1988; Oyama, 1989; Thelen, 1989) is well illustrated in the development of early intersensory functioning. Indeed, as noted over 20 years ago by Gottlieb (1968, 1971b), a pioneering investigator of embryonic sensory experience, the onset and subsequent development of each sensory system affords a potentially fertile testing ground for many of our conceptions regarding the process of epigenesis. All sensory systems begin to develop prenatally and in some precocial animal species are structurally mature before birth. Importantly, onset of function within the various sensory modalities appears to proceed in an invariant pattern among vertebrate species. This temporal sequence of onset of sensory function (tactile → vestibular → chemical → auditory → visual) appears to hold whether the young of a particular species are born in a precocial or an altricial condition (Alberts, 1984; Bradley & Mistretta, 1975; Gottlieb, 1968, 1971b). Of course, in precocial infants the capacity for auditory and visual function develops prenatally, whereas in most altricial infants auditory and visual sensitivity does not develop until after birth or hatching.

The fact that the sensory systems of birds and mammals do not become functional at the same time in development raises the interesting question of how sensory systems and their respective stimulative histories might influence one another, especially during the prenatal period. For example, it is possible that sensory deprivation (or sensory enhancement) within a late-developing system (i.e., the visual system) could potentially result in either the acceleration or deceleration of the development of behavior mediated by earlier developing sensory systems (Gottlieb, 1971b, 1973a; Tees, 1976, 1986). Of course, manipulations of early sensory experience may have greater or lesser impact depending on what kind of sensory input to specific modalities is manipulated relative to the developmental sequence of sensory competence (Burnstine, Greenough, & Tees, 1984; Radell & Gottlieb, 1992).

One method for studying the influence of timing of onset of sensory input on early perceptual development is to withhold or provide input to a particular modality at atypical times, thereby temporally rearranging the experiential opportunities among emerging sensory systems (Gottlieb, 1973b; Turkewitz & Mellon, 1989). To date, the vast majority of studies concerned with the experimental manipulation of perinatal sensory experience have focused on the effects of sensory deprivation (see Burnstine et al., 1984; Riesen & Zilbert, 1975; Tees, 1976, 1986, 1990; Tees & Symons, 1987). On the other hand, relatively little attention has been paid to the consequences of providing sensory experience earlier in development than when it would ordinarily be available. Although there are a number of plausible reasons for this disparity, it is certainly the case that experiments involving unusually early sensory experience are often difficult to conduct, especially when prenatal manipulations are required.

Despite the fact that there has been little experimental concern with the impact of unusually early sensory experience on perceptual development, several interesting and testable hypotheses regarding the role of timing of sensory experience have emerged in recent years. For example, Turkewitz and Kenny (1982, 1985) offered a theory of early perceptual development that centers around the role of developmental limitations of sensory/perceptual experience. Turkewitz and Kenny argued that sensory limitations during early development both reduce information and mediate the timing of the introduction of information, thereby reducing the amount of competition between maturing sensory modalities. As discussed earlier, under undisturbed or natural conditions these limitations on sensory experience are not random, but rather are regular and orderly, as the sensory systems become functional in an invariant sequence in both birds and mammals, including humans. Without this pattern of limited sensory functioning, a later developing system could interfere with earlier developing systems when the latter are still undergoing development. From Turkewitz and Kenny's perspective, limitations on sensory experience during early stages of development are thus not handicaps or deficiencies to be overcome by the infant, but rather provide an important source of structure and order that help to determine the nature of early intersensory relationships. In particular, limitations of sensory input may serve to reduce the quantity and/or quality of sensory stimulation available to the young organism at sensitive stages of perinatal development. If this is indeed the case, then altering the timing of onset of function of a sensory system during prenatal development could result in a change in the nature of early postnatal intersensory relationships.

In this chapter we review a number of recent studies that have employed this approach with precocial birds and that have demonstrated the importance of asynchronous sensory system development to early perceptual organization. In particular, these studies have established the value of an "early exposure" procedure during the perinatal period to the investigation of how particular sensory experiences at particular times impact the nature of both intrasensory and intersensory perceptual development. Work with mammalian infants has also found similar results, but is not reviewed here (e.g., see Foreman & Altaha, 1991; Kenny & Turkewitz, 1986). Just as importantly, the studies reviewed in this chapter also serve to illustrate the dynamic, constructive nature of early perceptual development and lend empirical support to the notions of diffuse control and reciprocal determination central to a "developmental systems" perspective of development.

THE EARLY EXPOSURE PROCEDURE

Because their prenatal development takes place in an egg rather than *in utero*, birds are obviously more accessible to embryonic manipulations than are mammalian species. In addition, precocial birds' auditory systems begin functioning embryonically, overlapping with the later onset of visual capability (Gottlieb, 1968, 1971b; Freeman & Vince, 1974; Heaton, 1972; Konishi, 1973). Although the precocial avian embryo is responsive to visual stimulation embryonically (Heaton, 1973; Oppenheim, 1968), the embryo does not ordinarily experience patterned visual stimulation until after hatching from the egg. It is possible, however, to remove this constraint typically present in the embryo's developmental context and to provide precocial avian embryos unusually early exposure to patterned visual stimulation and/or altered auditory stimulation. This can be accomplished by the relatively simple experimental procedure of removing the shell and inner-shell membrane over the air space at the large end of the egg several days prior to hatching (see Oppenheim, Levin, & Harth, 1973). The embryo's bill normally penetrates the air space during this period of incubation, and the embryo becomes capable of pulmonary respiration; the embryo's head can thus be exposed at this time without negatively affecting the bird's survivability or hatchability (Gottlieb, 1971a, 1988; Heaton & Galleher, 1981; Lickliter, 1990a, 1990b). This egg opening procedure allows enhancement or augmentation of embryonic auditory stimulation and/or visual stimulation during the days prior to hatching (Gottlieb et al., 1989; Lickliter, 1990a, 1990b; Lickliter & Hellewell, 1992; Lickliter & Stoumbos, 1991).

Over the last several years our laboratory has utilized this procedure with bobwhite quail (*Colinus virginianus*), a small but highly precocial bird. Bobwhite quail chicks are particularly well suited to the investigation of early intersensory development. Like many other precocial birds, incubator-hatched quail chicks exhibit a naive attraction to their maternal call and are capable of discriminating between it and similar conspecific vocalizations in the period shortly before as well as immediately after hatching (Heaton & Galleher, 1981; Heaton, Miller, & Goodwin, 1978; Lickliter & Virkar, 1989). This species-specific auditory responsiveness provides a useful and reliable means of assessing the impact of both altered auditory experience and unusually early visual experience on chicks' normal auditory functioning. In addition, unlike most other precocial birds, bobwhite quail are able to synchronize their hatching with that of their broodmates. This hatching synchrony appears to depend on the bird's prenatal exposure to auditory stimulation from neighboring embryos of their clutch (Vince, 1972, 1973), indicating a high degree of sensitivity on the part of bobwhite chicks to the stimulative aspects of their auditory environment even before hatching.

The fact that the quail chick's auditory system has had more prenatal experience at the time of hatching than has the visual system suggests that the quail hatchling's auditory system should be more fully developed and functional than its visual system in the period immediately following hatching. In addition, the prenatal experiential precedence of the auditory over the visual system suggests that quail hatchlings might initially utilize auditory over visual cues in the immediate posthatch period. Later, as the visual system becomes more fully functional and experienced, hatchlings are likely to require integrated audiovisual cues to control their early perceptual and social preferences. Recent evidence from studies conducted in our laboratory and discussed later supports the existence of such a functional "cue hierarchy" and indicates that the bobwhite quail is both an appropriate and useful model for the study of the prenatal mechanisms underlying early intersensory integration.

PERINATAL SENSORY DOMINANCE PATTERNS

The auditory and visual modalities are known to play an important role in the control of early social behavior of precocial birds (Boyd & Fabricius, 1965; Gottlieb, 1971a; Smith & Bird, 1963). Nonetheless, the nature of the relationship between the auditory and visual systems and the ways in which these two later developing sensory modalities interact during the course of development have received little experimental attention. A study conducted by Lickliter and Virkar (1989) addressed this issue and examined the interaction between normally occurring auditory and visual stimulation in the control of social preferences in bobwhite quail hatchlings. The results of these experiments reveal a hierarchy in the functional priority of the auditory and visual systems in the days immediately following hatching. At 1 and 2 days of age, species identification was found to depend on the auditory component of maternal stimulation. Chicks consistently required only the maternal call to direct their filial behavior at 24 and 48 hr following hatching. At 3 and 4 days of age, combined maternal auditory and visual stimulation was found to be necessary to direct chicks' social preferences. However, even at these later ages the auditory modality remained dominant over the visual modality in eliciting responsiveness to the maternal hen. Chicks consistently responded to species-typical auditory cues (the maternal call) in preference to species-typical visual cues (a stuffed hen) during the days immediately following hatching (Lickliter & Virkar, 1989). In addition, chicks did not respond to species-specific visual cues when presented alone (i.e., without auditory cues) at any of the ages tested.

These findings conform well to what is known about the neuroembryological development of the sensory systems; as discussed earlier, the auditory system develops in advance of the visual system (Bradley & Mistretta, 1975; Gottlieb, 1968, 1971b; Mistretta & Bradley, 1978). As a result, at the time of birth or hatching these two sensory systems have had different amounts of prenatal experience. This precedence of auditory over visual experience may help to explain why precocial avian hatchlings initially utilize auditory over visual cues in directing their early perceptual and social preferences. For example, we found that the bobwhite maternal call is an extremely compelling stimulus for young quail hatchlings, easily outweighing the effects of species-typical visual cues during early postnatal development. A similar pattern of early auditory dominance has also been reported for other precocial birds, including domestic chicks (Gottlieb, 1971a; Gottlieb & Simner, 1969) and ducklings (Gottlieb, 1971a; Johnston & Gottlieb, 1981, 1985; Storey & Shapiro, 1979). We wondered to what extent this pattern of early sensory dominance is influenced by the nature of prenatal sensory experience.

EFFECTS OF UNUSUALLY EARLY VISUAL EXPERIENCE ON SENSORY DOMINANCE PATTERNS

Turkewitz and Kenny (1985) proposed that differences in the functional relationship between sensory systems (i.e., dominance hierarchies) could stem from differences in the time of the development of the various systems in relation to each other. If this is indeed the case, then altering the asynchronous onset of function of the auditory and visual systems should potentially result in a change in the nature of early intersensory relationships. Specifically, accelerating the onset of function of the visual system so that it becomes experienced prenatally should potentially alter the usual prepotence of the auditory system during early postnatal development. In this light, a study was designed to assess the impact of unusually early (prenatal) visual experience on the bobwhite quail's species-typical pattern of early sensory dominance (Lickliter, in press).

Maternally naive, incubator-hatched bobwhite quail chicks served as subjects. The typical incubation period of bobwhite quail is 23 days. The embryo's bill normally penetrates the air space of the egg early on Day 21 of incubation, and it is at this time that the embryo begins to respire through its lungs and vocalize (Freeman & Vince, 1974). We removed a portion of the shell and inner shell membrane over the air space of the egg of each subject during the second half of the 21st day of incubation. Following removal of the shell, opened eggs were placed in a portable incubator until hatching on Day 23. This incubator was equipped with a clear Plexiglas top, allowing both observation and external visual stimulation of the embryos. A preliminary experiment established that simply removing a portion of the eggshell does not alter subsequent species-typical patterns of early sensory dominance. That is, hatchlings that had undergone the egg opening procedure but did not receive exposure to prenatal visual stimulation performed as normal, unstimulated controls and demonstrated a significant preference for species-specific maternal auditory cues over species-specific maternal visual cues.

To provide unusually early visual experience, experimental embryos were exposed to a 15-watt light, pulsed at 3 cycles per second following the egg opening procedure. Depending on when they hatched, embryos were exposed to this patterned light in their incubator for a minimum of 24 hr and a maximum of 36 hr prior to hatching. As a result of this manipulation, the stimulation histories of the auditory and visual modalities were made to coincide during the final stage of the prenatal period.

Following hatching, individual chicks were given a simultaneous choice test at either 24, 48, 72, or 96 hr of age between a bobwhite maternal call paired with a stuffed model of a scaled quail (*Calipepla squamata*) hen and a chicken maternal call paired with a stuffed model of a bobwhite (*Colinus virginianus*) hen. The scaled quail and the bobwhite quail are different quail species that are similar in size, but not similar in markings or color (see Fig. 1, Lickliter & Virkar, 1989). Under these testing conditions, chicks were presented with both auditory and visual cues, but the species-specific maternal call was placed in conflict with the visual features of the species-specific hen. This required chicks to choose one sensory cue over the other in order to demonstrate a species-specific preference.

The results of interest in this experiment were the preferences for the maternal auditory and visual stimuli presented during simultaneous choice test trials. A measure of preference was derived from the duration of response to the test stimuli; an individual preference was assigned to any chick that stayed in proximity to one stimulus array for more than twice as long as the other during the course of a 5-min trial (see Lickliter & Virkar, 1989, for details).

Results of testing reveal that prenatally (visually) stimulated chicks exhibited a significant preference for the bobwhite maternal call paired with the species-atypical scaled quail hen at 24, 48, 72, and 96 hr following hatching (Lickliter, in press). At no ages did chicks respond to the bobwhite hen paired

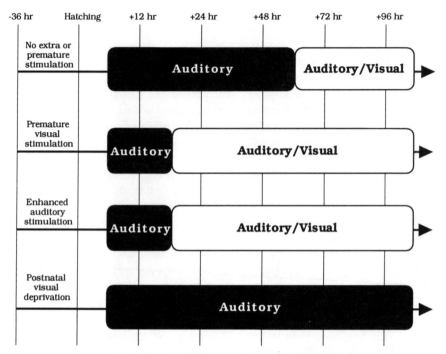

FIG. 4.1. From Banker and Lickliter (1993), Lickliter (1990a, 1990b), Lickliter
and Stoumbos (1992), Lickliter and Vikar (1989). Reprinted by permission.

with the species-atypical chicken call. In other words, the visual features of
the bobwhite hen were not sufficient to direct the chicks' social preferences
at any of the ages tested. These results demonstrate that quail hatchlings that
received unusually early visual stimulation as embryos continue to demonstrate postnatal auditory dominance in directing their early social preferences;
like normal unmanipulated chicks, prenatally stimulated chicks preferred the
bobwhite maternal call regardless of the static visual cues with which it was
paired.

One possible explanation for the apparent lack of effect found in this
experiment is that the testing situation may have provided less than adequate
visual cues, as the visual stimuli presented in the test trials were motionless
(inanimate, stationary models of hens) rather than kinetic (live, moving
hens). For example, recent work by Lewkowicz (1991, 1992) with human
infants shows an absence of early auditory dominance when the visual
component of a compound stimulus is kinetic rather than static.

Thus, a subsequent experiment employed the same procedures as described earlier, with the exception that subjects were tested in a simultaneous
choice test between the bobwhite call paired with a live scaled hen versus the
chicken maternal call paired with a live bobwhite hen. Unlike the stuffed hen

models used in the previous experiment, these live hens provided animate, kinetic visual cues to subjects in the choice test. Although control chicks continued to exhibit a significant preference for the bobwhite call paired with the scaled hen at all ages tested, chicks that received prenatal visual experience did not demonstrate a preference for either stimulus array at 72 hr following hatching and showed a significant preference for the bobwhite hen paired with the chicken maternal call at 96 hr following hatching (Lickliter, in press). These results indicate an alteration in the hierarchical relationship between the auditory and visual modalities as a result of unusually early visual experience.

EFFECTS OF UNUSUALLY EARLY VISUAL EXPERIENCE ON AUDITORY AND VISUAL RESPONSIVENESS

The fact that unusually early visual experience appeared to affect postnatal sensory dominance patterns, at least under certain conditions, prompted us to undertake another series of experiments to further examine the effects of unusually early visual experience on early perceptual organization. Specifically, rather than focusing on sensory dominance patterns, we focused on the influence of prenatal visual stimulation on later auditory, visual, and audiovisual functioning in bobwhite quail chicks (Lickliter, 1990a, 1990b). In these studies, quail embryos were provided visual stimulation with patterned light during the last 24–36 hr of incubation by removing the upper portions of the egg shell and exposing their heads as described in the previous experiment. As in the previous experiment, this procedure resulted in embryos receiving both normal auditory and abnormally early visual experience prior to hatching, thereby altering the typical prenatal pattern of reduced competition between the emerging auditory and visual systems. Following hatching, chicks were tested in simultaneous choice tests between various combinations of maternal auditory and visual cues, as described earlier.

The results of this work showed that when unusually early patterned visual stimulation is provided to embryos during the period immediately prior to hatching, chicks subsequently exhibit postnatal auditory and visual preferences different from those of unstimulated chicks. For example, when only maternal auditory cues were present during testing, quail chicks that prematurely experienced patterned light during the last 24–36 hr of incubation did not exhibit an auditory preference for the species-specific bobwhite maternal call over a species-atypical chicken maternal call at 24 hr following hatching (Lickliter, 1990a). This is in contrast to normal quail hatchlings, which show a strong auditory preference for the bobwhite maternal call over non-conspecific maternal calls (when both are presented without visual cues) at both 24 and 48 hr following hatching (Heaton, Miller,

& Goodwin, 1978; Lickliter & Virkar, 1989). Thus, it appears that earlier than normal availability of visual input can, at least under some conditions, interfere with normal functioning in the earlier developing auditory modality (see also Gottlieb et al., 1989, for an example with ducklings).

A related study examined the effects of unusually early visual experience on intersensory functioning by utilizing both maternal auditory and visual cues in the testing situation. Specifically, bobwhite chicks were presented with the bobwhite maternal call paired with a bobwhite hen model versus a chicken maternal call paired with a scaled quail hen model. This choice test thus placed species-typical maternal auditory and visual cues in competition with species-atypical auditory and visual cues. Interestingly, whereas auditory responsiveness to the maternal call was found to be reduced, intersensory functioning in quail chicks appeared accelerated by the experience of premature visual stimulation (Lickliter, 1990b). That is, birds that received patterned visual stimulation prenatally required maternal audiovisual cues to direct their social preferences as early as 24 hr following hatching (i.e., they demonstrated a significant preference for the bobwhite call paired with the bobwhite hen). In contrast, normally hatched chicks do not require maternal visual cues at this stage of postnatal development; rather, they readily direct their filial behavior on the basis of auditory cues alone at 24 and 48 hr of age. However, later in development normal chicks also require combined auditory and visual cues by 72 and 96 hr of age (Lickliter & Virkar, 1989).

Thus, by way of comparison, chicks that received visual experience as embryos exhibited intersensory capabilities at 24 hr of age comparable to those seen in unstimulated chicks at 72 hr of age. This accelerated pattern of intersensory functioning provides a clear example of sensory stimulative histories having an important influence on subsequent intersensory relationships and early perceptual organization. Providing quail chicks patterned visual stimulation prenatally resulted in species-atypical patterns of responsiveness to both maternal auditory and maternal visual cues. In keeping with the developmental systems perspective, it seems that the restricted visual experience of normally hatched embryos accounts, at least in part, for their species-typical patterns of perceptual organization.

To further examine the impact of unusually early visual experience on aspects of subsequent visual responsiveness, a related experiment tested prenatally stimulated chicks in simultaneous choice tests with species-specific auditory and visual cues, as in the previous experiment. However, the testing situation was arranged in such a way that the auditory cues presented did not permit a choice to be made. Specifically, subjects were presented with a choice test in which identical species-typical auditory cues (the same bobwhite maternal call) were paired with a stuffed bobwhite hen on one side of the testing arena and a stuffed scaled quail hen on the other side of the testing arena. This simultaneous choice test configuration required chicks to choose on the basis of available visual cues provided by the different adult hens in order to demonstrate a species-specific maternal preference, as the auditory cues did not allow a basis for decision.

The results of this experiment (Lickliter, 1990b) reveal that prenatally visually stimulated bobwhite chicks are able to utilize species-specific visual cues to direct their social preferences as early as 24 hr following hatching. On the other hand, normally hatched chicks do not utilize maternal visual cues to direct their filial behavior at either 24 or 48 hr of age. However, normally hatched chicks are able to use species-specific visual cues by 72 and 96 hr of age (Lickliter & Virkar, 1989), indicating that unusually early visual experience accelerated the use of visual information in the early postnatal period. In other words, embryonically stimulated chicks are more visually oriented than normally hatched chicks during the days immediately following hatching, even though the auditory modality remains dominant in directing perceptual preferences. It is important to remember that chicks are unable to direct their filial preferences on the basis of visual cues alone, whether or not they have received unusually early visual experience (Lickliter, 1990a; Lickliter & Virkar, 1989). Rather, all chicks require both maternal auditory and visual cues by 72 hr following hatching. Thus, although the findings of this study indicate that chicks that receive unusually early visual experience are more visually oriented than normally hatched chicks, this does not mean the auditory information is unnecessary or is ignored during the early postnatal period.

EFFECTS OF ENHANCED AUDITORY EXPERIENCE ON POSTNATAL VISUAL RESPONSIVENESS

The results of a related study from our laboratory went on to demonstrate that postnatal visual responsiveness can also be facilitated by intermodal sensory stimulation (Lickliter & Stoumbos, 1991). In this study, providing bobwhite quail embryos enhanced prenatal auditory experience altered the nature of their postnatal responsiveness to species-specific visual cues. Specifically, chicks that received exposure to increased amounts of their own embryonic vocalizations prior to hatching showed an accelerated pattern of using maternal visual cues after hatching, directing their social preferences on the basis of maternal visual cues (presented with maternal auditory cues as in the previous experiment) as early as 24 hr of age. This finding parallels the results obtained from chicks that received early visual experience as embryos, in that when the maternal auditory cues did not allow a basis for decision, subjects were able to utilize species-specific visual cues some 48 hr earlier than normally reared birds. This finding indicates that acceleration of function within the visual modality of quail chicks can be achieved in several different ways. In particular, it appears that early visual responsiveness can be facilitated by both intramodal and intermodal stimulation during the prenatal period, again illustrating the dynamic nature of early perceptual development.

This apparent lack of stimulation specificity also suggests that when a certain threshold level of sensory input is achieved, regardless of the specific modality of input, new perceptual functions can appear from antecedent conditions that do not necessarily contain those specific functions (see also Radell & Gottlieb, 1992, for a discussion of optimal threshold levels of sensory input). In other words, as described for other developmental systems, the experiential precursors to a particular phenotypic outcome are often nonlinear or nonobvious (Gottlieb, 1991), or, said another way, the control parameters involved in a developmental shift in perceptual functioning may be nonisomorphic with its effects (Thelen, 1988).

EFFECTS OF DELAYED VISUAL EXPERIENCE ON INTERSENSORY DEVELOPMENT

Because altering prenatal auditory or visual experience was found to impact aspects of postnatal auditory and visual functioning, we decided to further investigate the role of timing of onset of sensory experience to intersensory development. By way of a brief review, bobwhite quail chicks initially direct their social preferences on the basis of available maternal auditory cues. However, by 72 hr following hatching maternal vocalizations are not sufficient to direct the chicks filial behavior. Rather, at that age, chicks require both maternal auditory and maternal visual cues to direct their social preferences (Lickliter & Virkar, 1989). As a first step in examining the role of postnatal experience in this shift from auditory to intersensory functioning, we conducted an experiment that deprived chicks of postnatal visual experience during the period from hatching until testing (we did not manipulate visual experience prenatally). Specifically, we occluded the eyes of each chick immediately following hatching by means of an adhesive tape strip applied to its facial region (Banker & Lickliter, 1993). This tape strip completely covered both eyes of the young hatchling, allowing subjects to hear but not see other chicks in the period between hatching and testing. Each chick was tested individually in a simultaneous auditory choice test at either 24, 48, or 72 hr of age between the species-typical bobwhite maternal call and a chicken maternal call. The tape strip was removed from each chick 10–15 min prior to testing.

Chicks denied postnatal visual experience from hatching to testing demonstrated a significant preference for the bobwhite maternal call at all ages tested. In contrast, normally reared chicks fail to respond to maternal auditory cues (when presented without visual cues) at 72 hr following hatching (Lickliter & Virkar, 1989). The results of this experiment thus indicate that chicks denied postnatal visual stimulation show a delay in the emergence of auditory–visual functioning. This interpretation was further supported by the results of a related experiment (Banker & Lickliter, 1993). In this experiment, chicks that had their eyes occluded from hatch to testing failed to demonstrate a significant preference for species-specific visual cues (paired with species-specific auditory cues) at either 24, 48, or 72 hr following hatching. In contrast, normally reared chicks are able to rely on species-specific visual cues (if presented with auditory cues, as in this experiment) by 72 hr following hatching (Lickliter & Virkar, 1989). The fact that chicks denied postnatal visual experience did not display such a pattern of visual responsiveness likewise indicates a delay in the emergence of typical or normal intersensory functioning and suggests that postnatal visual experience is involved in the achievement of species-typical perceptual organization.

EFFECTS OF EARLY AND DELAYED VISUAL EXPERIENCE ON INTERSENSORY DEVELOPMENT

Because a delay in postnatal visual experience was found to result in a change in both species-typical auditory and species-typical visual responsiveness in quail chicks, we next conducted an experiment that manipulated the timing of the onset of visual function both prenatally and postnatally (Banker & Lickliter, 1993). Specifically, we provided subjects both unusually early (prenatal) visual experience as embryos and delayed (postnatal) visual experience as hatchlings. In other words, a limitation of sensory experience that is normally present in early development (no patterned visual stimulation prenatally) was removed, and a limitation of sensory experience that is not normally present in early development (no patterned visual stimulation postnatally) was provided to the same subjects. This experimental manipulation served to effectively reverse the normally occurring pattern of experience from the emerging auditory and visual modalities during the perinatal period. Chicks were subsequently tested for both auditory and visual responsiveness, as in the previous experiments.

Chicks that received both unusually early prenatal visual experience and delayed postnatal visual experience exhibited a pattern of auditory and visual responsiveness that was different from chicks that received only one visual manipulation. Specifically, chicks displayed species-typical patterns of auditory and visual responsiveness during the first 3 days following hatching, responding to maternal auditory and visual cues like normally reared, unmanipulated chicks. That is, the two visual experience manipulations we employed (one of which is known to accelerate intersensory functioning and one of which is known to delay intersensory functioning) appeared to cancel the effects of one another. This canceling effect resulted in the birds' demonstration of a normal or species-typical pattern of auditory and visual responsiveness, despite our prenatal and postnatal experimental manipulations. In other words, when the pattern of competition between the auditory and visual modalities was reversed, there was no apparent effect on the perceptual abilities tested. This finding suggests that, at least under these particular conditions, the influences of early and delayed visual experience during the perinatal period are relatively comparable, in that the influence of each overrode the known impact of the other. These results emphasize the importance of both the nature of the organism and the nature of sensory experience (limitation or enhancement) to our attempts to characterize the possible mechanisms of early perceptual development. The effectiveness of manipulations of sensory experience appears to depend on an array of nested variables, including those associated with the organism, the sensory stimulation provided or denied, and the larger developmental context (Lickliter, in press; Radell & Gottlieb, 1992).

Related work recently performed in our laboratory has continued to employ this developmental systems approach and has examined the effects of prenatal and postnatal sensory experience on early auditory learning. The results obtained and reviewed later in this chapter suggest that the normally occurring sequence of sensory system development and the resulting limitation of sensory experience in the later developing visual modality prior to hatching have important implications for the ways in which the young precocial bird learns the auditory features of its perinatal environment.

TEMPORAL AND CONTEXTUAL FEATURES
OF PERINATAL AUDITORY LEARNING

As discussed earlier, the auditory system of precocial birds (and mammals) is functional during the later stages of prenatal development. In addition, the embryos of a number of avian and mammalian species are capable of learning the individually distinctive auditory features of their parents' vocalizations before birth or hatching (Bailey & Ralph, 1975; DeCasper & Fifer, 1980; Falt, 1981; Gottlieb, 1988; Impekoven, 1976). However, if precocial duck embryos are exposed to unusually early visual stimulation during prenatal exposure to the parental calls, they are unable to learn the individually distinctive auditory features of these vocalizations (Gottlieb et al., 1989). Such intersensory interference appears to be the result, at least in part, of simultaneous sensory stimulation. Simultaneous stimulation increases experiential competition between the auditory and visual modalities when both are still undergoing maturation and thereby may overtax the attentional capacities of the young organism. Support for this interpretation was provided by the fact that when premature visual experience was made to alternate with exposure to the maternal call, duck embryos in the study by Gottlieb and colleagues were capable of learning the call, as evidenced by their auditory choice test preferences after hatching.

A recent series of experiments from our lab has also examined the relationship between early auditory learning and the timing of intersensory function (Lickliter & Hellewell, 1992). In this study, the ability of bobwhite quail embryos and hatchlings to learn an individual bobwhite maternal call was examined. To our surprise, embryos demonstrated clearer evidence of early auditory learning than older, more mature hatchlings. Specifically, communally incubated embryos could learn an individual bobwhite maternal call and remember that call for at least 24 hr following exposure. On the other hand, group-reared hatchlings exposed postnatally to an individual maternal call did not show a preference for that familiar call over an unfamiliar maternal call at 24 hr following exposure.

One plausible explanation for this rather surprising and unexpected difference in performance between embryos and hatchlings is that the more complex environment of the hatchling (when compared to that of the embryo) somehow disrupts or interferes with early auditory learning. To assess this possibility, a subsequent experiment reared chicks under conditions of reduced visual and social experience during postnatal exposure to an individual maternal call (Lickliter & Hellewell, 1992). Unlike group-reared hatchlings, these isolation-reared chicks did exhibit a significant preference for the familiar maternal call 24 hr following exposure, suggesting that the perceptual and social complexity of postnatal rearing conditions somehow interferes with the young chick's early auditory learning.

Additional support for this interference notion was provided by the finding that embryos also fail to exhibit a preference for an individual maternal call if the call is paired with patterned visual experience during the period prior to hatching. This finding parallels the negative results obtained from group-reared hatchlings and suggests that either increasing the complexity of the prenatal environment by providing visual experience in the egg or hatching into the more visually and socially complex postnatal environment can effectively distract the embryo and hatchling, thereby disrupting the development of a preference for an individual maternal call. Taken together, the results of the Lickliter and Hellewell (1992) study and the Gottlieb et al. (1989) study support the idea that limitation of visual experience during the prenatal period serves to reduce competition between the emerging auditory and visual modalities and can thus contribute to the prenatal auditory learning observed in a variety of precocial animal infants.

A recent study by Radell and Gottlieb (1992) also focused on intersensory interference of early auditory learning. In particular, this study examined whether enhanced stimulation of earlier developing sensory systems (tactile–

vestibular) would interfere with the functioning of the later developing auditory system. Results revealed that duck embryos experiencing concurrent tactile–vestibular and auditory stimulation failed to learn an individual mallard duck maternal call. In contrast, normally reared ducklings are capable of learning the distinctive features of an individual maternal call as embryos (Gottlieb, 1988). These results parallel those of Gottlieb et al. (1989) and Lickliter and Hellewell (1992), in that intersensory interference (i.e., lack of early auditory learning) occurred only when two or more sensory systems were concurrently stimulated prenatally. Radell and Gottlieb (1992) suggested that such intersensory interference is likely to occur when immature sensory systems are stimulated simultaneously. They proposed that the embryo is not capable of adequately attending to simultaneous sensory stimulation, in that the complexity and/or amount of simultaneous stimulation effectively overwhelms the young organism's attentional capabilities.

Although additional research is certainly needed to further examine and test this "embryonic attention" hypothesis, it does fit nicely with the notion of the importance of limitation of sensory input proposed by Turkewitz and Kenny (1982, 1985). As discussed earlier, these authors argued that sensory limitations of embryos and many newborn animals reduce the amount of information neonates have to deal with and in doing so aid in constructing a simplified contextual/experiential milieu during the perinatal period. In other words, sensory limitation may help to initially provide the neonate with a relatively simple, orderly world, which does not overly tax its relatively undeveloped attentional abilities.

Of course, limitation of sensory input stems not only from the limited functioning of immature sensory systems, but also from the buffered, protected nature of the prenatal environment. Because the embryo is constrained within the buffered and relatively less variable stimulative system of the egg or uterus, stimulation involving light, sound, temperature, and chemical cues is typically attenuated prior to reaching the developing embryo. It is important to emphasize that we are not proposing that the avian or mammalian embryo does not receive an array of sensory stimulation prenatally. There is an ever-growing body of data to document the fact that embryos receive ongoing sensory stimulation prenatally; in addition, avian and mammalian embryos are known to be responsive to a variety of tactile, acoustic, and chemosensory cues prior to birth or hatching (e.g., Gottlieb, 1971b; Hepper, 1988; Lecanuet, Granier-Deferre, Jaquet, & Busnel, 1992; Lickliter & Stoumbos, 1992; Radell & Gottlieb, 1992; Smotherman & Robinson, 1987, 1992). We are simply pointing out that by the very design of the egg or uterus, the developing embryo resides in a relatively cloistered environment, and this simplified environment can itself contribute to the development and organization of early perceptual capabilities. In more general terms, the organism–environment relationship is one that is structured on both sides. Both limited sensory capacities and a constrained developmental context combine to minimize the simultaneous presentation of multiple "sources" of information to the developing embryo. As a result, the demands placed on the embryo's allocation of attention are controlled or attenuated (see Kinchla, 1992, for a recent discussion and review of the study of attention). This control of attentional demands appears to influence the nature of intersensory relationships in the perinatal period; in particular, it appears to favor the initial prepotence of auditory cues over visual cues in directing the infant's behavior following birth or hatching (for examples see Gottlieb, 1971a; Lewkowicz, 1988; Lickliter & Virkar, 1989).

SUMMARY AND CONCLUSIONS

The studies reviewed in this chapter underscore the dynamic nature of early perceptual organization in precocial birds. Related studies from our laboratory have, for example, accelerated (or decelerated) the emergence of intersensory functioning in bobwhite quail chicks by providing embryos or hatchlings early (or delayed) sensory experience during the perinatal period (Fig. 4.1). Under normally occurring conditions, the order and constraint typically supplied by the sequential onset of sensory functioning prenatally serve to minimize or reduce the possible degrees of freedom contributing to early perceptual organization (see Gottlieb, 1991). More specifically, limited sensory functioning during early development reduces available sensory input or experience from particular modalities at particular times, thereby decreasing experiential competition between emerging systems during the perinatal period (Turkewitz & Kenny, 1982). This condition produces a reliable order and structure to prenatal sensory experience, minimizes the quantity and/or complexity of prenatal sensory experience, and reduces the attentional demands placed on the developing embryo. For example, normally occurring limitations in visual experience during prenatal development were found to play an important role in the processing of auditory information in the perinatal period in both quail chicks and ducklings.

In the more general sense, the demonstration that the timing of sensory function provides order and modulates competition between emerging sensory systems is consistent with a view of development that recognizes that the organism–environment relationship is one that is structured on both sides. That is, it is a relation between a structured organism and a structured environment (for a more detailed discussion of this view see Lickliter, Dyer, & McBride, 1993; West & King, 1987). As the discussion of the results of the various studies considered in this chapter attempts to make clear, the epigenetic emergence of early perceptual organization is constrained (and directed) by features of both the organism's characteristics and those of its developmental context. In the case of precocial birds, the order, regularity, and constraint of the onset of sensory system function and the relatively closed system of the avian egg provide a stable framework within which species-typical intersensory relationships become manifest. For example, bobwhite embryos reared in their typical developmental context (one in which ongoing patterned visual stimulation is not present) are capable of learning an individual bobwhite maternal call; on the other hand, embryos provided with a different developmental context (one in which patterned visual stimulation is made available) do not learn an individual maternal call. In this particular example, the effectiveness of ongoing prenatal exposure to an individual maternal call is dependent on other features of the developmental system, namely, the absence of ongoing exposure to concurrent visual stimulation (for similar examples see Gottlieb et al., 1989; Turkewitz & Devenny, 1992).

We believe that an important requirement for future research in the area of early perceptual development will be the use of a combination of broadly based behavioral measures to more precisely assess the mechanisms and processes underlying the embyro's and neonate's emerging perceptual competence. Although the early exposure paradigm employed in the studies reviewed in this chapter has certainly proven to be a useful addition to traditional "early deprivation" studies in the investigation of the effects of altered developmental histories on intersensory development, future work concerned with the mechanisms of perinatal perceptual organization will need to include a wider variety of behavioral probes aimed at assessing the attentional, experiential, motivational, and temporal features underlying intersensory development. Given that there are undoubtedly different types of intersensory functioning at different times in development (Botuck & Turkewitz, 1990; Lewkowicz, chap. 8, this volume; Spear & McKinzie, chap. 7, this volume; Turkewitz, chap. 1, this volume), further descriptive and experimental studies are clearly needed to better understand how sensory experience serves to maintain, facilitate, or interfere with the normal course of early intersensory development.

ACKNOWLEDGMENTS

This chapter was supported by NIMH Grant MH48949 awarded to Robert Lickliter. We thank Robin Panneton Cooper, Gilbert Gottlieb, and David Lewkowicz for their constructive comments on an earlier version of this chapter.

REFERENCES

Alberts, J. R. (1984). Sensory-perceptual development in the Norway rat: A view toward comparative studies. In R. Kail & N. S. Spear (Eds.), *Comparative perspectives on memory development* (pp. 65–101). Hillsdale, NJ: Lawrence Erlbaum Associates.

Anokhin, P. K. (1964). Systemogenesis as a general regulator of brain development. *Progress in Brain Research, 9*, 54–86.

Bailey, E. D., & Ralph, K. M. (1975). The effects of embryonic exposure to pheasant vocalizations in later call identification by chicks. *Canadian Journal of Zoology, 53*, 1028–1034.

Banker, H., & Lickliter, R. (1993). Effects of early and delayed visual experience on intersensory development in bobwhite quail chicks. *Developmental Psychobiology, 26*, 155–170.

Botuck, S., & Turkewitz, G. (1990). Intersensory functioning: Auditory-visual pattern equivalence in younger and older children. *Developmental Psychology, 26*, 115–120.

Boyd, H., & Fabricius, E. (1965). Observations on the incidence of following visual and auditory stimuli in naive mallard ducklings. *Behaviour, 25*, 1–15.

Bradley, R. M., & Mistretta, C. M. (1975). Fetal sensory receptors. *Physiological Reviews, 55*, 352–382.

Burnstine, T. H., Greenough, W. T., & Tees, R. C. (1984). Intermodal compensation following damage or deprivation. In C. R. Almli & S. Finger (Eds.), *The behavioral biopsychology of early brain damage* (pp. 3–34). New York: Academic Press.

Carmichael, L. (1933). Origin and prenatal growth of behavior. In C. Murchison (Ed.), *A handbook of child psychology* (pp. 31–159). Worcester, MA: Clark University Press.

Coghill, G. E. (1929). *Anatomy and the problem of behavior*. New York: Cambridge University Press.

DeCasper, A. J., & Fifer, W. P. (1980). Of human bonding: Newborns prefer their mothers' voices. *Science, 208*, 1174–1176.

DeCasper, A. J., & Spence, M. J. (1986). Prenatal maternal speech influences newborns' perception of speech sounds. *Infant Behavior and Development, 9*, 133–150.

Falt, B. (1981). Development of responsiveness to the individual maternal "clucking" by domestic chicks. *Behavioral Processes, 6*, 303–317.

Fifer, W. P. (1987). Neonatal preference for mother's voice. In N. A. Krasnegor, E. M. Blass, M. A. Hofer, & W. A. Smotherman (Eds.), *Perinatal development: A psychobiological perspective* (pp. 111–124). New York: Academic Press.

Foreman, N., & Altaha, M. (1991). The development of exploration and spontaneous alteration in hooded rat pups: Effects of unusually early eyelid opening. *Developmental Psychobiology, 24*, 521–537.

Freeman, B. M., & Vince, M. A. (1974). *Development of the avian embryo*. London: Chapman and Hall.

Gottlieb, G. (1968). Prenatal behavior of birds. *Quarterly Review of Biology, 43*, 148–174.

Gottlieb, G. (1971a). *Development of species identification in birds*. Chicago: University of Chicago Press.

Gottlieb, G. (1971b). Ontogenesis of sensory function in birds and mammals. In E. Tobach, L. Aronson, & E. Shaw (Eds.), *The biopsychology of development* (pp. 67–128). New York: Academic Press.

Gottlieb, G. (1973a). *Behavioral embryology*. New York: Academic Press.

Gottlieb, G. (1973b). Neglected developmental variables in the study of species identification in birds. *Psychological Bulletin, 79*, 362–372.

Gottlieb, G. (1985). Development of species identification in ducklings: XI. Embryonic critical period for species-typical perception in the hatchling. *Animal Behaviour, 33*, 225–233.

Gottlieb, G. (1988). Development of species identification in ducklings: XV. Individual auditory recognition. *Developmental Psychobiology, 21,* 509–522.

Gottlieb, G. (1991). Experiental canalization of behavioral development: Theory. *Developmental Psychology, 27,* 35–39.

Gottlieb, G., & Simner, M. L. (1969). Auditory versus visual flicker in directing the approach response of domestic chicks. *Journal of Comparative and Physiological Psychology, 67,* 58–63.

Gottlieb, G., Tomlinson, W. T., & Radell, P. L. (1989). Developmental intersensory interference: Premature visual experience suppresses auditory learning in ducklings. *Infant Behavior and Development, 12,* 1–12.

Hamburger, V. (1963). Some aspects of the embryology of behavior. *Quarterly Review of Biology, 38,* 342–365.

Heaton, M. B. (1972). Prenatal auditory discrimination in the wood duck. *Animal Behaviour, 20,* 421–424.

Heaton, M. B. (1973). Early visual function in bobwhite and Japanese quail embryos as reflected by pupillary reflex. *Journal of Comparative and Physiological Psychology, 84,* 134–139.

Heaton, M. B., & Galleher, E. (1981). Prenatal auditory discrimination in the bobwhite quail. *Behavioral and Neural Biology, 31,* 242–246.

Heaton, M. B., Miller, D. B., & Goodwin, D. G. (1978). Species-specific auditory discrimination in bobwhite quail neonates. *Developmental Psychobiology, 11,* 13–21.

Hepper, P. G. (1988). Adaptive fetal learning: Prenatal exposure to garlic affects postnatal preferences. *Animal Behaviour, 36,* 935–936.

Herrick, C. J., & Coghill, G. E. (1915). The development of reflex mechanisms in *Amblystoma*. *Journal of Comparative Neurology, 25,* 65–85.

Hooker, D. (1952). *The prenatal origin of behavior.* Lawrence: University of Kansas Press.

Impekoven, M. (1976). Responses of laughing gull chicks (*Larus atricilla*) to parental attraction and alarm calls, and effects of prenatal auditory experience on the responsiveness to such calls. *Behaviour, 61,* 250–278.

Johnston, T. D., & Gottlieb, G. (1981). Development of visual species identification in ducklings: What is the role of imprinting? *Animal Behaviour, 29,* 1082–1099.

Johnston, T. D., & Gottlieb, G. (1985). Effects of social experience on visually imprinted maternal preferences in Peking ducklings. *Developmental Psychobiology, 18,* 261–271.

Kenny, P., & Turkewitz, G. (1986). Effects of unusually early visual stimulation on the development of homing behavior in the rat pup. *Developmental Psychobiology, 19,* 57–66.

Kinchla, R. A. (1992). Attention. *Annual Review of Psychology, 43,* 711–742.

Konishi, M. (1973). Development of auditory neuronal responses in avian embryos. *Proceedings of the National Academy of Sciences, 70,* 1795–1798.

Kuo, Z.-Y. (1976). *The dynamics of behavioral development.* New York: Plenum.

Lecanuet, J. P., Granier-Deferre, C., Jacquet, A.-Y., & Busnel, M.-C. (1992). Decelerative cardiac responsiveness to acoustical stimulation in the near term fetus. *Quarterly Journal of Experimental Psychology, 44B,* 279–304.

Lewkowicz, D. J. (1988). Sensory dominance in infants: 1. Six-month-old infants' response to auditory-visual compounds. *Developmental Psychology, 24,* 155–171.

Lewkowicz, D. J. (1991). Development of intersensory functions in human infancy: Auditory/visual interactions. In M. J. Weiss & P. R. Zelazo (Eds.), *Newborn attention: Biological constraints and the influence of experience* (pp. 308–338). Norwood, NJ: Ablex.

Lewkowicz, D. J. (1992). Responsiveness to auditory and visual components of a sounding/moving compound stimulus in human infants. *Perception and Psychophysics, 52,* 519–528.

Lewontin, R. C., & Levins, R. (1988). Aspects of wholes and parts in population biology. In G. Greenberg & E. Tobach (Eds.), *Evolution of social behavior and integrative levels* (pp. 31–52). Hillsdale, NJ: Lawrence Erlbaum Associates.

Lickliter, R. (1990a). Premature visual stimulation accelerates intersensory functioning in bobwhite quail neonates. *Developmental Psychobiology, 23,* 15–27.

Lickliter, R. (1990b). Premature visual experience facilitates visual responsiveness in bobwhite quail neonates. *Infant Behavior and Development, 13,* 487–496.

Lickliter, R. (in press). Prenatal visual experience alters postnatal sensory dominance hierarchy in bobwhite quail chicks. *Infant Behavior and Development.*

Lickliter, R., & Berry, T. D. (1990). The phylogeny fallacy: Developmental psychology's misapplication of evolutionary theory. *Developmental Review, 10,* 322–338.

Lickliter, R., Dyer, A. B., & McBride, T. (1993). Perceptual consequences of early social experience in precocial birds. *Behavioural Processes, 30,* 185–200.

Lickliter, R., & Hellewell, T. B. (1992). Contextual determinants of auditory learning in bobwhite quail embryos and hatchlings. *Developmental Psychobiology, 25,* 17–31.

Lickliter, R., & Stoumbos, J. (1991). Enhanced prenatal auditory experience facilitates postnatal visual responsiveness in bobwhite quail chicks. *Journal of Comparative Psychology, 105,* 89–94.

Lickliter, R., & Stoumbos, J. (1992). Modification of prenatal auditory experience alters postnatal auditory preferences of bobwhite quail chicks. *Quarterly Journal of Experimental Psychology, 44B,* 199–214.

Lickliter, R., & Virkar, P. (1989). Intersensory functioning in bobwhite quail chicks: Early sensory dominance. *Developmental Psychobiology, 22,* 651–667.

Mistretta, C. M., & Bradley, R. M. (1978). Effect of early sensory experience on brain and behavioral development. In G. Gottlieb (Ed.), *Early influences* (pp. 215–247). New York: Academic Press.

Oppenheim, R. W. (1968). Light responsivity in chick and duck embryos just prior to hatching. *Animal Behaviour, 16,* 276–280.

Oppenheim, R. W. (1982). Preformation and epigenesis in the origins of the nervous system and behavior: Issues, concepts, and their history. In P. P. G. Bateson & P. H. Klopfer (Eds.), *Perspectives in ethology* (Vol. 5, pp. 1–100). New York: Plenum.

Oppenheim, R. W., Levin, H. L., & Harth, M. S. (1973). An investigation of various egg-opening techniques for use in avian behavioral embryology. *Developmental Psychobiology, 6,* 53–68.

Oyama, S. (1985). *The ontogeny of information: Developmental systems and evolution.* New York: Cambridge University Press.

Oyama, S. (1989). Ontogeny and the central dogma: Do we need the concept of genetic programming in order to have an evolutionary perspective? In M. R. Gunner & E. Thelen (Eds.), *Systems and development* (pp. 1–34). Hillsdale, NJ: Lawrence Erlbaum Associates.

Preyer, W. (1885). *Specielle Physiologie des Embryo.* Leipzig: Grieben.

Radell, P. L., & Gottlieb, G. (1992). Developmental intersensory interference: Augmented prenatal sensory experience interferes with auditory learning in duck embryos. *Developmental Psychology, 28,* 795–803.

Riesen, A. H., & Zilbert, D. E. (1975). Behavioral consequences of variations in early sensory development. In A. H. Riesen (Ed.), *The developmental neuropsychology of sensory deprivation* (pp. 211–252). New York: Academic Press.

Smith, F. V., & Bird, M. W. (1963). The relative attraction for the domestic chick of combinations of stimuli in different sensory modalities. *Animal Behaviour, 11,* 300–305.

Smotherman, W. P., & Robinson, S. R. (1985). The rat fetus in its environment: Behavioral adjustments to novel, familiar, aversive, and conditioned stimuli presented in utero. *Behavioral Neuroscience, 99,* 521–530.

Smotherman, W. P., & Robinson, S. R. (1987). Psychobiology of fetal experience in the rat. In N. A. Krasnegor, E. M. Blass, M. A. Hofer, & W. P. Smotherman (Eds.), *Perinatal development: A psychobiological perspective* (pp. 39–60). New York: Academic Press.

Smotherman, W. P., & Robinson, S. R. (1992). Habituation in the rat fetus. *Quarterly Journal of Experimental Psychology, 44B,* 215–230.

Storey, A. E., & Shapiro, L. J. (1979). Development of preferences in white Peking ducklings for stimuli in the natural post-hatch environment. *Animal Behaviour, 27*, 411–416.

Tees, R. C. (1976). Perceptual development in mammals. In G. Gottlieb (Ed.), *Neural and behavioral specificity* (pp. 281–326). New York: Academic Press.

Tees, R. C. (1986). Experience and visual development: Behavioral evidence. In W. T. Greenough & J. M. Juraska (Eds.), *Developmental neuropsychobiology* (pp. 317–361). New York: Academic Press.

Tees, R. C. (1990). Experience, perceptual competencies, and at cortex. In B. Kolb & R. C. Tees (Eds.), *The cerebral cortex of the rat* (pp. 507–536). Cambridge, MA: MIT Press.

Tees, R. C., & Symons, L. A. (1987). Intersensory coordination and the effects of early sensory deprivation. *Developmental Psychobiology, 20*, 497–508.

Thelen, E. (1988). Dynamical approaches to the development of behavior. In J. A. S. Kelso, A. Mandell, & M. Shlesinger (Eds.), *Dynamic patterns in complex systems* (pp. 348–369). Singapore: World Scientific.

Thelen, E. (1989). Self-organization in developmental processes: Can systems approaches work? In M. G. Gunnar & E. Thelen (Eds.), *Systems and development* (pp. 77–117). Hillsdale, NJ: Lawrence Erlbaum Associates.

Turkewitz, G., & Devenny, D. A. (1993). *Developmental time and timing.* Hillsdale, NJ: Lawrence Erlbaum Associates.

Turkewitz, G., & Kenny, P. A. (1982). Limitations on input as a basis for neural organization and perceptual development: A preliminary theoretical statement. *Developmental Psychobiology, 15*, 357–368.

Turkewitz, G., & Kenny, P. A. (1985). The role of developmental limitation of sensory input on sensory/perceptual organization. *Journal of Developmental and Behavioral Pediatrics, 6*, 302–306.

Turkewitz, G., & Mellon, R. C. (1989). Dynamic organization of intersensory function. *Canadian Journal of Psychology, 43*, 286–307.

Vince, M. A. (1972). Communication between quail embryos and the synchronization of hatching. *Proceedings of the XV International Ornithological Congress*, 357–362.

Vince, M. A. (1973). Some environmental effects on the activity and development of the avian embryo. In G. Gottlieb (Ed.), *Behavioral embryology* (pp. 285–323). New York: Academic Press.

West, M. J., & King, A. P. (1987). Settling nature and nurture into an ontogenetic niche. *Developmental Psychobiology, 20*, 549–562.

Windle, W. F. (1944). Genesis of somatic motor function in mammalian embryos: A synthesizing article. *Physiological Zoology, 17*, 247–260.

CHAPTER FIVE

Development and Neural Basis of Multisensory Integration

Barry E. Stein
Bowman Gray School of Medicine, Wake Forest University

M. Alex Meredith
Medical College of Virginia, Virginia Commonwealth University

Mark T. Wallace
Bowman Gray School of Medicine, Wake Forest University

INTERSENSORY BIASES

The literature is replete with examples in which information in one sense changes perception in another. Specifically, a visual cue can significantly alter one's judgments about proprioceptive and auditory cues, and proprioceptive cues can bias judgments regarding the location of an auditory stimulus (Held, 1955; Pick, Warren, & Hay, 1969; Shelton & Searle, 1980; Thurlow & Rosenthal, 1976; Warren, Welch, & McCarthy, 1981; Welch & Warren, 1980). For example, the magnitude of intersensory influences is made quite evident when watching some of the films now shown in planetariums. One that was played at the theater in the Science Museum of Virginia simulated the visual cues one would experience in an Alaskan bush plane flying through a rugged mountain range. The vestibular sensations initiated by the rapidly shifting visual images were quite vivid, and the secondary gastrointestinal changes they produced were ever so real.

It is because the sensory systems have evolved to work synergistically that misperceptions occur when the cues they provide conflict with one another. An excellent example is to be found in studies of speech perception. When nonmatching visual (e.g., the mouth forms the sound "ga-ga") and auditory (e.g., the sound "ba-ba") stimuli are combined, the resultant perception is a synthesis of the two inputs: neither "ba-ba" nor "ga-ga", but "da-da" (McGurk & MacDonald, 1976). A wealth of different examples of such intersensory biases can be found throughout this volume and elsewhere (e.g., Welch & Warren, 1986). Yet, despite the overwhelming number of situations in which intersensory effects are evident in controlled experiments, most of us are quite unaware of the operation of these biases during our daily lives. The objective judgments we make about modality-specific sensations seem to be unchanged by the presence of cues from other modalities. Furthermore, the subjective properties of the senses (e.g., hue, pitch, tickle) appear to be tightly constrained within modality-specific boundaries.

However, for some individuals, called *synesthetes*, the situation is far different. Sensory experiences are much less discrete and, for example, a stimulus in one modality may elicit an entire complex of impressions that readily cross intersensory boundaries. A provocative example that has recently been cited (see Ackerman, 1990) is that of a woman who tasted baked beans whenever she heard the word *Francis*.

Synesthesia literally means "joining the senses," and it has been said to reflect "an involuntary joining in which the real information of one sense is accompanied by a perception in another sense" (Cytowic, 1989, p. 1; also see Marks, 1975, 1978). There is no adequate neural explanation for this seemingly odd syndrome, but to some, the synesthete represents less of an oddity than a case of arrested sensory development.

These investigators believe that the normal neonate has sensory impressions that are poorly differentiated from one another and that form a "primitive unity" (see Bower, 1977; Gibson, 1966; Marks, 1978; Ryan, 1940; Turkewitz & Mellon, 1989; von Hornbostel, 1938), so that a single, modality-specific stimulus can produce "sensations (that) spill from one sensory system into another" (Maurer & Maurer, 1988, p. 164). Although some researchers believe the sensory modalities are well differentiated at birth and associations among them must be learned (e.g., Piaget, 1952; von Helmholtz, 1884/1968), a number of recent observations provide serious challenges to assumptions about the gradual maturation of intersensory capabilities. These make one wonder whether explanations based on traditional association phenomena are adequate to explain them. Perhaps the most dramatic of these is that of Meltzoff and colleagues (e.g., Meltzoff & Moore, 1977, 1983a, 1983b), who showed that newborn babies could "imitate" the facial expressions of the investigator despite never having had the opportunity to develop associations between what they were seeing and what they were doing (see Meltzoff & Kuhl, chap. 14, this volume). Some suggest that the babies can match the visual images with their tactile or proprioceptive sensations directly (e.g., Maurer & Maurer, 1988) because normal babies are synesthetic, a process that Meltzoff refers to as *active intermodal mapping*. That a normal infant is compelled to mimic an experimenter's facial expression is a significant puzzle itself. However, at least it helps explain why so many adults will screw their faces into the strangest contortions and present them as close as possible to the infant—and are disappointed if they are ignored.

That intersensory influences are already operative at neonatal stages in species other than humans is indicated by studies in which patterned visual input is provided before it normally occurs (e.g., by opening the eyelids in mammals [Turkewitz & Mellon, 1989], or making it possible for bird embryos to see beyond their shells [Gottlieb, Tomlinson, & Radell, 1989; Lickliter, 1990]). In both examples, the earlier-than-normal visual experience affects the animals' use of their other sensory systems. Whether comparable effects of early usage apply to human infants is not yet known. However, on the basis of the animal literature, one could support the claim that hypotheses of prenatal intersensory linkages are more conservative than those requiring all intersensory connections to be established postnatally. As discussed later, experience seems to play its primary roles in determining which convergence patterns will survive.

The suggestion that the substrate for some form of intersensory interaction is established prenatally is consistent with recent neuroanatomical findings. Some rodents and carnivores are now known to come into the world with inputs from different sensory modalities converging on the same target structures, presumably synapsing onto the same neurons. Many of these inputs are "inappropriate" (e.g., visual inputs to auditory and somatosensory thalamus), as they are not maintained into adulthood. Thus, from an anatomical perspective, the fetal and newborn brains of some animals are more multisensory than when they become mature. Presumably, the inappropriate inputs to these structures are at a competitive disadvantage and normally are retracted during early development unless extraordinary surgical means are taken to eliminate more competitive, and thus more "appropriate," inputs (Asanuma, Ohkawa, Stanfield, & Cowan, 1988; Frost, 1984; Innocenti & Clarke, 1984; Sur, Garraghty, & Roe, 1988).

A MODEL MULTISENSORY NEURAL STRUCTURE: THE CAT SUPERIOR COLLICULUS

How do the inputs from the different senses normally interact in the brain? Despite the fundamental nature of this question, there has been a surprising lack of information available. This is not due to a paucity of potential sites in the brain to study. There are many regions in the mammalian brain where inputs from two or more sensory systems converge on single neurons, thereby rendering them *multisensory* (see Meredith & Stein, 1986a, for a brief review), and many of these multisensory neurons are retained in adulthood. It seems quite reasonable to expect that these multisensory neurons provide the essential basis for integration among sensory modalities.

Perhaps the best known among the multisensory areas is the superior colliculus, a midbrain structure in which visual, auditory, and somatosensory inputs converge (Stein, 1984b), and which plays an important role in attending and orienting to these sensory stimuli (e.g., Casagrande, Harting, Hall, & Diamond, 1972; Goodale & Murison, 1975; Meredith, Wallace, & Stein, 1992; Schneider, 1969; Sparks, 1986; Sprague & Meikle, 1965; see Fig. 5.1). A number of years ago we began studying the development of the sensory properties of superior colliculus neurons in the cat, and how these neurons dealt with unimodal and multisensory stimuli. However, before describing what we know of how these neurons synthesize multisensory information, it is important to review briefly the organization of the superior colliculus and how its sensory properties develop.

Sensory Topographies and Alignment Among Maps

Visual, auditory, and somatosensory inputs innervate the superior colliculus, and each modality is represented in this structure by a map of sensory space. The different maps overlap each other and share similar axes. Consequently, points in frontal space are represented toward the front of the superior

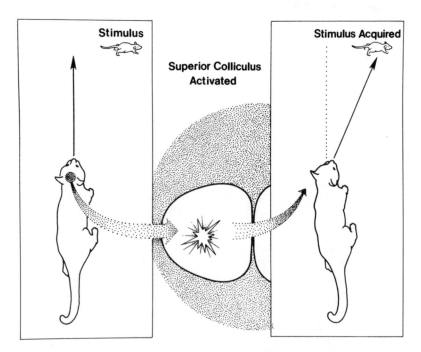

FIG. 5.1. The behavioral role of the superior colliculus. (Left) The rat is a stimulus in the peripheral field of the cat. This stimulus evokes neural activity in a specific region of the superior colliculus (center). This same region of the superior colliculus directs the animal's orientation toward the location of the stimulus (right).

colliculus, and those toward the rear of the animal are represented caudally; those in upper space are located medially and those in lower space are represented laterally (e.g., Chalupa & Rhoades, 1977; Cynader & Berman, 1972; Drager & Hubel, 1975; Feldon, Feldon, & Kruger, 1970; Finlay, Schneps, Wilson, & Schneider, 1978; Graham, Pearson, Berman, & Murphy, 1981; Schaefer, 1970; Siminoff, Schwassman, & Kruger, 1966; Stein & Dixon, 1979; Stein, Magalhaes-Castro, & Kruger, 1976). Together, these overlapping maps generate a comprehensive multisensory map (see Fig. 5.2).

This organizational pattern allows stimuli originating from the same source (e.g., the sound and sight of a bird) to activate the same region of the superior colliculus: an efficient way of combining the various sources of sensory information to produce a focus of high neural activity. Because the sensory representations are also in register with motor representations (see Harris, 1980; Sparks, 1986; Stein, Goldberg, & Clamann, 1976; also see Fig. 5.2), the

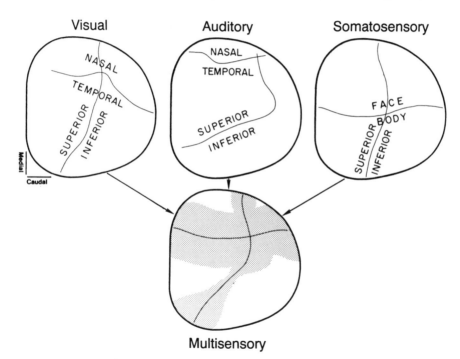

FIG. 5.2. The individual representations of sensory space (top) are aligned in the superior colliculus to form a unified, multisensory map (bottom). The line that divides nasal from temporal visual and auditory space, or the front (face) from the rear of the body, runs from medial to lateral across the superior colliculus. The line that divides superior from inferior visual and auditory space, and dorsal from ventral body surface, runs from rostral to caudal on the structure. Because these axes are in general register with one another, a common representation of multisensory space is effected.

different sensory inputs have access to common motor circuits and can produce identical behaviors (Stein, Magalhaes-Castro, & Kruger, 1976). Thus, inputs from upper sensory space produce a high level of activity in the medial superior colliculus, a locus from which upward orientations of the eyes, ears, and head are initiated. The consequent movement of these sensory organs results in them centering on the stimulus (Fig. 5.2).

Development of Sensory and Motor Activity

At birth, kittens are poor representatives of the remarkable sensory integration and sensorimotor capabilities of an adult cat. They are born at a relatively early stage of development, and are altricial in nature. Although the inputs that form the sensory representations are established during fetal stages, many of their constituent neurons are not responsive to natural stimuli until several days after birth. Therefore, they can play no role in transforming stimuli into coordinated behaviors. However, as if to prepare the kitten for its most immediate postnatal task of nuzzling its mother's fur in search of a source of milk, tactile-responsive neurons become active in late fetal stages (Stein, Labos, & Kruger, 1973a). This somatosensory responsiveness is critical for the kitten to find the nipple and get it into its mouth (Larson & Stein, 1984; see Fig. 5.3).

Nevertheless, the overall activity of the cat superior colliculus at birth is quite low. The responses of these first somatosensory neurons are weak and

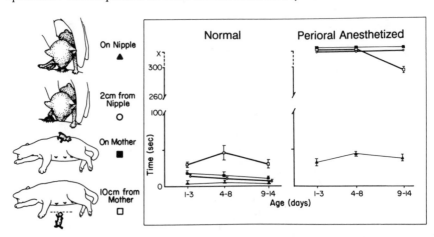

FIG. 5.3. Somatosensory cues are essential to neonatal localization. Kittens placed on the mother's nipple, near the nipple, on the mother's back, or on the floor 10 cm from the mother all localized the nipple and began suckling within a short period of time (center graph). However, when the perioral region was anesthetized with lidocaine, only those placed directly on the nipple were able to find it and suckle. From Larson and Stein (1984). Adapted by permission.

fatigue readily. Within about 5 days after birth neurons reponsive to auditory stimuli first appear (Stein, Labos, & Kruger, 1973a), and within 6–7 days the first visual neurons become responsive (Kao, McHaffie, Meredith, & Stein, 1991; Stein, Labos, & Kruger, 1973a; see Fig. 5.4). Multisensory neurons are first found at about 10 days of age. Although all of these sensory neurons undergo developmental changes in their responsiveness, the visual properties of superior colliculus neurons seem to have a particularly protracted developmental time course, requiring 6–8 weeks to become adult-like (Norton, 1974; Stein, 1984a; Stein, Labos, & Kruger, 1973a, 1973b). However, this peculiarity of visual responses may simply reflect the fact that we know far more about these visual properties, and will therefore be more sensitive to subtle developmental changes in them.

Although there is no way to be sure, it is possible that the sensory inputs produce superior colliculus-mediated behaviors at this early developmental stage. Some motor responses can already be effected via electrical stimulation of the superior colliculus at 2 days postnatal. Although the threshold for activation is comparatively high, and only a few sites are effective, focal electrical stimulation of the superior colliculus at this time can produce brisk, saccade-like movements of the eyes (often accompanied by appropriate movement of the ears, neck, whiskers, and limbs; Stein, Clamann, & Goldberg, 1980). These movements are topographically correct, so that stimulating in the left superior colliculus moves the two eyes rightward, and stimulation of the homotopic site in the other superior colliculus produces a mirror-image leftward eye movement, as in the adult (Stein, Goldberg, & Clamann, 1976a; see Fig. 5.5).

The presence of an incomplete motor organization in young animals has important implications for theories of visuomotor development. For example, an image can move across the retina when the object itself moves, or when the eyes move. However, it appears that movement of the eyes is critical if the animal is ever to make sense of the visual input (Hein, Vital-Durand, Salinger, & Diamond, 1979). The fact that eye movements can be evoked from the superior colliculus before visual inputs can drive its cells is consistent with this sort of motor–sensory chronology. However, it also raises the issue of which natural stimuli first initiate eye movements in kittens to set the stage for the animal making sense of the visual cues it now scans. Because somatosensory and auditory inputs are effective before visual inputs are, and because all the modalities appear to have access to the same motor outputs that orient the sensory organs, these cues could be essential for the formation of visuomotor associations somewhat later in development.

These observations also have direct bearing on studies with human infants. Auditory as well as visual stimuli can elicit eye movements in infants (for a detailed discussion see Butterworth, 1981). At least one case has been described in which an infant would make coordinated eye movements

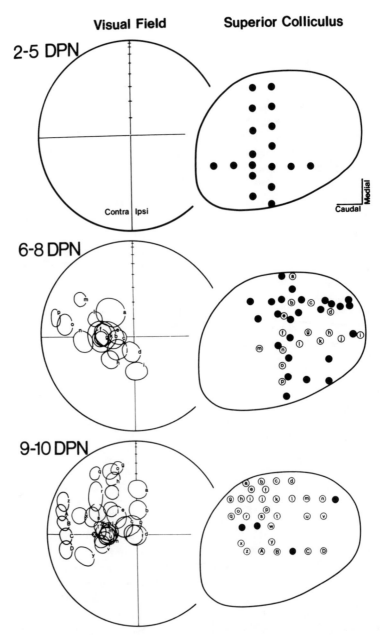

FIG. 5.4. Development of the visual map in the superficial layers of the superior colliculus. Although no visual activity was identified in very young animals (2–5 days postnatal, DPN), the incidence of visual responsiveness progressively increased with age (6–8; 9–10 DPN). Open circles indicate recording sites at which visual activity was observed (numbering indicates matching of recording site with receptive field location). Filled circles represent electrode penetrations in which no visual activity was recorded. Note that both central and peripheral portions of the visual field are represented even at the earliest stages of activity. From Kao et al. (1991). Adapted by permission.

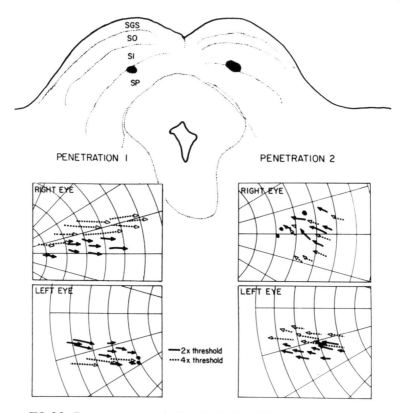

FIG. 5.5. Eye movements evoked by stimulation of the superior colliculus in a 2-day-old kitten. Stimulation of the nearly homotopic regions of the left (penetration 1) and right (penetration 2) colliculi elicited contralateral, contraversive eye movements that were approximated mirror images of one another. Marking lesions at the stimulation sites are indicated by the dark ovals. Direction of arrow indicates the direction of an eye movement; the length of the arrow represents two-times the actual magnitude of movement. Abbreviations: SGS, stratum griseum superficiale; SO, stratum opticum; SI, strata intermediale; SP, strata profunda. From Stein et al. (1980). Reprinted by permission.

toward a sound within moments of birth, and another in which a congenitally blind infant's eyes converged to approaching sounds and diverged to receding sounds. These observations are not explainable by mere arousal effects or traditional learning theories, and suggest a prenatal link between vision and audition, at least in terms of their spatial relations. Given observations that nonvisual inputs drive neurons in the superior colliculus of a newborn animal less well developed than the human infant, and that these inputs have access to neurons that project to brainstem areas that control eye movements in adult animals (e.g., Stein & Meredith, 1991), the presence of nonvisually evoked eye movements in human infants should not be terribly surprising. In fact, because the different sensory representations share the same map-like representations in the superior colliculus, nonvisually evoked eye movements would be expected to be directed toward the source of the stimulus just as they would if evoked visually. One would predict, however, that the use of this circuit would produce less accurate eye movements in response to auditory than to visual cues because of the comparatively large auditory receptive fields in the superior colliculus. When Spelke compared the eye movement accuracy to auditory versus visual stimuli in human infants (Spelke, 1987), and when Hartline and Northmore (1986) did the same thing in cats, they found that accuracy was lower to auditory targets.

The development of the sensory inputs and motor outputs of the superior colliculus takes place over approximately the same period. Both appear to become adult-like at about the second postnatal month. At this time vigorous sensory responses and overt orienting movements can be evoked from the superior colliculus, and the sensory and motor maps are in close topographic register.

Development of Alignment Among Sensory Maps

The alignment of the visual, auditory, and somatosensory maps in the superior colliculus proves to be essential for its neurons to engage in meaningful multisensory integration (this statement is explained in detail later; see The Rules of Multisensory Integration). Yet the fact that the alignment actually develops the way it does appears to be more than fortuitous. There are active processes at work to make sure that the various maps align with one another. This is apparent from studies in which sensory inputs are altered experimentally.

If an animal is raised with a plug in one ear, so that the inputs from that ear are limited, the inputs from the other ear will be far more effective in driving neurons in the central nervous system. However, because the relative timing and intensity of inputs to the two ears are critical cues in the formation of a computational map of auditory space, the brain must "correct" for the asymmetry of the two inputs by changing their relative weights. At least, it must do this if it is to build what looks like a normal map (see Fig. 5.6). Strangely enough, it does just that, and the auditory map that develops in ear-occluded animals is in surprisingly good register with the visual map (King, Hutchings, Moore, & Blakemore, 1988; Knudsen, 1983; see Fig. 5.6).

Apparently, the brain uses the visual map to determine how to weight the inputs from the two ears in order to produce an auditory map that matches the visual. Consequently, multisensory neurons develop receptive fields that

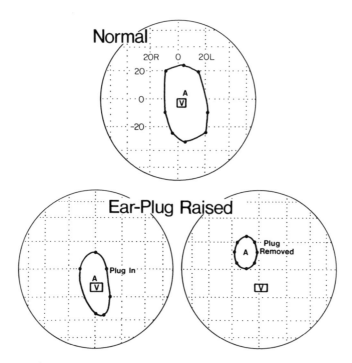

FIG. 5.6. Normal auditory–visual registry develops in owl optic tectum even when one ear is occluded, although removing the ear plug from an adult owl disrupts this multisensory alignment. The auditory and visual receptive fields are closely aligned in neurons in the optic tectum of a normal barn owl (top). Similarly, the auditory and visual receptive fields closely correspond in owls that have been raised with a sound-attenuating plug in one ear (bottom left). However, if this plug is removed as an adult, the auditory and visual receptive fields become misaligned (bottom right). From Knudsen (1982, 1983). Adapted by permission.

are in spatial register with one another, just as in normally reared animals (Fig. 5.6). This sort of alignment plasticity does not last forever, and after a period of experience in this situation the maps are fixed relative to one another. Thus, removing the ear plug when the animal becomes an adult disrupts the visual–auditory alignment. The auditory map shifts because the initial computation used in establishing visual–auditory alignment is now incorrect and the brain is no longer capable of readjusting to this new condition (Fig. 5.6). Its sensitive period for rearranging the auditory map is over.

The auditory system's use of the visual map as a developmental template is also evident from studies in which the visual map is displaced by ocular prisms early in life. The auditory map matches the altered visual map (King et al., 1988; Knudsen & Knudsen, 1989). Similarly, depriving the animal of the possibility of linking specific visual and auditory cues in space and time (e.g., by raising them in darkness or with omnidirectional sound) precludes the formation of an auditory map (Withington-Wray, Binns, & Keating, 1990; Withington-Wray, Binns, Dhanjal, Brickley, & Keating, 1990). Of the three maps in the superior colliculus, the auditory map is the most plastic, perhaps because, unlike the visual and somatosensory maps, it is derived via a computation rather than via a simple spatial transformation of inputs from the receptors.

It should be obvious from the discussion thus far that a good deal of biological energy is expended toward ensuring that the maps of the different senses align with one another. We believe that this has tremendous adaptive value. The spatial relationships among these maps are critical for determining how multisensory inputs are integrated in the same neuron. Furthermore, by pooling inputs with similar spatial coordinates onto common motor circuits, a most economical system is constructed for evoking the same behaviors regardless of the modality of the cue. These advantages should become clear from the discussion of the rules of multisensory integration presented next.

The Rules of Multisensory Integration:
Physiological Studies

Multisensory neurons are quite common in the superior colliculus (also see Gordon, 1973; King & Palmer, 1985; Meredith & Stein, 1983, 1986a; Stein & Arigbede, 1972; Stein, Magelhaes-Castro, & Kruger, 1976b), with the most common multisensory cell being responsive to both visual and auditory input.

The dramatic consequences of combining inputs from different modalities were evident from the first multisensory superior colliculus neuron we examined (Meredith & Stein, 1983). Weak responses to the most effective visual stimulus could be enhanced 1200% or more by combining it with an auditory stimulus, as shown in Fig. 5.7. In some cases, neurons that were unresponsive to either of two stimuli individually responded very well to their combination, a rather dramatic demonstration of the multiplicative effects of multisensory stimulus combinations. The near opposite was also found. In these cases, the neuron exhibited a vigorous response to one stimulus and seemed unresponsive to another. Combining them, however, resulted in a loss of the effectiveness of the first stimulus. The neuron simply failed to respond.

To explore how these opposite tendencies might relate to the properties of the particular neuron studied, to the physical nature of the stimuli, and, ultimately, to behavior, we posed a number of questions that lent themselves to experimental examination:

1. Do specific modality combinations invariably produce enhancement as opposed to depression? Or,

2. Can the same neuron exhibit enhancement *and* depression? If so,

3. What factors control enhancement and depression? (a) Is it necessary for the different stimuli to occur at the same time for an interaction to be produced? If not, (b) How long can the intervals between stimuli be, and how does the interaction change as the intermodality stimulus intervals increase? (c) How do the spatial relationships among the stimuli and the neuron's receptive field influence these processes?

4. Are the principles governing multisensory integration at the level of the single neuron applicable to overt behavior?

To deal with these and other questions, we began by systematically manipulating the parameters of the stimuli after documenting the unimodal

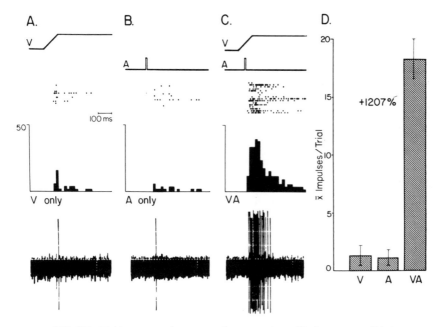

FIG. 5.7. Multisensory enhancement in a superior colliculus neuron. (A) A visual stimulus (ramp labeled V) was weakly excitatory, as evidenced by the dot raster (1 dot = 1 impulse, each row = 1 presentation) and the peristimulus histogram (sum of rasters). (B) An auditory stimulus (square wave labeled A) was an even less effective stimulus. (C) However, when the same stimuli were presented together, not only was activity evoked on each presentation, but also the number of impulses elicited each time was dramatically increased. (D) The combined-modality stimuli produced a 1207% enhancement of activity over that elicited by the best single-modality stimulus, as illustrated in the bar graph. Oscillograms indicate that the spike amplitude of the neuron was identical throughout each of the stimulus conditions and demonstrate that the activity was evoked by a single neuron. From Meredith and Stein (1986a). Reprinted by permission.

response properties of every neuron encountered (Meredith & Stein, 1983, 1986a; Meredith, Nemitz, & Stein, 1987). The results of these studies produced a set of very reliable guidelines, and are referred to here, for descriptive convenience, as integrative "rules."

Temporal Rules. Each of the sensory inputs to the superior colliculus has its own latency. Auditory inputs are the fastest (6–25 msec), somatosensory next (12–30 msec), and visual are the slowest (40–120 msec). This difference in timing would seem to render the system poorly suited to dealing with real-world events. However, interactions among the modalities are common occurrences in these neurons. It turns out that most stimuli initiate excitatory or inhibitory events that last far longer than intersensory differences in input latencies. In fact, the temporal "window" during which interactions among the sensory inputs take place sometimes exceeds 1.5 sec. In many neurons a long temporal window allows simultaneous visual and nonvisual stimuli to have striking interactions despite their significant differences in input latencies (Meredith et al., 1987). However, maximal interactions have less to do with matching the onset of the stimuli than with how their individual discharge trains overlap one another. The key is to overlap their periods of peak activity. In some cases this is achieved with simultaneous stimuli because their individual peak activities occur at different positions within their respective discharge trains, but their differing input latencies allow the peaks to overlap. In other cases, the peaks are overlapped only when one stimulus precedes the other by 50–100 msec. The flexibility in the timing of the inputs and the wide temporal window for multisensory interactions have very real consequences for dealing with external events. If the influences of visual and auditory stimuli had to reach a neuron at the same time for integration to be achieved, the cues initiated by the rodent in the example shown in Fig. 5.8 could influence one another from only a limited range of distances. However, the multisensory integrative system markedly expands this range.

Spatial Rules. In exploring how temporal factors affect multisensory integration, the two stimuli (e.g., visual, auditory) were presented at the same location in space. However, spatial factors play a critical role in this integration. As noted earlier, the spatial registry among sensory maps in the superior colliculus (and thus among the receptive fields of each multisensory neuron) is a key determinant of multisensory integration. For example, a visual and an auditory stimulus originating from the same location will fall within the excitatory receptive fields of the same multisensory neuron. This spatially coincident stimulus combination enhances the neuron's responses far above those to either stimulus alone. On the other hand, when a stimulus (e.g., the auditory stimulus) is moved to a location outside its excitatory

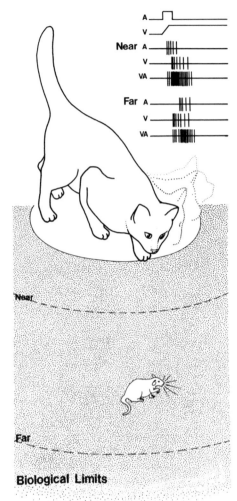

FIG. 5.8. Response enhancement can occur whenever the discharge trains evoked by each of a pair of stimuli overlap. Sound and light travel at significantly different velocities, and there are substantial latency differences for responses to visual and auditory stimuli. Because of these factors, the biological limits within which the effects of sensory stimuli can overlap to produce orientation behaviors are extremely broad and are not restricted to that area of space in which latencies to simultaneous stimuli can match. From Meredith et al. (1987). Adapted by permission.

receptive field, it is no longer capable of enhancing the neuron's activity, and if it falls within an inhibitory region, it will depress the neuron's responses to the visual stimulus (Meredith & Stein, 1986b). Therefore, enhancement and depression are dynamic properties, and depend on the relative spatial relationships of stimuli (see Fig. 5.9).

Magnitude or Inverse Effectiveness Rule. In most cases the multisensory enhancements were found to be multiplicative rather than additive. That is, one sensory input could produce a single impulse, a second stimulus could also produce only one impulse, but when combined they could elicit 12 impulses. In the most dramatic examples, the combination of an ineffective

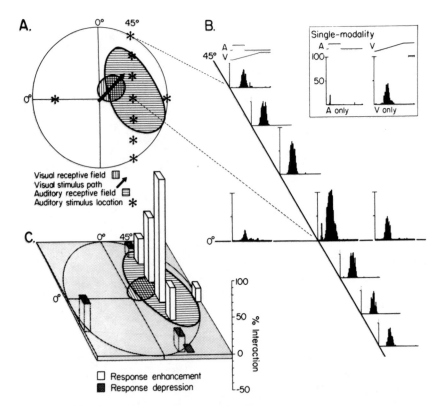

FIG. 5.9. Multisensory interactions are determined by the spatial relationships of the components of a multisensory stimulus. (A) The locations of the visual and auditory receptive fields of this neuron are projected onto a representation of visual/auditory space. A visual stimulus (arrow) was always moved across the visual receptive field. The auditory stimulus (asterisk) was presented in combination with the visual stimulus at specified locations within and outside the auditory receptive field. The resultant activities from these stimulus combinations are shown in (B), where the location of each histogram corresponds to the position of the auditory stimulus during that set of presentations. Note that the magnitude of the interaction varied with the position of the auditory stimulus. These interactions are displayed in perspective in (C) in order to admit a third axis: the percent of response interaction plotted at the location at which the auditory stimulus was presented. Clearly, response enhancement was produced when the auditory stimulus was presented within its receptive field, and response depression was elicited when the auditory stimulus fell outside of it. From Meredith and Stein (1986b). Reprinted by permission.

visual stimulus and an ineffective auditory or somatosensory stimulus reliably evokes responses (Meredith & Stein, 1986a). In some neurons it was possible to vary the effectiveness of the individual stimuli by changing their sizes or intensities. It soon became evident that the more effective the unimodal stimuli were, the lower the magnitude of the enhancement they were capable of generating by combination. This proved to be a reliable effect, and one could regularly manipulate the magnitude of the interaction this way. Apparently, there is an inverse relationship between unimodal stimulus effectiveness and multisensory enhancement. In behavioral terms the organism benefits most from the combination of weak stimuli, an effect that may have significant survival value in hunting (or hunted) animals. In contrast, potent unimodal stimuli need no enhancement to be effective.

Receptive Field Preservation Rule. Despite the profound effects that have been demonstrated, the unimodal receptive field properties of superior colliculus neurons are not altered during multisensory integration. For example, although the absolute level of a visually responsive neuron's activity may change dramatically in the presence of a nonvisual stimulus, it retains its visual receptive field borders, its directional and velocity selectivity, and its specificity for stimulus size (Stein, Meredith, & Wallace, 1993). The invariance of a neuron's unimodal receptive field properties seems essential if the nervous system is to maintain a constant code for stimulus features in a very changeable sensory world.

The Rules of Multisensory Integration: Behavioral Studies

Because the axons of multisensory neurons are a major component of the output pathways by which the superior colliculus effects orientation (Meredith & Stein, 1985), the relevant neural messages carried by this pathway are likely to be multisensory. To evaluate whether overt orientation behaviors would follow rules of multisensory integration similar to those seen at the cellular level in the superior colliculus, the orientation behavior of cats was examined in response to single-modality and multisensory stimuli.

   The animals were trained in a perimetry device in which pairs of speakers and light-emitting diodes (LEDs) were spaced at 30° intervals from the midline to 90° on either side. The animal's task was to orient toward the one LED that was illuminated on a particular trial. The LEDs were quite dim and the task was a demanding one. The animals were also presented with brief, low-intensity noise bursts from one of the speakers. The active speaker could be anywhere along the perimetry device. In one paradigm animals were taught to orient to the noise bursts, and in another they were taught to ignore them regardless of their location in space. Yet these differences in training made little difference in the behavioral product that was observed. Each animal showed a significantly enhanced capability to detect and orient to the visual stimulus when the auditory stimulus was presented at the same location (e.g., spatially coincident—see Fig. 5.10) and at the same time. In contrast, when a noise burst was presented simultaneously with the LED but at a different location (e.g., spatially disparate, see Fig. 5.10), significantly depressed responses occurred. Often the animal stood there as if it was unaware that a stimulus was presented or it wandered aimlessly in the apparatus; sometimes it went to a location halfway between the speaker and the LED, as if a "phantom" stimulus were perceived.

The product of the multisensory enhancements seen in these behavioral paradigms was not a simple addition of the responses to each unimodal stimulus, but was multiplicative. Thus, the spatial principle and the multiplicative nature of multisensory integration found at the level of the single neuron were also operative at the behavioral level.

The Rules Of Multisensory Integration Are the Same in Polysensory Cortex

These behavioral data suggested a general applicability of the rules governing multisensory integration, for it seemed quite unlikely that these complex overt behaviors depend solely on the superior colliculus, or that the animals' reactions were elicited without parallel perceptual processes that would involve multisensory circuits in cortex. Our guess was that similar rules of multisensory integration would be present in cortical neurons even though these neurons might be involved in processes of a "higher order" than those mediating immediate overt reactions. To examine this possibility, we began a series of recording studies in two polysensory cortices—specifically, the anterior ectosylvian sulcus (AES), and the rostral lateral suprasylvian sulcus (r-LS).

The AES has three sensory representations distributed along its banks: Rostral on the dorsal bank is a representation of the body surface (SIV; see Clemo & Stein, 1982), on the ventral bank is a visual representation (AEV; see Mucke, Norita, Benedek, & Creutzfeldt, 1982; Olson & Graybiel, 1987), and furthest caudal is an auditory representation (Field AES, FAES; see Clarey & Irvine, 1990). Near the borders of the unimodal areas are clusters of multisensory neurons (Clemo, Meredith, Wallace, & Stein, 1991), which typically reflect the modalities represented in the adjacent unimodal areas (e.g., auditory–somatosensory neurons are generally found near the border between FAES and SIV). We have examined a number of these neurons, and all exhibit the same kinds of cross-modal receptive field register as already described for multisensory neurons in the superior colliculus, as well as abiding by the same integrative rules.

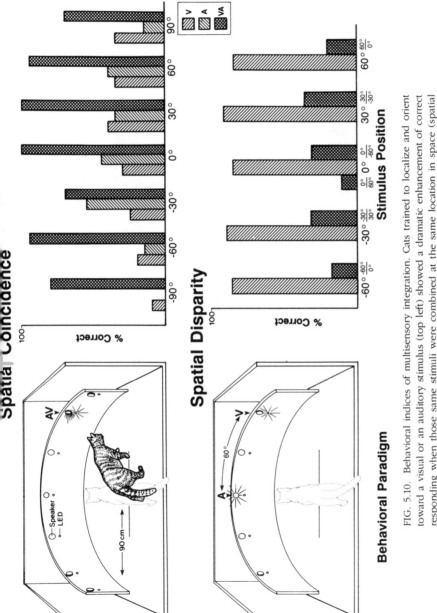

FIG. 5.10. Behavioral indices of multisensory integration. Cats trained to localize and orient toward a visual or an auditory stimulus (top left) showed a dramatic enhancement of correct responding when those same stimuli were combined at the same location in space (spatial coincidence; top right). In contrast, cats trained only to respond to visual stimuli (bottom left) showed a profound depression in correct responding to a visual stimulus when it was combined with an auditory stimulus that was 60° disparate to it (spatial disparity; bottom right). Adapted from Stein et al. (1989).

99

An example of integration in a multisensory AES neuron is described in Fig. 5.11. Its somatosensory and auditory receptive fields have the characteristic spatial overlap in contralateral space. Although the neuron responded to both unimodal stimuli, their simultaneous presentation within their receptive fields produced a significantly enhanced response. However, when the two stimuli were spatially disparate, so that one fell outside its receptive field, the response was depressed. Thus, the spatial rule was also applicable to cortical multisensory neurons. Temporal manipulations of the stimuli also demonstrated that the largest enhancements were achieved when the maximal periods of unimodal responses were overlapped. The combination of two weak unimod-

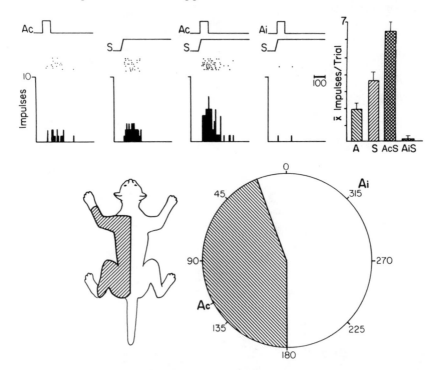

FIG. 5.11. Multisensory integration in a cortical (anterior ectosylvian sulcal cortex) neuron. This neuron was responsive to a contralateral auditory stimulus (square wave labeled Ac) and to a somatosensory stimulus placed on the hindlimb (ramp labeled S). When these stimuli were combined, responses were markedly enhanced. However, when an ipsilateral auditory stimulus was presented (square wave labeled Ai, which itself evoked no impulses), responses to the somatosensory stimulus were profoundly depressed. This activity is summarized in the bar graphs (right). The somatosensory receptive field is shown at the bottom left. The auditory receptive field, plotted on the horizontal plane through auditory space (0° is directly ahead of the animal, 90° is contralateral), is illustrated at the bottom right where the positions of the auditory stimuli (Ac, Ai) are also denoted.

al stimuli generally resulted in the largest interaction, demonstrating that the inverse effectiveness rule was applicable. In no case were the receptive field properties of a cortical neuron altered during the presentation of multisensory stimuli. Similar results were obtained in a small sample of neurons recorded in r-LS. In short, the same rules of multisensory integration were operative in the superior colliculus and polysensory cortex.

To examine whether similar effects can be seen in the cortex of primates, we have begun studies in the superior temporal sulcus (STS) and portions of the intraparietal sulcus (IPS) of the rhesus monkey. These areas have previously been shown to be polymodal (e.g., Bruce, Desimone, & Gross, 1981; Duhamel, Colby, & Goldberg, 1989; Mistlin & Perrett, 1990; Watanabe & Iwai, 1991). Although only preliminary data have been generated thus far, those neurons found to be multisensory ($n = 6$), were also found to exhibit multisensory enhancement and/or depression during quantitative evaluation. Both visual–somatosensory and auditory–somatosensory neurons were encountered (Stein et al., 1992).

CONCLUDING REMARKS

As infants, we are subject to a "booming, buzzing confusion" of sensory stimuli. Learning to sort and relate among peripheral stimuli becomes an essential task if we are ever to make sense of the external world. Much remains to be learned of the ontogenetic events that facilitate this process. However, the existence of specialized sensory systems provides us with a means of dissociating stimuli by modality, and the convergence of different inputs in the central nervous system provides us with a mechanism for identifying related events. The data generated in animal subjects suggest that the register among the receptive fields of multisensory neurons and their temporal properties provide a neural substrate for enhancing responses to meaningful stimuli (stimuli that covary in space and time) and for inhibiting responses to unrelated, distracting stimuli (stimuli that are not spatially and temporally related). Preliminary work with human subjects (e.g., see Costin, Neville, Meredith, & Stein, 1991) suggests that the same principles are operative in us.

The data available demonstrate that multisensory integration is a dynamic process and suggest that the interplay of stimuli from different modalities will normally depend on the physical properties of the stimuli as well as the genetic and experiential history of the organism. Nevertheless, these factors are likely to operate within the fundamental spatial and temporal rules that have already been described. Although different neural structures appear to synthesize multisensory information in very similar ways, the results of these syntheses must surely have very different impacts on behavior and perception. But it is likely that the use of similar integrative processes is necessary to link the kinds of immediate behaviors mediated by the superior colliculus, with the "higher" perceptual and cognitive processes mediated by cortex, and even with emotive processes mediated by the limbic system. In this way the brain can increase or decrease the salience of the same complex of stimuli at all levels of information processing.

REFERENCES

Ackerman, D. (1990). *A natural history of the senses.* New York: Random House.

Asanuma, C., Ohkawa, R., Stanfield, B. B., & Cowan, W. M. (1988). Observations on the development of certain ascending inputs to the thalamus in rats. I. Postnatal development. *Developmental Brain Research, 41,* 159–170.

Bower, T. G. R. (1977). *A primer of infant development.* San Francisco: Freeman.

Bruce, C., Desimone, R., & Gross, C. G. (1981). Visual properties of neurons in a polysensory area in superior temporal sulcus of the macaque. *Journal of Neurophysiology, 46,* 369–384.

Butterworth, G. (1981). The origins of auditory-visual perception and visual proprioception in human development. In R. D. Walk & L. H. Pick, Jr. (Eds.), *Intersensory perception and sensory integration* (pp. 37–70). New York: Plenum.

Casagrande, V. A., Harting, J. K., Hall, W. C., & Diamond, I. T. (1972). Superior colliculus of the tree shrew: a structural and functional subdivision into superficial and deep layers. *Science, 177,* 444–447.

Chalupa, L. M., & Rhoades, R. W. (1977). Responses of visual, somatosensory, and auditory neurones in the golden hamster's superior colliculus. *Journal of Physiology (London), 207,* 595–626.

Clarey, J. C., & Irvine, D. R. F. (1990). The anterior ectosylvian sulcal auditory field in the cat: I. An electrophysiological study of its relationship to surrounding auditory cortical fields. *Journal of Comparative Neurology, 301,* 289–303.

Clemo, H. R., Meredith, M. A., Wallace, M. T., & Stein, B. E. (1991). Is the cortex of cat anterior ectosylvian sulcus a polysensory area? *Society for Neuroscience Abstracts, 17,* 1585.

Clemo, H. R., & Stein, B. E. (1982). Somatosensory cortex: A "new" somatotopic representation. *Brain Research, 235,* 162–168.

Costin, D., Neville, H. J., Meredith, M. A., & Stein, B. E. (1991). Rules of multisensory integration and attention: ERP and behavioral evidence in humans. *Society for Neuroscience Abstracts, 17,* 656.

Cynader, M., & Berman, N. (1972). Receptive-field organization of monkey superior colliculus. *Journal of Neurophysiology, 35,* 187–201.

Cytowic, R. E. (1989). *Synesthesia: A union of the senses.* New York: Springer-Verlag.

Drager, U. C., & Hubel, D. H. (1975). Responses to visual stimulation and relationship between visual, auditory and somatosensory inputs in mouse superior colliculus. *Journal of Neurophysiology, 38,* 690–713.

Duhamel, J.-R., Colby, C. L., & Goldberg, M. E. (1989). Congruent visual and somatosensory response properties of neurons in the ventral intraparietal area (VIP) in the alert monkey. *Society for Neuroscience Abstracts, 15,* 162.

Feldon, S., Feldon, P., & Kruger, L. (1970). Topography of the retinal projection upon the superior colliculus of the cat. *Vision Research, 10,* 135–143.

Finlay, B. L., Schneps, S. E., Wilson, K. G., & Schneider, G. E. (1978). Topography of visual and somatosensory projections to the superior colliculus of the golden hamster. *Brain Research, 142,* 223–235.

Frost, D. O. (1984). Axonal growth and target selection during development: Retinal projections to the ventrobasal complex and other "nonvisual" structures in neonatal Syrian hamsters. *Journal of Comparative Neurology, 230*, 576–592.

Gibson, J. J. (1966). *The senses considered as perceptual systems.* Boston: Houghton-Mifflin.

Goodale, M. A., & Murison, R. C. C. (1975). The effects of lesions of the superior colliculus on locomotor orientation and the orienting reflex in the rat. *Brain Research, 88*, 243–261.

Gordon, B. G. (1973). Receptive fields in the deep layers of the cat superior colliculus. *Journal of Neurophysiology, 36*, 157–178.

Gottlieb, G., Tomlinson, W. R., & Radell, P. L. (1989). Developmental intersensory interference: Premature visual experience suppresses auditory learning in ducklings. *Infant Behavior and Development, 12*, 1–12.

Graham, J., Pearson, H. E., Berman, N., & Murphy, H. E. (1981). Laminar organization of superior colliculus in the rabbit: A study of receptive-field properties of single units. *Journal of Neurophysiology, 45*, 915–932.

Harris, L. R. (1980). The superior colliculus and movements of the head and eyes in cats. *Journal of Physiology, 300*, 367–391.

Hartline, P., & Northmore, D. (1986). Precision of sound localization and coordination of eye and pinna movements by cats presented with visual and auditory targets. *Society for Neuroscience Abstracts, 12*, 1277.

Hein, A., Vital-Durand, F., Salinger, W., & Diamond, R. (1979). Eye movements initiate visual-motor development in the cat. *Science, 204*, 1321–1322.

Held, R. (1955). Shifts in binaural localization after prolonged exposures to atypical combinations of stimuli. *American Journal of Psychology, 68*, 526–548.

Innocenti, G. M., & Clarke, S. (1984). Bilateral transitory projection to visual areas from auditory cortex in kittens. *Developmental Brain Research, 14*, 143–148.

Kao, C.-Q., McHaffie, J. G., Meredith, M. A., & Stein, B. E. (1991). Physiological maturation of the visual topography in the cat superior colliculus. *Society for Neuroscience Abstracts, 17*, 1378.

King, A. J., Hutchings, M. E., Moore, D. R., & Blakemore, C. (1988). Developmental plasticity in the visual and auditory representations in the mammalian superior colliculus. *Nature, 332*, 73–76.

King, A. J., & Palmer, A. R. (1985). Integration of visual and auditory information in bimodal neurones in the guinea-pig superior colliculus. *Experimental Brain Research, 60*, 492–500.

Knudsen, E. I. (1983). Early auditory experience aligns the auditory map of space in the optic tectum of the barn owl. *Science, 222*, 939–942.

Knudsen, E. I., & Knudsen, P. F. (1989). Vision calibrates sound localization in developing barn owls. *Journal of Neuroscience, 9*, 3306–3313.

Larson, M., & Stein, B. E. (1984). The use of tactile and olfactory cues in neonatal orientation and localization of the nipple. *Developmental Psychobiology, 17*, 423–436.

Lickliter, R. (1990). Premature visual stimulation accelerates intersensory functioning in bobwhite quail neonates. *Developmental Psychobiology, 23*, 15–27.

Marks, L. E. (1975). On colored-hearing synesthesia: Cross-modal translations of sensory dimensions. *Psychological Bulletin, 82*, 303–331.

Marks, L. E. (1978). *The unity of the senses: Interrelations among the modalities.* New York: Academic Press.

Maurer, D., & Maurer, C. (1988). *The world of the newborn.* New York: Basic Books.

McGurk, H., & MacDonald, J. (1976). Hearing lips and seeing voices. *Nature, 264*, 746–748.

Meltzoff, A. N., & Moore, M. K. (1977). Imitation of facial and manual gestures by human neonates. *Science, 198*, 75–78.

Meltzoff, A. N., & Moore, M. K. (1983a). The origins of imitation in infancy: Paradigm, phenomena, and theories. In L. P. Lipsitt (Ed.), *Advances in infancy research* (Vol. 2, pp. 265–301). Norwood, NJ: Ablex.

Meltzoff, A. N., & Moore, M. K. (1983b). Newborn infants imitate adult facial gestures. *Child Development, 54,* 702–709.

Meredith, M. A., Nemitz, J. W., & Stein, B. E. (1987). Determinants of multisensory integration in superior colliculus neurons. I. Temporal factors. *Journal of Neuroscience, 10,* 3215–3229.

Meredith, M. A., & Stein, B. E. (1983). Interactions among converging sensory inputs in the superior colliculus. *Science, 221,* 389–391.

Meredith, M. A., & Stein, B. E. (1985). Descending efferents from the superior colliculus relay integrated multisensory information. *Science, 227,* 657–659.

Meredith, M. A., & Stein, B. E. (1986a). Visual, auditory, and somatosensory convergence on cells in superior colliculus results in multisensory integration. *Journal of Neurophysiology, 56,* 640–662.

Meredith, M. A., & Stein, B. E. (1986b). Spatial factors determine the activity of multisensory neurons in cat superior colliculus. *Brain Research, 365,* 350–354.

Meredith, M. A., Wallace, M. T., & Stein, B. E. (1992). Visual, auditory and somatosensory convergence in output neurons of the cat superior colliculus: Multisensory properties of the tecto-reticulospinal projection. *Experimental Brain Research, 88,* 181–186.

Mistlin, A. J., & Perrett, D. I. (1990). Visual and somatosensory processing in the macaque temporal cortex: The role of "expectation." *Experimental Brain Research, 82,* 437–450.

Mucke, L., Norita, M., Benedek, G., & Creutzfeldt, O. (1982). Physiologic and anatomic investigation of a visual cortical area situated in the ventral bank of the anterior ectosylvian sulcus of the cat. *Experimental Brain Research, 46,* 1–11.

Norton, T. T. (1974). Receptive-field properties of superior colliculus cells and development of visual behavior in kittens. *Journal of Neurophysiology, 37,* 674–690.

Olson, C. R., & Graybiel, A. M. (1987). Ectosylvian visual area of the cat: Location, retinotopic organization, and connections. *Journal of Comparative Neurology, 261,* 277–294.

Piaget, J. (1952). *The origins of intelligence in children.* New York: International Universities Press.

Pick, H. L., Jr., Warren, D. H., & Hay, J. C. (1969). Sensory conflict in judgements of spatial direction. *Perceptual Psychophysiology, 6,* 203–205.

Ryan, T. A. (1940). Interrelations of the sensory systems in perception. *Psychological Bulletin, 37,* 659–698.

Schaefer, K. P. (1970). Unit analysis and electrical stimulation in the optic tectum of rabbits and cats. *Brain Behavior and Evolution, 3,* 222–240.

Schneider, G. E. (1969). Two visual systems: Brain mechanisms for localization and discrimination are dissociated by tectal and cortical lesions. *Science, 163,* 895–902.

Shelton, B. R., & Searle, C. L. (1980). The influence of vision on the absolute identification of sound-source position. *Perceptual Psychophysiology, 28,* 589–596.

Siminoff, R., Schwassmann, O., & Kruger, L. (1966). An electrophysiological study of the visual projection to the superior colliculus of the rat. *Journal of Comparative Neurology, 127,* 435–444.

Sparks, D. L. (1986). Translation of sensory signals into commands for control of saccadic eye movements: Role of primate superior colliculus. *Physiological Reviews, 66,* 116–177.

Spelke, E. S. (1987). The development of intermodal perception. In P. Salapatek & L. Cohen (Eds.), *Handbook of infant perception* (Vol. 2, pp. 233–273). New York: Academic Press.

Sprague, J. M., & Meikle, T. H., Jr. (1965). The role of the superior colliculus in visually guided behavior. *Experimental Neurology, 11,* 115–146.

Stein, B. E. (1984a). Development of the superior colliculus. *Annual Review of Neuroscience, 7,* 95–125.

Stein, B. E. (1984b). Multimodal representation in the superior colliculus and optic tectum. In H. Vanegas (Ed.), *Comparative neurology of the optic tectum* (pp. 819–841). New York: Plenum.

Stein, B. E., & Arigbede, M. O. (1972). Unimodal and multimodal response properties of neurons in the cat's superior colliculus. *Experimental Neurology, 36,* 179–196.

Stein, B. E., Clamann, H. P., & Goldberg, S. J. (1980). Superior colliculus: Control of eye movements in neonatal kittens. *Science, 210,* 78–80.

Stein, B. E., & Dixon, J. P. (1979). Properties of superior colliculus neurons in the golden hamster. *Journal of Comparative Neurology, 183,* 269–284.

Stein, B. E., Goldberg, S. J., & Clamann, H. P. (1976). The control of eye movements by the superior colliculus in the alert cat. *Brain Research, 118,* 469–474.

Stein, B. E., Labos, E., & Kruger, L. (1973a). Sequence of changes in properties of neurons of superior colliculus of the kitten during maturation. *Journal of Neurophysiology, 36,* 667–679.

Stein, B. E., Labos, E., & Kruger, L. (1973b). Determinants of response latency in neurons of superior colliculus in kittens. *Journal of Neurophysiology, 36,* 680–689.

Stein, B. E., Magalhaes-Castro, B., & Kruger, L. (1976). Relationship between visual and tactile representation in cat superior colliculus. *Journal of Neurophysiology, 39,* 401–419.

Stein, B. E., & Meredith, M. A. (1991). Functional organization of the superior colliculus. In A. G. Leventhal (Ed.), *The neural basis of visual function* (pp. 85–110). Hampshire, UK: Macmillan.

Stein, B. E., Meredith, M. A., & Wallace, M. T. (1993). The visually responsive neuron and beyond: Multisensory integration in cat and monkey. *Progress in Brain Research, 95,* 79–90.

Sur, M., Garraghty, P. E., & Roe, A. W. (1988). Experimentally induced visual projections into auditory thalamus and cortex. *Science, 242,* 1437–1441.

Thurlow, W. R., & Rosenthal, T. M. (1976). Further study of existence regions for the "ventriloquism effect." *Journal of the American Audiology Society, 1,* 280–286.

Turkewitz, G., & Mellon, R. C. (1989). Dynamic organization of intersensory function. *Canadian Journal of Psychology, 43,* 286–307.

von Helmholtz, H. (1968). The origin of the correct interpretation of our sensory impressions. In R. M. Warren & R. P. Warrent (Eds.), *Helmholtz on perception: Its physiology and development* (pp. 247–266). New York: Wiley. (Original work published 1884)

von Hornbostel, E. M. (1938). The unity of the senses. In W. D. Ellis (Ed.), *A sourcebook of Gestalt psychology* (pp. 211–216). New York: Harcourt Brace.

Warren, D. H., Welch, R. B., & McCarthy, T. J. (1981). The role of visual-auditory "compellingness" in the ventriloquism effect: Implications for transitivity among the spatial senses. *Perceptual Psychophysiology, 30,* 557–564.

Watanabe, J., & Iwai, E. (1991). Neuronal activity in visual, auditory and polysensory areas in the monkey temporal cortex during visual fixation task. *Brain Research Bulletin, 26,* 583–592.

Welch, R. B., & Warren, D. H. (1980). Immediate perceptual response to intersensory discrepancy. *Psychological Bulletin, 88,* 638–667.

Welch, R. B., & Warren, D. H. (1986). Intersensory interactions. In K. R. Boff, L. Kaufman, & J. P. Thomas (Eds.), *Handbook of perception and human performance, Volume I: Sensory processes and perception* (pp. 25-1–25-36). New York: Wiley.

Withington-Wray, D. J., Binns, K. E., & Keating, M. J. (1990). The maturation of the superior collicular map of auditory space in the guinea pig is disrupted by developmental visual deprivation. *European Journal of Neuroscience, 2,* 682–692.

Withington-Wray, D. J., Binns, K. E., Dhanjal, S. S., Brickley, S. G., & Keating, M. J. (1990). The maturation of the collicular map of auditory space in the guinea pig is disrupted by developmental auditory deprivation. *European Journal of Neuroscience, 2,* 693–703.

CHAPTER SIX

Early Stimulation History, the Cortex, and Intersensory Functioning in Infrahumans: Space and Time

Richard C. Tees
University of British Columbia

The ontogeny of intersensory competencies, their plasticity, and the neural/psychological mechanisms that might underlie multisensory integrative behaviour have become issues of importance for both developmental neurobiologists and psychologists working with young (and adult) humans and nonhumans (Mendelson, 1979; Tees & Buhrmann, 1989; Turkewitz, chap. 1, this volume; Turkewitz & Mellon, 1989). In this regard there are several kinds of cross-modal phenomena that have been under investigation in developing organisms.

One line of inquiry has been the extent to which processing modality-specific signals in one sensory system by neonates influences their processing of signals in another system, either by facilitation, inhibition, or alteration of their effectiveness in some fashion. An example of such research is the classic study of Lewkowicz and Turkewitz (1981) in which they looked at the effect of auditory stimulation on human neonates either immediately prior to or concurrent with measures of visual preferences. They found that infants showed a preference for less intense visual stimulation if auditory stimulation immediately preceded or was presented concurrently with visual test stimuli. Similarly, Gottlieb, Tomlinson, and Radell (1989), looking at the effects of concurrent visual stimulation, showed that it interferes with the ability of mallard duck embryos to learn the auditory maternal assembly call. A second class of cross-sensory functioning or multimodal interaction under investigation has been called by Turkewitz and Mellon (1989) *concurrent polymodal input* and involves simultaneous input from different sensory receptors, which is the result of a reaction to stimulation in one

107

modality. For example, newborn infants turn their eyes and/or head in the direction of an auditory stimulus, which provides concomitant visual stimulation. The same kind of response-initiated coordination of sensory information has been examined in other species (Knudsen, 1984; Whittington, Hepp-Reymond, & Flood, 1981). B. E. Stein and Meredith (1990) also reported on behavioral studies of cats trained to orient to visual stimuli in different locations while ignoring noise bursts. These animals exhibited an enhanced capacity to orient to the visual stimuli if the auditory stimulus was presented simultaneously in the same general location, whereas their visual orientation was less accurate when noise bursts occurred in spatially disparate locations. One can view these cumulative multimodal effects on the cats in terms of intersensory facilitation and inhibition or in terms of concurrent polymodal input, but clearly they reflect multimodal interactions of a sort (see Stein, Meredith, & Wallace, chap. 5, this volume).

Another type of multisensory association or coordination, which has been examined in a variety of developing organisms, involves more or less arbitrary associations between modality-specific visual, auditory, tactile, olfactory, or gustatory characteristics of objects and events. Studies of this type of functioning are exemplified by Lawson's (1980) study of conditions required for 6-month-old infants to form auditory-visual associations. Studies by Spear and his colleagues exemplified this kind of functioning in developing rats (Spear & McKinzie, chap. 7, this volume) or brain-damaged organisms of various species (e.g., Pinto-Hamuy et al., 1987). In the case of developing rats, some studies have indicated age-related differences in intersensory functioning in which the neonatal period is characterized by greater responsiveness to the overall stimulus intensity, and adulthood is characterized by more complex responsiveness. (However, preweanling animals, given appropriate early stimulation history also seem to evidence adult-like perceptual "complexity" [Spear & McKinzie, chap. 7, this volume; Mellon, Kraemer, & Spear, 1991].) In any event, the primary focus of this review is on another kind of sensory integrative behavior.

AMODAL ATTRIBUTES

Another type of intersensory processing that plays a major role in perception is the detection of amodal properties or attributes that are not specific to any modality but are or can be abstracted from modality-specific stimuli. The ability to recognize these kinds of intersensory equivalencies has been subjected to the most intense study. Mendelson (1979) provided a scheme or list of such amodal properties. These amodal properties relate to space and time and involve points along a continuum (e.g., location), intervals within continuum (e.g., duration), patterns of intervals (e.g., form), rates of patterns (e.g., tempo), or changes of rate (e.g., texture gradients). Other cross-modal correspondences such as numerosity or intensity also have been examined. Although most of the investigations have focused on amodal spatial/temporal properties involving auditory/visual correspondences, some investigators (e.g., Streri & Molina, chap. 12, this volume; Rose, chap. 11, this volume) examined infants' response to amodal attributes across the visual and haptic modalities.

A fundamental empirical issue for studies of intersensory perception has been whether and when human infants show or develop the ability to recognize particular crossmodal intersensory equivalences. It has been clear that one set of researchers, including Birch and Lefford (1963), have emphasized separate development of sensory systems and a later emergence of the ability for sensory integration. Similarly, Gottlieb (1971, 1983) emphasized the somewhat invariant sequence of sensory systems development in most vertebrates and also has predicted delayed recognition of intersensory equivalences. On the other hand, others (Bower, 1978; Gibson, 1969) have highlighted the primitive unity of sensory systems with respect to objects and events and suggested that the ability to recognize these intersensory equivalences should be both less dependent on experience and emerge earlier in development. Whatever the researcher's perspective, all seem to assume that neonates must be or soon become sensitive to these important spatiotemporal, nonarbitrary correspondences because they provide a basis for learning more arbitrary relationships. Another assumption of all viewpoints (except Gottlieb's) has been that sensory systems start on an equal basis. Yet, given the evidence that structural and functional aspects of sensory systems develop unevenly (Bronson, 1982; Gottlieb, 1971), it is possible that specific sensory dominance hierarchies operate in early development and change with age. Another prevalent assumption that we considered worth examining is whether the story on ontogeny and experience would unfold in a similar fashion no matter which intersensory equivalence was at issue.

Our own work in this area has been concerned with investigating questions related to plasticity and neural mechanisms underlying intersensory functions in young and adult rodents. We have argued that, because of the skepticism about the intersensory perceptual/cognitive abilities of infrahumans (particularly rodents), the paradigms and evidence that have been judged as acceptable for demonstrating the intersensory competency of human infants have not been judged as acceptable in the case of nonhumans. As far as tests of human neonates are concerned, infants of various ages typically are presented with two side-by-side visual stimuli, and the extent of a preference for the visual stimulus that matches a concurrently presented sound in terms of some amodal attribute is measured. Alternatively, an habituation/dishabituation procedure is employed in which subjects are habituated to an auditory/visual compound stimulus first and then their responsiveness to elements of the compound stimulus is examined in a dishabituation phase. Preferential looking (or even significant nonlooking) at the matched visual stimulus in the visual preference studies is taken as evidence of recognition of the amodal attribute. Is such a claim reasonable? Is the failure to show preferential looking or even dishabituation unambiguous as far as demonstrating the inability to detect equivalence?

TESTING FOR TRANSFER: THE RAT

Although it is evident to us that the rat does not represent a complete model for human neonatal perceptual/cognitive processes, we believe that the comparison of similarities and differences for these two related species can be illuminating as far as understanding intersensory functioning is concerned. One of the positive aspects of contemporary animal research (e.g., Kesner & Olton, 1990) is to show that procedures used to study human cognition can also be used in animal studies. This is not a one-way street. Procedures used for testing animals can, and should, be used to understand human infant perception/cognition and its important features. The paradigms typically utilized in animal research have involved transfer testing. For example, Over and Mackintosh (1969) reported that normally reared adult rats, trained to discriminate between high and low intensities of either light or sound, showed transfer when presented with stimuli differing along that same dimension in the other modality. The amount of transfer observed in this and other early studies, however, was actually very small. More importantly, virtually all of these studies inferred cross-modal transfer (CMT) by comparing the transfer of performance in a nonreversal (or consistent) conditions with that of animals tested in a reversal (or inconsistent) condition. As Church and Meck (1983) argued in their review of the early literature on cross-modal equivalence in animals, the idea that these animals recognize and use amodal correspondences between, for example, optical and acoustical information would be more persuasive if positive transfer displayed by animals being tested under rule-consistent conditions and negative transfer observed for animals being tested under rule-inconsistent conditions were both significantly different from chance performance (see Fig. 6.1). Otherwise the results can be accounted for in terms of mediation by bridging stimuli present during training and transfer tests.

Let us assume that after a specific auditory temporal pattern has been established as a discriminative conditioned stimulus for a classically or instrumentally conditioned response of an animal, a visual stimulus of the same temporal pattern turns out to be a conditioned stimulus or warning signal in a subsequent transfer phase. If one focuses on the light and tone patterned stimuli, there appears to be a cross-modal transfer of the amodal property of

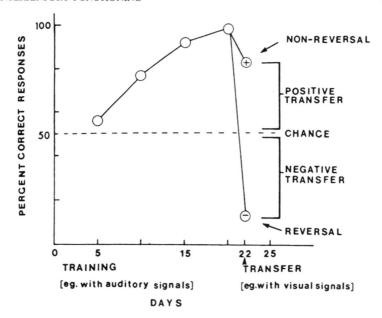

FIG. 6.1. Hypothetical performance of animals displaying incomplete but significant evidence of CMT after learning a modality-specific discrimination involving a property (e.g., location) of signals. Positive transfer would be expected under rule-consistent (nonreversal) conditions and negative transfer under rule-inconsistent (reversal) conditions.

rate (or pattern). If one focuses on the background, there does not. In training and transfer there are identical backgrounds that are interrupted 8, 10, 75 (or whatever) times a minute. The animal may not be making the same response to three flashes of light per second and three pulses of noise per second; instead it may be making the same response to three occurrences per second of identical background whether interrupted by a light or noise.

Alternative interpretations of early studies of CMT involving intensity could be mounted in a similar fashion. Once again, the animal's task is to identify a particular cue in training that is also present in the transfer test. Over and Mackintosh (1969) trained rats in a simple discrimination in which responses to one intensity of a signal were reinforced on a variable interval schedule and responses to another were unreinforced. After discrimination training on high versus low intensity signals in one modality (visual or auditory), rats subsequently learned a discrimination between high and low signals in the other modality more readily when the positive signals in both tasks were the same intensity (e.g., "high") than when they were different. This original study was then replicated by Yeterian, Waters, and Wilson (1976). Church and Meck (1983) pointed out that the "positive" stimuli were actually compound stimuli of both light and noise and the animals could have been responding to the similarity between such a compound positive stimulus during training and the corresponding compound positive stimulus during testing. The auditory signals in the Over and Mackintosh study were 62 and 95 dB, presented in a background light of 0.6 foot candles (ft-c). The visual signals were 0.05 and 14 ft-c, presented with background noise of 79 dB. The intensities of background light and sound during training were not halfway between the test stimuli on a psychological scale. For example, the background noise intensity (79 dB) was probably closer in intensity to the high-intensity noise (95 dB) than the low-intensity noise (62 dB). The background light was probably closer to the high-intensity light than to the low-intensity light stimulus.

Let's assume the animals were treating the stimuli as compound stimuli and that their performance during transfer was related to the similarity of the elements of one of the two (compound) transfer stimuli to the elements of the original positive stimulus used in training. We would expect, for example, that (Group 2) animals trained with the less intense (0.05 ft-c) light (and a "higher" 79-dB background noise) as the positive stimulus, when confronted with the high 95-dB noise stimulus (and 0.6 ft-c background light) would find that compound more similar to the original positive stimulus than the new negative stimulus (0.62 dB noise, 0.6 ft-c light) and display some transfer (see Table 6.1). The amount of transfer for Group 2 should be more than that displayed by Group 3 animals, who were transferring from a positive stimulus (0.6 ft-c, 79 dB) more similar to the new negative stimuli (0.6 ft-c, 95 dB) than the positive stimulus (0.6 ft-c, 62 dB). The cross-modal predictions would be that animals transferring from high-intensity light to high-intensity noise (Group 1) and low-intensity light to low-intensity noise (Group 3) would both show high levels of transfer compared to "reversed" groups (Groups 2 and 4). As Church and Meck (1983) argued, examination of the performance of the animals in these early studies revealed that the number of responses made to the new positive stimuli fit better a compound element analysis rather then a cross-modal analysis (see Table 6.1). Ironically, many of the experiments involving successful CMT in human infants could also be criticized for failing to determine whether or not there are common bridging elements or even what are alternative explanations for preferential looking, and so forth. In fact, not surprisingly, nonspecific arousal/intensity-related processes have been recognized as potential mediators of instances in which young infants appear to recognize some intersensory equivalences (e.g., Lewkowicz & Turkewitz, 1980; Turkewitz & Mellon, 1989). In any event, Meck and Church (1982), as well as Roberts (1982), did proceed to demonstrate unambiguous cross-modal use of duration information by rodents. These animals abstracted temporal attributes from modality-specific signals, measuring and remembering the duration of lights and sounds using some kind of common clock mechanism.

TABLE 6.1
Predicted and Actual Performance of Groups:
Properties of Responses During CMT to New Positive Stimulus

		Predicted		Actual	
Group[a]		Cross-modal	Element	Over & Mackintosh (1969)	Yeterian, Waters, & Wilson (1976)
1	Ll-Nn	1.5	1	1	1
2	lL-Nn	3.5	2	2	2
3	lL-nN	1.5	3	3	3
4	Ll-nN	3.5	4	4	4

Note. From Church and Meck (1983). Adapted by permission.
[a]L = 14ft.c. light (79db background noise); N = 95 db noise (.6 background light); l = 05ft.c. light (79db background noise); n = 62 db noise (.6 background light).

CROSS-MODAL TRANSFER: THE ROLE OF EXPERIENCE

Although these researchers (e.g., Meck & Church) viewed these abilities as involving genetically determined neural circuitry, no one actually had looked at the potential role played by early stimulation history. In early work we showed (Tees & Cartwright, 1972) that dark-reared (DR) rats benefited less than light-reared (LR) controls from a brief multimodal (auditory–visual) sensory preconditioning (SPC) experience. No such differences in impact were found with an intramodal (auditory) SPC experience. In a more recent study of rodents (Tees & Symons, 1987), we attempted to reexamine the issue by assessing the impact of early temporary visual deprivation (e.g., dark rearing from birth through to the end of testing) using similar procedures to those of Meck and Church (1982).

First, we found that all of our rats were somewhat more successful in acquiring the auditory discrimination (2 vs. 6 s) than the visual discrimination between these two durations during the initial training phase. In a comparable context, Lewkowicz (1988a, 1988b) also reported attentional dominance by auditory signals in 6- and 10-month-old human infants. In Lewkowicz's situation, infants were habituated to temporally modulated auditory/visual compound stimuli and were tested (i.e., dishabituated) in a series of trials in which one or two temporal attributes of the visual, auditory, or both compounds were changed.

In describing and interpreting comparable findings with human adult subjects, Posner (1978) argued that under certain conditions, acoustic signals had "automatic access" to central information processing and/or attentional mechanisms and took less time to process than visual signals. Intuitively, it seems one might need to learn to direct attention to visual stimuli in a situation whereas no such learning would be needed for acoustical events. In any event, such was the case with respect to the performance of both our LR and DR animals during the original training phase. More significantly, lack of experience did not adversely affect the ability of visually naive animals to recognize temporal auditory/visual correspondence. The LR and DR animals both showed incomplete but significant appropriate positive and negative transfer during the first session of the CMT testing (Day 22) under either nonreversal and reversal conditions (see Fig. 6.2). The most striking observation made in this initial investigation was that visually naive rats were as able as visually experienced animals to abstract temporal attributes from modality-specific aspects of acoustical signals and to relate these to visual events during their very first experience with such signals. That is to say, as Church and others seem to have assumed, an early visual stimulation history may well play less of a role in the case of intersensory coordination related to the attribute of duration than we and some other researchers would have predicted. The ability to recognize intersensory equivalence involving duration information may prove to be less sensitive to manipulations of visual and auditory experience in other mammals, including human infants (even if and when more stringent testing is done than has been to date).[1]

In the Tees and Symons (1982) study, we did observe differences in performance due to lack of an early visual stimulation history. For example, after demonstrating comparable negative transfer, the visually naive DR animals were less effective than their LR counterparts in adjusting to the "new world" during a cross-modal retraining phase. One interpretation of this difference is that it reflects a nonvisual spatial deficit seen in DR animals in other contexts (e.g., Tees, Midgeley, & Nesbitt, 1979). Hence, the second question we addressed (Tees & Buhrmann, 1989) was whether or not inexperienced animals would be able to recognize other correspondences, particularly the correspondence between the location of visual and auditory events. Would the animals' ability be affected by a lack of stimulation history? This question has been investigated in human infants (see Spelke, 1987). One might expect developmental differences in competencies related to cross-modal nonarbitrary equivalences involving different dimensions.

With respect to performance during the initial training phase, we found that the modality of the signals and the arrangement of the side of response vis-à-vis the stimulus did make a difference. Again, the rats were more successful overall, acquiring the discrimination between 2-s (pulsing) acoustical stimuli presented to the left and to the right, than they were when trained with

---

[1]Lewkowicz (1986) provided some evidence that 3-month-old infants do not respond to cross-modal equivalence of duration whereas older babies do, and speculated (Lewkowicz, 1992) on a developmental timetable for the differentiation of intersensory temporal capacities in which responsiveness to duration is of "later onset" than responsiveness to temporal synchrony. I'm arguing that his data are open to alternative interpretations.

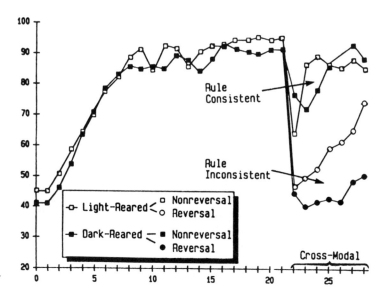

A: Signal Duration: Auditory Visual Correspondence

B. Signal Duration: Visual Auditory Correspondence

Test Days

FIG. 6.2. Performances of LR and DR rats during the initial acquisition of a duration discrimination involving auditory (A) and visual (B) events, and during the subsequent phases of CMT, signal omission, retraining, and transfer testing. From Tees and Symons (1987). Adapted by permission.

comparable visual events. Interestingly, researchers interested in the development of auditory and visual localization in human infants during their first 12 months emphasized the notion that, throughout this period, infants attach low attentional priority to acoustical spatial information in the perception of objects and events (e.g., Field, 1987). Only Lewkowicz (1988a, 1988b) suggested that signals from a visual modality might play a subordinate role to the auditory modality in human infants in their early intersensory functioning, at least when the visual information is spatially static.

As far as performance of our rats was concerned, auditory signals were more effective and more salient in terms of establishing stimulus/response associations from day 1 of their training. [Further, those animals trained to respond ipsilaterally (e.g., to a signal on the left by pressing the left lever) made significantly more correct responses than those trained to respond contralaterally to the location of a stimulus (e.g., to the left stimulus by reacting to the right lever). It is not surprising that the contiguity between the location of the stimulus and the response would have an impact on initial performance, because such a relationship has been observed in many other situations (e.g., Roitblat, 1987).]

Our major finding involved the relative CMT of initial modality-specific location discrimination observed in DR versus LR rats. After reaching comparable levels of performance during their initial training with either visual or auditory signals, visually naive DR rats failed to demonstrate as much CMT (especially negative transfer under reversal conditions) as their visually experienced LR counterparts. Moreover, the inferior performance of the DR rats was not only observed in those instances in which they were confronted with visual signals for the very first time (after initial auditory training). Their difficulties were evident when the transfer involved a switch from visual to auditory, as well as from auditory to visual events. (Both LR and DR rats evidently found the switch from visual to auditory easier, underlining the point made earlier about the salience or automatic access of acoustical events in such conditions.) We now had evidence for an experience-related difference as far as cross-modal equivalences involving different attributes were concerned. Lack of visual experience did not affect the development and/or maintenance of a common timing or clock mechanism that is likely to be in operation when an animal is measuring and remembering the duration of light and sound stimuli (Tees & Symons, 1987). It did, however, affect recognition of intermodal equivalences involving the location of signals in space, and this finding has strengthened our idea that the visually deprived rodent exhibits less effective use of both visual and nonvisual spatial information (Tees, 1990). Several researchers, including Warren (1978), reported on superior spatial abilities in blind persons who had experienced a period of early vision, relative to those with congenital blindness. We and others have contended that an early visual stimulation history facilitates the establishment of an organizational framework for spatial ability even with respect to responses to signals in other modalities (Burnstine, Greenough, & Tees, 1984; Tees, 1990; Turkewitz & Kenny, 1982; Stein, Meredith, & Wallace, chap. 5, this volume). Our perspective about differential effects of early stimulation history has been strengthened by the data from a recently completed study. We have found that a multimodally enriched stimulation history (i.e., complex rearing) facilitates the development of the ability to recognize location on the basis of modality-specific visual or auditory signals even though having little effect on CMT involving duration (Tees, in preparation).

In reviewing their approach to the evidence of intersensory function in human infants and developing rodents, Turkewitz, Lewkowicz, and Gardner (1983) reasoned that stimulation from different modalities could be viewed as additive. They argued that young infants ignore differences between inputs in different modalities and respond to these inputs as equivalent when their effective intensity is the same (see also Lewkowicz, chap. 8, this volume).[2] In a narrow sense, this position is reminiscent of the view that development proceeds as a process of differentiation of an initial supramodal unity (e.g., Bower, 1978). This would suggest that the success of our rats in recognizing the attribute of duration of signals should be reinterpreted (which would involve some difficulty) as simply reflecting the perception of long visual and auditory signals as more intense than short signals. However, such an intensity-based interpretation of the CMT of the location of signals shown by our LR rats is not plausible (Tees & Buhrmann, 1989). Although the LR rats showed reasonably good CMT of location overall, their performance during other kinds of transfer tests suggests that modality-specific spatial information is influential as well. If performance by LR rats on CMT indicated incomplete but significant recognition of the correspondence between visually and auditorily signaled "locations," then their performance later in the transfer testing made it clear that they also remembered the original association between a specific response with the modality-specific signal. When confronted with a choice and a conflict, they consistently responded in accordance with their original training. Presumably the amodal correspondence involving the location attribute is recognizable but less salient for the rats. Although this adds to the complexity of possible interpretations of our own data, it should be pointed out, once again, that we don't have comparable, detailed examination of CMT in human infants. If we did, we might well have equally complex data to interpret.

We do know that intersensory functioning can be altered by earlier than normal availability of visual and other kinds of sensory input, accelerating or

---

[2]As mentioned earlier, preweanling rats given differential reinforcement exhibit nonadditive, non-intensity-based intermodal responding (Mellon et al., 1991). Perhaps young human infants are also able to respond to other intermodal properties besides intensity with appropriate motivation. The key experiment hasn't been undertaken.

decelerating the onset of species-typical auditory/visual intermodal responsiveness in birds (Lewkowicz & Lickliter, chap. 16, this volume; Lickliter, 1990). Although such demonstrations emphasize the importance of normally occurring developmental limitations of sensory input to early perceptual organization, the evidence to date on such effects represents short-lived, temporary consequences measured by preferential responding. Failure to demonstrate preferences for particular stimuli may not reflect processing inadequacies. Nonetheless, it is certainly evidence for a weak form of the developmental intersensory interference hypothesis of Turkewicz and Kenny (1982) in that momentary attentional difficulties are caused by concurrent, inappropriate stimulation of a neonate's immature system.

CROSS-MODAL RECOGNITION: NEURAL SYSTEMS

I have argued elsewhere (Tees, 1990) that the impact of experience (as reflected in the outcome of controlled rearing experiments) is more diffuse than that observed with specific cortical lesions. However, some kinds of processing "modules" appear to be more affected by manipulations of experience than others. Those modules that are involved in competencies or operations that require more information integration and appear more dependent on memorial and selective attentional processes seem to be vulnerable to changes in stimulation history. For example, the ability to acquire and remember a spatial map of an environment and to navigate to invisible targets, the ability to recognize stationary patterns on the basis of the relationships between the lines, the ability to orient to spatial and temporal changes in patterned (auditory or visual) events, and CMT involving location all appear to be influenced by stimulation history. All could be characterized as requiring trade-offs between an appreciation of aspects of the environment and remembering some specific features of the environment, while ignoring others. My own view is that there is a fundamental difference in the role played by experience in the ontogeny and the nature of the neural substrates for "clock" and "map" perceptual mechanisms. In this regard, mechanisms underlying the recognition of some other attributes, including intensity, would resemble that underlying duration. The recognition of patternlike attributes would be similar to cross-modal recognition of location. Because these latter competencies involve memory, attention, appreciation of spatial aspects of the environment, the extrastriate (Oc2M, Oc2L), secondary auditory (TE3), parietal (PPC), and temporal (Te2) areas of cortex seem likely to us to be implicated as far as the underlying neural circuitry is concerned. The cortical tissue necessary for these kinds of operations could well be late developing and thus logically would be more vulnerable to manipulations of early stimulation history. There is, of course, a reasonable alternative view to this. It could well be that the controlled rearing affects every operation somewhat and equally. The more operations there are, the more modules are required for the successful performance of a perceptual task, the greater the impact of controlled rearing would appear to be. Thus, the small but real effects on the animal's ability to resolve detail, to orient, to process, to remember, and so forth, would produce cumulative and sizeable effects on those cortical-dependent behaviors that rely on many of these operations. The two views are not mutually exclusive and our ability to distinguish these alternatives is limited. In any event, we have tried to focus on the first of these alternatives.

Some time ago, Yeterian (1977) looked at the impact of visual/striate and auditory/temporal cortical lesions in rodents on CMT involving the intensity of visual and auditory stimuli. Although, as I've indicated, there are some problems in the design of the experiment, the effects of his relatively sizeable visual or auditory posterior cortical lesions were such that modality-specific auditory and visual intensity discriminations were unaffected by either lesion. On the other hand, all lesioned animals failed to show any evidence of CMT of intensity. Yeterian argued for convergence of auditory and visual inputs into "secondary" portions of visual (e.g., possibly Oc2M) and auditory (e.g., possibly Te3) cortex, suggesting that the damage to either of these regions resulted in a failure to recognize the attribute and show CMT.

One alternative to this idea is that the critical region for convergence is a different area of neocortex whose input and cortical interconnections would be disrupted by either sensory cortical lesion. Polysensory neurons, responsive to visual, tactile, and/or auditory events, have been observed in the association cortex (as well as the colliculus and hippocampus) of normally reared rodents and have been found to be late developing (Drager & Hubel, 1976; Meikle, 1968). In fact, in a better designed study of the role played by primary cortex, Salazar, Wallace, and Baker-Salazar (1991) found neither a (more restricted) primary auditory nor a visual cortical lesion affected CMT of intensity. Further, Thompson and Kraemer (1965) found that posterior association cortical lesions and not primary sensory lesions affected learned auditory–visual associations in rats.

Obviously, a third possibility is that the critical convergence involves connections to subcortical structures such as the superior colliculus (Drager & Hubel, 1976), which is clearly a polysensory/motor processing structure (see Stein, Meredith, & Wallace, chap. 5, this volume). Unfortunately, the evidence available from 2DG measurement and the effects of lesions on learned cross-modal tactile/visual recognition stimuli have not given us a clear picture of which subcortical and cortical structures are critically involved in processing such information (Ettlinger & Garcha, 1980; Hörster et al., 1989; Streicher & Ettlinger, 1987).

As far as polysensory subcortical and cortical neural development is concerned, there is an exciting literature emerging about how sensitive these perceptual/neural systems are—at least the multimodal structures that might underlie localizing and cross-modal pattern recognition—to the effects of early experience. Experience-dependent plasticity in the auditory–visual space map has now been assessed in several species, either by examining the effects of sensory deprivation or by selectively altering the spatial information provided by the ears and eyes (see review by King & Moore, 1991). Rearing barn owls and ferrets with abnormal binaural cues (i.e., with ear plugs) leads to compensatory adjustments in the auditory map so that the alignment with the visual map is preserved. A surgically induced lateral deviation of one eye in ferrets results in a corresponding change in the auditory map of the contralateral superior colliculus (SC), again maintaining registration with the visual map. Guinea pigs of different ages have been placed in an environment of omnidirectional white noise, and this form of selective exposure/deprivation can prevent the formation of auditory/visual maps. Visual or auditory deprivation itself also prevents the emergence of the electrophysiological (and behavioral) map of auditory space in the guinea pig (Withington-Wray & Keating, 1989). This developmental plasticity found in centrally synthesized maps of auditory/visual space enables the brain to adjust to growth-related changes in the relative geometry of different sense organs. The developmental requirement for coincidental visual and auditory sensory input also makes clear that polysensory structures, such as the superior colliculus, could represent candidates for the neural substrate of CMT involving amodal location, particularly in young organisms. (The SC is relatively mature in human infants at birth, and the postnatal plasticity of maps demonstrated in infrahumans may not be as relevant.) In any event, it has been suggested that newborn human infants map sensory information from one modality onto sensory information from another almost automatically by these collicular mechanisms (Diamond, in B. E. Stein & Meredith, 1990). Stein, Meredith, and Wallace (chap. 5, this volume) argue that there is nothing special about the multisensory integration that goes on in the colliculus, arguing for a more widespread representation of polysensory neurons (which could form the substrate for crossmodal transfer). In the cat, Rauschecker and Harris (1983) showed that visual deprivation only produces modest changes in visual responsiveness as far as neurons in the SC are concerned, but it does produce evidence of auditory compensation. They provided data to suggest that compensatory processes are activated that lead to a visually deprived adult animal being more capable of localizing peripheral sounds as a result of unimodal visual deprivation. Detailed, systematic behavioral investigation of compensatory effects has not yet been undertaken (however, see Neville, 1990). In any event, although these unimodal restrictions of sensory input have been shown to have intersensory effects, no one has shown that one of these is the facilitation of CMT involving properties of previously "undeprived" sensory input of other modalities.

In discussing the organization of the posterior cortex of the rat, Kolb and Tees (1990) speculated that the posterior parietal (PPC) region might be a key structure in respect to intermodal recognition. In that review, our focus was on the learning of arbitrary intermodal signals. The pattern of connections between PPC and other regions of cortex is similar in general plan to that of the monkey, but still there are some identifiable differences. For example, in the case of the rat, there are direct projections from auditory cortical areas (see Fig. 6.3). In any event, this PPC represents a region of posterior cortex that receives inputs from visual, auditory, somatosensory cortical regions and has reciprocal connections with prefrontal cortex. (One interesting aspect of this PPC area is its close relationship with the extrastriate region [Oc2M] that itself has a retinotopic map, as well as significant connections with the SC.) Rats with PPC lesions are impaired on a task in which they have to learn to match a tactile cue (roughness of the floor) with a visual cue (Pinto-Hamuy et al., 1987). Rats with lesions of auditory or visual cortex are not similarly impaired. In this study, the rats had to learn, for example, that a smooth floor was associated with reward when paired with one visual stimulus and not with

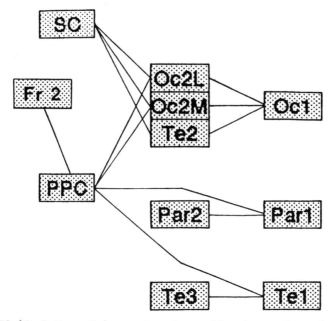

FIG. 6.3. Cortico-cortical connections of some of the primary and secondary sensory regions to the positive posterior parietal cortex (PPC) of the rat. Oc1 (occipital), Par 1 (parietal/somatosensory), and Te1 (temporal/auditory) are primary sensory cortical regions (Zilles, 1990). Oc2L, Oc2M, Te2, Par 2, and Te3 are secondary visual somatosensory and auditory cortical regions. The connections to prefrontal (Fr2) cortex and the subcortical superior colliculus (SC) are also indicated.

another, while the relationship between a rough floor and the visual stimuli was the opposite. Certainly the ability to learn cross-modal (arbitrary) associations between stimuli from different modalities represents a test of intermodal integrative ability. The posterior parietal cortex (PPC) could enable the animal to encode and associate stimuli, at least from the somatic, auditory, and visual modalities, as has been suggested for the primate (see Kolb & Whishaw, 1990). Farah, Wong, Monheit, and Morrow (1989) examined parietal cortically damaged human patients and their data argue for a PPC-based supramodal attentional system that is automatically engaged by at least auditory and visual stimuli.

Rodents with PPC lesions have also been tested under a wide range of maze tasks, and they appear to be impaired in virtually every type of maze employed. The deficits vary considerably with severity, with the largest deficits being evident on the Hebb-Williams Maze. The most likely explanation of the deficit appears to be that they have difficulty perceiving the spatial relationships between objects and do not orient themselves accurately with respect to that spatial information (Kolb, 1990). Dimattia and Kesner (1988) argued that the parietal cortex plays an important role in the processing of information about space that is allocentric or external to the body. On the other hand, on the basis of changes in the exploratory behavior in an environment in which stimuli are moved, taken away, or introduced, Foreman, Save, Thinus-Blanc, and Buhot (1992) argued that rat parietal cortex is not essential for redirection of attention to multimodal stimuli notable for their unexpected presence or absence. They argue that the parietal cortex functions to resolve interhemispheric competition, playing a role in making decisions about where attention should be directed when lower structures such as the bilateral SC are equally and symmetrically stimulated. Save, Poucet, Foreman, and Buhot (1992), looking at differences between the effect of lesions of either the anterior and posterior regions in the PPC on exploration of objects in an open field, concluded that the anterior portion was involved in an attentional effort itself and that the posterior region was involved in multimodal spatial information processing necessary to represent the features of the field. The experimental evidence for such speculations is weak. It is also unfortunate that in virtually every instance the investigative emphasis has been on relationships between visual cues rather than cues of different modalities. However, the idea that such a structure in the cortex may mediate higher levels of multimodal selective attention seems like a promising one. Very recently, we have examined the impact of selective PPC lesions on the ability to show CMT of nonarbitrary associations (i.e., amodal attributes) of auditory and visual signals (Tees, Johnston, Sivucha, & Kwan, in preparation). The specific PPC lesions had little or no effect on the cross-modal recognition of duration, but did have a considerable effect on cross-modal recognition of location. That is to say, animals with PPC lesions have difficulty, after being trained to respond to left and right (e.g., auditory signals), transferring when presented with two visual signals presented in similar locations. It is possible that the PPC is one critical part of the neural circuitry underlying intermodal processing of location signals, but not intermodal processing in general.

With respect to the neural substrate that might underlie cross-modal recognition of nonarbitrary attributes such as duration and location, we have emphasized the role that might be played by posterior association neocortex. There is certainly another research literature that would predict prefrontal cortex to be a part of the neural circuitry (Kolb & Walkey, 1987). We have not tested prefrontal rats on any CMT test. We have viewed the descending connections of the posterior regions to SC as representing neural tissue that is more likely to be of significance for the rat's ability to integrate information about both time and space. Such an emphasis certainly would be consistent with our view that intermodal spatial and temporal sensitivity requires both polymodal single-neuron topography (Stein et al., chap. 5, this volume) and a link to orientation systems in which, for example, movements of the stimulus events trigger integrative behavioral output. Our very preliminary data suggest that combined bilateral lesions of SC, Oc2M, and PPC eliminate CMT of both direction and location. In contrast, such lesions do not affect modality-specific acquisition.

What other evidence is available to specify which neural structures are not important for cross-modal abilities involving the abstraction of duration of location and other basic amodal attributes such as rate, intensity, location, and number? Meck, Church, and Olton (1984) examined rats with hippocampal lesions, as well as unlesioned controls, and found that all animals demonstrated CMT of the duration and rate of auditory signals used in training to the visual signals used in testing. It seems that their hippocampal rats were performing the CMT on the basis of a central timing mechanism that was independent of stimulus modality, and the brain damage did not affect the ability to transfer information from one modality to another. It seems somewhat surprising that the processing of duration and rate (i.e., temporal information and the related CMT) did not require a hippocampus or working memory. Our prediction would be that the CMT involving location would be adversely affected by hippocampal damage.

In investigations of numerical competency (Davis & Pérusse, 1988), a great deal of evidence has emerged that rats can count. For example, Fernandes and Church (1982) demonstrated that rats could be trained to press a lever following two successive sounds and to press another for four successive sounds. Classification of other novel sound sequences suggests that the animals either were using "number" or "sum of sound durations" in a sequence as a relevant cue. When this total sound duration was put in conflict with number, the rats classified by number. The conclusion reached by Fernandes and Church was that rats could discriminate number, even when temporal cues were controlled. Those engaged in research on "animal counting" have agreed that the best test of ability would involve intermodal transfer. That is to say, evidence of intermodal transfer would provide the operational basis for a claim that a given example of numerical ability was modality-abstract or free. Indeed, Church and Meck (1984) retrained Fernandes and Church's animals on their auditory numbers and found evidence for CMT to numbered visual stimuli.

In Meck and Church's account (e.g., Meck et al., 1984), the recognition of rate, time, and number involves either the same neural system, or has a common neural element that affects the separate networks. In order to demonstrate this, Church and Meck (in a series of papers; e.g., Church & Meck, 1984) utilized pharmacological manipulation to show that chemicals such as methamphetamine would alter both timing and counting—that is, the recognition of the amodal property of duration and number.

What sort of research has been done on recognition of numerical information by infants? Starky, Spelke, and Gelman (1983) claimed that 7-month-old infants can extract an abstract dimension such as number across two different sensory modalities. When confronted with two arrays of visual objects, infants preferred to look at an array that corresponded in number to a sequence of sounds (e.g., drumbeats). Davis, Albert and Barron (1985) argued strongly that the evidence provided by Starky et al. did not demonstrate detection of intermodal numerical correspondences and that their data could be more parsimoniously described as showing an intermodal discrimination of "more numerous" to "less numerous" discrete quantities. There may be, however, nothing to account for as far as evidence on human neonate's ability. Moore, Beninnsen, Resnick, Peterson, and Kagan (1987) replicated the original Starkey et al. study and their data seemed to support the idea that, if anything, infants look longer at noncorresponding displays when slides of two or three objects are presented with either two or three drumbeats. The data they collected did not support a claim that 7-month-old infants prefer to look at arrays that corresponded to a specific number of sounds (Moore et al., 1987). Their data revealed an infant preference for greater contour density and a tendency to habituate to repeatedly presented stimuli. They considered a simple conclusion about their results suggested originally by Lewkowicz and Turkewitz (1981), namely, that infants generally seek an optimum level of stimulation across all modalities. Infants who hear three beats may be driven to visually explore the less simulating display of two objects, whereas infants who hear two beats are driven to explore the more stimulating display of three objects. In my view, neither the original demonstration reported in *Science* (Starkey et al., 1983) nor the subsequent attempt to replicate this study would have constituted even weak evidence for intermodal recognition of number had the experiment been undertaken with any other species (see Davis & Pérusse, 1988, for a more complete account).

CONCLUDING REMARKS

In this chapter I have discussed the role played by early stimulation history and by particular neural systems in the development of intermodal functions related to the detection of location and time. I've tried to contrast the procedures utilized to establish intersensory abilities in the rat and human infant. Clearly the rat does not represent a complete model for human neonatal perceptual cognitive processes; however, comparison of similarities and differences between these two related species can be illuminating as far as understanding intersensory functioning. I believe the procedures used in animal studies can and should be applied to help understand human infant perception/cognition. The animal cognitive literature should be a rich source of ideas about research paradigms. For instance, Tomie and Whishaw (1990) showed that rats of various ages can be trained easily to pull up strings to obtain attached food pellets and can utilize compound stimuli involved in the string's size, texture, olfactory, and visual characteristics. Rudy (1991) has also shown the value of moving back and forth between experiments involving young children and different aged and brain-damaged rats in his studies of differences between learned elemental and configural associations. A series of experiments demonstrated that animals with hippocampal damage, preweanling rats, and children less than 55 months of age were significantly impaired on tasks that required solving configurational associations, arguing for separate neural systems available to support "elemental" and "configural" learning, with the configural one depending on the integrity of the hippocampal formation (see Rudy, 1991). Cross-modal transfer (CMT), number, and duration apparently do not depend on the hippocampus (Meck et al., 1984). If that is the case, we know that at least the "clock" function has a different neural and perhaps developmental history. We need to develop a better idea about the extent of neural systems underlying other functions and differences in these with respect to other important amodal properties. We have tried to emphasize that the data to date suggest that map and clock functions really involve different neural systems, and that the map or location system may include polysensory cortex, Oc2M, and PPC and subcortical structures including the SC. One approach we plan to take to better understand the neural systems underlying these abilities is the use of chemical manipulation. Church's clever use of drugs to show the common effects on clock and number responsiveness in rats could also be used to dissociate other competencies from these. Along a related track, we have already (Tees & Johnston, 1992) altered cholinergic neural systems neonatally and have shown that such dietary supplementation affects spatial CMT in adult animals.

Although polysensory cortical structures are involved in these multimodal abilities, it is certainly highly probable that newborn human infants, as well as rats, could map sensory information from one modality onto sensory information from another modality automatically by collicular mechanisms. The argument could be made that older infants and adults, who have more mature cortical areas to inhibit the colliculus, may do some of that same mapping (as well as recognizing more sophisticated equivalences) with association cortex-based mechanisms. Not only might the SC be capable of serving multisensory integration needed for young infants and for rats to succeed at many intermodal tasks, but the colliculus is also capable of associating perceptual recognition with action (see Stein et al., chap. 5, this volume). For instance, a neonate perceives a facial gesture and then automatically acts to imitate it (Meltzoff & Kuhl, chap. 14, this volume). The SC might help mediate this integrative behavior. However, on the face of it, facial imitations and cross-modal speech responsiveness (see Meltzoff, 1990) would seem to require inputs from cortical regions. Unfortunately, the evidence suggests that these regions perhaps are not sufficiently mature to provide the modulation the SC would need to regulate the complex multimodal responsiveness that Meltzoff documents in human infants (Kolb & Fantie, 1989).

The issue of whether exuberant cross-modal neural projections might mediate early multimodal abilities seems more tenuous to me. It is true (Sur, Pallas, & Roe 1990) that very early in development there are connections between different sensory systems that will later disappear. It is now widely recognized that the normal development of the central nervous system is a destructive as well as a constructive process. There is an overproduction and subsequent elimination of sensory perceptually related neurons and their connections. The argument would go that these could subserve the multimodal abilities demonstrated by developing infants (and rats). We do know from Frost's work (1990), in which he stabilizes normally retracting exuberant projections from one sensory system to another, that they are functional physiologically and behaviorally at least in adult rodents. In my view, however, there is no evidence to suggest that these exuberant projections exist or function in cross-modal performance observed in human infants. These exuberant connections seem to have more to do with the evidence for intermodal compensation evident in congenitally deaf or visually deprived adult humans and animals (Burnstine, Greenough, & Tees, 1984; Neville, 1990).

One observation that I would like to reinforce was originally made by David Lewkowicz. Many events in the world require that we associate multimodal inputs that are not explicitly related by some amodal invariant or property but that co-occur (e.g., the visual, auditory, and tactile characteristics of a puppy dog). In these kinds of cases, the ability to detect amodal and intersensory equivalents seems irrelevant. It seems that the amodal invariances we are investigating must play a calibrating role as far as other modalities are concerned and a critical role in early intermodal perceptual learning.

Finally, we can conclude on the basis of available evidence that nonhumans, including rodents, are capable of detecting intersensory equivalences based on a variety of amodal stimulus attributes. Time, number, rate, and location all seem to have been reasonably well established as far as these cross-modal competencies are concerned. There are both similarities and clear differences about the neural systems underlying these different abilities and the role played by early stimulation history in their development. This is an exciting time to be trying to understand the ontogeny of these competencies and their neural substrates.

ACKNOWLEDGMENTS

This chapter was supported by Natural Sciences and Engineering Council of Canada Grant AP0179. The assistance of Lucille Hoover and the patient David Lewkowicz is gratefully acknowledged.

REFERENCES

Birch, H. G., & Lefford, A. (1963). Visual differentiation, intersensory integration, and voluntary control. *Monographs of the Society for Research and Child Development, 32* (Serial No. 110).

Bower, T. G. R. (1978). Perceptual development: Object and space. In E. C. Carterette & M. P. Friedman (Eds.), *Handbook of perception* (Vol. VIII, pp. 83–103). New York: Academic Press.

Bronson, G. W. (1982). Structure, states, and characteristics of the nervous system and birth. In P. Stratton (Ed.), *Psychobiology of the human newborn* (pp. 99–118). Chichester: Wiley.

Burnstine, T. H., Greenough, W. T., & Tees, R. C. (1984). Intermodal compensation following damage or deprivation. In C. R. Almli & S. Finger (Eds.), *The behavioural biopsychology of early brain damage* (pp. 3–34). New York: Academic Press.

Church, R. M., & Meck, W. H. (1983). Acquisition and cross-modal transfer of classification rules for temporal intervals. In M. L. Commons, R. J. Herrnstein, & A. R. Wagner (Eds.), *Quantitative analysis of behaviour: Discrimination processes* (Vol. 4, pp. 75–97). Cambridge, MA: Ballinger.

Church, R. M., & Meck, W. H. (1984). The numerical attribute of stimuli. In H. L. Roitblat, T. G. Bever, & H. S. Terrace (Eds.), *Animal cognition* (pp. 445–464). Hillsdale, NJ: Lawrence Erlbaum Associates.

Davis, H., & Pérusse, R. (1988). Numerical competence in animals. *Behavioural and Brain Sciences, 11,* 561–615.

Davis, H., Albert, M., & Barron, R. W. (1985). Detection of number or numerousness in human infants. *Science, 228,* 1222.

Dimattia, B. D., & Kesner, R. P. (1988). Spatial cognitive maps: Differential role of parietal cortex and hippocampal formation. *Behavioural Neuroscience, 102,* 471–480.

Drager, U. C., & Hubel, D. H. (1976). Topography of visual and somatosensory projections to mouse superior colliculus. *Journal of Neurophysiology, 39,* 91–101.

Ettlinger, G., & Garcha, H. S. (1980). Crossmodal recognition by the monkey: The effect of cortical removals. *Neuropsychologia, 18,* 685–692.

Farah, M. J., Wong, A. B., Monheit, M. A., & Morrow, L. A. (1989). Parietal lobe mechanisms of spatial attention: Modality-specific or supramodal? *Neuropsychologia, 27,* 461–470.

Fernandes, D. M., & Church, R. M. (1982). Discrimination of the number of sequential events by rats. *Animal Learning and Behaviour, 10,* 171–176.

Field, J. (1987). The development of auditory-visual localization in infancy. In D. E. McKenzie & R. H. Day (Eds.), *Perceptual development in early infancy: Problems and issues* (pp. 175–198). Hillsdale, NJ: Lawrence Erlbaum Associates.

Foreman, N., Save, E., Thinus-Blanc, C., & Buhot, M. (1992). Visually guided locomation, distractibility, the missing-stimulus effect on hooded rats with unilateral or bilateral lesions of parietal cortex. *Behavioural Neuroscience, 106,* 529–538.

Frost, D. O. (1990). Sensory processing in novel, experimentally induced crossmodal circuits. In A. Diamond (Ed.), The development and neural bases of higher cognitive functions. *Annals of the New York Academy of Sciences, 608,* 92–112.

Gibson, E. J. (1969). *Principles of perceptual learning and development.* Englewood Cliffs, NJ: Prentice-Hall.

Gottlieb, G. (1971). Ontogenesis of sensory functions in birds and mammals. In E. Tobach, L. R. Aronson, & E. Shaw (Eds.), *The biopsychology of development* (pp. 67–128). New York: Academic Press.

Gottlieb, G. (1983). The psychobiological approach to developmental issues. In P. H. Mussen (Ed.), *Handbook of child psychology: Vol. 1. Infancy and developmental psychobiology* (pp. 1–26). New York: Wiley.

Gottlieb, G., Tomlinson, W. T., & Radell, D. L. (1989). Developmental intersensory interference: Premature visual experience suppresses auditory learning in ducklings. *Infant Behaviour and Development, 12,* 1–12.

Hörster, W., Rivers, A., Schuster, B., Ettlinger, G., Skreczek, W., & Hesse, W. (1989). The neural structures involved in crossmodal recognition and tactile discrimination performance: An investigation using 2-DG. *Behavioural Brain Research, 33,* 209–227.

Kesner, R. P., & Olton, D. S. (1990). *Neurobiology of comparative cognition.* Hillsdale, NJ: Lawrence Erlbaum Associates.

King, A. J., & Moore, D. R. (1991). Plasticity of auditory maps in the brain. *Trends in Neuroscience, 14,* 31–37.

Kolb, B. (1990). Posterior parietal and temporal association cortex (pp. 459–471). *The cerebral cortex of the rat.* Cambridge, MA: MIT Press.

Kolb, B., & Fantie, B. (1989). Development of a child's brain and behavior. In C. R. Reynolds & E. Fletcher Jenzen (Eds.), *Handbook of clinical child neuropsychology* (pp. 17–39). New York: Plenum.

Kolb, B., & Tees, R. C. (1990). *The cerebral cortex of the rat.* Cambridge, MA: MIT Press.

Kolb, B., & Walkey, J. (1987). Behavioural and anatomical studies of the posterior parietal cortex in the rat. *Behavioural Brain Research, 23,* 127–145.

Kolb, B., & Whishaw, I. Q. (1990). *Fundamentals of human neuropsychology* (3rd ed.). New York: Freeman.

Knudsen, E. F. (1984). The role of auditory experience in the development and maintenance of sound localization. *Trends in Neuroscience, 7,* 326–330.

Lawson, K. R. (1980). Spatial and temporal congruity and auditory integration in infants. *Developmental Psychology, 16,* 185–192.

Lewkowicz, D. J. (1986). Developmental changes in infants' bisensory response to synchronous durations. *Infant Behaviour and Development, 9,* 335–353.

Lewkowicz, D. J. (1988a). Sensory dominance in infants. I. Six-month old infant responses to auditory-visual compounds. *Developmental Psychology, 24,* 155–171.

Lewkowicz, D. J. (1988b). Sensory dominance in infants. II. Ten-month old infants' response to auditory-visual compounds. *Developmental Psychology, 24,* 172–182.

Lewkowicz, D. J. (1992). The development of temporally-based intersensory perception in human infants. In F. Macar, V. Pouthas, & W. J. Friedman (Eds.), *Time, action and cognition: Towards bridging the gap* (pp. 33–43). Dordrecht: Kluwer.

Lewkowicz, D. J., & Turkewitz, G. (1980). Cross modal equivalence in early infancy: Auditory-visual intensity matching. *Developmental Psychology, 16,* 597–607.

Lewkowicz, D. J., & Turkewitz, G. (1981). Intersensory interaction in newborns: Modification of visual preferences following exposure to sound. *Child Development, 52,* 827–832.

Lickliter, R. (1990). Premature visual stimulation accelerates intersensory functioning in bobwhite quail neonates. *Developmental Psychobiology, 23,* 15–27.

Meck, W. H., & Church, R. M. (1982). Abstraction of temporal attributes. *Journal of Experimental Psychology: Animal Behaviour Processes, 8,* 226–243.

Meck, W. H., Church, R. M., & Olton, D. S. (1984). Hippocampus, time, and memory. *Behavioural Neuroscience, 98,* 3022

Meikle, M. B. (1968, April). *Unit activity in rat association cortex in response to auditory, visual and tactile stimulation.* Paper presented at the meeting of the Western Psychological Association, San Diego.

Mellon, R. C., Kraemer, P. J., & Spear, N. E. (1991). Development of intersensory function: Age related differences in stimulus selection of multimodal compounds in rats as revealed by pavlovian conditioning. *Journal of Experimental Psychology: Animal Behaviour Processes, 17,* 448–464.

Meltzoff, A. N. (1990). Towards a developmental cognitive science. In A. Diamond (Ed.), The development and neural bases of higher cognitive functions. *Annals of the New York Academy of Sciences, 608,* 1–37.

Mendelson, M. J. (1979). Acoustic-optical correspondences of auditory-visual coordination in infancy. *Canadian Journal of Psychology, 33,* 334–346.

Moore, D., Benenson, J., Reznick, J. S., Peterson, M., & Kagan, J. (1987). Effect of auditory numerical information on infants' looking behaviour: Contradictory evidence. *Developmental Psychology, 23,* 665–670.

Neville, H. J. (1990). Intermodal competition and compensation in development: Evidence from studies of the visual systems in congenitally deaf adults. In A. Diamond (Ed.), The development and neural bases of higher cognitive functions. *Annals of the New York Academy of Sciences, 608,* 71–91.

Over, R., & MacIntosh, N. J. (1969). Cross-modal transfer of intensity discrimination by rats. *Nature, 224,* 918–919.

Pinto-Hamuy, T., Olavarria, J., Guic-Robles, E., Morgues, M., Nassal, O., & Petit, D. (1987). Rats with lesions in anteromedial extrastriate cortex fail to learn a visuosomatic conditional response. *Behavioural Brain Research, 25,* 221–231.

Posner, M. I. (1978). *Chronometric explorations of the mind.* Hillsdale, NJ: Lawrence Erlbaum Associates.

Rauschecker, J. P., & Harris, L. R. (1983). Auditory compensation of the effects of visual deprivation in the cat's superior colliculus. *Experimental Brain Research, 50,* 69–83.

Roberts. S. (1982). Cross-modal use of an internal clock. *Journal of Experimental Psychology: Animal Behaviour Processes, 8,* 2–22

Roitblat, H. L. (1987). *Introduction to comparative cognition.* San Francisco: Freeman.

Rudy, J. W. (1991). Elemental and configural associations, the hippocampus and development. *Developmental Psychobiology, 24,* 221–236.

Salazar, R. A., Wallace, R. B., & Bake-Salazar, G. L. (1991). Visual and auditory cortex ablations following cross-modal transfer and recovery of function in the rat. *Society of Neuroscience Abstracts, 17,* 848.

Save, E., Poucet, B., Foreman, N., & Buhot, M. (1992). Object exploration and reactions to spatial and nonspatial changes in hooded rats following damage to parietal cortex or hippocampal formation. *Behavioural Neuroscience, 106*, 447–456.

Spelke, E. (1987). The development of intermodal perception. In P. Salapetek & L. Cohen (Eds.), *Handbook of infant perception: From perception to cognition* (pp. 233–273). New York: Academic Press.

Starkey, P., Spelke, E. S., & Gelman, R. (1983). Detection of intermodal numerical correspondences by human infants. *Science, 222*, 179–181.

Stein, B. E., & Meredith, M. A. (1990). Multisensory integrative neural and behavioural solutions for dealing with stimuli from different modalitiees. In A. Diamond (Ed.), The development and neural bases of higher cognitive functions. *Annals of the New York Academy of Sciences, 668*, 51–70.

Streicher, M., & Ettlinger, G. (1987). Crossmodal recognition of familier and unfamilier objects by the monkey: The effect of ablation of polysensory neocortex or of the amydaloid complex. *Behavioural Brain Research, 23*, 95–107.

Sur, M., Pallas, S. L., & Roe, A. W. (1990). Crossmodal plasticity in cortical development: Differentiation and specification of sensory cortex. *Trends in Neuroscience, 13*, 227–233.

Tees, R. C. (in preparation) The effect of early stimulation history on cross modal transfer of spatial information in rats.

Tees, R. C. (1990). Experience, perceptual competencies and rat cortex. In B. Kolb & R. C. Tees (Eds.), *The cerebral cortex of the rat* (pp. 507–536). Cambridge, MA: MIT Press.

Tees, R. C., & Buhrmann, K. (1989). Parallel perceptual/cognitive functions in humans and rats: Space and time. *Canadian Journal of Psychology, 43*, 266–285.

Tees, R. C., & Cartwright, J. (1972). Sensory preconditioning in rats following early visual deprivation. *Journal of Comparative and Physiological Psychology, 81*, 12–20.

Tees, R. C., & Johnston, J. (1992). Effect of pre- and/or postnatal choline supplementation on working and reference memory (spatial and nonspatial) and open field behavior in the rat. *Society of Neuroscience Abstracts, 18*, 1203.

Tees, R. C., Johnson, J., Sivuck, G., & Kwan, T. (in preparation). The effect of selective cortical lesions and early dietary choline supplementation on the adult rat's intersensory spatial competences.

Tees, R. C., Midgley, G., & Nesbit, J. C. (1979). The effect of early visual experience on spatial maze learning in rats. *Developmental Psychobiology, 14*, 425–438.

Tees, R. C., & Symons, L. A. (1987). Intersensory coordination and the effect of early sensory deprivation. *Developmental Psychobiology, 23*, 497–507.

Thompson, R. F., & Kramer, R. (1965). Role of association cortex in sensory preconditioning. *Journal of Comparative and Physiological Psychology, 60*, 186–191.

Tomie, J., & Whishaw, I. Q. (1990). New paradigm for tactile discrimination studies with the rat: Methods for simple, conditional, and configural discriminations. *Physiology and Behaviour, 48*, 225–231.

Turkewitz, G., & Kenny, P. A. (1982). Limitations on input as a basis for neural organization and perceptual development: A preliminary theoretical statement. *Developmental Psychobiology, 15*, 357–368.

Turkewitz, G., Lewkowicz, D. J., & Gardner, J. M. (1983). Determinants of infant perception. In J. S. Rosenblatt, R. A. Hinde, C. Beer, & M. C. Busnel (Eds.), *Advances in the study of behaviour* (Vol. 13, pp. 40–62). New York: Academic Press.

Turkewitz, G., & Mellon, R. C. (1989). Dynamic organization of intersensory function. *Canadian Journal of Psychology, 43*, 286–301.

Warren, D. H. (1978). Perception of the blind. In E. C. Carterette & M. P. Friedman (Eds.), *Handbook of perception* (Vol. 10, pp. 65–90). Orlando, FL: Academic Press.

Whittington, D. A., Hepp-Raymond, M. C., & Flood, W. (1981). Eye and head movements to auditory targets. *Experimental Brain Research, 41*, 358–363.

Withington-Wray, D. J., & Keating, M. J. (1989). Visual or auditory deprivation of an electrophysical map of auditory space in the guinea pig. *Society for Neurosciences Abstracts, 15*, 291.

Yeterian, E. H. (1977). The effects of visual or auditory cortical lesions on specific cross-modal transfer in the rat. *Neuropsychologia, 15*, 517–526.

Yeterian, E. H., Waters, R. S., & Wilson, W. A. (1976). Posterior cortical lesions and specific crossmodal transfer of the rat. *Physiological Psychology, 4*, 281–284.

Zilles, K. (1990). Anatomy of the neocortex: Autoarchitecture and myeloarchitecture. In B. Kolb & R. C. Tees (Eds.), *The cerebral cortex of the rat* (pp. 77–112). Cambridge, MA: MIT Press.

CHAPTER SEVEN

Intersensory Integration in the Infant Rat

Norman E. Spear
David L. McKinzie
Binghamton University

A dilemma with which infants must contend from birth is the organization of neural input arising simultaneously from different sensory routes. The prototypic instance is an object, just about any object. When dealing with its milk bottle, the human infant must accommodate differences in the neural activity arising from the bottle's visual appearance, its smell, the tactile sensations associated with the nipple and the bottle itself that may occur simultaneously through the mouth and hands, how it tastes, and perhaps what it sounds like when manipulated. Despite all these potentially separate sensations and sites of neural activity, the infant's task is to treat them as functionally equivalent in terms of a single object, the bottle. Research discussed in the present chapter is directed toward understanding age-related differences in learning about multiple sensory events that occur simultaneously; it is hoped that this might help us understand the processes through which infants learn about objects.

Our studies have involved the developing rat, in order to take advantage of the conventional benefits this animal provides for ontogenetic research—experiential and genetic control, the opportunity for precise variation in age, an abundance of background data on how this animal develops behaviorally and neurophysiologically, the opportunity to supplement environmental manipulations and behavioral measures with neurophysiological manipulations and measures, and a variety of techniques that have become available for testing of multi-event learning in such an animal. The techniques we employ are derivations of basic Pavlovian conditioning that allow precise evaluation of what is learned about a multiple event episode. The most basic of these techniques is compound conditioning: A conditioned stimulus (CS) consisting of two or more stimulus elements is paired with an unconditioned stimulus (US) such as an infusion of a sweet taste or an aversive footshock. [Footshock is the most commonly used US for testing the ontogeny of learning because the psychophysics of its reinforcing properties in relation to age is relatively well understood (Campbell, 1967). Only a few footshocks are applied in the tests we discuss; they inflict no physical damage and are startling but not painful to human touch.] To compose a multi-event CS, a light and tone might be presented simultaneously, or an odor and a taste, or an odor and a tone, or two odors.

If the CS and US are presented relatively simultaneously—we continue here with the analogy of learning about objects—one might conceptualize this as an object that is particularly aversive or particularly pleasant (depending on whether the footshock or sweet taste is the US). There are reasons to expect, however, that learning involving a conventional reinforcer or US may differ in its characteristics from learning involving only relatively neutral stimuli (e.g., Holland, 1979; Rudy & Wagner, 1975). So we also use two different techniques to study the learning of multiple-event episodes that do not include a US. The first technique has been termed *sensory conditioning* and the second *latent inhibition*.

Sensory Conditioning

For sensory conditioning an animal first is merely presented with the multi-event "object," such as a light and a tone. To determine whether the animal has learned to treat the light and tone as functionally equivalent (probably through associative mechanisms), the value of one of the two elements is changed by pairing it with a US. If the animal then treats the value of the other element as changed in the same way, we infer that the animal had functionally equated (associated) the two elements. For instance, after the light and tone have been presented together, the tone may be paired with an aversive US and the consequential aversion to the light tested. Alternatively, we might pair the tone with an appetitive US and test whether the light has become more preferred as a consequence. Although a US is used to confirm learning of the relationship between two stimulus elements, that learning itself takes place in the absence of a US.

Latent Inhibition

Latent inhibition involving a multiple-event episode is similar in form to sensory conditioning. In this case, the light and tone are presented alone to the animal, followed by pairing of, say, the tone and a US. We then measure the extent to which the tone is changed in its value as a consequence of being paired with the US. If conditioning of the tone is reduced by prior presentation of the light–tone combination (relative to animals that did not receive this prior presentation), then latent inhibition of the tone is said to occur. We may then test to what extent the presence of the preexposed light affects the tone's capacity to induce latent inhibition in subsequent conditioning to the same tone. This would permit inferences about the animal's organization of the preexposed multiple-event stimulus, light + tone.

Two other relatively technical issues must be discussed before we consider how infants organize multi-event stimuli, but these technical points have some intrinsic interest of their own.

Functional Differences in Learning With and Without a US

We now have clear evidence of four functional differences in infant behavior with episodes that do and do not involve a US. These take the form of different effects observed in sensory conditioning and primary conditioning among infant rats. The first functional difference is in the effect of age: In circumstances in which there are no age-related differences in learning an association between an odor and a footshock during the second, third, and fourth postnatal weeks, rats during the second and third postnatal weeks are more effective in the sensory conditioning of two simultaneously presented odors than are rats during the fourth postnatal week and older (e.g., Chen, Lariviere, Heyser, Spear, & Spear, 1991). In other words, preweanlings learn the relationship between two odors more rapidly than older animals, even though the relationship between an odor and a footshock is learned at the same rate by preweanlings and older animals. Second, in circumstances in which a given dose of ethanol has no effect on conditioning involving pairing of an odor and footshock, the same dose of ethanol facilitates odor–odor sensory conditioning among preweanlings and young postweanlings (Chen, Spear, & Spear, 1992). Third, although perinatal administration of the drug DSP4, which acts to drastically interfere with the action of norepinephrine as a neurotransmitter, has no effect on odor–footshock primary conditioning, it does significantly impair odor–odor sensory conditioning (Chen, Spear, & Spear, 1993). Finally, prenatal exposure to cocaine has no effect on odor–footshock primary conditioning at certain preweanling ages, but at the same ages odor–odor sensory conditioning is significantly impaired among animals exposed prenatally to cocaine (Heyser, Chen, Miller, Spear, & Spear, 1990).

The point of these examples is to illustrate the likelihood that principles governing the developing animal's organization of multi-event episodes could depend on the nature of the events. These examples suggest that some characteristic of footshock (e.g., its intensity or aversiveness) might engage special organizational characteristics in developing animals. We cannot be conclusive due to other differences in the odor–odor and odor–shock pairings (e.g., temporal parameters of the events, and number of sensory modalities required).

What Attributes are Learned?

The final semitechnical issue is how one determines what "events" are in fact processed by the animal in a given multi-event episode. Continuing with the simple example of learning about a simultaneously occurring light and tone, it is not immediately obvious what dimensions of the light and tone will be used by the animal to establish their relationship. Rather than learning that light belongs with tone, the animal might learn, for instance, that two novel events belong together, or that a moderately intense event and a very intense event belong together. It is also possible that the light and tone are not actually perceived as separate elements by the animal but are treated in integral fashion as a configuration (e.g., "bright noise").

We turn now to experimental examples in which the animal's treatment of intersensory information can determine the amount of conditioning that occurs. We have observed a fundamental difference in the behavior of infant and older animals in conditioning with multi-event, *compound* stimuli, which we believe is attributable to an infantile manner of intersensory integration.

AGE-RELATED DIFFERENCES IN THE ORGANIZATION OF CS EVENTS FOR PAVLOVIAN CONDITIONING

A conventional means for analyzing an animal's organization of a multi-event episode has been to compare Pavlovian conditioning with a compound stimulus involving two elements to the same conditioning with only one of the elements. If the compound CS includes both A and B, we test the consequences of the interaction between A and B by comparison with conditioning to A alone. If A is learned less effectively when presented with B than when presented alone, we say that *overshadowing* has occurred. If A is learned more effectively in the presence of B than when it appears alone, we say that *potentiation* has occurred.

In our first study of compound stimulus conditioning we tested conditioning to one or both of two flavors (coffee and sucrose) in preweanling (18 days old) and young adult (60 days old) rats. Conditioning was accomplished by pairing consumption of one or both flavors with an illness-inducing injection of lithium chloride. With a technique that allowed tight experimental control over rate and duration of the consumption of a flavor, we arranged parameters so that conditioning to a single flavor was roughly equivalent for the two ages.

In a large study involving a wide variety of experimental and control conditions, David Kucharski found that preweanlings were more likely to exhibit potentiation whereas adults were more likely to exhibit overshadowing (Kucharski & Spear, 1984, 1985). Although the presence of flavor B (e.g., coffee) in solution with A (e.g., sucrose) markedly facilitated conditioning to A among the preweanlings, it tended to impair conditioning of A in the adults. This effect was found for a variety of flavors in a variety of circumstances, as long as the flavors were presented simultaneously. If presented sequentially, infants as well as adults tended toward overshadowing (for reviews see Spear & Kucharski, 1984a, 1984b).

We were surprised that the simultaneous presence of a second stimulus would facilitate conditioning to the first stimulus to a greater extent in infants than in adults. It implied that extra information (stimulus B) continued to be processed longer for infants than for adults, and was used by the infants to promote conditioning of A. This seemed contrary to the presumably limited capacity for processing information in the younger animal (e.g., the 18-day-old rat has only 15–20% as many synapses in the neocortex as the adult). How was the information from the two elements organized by the infant to accomplish this?

Two explanations for potentiation in such adults have been suggested by Rescorla and Durlach (1981). These explanations differ in whether the elements in the stimulus compound are assumed to be configured or analyzed. If processed as separable units, A is assumed in one explanation to be associated with the US and also with B, which itself is associated with the US. Therefore, A would acquire aversion not only from its association with the US but also from its association with B, which itself has become aversive through its own association with the US. Hence the conditioned aversion to A is stronger in this situation than if only A had been paired with the US. In contrast, if the AB compound were processed in integral fashion, as a Gestalt-like configuration, potentiation is assumed in the second explanation to occur because the net intensity of the configured A and B is greater than that of A alone, and more intense stimuli condition more strongly (a general principle reviewed, e.g., by Kimble, 1961; for infant rats, see Mellon, Kraemer, & Spear, 1991). The drawback to this mode of processing is that after conditioning with AB the animal is tested with A alone, and such stimulus change reduces the expression of conditioning (*generalization decrement*). In order for potentiation to be seen, the advantage of conditioning to the relatively intense compound must more than compensate for the generalization decrement expected when only one of the elements of the stimulus compound is tested.

Although a definitive test of the distinction between these two interpretations is difficult to imagine (see Rescorla, 1981), other evidence seemed to us to indicate that infants process the stimulus compound in integral fashion, favoring the second interpretation (henceforth termed the *integral* interpretation) over the first (the *separable* interpretation; these terms are based on the distinctions between integral and separable processing applied by Garner, 1970, 1974, and by Shepp, 1978, 1989). This was in part because with the separable interpretation, greater potentiation by infants than adults would imply greater strength of the association between A and B or between B and the US for the infants, and there was no evidence to confirm this. Most tests have indicated the opposite, that associative strength would be weaker for infants than adults (Rudy, Vogt, & Hyson, 1984; Spear & Rudy, 1991; but see Spear, McKinzie & Arnold, in press, for apparently contrary evidence). We did, however, have evidence to support the assumptions required by the integral interpretation—that infants are more likely than adults to configure such flavor–flavor stimulus compounds and are less likely to show generalization decrement when tested with a taste different from that used for conditioning (for further discussion of these issues see Spear, 1984; Spear & Kucharski, 1984a, 1984b).

We tested the integral hypothesis further, with CSs more amenable to variation in intensity (tones and lights). The hypothesis was that infant rats would tend to configure a stimulus compound consisting of a light and tone, encode that configuration in terms of its net intensity, and be relatively unaffected by the generalization decrement potentially encountered when tested with only the tone. One might think that we would be at a disadvantage when testing this hypothesis when intersensory integration was required (i.e., with stimulus elements processed by two different sensory modalities—vision and audition). Given the evidence that greater similarity between elements in a compound promotes their configuration or the acquisition of associations between the elements (e.g., Rescorla, 1980, 1981), the intermodal integration involving lights and tones would seem less likely than the intramodal integration involving two flavors. This did not discourage us, however, because we also had evidence that infants are unlikely to judge similarity on the basis of sensory modality, and perhaps more likely than adults to use amodal encoding (Spear & Molina, 1987; see Turkewitz, Lewkowicz, & Gardner, 1983).

Tests of the Integral Hypothesis

Two immediate sets of predictions arise from the integral hypothesis, one dealing with the effects of variation in intensity within a sensory modality and the other with integration between sensory modalities.

Effects of Stimulus Intensity on Conditioning. If conditioned with a more intense stimulus than is used for testing, preweanlings should, according to the integral hypothesis, exhibit stronger conditioning than if they had been conditioned with the same stimulus used during testing. Adults, however, would not be expected to show this benefit from conditioning with a relatively high-intensity stimulus and might be impaired on the test with a low-intensity stimulus due to their greater susceptibility to generalization decrement. These predictions were tested with preweanlings (17 days old) and adults. Conditioned aversions to a 48-dB tone (2000 Hz) were compared for animals previously given pairings of this tone presented at 89, 73, or 48 dB and footshock. The results confirmed the predictions. Relative to animals conditioned with the same 48-dB tone used for testing, preweanlings conditioned with a more intense tone exhibited stronger conditioning, whereas adults conditioned with a more intense tone exhibited weaker conditioning (see Fig. 7.1; Mellon et al., 1991). The result is consistent with the integral explanation of why greater potentiation is observed in younger animals. In particular, it is consistent with the notion that facilitation in the expression of conditioning to an element in a compound stimulus can be expected for preweanlings that encode a compound stimulus as a more intense unit than the element.

Effects of Presenting a Light with the Tone. The integral hypothesis predicts that a light presented along with a low-intensity tone CS will be encoded by infants as a relatively intense event, comparable to a more intense tone. We should therefore expect infants to express substantial conditioning to an intense tone after pairings of this compound CS (light + low-intensity tone) and a US. Adults, however, should express relatively little conditioning in this situation, given the likelihood that they will analyze the light–tone compound into its elements and allocate their processing of these elements differentially so that conditioning to the low-intensity tone will be overshadowed by the light.

The conditioning exhibited to a 73-dB tone by preweanlings and adults was compared following conditioning to either a 48-dB tone alone or the 48-dB tone plus a simultaneously occurring light. The predictions were confirmed. For preweanlings, adding the light to the low-intensity tone markedly enhanced conditioning expressed to the higher intensity tone. For the adults, however, the addition of the light significantly decreased the conditioning expressed to the higher intensity tone (see Fig. 7.2; Mellon et al., 1991). This supports the idea that the preweanlings encoded the light-tone combination as a unit similar to the more intense tone (i.e., that the light–tone combination was encoded configurally as a more intense event than either element alone, and so more similar to the relatively loud tone), whereas adults analyzed the light–tone compound into its elements, and in so doing, the light overshadowed conditioning to the low-intensity tone.

Do Infants Have the Capacity for Discriminating the CSs? Perhaps, however, the 17-day-old rats were merely incapable of discriminating the light–tone stimulus compound from the 73-dB tone. Perhaps animals of this

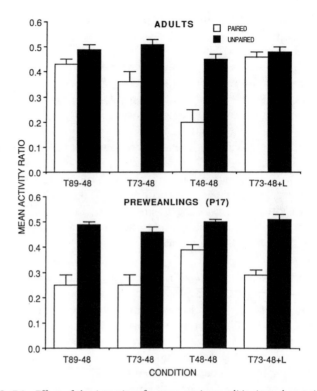

FIG. 7.1. Effect of the intensity of a tone on its conditioning when paired with an aversive US (footshock). Adult rats (upper panel) and preweanling rats (lower panel) are compared with respect to the change in activity induced by a 48-dB tone, or a 48-dB tone in addition to a light (far right bars), following conditioning with either an 89-, 73-, or 48-dB tone as the CS (the first number indicating each condition refers to the intensity of the CS and the second number to the intensity of the test stimulus). The lower the activity ratio, the greater the stimulus-induced suppression of activity. The greater the difference between the scores of animals given pairings of the CS and US (white bars) and those given unpaired presentations of the CS and US (black bars), the greater the conditioning. From Mellon, Kraemer, and Spear (1991). Adapted by permission.

age, which only recently have begun to see and hear, just do not possess sufficiently sophisticated sensory systems to allow discrimination between a light and a tone. We tested whether 17-day-old animals could learn such discriminations if given differential reinforcement. Preweanlings were presented reinforced occurrences of the stimulus compound consisting of a light and a 48-dB tone interspersed with nonreinforced exposures to either a 48-dB tone, a 73-dB tone, or an 89-dB tone. Discrimination learning was extremely effective and roughly equivalent in all three conditions (see Fig. 7.3; Mellon

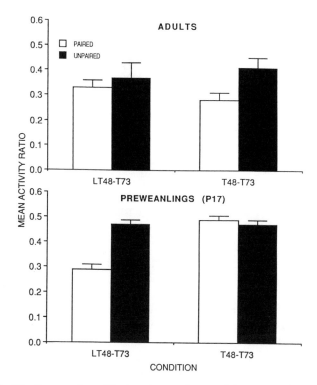

FIG. 7.2. Degree of conditioning expressed to a 73-dB tone is shown for adults (upper panel) and preweanlings (lower panel) given pairings of the US and either a 48-dB tone (right bars) or the 48-dB tone in simultaneous compound with a flashing light (left bars). Degree of conditioning is indicated by the difference between the scores of subjects in the paired and unpaired conditions. (For further details of the measure see Fig. 7.1 and text.) From Mellon et al. (1991). Adapted by permission.

et al., 1991). A similar experiment tested the preweanlings' capacity to discriminate between a light and a 73-dB tone, and this learning was also effective (see Fig. 7.4: Mellon et al., 1991). We conclude that the substantial transfer between conditioning with a simultaneously occurring low-intensity tone and a light and testing with the high-intensity tone did not occur merely because preweanling rats lack the capacity to discriminate between these events.

Three Additional Examples of Intersensory Integration by Infants

We mentioned earlier that in learning associations between two stimuli adult animals are more effective the greater the similarity between them, and in that sense are less likely to exhibit interstimulus integration with stimuli

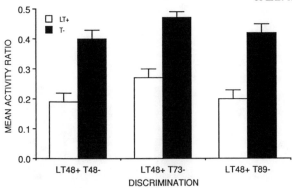

FIG. 7.3. The expression of a conditioned discrimination between a compound stimulus (simultaneously occurring light and 48 dB tone) and a tone of either 48, 73, or 89 dB is shown in terms of stimulus-induced suppression of activity (lower scores indicate greater suppression). A difference in suppression to the stimulus compound and the tone indicates that a discrimination between these events was formed by the preweanlings. From Mellon et al. (1991). Adapted by permission.

processed by different sensory modalities (i.e., intersensory integration). It is therefore striking that infant animals are so effective in intersensory integration. Our data indicate that preweanling rats proficiently accomplish intersensory integration in three circumstances: a paradigm that simulates acquired equivalence; sensory conditioning; and second-order conditioning. In each case infant rats during their first 2 postnatal weeks have been quite effective in integrating intersensory information processed through olfactory and cutaneous receptors.

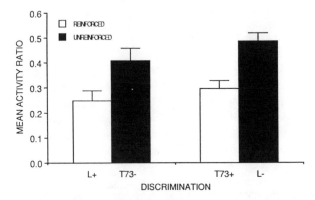

FIG. 7.4. Degree of suppression of activity (lower numbers indicate greater suppression) is shown to a light and to a 73-dB tone that had been either paired (+) or not paired (−) with the US. It can be seen that in both conditions the preweanling rats formed a discrimination between the light and the tone. From Mellon et al. (1991). Adapted by permission.

Acquired "Equivalence." After two odors are presented simultaneously for a short period (3 min), rat pups treat the odors as if they were functionally equivalent or associated, but not if the odors were presented sequentially with a substantial interval (e.g., 20 min) between their occurrence (Chen et al., 1991). Wei-Jung Chen found, however, that functional equivalence between such temporally disparate odors could be induced if each was presented in combination with the same novel texture (a particular style of carpet flooring; Chen & Spear, 1991). In other words, it was possible to produce an association between two temporally disparate odors if each was associated with a common tactile stimulus.

A previous instance of such simulated acquired equivalence in the preweanling rat was achieved in studies by Drew Smoller (Spear, Kraemer, Molina, & Smoller, 1988). In these experiments, 1-week-old rats were presented intraoral infusions of sucrose solution while being exposed to a novel texture. Next they were presented the same intraoral sucrose infusion in the presence of a novel odor (without the novel texture). When the value of the odor subsequently was decreased by pairing it with a footshock, the value of the texture decreased similarly. This indicates that exposure to the common element (sucrose) led to a functional equation of the associated texture and odor elements.

Sensory Conditioning and Second-Order Conditioning. Intersensory integration with odors and textures also is readily achieved in preweanling rats in terms of sensory conditioning. Seven-day-old rats were exposed simultaneously to a novel texture and a novel odor, then the value of the odor was reduced by pairing it with footshock. Consequently, the animal's preference for the novel texture decreased significantly, indicating an acquired association between the odor and texture (Smoller & Spear, 1988).

Finally, intersensory integration has been found to occur readily in preweanling animals in terms of second-order conditioning. Preweanling rats (4 or 8 days of age) were given pairings of a novel odor and illness-inducing LiCl. When that odor subsequently was paired with a novel texture, the novel texture in turn became significantly aversive to the infant rat, in a wide variety of circumstances (Miller, Molina, & Spear, 1990). In addition, we have found that slightly older preweanling rats integrate olfactory and visual information. Following pairings of an odor and footshock to induce a conditioned aversion to the odor, brief presentation of that odor in a black location for 20 sec resulted in a significant aversion to that location in 16-day-old rats. In contrast, older, postweanling rats did not exhibit this degree of second-order conditioning involving intersensory integration (McKinzie, Smoller, & Spear, in preparation).

These instances of intersensory association (integration of stimuli so dissimilar that they are processed by different sensory modalities) are interesting in view of the sensitivity of older animals to interstimulus similarity in similar cases. The effectiveness of sensory conditioning and second-order conditioning in the adult rat and pigeon has seemed proportional to the degree of similarity between the stimuli that are to be associated (Rescorla, 1980, 1981). Preweanling rats, however, apparently view differences in the energy source through which sensory detection occurs as relatively inconsequential for stimulus similarity—a tone and a light may be viewed as similar at this age, but as less similar later in development. This is consistent with other evidence suggesting that preweanlings are more likely than older rats to encode amodally, and so would determine similarity on the basis of attributes such as intensity, novelty, affect, or temporal characteristics, rather than in terms of the sensory modality through which a stimulus is processed (Spear et al., 1988; Spear & Molina, 1987; Turkewitz et al., 1983). It is difficult, however, to attain the experimental control necessary for direct comparison of the most effective dimensions of stimulus similarity in infants and older animals, and more direct evidence is needed.

Summary

The evidence reviewed so far points to three somewhat surprising characteristics of the infant rat's information processing. Each is observed in the processing of multimodally specified objects—a situation normally encountered by the rat in its everyday environment. First, infant rats do not treat different sensory characteristics of an episode as functioning competitively. Instead, they respond to them as complementary, such that the learning of a particular characteristic of an episode is facilitated by the simultaneous presence of a different characteristic. This effect—potentiation of the learning of stimulus A by the presence of stimulus B—is opposite to the effect observed most often in adult animals. In adults, overshadowing usually is observed, such that learning of stimulus A is impaired by the presence of stimulus B. It is notable that overshadowing is so prevalent in the adult animal that virtually all theories of conditioning and learning predict its occurrence (which should not be surprising since the assumptions on which these theories are based were derived from experiments with adult animals). The tendency in infants for the learning of stimulus A to be facilitated by the presence of B implies more extensive active processing of B than would be needed if the presence of B would impair learning of A. Infants apparently are predisposed to actively process redundant events.

A second characteristic of infant rats is their disposition to configure simultaneous events, in the sense originally suggested by Gestalt psychologists. This conclusion is based more on inference from alternative theories than by direct tests of configuration, which are difficult to achieve. This tendency in infants does not seem to be attributable to their inability to discriminate between alternative sensory events that might occur simultaneously. Once configured, the components of the compound stimulus tend to be encoded in terms of their intensity, an amodal attribute that has special significance for developing animals and humans (Turkewitz et al., 1983).

The third characteristic of infant rats is that integration of information from simultaneously occurring stimuli is surprisingly independent of the extent to which these stimuli are similar to one another in terms of the energy sources that define the stimuli. Direct tests of this conclusion are limited, but it seems justified in view of the variety of examples of intersensory integration observed in preweanling rats.

Before discussing the implications of these characteristics, we present two recent sets of data that are consistent with them. These examples are striking because they are at odds with predictions based on conventional theories of learning and at odds with a great deal of evidence gathered with adult animals. They also provide further evidence that the characteristics of intersensory integration are unique for preweanling rats and markedly different from those of adult animals.

INFANTILE INTERSENSORY INTEGRATION LEADS TO CONDITIONING UNCHARACTERISTIC OF ADULTS

Intersensory Integration of Contextual and Target Information

The conventional assumption of most theories of conditioning is that learning about the context competes with learning about a target event within that context. If processing is directed toward acquiring an association between the context and the US, learning about the relationship between a target event within that context and the US would be expected to suffer. Accordingly, procedures that promote processing of the relationship between CS and US are expected to decrease learning about the relationship between context and US. This notion has seemed reasonable, assuming that the animal has limited resources with which to process several stimuli. We were surprised, therefore, to discover that quite the opposite occurs in the infant rat's learning of contextual and target information.

In an extensive study by David McKinzie, preweanling rats were conditioned and tested in either a typical test chamber or a "rich" context that included the presence of a novel odorant, black Plexiglas walls, and a flashing light. Effects of interest here were seen most clearly with the rich context and so we focus on these.

Seventeen-day-old rats were given pairings of a tone and footshock and then were tested 24 hr later for the strength of the aversions they had acquired to the context and to the tone. Conditioning to the context was determined by the degree to which activity in that context was suppressed relative to that of control animals given footshock in a distinctly different context. The surprising result was that unlike adults, infants given pairings of the tone and footshock conditioned more strongly to the context than did those given unpaired presentations of the tone and footshock in the same context. Moreover, among infants given pairings of the tone and footshock, those given less of a delay between these two events (and hence, better conditioning to the CS) showed the strongest conditioning of all to the context.

In short, context learning was facilitated by CS learning among infants but impaired by CS learning among adults. This indicates integration of context and CS information in infants, but competition between the processing of CS and context information in adults. Integration between context and CS information in infants also was indicated in terms of the degree of conditioning to the tone that served as the CS; conditioning to the tone was greater for infants conditioned in the rich context than for those conditioned in the normal context, and generally, conditions that enhanced context learning correspondingly enhanced CS learning. Especially striking was the finding that the rich context enabled the infants to show CS conditioning despite a long trace interval between CS and US that precluded CS conditioning in the plain context.

These findings are of interest for theories of conditioning because precisely the opposite has been reported with adults: Conditioning to context is less effective under circumstances in which conditioning to the CS is greater (e.g., Marlin, 1981; Odling-Smee, 1975). It is of special interest here because the CS and context were processed by different sensory modalities, yet the information they provided was integrated such that the conditioning of one facilitated conditioning of the other. This is another instance in which the infant integrates information from simultaneously occurring events, even when these events are processed by quite different sensory modalities.

McKinzie's striking evidence of integration between contextual and target information parallels previous data that led us to expect infants to be relatively good at processing redundant information such as that represented by context. In two previous studies, preweanling rats were found to be more affected by redundant context than were adults (Lariviere, Chen, & Spear, 1990; Solheim, Hensler, & Spear, 1980). In one of these studies, conditioning to the context was found to be greater in the preweanlings than in adults, and there were indications of integration between contextual (olfactory) and target (largely visual) information, in that extinction of one tended to decrease the associative strength of the other (Lariviere et al., 1990).

Latent Inhibition

Latent inhibition is said to occur if nonreinforced presentations of a stimulus retard subsequent conditioning of that stimulus. Although this is a well-established effect in adult animals (for a thorough review see Lubow, 1992), its ontogeny has been much less studied. Recently, however, due in part to its suggested use as a marker of hippocampal development, interest in the developmental aspects of latent inhibition has grown (Kraemer & Randall, 1992).

Tests of latent inhibition in developing animals have yielded results sufficiently interesting to question interpretations of the effect. Although most theories of latent inhibition have interpreted it as an acquisition deficit, tests with preweanlings have agreed with those of adults in suggesting postacquisition processes as the locus of the latent inhibition effect. These tests by Kraemer and his colleagues have indicated that the effect is not permanent but dissipates after a long retention interval (e.g., Kraemer, Hoffmann, & Spear, 1988; Kraemer & Roberts, 1984; Kraemer & Spear, 1993). Although it is now clear that preweanling rats are capable of exhibiting latent inhibition despite having an incompletely developed hippocampus, it is also established that in some circumstances latent inhibition is not only stronger among older preweanlings, but that the opposite effect—latent facilitation—can be observed in very young infants (Hoffmann & Spear, 1989; Spear & Smith, 1978). The latter follows from the notion that prior exposure to a stimulus that is relatively complex and unfamiliar might help the subject integrate its parts and "learn" the stimulus by forming a stable representation of it (Hall, 1991). On this basis one might expect that infant animals, which presumably require more perceptual learning than adults, would have less latent inhibition and perhaps even latent facilitation following preexposure to more complex stimuli.

Intersensory Integration in Latent Inhibition. Kraemer and Randall (1992) reported that substantial latent inhibition could occur in preweanlings preexposed to a light–tone compound and conditioned with that same compound. This procedure was incorporated into a large and relatively complicated study by Wei-Jung Chen (1992) in our laboratory. We refer here only to Chen's behavioral tests of latent inhibition, although we have occasion later to mention his other experiments involving sensory conditioning and some psychopharmacological manipulations.

Chen (1992) gave preweanling (17 days old) and periadolescent (35 days old) rats eight prior exposures to a simultaneous light–tone compound before eight pairings of either the tone and footshock or the light and footshock. The two conditioned stimuli (light and tone) yielded the same general results, and it is simplest to focus on the results of conditioning to a tone following nonreinforced presentations of a light-tone stimulus compound.

For 17-day-olds, latent inhibition was quite strong in each of three separate experiments, but only in certain conditions. For instance, prior exposures to the light–tone compound yielded substantial latent inhibition in conditioning of the tone, but in these circumstances prior exposures to that tone alone did not (see Fig. 7.5). It was as if the consequences of nonreinforced occurrences of the tone before conditioning were potentiated by presenting the light as well. In contrast, tests with adults have suggested that the consequences of presenting stimulus A prior to conditioning stimulus A are overshadowed by prior presentations of stimulus B in compound with A (Mackintosh, 1973; a careful review by Hall, 1991, concluded that in some circumstances this effect does not occur). It seemed that for infants, the effect of preexposing a stimulus processed by one sensory modality was increased by pairing it with a stimulus processed by a different stimulus modality, whereas for adults, the effect of preexposing a stimulus of one modality was often decreased by pairing it with a stimulus of another modality. When Chen tested periadolescent rats (between infancy and adulthood, about the age of puberty), the results were intermediate. But even aside from age-related comparisons, the intermodal facilitation in infants observed in Chen's experiments, without the concurrent presence of a reinforcer, extends the generality of the effect.

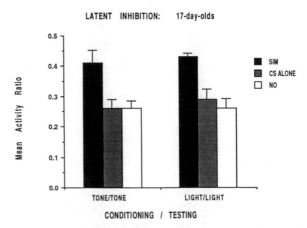

FIG. 7.5. Suppression of activity in the presence of a tone (left bars) and a light (right bars) is shown for preweanling rats previously given either of three kinds of treatment prior to pairings of the tone (left bars) or light (right bars) with the aversive US (footshock). Prior to conditioning, these rats were given nonreinforced presentations of either a compound stimulus consisting of the tone and light presented simultaneously (SIM), or the stimulus to which they would later be conditioned and tested (CS alone), or they were given no preexposure at all (NO).

We referred earlier to evidence that potentiation in conditioning could be simulated by conditioning with a very intense element of the stimulus compound rather than the stimulus compound itself. This result had been suggested by the hypothesis that infants encode a stimulus compound as a more intense event than one of its elements (Mellon et al., 1991). David McKinzie tested the related hypothesis that latent inhibition in conditioning of a tone would be increased by prior nonreinforced presentation of a relatively intense tone presented alone or in compound with a light. The results confirmed this prediction. Conditioning of a 70-dB tone was retarded more by prior nonreinforced preexposure to an 89-dB tone than to similar preexposure to the same 70-dB tone, whether the prior nonreinforced presentations included a stimulus compound consisting of the 89-dB tone and a light or of the tone alone. Although the effect was not as strong as we had anticipated, the main effect of preexposure intensity of the tone was significant, and there was no interaction with the number of elements in the CS (tone alone vs. tone-plus-light).

These results present two major puzzles. The first is why, for preweanlings, any latent inhibition resulted from prior exposure to the relatively complex stimulus compound, in view of the previous suggestions that latent inhibition at this age should be weak or that latent facilitation might occur following prior presentations of a relatively complex stimulus. The second puzzle is why preexposure to an intense stimulus should yield greater latent inhibition in conditioning to a less intense stimulus than does preexposure to the less intense stimulus itself. This might be attributed to a perceptual contrast effect. If the moderately intense tone used for conditioning is perceived as less intense due to the animal's prior exposure to the more intense tone, conditioning to it would be expected to be weakened, through whatever processes cause more intense CSs to be more strongly conditioned. Perceptual contrast effects are of course widely recognized in animals as well as humans (Sarris, 1990). Although similar effects of preexposure intensity also have been observed with adults (Schnur & Lubow, 1976), the present effect is not sufficiently understood to allow more speculation about the underlying mechanism.

ORIGIN AND SIGNIFICANCE OF INTERSENSORY INTEGRATION IN THE INFANT RAT

We now review the six instances of intersensory integration observed in the developing rat within the context of basic Pavlovian conditioning, before considering their implications. The first case was potentiation in the conditioning of element A by the simultaneous occurrence of element B. That infants tend to learn more about A in this situation than when A is presented alone contrasts with the typical observation with adults. Among adults in comparable circumstances, the presence of B results in the expression of less learning of A than if A alone is paired with the US. Such potentiation has been observed in infants when A and B are two flavors, an odor and a flavor, a light and a tone, or an odor and a tone. The explanation that seems to be most consistent with this broadly generalizable effect and some analytic experiments is that infants tend to treat A and B as a unit that is encoded in terms of its net intensity, whereas adults treat the different sensory inputs from A and B separately, do not integrate their respective information, and instead process B at the expense of processing A.

A second and related instance is in the conditioning of contextual events. In infant rats, conditioning to the context is potentiated by conditioning of target stimuli within that context. In the specific test, the CS was a tone and the primary component of the context was an odor, suggesting auditory–olfactory integration. Adults did not exhibit potentiation of context learning by CS learning in the same circumstances; rather, they tended to learn the CS only at the expense of learning the context.

The third instance of intersensory integration comes from studies of latent inhibition to lights and tones. Conditioning to a tone was mildly retarded for infant rats by prior nonreinforced presentations of a loud version of that tone, and retarded by prior nonreinforced presentations of that tone in simultaneous combination with a light. In contrast, in previous tests with adults, we and others (e.g., Mackintosh, 1983) have observed less retardation of the conditioning of a tone if prior nonreinforced presentations of stimulus A (e.g., tone) are accompanied by Stimulus B (e.g., light) than if not accompanied by B. Like the former two instances of potentiation, this qualifies as a case of intersensory function as defined by Turkewitz and his colleagues (Botuck & Turkewitz, 1990; Turkewitz & Mellon, 1989).

The fourth and fifth cases of intersensory integration in infants have have been found in two closely related paradigms of Pavlovian conditioning. In both sensory conditioning and second-order conditioning, when two relatively neutral stimuli occur simultaneously—for example, a texture and an odor, or a distinctive location and an odor—they are treated thereafter as if functionally equivalent, apparently because an association has been acquired. The final and sixth case in which stimuli processed by different sensory modalities become readily treated as if functionally equivalent has been termed *acquired equivalence* (although "equivalence" is probably too strong a term until further tests are conducted). In this case two events such as a texture and an odor become treated as if functionally equivalent even if they do not occur simultaneously, as long as the same novel event is presented in association with each of them (e.g., intraoral infusion of sucrose solution). The last three instances qualify as examples of intersensory function in terms of the Turkewitz et al. category of intersensory equivalence.

Does the Intersensory Integration of Infants Differ from That of Adults?

The six cases of intersensory integration just described are interesting because in several of these circumstances adults behave quite differently. First, in conditioning to one of two elements of a compound stimulus, adults are impaired or unaffected (overshadowing) in the same circumstances in which infants' responsiveness is facilitated by the presence of the second element (potentiation). In circumstances in which the facilitation for infants is less clear, the impairment for adults is more clear. Although direct comparisons of infant and adult behavior are subject to methodological difficulties (e.g., Campbell, 1967), validity of the age-related comparisons in these experiments has been promoted by conditions that ensured equivalent conditioning to a single element for infants and adults (Kucharski & Spear, 1985; Mellon et al., 1991). Differences between infants and adults in potentiation and overshadowing have seemed apparent whether the two elements of the conditioned stimulus are processed by the same or different sensory modalities. Implications of this age-related difference in intersensory function have been discussed by Turkewitz and Mellon (1989) in terms of "intersensory inhibition and facilitation."

Adult subjects also differ in that their conditioning to a contextual cue is impaired to the extent that CS conditioning occurs within that context, whereas for infants, greater CS conditioning leads to greater context conditioning. Similarly among infants, nonreinforced preexposure to a two-element compound decreases subsequent conditioning of one of the elements, with an effect greater than when preexposure is given only the element being conditioned (Chen, 1992). In contrast, adult conditioning to a stimulus is more impaired following preexposure to only that stimulus than following preexposure to that stimulus and another in compound (Honey & Hall, 1988). The age-related differences in this case are less secure, but this is not surprising in view of the uncertainty as to when latent inhibition in conditioning of A in adults will be impaired by the simultaneous nonreinforced presentation of a second element B and when there is no effect (as mentioned earlier; Honey & Hall, 1988).

Age-related differences in sensory conditioning are quite clear—younger animals are more effective than adults (with simultaneous elements; see next section). So far, the best examples of this are for learning of the relationship between two stimuli processed by the same sensory modality (two odors; e.g., Chen et al., 1991; there is preliminary evidence, however, that infants readily acquire intersensory relationship on the same basis; Smoller & Spear, 1988). In second-order conditioning, preweanlings are more effective than older rats in an instance requiring intersensory integration between vision and olfaction (reported in Spear, McKinzie, & Arnold, in press). Finally, in a case of apparent acquired equivalence reported by Molina et al. (1991), infants also seem more effective than adults in functionally equating information acquired from olfactory and visual processing. Integration in this case was in terms of transfer from learning of an olfactory event to learning of a visual event.

In short, there is evidence in each of these cases that infants might, if anything, be more effective than adults in intersensory integration. This suggestion must be taken with the greatest caution, however, for at least three reasons. The first is the well-known difficulty of achieving methodologically clear comparisons of learning or memory between different ages. Second, the circumstances of these tests may be limited in their generality. Finally, the nature of this intersensory integration tested is of the simplest variety. It is no doubt because of this relatively low-level category of intersensory integration—and there surely are different categories (Botuck & Turkewitz, 1990; Turkewitz & Mellon, 1989)—that infants seem more effective than older animals, rather than vice versa. When infants do and do not excel in intersensory integration can now be considered, albeit in preliminary fashion.

What Enables Infants to be Effective in Intersensory Integration?

We believe that there are at least two characteristics of infants that promote intersensory integration: relatively poor differentiation among stimuli, and a disposition to encode events amodally and ignore their source of energy. We also discuss a task variable that determines interstimulus integration in infants—degree of temporal disparity between stimuli.

Differentiation. There seems little doubt that the generally limited ability of infants to differentiate stimuli perceptually is in part responsible for the instances of intersensory integration reviewed in this chapter. There is no need to cite the overwhelming evidence on this point. This age-related deficiency in differentiation applies not only to sensory modalities that are new because they have recently emerged for an infant's use, such as vision and audition for the 17-day-old rat. For instance, the developing rat is pretty much of an olfactory expert by its first postnatal week, having processed olfactory information critical to its adaptation (e.g., how to find its first postnatal meal) since before birth. Yet, measures of olfactory differentiation indicate that the rat continues to improve in this respect almost until the time that its brain has achieved adultlike status (for reviews see Alberts, 1981; Leon, 1986). More generally, the infant's struggles with differentiation and the consequences of this for some cases of intersensory integration have been discussed thoroughly by Gibson (1969, 1983). It should be clear, however, that the failure to differentiate two events does not necessarily imply the lack of a capacity to discriminate those events. Differentiation is presumed to be a consequence of the animal's disposition for organizing events, whereas capacity for discrimination implies a genuine limitation on sensory receptors or cognition. We have already mentioned examples in which a clear lack of differentiation in infants was independent of their ability to discriminate (e.g., Mellon et al., 1991).

Amodal Encoding. Infant rats tend to ignore the energy source of a stimulus. The source of stimulus energy determines the sensory modality through which a stimulus is processed, so this is simply another way of saying that the sensory modality through which an event is processed is not treated by infants as an important attribute of that event for encoding and memory. The evidence for this is limited. Although it seems supported by the number of instances of intersensory integration more likely found in infants than adults, it is circular to account for these instances, in turn, by this hypothetical infantile disposition to ignore energy source.

The best evidence for an infant's disposition to ignore energy sources would be cases in which novel events processed by two different sensory modalities are treated as functionally equivalent although potentially discriminable. Two such instances have appeared in our research. The first is within an extensive series of studies by Juan Molina and his colleagues testing age-related differences in response to alcohol as a stimulus (Molina, Hoffmann, & Spear, 1986; Molina, Serwatka, & Spear, 1984, 1986; Serwatka, Molina, & Spear, 1986). The general finding in these experiments was that relative to adults, preweanlings show greater direct transfer between olfactory and gustatory responses to ethanol. Preweanlings for which an aversion was conditioned to the odor of ethanol drank less ethanol, and those for which a preference was conditioned for the odor of ethanol drank more ethanol; comparable conditioning to the odor of ethanol among adult animals had no influence on their drinking of ethanol. This age-related disposition for the infant to treat a taste as if it were an odor may be limited to the case of ethanol; Pamela Hunt in our laboratory was unable to find comparable transfer between the odor and taste of other substances in preweanling rats. A similar instance of such direct intermodal transfer between a tone and a light was found with infants by Mellon et al. (1991). These experiments indicated a tendency for a light to be treated as if it were a conditioned tone, and vice versa, among preweanling rats that were quite capable, however, of discriminating this same tone and light when differential reinforcement required it. Adults did not show this direct transfer between conditioning of a tone and response to a light, nor vice versa. The effects with infants were, however, relatively weak, of borderline significance, and not consistently replicated in our laboratory.

The possibility of an infantile disposition for amodal encoding is encouraged nevertheless by other sources of evidence for direct intermodal transfer or intermodal equivalence in developing animals or people. The first evidence of the unique role played by intensity for intersensory equivalence in early development was demonstrated in 3-week-old infants by Lewkowicz and Turkewitz (1980). They showed that infants, but not adults, spontaneously equated auditory and visual stimuli on the basis of their intensity. Another source of such evidence is synesthesia that has been observed with special prevalence, perhaps, in children (for a review, see Marks, 1978; Marks, Hammeal & Bornstein, 1987). By synesthesia is meant "the translation of attributes of sensation from one sensory domain to another" (Marks, 1975, p. 303) or "the transposition of sensory attributes from one modality to another" (Marks, 1978, p. 8). The neurological basis for synesthesia, although certainly not understood, may rest in the occurrence of a high percentage of cells in areas associated with perception (e.g., superior colliculus, medial geniculate) that respond to more than one source of energy (e.g., to both auditory or visual stimuli, or to tactile and vestibular stimuli). There is also a potential neurological basis for the apparent disposition of younger animals to show greater intersensory transfer than adults: Almli and Fisher (1984) found that the number of different sensory modalities capable of activating single cells in the hypothalamus of the rat is greater at postnatal day 5 than at postnatal day 15.

Substance is added in terms of the psychological basis for direct intersensory transfer. It seems likely, for example, that an odor and a taste or a light and a tone will be treated as equivalent to the extent that (a) they share common amodal attributes and (b) the animal is biased toward processing amodal rather than modal attributes of a stimulus. Net intensity of an event seems the most likely candidate for preferential encoding by infants (Lewkowicz & Turkewitz, 1980, 1981; Turkewitz et al., 1983), so we might expect that a light and tone perceived to be of equal intensity will be treated as equivalent. Other amodal attributes are less well established, but there is some evidence that these might include affect and novelty for the developing animal (Spear & Molina, 1987). On the other hand, Lewkowicz (1992) and Botuck and Turkewitz (1990) have suggested that rhythm is unlikely to be an effective amodal attribute processed by infants. In general agreement, unpublished studies in our laboratory by Robert Mellon, Wei-Jung Chen, and their colleagues have suggested that direct transfer between lights and tones by preweanling rats is unaffected by whether the lights and tones are presented with the same or different rhythm (this was a simple "rhythm" that included intersensory correspondence in synchrony, duration, and rate; e.g., continuous presentation vs. pulsed presentation at the rate of 0.25 sec off, 0.25 sec on or vs. 0.5 sec off, 0.5 sec on). We have discussed the issue of amodal encoding in the developing rat elsewhere, and have no substantive new data to present (Spear & Molina, 1987; Spear et al., 1988).

Degree of Temporal Disparity Between Stimuli. The major condition that seems to determine intersensory or intrasensory integration in infants is the temporal relationship of the stimuli to be integrated. Infants that readily integrate simultaneously occurring events have shown no indication of such integration when the same events occur sequentially. A small difference in degree of temporal disparity—if stimuli occur in immediate succession rather than simultaneously—can result in a major difference in the infant's processing of those stimuli. Stimuli occurring sequentially tend to be processed by infants as separate units, whereas those occurring simultaneously are processed together, or so it seems. Adults tend to behave differently. For instance, it is well known that adults do not readily evidence conditioning when the CS and US occur simultaneously. Yet we recently have found substantial simultaneous conditioning in preweanling rats tested in a rich context.

In other words, there is an apparent infantile disposition to treat events that occur in the same time and place as if they belong together and are to be treated as an undifferentiated unit. Whether this is the best characterization remains to be seen. A few examples will illustrate why, in terms of our current interpretations of these effects, this characterization seems reasonable.

Sensory conditioning provides the first example, albeit in terms of intra-sensory integration. Basic sensory conditioning to associate stimuli processed by different sensory modalities is readily achieved with infants, however, and there is no reason to expect that the effects of temporal disparity would differ whether the stimuli are processed by the same or different sensory modalities. We have already mentioned that infants (preweanlings) are significantly more effective than older rats in learning the association between two simultaneously occurring odors. If, however, the odors are presented sequentially, one immediately after the other, preweanlings and older animals learn their association with equivalent rates. As the temporal disparity between the two odors increases, the older animals' superiority in this learning emerges and increases until the disparity is so great that no learning is evident for either the older animals or the preweanlings (Chen & Spear, 1991; Lariviere, 1991). For instance, at 12 days of age the association between the two odors no longer is formed by the 12-day-old when the interval between the odors is as long as 20 min, although with that interval the 21-day-old still is effective in this learning; with the 30-min interval between odors, the 21-day-old also fails to exhibit this learning. Similarly, there are indications that periadolescent animals (35 days old) can learn the association between a light and a tone despite an interstimulus interval of over 2 min, whereas the 17-day-old rat shows no indications of learning with such a long interstimulus interval (Chen, 1992).

The processing of compound stimuli by infants differs in similarly dramatic fashion when the elements of the compound occur sequentially rather than simultaneously. The best evidence for this is also a case involving intrasensory integration, although again there is no reason to expect the facts to change with intersensory integration in view of the other common effects observed in infants with intra- and intersensory compound stimuli. Kucharski and Spear (1985) found that if two flavors were presented simultaneously as a compound (sucrose and coffee) and were paired with LiCl, the learning of either element was stronger than if only that element had been paired with LiCl; in other words, potentiation occurred. This effect was observed for infants but not adults. When, however, the flavors were presented in immediate succession or with an hour intervening between them, the infants exhibited adultlike overshadowing—conditioning of an element was impaired by the presence of another element in sequential compound with it—rather than potentiation.

The final example, with latent inhibition, involves intersensory integration. Prior to conditioning of a tone, Chen (1992) gave nonreinforced presentations of either that tone alone, a light and tone presented simultaneously, or a light and tone presented sequentially. For 17-day-old rats, whether subsequently conditioned with either a light or a tone, only simultaneous nonreinforced presentations of the light and tone yielded significant latent inhibition. There was no significant latent inhibition with either nonreinforced presentations of a light immediately following a tone (or vice versa) or explicitly unpaired presentations of light and tone (mean interstimulus interval of 135 sec). For animals conditioned with a tone, there was a tendency for nonreinforced sequential presentations to induce latent inhibition, but this was not statistically significant. Latent inhibition of conditioning to a tone also occurred for 35-day-olds only with prior nonreinforced simultaneous presentations of light and tone (not with either immediate-sequential or explicitly unpaired nonreinforced presentations of light and tone; for those conditioned to the light, latent inhibition was not induced under any circumstance). In other words, the results suggest a special status for a simultaneous compound that included the conditioned stimulus as one element. When presented without reinforcement prior to conditioning an element from the compound, the simultaneous compound induced more latent inhibition than did the same compound with the elements presented sequentially, one immediately following the other. The difference between the effects of simultaneous and sequential compounds was clearer for the infants, although it also was partly evident for the periadolescent animals, which are not yet sexually mature and are significantly younger (35 days old) than the animals we term adults (60 days of age or older).

Why developing animals should differ in the effectiveness of a simultaneous and sequential compound for latent inhibition is as yet unclear. As mentioned earlier, we view the effect as mediated by intensity encoding in the same way as conditioning with a simultaneous compound as the CS. This

implies that whatever is responsible for greater latent inhibition by nonreinforced presentations of more intense stimuli to developing animals, is also
responsible for the greater latent inhibition induced by simultaneous than
sequential compounds. In any case, this adds to the other evidence that the
behavior of infants in either intersensory or intrasensory integration may be
profoundly affected by the temporal disparity of the stimuli to be integrated.

INTERSENSORY INTEGRATION AND THE DEVELOPING RAT WITHIN THE CONTEXT OF GENERAL INTERSENSORY FUNCTION

The evidence we have described agrees with one central point of a large and
growing array of studies on perceptual development: As ontogeny progresses,
there is an increasing appreciation of differences in the source of energy of a
stimulus. There is likely a corresponding increase in the appreciation of how
different sources of energy emitted by an object are organized to result in their
equivalent treatment. It seems gratuitous to mention that especially with the
latter, some very fundamental issues remain to be answered. For instance, we
must learn to distinguish between instances in which events from different
sensory modalities are treated equivalently (as if they comprise a single object)
by design (e.g., because they share a common affordance) and by default (e.g.,
because the animal's sensory apparatus could not in any circumstance allow
for discrimination between the two events). We must also be aware that even
if discrimination could be achieved, one cannot infer that the different sources
of energy have been differentiated; discrimination could be achieved also on
the basis of common amodal attributes of the events.

A particular advantage of our studies with animals is the use of reasonably
comparable tests of intersensory integration across a wide range of ages.
These have provided an array of converging findings indicating that infants
respond to intersensory information (and intrasensory information) differently than adults. Surprisingly, the infantile manner of response is advantageous from the standpoint of learning. Infants are more likely than adults
to accept information from different sources of energy as equivalent, and
they also are more likely than adults to use information provided by one
energy source to aid in learning about information provided by another
source. The important qualification is that each effect is more likely when
the elements of the intersensory information are presented simultaneously
or, if not simultaneously, have been associated in common with the same
distinctive event. If asked to speculate, we would suggest that the infant's
advantage in these situations is linked to the developing animal's need to
learn that objects are defined by multiple sensory input that is either
simultaneous experientially or associated in common with the same event.

These and other infantile dispositions in rats share features of development observed with humans in terms of, for example, distinctions between integral and separable processing (Shepp, 1978, 1989), synesthesia (Marks, 1978; Marks et al., 1987), and amodal encoding (Lewkowicz & Turkewitz, 1981; Turkewitz et al., 1983). These examples of possibly general features of cognitive development are discussed in detail elsewhere (Spear, 1984, 1988; Spear & Molina, 1987; Spear et al., 1988).

ACKNOWLEDGMENTS

This research was supported in part by grant 5 R37 MH35219 from the National Institute of Mental Health to Norman E. Spear. The authors would like to thank Teri Tanenhaus for secretarial assistance and Norman Richter for technical assistance.

REFERENCES

Alberts, J. R. (1981). Ontogeny of olfaction: Reciprocal roles of sensation and behavior in the development of perception. In R. N. Aslin, J. R. Alberts, & M. R. Peterson (Eds.), *The development of perception: Psychobiological perspectives, Vol. 1: Audition, somatic perception and the chemical senses.* New York: Academic Press.

Almli, C. R., & Fisher, R. S. (1984). Postnatal development of sensory influences on lateral hypothalamic neurons of the rat. *Developmental Brain Research, 12,* 55–75.

Botuck, S., & Turkewitz, G. (1990). Intersensory functioning: Adult visual pattern equivalence in younger and older children. *Developmental Psychology, 26,* 115–120.

Campbell, B. A. (1967). Developmental studies of learning and motivation in infraprimate mammals. In H. W. Stevenson, E. H. Hess, & H. L. Rheingold (Eds.), *Early behavior: Comparative and developmental approaches* (pp. 43–72). New York: Wiley.

Chen, W. J. (1992). *The effects of ethanol agonist (RO15-4513) on nonreinforced associative learning in preweanling and periadolescent rats.* Unpublished PhD dissertation, Binghamton University.

Chen, W. J., Lariviere, N. A., Heyser, C. J., Spear, L. P., & Spear, N. E. (1991). Age-related differences in sensory conditioning in rats. *Developmental Psychobiology, 24,* 307–325.

Chen, W. J., & Spear, N. E. (1991, November). *A novel texture can mediate the association of temporal disparate stimuli in developing rats.* Presented at meetings of the International Society for Developmental Psychobiology.

Chen, W. J., Spear, L. P., & Spear, N. E. (1992). Enhancement of sensory preconditioning by a moderate dose of ethanol in infant and juvenile rats. *Behavioral & Neural Biology, 57,* 44–57.

Chen, W. J., Spear, L. P., & Spear, N. E. (1993). Disruptive influence of norepinephrine depletion on sensory preconditioning, but not primary conditioning, in preweanling rats. *Behavioral and Neural Biology, 60,* 110–117.

Garner, W. R. (1970). The stimulus in information processing. *American Psychologist, 25,* 350–358.

Garner, W. R. (1974). *The processing of information as structure.* Hillsdale, NJ: Lawrence Erlbaum Associates.

Gibson, E. J. (1969). *Principles of perceptual learning and development.* New York: Appleton-Century-Crofts.

Gibson, E. J. (1983). Development of knowledge about intermodal unity: Two views. In L. S. Liben (Ed.), *Piaget and the foundations of knowledge* (pp. 19–41). Hillsdale, NJ: Lawrence Erlbaum Associates.

Hall, G. (1991). *Perceptual and associative learning.* New York: Oxford University Press.

Heyser, C. J., Chen, W.J., Miller, J. S., Spear, N. E., & Spear, L. P. (1990). Prenatal cocaine exposure induces deficits in Pavlovian conditioning and in sensory preconditioning among infant rat pups. *Behavioral Neuroscience, 104,* 955–963.

Hoffmann, H., & Spear, N. E. (1989). Facilitation and impairment of conditioning in the preweanling rat after prior exposure to the conditioned stimulus. *Animal Learning & Behavior, 17,* 63–69.

Holland, P. C. (1979). Differential effects of omission contingencies on various components of Pavlovian appetitive conditioned responding in rats. *Journal of Experimental Psychology: Animal Behavior Processes, 5,* 178–193.

Honey, R. C., & Hall, G. (1988). Overshadowing and blocking procedures in latent inhibition. *Quarterly Journal of Experimental Psychology, 40B,* 163–186.

Kimble, G. A. (1961). *Hilgard and Marquis' conditioning and learning.* New York: Appleton-Century-Crofts.

Kraemer, P. J., Hoffmann, H., & Spear, N. E. (1988). Attenuation of the CS preexposure effect after a retention interval in preweanling rats. *Animal Learning & Behavior, 16,* 185–190.

Kraemer, P. J., & Randall, C. K. (1992). Latent inhibition in preweanling rats. *Psychobiology, 20,* 81–84.

Kraemer, P. J., & Roberts, W. A. (1984). Short-term memory for visual and auditory stimuli in pigeons. *Animal Learning & Behavior, 12,* 275–284.

Kraemer, P. J., & Spear, N. E. (1993). Retrieval processes and conditioning. In T. Zentall & W. Maki (Eds.), *Animal cognition: Essays in honor of Donald A. Riley* (pp. 87–107). Hillsdale, NJ: Lawrence Erlbaum Associates.

Kucharski, D., & Spear, N. E. (1984). Conditioning of aversion to an odor paired with peripheral shock in the developing rat. *Developmental Psychobiology, 17,* 465–479.

Kucharski, D., & Spear, N. E. (1985). Potentiation and overshadowing in preweanling and adult rats. *Journal of Experimental Psychology: Animal Behavior Processes, 11,* 15–34.

Lariviere, N. A. (1991). *The effects of early experience on subsequent learning in preweanling rats.* Unpublished PhD dissertation, SUNY Binghamton.

Lariviere, N. A., Chen, W. J., & Spear (1990). Effects of Pavlovian conditioning context on preweanling and adult rats. *Animal Learning & Behavior, 18,* 179–190.

Leon, M. (1986). Development of thermoregulation. In E. M. Blass (Ed.), *Handbook of behavioral neurobiology* (Vol. 8). New York: Plenum.

Lewkowicz, D. J. (1992). The development of temporally based intersensory perception in human infants. In F. Macar, V. Pouthas, & W. J. Friedman (Eds.), *Time, action, & cognition: Towards bridging the gap.* Dordrecht: Kluwer Academic Publishers.

Lewkowicz, D. J., & Turkewitz, G. (1980). Cross-modal equivalence in early infancy: Auditory-visual intensity matching. *Developmental Psychology, 16,* 597–607.

Lewkowicz, D. J., & Turkewitz, G. (1981). Intersensory interaction in newborns: Modification of visual preferences following exposure to sound. *Child Development, 52,* 827–832.

Lubow, R. E. (1973). Latent inhibition. *Psychological Bulletin, 79,* 398–407.

Mackintosh, N. J. (1983). *Conditioning and associative learning.* New York: Oxford University Press.

Marks, L. E. (1975). On color-hearing synesthesia: Cross-modal translation of sensory dimensions. *Psychological Bulletin, 82,* 303–331.

Marks, L. E. (1978). *The unity of the senses: Interrelations among the modalities.* New York: Academic Press.

Marks, L. E., Hammeal, R. J., & Bornstein, M. H. (1987). Perceiving similarity and comprehending metaphor. *Monographs of the Society for Research in Child Development, 52*, 1–92.

Marlin, N. A. (1981). Contextual associations in trace conditioning. *Animal Learning & Behavior, 9*, 519–523.

McKinzie, D. L. (1992). *Ontogenetic differences in the expression of context and CS conditioning as a function of context saliency and CS-US interval.* Unpublished M.A. thesis, Binghamton University.

McKinzie, D. L., Smoller, D. E., & Spear, N. E. (in preparation). *Ontogenetic differences in cross-sensory second-order conditioning in rats.*

Mellon, R. C., Kraemer, P. J., & Spear, N. E. (1991). Intersensory development and Pavlovian conditioning: Stimulus selection and encoding of lights and tones in the preweanling rat. *Journal of Experimental Psychology: Animal Behavior Processes, 17*, 448–464.

Miller, J. S., Molina, J. C., & Spear, N. E. (1990). Ontogenetic differences in the association of odor-aversion leaning in 4- and 8-day old rats. *Developmental Psychobiology, 23*, 319–330.

Molina, J. C., Hoffmann, H., & Spear, N. E. (1986). Conditioning of aversion to alcohol orosensory cues in 5- and 10-day old rats: Subsequent reduction in alcohol ingestion. *Developmental Psychobiology, 19*, 175–183.

Molina, J. C., Hoffmann, H., Serwatka, J., & Spear, N. E. (1991). Establishing intermodal equivalence in preweanling and adult rats. *Journal of Experimental Psychology: Animal Behavior Processes, 17*, 433–447.

Molina, J. C., Serwatka, J., & Spear, N. E. (1984). Changes in alcohol intake resulting from prior experience with alcohol odor in young rats. *Pharmacology, Biochemistry and Behavior, 21*, 387–391.

Molina, J. C., Serwatka, J., & Spear, N. E. (1986). Alcohol drinking patterns of young adult rats as a function of infantile aversive experiences with alcohol odor. *Behavioral & Neural Biology, 46*, 257–271.

Odling-Smee, F. J. (1975). The role of background stimuli during Pavlovian conditioning. *Quarterly Journal of Experimental Psychology, 27*, 201–209.

Rescorla, R. A. (1980). Simultaneous and successive associations in sensory preconditioning. *Journal of Experimental Psychology: Animal Behavior Processes, 6*, 207–216.

Rescorla, R. A. (1981). Simultaneous associations. In P. Harzum & M. D. Zeiler (Eds.), *Predictability, correlation and contiguity* (pp. 47–80). New York: Wiley.

Rescorla, R. A., & Durlach, P. J. (1981). Within-event leaning and Pavlovian conditioning. In N. E. Spear & R. R. Miller (Eds.), *Information processing in animals: Memory mechanisms* (pp. 81–110). Hillsdale, NJ: Lawrence Erlbaum Associates.

Rudy, J. W. (1991). Elemental and configural associations, the hippocampus and development. *Developmental Psychobiology, 24*, 224–236.

Rudy, J. W., Vogt, M. B., & Hyson, R. L. (1984). A developmental analysis of the rat's learned reaction to gustatory and auditory stimulation. In R. Kail & N. E. Spear (Eds.), *Comparative perspectives on the development of memory* (pp. 181–208). Hillsdale, NJ: Lawrence Erlbaum Associates.

Rudy, J. W., & Wagner, A. R. (1975). Stimulus selection in associative learning. In W. K. Estes (Ed.), *Handbook of learning and cognitive processes* (Vol. 2, pp. 269–304). Hillsdale, NJ: Lawrence Erlbaum Associates.

Sarris, V. (1990). Contextual effects in animal psychophysics: A comparative analysis of the chicken's perceptual relativity. *European Bulletin of Cognitive Psychology, 10*, 475–489.

Schnur, P., & Lubow, R. E. (1976). Latent inhibition: The effects of ITI and CS intensity during preexposure. *Learning and Motivation, 7*, 540–550.

Serwatka, J., Molina, J. C., & Spear, N. E. (1986). Weanlings' transfer of conditioned ethanol aversion from olfaction to ingestion depends on the unconditioned stimulus. *Behavioral & Neural Biology, 45*, 57–70.

Shepp, B. E. (1978). From perceived similarity to dimensional structure: A new hypothesis about perspective development. In E. Rosch & B. B. Lloyd (Eds.), *Cognition and categorization.* Hillsdale, NJ: Lawrence Erlbaum Associates.

Shepp, B. E. (1989). On perceiving objects: Holistic versus featural properties. In B. E. Shepp & S. Ballesteros (Eds.), *Object perception: Structure and process* (pp. 203–233). Hillsdale, NJ: Lawrence Erlbaum Associates.

Smoller, D. E., & Spear, N. E. (1988, October). *Sensory preconditioning and "unitization" in the developing rat.* Presented at meetings of the International Society for Developmental Psychobiology.

Solheim, G. S., Hensler, J. G., & Spear, N. E. (1980). Age-dependent contextual effects on short-term active avoidance retention in infants. *Behavioral & Neural Biology, 30,* 250–259.

Spear, N. E. (1984). Ecologically determined dispositions control the ontogeny of learning and memory. In R. Kail & N. E. Spear (Eds.), *Comparative perspectives on the development of memory* (pp. 227–252). Hillsdale, NJ: Lawrence Erlbaum Associates.

Spear, N. E. (1988, October). *Infantile learning and memory in the rat.* President Address, Meetings of the International Society of Developmental Psychobiology.

Spear, N. E., Kraemer, P. J., Molina, J. C., & Smoller, D. E. (1988). Developmental change in learning and memory: Infantile disposition for "unitization." In J. Delacour & J. C. S. Levy (Eds.), *Systems with learning and memory abilities: Proceedings of the workshop held in Paris, June 15–19, 1987.* Amsterdam: Elsevier/North Holland.

Spear, N. E., & Kucharski, D. (1984a). Ontogenetic differences in the processing of multi-element stimuli: Potentiation and overshadowing. In H. Roitblat, T. Bever, & H. Terrace (Eds.), *Animal cognition* (pp. 545–567). Hillsdale, NJ: Lawrence Erlbaum Associates.

Spear, N. E., & Kucharski, D. (1984b). Ontogenetic differences in stimulus selection during conditioning. In R. Kail & N. E. Spear (Eds.), *Comparative perspectives on the development of memory* (pp. 227–252). Hillsdale, NJ: Lawrence Erlbaum Associates.

Spear, N. E., McKinzie, D. L., & Arnold, H. M. (in press). Suggestions from the infant rat about brain dysfunction and memory. In J. Delacour (Ed.), *The memory system of the brain.* Singapore: World Scientific Publishing.

Spear, N. E., & Molina, J. C. (1987). The role of sensory modality in the ontogeny of stimulus selection. In N. Krasnegor, E. M. Blass, M. A. Hofer, & W. P. Smotherman (Eds.) *Perinatal development: A psychobiological perspective* (pp. 83–110). Orlando, FL: Academic Press.

Spear, N. E., & Rudy, J. W. (1991). Tests of learning and memory in the developing rat. In H. N. Shair, G. A. Barr, & M. A. Hofer (Eds.), *Developmental psychobiology: Current methodological and conceptual issues* (pp. 84–113). New York: Oxford University Press.

Spear, N. E., & Smith, G. J. (1978). Alleviation of forgetting in neonatal rats. *Developmental Psychobiology, 11,* 513–530.

Turkewitz, G., Lewkowicz, D. J., & Gardner, J. M. (1983). Determinants of infant perception. In H. S. Rosenblatt, R. A. Hinde, C. Beer, & M. C. Busnel (Eds.), *Advances in the study of behavior* (Vol. 13, pp. 39–62). New York: Academic Press.

Turkewitz, G., & Mellon, R. C. (1989). Dynamic organization of intersensory function. *Canadian Journal of Psychology, 43,* 286–301.

PART THREE

INTERSENSORY INTERACTIONS
IN HUMAN DEVELOPMENT

CHAPTER EIGHT

Development of Intersensory Perception in Human Infants

David J. Lewkowicz
New York State Institute for Basic Research in Developmental Disabilities

Although each of our sensory modalities uniquely specifies different kinds of sensory experiences, there are many dimensions of experience that correspond across the modalities. The phenomenon of intersensory correspondence and its meaning to perception and cognition has been of interest since the time of the Greek philosophers (Marks, 1978). What possible advantage can we gain from having multimodal sources of information about objects and events? Some have considered this question from an evolutionary perspective and have suggested that the ability to use multimodal information allows greater plasticity in behavior and that this, in turn, leads to greater adaptability to one's ecological niche (Maier & Schneirla, 1935). For example, a predator is far more accurate in localizing a prey when both auditory and visual cues specify the prey than when only a unimodal cue specifies it (Stein & Meredith, 1993). Others have considered this question from a functional perspective and have suggested that the specification of an object or event in terms of several concurrent and corresponding attributes is advantageous because the resulting redundancy makes identification of the object or event more certain and the correspondences make perceptual integration possible (J. J. Gibson, 1966; Welch & Warren, 1986). For example, adult subjects are considerably more accurate in their identification of linguistic information when it is specified by both visible and audible information than they are when the linguistic information is specified only by audible information (Massaro & Cohen, 1990; Summerfield, 1979).

In general, there are two classes of stimulus attributes: *amodal* (or also referred to by some as intermodal) and *modality-specific*. Amodal attributes are those that can be represented equally well in different modalities. Examples of amodal attributes are duration, rhythm, shape, intensity, and spatial extent. Modality-specific attributes are those attributes that can be represented only in a single modality because their specification depends on the unique transduction properties of that modality. Examples of modality-specific attributes are color, odor, temperature, and pitch.

Adults possess a variety of perceptual mechanisms that enable them to deal with multimodal inputs. They can detect equivalent attributes in different sensory modalities and integrate them into a unified percept, use modality-specific attributes in different modalities in an integrated manner for more accurate perception, and resolve discrepancies between conflicting inputs to different modalities by responding selectively to input in one modality and ignoring inputs in other modalities. What might be the developmental origins of such perceptual abilities? Thanks to an explosion of research into infants' intersensory abilities in the last 20 years we have come a lot closer to answering this question. The bulk of this research, however, has focused on infants' detection of intersensory equivalence and various aspects of intersensory integration, such as integration of modality-specific inputs, and selective responsiveness to multimodal signals still await investigation.

The early work on intersensory development was framed in terms of one of two opposing theoretical views: the *integration view* (Birch & Lefford, 1963, 1967; Piaget, 1952) or the *differentiation view* (Bower, 1974; E. J. Gibson, 1969; Werner, 1973). The integration view, which is constructivist in nature, assumes that the senses operate as separate avenues of sensory input at birth and that slowly, either over many months, or over several years, the liaisons among the senses develop. In contrast, the differentiation view holds that we are born with the ability to perceive intersensory relations. There are two variants of the differentiation view. One (Bower, 1974; Werner, 1973) argues that we are born with a single, supramodal sense modality, and that as development progresses the different sensory modalities are differentiated from one another. The second, known as invariance-detection theory (E. J. Gibson, 1969; Bahrick & Pickens, chap. 9, this volume), argues that there is a great deal of unimodal and multimodal structure in the environment, that the senses can "pick up" this structure right from birth, and that as development progresses, increasingly finer and more complex amodal invariants are picked up.

My initial work on the development of intersensory perception in infants was guided by what has come to be known as the Intensity Hypothesis (Lewkowicz & Turkewitz, 1980; Schneirla, 1959; Turkewitz, Lewkowicz, & Gardner, 1983). The basic premise of the Intensity Hypothesis, and one that has unique consequences for intersensory responsiveness during early development, is that during the first few months of life infants' responsiveness to stimulation in all modalities is dominated by the quantitative aspects of stimulation. Some time after this initial period, domination by the quantitative aspects of stimulation diminishes and responsiveness to the qualitative aspects of stimulation emerges. An implicit assumption of the Intensity Hypothesis is that the initial immaturity of the nervous system makes infants responsive to what is commonly considered to be the lowest common denominator of stimulation. As development progresses, the reciprocal interaction of factors intrinsic and extrinsic to the infant results in the emergence of more advanced response mechanisms capable of responding to the qualitative aspects of stimulation. An explicit assumption of the Intensity Hypothesis is that both integration and differentiation processes are involved in the developmental process that leads up to the emergence of these more advanced response mechanisms.

If the notion that young infants respond primarily to the quantitative aspects of stimulation is accepted, then it should be possible to demonstrate that young infants respond to quantitative variations but that they do not respond to qualitative ones. With specific regard to intersensory responsiveness, it should be possible to demonstrate that (a) young infants perceive inputs in different modalities as equivalent if the intensity of the inputs is the same, and (b) young infants' responsiveness to quantitative variations in one modality should be affected in a predictable and systematic manner by concurrent quantitative variations in a second modality. There is considerable empirical support for these predictions. First, with regard to intrasensory responsiveness, 4-month-old infants respond to the quantitative aspect of temporally varying visual stimulation and disregard the temporal variations per se, whereas 6-month-old infants respond to the specific temporal variations but not to the quantitative ones (Lewkowicz, 1985b). Second, with regard to intersensory responsiveness, 3-week-old infants spontaneously equate auditory and visual stimuli on the basis of their quantitative equality (Lewkowicz & Turkewitz, 1980), whereas adults do not. Third, with regard to generalized effects of quantitative variations in one modality on responsiveness to stimulation in another modality, we have shown that quantitative variations in one modality produce systematic changes in response to quantitative variations in another modality. Thus, we have found that newborn and 4-month-old infants shift their looking toward lower levels of visual stimulation when concurrent auditory stimulation is presented (Gardner, Lewkowicz, Rose, & Karmel, 1986; Lewkowicz, 1985a; Lewkowicz & Turkewitz, 1981). Finally, recent studies of young infants' response to visual stimuli specified either by configural or quantitative variations have shown that infants younger than 2 months of age respond to the quantitative characteristics of the stimuli (Kleiner, 1987; Kleiner & Banks, 1987).

The research that my colleagues and I have conducted over the past several years with human infants has provided a good deal of support for Schneirla's original idea that intensity was important for behavioral functioning in early development. Since then, results from studies of nonhuman species (Spear & McKinzie, chap. 7, this volume) also have provided evidence in support of the Intensity Hypothesis. Thus, the Intensity Hypothesis appears to be a useful conceptual approach to understanding early intersensory functioning. Indeed, Maurer (1993) recently put forth the suggestion that much of the evidence on intersensory matching in very young infants can be accounted for in terms of a "confusion" or synesthesia of the senses, rather than true intersensory matching. She based her argument on the notion, originally proposed by my colleagues and myself, that infants respond to the overall amount of stimulation, rather than to the qualitative nature of stimulation. Unfortunately, Maurer (1993) contradicted her major thesis when she concluded that the Intensity Hypothesis cannot account for early cross-modal matching. On the contrary, one of the early studies that examined the implications of the Intensity Hypothesis for intersensory functioning in human infants (Lewkowicz & Turkewitz, 1980) was specifically and explicitly designed to test the prediction, generated uniquely by the Intensity Hypothesis, that one should be able to find evidence of intersensory matching based on intensity if very young infants respond to the world primarily in terms of intensity. To quote Lewkowicz and Turkewitz (1980): "If young infants are indeed primarily attentive to the quantitative aspects of stimulation rather than to their qualitative aspects, it is possible that they may respond to stimuli as equivalent or not equivalent based on the degree of similarity of the stimuli with regard to their intensity" (p. 598). The results of that study were fully consistent with the prediction.

Although evidence of intensity-based intersensory matching was found, Lewkowicz and Turkewitz (1980) offered an important caveat in their discussion of the results by stating that "care be taken to distinguish between various types of cross-modal equivalence" (p. 606) and that "some equivalences may be based on primitive and undifferentiated functioning, whereas others may represent the highest levels of cross-modal functioning and may involve perceptual and cognitive as well as sensory mechanisms" (p. 606). Given that intensity-based response mechanisms can provide the initial basis for intersensory integration, it is likely that the higher level kinds of intersensory functions that appear later in development differentiate out of the functional organization laid down as a consequence of intensity-based responsiveness. This would suggest that differentiation is an important process in intersensory development. At the same time, however, the fact that infants are capable of performing some intersensory integration as early as the first month of life certainly rules out a strong version of the integration view (Rose & Ruff, 1987). Yet, integration of certain perceptually and/or cognitively complex amodal attributes does not occur until later in development and appears to depend on the elaboration of perceptual mechanisms responsive to lower level forms of amodal attributes. For example, recognition of the dimensional similarity of pitch and brightness and of loudness and brightness appears as early as 3 years of age (whether it appears earlier is not known because it has not been studied earlier), whereas recognition of the cross-dimensional similarity of pitch and size does not appear until 11 years of age (Marks, Hammeal, & Bornstein, 1987).

From a theoretical point of view, the emergence of different intersensory perceptual capacities at different points in development, and the role that the earlier ones can play in the emergence of the later ones, can be best understood in terms of a process-oriented approach. This approach views development as a set of complex epigenetic interactions between the external environment and the organism (Edelman, 1992; Gottlieb, 1991; Johnston, 1987). According to this view, the changing functional properties of the sensory systems, the differential effects of experience, and the processes of differentiation and integration all contribute to the development of specific intersensory functions through an intricate process of interaction among all of these factors. These complex interactions are often likely to lead to nonlinear effects (Thelen, 1990) and, as a result, predictions based on end point (i.e., adult) performance are inappropriate and can lead to false predictions (Smith, 1991). This approach makes the question of whether intersensory functions are innate or learned moot. Posing the problem in terms of the learned/innate dichotomy is fruitless because it does not address the key developmental issue: What developmental process leads to the production of the function under scrutiny?

My investigations of infants' intersensory perception have been framed around the process-oriented, epigenetic approach outlined earlier. The investigations have addressed two aspects of infants' perception of temporal auditory–visual (A-V) relations: (a) response to intersensory equivalence based on rate, duration, and synchrony, and (b) infants' response to temporally related components of A-V compound stimuli.

RELEVANCE OF TEMPORAL VARIATIONS
TO INTERSENSORY FUNCTIONING
AND TYPES OF TEMPORAL A-V RELATIONS

Temporal stimulus attributes are ubiquitous and are ideally suited for intersensory integration. Events occur in space and time, and objects move through space and time. As a result, events and objects can be described not only in terms of their unique static properties but also in terms of their temporal properties. It turns out that infants are especially sensitive and responsive to temporal information early in development (Kellman, 1988). This is fortuitous because the perception of the temporal aspects of the environment and the performance of behaviors that are temporally organized play a critical role in the development of a variety of skills such as social interaction, linguistic communication, and sensory-motor control (Ashton, 1976; Lashley, 1951; Miller & Byrne, 1984).

In order to understand how information in the visual and auditory modalities can be temporally related, one must first consider the different ways in which visual and auditory information can vary in the temporal dimension. Visual objects can be either spatially static or spatially dynamic. A spatially static object can appear and disappear in an alternating fashion, and the way it does so over time determines its temporal characteristics. A spatially dynamic object derives its temporal characteristics from the way it moves over time. Finally, an auditory stimulus derives its temporal characteristics from the way it occurs over time.

The two types of visual events can be related to auditory events in one of three ways:

1. A spatially static visual stimulus and a sound can pulse on and off synchronously.
2. An object can move through space and a sound can accompany the motion of that object continuously from the moment it begins to move to the moment that it ceases its motion.
3. An object can move through space and a punctate sound can occur when the object's motion path is altered either due to some obstacle that it comes into contact with, or due to some inherent property of the object.

Common examples of these three types of relations abound. An example of a spatially static visual stimulus is a flashing light and an accompanying sound. Examples of moving objects and continuous sounds are the sight and sound of a car moving along a road, the sight and sound of a person talking, or the sight and sound of a bow being drawn across the strings of a violin. Common examples of moving objects accompanied by punctate sounds are the sight and sound of a ball bouncing on the floor, drumsticks beating on a drum, or the sight and sound of a flamenco dancer's feet.

From a perceptual point of view, the key feature in all of these examples is the availability of a temporal attribute that is common to the auditory and visual aspects of an event. The common temporal attribute makes it possible for an observer to integrate the auditory and visual aspects of the event into a unified and coherent event. The ability to integrate the information in this way makes it possible for the observer to distinguish objects and events from one another. For example, a naive observer, who is watching an orchestra and knows nothing about the kinds of sounds that different instruments make, can tell through the use of his intersensory integration skills that the drum roll he is hearing is produced by the person playing the drum rather than by the person playing the violin. The information that makes it possible for the observer to correctly identify the instruments and distinguish them from one another is that (a) the sound occurs each time there is a drum beat, (b) the sound that emanates from the violin is continuous, rather than punctate, and (c) the duration of the audible and visible aspects of the violin is the same, whereas this is not the case for the drum beat.

DEVELOPMENTAL DIFFERENCES IN INFANTS' INTERSENSORY RESPONSE TO A-V EQUIVALENCE

Based on the process-oriented, epigenetic interaction view, it is not unreasonable to expect developmental changes in intersensory functions in infancy. In this section I describe findings from studies that asked whether infants are sensitive to and respond to intersensory equivalence based on such temporal attributes as duration, rate, and synchrony. These findings show that developmental changes in responsiveness to these different temporal attributes occur during infancy.

Intersensory Response to Rate/Synchrony: Spatially Static Visual Stimuli

Two important findings on infants' integration of temporal A-V relations were published in the late 1970s. One finding (Allen, Walker, Symonds, & Marcell, 1977) was that 7-month-old infants could recognize a rhythmic pattern produced by flashing lights as the same as that produced by a sequence of sounds. A second finding (Spelke, 1979) was that 4-month-old infants recognize the correspondence between a punctate sound and the motion characteristics of a bouncing object (Spelke, 1979). These findings were important for two reasons: they suggested (a) that infants were capable of recognizing temporal A-V correspondences regardless of whether they were produced by spatially static or spatially dynamic visual stimuli, and (b) that in the case of moving objects, infants can use temporal correspondences to unify diverse object properties into coherent and meaningful percepts.

Given the Allen et al. demonstration of cross-modal transfer with spatially static visual stimuli, I reasoned that if Spelke's findings reflected a general capacity on the part of infants to integrate A-V events on the basis of their temporal relations, then infants should be able to recognize intersensory temporal relations when the visual information is specified by spatially static visual stimuli. Findings from studies of adults' response to the temporal relation between spatially static visual stimuli (i.e., flashing lights) and sounds that pulse on and off synchronously with the lights indicated that they have little difficulty in detecting such relations (Myers, Cotton, Hilp, 1981; Rubinstein & Gruenberg, 1971). Of course, adult capacities do not predict infant capacities, but the adult findings suggest that the capacity to detect the temporal relation emerges sometime in development. Thus, I carried out a series of studies (Lewkowicz, 1985a) with 4-month-old infants to determine if they would detect the relation between the temporal properties of a flashing visual stimulus and a pulsing sound. The infants were given a series of 30-sec trials during which they saw pairs of identical checkerboard patterns that flashed on and off at different rates. During the first six trials the checkerboards flashed in silence. All possible pairings of three different flash rates (2, 4, or 8 Hz), counterbalanced for side of presentation, were administered across the six trials. During the next 12 trials, the flashing checkerboards were presented together with a tone whose onset and offset was synchronous with the onset and offset of one member of the pair of visual stimuli; as a result, the pulse rate of the sound corresponded to the pulse rate of the synchronous checkerboard. Given these sound/checkerboard pairings, it was possible to ask whether the infants would choose to look at a visual stimulus that corresponded temporally to the concurrent sound across a range of temporal rates.

In the first study, the auditory and visual stimuli were presented at a 50% on/off ratio. This insured that regardless of the specific rate at which a stimulus was presented, it was on and off for an equal amount of time and that, as a result, the total amount of stimulation was equal across different rates of presentation. This control was important because data from our earlier studies (Gardner et. al., 1986; Lewkowicz & Turkewitz, 1980, 1981) indicated that young infants respond differentially to different amounts of stimulation across modalities. Contrary to expectations based on Spelke's (1979) findings, the auditory stimulus had no effect on the infants' visual fixations. Given this result, and given prior findings indicating that young infants' intersensory response can be affected by the overall amount of stimulation, a second study was conducted where explicit intensity variations were provided. It was reasoned that if the intensity-based intersensory response mechanism still operated at 4 months of age, the same types of generalized, nonspecific A-V interactions that we had previously found in neonates (Gardner et al., 1986; Lewkowicz & Turkewitz, 1980, 1981) could be expected in 4-month-old infants. Thus, in the second study, infants were tested with stimuli whose on duration was kept constant across different rates of stimulation. Keeping the on duration constant meant that as rate increased, so did the overall amount of stimulation.

Although, once again, no evidence of A-V matching was found, the auditory stimulus had a generalized effect on visual attention similar to the type found in neonates; the infants spent less time looking at the fastest visual stimulus and more time looking at the slower visual stimulus in the presence of the auditory stimulus. To further determine whether a general, intensity-based response mechanism was responsible for the observed shift in looking, a third study was conducted where infants were presented with stimuli whose rate was kept constant but whose duration, and thus overall intensity, differed. Once again, a generalized shift in looking was found; the infants looked less at the long visual stimulus and more at the short one when they heard the long and the medium-duration sound. Other investigators utilizing very similar procedures also have failed to obtain intersensory matching. For example, Humphrey and Tees (1980) presented pairs of LED lights to 3-, 7-, and 10-month-old infants. The members of the pairs flashed at different rates and a tone that was temporally synchronous with one of the lights was presented at the same time. Neither the 3- nor the 7-month-old infants exhibited any intersensory matching and the 10-month-old infants exhibited only marginal evidence of intersensory matching. Moore and Gibbons (1988) failed to find intersensory matching with stimuli similar to those used by Lewkowicz (1985a) when they tested 4-month-old infants. Finally, in some subsequent unpublished studies in our laboratory (Lewkowicz, 1989a) we failed to obtain intersensory matching of rate in infants tested at 6, 8, and 10 months of age.

Intersensory Response to Duration/Synchrony

Duration is actually a more basic temporal feature of stimulation than rate, because it is the differences in both the duration of stimulation and the duration of interstimulus intervals that give rise to differences in rate. Therefore, to determine if the intersensory detection of duration might be easier, in this study (Lewkowicz, 1986), pairs of checkerboards that flashed at the same rate but for different durations were presented in silence as well as together with a sound. All possible pairs of three different durations (400, 800, or 1600 msec) were presented. During the trials accompanied by the sound, the onset and offset of the sound was synchronous with the onset and offset of one of the visual stimuli. As a result, its duration corresponded to the duration of one member of the pair of visual stimuli. Separate groups of 3-, 6-, and 8-month-old infants were tested.

The 3-month-old infants did not make intersensory matches, but the 6- and the 8-month-old infants did when presented with the 400–1600 msec and the 800–1600 msec pairs. When presented with the 400–1600 msec pair, the infants at each of the two older ages looked longer at the 1600-msec stimulus when it was presented together with the 1600-msec sound than when it was presented either in silence or together with the 400-msec sound. Likewise, when presented with the 800–1600 msec pair, the infants at the two older ages looked longer at the 1600-msec stimulus when it was presented together with the 1600-msec sound than when it was presented either in silence or together with the 800-msec sound.

The fact that the onset and offset of the sound was synchronized with the onset and offset of the matching visual stimulus made it possible that the intersensory matching that we found was based on synchrony and not on duration. To test this possibility, a new group of 8-month-old infants was given the identical stimuli except that the onset and offset of the sound was delayed with respect to the onset and offset of the corresponding visual stimulus by 300 msec. Results from this study indicated that synchrony did, in fact, mediate the intersensory matching found in the first study; when the auditory and visual stimuli were no longer in synchrony the infants no longer exhibited evidence of matching. Together, the results from these two studies indicate that detection of duration-based intersensory correspondence is possible by 6 months of age when A-V synchrony defines the correspondence in duration. In contrast, the results from the rate matching studies indicate that detection of rate-based intersensory correspondence is not possible even as late as 10 months of age and even when synchrony covaries with rate.

**Intersensory Response to Rate/Synchrony Specified
by Spatially Dynamic Visual Stimuli**

Given that infants are highly responsive to motion cues very early in development (Kaufmann, Stucki, & Kaufmann-Hayoz, 1985; Kremenitzer, Vaughan, Kurtzberg, & Dowling, 1979; Volkman & Dobson, 1976), it is possible that motion plays an important role in specifying temporal intersensory relations early in development. It is possible that the absence of motion in our rate matching studies may have been responsible for the failure to find intersensory matching. We addressed this possibility in the next set of studies where we investigated infants' response to the temporal relation between moving visual stimuli and temporally varying sounds.

Detection of the temporal relation between a moving object and a corresponding sound only requires that the infant recognize the relation between the discontinuity of motion and the occurrence of the sound. The infant does not have to attend to the specific properties of the visual object such as its texture, color, or shape, or to the specific properties of the sound such as its pitch or timbre. In other words, detection of an A-V relation based solely on the temporal properties of the information in the respective modalities should be relatively easy, and it might be reasonable to expect that it would be present relatively early in development. As already seen, this prediction is not supported for A-V relations when the visual information is spatially static. The purpose of our next set of studies (Lewkowicz, 1992a) was to test the prediction for spatially dynamic visual stimuli. One of the features of these studies was that the examination of the intersensory capacities reported by

Spelke (1979) was expanded in order to examine responding beyond 4 months of age and in order to examine responding to a broader range of rate variations.

Intersensory Detection of Rate. On each trial, 4- and 8-month-old infants saw two circular, two-dimensional images moving on each side of a TV screen. At the beginning of each trial, the two visual stimuli appeared at the top of the screen and began to move down. In the first study, one stimulus always moved at a different rate of speed than did the other. When each stimulus reached the bottom of the screen, it reversed direction and moved up. Once each stimulus returned to its starting point, it reversed direction once again and began moving down. This up and down movement of each stimulus continued for the duration of the trial (30 sec). Each time one of the visual stimuli bounced at the bottom of the screen, a tone was sounded. The tone was a harmonically complex sound, with a fundamental frequency of 62.5 Hz. The impression created by this display was that of two balls bouncing at different rates, with one of the balls producing a sound each time it hit bottom. All possible pairs of stimuli moving at one of three different rates (0.22, 0.42, or 0.98 Hz) were presented. Across trials, the presentation of the sound was synchronized with the bounce of both the slow and the fast member of each unique pair of visual stimuli. Because the presentation of the sound was synchronized with the bounce of the visual stimulus, its pulse rate was the same as the rate at which the visual stimulus bounced. Contrary to our expectations, we found no evidence of intersensory matching. Examination of both the total duration of looking and of the frequency or duration of first looks revealed no differential effects of the sound on visual preferences.

Detection of A-V Synchrony. One question that the failure to obtain intersensory matching raised was whether the infants could detect the synchrony between the matching auditory and visual stimuli. To answer this question, we first habituated 4- and 8-month-old infants to a single bouncing visual stimulus and a sound that pulsed in synchrony with the bounce. Then, during the test trials, we either disrupted the A-V synchrony or eliminated the sound altogether to see if the infants would detect the change.

The 4-month-old infants' response to the asynchronous test trial depended on whether this test trial was presented first or second. They exhibited significant recovery of responsiveness when the asynchronous test trial was administered first but did not when it was administered second. They did not exhibit any evidence of discrimination in the silent test trial. In contrast, the 8-month-old infants exhibited clear discrimination of each type of change and discriminated the disruption of the A-V synchrony regardless of the order in which the asynchronous test trial was administered. These results make it clear that infants as young as 4 months of age have the capacity to detect A-V synchrony. Consequently, the failure to obtain intersensory matching in the previous paired-preference study could not have been due to the infants' failure to detect the A-V synchrony.

Detection of A-V Equivalence in the Absence of Rate Variations. It is possible that the paired-preference task in the rate-matching study imposed demands on the infants' information-processing capacities that exceeded their ability to process the information. Specifically, the infants were required to make a choice between one of two competing visual stimuli on the basis of their relation to the sound. It may have been difficult for them to make this choice when the relation between one of the visual stimuli and the sound was based on both rate and synchrony, even though the two temporal attributes were perfectly correlated. Support for this possibility comes from some of our earlier studies (Lewkowicz, 1988a, 1988b) in which we found that the availability of more than one discriminative cue adversely affected infants' discriminative performance. Thus, it may be that the rate difference of the two visual stimuli in the paired-preference study overshadowed the synchrony between the matching auditory and visual stimuli.

To determine if this was the case, we repeated the paired-preference study except that this time the visual stimuli did not move at different rates. As a result, the only temporal attribute that united one of the visual stimuli and the sound was synchrony. Because the two visual stimuli moved at the same rate, it was necessary to move them out of phase with respect to each other in order to permit synchronization of the sound with one but not the other. As a result, each trial began with the appearance and motion of one visual stimulus (named the leading visual stimulus) followed a short time later by the appearance and motion of a second identical visual stimulus (the lagging stimulus) on the other side of the screen. On a given trial, the visual stimuli moved at one of three rates: 0.32 Hz (slow), 0.49 Hz (medium), or 0.73 Hz (fast). Each infant received two blocks of trials. In one block of trials, the occurrence of the sound was synchronized with the direction reversal of the leading visual stimulus, whereas in the other block it was synchronized with the direction reversal of the lagging visual stimulus.

Evidence of intersensory matching was found at both ages when the stimuli moved at the slow and the medium rate, although the effects were more robust at 8 months of age. When the visual stimuli moved at the slow rate, the 4-month-old infants looked longer at the sounding/leading stimulus than at the silent/lagging stimulus only when the sound was synchronized with the leading stimulus in the first block of trials. The 8-month-old infants looked longer at the sounding/leading stimulus in both blocks of trials. When the visual stimuli moved at the medium rate, both the 4- and the

8-month-old infants looked longer at the leading/sounding stimulus than at the lagging/silent stimulus in each block of trials. We found no differential effects when the sound was associated with the lagging stimulus. The fact that the infants only preferred the leading stimulus when the sound corresponded to it but not when it did not shows that the preference for the leading stimulus in the presence of the corresponding sound reflected intersensory matching.

These results support the previously proposed hypothesis that the concurrent presence of two cues in the first study contributed to the infants' failure to make intersensory matches. Once the two members of a pair of visual stimuli no longer differed in terms of rate, infants at both ages exhibited evidence of intersensory matching. It is interesting to note that the strongest and most consistent differential effects were found in the first block of trials, and those were primarily evident in a preference for the leading stimulus when it bounced in synchrony with the sound. Although our results from the 4-month-old infants confirmed, in part, previous findings (Spelke, 1979; Spelke, Born, & Chu, 1983), they differed in that we only obtained evidence of intersensory matching when the intersensory correspondence was specified by synchrony, but not when it was specified by rate. One interesting finding, not previously reported in studies of infants' auditory-visual integration, was that when two objects begin to move at slightly different times, it is only the object that captures the subject's attention first that becomes integrated with corresponding auditory information.

Do the data from this set of experiments allow us to answer the question of whether motion facilitates intersensory matching? The answer is a qualified yes. On the one hand, they show that infants can recognize the relation between auditory and visual information when the correspondence is based on synchrony between a moving object and a synchronous sound. On the other hand, the data so far presented show that motion per se does not facilitate the recognition of all types of temporally based intersensory relations because when the relation is based on rate variations infants did not exhibit intersensory matching.

Effects of Prior Familiarization with the A-V Relation on Detection of Equivalence.   It is possible that rate-based intermodal matching is more difficult and that the intersensory paired-preference task is not the most sensitive way to test for it. It may be that the difficulty of the problem requires that infants have the opportunity to become more familiar with the nature of the auditory-visual relation before they are tested for recognition of that relation. This possibility is suggested by the results from a series of studies by Bahrick (1987, 1988) on infants' response to temporal A-V relations. Bahrick (1987) found that when infants were tested for recognition of A-V correspondence based on synchrony, 3-month-old infants did not exhibit intersensory matching whereas older infants did when tested with an intersensory paired-preference test. Following initial familiarization to the A-V relation (Bahrick, 1988), however, 3-month-old infants recognized this relation in a subsequent intersensory paired-preference test.

Given Bahrick's findings, we (Lewkowicz, in press b) conducted a series of studies where we provided infants with the opportunity to become familiar with a rate-based intersensory relation first to see if they also might exhibit recognition of that relation in a subsequent test. Thus, 4-, 6-, and 8-month-old infants first were familiarized with a single auditory/visual event until they reached a predetermined familiarization criterion. To make direct comparisons with our initial intersensory rate study possible, we familiarized the infants with the same auditory/visual compound stimulus presented in the original (Lewkowicz, 1992a) study. Thus, the visual stimulus moved up and down on the screen and a sound occurred each time the stimulus bounced. At each age, half the infants were familiarized with a slowly moving and sounding compound stimulus and half with a rapidly moving and sounding one. Following familiarization, we administered the intermodal paired-preference test during which the infants could see a slowly moving stimulus on one side of a screen and a rapidly moving stimulus on the other side and could hear the slowly occurring sound on one trial and the rapidly occurring sound on the other trial. Contrary to expectations, and despite the opportunity to become familiar with the intersensory relation, the infants exhibited no evidence of intersensory matching. Instead, those infants who were familiarized with the slow compound stimulus looked longer at the rapid visual stimulus, whereas those who were familiarized with the rapid compound stimulus looked longer at the slow visual stimulus.

Although these results indicated that the test-phase sound did not influence looking preferences, we could not determine from these results whether the familiarization-phase sound played any role in subsequent responsiveness. To determine if it did, we conducted two new studies. In one, we familiarized 4-, 6-, and 8-month-old infants with a temporally discordant compound stimulus and in the other we familiarized a different set of 4-, 6-, and 8-month-old infants with a silently moving visual stimulus. In the study with the discordant compound stimulus, we familiarized half the infants with a rapidly moving visual stimulus and a slowly sounding auditory stimulus, and half with a slowly moving visual stimulus and a rapidly sounding auditory stimulus. In the study with the silent visual stimulus, we familiarized half the infants with the rapidly moving visual stimulus and half with the slowly moving visual stimulus. The test trials again involved the presentation of two visual stimuli moving at two different rates and a sound pulsing either at the slow rate or at the rapid rate. Once again, we found that the infants preferred the novel visual stimulus.

Because the infants in Bahrick's studies (1988) were familiarized with both kinds of intermodal relations before they were tested for response to temporal correspondence, in our last study we familiarized infants with both intermodal relations. Thus, we familiarized separate groups of 4-, 6-, and 8-month-old infants with the slow auditory/visual compound stimulus until they reached criterion and then with the rapid compound stimulus until they reached criterion. Despite the differential familiarization, we did not obtain evidence of intermodal matching and only found the novelty preference. The possibility that the infants' failure to make intermodal matches was due to the auditory stimulus being subthreshold was ruled out in prior studies by the fact that the identical auditory stimulus was highly effective in eliciting discrimination of the rate at which it pulses (Lewkowicz, 1992b) and by the fact that it elicited auditory–visual matching (Lewkowicz, 1992a).

The most likely factor that might account for the difference in outcome between our familiarization studies and Bahrick's studies is the nature of the cues that specified the A-V temporal correspondence in the two sets of studies. In Bahrick's studies, the two auditory/visual events were highly distinctive. The events differed in a number of ways, in terms of both their visual and their auditory characteristics. One event was a film of a single, large, blue and yellow marble moving back and forth inside a transparent tube. The other was a film of 43 small marbles, 15 of which were blue and 28 of which were yellow, moving back and forth inside the tube. Thus, the two visual events differed in terms of the size of the individual elements making up the event, the overall number of elements comprising each event, and the color of each individual element comprising the event. The sound that the large marble made was a discrete impact sound, which was the result of the marble making repeated contact with one end of the tube as the tube was abruptly rotated in an arc-shaped trajectory. The other sound consisted of a more prolonged ensemble of sounds produced by the many small marbles coming into contact with the end of the tube. In addition to the distinctive visual and auditory characteristics, the temporal characteristics of the two events differed. The tube was moved in an erratic and unpredictable manner and, as a result, the visible and audible temporal patterns of the two events differed.

In contrast to Bahrick's stimulus events, the events presented in our familiarization studies were much more similar to each other. The visual stimuli in each case were identical and the only cue that differentiated them from one another was the rate at which each moved. The auditory stimuli in each case also were identical and the only cue that differentiated them was the rate at which each was pulsed on and off. As a result, even when the infants had the opportunity to learn about two different audible and visible events during familiarization, the only available cue that permitted differentiation of the two events was rate, and the only cues that permitted identification of the visual stimulus that corresponded to the auditory stimulus were rate and synchrony. Obviously, the task facing the infants in our studies was far more difficult than the task facing the infants in Bahrick's studies. In our studies, infants only had the intermodal cues of synchrony and rate available to them, whereas the infants in Bahrick's studies had intermodal temporal cues, as well as a host of modality-specific cues available to them to help in the detection of the auditory–visual relation. Indeed, it is likely that the infants in Bahrick's studies learned to associate the various modality-specific cues during the initial familiarization phase and then were able to recognize the intersensory correspondence on the basis of these associations.

Thus, it appears that integration of auditory and visual inputs is possible by 4 months of age when the two inputs are related in terms of synchrony. In contrast, it appears that integration of auditory and visual inputs that have identical physical characteristics and only differ in terms of a single temporal attribute is much more difficult, and does not emerge until sometime after 8 months of age, when the temporal basis for uniting them is rate. This timetable is consistent with other findings on infants' integration of auditory and visual information on the basis of temporal attributes. Thus, our findings, as well as those of Bahrick (1988), Spelke (1979) and Spelke et al. (1983), all agree that integration on the basis of synchrony is possible by 4 months of age. The data on response to rate also are consistent in that Lewkowicz (1985a, 1992a), Moore and Gibbon (1988), and Humphrey and Tees (1980) all failed to find matching of rate as late as 8 months of age. Although Spelke's (1979) initial report of rate-based matching at 4 months of age would place intersensory integration on the basis of rate earlier, a careful examination of the original results (Lewkowicz, in press a) reveals that the infants in that study only exhibited matching in the fast but not the slow sound condition. This suggests, at best, a limited ability to make rate-based matches at 4 months of age. Indeed, Spelke recently has decried her initial overemphasis of the positive results of that study (Spelke, in press).

In conclusion, the results from the studies reviewed in this section indicate that synchrony plays an important role in infants' detection of intersensory relations and that its role is dependent on what other temporal attributes covary with it. When synchrony covaries with rate it does not appear to facilitate detection of intersensory correspondence. This is true regardless of whether rate variations occur in a spatially static or spatially dynamic manner in the visual modality. In contrast, when synchrony covaries with duration, it does facilitate intersensory matching and does so in the absence of motion. Based on such findings, I recently proposed that differentiation of several different intersensory temporal attributes proceeds in a sequential manner (Lewkowicz, 1992b). Based on the evidence just reviewed, I proposed that intersensory responsiveness to synchrony differentiates first in development and that synchrony then provides the basis for the subsequent sequential differentiation of responsiveness to duration, rate, and rhythm.

RESPONSE TO COMPONENTS OF A-V COMPOUND STIMULI

Response to A-V Compounds Composed of a Spatially Static Visual Component

The general problem of the perceiver's response to multimodal sources of information is multifaceted. The most obvious and most studied aspect of the problem is how the perceiver detects the equivalence of multimodal inputs and thus perceives the unity of information regardless of its source. What if, however, the perceiver has equivalent information available in different modalities but is not yet able to respond to the equivalence because the ability to do so has not yet developed? As our data show, this appears to be the case for intersensory perception of rate even as late as 10 months of age. How will the perceiver respond to the multimodal information then? Could it be that the infants' inability to respond to rate intermodally is due to differential responsiveness to input in the different modalities? Does greater responsiveness to input in one modality prevent the infant from responding to intersensory equivalence? These were the questions that I asked in a series of studies (Lewkowicz, 1988a, 1988b).

In order to answer these questions I had to devise a method that would permit separate assessment of responsiveness to the components of a compound multimodal stimulus. The method consisted of first habituating infants to a compound stimulus and then administering a series of test trials where the components making up the compound stimulus were changed systematically. If the infants discriminated a particular type of change, then it was expected that they would exhibit a significant recovery of responsiveness on the test trial involving that change.

My initial conceptualization of the problem of differential responsiveness to inputs in the different modalities was based on the fact that the sensory modalities develop in a sequential manner (Gottlieb, 1971). In humans, the auditory modality has its functional onset some time during the last trimester of pregnancy whereas the visual modality has its functional onset at birth. Given that the auditory modality has a more extensive developmental history, I reasoned that young infants should be more responsive to auditory input. Given that the visual modality develops very rapidly during the first months of postnatal life (Banks & Salapatek, 1983), I also reasoned that older infants should be equally responsive to inputs in both modalities.

In the first experiment, 6- and 10-month-old infants were habituated with an A-V compound stimulus composed of a flashing checkerboard and a pulsing tone. Then each infant was given three separate test trials to determine what aspects of the compound stimulus the infant had learned about during the habituation phase. The three types of test trials were an auditory (A) test trial during which some temporal aspect of the auditory component was changed while the visual component remained unchanged, a visual (V) test trial where some temporal aspect of the visual component was changed while the auditory component remained unchanged, and an auditory–visual (A-V) test trial where some temporal aspect of both components was changed simultaneously. The temporal aspect of the components that changed was either rate, duration, or rate and duration together.

6-Month-Old Infants. As a whole, the studies with the 6-month-old infants indicated that infants at this age are more responsive to auditory input than to visual input. This conclusion was reached through a series of six studies. In the first study, half the infants were habituated with a compound stimulus consisting of a checkerboard flashing at a temporal rate of 2 Hz and a tone pulsing in synchrony with the checkerboard, whereas the other half were habituated with a checkerboard/tone combination presented at 4 Hz. For those infants who were habituated with the 2-Hz compound stimulus, the rate changed to 4 Hz during the test trials, whereas for those habituated with the 4-Hz compound stimulus, the rate changed to 2 Hz. The on time of the components was the same (150 msec) for both temporal rates. To determine whether the infants detected the changes during the test trials, a recovery score was calculated by comparing the response during the specific test trial versus the response during the terminal part of the habituation phase. Results indicated that the infants discriminated the combined A-V change but that they did not discriminate the change in either component alone.

Each unimodal change represented a disruption of A-V equivalence. Had the infants perceived the two components as temporally equivalent, then they should have responded to each unimodal change. The failure to do so may have reflected the fact that the temporal similarity of the auditory and visual components during the habituation phase made it difficult for the infants to learn about the temporal attributes of each of the components sufficiently well to enable them to discriminate a change in their respective temporal characteristics. To provide infants with an opportunity to learn about the temporal characteristics of the constituent components, in the next study they were habituated with a temporally discordant compound stimulus. Thus, half the infants were habituated with a compound stimulus consisting of a 2-Hz visual component and a 4-Hz auditory component, and half were habituated with a compound stimulus consisting of a 4-Hz visual component and a 2-Hz auditory component. This time, the infants not only discriminated the simultaneous change in both components, but also discriminated the change in the auditory component. They did not, however, discriminate the change in the visual component.

Although the greater temporal distinctiveness of the components in the habituation phase made it easier for the infants to make the discrimination, the failure to discriminate the visual change suggested that the temporal difference between the components may still not have been sufficient. Another way to facilitate discrimination of changes in the constituent components was to increase the number of cues that served to signal the change from the habituation to the test phase. This was done in the next study by changing both rate and duration when going from the habituation to the test phase. In order to change rate and duration simultaneously the stimuli have to be pulsed according to a 50% duty cycle. This means that the stimuli were on and off for equal proportions of a cycle regardless of rate—a 2-Hz stimulus was on for 250 msec and off for 250 msec, whereas a stimulus presented at 4 Hz was on for 125 msec and off for 125 msec. Consequently, when the rate of a component changed from one to the other, the duration of the component also changed. Results indicated that enhancing the temporal distinctiveness of the change from the habituation to the test phase was not as effective as increasing the temporal distinctiveness of the habituation-phase components. As before, the infants discriminated the combined change in the two components, but they only exhibited marginal discrimination of the change in the auditory component.

The failure of the infants to respond to the visual component changes and their successful response to the auditory changes in the second study suggested some form of auditory dominance. It was still possible, however, that further enhancement of the temporal distinctiveness of the components might enable the infants to discriminate the visual changes. Thus, in the next study we habituated infants to a temporally discordant compound stimulus where the components were presented according to a 50% duty cycle. This meant that the components differed both in duration and rate during the habituation phase and that whenever the rate of a component changed during a test trial so did its duration. Results indicated that the availability of two concurrent discriminative cues was not effective because the infants only discriminated the change in the A-V test trial. This finding suggested that concurrent variation in two temporal discriminative cues actually made it more difficult for the infants to process the temporal characteristics of the components; they not only had to encode simultaneous differences in rate and duration during the habituation phase but they also had to determine which attribute changed and which did not during the test phase.

The consistent failure of the infants to discriminate the change in the visual component raised several questions. First, did it reflect a general inability of infants at this age to discriminate rate differences visually, or did it reflect an inability to process visual rate changes when concurrent auditory input was present? Second, was the failure to respond to the visual component change due to its being less salient than the auditory component? The latter possibility was likely because no a priori matching of the two components was done.

To answer the first question, the same testing method was used, except that the infants were habituated with the visual component only, and then were tested with a change in the rate at which the visual component flashed. Results showed that the infants exhibited significant discrimination, indicating that their failure to discriminate the change in the V test trial in the prior studies was specifically due to the simultaneous presence of the auditory component. To answer the second question about relative salience, infants were once again habituated with a temporally concordant compound stimulus whose components were presented at a 50% duty cycle. This time, however, the salience of the visual component was increased by increasing its intensity. The infants still did not discriminate the change in the V test trial; they only discriminated the changes in the A-V and A test trials. At the same time, however, there were indications that the visual component played a role in responsiveness. First, the magnitude of response in the A-V test trial was significantly greater than the magnitude of response in the A test trial; this was not the case in the identical previous study in which the low-intensity visual component was presented. Second, the discrimination in the A test trial in this study was statistically reliable, whereas it was only marginally so in the previous study with the low-intensity visual component. This suggests that the higher intensity visual component provided an important backdrop for the auditory component. Despite this indirect evidence, however, the basic finding in all of these studies was that when a visual component had to compete with an auditory component for the infants' attention, they did not respond to the visual component in a clear and unequivocal manner.

10-Month-Old Infants. With one exception, we conducted the same series of studies with 10-month-old infants. We found that in addition to being able to discriminate the A and the A-V changes, the older infants also responded to changes in the visual component. Specifically, when the 10-month-old infants were habituated with the temporally concordant compound stimulus that consisted of equal-duration components across different rates (i.e., on for 150 msec regardless of rate), they, like the younger infants, did not discriminate the visual change. They did, however, discriminate the change in the A-V and the A test trials. When they were habituated with the temporally discordant compound stimulus with equal-duration components, they not only discriminated the change in the A-V and in the A test trials, but, unlike the younger infants, also discriminated the change in the V test trial. Finally, in contrast to the younger infants, when the older infants were habituated with the temporally concordant compound stimulus consisting of components presented at a 50% duty cycle, they discriminated all three types of changes.

The one interesting similarity in outcome between the younger and older infants was that when the older infants were habituated with the temporally discordant compound stimulus made up of unequal-duration components they also only discriminated the change in the A-V test trial. This suggested that the older infants also found it more difficult to process two temporal cues simultaneously. Nonetheless, there were reasons to suspect that even in this last study the visual component was involved indirectly in responsiveness. First, the data from the other studies showed that the older infants could discriminate visual component changes. Second, a significant discrimination in the A-V test trial, and the absence of a discrimination in the A test trial, means that the visual component must have contributed in some way to responsiveness. Given that the older infants could discriminate visual component changes when they only had to process one temporal cue, we reasoned that the failure to respond to the visual component when the information load was greater might be made easier by enhancing the visual component. Thus, the last study was repeated but this time the intensity of the visual component was increased. As expected, the infants not only discriminated the A-V change but also discriminated the change in the A and in the V test trials. Thus, the increased intensity of the visual component helped the older infants to overcome the increased information load of the task, which was not the case for younger infants. At the same time, however, the infants responded more to the change in the auditory component, indicating that the auditory information was still more salient.

Response to A-V Compounds Composed of a Spatially Dynamic Visual Component

As noted earlier, motion is a very important visual cue and infants are highly responsive to it. The data from the preceding series of studies suggested that auditory dominance operated in early development and that by the end of the first year of life it began to wane. This conclusion, however, was based on results from studies with spatially static visual stimuli. Given the ubiquity and importance of motion in the visual modality, it was important to determine whether the developmental trends observed in the previous studies reflected a general process. If they did, then a similar pattern of findings should be obtained with moving/sounding stimuli. To find out if this was the case, we (Lewkowicz, 1992c) conducted a new series of studies that were identical in design but this time the visual component was spatially dynamic. The actual visual and auditory stimuli that were used were the same ones that were used in the previously discussed studies of intersensory matching (Lewkowicz, 1992a).

Groups of 4-, 6-, 8-, and 10-month-old infants were habituated with the bouncing/sounding compound stimulus and then tested with changes in the auditory component alone, in the visual component alone, and in both components together. At each age, half the infants were habituated with a slow compound stimulus moving and sounding at 0.32 Hz and half were habituated with a fast compound stimulus moving and sounding at 0.73 Hz. For those infants habituated with the slow compound stimulus, the rate of stimulus presentation during the test trials changed to the fast one, whereas for those habituated with the fast compound stimulus the rate changed to the slow one.

In contrast to the findings from the studies with spatially static visual stimuli (Lewkowicz, 1988a, 1988b), the findings from this study showed that even the youngest infants responded in a very robust manner to the change in the movement rate of the visual stimulus. In fact, in a subsequent unpublished study, we have found that infants as young as 2 months of age respond to the change in the movement rate of the visual stimulus. Overall, no age differences in responsiveness to any of the three changes were found, as infants at all ages had no problem discriminating any of the changes. In addition, the infants not only responded more to the bimodal change than to the change in the A test trial, but in contrast to the findings from the original studies, they responded more to the change in the visual component than they did to the change in the auditory component.

One of the problems inherent in the design of this study is that whenever rate changed in the A and V test trials, the sound became desynchronized with respect to bounce of the visual stimulus. As a result, a second, identical study was conducted with separate groups of 4-, 6-, 8-, and 10-month-old infants except that this time the A-V test trial was replaced by a new test trial where only the temporal relation between the A and V components was changed. This was done by having the sound occur when the visual stimulus reached the midpoint of its motion trajectory. Once again, the infants exhibited very robust discrimination of the unimodal changes. They also discriminated the desynchronization of the A and V components. The magnitude of response recovery in the desynchronization trial was, however, significantly smaller than the magnitude of response recovery in the A-V test trial in the preceding study. This indicated that the concurrent change in the rate of both components was more discriminable than was the change from synchrony to asynchrony.

The original postulation of the operation of a sensory dominance process was in no way meant to imply that the hierarchical relationship between the senses was fixed during development. Indeed, the findings from this latest set of studies with moving stimuli further confirm this idea and suggest that the hierarchical relationship of the different sensory modalities is quite fluid. The fluidity is illustrated by the finding that infants as old as 6 months of age did not respond to temporal changes in the visual modality when the changes were produced by a spatially static visual component, but that infants as young as 2 months of age did respond to temporal changes when they were produced by a spatially dynamic visual component. In addition to showing how much responsiveness to visual information depends on the nature of the information, it also illustrates the primacy of motion cues for the visual modality. As already noted, the visual modality is highly responsive to motion right at birth. In addition, motion and temporal detection mechanisms become differentiated earlier and are more adultlike earlier than are spatial detection mechanisms (Banks & Salapatek, 1983; Freedland & Dannemiller, 1987). In general, motion is such a fundamental property of the visual world that mechanisms for the detection of motion are found at many phylogenetic levels where mechanisms for the detection of pattern are either not present at all, or are very rudimentary (Nakayama, 1985).

Similar to the primacy of motion for the visual modality, the primacy of temporal variations for the auditory modality is illustrated by the finding that infants as old as 10 months of age were more responsive to changes in the temporal attributes of an auditory component than to changes in the temporal attributes of a spatially static visual component. In this particular case, it appears that when temporal variations in the auditory modality compete with temporal variations in the visual modality when motion cues are absent, responsiveness to the auditory input is greater. This general pattern of findings, indicating differential relative responsiveness of the auditory and visual modalities when inputs from both modalities compete for the subject's attention, is consistent with what has come to be known as the modality appropriateness hypothesis.

Although this hypothesis has been largely used to account for modality biasing effects in adults (Freides, 1974; Lederman, Thorne, & Jones, 1986; O'Connor & Hermelin, 1972; Welch & Warren, 1986), it can be adapted easily as an explanatory concept for modality interactions in early development. The basic concept behind this hypothesis is that each modality is specialized for responding to specific stimulus features, and when inputs from different modalities are present at the same time, the perceiver will utilize and/or favor the modality best suited to the processing of the incoming information. In general, vision is best at processing spatial information whereas audition is best at processing temporal information (Kubovy, 1988).

Caveat. One very important caveat regarding the results from the A-V compound studies must be noted. The results from these studies do not permit a determination of the relative standing of the sensory modalities because the relative salience of the components was not matched in either set of studies. This is a difficult, if not an intractable, problem. Many investigators studying adult observers' response to intersensory discrepancy have used a discrepancy technique that involves presenting conflicting information in two different modalities and observing the subject's response (Welch & Warren, 1980). Because the normal tendency of the perceptual system is to achieve a unified perceptual experience, discrepancies usually lead to strong biasing effects. The direction of the bias has been used to infer the relative dominance of one modality over another in situations involving intersensory interactions. In studies employing discrepancy methods, investigators have typically ignored questions regarding the subjective equality of concurrent inputs in different modalities. In contrast, in studies employing reaction-time methods, investigators have been concerned with equivalence but their solution has been to match the auditory and visual stimuli only in terms of their intensity.

Although establishing subjective equality in terms of intensity may be important, it actually may be irrelevant, or it may not solve the problem at all. This is illustrated by the fact that intersensory biasing effects in adults remain the same whether the auditory and visual components of a compound stimulus are matched in terms of intensity or not (Colavita, 1974), and by the fact that biasing effects remain the same in infants even when the relative intensity of an auditory and visual component is changed (Lewkowicz, 1988a). The fallacy that a priori matching might solve the problem is illustrated best when one wants to form an auditory/visual compound stimulus from two equivalent components. As soon as the components are combined, the value of each is changed by the value of the other. A case in point is the well-known phenomenon of auditory "driving" in adults (Gebhard & Mowbray, 1959; Myers et al., 1981; Shipley, 1964). When subjects are asked to match rates of visual flicker with rates of auditory flutter, the auditory flutter appears to drive the visual flicker. As a result, the visual flicker appears to increase as the auditory flutter increases, even though the rate of the visual stimulus remains constant. Thus, a priori matching of the components on the basis of intensity, or on the basis of some other attribute, either may be irrelevant if some other dimension governs responsiveness, or may be inappropriate due to interaction effects.

A SYNTHESIS AND A PRELIMINARY MODEL
OF INTERSENSORY TEMPORAL PROCESSING

The body of data reviewed so far suggest that infants:

1. Are sensitive to A-V relations based on synchrony beginning around the fourth month of life.
2. Become sensitive to A-V relations based on the combination of duration and synchrony between the third and sixth month of life.

3. Are not sensitive to A-V relations based on rate up through the eighth month of life.
4. Are sensitive to unimodal differences in rate.

Figure 8.1 summarizes the findings on temporally based intersensory responsiveness and shows the relative emergence of responsiveness to these various temporal attributes during infancy.

Why might the differentiation of responsiveness to the four intersensory temporal attributes be ordered as depicted in Fig. 8.1? In my view, the reasons have to do with the kinds of mechanisms that are required for responsiveness to each of the four temporal attributes. The developmental primacy of the emergence of responsiveness to intersensory synchrony is probably due to two facts. First, the mechanisms required to detect synchrony need not be very complicated; they only need to be sensitive to temporal contiguity. Second, the contiguous events don't even have to be precisely time-locked to be perceived as belonging together. As Fraisse (1982) pointed out, we operate within what he called the "psychological present," which is a window of time during which two events can occur and be perceived as simultaneous despite the fact that, technically, they are temporally noncontiguous. With specific regard to multimodal events, the psychological present for adults depends on the sequential order in which the two events occur. When an auditory event precedes a visual event, the two events can be separated by nearly 80 msec and still be perceived as unified. In contrast, when an auditory event follows a visual event, the two events can be separated by nearly 140 msec and still be perceived as unified (Dixon & Spitz, 1980; McGrath & Summerfield, 1985).

Recent data from studies in my laboratory (Lewkowicz, 1993) indicate that the psychological present is considerably longer in infants. In these studies, separate groups of 2-, 4-, 6-, and 8-month-old infants were first habituated to a compound auditory/visual stimulus consisting of a bouncing visual stimulus and a sound that occurred in synchrony with the bounce. During several different test trials, the synchrony between the bounce and the sound was disrupted to different degrees. Results indicated that regardless

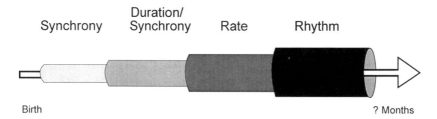

FIG. 8.1. Developmental sequence of the emergence of responsiveness to four types of intersensory temporal attributes.

of age, the infants discriminated the change from synchrony to asynchrony only when the magnitude of the asynchrony interval was at least 350 msec when the sound preceded the bounce, and at least 450 msec when the sound followed the bounce. These findings indicate that, compared to adults, the interval over which contiguity is acceptable to infants is considerably longer.

In contrast to the detection of synchrony, the detection of A-V relations on the basis of rate is more difficult. There are two reasons for the greater difficulty. First, the infant must be able to detect the specific rate in each modality. Second, some sort of a comparator process that determines whether the two rates in the two modalities are equal or not must operate. At sufficiently slow rates—rates that have a longer cycle time than the infant's psychological present (less than roughly 2 Hz)—these two requirements do not have to be met because the infants should be able to perform the matches purely on the basis of synchrony. In other words, at slow enough rates, what might appear to be rate matches are in reality matches that are made on the basis of synchrony. This idea is illustrated in the top part of Fig. 8.2, which shows in schematic form the temporal distribution of what might be a real-life event like a ball that is bouncing repeatedly at some constant rate. If the ball is bouncing at a rate of approximately 2 Hz, the sound will be perceived as belonging to the ball, even if the sound and the bounce are not precisely time-locked but occur within the psychological present. If, however, the ball begins to bounce at a higher rate (see the bottom part of Fig. 8.2), the infant no longer can integrate the auditory and visual aspects of that compound stimulus on the basis of synchrony alone. This is because each bounce of the ball occurs too close in time to the next

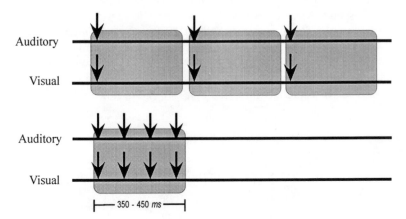

FIG. 8.2. Differential consequences of the infant's psychological present for the processing of temporally distributed multimodal events. The grey rectangle represents the psychological present.

one, and, as a result, the four instances of the bounce fall within a single psychological present. In other words, a kind of "temporal smearing" results if the infant were to attempt to integrate the auditory and visual streams purely on the basis of synchrony alone.

It seems that a more reasonable solution to this problem of integration is that the infant have the capacity to respond to the specific rate (i.e., speed) at which each event occurs, compare the rates of the two events, and decide whether they are the same or different. The evidence already reviewed shows that infants are capable of responding to rate differences. As a result, infants' failure to integrate rate must be due to the fact that (a) the infant's nervous system is incapable of determining precisely the temporal rate of a given event, (b) the comparator mechanism is absent, or (c) the comparator mechanism is not fully functional yet.

Employing the concept of the psychological present, it is also possible to account for the relatively early emergence of intersensory integration based on duration/synchrony. The model would predict that the easiest duration/synchrony-based intersensory matches should be those involving durations that are longer than the psychological present (i.e., 350–450 msec). In an earlier study (Lewkowicz, 1986) I showed that 6- and 8-month-old infants matched on the basis of duration/synchrony when presented with a 400–1600 msec pair and an 800–1600 msec pair, but not when presented with a 400–800 msec pair. To account for these findings, the model makes three assumptions: (a) the critical events are the on and off energy transitions in each modality, (b) the psychological present begins at the point of energy transition, and (c) the size of the psychological present depends on whether the energy transition of the auditory stimulus occurs prior to or after the occurrence of the energy transition of the visual stimulus; it is 350 msec if the auditory stimulus precedes the visual stimulus and 450 msec if it follows it. Given these assumptions, Fig. 8.3 shows how the model might account for the differential effects. In the case of successful matching, the top part of Fig. 8.3 shows that the matching is performed on the basis of the offset of the stimuli in the two modalities. The psychological present begins with the offset of the short auditory and visual stimuli and continues for between 350 and 450 msec. According to the model, these two stimuli will be perceived as belonging together because they fall within the same psychological present, whereas the long visual stimulus will not be because it falls outside of the psychological present. The bottom part of Fig. 8.3 shows why matching was not possible in the case of the 400–800 msec pair; the offset of both visual stimuli occurred within the same psychological present in which the offset of the auditory stimulus occurred and, as a result, the infant had no basis for distinguishing between the two visual stimuli in relation to the auditory stimulus.

In contrast to synchrony, duration/synchrony, and rate, a response to rhythm requires an additional, and even more complex, perceptual mecha-

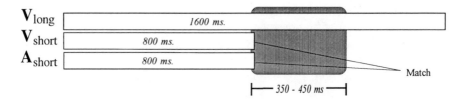

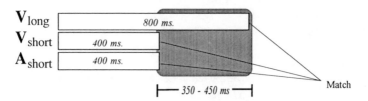

FIG. 8.3. The effect of the psychological present on intersensory matching based on duration/synchrony. The grey rectangle represents the psychological present.

nism. Rhythm is a special case of a periodic process because the intervals separating the elements constituting a single rhythmic sequence are unequal, and the longest interval usually serves to segregate multi-element sequences into separate but identical perceptual units. Thus, although the elements that comprise each individual unit have their own periodicity, the unique aspect of a rhythmic sequence is that there is an overriding temporal structure that manifests itself by way of the larger multi-element units. As in the case of rate, the periodicity of the elements making up a single rhythmic unit is shorter than the psychological present. Consequently, the mechanism that would be needed to integrate the audible and visible aspects of a rhythmic unit would not only have to be sensitive to periodicity, but would (a) have to posses a comparator process to determine the equality of the specific periodicity of the information in each modality, and (b) have to be sensitive to the overriding temporal structure of the rhythmic units.

The sequential order depicted in Fig. 8.1 was derived from empirical findings. It should be noted, however, that this order also could have been predicted a priori given the requirement that increasingly more complex mechanisms are likely to be involved in the integration of multimodal inputs based on synchrony, duration/synchrony, rate, and rhythm. One important feature of Fig. 8.1 is the depiction of the sequential emergence of responsiveness as a set of increasingly larger pipes. This is intended to capture the idea that responsiveness to the developmentally later aspects of temporal experience is dependent on perceptual differentiation of mechanisms responsive to developmentally earlier aspects of temporal experience.

In other words, once infants become adept at responding to a given intersensory temporal attribute (e.g., synchrony), they then can rely on that attribute to "discover" the next and more complex temporal attribute. As a result, responsiveness to complex temporal structure, as exemplified in a rhythmic unit, would not be expected to emerge until the infant perceptually differentiated the other three temporal attributes. This idea of an incremental developmental process resulting in the construction of increasingly more sophisticated perceptual mechanisms is consistent with the results from research in other domains of perceptual development (Cohen, 1991).

In sum, the length of the infant's psychological present, and the different kinds of mechnisms required for intersensory integration, appear to be good predictors of the sequential emergence of responsiveness to what appear to be qualitatively different temporal features of the world. The psychological present seems to reflect some basic underlying periodicity of the nervous system that gives rise to a variety of heretofore seemingly disparate phenomena and provides a unifying principle for understanding the developmental changes observed in infants' intersensory responsiveness to temporally distributed events. The length of the psychological present, the consequences of its specific length for responsiveness to synchrony versus rate, or synchrony versus duration/synchrony, and the different kinds of mechanisms required for intersensory integration on the basis of different intersensory temporal attributes all provide some general principles that can be used to formulate the foregoing model. The advantage of this model is that it provides specific mechanisms that permit specific predictions regarding the kinds of temporal intersensory relations that infants should be sensitive to at various points in development. For example, based on adult data, we already know that the length of the psychological present slowly becomes shorter with development. This is probably due to myelination in the nervous system, making conduction velocity faster. What might be the consequences of a shorter psychological present? This feature of the model gives it a distinct advantage over the Gibsonian invariance detection view; the latter assumes that infants come into this world ready to pick up amodal invariants, but does not specify what those invariants are nor when they can be expected to emerge in development.

The predictive nature and emprical testability of the model can be illustrated in two ways. For example, so far, no clear-cut, convincing demonstrations of infants' intersensory perception of rhythm have been published (see Lewkowicz, 1989b, for criticism of the available data). The model predicts a priori that intersensory responsiveness to rhythm should emerge last. Given that infants have been shown to be responsive to relatively complex rhythmic patterns in the auditory modality at 12 months but not earlier (Morrongiello, 1984), it would be reasonable to expect responsiveness to intersensory relations based on rhythm to emerge at 1 year of age or later. Demonstration of intersensory responsiveness to rhythm earlier than that would refute the developmental requirements of the model that responsiveness to the other temporal attributes differentiate first and provide a necessary foundation for the differentiation of responsiveness to rhythm. Earlier-than-predicted responsiveness to rhythm could be due to the fact that the kind of structure inherent in rhythmic events is processed in a wholistic fashion and does not need to be built up from an appreciation of the more elementary aspects of temporal information such as periodicity. On the other hand, the failure to respond to rhythm would require that discriminability in each modality be established first before the failure of the comparator process is implicated.

In addition to the prediction regarding responsiveness to rhythm, the model would predict that a nervous system that operates at a slower time constant would have a longer psychological present. A number of studies have shown that infants with various insults to their nervous system process information more slowly (Landry, Leslie, Fletcher, & Francis, 1985; Lewis & Bendersky, 1989; Ross, Tessman, Auld, & Nass, 1992). According to the model, this would mean that given that intersensory integrative mechanisms were not damaged, brain-injured infants should display a longer asynchrony threshold than do normal infants.

RESPONSE TO NATURALISTIC A-V COMPOUNDS COMPOSED OF FACES AND VOICES

One of the major underlying goals of my research has been to determine whether it would be possible to generate a set of general principles that might describe and explicate the development of intersensory perceptual mechanisms in human infants. The model just presented is an attempt to do so, but it only accounts for intersensory integration on the basis of temporal information. Obviously, intersensory integration can occur on many levels and can utilize a variety of stimulus features besides temporal ones. For example, intensity or location also can serve as a basis for integration in the auditory and visual modalities. Even such attributes as the pitch of the voice and the degree of movement of the head can serve as cues for integrating the multimodal properties of the face. For other pairs of modalities, such as the visual and tactual, for example, shape and texture are the principal attributes subserving integration.

Although the data from our work on infants' response to different types of A-V compounds suggests that the nature of the information represented by an A-V compound greatly affects how infants will respond to the components of the compound stimulus, more empirical information is needed before general principles can be generated. This kind of approach is consistent with Kluver's

(1933) insistence on studying responsiveness to as wide a range of stimuli as possible if one wants to understand the mechanisms underlying a given response function. Kluver's method of equivalent and nonequivalent stimuli requires that one identify a set of stimuli that elicit the same response from a subject (equivalent set) as well as a set of stimuli that elicit a different response (nonequivalent set). A comparison of the properties of the two sets of stimuli then enables the investigator to identify a property that is present and common to the stimuli in the equivalent set but absent in the nonequivalent set. This property makes it possible for the investigator to make inferences regarding the mechanisms mediating that particular behavior. My approach to the study of infants' intersensory responsiveness has been guided by Kluver's method of equivalent and nonequivalent stimuli and by the desire to cast as wide a net over infants' response to multimodal information as possible in order to generate some general principles. As a result, in our most recent work currently in progress in our laboratory, we have been examining infants' responsiveness to dynamic human faces and voices.

There is no doubt that human faces and voices have a special status for human infants. Given their special status, it is highly desirable to examine infants' responsiveness to multimodally represented faces. In addition, given their special status, it might be reasonable to postulate that the visual and auditory attributes of the human face might be integrated earlier in development than other less meaningful or ubiquitous events. Unfortunately, the evidence that would permit an evaluation of this possibility is currently not available. Certainly, the data already available and reviewed earlier would suggest that such a possibility is likely because infants as young as 1 month of age can integrate information intermodally (Lewkowicz & Turkewitz, 1980). On the other hand, integration of continuous, linguistically complex auditory information with dynamic visual information of a visually complex stimulus might not emerge until later. This is suggested by the fact that visual face recognition does not emerge until the fifth month of life (Nelson, 1987). Of course, intersensory integration of the multimodal properties of a face also could be done on a much lower level, not involving the response to the holistic properties of the face and voice. At the moment, data to answer this question are not available; the only data that are available are from studies of infants' response to static human faces.

Our studies of infants' response to dynamic face/voice compounds utilize a method very similar to the one used in the other two sets of studies examining infants' responsiveness to compound A-V stimuli. First, during the habituation phase, we present a series of 12, 20-sec videotaped segments of a person reciting a prepared script. Then, during the test phase, we present a familiar test trial and three test trials. The familiar test trial involves presentation of the face and voice seen and heard during the habituation phase. The three test trials consist of (a) the A test trial, where a new script recited by a new voice is heard while the face remains unchanged, (b) the V test trial, where a new face is seen reciting a different script while the voice and script remain unchanged, and (c) the A-V test trial, where a new script, voice, and face are seen and heard. To check for possible fatigue effects, a pre- and a posttest trial, consisting of a 20-sec segment of a color cartoon, is presented prior to the start of the habituation phase and following the administration of the last test trial, respectively. If the infants fail to exhibit a response recovery to a change in a given test trial but do exhibit response recovery during the posttest trial, then fatigue can be ruled out.

In the first study, separate groups of 32 infants aged 4, 6, and 8 months were habituated with a female face/voice compound stimulus and tested with changes to auditory and visual aspects of another female. In both phases, the females spoke with a minimum amount of intonation and moved their head as little as possible in order to resemble what might be considered as adult directed talk (ADT). The results from the three test trials differed across age. The 4-month-old infants only discriminated the change in the A-V test trial. In contrast, both the 6-month-old and the 8-month-old infants discriminated the change in the A-V test trial and the change in the V test trial. Discrimination of the A-V change is not surprising. Discrimination of the face change in the V test trial by the two older groups is consistent with the general finding that face recognition emerges around the fifth month of life. The failure of infants at all ages to discriminate the auditory change was, however, surprising because three aspects of the compound stimulus changed during the A test trial: (a) the face and voice became asynchronous, (b) the script changed, and (c) the voice changed.

Despite the fact that the A test trial involved changes in three aspects of the stimulus, it seems that these changes are not representative of the salient aspects of a face/voice compound stimulus to infants. Recent research on infants' auditory responsiveness has shown that infants are most responsive to the human voice when its properties are highly exaggerated. The exaggeration, usually observed in an adult speaking to an infant, has been named infant-directed talk (IDT). It involves a modification of the prosodic characteristics of an utterance resulting in a higher overall fundamental frequency, greater pitch modulation, and greater rhythmicity (Fernald, 1985; Fernald & Kuhl, 1987; Papousek, Papousek, & Bornstein, 1985). Although studies have shown that infants prefer to listen to IDT over ADT (Werker & McLeod, 1989), no studies to date have examined infants' response to multimodally represented IDT. To increase the salience of the face/voice compound stimulus and to examine infants' response to IDT, in the next study we habituated infants to a male face/voice combination and tested them with a female face/voice combination where the female spoke in IDT. As expected, the increased salience of the test compound stimulus made it possible for the two older groups of infants to make the auditory discrimination. For the youngest group, the increase in salience made it possible to discriminate the face change in the V test trial but not the auditory change.

It is possible, of course, that the improved performance in the IDT study was due to the concurrent change in the person's gender. To determine if this was the case, we conducted another study where we habituated them with a male face/voice and tested them with a female face/voice, but this time both people spoke the script in ADT. Results indicated that a gender change by itself did not contribute to the enhancement of auditory responsiveness in the IDT study. We found no discrimination of the change in the A test trial at any age. The gender change did, however, appear to make a difference for visual responsiveness because the 4-month-olds in this study did respond to the change in the V test trial.

The successful discrimination of the script/voice change by the two older groups indicates that exaggerated audible prosody cues are a salient aspect of multimodal speech by 6 months of age but not earlier. The successful discrimination of the face as early as 4 months of age indicates that exaggerated visible cues associated with IDT and/or a change in the gender of the person are a salient aspect of multimodal speech for infants by 4 months of age (or maybe even earlier). The successful discrimination of the auditory change by the older infants could not have been due to a gender change because the results from the second study showed that a gender change was not discriminable.

Recent research has shown that infants prefer to listen to highly modulated speech patterns as early as 1 month of age (Cooper & Aslin, 1990). The results from the IDT study indicate that selective attention to IDT appears later in development when it occurs in a multimodal context. This finding is consistent with our results from the original A-V compound stimulus studies (Lewkowicz, 1988a, 1988b) in showing that responsiveness to information in one modality is affected by the concurrent presence of information in another modality. Therefore, we must consider the joint influence of visual and auditory sources of input on linguistic learning in infants because the great majority of infants' linguistic experiences are multimodal in nature and because visual information has been shown to contribute to speech perception (Summerfield, 1979; Massaro & Cohen, 1990).

To broaden the scope of our inquiry into the determinants of auditory responsiveness in a multimodal context, we conducted two more studies where we enhanced the discriminability of the auditory change. This time one set of infants at each of the three ages was habituated with a male face/voice/script (in ADT) and tested with attributes of a female who sang a portion of a song (the song was "Oh What a Beautiful Morning" from the musical "Oklahoma"). Another set of infants at the three ages was habituated with a female face/voice/script (in ADT) and tested with the same singing female. Singing is a highly salient event for infants probably because it has so many of the same characteristics that IDT has. As expected, regardless of whether the change involved a concurrent change in gender and speech to singing, or just a change from speech to singing, infants at all three ages discriminated all three types of changes. What is interesting about this set of results is that evidence of discrimination in the A test trial was obtained for the first time as early as 4 months of age. This suggests that the attributes that contribute to the difference between adult-directed speech and singing are even more salient than those that contribute to the difference between ADT and IDT.

Obviously these studies are only a beginning in this complex area of research. They raise a number of questions that will have to be answered next. For example, in every test trial there are changes in multiple characteristics. Moreover, in each of the unimodal test trials, the change in the attribute being changed is always accompanied by a change in the temporal relation between the auditory and visual components—the two components become asynchronous. Despite these confounds, however, the results from the studies form a coherent pattern that is meaningful and informative about developmental differences in infants' responsiveness to the multimodal components of human faces and broaden our understanding of infants' responsiveness to the multimodal properties of their world.

FUTURE DIRECTIONS

There is no longer any doubt that infants are sensitive to intersensory equivalence across a variety of stimulus attributes, and across different sets of modalities. Yet, demonstration of this fact is only the first step in understanding the development of intersensory integration. It has now become clear that intersensory integration is a complex process that depends on the level of processing required by the subject, the way we test for its presence, and on the interaction of modality-specific and amodal cues. Future work will have to explicate the mechanisms that mediate intersensory integration at various levels of stimulus complexity. The new findings reviewed in this chapter suggest that the available theoretical conceptions of intersensory development are no longer adequate. There is no doubt that invariance-detection theory has served an important role in our investigations of intersensory perception in early development by helping us focus on the critical aspects of the infant's perceptual world. Its drawback, however, is that it is only concerned with the identification of the types of perceptual structure that younger and older infants can pick up; it offers few suggestions about the mechanisms that might underlie developmental changes in subjects' response to perceptual structure during development (Smith, 1991). In addition, the implicit assumption of invariance-detection theory is that the perceptual structure inherent in the observer's environment is unaffected by the developmental status of the organism. This assumption ignores the fact that sensory qualities are as much a result of sensory function as they are of the stimulus itself. This point is particularly important for developmental studies because the *umwelt* (von Uexküll, 1957) of the infant is likely to be different than that of the child or adult. The infant is likely to have a qualitatively different picture of the world and its structure as the status of his sensory systems changes during development.

A process-oriented approach to intersensory development differs from invariance-detection theory because it focuses on (a) the mechanisms that mediate responsiveness at a given point in development, (b) the way these mechanisms change with development, and (c) uncovering the factors that are responsible for the changes. One way in which this approach attempts to explicate the development of intersensory perception is by asking how sensory/perceptual differentiation in one modality affects sensory/perceptual differentiation in a second modality within a strictly developmental context. An excellent example of this type of approach is Lickliter's (1993, Lickliter & Banker, chap. 4, this volume) work on the timing of specific developmental experience in one modality on responsiveness to input in another modality. Although studies of human infants cannot manipulate the kind and timing of developmental experience, studies of special populations (e.g., infants with different types of nervous system damage) or of infants with specific sensory experiences can indicate how intersensory organization is affected by modifications in the kind and timing of sensory/perceptual experience. Our investigations of the way input in one modality affects responsiveness to input in a second modality represent the first step in our attempt to broaden the scope of our inquiry into problems of intersensory integration beyond those concerned with the detection of intersensory equivalence. It is our belief that by doing so we will arrive at a fuller understanding of the development of intersensory integration.

REFERENCES

Allen, T. W., Walker, K., Symonds, L., & Marcell, M. (1977). Intrasensory and intersensory perception of temporal sequences during infancy. *Developmental Psychology, 13*, 225–229.
Ashton, R. (1976). Aspects of timing in child development. *Child Development, 47*, 622–626.
Banks, M. S., & Salapatek, P. (1983). Infant visual perception. In M. M. Haith & J. J. Campos (Eds.), *Handbook of child psychology* (pp. 435–571). New York: Wiley.
Bahrick, L. E. (1987). Infants' intermodal perception of two levels of temporal structure in natural events. *Infant Behavior and Development, 10*, 387–416.
Bahrick, L. E. (1988). Intermodal learning in infancy: Learning on the basis of two kinds of invariant relations in audible and visible events. *Child Development, 59*, 197–209.
Birch, H. G., & Lefford, A. (1963). Intersensory development in children. *Monographs of the Society for Research in Child Development, 28*(5).

Birch, H. G., & Lefford, A. (1967). Visual differentiation, intersensory integration, and voluntary motor control. *Monographs of the Society for Research in Child Development, 32*(2).

Bower, T. G. R. (1974). *Development in infancy.* San Francisco: Freeman.

Cohen, L. B. (1991). Infant attention: An information processing approach. In M. J. Weiss & P. R. Zelazo (Eds.), *Newborn attention: Biological constraints and the influence of experience* (pp. 1–21). Norwood, NJ: Ablex.

Colavita, F. B. (1974). Human sensory dominance. *Perception and Psychophysics, 16,* 409–412.

Cooper, R. P., & Aslin, R. N. (1990). Preference for infant-directed speech in the first month after birth. *Child Development, 61,* 1584–1595.

Dixon, N. F., & Spitz, L. (1980). The detection of auditory visual desynchrony. *Perception, 9,* 719–721.

Edelman, G. M. (1992). *Bright air, brilliant fire: On the matter of the mind.* New York: Basic Books.

Fernald, A. (1985). Four-month-old infants prefer to listen to "motherese." *Infant Behavior and Development, 8,* 181–195.

Fernald, A., & Kuhl, P. (1987). Acoustic determinants of infant preference for motherese speech. *Infant Behavior and Development, 10,* 279–293.

Fraisse, P. (1982). Rhythm and tempo. In D. Deutch (Ed.), *The psychology of music* (pp. 149–180). New York: Academic Press.

Freedland, R. L., & Dannemiller, J. L. (1987). Detection of stimulus motion in 5-month-old infants. *Journal of Experimental Psychology: Human Perception and Performance, 13,* 566–576.

Freides, D. (1974). Human information processing and sensory modality: Cross-modal functions, information complexity, memory, and deficit. *Psychological Bulletin, 81,* 284–310.

Gardner, J. M., Lewkowicz, D. J., Rose, S. A., & Karmel, B. Z. (1986). Effects of visual and auditory stimulation on subsequent visual preferences in neonates. *International Journal of Behavioural Development, 9,* 251–263.

Gebhard, J. W., & Mowbray, G. H. (1959). On discriminating the rate of visual flicker and auditory flutter. *American Journal of Psychology, 72,* 521–528.

Gibson, E. J. (1969). *Principles of perceptual learning and development.* New York: Appleton-Century-Crofts.

Gibson, J. J. (1966). *The senses considered as perceptual systems.* Boston: Houghton Mifflin.

Gottlieb, G. (1971). Ontogenesis of sensory function in birds and mammals. In E. Tobach, L. R. Aronson, & E. Shaw (Eds.), *The biopsychology of development* (pp. 67–128). New York: Academic Press.

Gottlieb, G. (1991). Experiential canalization of behavioral development: Theory. *Developmental Psychology, 27,* 35–39.

Humphrey, K., & Tees, R. C. (1980). Auditory-visual coordination in infancy: Some limitations of the preference methodology. *Bulletin of the Psychonomic Society, 16,* 213–216.

Johnston, T. D. (1987). The persistence of dichotomies in the study of behavioral development. *Developmental Review, 7,* 149–182.

Kaufmann, F., Stucki, M., & Kaufmann-Hayoz, R. (1985). Development of infants' sensitivity for slow and rapid motions. *Infant Behavior and Development, 8,* 89–98.

Kellman, P. J. (1988). Theories of perception and research in perceptual development. In A. Yonas (Ed.), *Perceptual development in infancy: The Minnesota symposia on child psychology* (Vol. 20, pp. 267–281). Hillsdale, NJ: Lawrence Erlbaum Associates.

Kleiner, K. A. (1987). Amplitude and phase spectra as indices of infants' pattern preferences. *Infant Behavior & Development, 10,* 49–59.

Kleiner, K. A., & Banks, M. S. (1987). Stimulus energy does not account for 2-month-old preferences. *Journal of Experimental Psychology: Human Perception and Performance, 13,* 594–600.

Kluver, H. (1933). *Behavior mechanisms in monkeys.* Chicago: University of Chicago Press.

Kremenitzer, J., Vaughan, H., Kurtzberg, D., & Dowling, K. (1979). Smooth-pursuit eye movements in the newborn infant. *Child Development, 50,* 442–448.

Kubovy, M. (1988). Should we resist the seductiveness of the space:time::vision:auditory analogy? *Journal of Experimental Psychology: Human Perception and Performance. 14,* 318–320.

Landry, S. H., Leslie, N. A., Fletcher, J. M., & Francis, D. J. (1985). Visual attention skills of premature infants with and without intra-ventricular hemorrhage. *Infant Behavior and Development, 8,* 309–321.

Lashley, K. S. (1951). The problem of serial order in behavior. In L. A. Jeffress (Ed.), *Cerebral mechanisms in behavior* (pp. 112–136). New York: Wiley.

Lederman, S. J., Thorne, G., & Jones, B. (1986). Perception of texture by vision and touch: Multidimensionality and intersensory integration. *Journal of Experimental Psychology: Human Perception and Performance, 12,* 169–180.

Lewis, M., & Bendersky, M. (1989). Cognitive and motor differences among low birthweight infants: Impact of intraventricular hemorrhage, medical risk, and social class. *Pediatrics, 83,* 187–191.

Lewkowicz, D. J. (1985a). Bisensory response to temporal frequency in 4-month-old infants. *Developmental Psychology, 21,* 306–317.

Lewkowicz, D. J. (1985b). Developmental changes in infants' response to temporal frequency. *Developmental Psychology, 21,* 858–865.

Lewkowicz, D. J. (1986). Developmental changes in infants' bisensory response to synchronous durations. *Infant Behavior and Development, 9,* 335–353.

Lewkowicz, D. J. (1988a). Sensory dominance in infants 1: Six-month-old infants' response to auditory-visual compounds. *Developmental Psychology, 24,* 155–171.

Lewkowicz, D. J. (1988b). Sensory dominance in infants 2: Ten-month-old infants' response to auditory-visual compounds. *Developmental Psychology, 24,* 172–182.

Lewkowicz, D. J. (1989a, April). *Infants' auditory/visual matching of rate with spatially-static visual stimuli.* Paper presented at the meeting of the Society for Research in Child Development, Kansas City, MO.

Lewkowicz, D. J. (1989b). The role of temporal factors in infant behavior and development. In I. Levin & D. Zakay (Eds.), *Time and human cognition: A life-span perspective* (pp. 9–62). Amsterdam: North Holland.

Lewkowicz, D. J. (1992a). Infants' response to temporally based intersensory equivalence: The effect of synchronous sounds on visual preferences for moving stimuli. *Infant Behavior and Development, 15,* 297–323.

Lewkowicz, D. J. (1992b). The development of temporally-based intersensory perception in human infants. In F. Macar, V. Pouthas, & W. J. Friedman (Eds.), *Time, action, & cognition: Towards bridging the gap* (pp. 33–43). Dordrecht: Kluwer.

Lewkowicz, D. J. (1992c). Responsiveness to auditory and visual components of a sounding/moving compound stimulus in human infants. *Perception & Psychophysics, 52,* 519–528.

Lewkowicz, D. J. (1993, November). *Defining the multimodal, psychological present in human infants.* Poster presented at the meeting of the International Society for Developmental Psychobiology, Alexandria, VA.

Lewkowicz, D. J. (in press a). Reflections on infants' response to temporally based intersensory equivalence: Response to Spelke. *Infant Behavior and Development.*

Lewkowicz, D. J. (in press b). Limitations on infants' response to rate-based auditory-visual relations. *Developmental Psychology.*

Lewkowicz, D. J., & Turkewitz, G. (1980). Cross-modal equivalence in early infancy: Auditory-visual intensity matching. *Developmental Psychology, 16,* 597–607.

Lewkowicz, D. J., & Turkewitz, G. (1981). Intersensory interaction in newborns: Modification of visual preferences following exposure to sound. *Child Development, 52,* 827–832.

Lickliter, R. (1993). Timing and the development of perinatal perceptual organization. In G. Turkewitz & D. A. Devenny (Eds.), *Timing as an initial condition of development* (pp. 105–123). Hillsdale, NJ: Lawrence Erlbaum Associates.

Maier, N. R. F., & Schneirla, T. C. (1935). *Principles of animal psychology.* New York: McGraw-Hill.

Marks, L. E. (1978). *The unity of the senses: Interrelations among the modalities.* New York: Academic Press.

Marks, L. E., Hammeal, R. J., & Bornstein, M. H. (1987). Perceiving similarity and comprehending metaphor. *Monographs of the Society for Research in Child Development, 52*(1).

Massaro, D. W., & Cohen, M. M. (1990). Perception of synthesized audible and visible speech. *Psychological Science, 1,* 55–63.

Maurer, D. (1993). Neonatal synesthesia: Implications for the processing of speech and faces. In B. de Boysson-Bardies, S. de Schonen, P. Jusczyk, P. McNeilage, & J. Morton (Eds.), *Developmental neurocognition: Speech and face processing in the first year of life* (pp. 109–124). Dordrecht: Kluwer.

McGrath, M., & Summerfield, Q. (1985). Intermodal timing relations and audio-visual speech recognition by normal-hearing adults. *Journal of the Acoustical Society of America, 77,* 678–685.

Miller, C. L., & Byrne, J. M. (1984). The role of temporal cues in the development of communication. In L. Feagans, C. Garvey, & R. Golinkoff (Eds.), *The origins and growth of communication* (pp. 77–101). Norwood, NJ: Ablex.

Moore, D. S. G., & Gibbons, J. L. (1988, April). *Early auditory and visual integration in 4-month-old infants.* Poster presented at the meeting of the International Conference on Infant Studies, Washington, DC.

Morrongiello, B. A. (1984). Auditory temporal pattern perception in 6- and 12-month-old infants. *Developmental Psychology, 20,* 441–448.

Myers, A. K., Cotton, B., & Hilp, H. A. (1981). Matching the rate of concurrent tone bursts and light flashes as a function of flash surround luminance. *Perception and Psychophysics, 30,* 33–38.

Nakayama, K. (1985). Biological image motion processing: A review. *Vision Research, 25,* 625–660.

Nelson, C. A. (1987). The recognition of facial expressions in the first two years of life: Mechanisms of development. *Child Development, 58,* 889–909.

O'Connor, N., & Hermelin, B. (1972). Seeing and hearing in space and time. *Perception and Psychophysics, 11,* 46–48.

Papousek, M., Papousek, H., & Bornstein, M. (1985). The naturalistic vocal environment of young infants: On the significance of homogeneity and variability in parental speech. In T. M. Field & N. Fox (Eds.), *Social perception in infants* (pp. 269–297). Norwood, NJ: Ablex.

Piaget, J. (1952). *The origins of intelligence in children.* New York: International Universities Press.

Rose, S. A., & Ruff, H. A. (1987). Cross-modal abilities in human infants. In J. D. Osofsky (Ed.), *Handbook of infant development* (pp. 318–362). New York: Wiley.

Ross, G., Tesman, J., Auld, P. A. M., & Nass, R. (1992). Effects of subependymal and mild intraventicular lesions on visual attention and memory in premature infants. *Developmental Psychology, 28,* 1067–1074.

Rubinstein, L., & Gruenberg, E. M. (1971). Intramodal and crossmodal sensory transfer of visual and auditory temporal patterns. *Perception and Psychophysics, 9,* 385–390.

Schneirla, T. C. (1959). An evolutionary and developmental theory of biphasic processes underlying approach and withdrawal. In M. R. Jones (Ed.), *Nebraska symposium on motivation* (Vol. 7, pp. 1–42). Lincoln: University of Nebraska Press.

Shipley, T. (1964). Auditory flutter-driving of visual flicker. *Science, 145,* 1328–1330.

Smith, L. B. (1991). Perceptual structure and developmental process. In G. R. Lockhead & J. R. Pomerantz (Eds.), *The perception of structure* (pp. 297–315). Washington, DC: American Psychological Association.

Spelke, E. S. (1979). Perceiving bimodally specified events in infancy. *Developmental Psychology, 15*, 626–636.

Spelke, E. S. (1994). Preferential looking and intermodal perception in infancy: Comment on Lewkowicz (1992). *Infant Behavior and Development, 17*(3).

Spelke, E. S., Born, W. S., & Chu, F. (1983). Perception of moving, sounding objects by four-month-old infants. *Perception, 12*, 719–732.

Stein, B. E., & Meredith, M. A. (1993). *The merging of the senses.* Cambridge, MA: MIT Press.

Summerfield, A. Q. (1979). Use of visual information in phonetic perception. *Phonetica, 36*, 314–331.

Thelen, E. (1990). Dynamical systems and the generation of individual differences. In J. Colombo & J. Fagen (Eds.), *Individual differences in infancy: Reliability, stability, prediction* (pp. 19–43). Hillsdale, NJ: Lawrence Erlbaum Associates.

Turkewitz, G., Lewkowicz, D. J., & Gardner, J. (1983). Determinants of infant perception. In J. Rosenblatt, C. Beer, R. Hinde, & M. Busnel (Eds.), *Advances in the study of behavior* (pp. 39–62). New York: Academic Press.

von Uexküll, J. (1957). A stroll through the world of animals and men. In C. H. Schiller (Ed.), *Instinctive behavior* (pp. 5–80). New York: International Universities Press.

Volkmann, F. C., & Dobson, M. V. (1976). Infant responses of ocular fixation to moving visual stimuli. *Journal of Experimental Child Psychology, 22*, 86–99.

Welch, R. B., & Warren, D. H. (1980). Immediate perceptual response to intersensory discrepancy. *Psychological Bulletin, 88*, 638–667.

Welch, R. B., & Warren, D. H. (1986). Intersensory interactions. In K. R. Boff, L. Kaufman, & J. P. Thomas (Eds.), *Handbook of perception and human performance, Vol. 1, Sensory processes and perception* (pp. 1–36). New York: Wiley.

Werker, J. F., & McLeod, P. J. (1989). Infant preference for both male and female infant directed talk: A developmental study of attentional and affective responsiveness. *Canadian Journal of Psychology, 43*, 230–246.

Werner, H. (1973). *Comparative psychology of mental development.* New York: International Universities Press.

CHAPTER NINE

Amodal Relations: The Basis for Intermodal Perception and Learning in Infancy

Lorraine E. Bahrick
Florida International University

Jeffrey N. Pickens
James Madison University

The Problem of Intermodal Perception

Put yourself in the place of an infant attempting to make sense of the world. Objects and events come and go within your perceptual field. Most are multimodal and evoke a diversity of sights, sounds, and tactile and olfactory impressions simultaneously. The sound of your mother's voice and the sight of her changing face; the feel of being picked up and of movement through space and the experience of a rapidly shifting visual field; the sounds of the radio and the smells of toast and coffee may all co-occur. How does the infant, like the adult, come to perceive a stable world of unitary objects and events from this continuously changing flux of stimulation? How does the infant determine which patterns of stimulation belong together and originate from a single event, and which are unrelated? How does she select stimulation that is relevant to her needs and actions?

Cognitive psychologists agree that perception and learning in the adult are guided by expectations, plans and prior knowledge. They have postulated that plans, goals, expertise, perceptual sets, schemas, scripts, and story grammars direct and constrain what we perceive, learn, and remember (see, e.g., Bartlett, 1932; Bower, 1976; Chase & Simon, 1973; Neisser, 1976; Schank & Ableson, 1977; Soloman, May, & Schwartz, 1981). These constructs describe how prior knowledge enables us to economically select from the vast flux of stimulation, information that is relevant, coherent, and meaningful to us, while ignoring the great majority of stimulation that is not. How, then, can the infant, with relatively little experience in the world, solve this problem? How can she select stimulation originating from unitary multimodal events rather than from unrelated streams of sights, sounds, and tactile impressions? How can she focus on information that is meaningful and relevant to her needs and actions, while ignoring information that is irrelevant?

In this chapter, we present evidence that this process is set in motion and guided by the detection of amodal invariant relations. Amodal invariant information is information that is not specific to a particular sensory modality; rather, it is completely redundant across one or more senses (E. J. Gibson, 1969; J. J. Gibson, 1966). Most audible and visible events occur over time and can thus be characterized by a temporal structure that is invariant across vision and audition. For example, the sights and sounds of a single event typically share a synchrony relation, a common tempo of action and a rhythm. The same rhythm, tempo, and synchrony may be picked up visually, acoustically or haptically. The different senses provide no unique information with respect to these properties. According to E. J. Gibson (1969), infants come into the world equipped to abstract amodal relations. Detection of amodal temporal relations is an ideal way to insure that perceptual differentiation will be veridical. Because the same temporal structure can be detected through two senses, it can specify that the audible and visible stimulation comes from a single event, and separate it from other co-occurring events that do not share the temporal structure. Initial sensitivity to temporal relations can selectively focus infant attention on meaningful, unitary events and serve as a buffer against learning the numerous wrong or meaningless relations one might detect. We believe that there is now sufficient evidence to conclude that young infants are at first selectively tuned to detect certain amodal relations. This initially substitutes for the prior knowledge that adult perceivers find so critical for directing meaningful perception, learning and memory. This chapter addresses this issue by examining and evaluating what we now know about the development of intermodal perception of audible and visual events in infancy. We evaluate the contribution of research from each of five different approaches toward understanding the nature and basis of perceptual development. Our discussion focuses primarily on infants' perception of auditory–visual relations.

Current Theories of Intermodal Perception

There are two essentially opposing schools of thought regarding the manner in which intersensory coordination develops during infancy:

1. *Integration theories*, which consider the senses to be independent at birth and postulate that intersensory coordination emerges gradually through development.

2. *Differentiation theories*, which suggest that the senses are unified early in development, and that perceptual development is characterized by differentiation of increasingly finer aspects of stimulation. Intersensory perception is thus possible from the beginning.

According to the intersensory integration hypothesis (e.g., Birch & Lefford, 1963, 1967; Blank & Bridger, 1964; Bryant, 1974), independent sensory systems are gradually integrated as infants and children learn to associate modality-specific sensations. For example, the visual image of a cube remains unrelated to the feel of the cube until visual and tactile impressions of the cube are associated over time. The senses are viewed as separate and uncoordinated at birth, and as a result cross-modal perception is assumed to be impossible during infancy. As we show, recent studies indicating that young infants are sensitive to intermodal relations appear to weaken some of the central assumptions of the "integration" position.

One of the most detailed accounts of infant sensory development has been offered by Jean Piaget (1952, 1954). Piaget suggested that intersensory perception develops gradually as the child organizes modality-specific actions into a coordinated representation of the world. Actions such as "touching a toy" gradually become coordinated with actions such as "looking at the toy" or "hearing the toy." Thus, "the first stages of development are marked by an absence of coordination between the sensory systems" (Piaget & Inhelder, 1969). Piaget's view is unique in adopting an "action centered" perspective that emphasizes the importance of the child's active experience with the environment for constructing intermodal knowledge. Infants are therefore incapable of intermodal coordination early in the sensorimotor period because motor behavior is not yet well developed. Thus, by assuming that initially independent sensory systems must be gradually coordinated through experience, Piaget's position is an example of an integration view.

In contrast to integration theories, which do not endow young infants with the capacity for intersensory coordination at first, differentiation theories suggest that at least some intermodal perceptual abilities are innate. E. J. Gibson's (1969) "invariant detection" view is the most popular current-day example of a differentiation theory and provides the theoretical context for this chapter. Gibson posits that the senses are unified at birth and that development is characterized as a process of progressive differentiation of increasingly finer levels of stimulation. Young infants have an innate capacity to perceive properties of objects that are *amodal* or invariant across sense modalities. Detection of these amodal relations enables the infant to perceive unified multimodal events from the beginning. According to the invariant detection framework, infants possess some intersensory capabilities very early, and continue to show perceptual learning as they differentiate increasingly finer and more complex multimodal relations. There is no stage where infants must "associate" or "integrate" information across the senses. Rather, amodal information inherently unites multimodal events, and need only be abstracted through a unified perceptual system. A more extreme version of this view (Bower, 1974) is that the sensory systems are totally undifferentiated at birth such that infants cannot distinguish between stimulation arising from the different senses. Through development, the infant must learn to differentiate the sense modalities. Intermodal relations would thus be detected at birth because the infant cannot yet distinguish among the senses.

The intensity hypothesis (Schneirla, 1959, 1965; Turkewitz, Lewkowicz, & Gardner, 1983) also adopts the view that intersensory coordination is possible in infancy, but differs from the invariant detection position with regard to the nature of the information hypothesized as the basis for the perception of intersensory equivalence. The intensity hypothesis suggests that very young organisms respond primarily to quantitative aspects of stimulation: those variables that contribute to the overall amount of stimulation. Thus, several properties of stimulation (size, brightness, loudness, duration, rate of stimulation, etc.) are undifferentiated by young infants. They are thought to respond to the effective intensity of stimulation, which is jointly determined by the physical intensity of external stimulation and the organism's state of arousal. When young infants match across modalities they are thought to do so by detecting equivalent stimulus intensities across modalities (e.g., Gardner, Lewkowicz, Rose, & Karmel, 1986; Lewkowicz & Turkewitz, 1980, 1981). Other stimulus features (such as rhythm, melody, texture or shape) are considered qualitative properties of stimulation, which infants are not predicted to differentiate until after 4 to 6 months of age (Lewkowicz, 1991). This position appears to share some of the assumptions of both the differentiation and integration views. Although multimodal relations are detected early in development and infants discern finer levels of stimulation with experience, detection of these relations progresses from quantitative to qualitative dimensions, and at least one mechanism for this is the integration of sensations from separate input modalities. In contrast, Gibson's (1969) invariant detection view posits that infants respond to both quantitative and qualitative aspects of stimulation from the start and discern meaningful properties of objects through the detection of invariant relations.

EVIDENCE FOR THE PRIMACY OF AMODAL AUDITORY–VISUAL RELATIONS

Young Infants Detect Amodal Relations

We have witnessed an explosion of research on the intermodal capabilities of infants during the past 20 years. As a whole, the research has shown that very young infants possess a surprisingly large and diverse repertoire of intermodal abilities. Infants' success in intersensory tasks was often found to be based on the detection of amodal relations. It was discovered that infants could match faces and voices on the basis of voice–lip synchrony (Dodd, 1979; Spelke & Cortelyou 1980; Walker, 1982), affective expressions including happy, sad, neutral, and angry (Walker, 1982; Walker-Andrews, 1986), speech sounds such as "a" versus "i" (Kuhl & Meltzoff, 1982, 1984), and gender of speaker (Walker-Andrews, Bahrick, Raglioni, & Diaz, 1991). Infants as young as 4 months of age were found to be sensitive to a number of temporal parameters unifying auditory and visual stimulation from natural events of objects moving through space. They detected the tempo of action uniting the sights and sounds of stuffed animals bouncing (Spelke, 1979), and the synchrony between the visual and acoustic impacts of objects striking against a surface (Bahrick, 1983, Spelke, 1979, 1981; Spelke, Born, & Chu, 1983). Infants were found to be sensitive to the common rhythm and duration uniting flashing lights with tones (Allen, Walker, Symonds, & Marcell, 1977; Lewkowicz, 1986) and the sight of puppets moving with the sounds they made (Mendelson & Ferland, 1982). Infants were found to detect the rigidity versus elasticity of substance for moving objects (Bahrick, 1983) and the composition of moving objects (whether they were composed of a single, unitary element or a cluster of smaller elements, Bahrick, 1987, 1988). Both substance and composition are thought to be properties of objects that are amodally specified across vision and audition through temporal information. By 4 months, selective attention to one of two superimposed films is guided by a synchronous and appropriate soundtrack (Bahrick, Walker, & Neisser, 1981). Finally, infants demonstrated sensitivity to the auditory and visible information of objects changing in depth (Pickens, in press; Walker-Andrews & Lennon, 1985). Thus, infants appear to be adept at perceiving a wide range of amodal invariant relations across a range of different events after only a few months of life.

Evidence of early detection of amodal relations weakens the integration views that suggest that intersensory perception is not possible until infants gradually learn to associate input from separate modalities. This body of research thus lends strength to E. J. Gibson's (1969) differentiation view, which posits that detection of amodal relations is central to the development of intermodal perception. However, to establish that these abilities exist is necessary but not sufficient for concluding that they are fundamental and regulate early perceptual differentiation. They could have come into existence through a number of processes. Converging evidence from several approaches is needed to evaluate the primacy of amodal relations in the development of intersensory perception. No single approach or set of studies can definitively speak to such a broad question. Thus, researchers have continued to explore these newly discovered abilities. They have investigated how these abilities developed, the nature of the intermodal learning process, constraints and boundary conditions for detection of amodal relations, and the developmental sequence in which different intermodal abilities emerged. These efforts are all discussed later in this chapter and evaluated with respect to the question of the basis for perceptual development.

Age-Related Changes in the Detection of Amodal Relations

Few studies have investigated changes in infant intersensory perception abilities across age. Of those that have, all have used cross-sectional approaches. These studies have for the most part found that intermodal abilities either are not evident at an early age and emerge at a later age, or show improvement with age.

The most common approach for assessing intermodal abilities for audible and visible events is some variant of the two-choice intermodal preference and search method (Spelke, 1976). In this method the infant views two films, side by side, along with a soundtrack that matches one of them. Then a soundtrack corresponding to the other film is played on a different trial. The soundtracks always emanate from a speaker centered between the two images so that infants cannot match on the basis of sound localization. Visual fixations are observed to determine whether the infant spends a greater proportion of the time exploring the film that matches the sound. A search procedure sometimes follows where infants again view the two films side by side along with intermittent bursts of sound from each. It is expected that infants will look first more often in the direction of the sound-matched film if they have learned which film goes with the sound.

Using this kind of procedure, Bahrick (1987) found that infants improved with age in their ability to match moving objects and sounds on the basis of two kinds of amodal temporal relations, temporal synchrony and temporal structure specifying object composition for single versus compound objects. (The internal temporal structure of each visual and acoustic impact specifies whether the object is single or compound.) Infants were shown two side-by-side films of rattlelike objects. One was a transparent cylinder with a single large marble, and the other was a transparent cylinder with a number of smaller marbles (see Fig. 9.1). The cylinders were abruptly turned back and forth in a erratic pattern, creating a clear impact sound with each turn. Results indicated that by 6 months, but not at 3 or $4\frac{1}{2}$ months, infants matched films and soundtracks on the basis of object composition. They looked significantly more to the film of the single marble when the single-impact sounds were played, and to the group of smaller marbles when the compound sounds were played, even though the motions of both cylinders were synchronized with each soundtrack. A second study found that making the sounds asynchronous with respect to the films disrupted the infants' detection of composition relations. Further, by $4\frac{1}{2}$ months infants

FIG. 9.1. Photograph of the single and compound stimuli used by Bahrick
(1987, 1988). Adapted by permission.

showed matching on the basis of motion–sound synchrony alone under
some conditions, and by 6 months this matching was more robust. Thus,
the ability to match one of two events with a single sound on the basis of
amodal temporal relations improves with age. These abilities emerge and
develop between the ages of $4\frac{1}{2}$ and 6 months.

The specific age at which different intermodal abilities appear to emerge
depends on differences in the stimuli and methods used. However, for any
developmental sequences uncovered within a single set of studies (same
stimuli and methods), the relative ordering of abilities should be constant and
generalizable. For example, in this set of studies there was some evidence that
detection of temporal synchrony ($4\frac{1}{2}$ months) preceded detection of information specifying object composition (6 months). This finding is consistent
with E. J. Gibson's (1969) increasing specificity view of perceptual development, because synchrony relations are characterized as more global whereas
temporal structure specifying object composition is an embedded relation (see
Bahrick, 1987). It is also consistent with a developmental sequence recently
proposed by Lewkowicz (1992a) where detection of intersensory temporal
synchrony is thought to emerge prior to the detection of other intersensory
temporal relations.

Accordingly, studies in progress in our lab suggest that when an infant-control habituation procedure (Horowitz, Paden, Bhana, & Self, 1972) is used, infants show detection of synchrony and composition relations at a much younger age than findings from the intermodal preference methods would suggest. Infants were habituated to two new events, a single and a compound object, striking a surface erratically and producing natural, synchronous impact sounds. Following habituation, experimental subjects received test trials in which the relation between the visual and acoustic information was changed: Either the synchrony relations were disrupted, or the wrong sounds were synchronized with the visual impacts, disrupting the composition relations. Controls received no change. Bahrick (1992, discussed in more detail in Detection of Amodal Versus Arbitrary Intermodal Relations) found that at $3\frac{1}{2}$ months, infants detected the changes in both synchrony and composition relations. They showed significant visual recovery to both types of test trials when compared with the performance of controls. More recent research from our lab using this method suggests that even infants as young as 6 and 10 weeks also detect these changes. In comparison with results of Bahrick (1987), the habituation method thus reveals sensitivity to these relations at much younger ages than does the intermodal preference method. This is not surprising because habituation is a discrimination task, whereas the intermodal preference procedure is a matching task, assumed to require greater attentional mobility and more sophisticated cognitive skills (Bahrick, 1992).

Intermodal functioning across age has also been investigated for infants' sensitivity to affective information available in both faces and voices (Walker 1982; Walker-Andrews, 1986, 1988). Using the intermodal preference method, Walker (1982) showed 5- and 7-month-old infants two films, side by side, of one woman speaking in a happy manner in one film versus a sad manner in the other. Results indicated that at both ages infants preferentially fixated the film whose matching soundtrack was played. Because voice–lip synchrony and affective information are typically confounded, Walker further investigated the independent contributions of each to infants' ability to match happy, neutral, sad, and angry filmed facial and vocal expressions. Seven-month-olds who were presented with inverted images of happy and angry faces along with a single synchronized soundtrack did not match the faces and voices, whereas those presented upright faces did. Because synchrony information was preserved and affective information is disrupted by showing faces upside down, these results suggest that infants' matching was not based predominately on synchrony information. Rather, infants apparently detected expressive information common to the movements of the face and sound of the voice. Further, when synchrony information was minimized by occluding the mouth area of the faces, 7-month-olds continued to show significant matching whereas 5-month-olds did not. Thus, detection of affective information common to the face and voice improves between 5 and 7 months of age and can be accomplished independent of voice–lip synchrony.

A developmental improvement between 4 and 6 months of age also has been found for infants' detection of intermodal relations specifying gender (Walker-Andrews, Bahrick, Raglioni, & Diaz, 1991). In two independent studies, 6-month-old infants showed matching of faces and voices of males and females speaking a nursery rhyme on the basis of speaker gender while voice–lip synchrony was controlled. Four-month-olds showed only an attenuated matching effect in one study.

A similar improvement in detection of intermodal relations uniting the faces and voices of children versus those of adults was found between 4 and 7 months of age in a recent study in our lab. Infants viewed video films of the faces of an unfamiliar child and adult of the same gender, side by side, speaking a nursery rhyme in synchrony with one another, along with the synchronized voice belonging to one of them. Seven-month-olds were able to match the appropriate faces and voices (Soutullo, Hernandez, & Bahrick, 1992), whereas the 4-month-olds showed only attenuated matching in one of the two trial blocks.

Another set of studies assessing developmental changes in the detection of amodal temporal relations has been conducted by Lewkowicz (1985, 1986, 1992b). With the exception of the most recent set of studies (Lewkowicz, 1992b), infants viewed pairs of spatially static stimuli consisting of flashing checkerboards and listened to a pulsing sound. When the bimodal stimuli were related by both synchrony and duration, 6- and 8-month-old infants performed intersensory matching but 3-month-olds did not (Lewkowicz, 1986). Because asynchrony disrupted the matching effect, synchrony was assumed to be the primary basis for matching. In a study utilizing the same methods and stimuli, where the bimodal stimuli were related by tempo and synchrony, 4-month-olds showed no matching (Lewkowicz, 1985). Similar results were reported by Humphrey and Tees (1980), who found that 3- and 7-month-olds did not match flashing lights with tones on the basis of synchrony and tempo combined, whereas 10-month-olds exhibited marginally significant matching. When infants were presented with spatially dynamic stimuli, both 4- and 8-month-olds were able to match a "bouncing" circle with a synchronous tone under limited conditions (when the sound corresponded with the stimulus that began to move first), but were unable to match on the basis of rate (Lewkowicz, 1992b).

Studies that have compared preterm and full-term infants' intermodal functioning suggest that preterm infants are initially at a disadvantage for detecting and learning about multimodal relations. Rose, Gottfried, and Bridger (1978) contrasted preterm and full-term infants' performance on a tactual–visual cross-modal transfer task. Both preterm and full-term infants exhibited equivalent visual discrimination, but only the full-term 1-year-olds were able to transfer shape information from the tactile to visual modalities. Pickens et al. (in press) investigated auditory–visual matching of faces and voices by preterm versus full-term infants. Side-by-side films of a woman's face were displayed along with a centrally presented soundtrack synchronized with the mouth movements of just one of the two videos. Full-term infants showed a significant looking preference for sound-specified films at 4 months of age, in agreement with prior studies. However, preterm infants did not show evidence of matching until 5 months (corrected for gestation time). One possible interpretation of the above studies is that preterm infants initially demonstrate a deficit in intersensory functioning, but that this deficit is overcome as a result of maturation and/or perceptual experience. New evidence suggests that intermodal perception deficits are more likely to persist for "higher risk" preterm infants with more severe health complications. For example, Lawson, Ruff, McCarton-Daum, Kurtzberg, and Vaughan (1984) showed that both low-risk and high-risk preterms demonstrated no evidence of detecting auditory–visual relations at 3 months of age; however, by 6 months of age, low-risk preterms "caught up" with full-term infants in the ability to associate an object and sound, whereas higher risk preterms continued to perform worse than full-terms. Thus, unlike low-risk infants, the high-risk infants were unable to overcome their initial intersensory perception deficits by 6 months of age. Therefore, further research must determine the extent to which prematurity and other perinatal risk factors, maturation, and perceptual experience all interact to determine infants' intermodal perceptual abilities.

In sum, intermodal matching improves with age. For dynamic, meaningful stimulus events, infants' matching on the basis of synchrony, information specifying object composition, speaker gender, child versus adult faces, and voice–face affect appears to emerge between the ages of 4 and 6 or 7 months of age. The ability to detect some of these amodal relations (e.g., synchrony and composition, tested thus far), however, appears to be present much earlier, as revealed by habituation studies. The apparent delay between the time infants detect amodal temporal relations (in a habituation paradigm) and match a soundtrack with one of two simultaneous films (in the intermodal preference method) may reflect a lag between noticing this information and the ability to use auditory information to guide visual exploration when several events are visible. Results from studies using spatially static and computer-generated stimuli are less clear. Similar improvements with age were found in detection of synchrony relations, although development appeared delayed and effects were more limited.

Although the improvement with age in detection of amodal relations is consistent with both the differentiation and the integration views, the early emergence of these abilities is difficult for integration views to accommodate. Simple association on the basis of co-occurrence seems inadequate to account for such well-developed intermodal abilities at such a young age, and coordination of action schemes is not yet possible due to the immature state of the infants' motor capabilities. Although improvement with age in infants' intermodal abilities would be expected by all theories, improvement characterized by detection of increasingly more specific relations with age would selectively support the differentiation view. The extent to which change across age conforms to this pattern is not yet clear and remains an important topic for future research.

**Constraints on Infants' Detection of Amodal
Audiovisual Relations**

Recently, Rose and Ruff (1987) argued that we do not yet know enough about the specific basis for the infants' responses on various intermodal tasks. More systematic experimental designs were needed to explore the mechanisms underlying infants' intersensory abilities. They described a method developed by Kluver (1933) known as "the method of equivalent and nonequivalent stimuli," which provides a technique for determining the stimulus information that serves as the basis for a subject's response on a given task. A series of different conditions must be systematically presented to establish the range of stimuli to which subjects do or do not respond. Early studies on intermodal perceptual functioning can be criticized in that most have shown (by employing only one or two isolated conditions) that infants detect a given intermodal relation at a given age. This approach cannot reveal the mechanism, boundary conditions, or developmental emergence and progression of intermodal capabilities. Researchers should test infants under a variety of conditions to establish the range of stimulation under which the subjects do or do not respond in a particular way. In this way we may better understand the critical stimulus variables underlying intermodal abilities.

Kluver's method has been applied to the study of infant's intermodal perception of auditory–visual relations. One such study was conducted by Spelke et al. (1983) to determine the basis for detecting sound–motion synchrony relations in 4-month-olds. Using a two-screen intermodal preference paradigm, they found that infants matched discrete sounds with a bouncing stuffed animal when (a) visible impacts were synchronized with the sounds, (b) pauses in midair along with reversals of trajectory were synchronized with the sounds, and (c) reversals in direction of a continuous circular motion were synchronized with the sounds. Thus, infants responded to auditory–visual synchrony when any change in trajectory co-occurred with a sound, regardless of whether it coincided with a visible impact. Spelke et al. (1983) further found that infants did not respond with matching when the discrete sounds were synchronized with objects moving in a continuous circle and arriving at a given spatial position at the time of each sound. Thus, infants do not respond to auditory–visual synchrony for continuously moving objects in the absence of a change in trajectory. In contrast, adults responded more selectively, matching only discrete sounds with visible impacts. By systematically presenting stimulus conditions that were sufficient versus insufficient to promote matching, Spelke et al. (1983) clarified the basis for infants' responding to synchronous sights and sounds.

Kuhl and Meltzoff (1982, 1984) found that 5-month-old infants could match faces and voices on the basis of spectral information in the vowel sounds "a" and "i." When infants viewed two films of two faces side by side along with each vowel sound synchronized with the motions of both, they looked significantly more to the face that produced lip movements appropriate to the sound they heard. However, they no longer showed matching when pure tones were played in precise synchrony with the lip movements. Thus, when spectral information was removed, the temporal information was not sufficient to produce intermodal matching.

Similar constraints on matching synchronous sights and sounds have been documented in our lab. Bahrick (1983) showed that $4\frac{1}{2}$-month-olds matched films and soundtracks on the basis of synchrony and on the basis of elasticity/rigidity of substance. However, they failed to match when sounds of the wrong substance were played in synchrony with the motions of the objects. Similarly, Bahrick (1988) found that infants learned to pair a film and soundtrack after hearing them played in synchrony with the correct sounds, but not when played in synchrony with sounds of the wrong composition. The studies reviewed demonstrate that infants do not respond equivalently to all conditions that present audiovisual synchrony. They show that there are meaningful constraints on the types of sounds that infants will perceive as related to the synchronous motions of objects.

Intermodal matching on the basis of changing distance is another area where Kluver's method has been successfully applied. Walker-Andrews and Lennon (1985) reported that infants were sensitive to auditory–visual relations corresponding to the changing distance of a sounding object. In an intermodal preference procedure, 5-month-old infants preferentially fixated films of an approaching object when the soundtrack of increasing amplitude was presented, and a retreating object when the soundtrack of decreasing amplitude was played. This study promoted further research to delineate what information was necessary versus sufficient for the infants' performance. For example, were the infants responding only to quantitative relations, such as overall auditory and visual intensity, or were they showing veridical perception of meaningful distances? Were some visual cues more important than others for matching?

To answer these questions, Kluver's approach was employed in a recent study of 5-month-olds' perceptions of auditory–visual distance relations

(Pickens, in press). Four conditions were presented wherein infants viewed side-by-side films along with a central soundtrack matching one of them. In Condition 1, infants viewed films of a toy train approaching and retreating over a natural landscape (depicted in Fig. 9.2). They were paired with engine sounds whose amplitude was either increasing ("approaching") or decreasing ("retreating"), with sound amplitude varying between 55 and 75 dB. Infants looked significantly longer to the approach film when the sound increased in intensity, and vice versa. Results are depicted in Fig. 9.3 along with those of the other conditions. Three other conditions were presented to assess the specificity of infants' performance. In Condition 2, infants viewed films of the train increasing and decreasing in size alone, along with the sounds that increased or decreased in amplitude. All background textures and landmarks were eliminated. Infants looked significantly more to the expanding film when the sound increased in amplitude, and vice versa. However, matching was significantly less robust than in Condition 1. This suggested that changing size was sufficient to allow matching; however, the availability of multiple depth cues facilitated matching beyond the level observed for changing size alone.

Two further conditions were included to test whether intensity relations alone, or more abstract stimulus relations, were sufficient to promote matching. Condition 3, the test of intensity relations, presented films of the train with no change in size, but with increasing and decreasing brightness, along with soundtracks of increasing or decreasing amplitude. Infants showed no evidence of matching on the basis of intensity alone. It is thus unlikely that auditory–visual intensity shifts played an important role in infants' matching under Conditions 1 or 2. Finally, in Condition 4 we tested infants' response to the image of the train moving up or down against a black background, paired with soundtracks of increasing and decreasing amplitude. Whereas adults consistently "matched" the up motion with the increasing sound amplitude, and vice versa, infants did not. This suggests that infants' matching behavior was specific to distance information and did not generalize to more global, metaphorical relations. Taken together, these results indicate that 5-month-old infants were sensitive to ecological auditory–visual relations specifying approach versus retreat, and that matching was specific to ecological depth information (where one important "cue" was changing size), and did not generalize to intensity relations, or metaphorical auditory–visual relations.

Two other studies examined infants' response to multimodal distance information. Morrongiello and Fenwick (1991) asked whether perception of changing distance relations changed during development. They examined infants' matching of increasing/decreasing amplitude sounds with films of static objects, objects moving laterally, and objects that expanded and contracted in size. Evidence for developmental differences was found: At 5 months of age infants performed audiovisual matching only when a static object was contrasted with a moving one. At 7 months infants matched when a static or

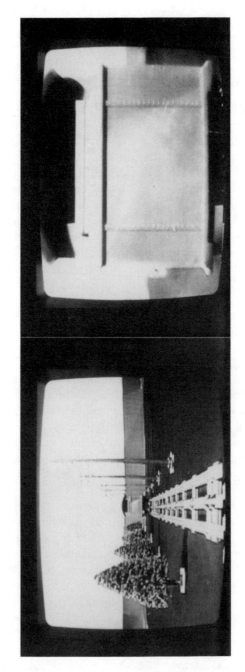

FIG. 9.2. An example of the approaching and retreating events used by Pickens (in press, Condition I).

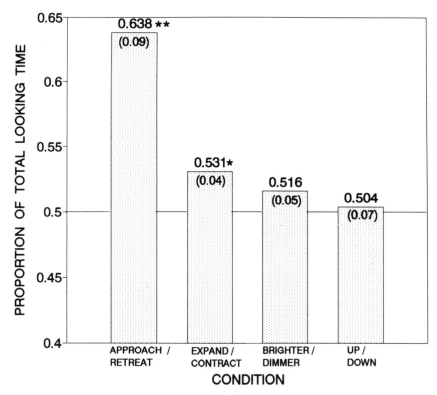

FIG. 9.3. Mean proportions of total looking time and standard deviations to the sound-specified events as a function of four stimulus conditions (Pickens, in press). Significant differences: *$p < .01$; **$p < .001$.

laterally moving object was contrasted with one moving in depth. Finally, at 9 months infants matched when an approaching object was contrasted with a retreating object. Thus, matching became increasingly more specific with age. In contrast with results of the prior studies, infants in this study could not match in the depth condition until the age of 9 months. This may be due to differences in stimulus events. The approach/retreat condition was created by using a zoom lens, and in this respect was not comparable to those of prior studies where objects translating real distances were filmed. The other study that examined perception of multimodal distance information was one by Schiff, Benasich, and Bornstein (1989), which extended the research on perception of changing distance to social stimuli. Schiff et al. found that 5-month-olds responded to coherent audiovisual relations when a speaking person was presented moving back and forth over a distance.

Taken together, the research reviewed in this section demonstrates that there are appropriate constraints on infants' intermodal perception of audio-visual spatial and temporal relations. Infants apparently respond to meaningful properties of objects such as changing distance, object unity, composition, substance, and spectral information. Although sights and sounds co-occurred and were synchronous under a number of conditions, they were perceived as related only under some conditions. These data are most clearly consistent with an invariant detection view of perceptual development. By the age of 4–7 months, infants' intermodal abilities become more specific and have progressed beyond the detection of synchronous relations to detection of more specific amodal relations specifying meaningful properties of objects. Taken together, this research underscores the primacy of amodal relations in directing intermodal perception.

This body of research also provides some direct evidence against the intensity matching view as a basis for intermodal matching after 3–4 months of age. It was shown that infants by 4 months responded to meaningful, qualitative properties of events rather than to simple quantitative aspects of stimulation. Matching on the basis of intensity alone was ruled out by Condition 3 of Pickens' (in press) study where infants failed to match under conditions which maximized intensity relations. It was eliminated as an explanation of matching in the Spelke et al. (1983) study because the sounds and objects were arbitrarily paired and counterbalanced and shared no common intensity relations. Further, although intensity relations were held constant in this study, matching occurred on the basis of synchrony under some conditions but not others. Given that the infants in these studies were 4–7 months of age, however, those supporting a more recent intensity matching view would argue that intensity-based matching occurs at younger ages and may already give way to matching on the basis of qualitative relations by the age of 4–6 months (see Lewkowicz, 1991). Thus, without testing infants of younger ages, one cannot determine how these abilities came into being. However, infants of 1 month and younger have shown cross-modal abilities for visual–tactile and visual–proprioceptive relations. One-month-olds are able to recognize the shape and substance of an object visually after only tactile experience (Gibson & Walker, 1984; Meltzoff & Borton, 1979). Even neonates demonstrate imitation of facial gestures, requiring intermodal visual–proprioceptive abilities (Field, Woodson, Greenberg, & Cohen, 1982; Meltzoff & Moore, 1977). Imitation is clearly an ability that cannot be accounted for on the basis of intensity matching.

Evidence against an integration-association view is also apparent. First, that infants show intermodal matching at such a young age is difficult for a view that posits gradual integration across sense modalities to account for. Second, results of studies using the intermodal preference method suggest that infants do not relate objects and sounds on the basis of mere co-occurrence because even synchronous sounds and sights are not perceived as related under many conditions. Because these studies typically tested infants of 4 months or older, it is still possible that many of these audiovisual relations were "integrated" and associated at younger ages. Infants may have generalized their experience with typically co-occurring sights and sounds to the new events used in the foregoing studies. However, results of studies that employed arbitrarily matched objects and sounds (e.g., Spelke et al., 1983) cannot be accounted for on these grounds. Further, without positing early detection of synchrony, one cannot explain how the infants' attention is focused on the correct object–sound relations in the first place. Thus, on balance, it is difficult for an integration view to accommodate the preceding findings.

Intermodal Learning

Another effective method for assessing the importance of detecting amodal relations in the development of perception is to investigate the process of learning directly. If it can be shown that detection of amodal relations guides intermodal learning, this will provide direct support for our hypothesis regarding the primacy of amodal relations. In the prior studies, the infants tested were already competent perceivers of intermodal relations. Bahrick (1988) examined the learning process directly in younger infants who showed no evidence of spontaneously detecting the amodal relations in question. Three-month-old infants viewed films of the single large marble and the group of smaller marbles, colliding against a surface in an erratic pattern (see Fig. 9.1). The sounds and moving objects shared two kinds of nested amodal temporal structure. Temporal synchrony (macrostructure) united the sights and sounds across impacts, and an embedded temporal structure (microstructure) specified the composition of the object at each impact (single vs. compound). Three-month-old infants were given the opportunity to learn the relationship between the objects and sounds by viewing single film and soundtrack pairings under a variety of familiariza-tion/training conditions where the object motions and sounds were either congruent or incongruent. Specifically, the films were accompanied by sounds that were (a) appropriate to the composition of the object and synchronous with its motions, (b) appropriate and asynchronous, (c) inappropriate and synchronous (the wrong sounds and films were synchro-nized), or (d) inappropriate and asynchronous. Then all subjects were tested in an intermodal matching test where the two events were presented side-by-side along with one soundtrack to determine under which familiari-zation conditions intermodal learning had occurred. Control subjects, who had received familiarization with irrelevant events, showed no matching. Thus, any results of the matching test could be attributed to learning during the familiarization phase of the experiment. Results are depicted in Fig. 9.4. They indicated that only subjects who had been familiarized with the appropriate and synchronous film and soundtrack pairs showed evidence of learning. They showed a visual preference for the film that, during training,

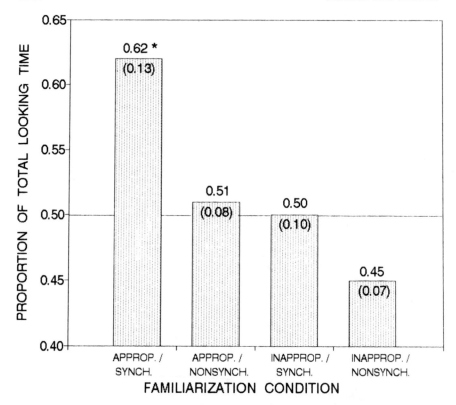

FIG. 9.4. Intermodal learning test (Bahrick, 1988): Two side-by-side films of objects were played along with a soundtrack that was synchronized with the motions of both objects but appropriate to the composition of only one. The results depict the mean proportions of total looking time and standard deviations to the film that, during familiarization, had been paired with the soundtrack infants were hearing. Significant difference: *$p < .05$. Adapted by permission.

had been paired with the soundtrack they were hearing, whereas infants in the other three training conditions showed no preference. Thus, infants learned to relate a film and soundtrack only when they shared two kinds of amodal temporal structure.

The Bahrick (1988) procedure provided an excellent test of the integration-association versus invariant detection views. Infants were given equal opportunity to associate the films and soundtracks during familiarization across the four conditions. However, learning only occurred when two kinds of amodal relations united the object motions and sounds. Learning did not occur through association, even when the film of a single object was played moving in synchrony with inappropriate sounds. The presence of an incongruent amodal relation (specifying object composition) was apparently sufficient to preclude learning under these conditions. Thus, by 3 months intermodal learning seems to be guided by the detection of amodal invariant relations. These relations already exert meaningful constraints on the types of synchronous sights and sounds that can be perceived as united.

Another approach to assessing intermodal learning has been to test older infants who can already detect the relations in question without special training. Under what conditions does the infant's experience with audible and visible events lead to knowledge about the relationship between specific visual and acoustic attributes? Spelke (1979, 1981) addressed this question by presenting infants with a visual search test to measure what they had learned during a prior intermodal preference phase. Four-month-old infants viewed films of two stuffed animals (a kangaroo and a donkey) bouncing side-by-side along with arbitrarily selected impact sounds (thuds or gongs) emanating from a central speaker during the preference phase. The sounds shared a common tempo and/or synchrony relation with the motions of one object and were unrelated to the motions of the other object. Next, a search test was conducted where the animals were again shown side-by-side along with intermittent sounds from each. Spelke (1979) found that infants searched first more often and eventually in the direction of the film that belonged with the sound they were hearing. Because the sounds and objects were arbitrarily paired, infants could only have learned which animal went with each sound by detecting amodal relations (synchrony and/or tempo) during the preference phases. Further, they did not learn by associating co-occurring objects and sounds, because each sound co-occurred with the presentation of both stuffed animals, yet only one of the animals was perceived as related to each sound. Thus, learning during the intermodal preference phase must have occurred on the basis of detecting amodal relations. These results were replicated and extended in a series of further studies (Spelke, 1981), which eliminated the possibilities that successful search behavior was based on "place learning" or on detection of synchrony during the search phase, rather than detection of amodal relations during the preference phase. Infants demonstrated learning of the arbitrary relations, even when the search phase was conducted with asynchronous sounds, the lateral positions of the animals had been switched, and the films and soundtracks were played successively.

The finding that intermodal learning occurred on the basis of detecting amodal relations was replicated and extended to different amodal relations. Bahrick (1983), using a similar method, showed $4\frac{1}{2}$-month-old infants films of wooden blocks banging and water-soaked sponges squishing. During a modified preference phase where synchrony was controlled, infants showed clear evidence of detecting the temporal information specifying rigidity and elasticity of substance. In the subsequent search phase, they were able to use this information to search first significantly more often to the sound-matched film. Infants apparently learned that the blocks made the banging sounds whereas the sponges made the squishing sounds.

Further, Bahrick (1987) conducted a developmental study using the films of the single large marble and the group of smaller marbles. By 6 months, infants were able to match the films and sounds in an intermodal preference phase solely on the basis of temporal information specifying object composition. By $7\frac{1}{2}$ months they were able to search successfully for the sound-specified object after abstracting this information in the preference phase. Because synchrony was controlled in both the preference and search phases, and because age-matched control subjects who received no preference phase were unable to search successfully, the search performance was attributed to intermodal knowledge acquired by detecting amodal relations specifying object composition in the preference phase. Infants must have learned something about the relation between the visual appearance of the object and the type of sound it produced.

Thus, taken together, the intermodal preference and search studies provide strong evidence that infants acquire knowledge about the relation between visual and acoustic aspects of events by detecting amodal audiovisual relations. Detection of amodal relations in the preference phase of each study described earlier (temporal synchrony, tempo of action, composition, and substance information) preceded and guided learning about modality-specific visual and acoustic relations. This knowledge enabled infants to search successfully for an object upon hearing the sound it was previously related to. Learning did not occur by integrating and associating co-occurring films and soundtracks, either when the soundtrack was played with a single film (Bahrick, 1988) or with two side-by-side (Bahrick, 1987; Spelke, 1979, 1981). That infants selectively learn about multimodal events on the basis of amodal relations (and not when amodal information is disrupted) constitutes a convenient buffer against learning the numerous possible inappropriate relations from unrelated sights and sounds. These studies provide evidence that detection of amodal temporal relations is an important basis for perceptual learning in early infancy.

Detection of Amodal Versus Arbitrary Intermodal Relations

A multimodal event makes a number of different intermodal relations available. Some, as we have discussed, are amodal and invariant across sense modalities, whereas others are arbitrary and not invariant across sense modalities. For any given event, one can abstract a number of arbitrary, modality-specific relations that may vary from one object or context to the next. For example, the relation between the sight of a person's face and the particular sound of their voice is arbitrary; or the color and shape of a moving object and the pitch of its impact sound; or the shape of a container and the smell, taste, or temperature of its contents. A red plastic toy may produce an impact sound that is high or low, or sharp or dull, depending on the type of surface it strikes. A tall green bottle could just as easily contain something sweet or sour, strong or mild, or hot or cold. Although amodal relations need not be learned through experience, arbitrary intermodal relations must be learned. Adults, however, seem to easily learn and remember a multitude of arbitrary relations in every day life.

When and under what conditions do infants detect and learn arbitrary intermodal relations? Does detection of these relations developmentally parallel, precede, or succeed detection of amodal relations in the same events? Empirical investigation of this question is another promising approach for evaluating the importance of amodal relations in the development of intermodal perception. Given the limited generalizability of arbitrary relations across objects and contexts, detection of these relations seems less important for perceptual development than detection of amodal relations. Very little research, however, has directly investigated the infant's sensitivity to arbitrary intermodal relations. One study (Spelke & Owsley, 1979) found that infants by the age of $3\frac{1}{2}$ months have already learned to relate the sight of their mother's face with the particular sound of her voice. Fernandez and Bahrick (in press) discovered that female infants at 4 months were able to learn the relation between the visual appearance of a toy and a distinctive odor. At 7 months, infants were able to learn the relationship between the color of a container and the taste of its food (Reardon & Bushnell, 1988). On the other hand, Bushnell (1986) found that infants of this age were unable to learn to pair the color of an object with its temperature. No clear pattern has yet emerged regarding the nature or timing of this developmental process.

How might arbitrary intermodal relations be learned? One possibility is that they are learned by association on the basis of co-occurrence. Bushnell (1986), consistent with the integration-association view, suggested that infants may treat arbitrary and amodal relations similarly. Both are experienced as "multimodal compounds," or as information in separate sense modalities that must be put together somehow. In contrast, our view is that only arbitrary or modality-specific relations must be learned through experience. Many events make both amodal and arbitrary relations available. Bahrick (1992) proposed that intermodal knowledge about arbitrary relations is differentiated only after amodal relations are detected. Several studies (Bahrick, 1983, 1987; Spelke, 1979, 1981, reviewed earlier) have shown that detection of amodal temporal relations during a preference phase made it possible for infants to detect the arbitrary relation between the visual appearance of the object and the particular sound that it produced, in a subsequent search phase. Further, Bahrick (1988) found that 3-month-olds learned to relate an object and a sound only after detecting two types of amodal invariant relations uniting their motions and sounds. We thus propose that detection of amodal invariants precedes and guides learning about arbitrary object–sound relations by directing infants' attention to appropriate object–sound pairings and then promoting sustained attention and further differentiation. Initial detection of an amodal relation (e.g., voice–lip synchrony, shared rhythm and tempo) enables the infant to focus on a unitary event (e.g., the mother's face and voice). This, in turn, may lead to differentiation of more specific, arbitrarily paired audible and visible attributes (e.g., the sound of the voice with the unique appearance of the face). In this way, detection of amodal relations can precede and guide learning about arbitrary relations. This pattern is consistent with an increasing specificity view of perceptual development (E. J. Gibson, 1969).

The studies reviewed in the prior section demonstrated that detection of amodal relations preceded and guided the acquisition of intermodal knowledge about arbitrary relations within a given testing session. Might there also be a developmental progression across age where infants detect amodal relations at a younger age than arbitrary relations from the same events? Only one recent set of studies has addressed this question. Bahrick (1992) presented 3-month-old infants with films of a single large object and a cluster of smaller objects, taken from one of six pairs (depicted in Fig. 9.5), striking a surface in an erratic pattern. The films portrayed two amodal invariant relations, temporal synchrony (SYNC) and temporal information specifying the composition of the objects (COMP), as well as one arbitrary, modality-specific relation, that between the pitch of the impact sounds and the color/shape of the objects (SOS). Infants were habituated to two of these events along with their natural, synchronous sounds, and then received test trials in which the relation between the visual and acoustic information was changed or mismatched. Infants showed significant visual recovery to a change in both amodal relations, but not to the change in the pairing of pitch with color/shape, relative to the performance of control subjects who received no change (see Fig. 9.6). Two further control studies demonstrated that the 3-month-olds could, in fact, discriminate the color/shape and pitch changes used. These findings suggested that by 3 months, infants were already sensitive to the amodal relations, but were not yet able to detect the arbitrary pitch–color/shape relations. It was thus proposed that detection of amodal temporal relations developmentally precedes detection of arbitrary relations.

At what age do infants detect the arbitrary relation between the pitch of an impact sound and the color/shape of an object? A further study using the same stimulus events (Bahrick, in press) revealed that it was not until 7 months of age that infants showed significant visual recovery to a change in these arbitrary relations. Three- and 5-month-olds did not. This suggests

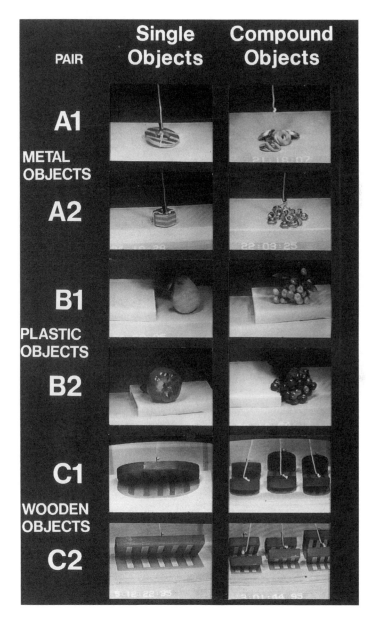

FIG. 9.5. The single and compound object pairs from Bahrick (1992). Reprinted by permission.

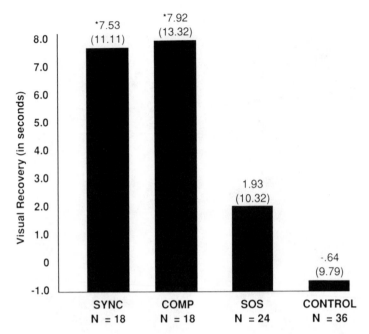

FIG. 9.6. Mean visual recovery and standard deviations to a change in synchrony (SYNC), composition (COMP), and color/shape-pitch (SOS) relations, as compared with no-change controls (from Bahrick, 1992). Significance: *p = or < .01 with respect to controls. Reprinted by permission.

a developmental lag between discrimination of unimodal stimulation and detection of arbitrary bimodal relations.

It is too early to determine how broad a phenomenon this developmental lag between detection of amodal and arbitrary relations will prove to be. To what other stimulus domains and conditions will it generalize? These are important questions for future research to address. Nevertheless, for the domains in which it does occur, this developmental lag is seen as adaptive in promoting the development of veridical perception. By detecting amodal relations first, infants can develop intermodal knowledge about persistent properties of objects and events prior to the acquisition of knowledge about more variable, idiosyncratic relations. This can provide appropriate constraints on learning about arbitrary relations that are typically context or stimulus specific. For example, by abstracting audiovisual synchrony and temporal information specifying composition, infants can learn and generalize that single objects produce single sounds and compound objects produce a more prolonged, "compound" sound. Detection of these relations can guide perceptual development appropriately. If infants learn that red, round objects produce a single sound, or a high-pitched sound, and attempt to generalize this across contexts, it would interfere with veridical perceptual development.

Thus, by first abstracting amodal relations, perceptual learning will be based on more permanent, context-free relations, and will not be disrupted by learning numerous relations that vary from one context to the next. In other words, detection of amodal relations in early development acts as a "buffer" against premature learning and inappropriate generalization of idiosyncratic relations.

CONCLUSIONS

The research reviewed in this chapter provides converging evidence from five domains that detection of amodal relations motivates and guides perceptual development in the first months of life. There is now abundant evidence that young infants detect a wide range of amodal relations in audible and visible stimulation, from temporal synchrony, and rhythm, to object substance, spectral information in speech, and changing distance relations. Nonetheless, the ability to detect many of these relations improves with age, and there are meaningful constraints on the perception of intermodal relations in infancy. Infants do not learn to pair just any co-occurring object and sound. Rather, they pair objects with sounds that are synchronous and "correct" with respect to the object's composition. Finally, amodal relations may be differentiated prior to arbitrary relations from the same event. Infants' unique sensitivity to amodal relations has been demonstrated across a diverse set of naturalistic events and different procedures, including the intermodal preference and search methods, infant-control habituation, or training and transfer, and across successive or simultaneous presentations of visual and acoustic stimulation. In our view, results of much of the research reviewed in this chapter seem inconsistent with the integration-association view, are difficult to explain on the basis of intensity matching, and occur too early in development to be accounted for on the basis of Piaget's action-centered view. Gibson's invariant-detection view appears to be most clearly consistent with all the research findings reviewed. However, none of the theories adequately describe what relations are detected first and how it is that inappropriate or irrelevant relations are not learned. What are the innate capacities of the infant that set the development of intermodal perception into motion such that it develops veridically within such a remarkably short period of time?

From our research and review of the literature we have elaborated a preliminary model that begins to address these questions. It is developed within the context of Gibson's invariant-detection theory and describes how detection of amodal relations can veridically guide perceptual development and intermodal learning:

1. Infants come into the world with a primitive intermodal coordination of audio-visual space (Wertheimer, 1961). How, though, does the infant

determine which of the many objects within his direction of gaze belong with the sound he is hearing?

2. Young infants are preadapted to selectively detect amodal relations and these relations guide perceptual exploration at first. By abstracting amodal relations, the infant explores and perceives unitary multimodal events.

3. Detection of further multimodal relations proceeds in order of increasing specificity (E. J. Gibson, 1969). That is, global, amodal relations may be differentiated prior to nested or more specific intermodal relations. This sequence may characterize the order in which infants abstract multimodal information in a given encounter with an event, as well as across age.

4. Selective tuning to amodal relations functions as a buffer against learning incongruent relations in early infancy. By detecting amodal relations first, learning will be based on more permanent, context-free relations that can be accurately generalized, whereas learning about arbitrary, idiosyncratic relations that do not generalize across contexts will be delayed until appropriate constraints are learned. Finally, once detection of amodal relations fulfills these functions, they presumably no longer play such a predominant role in directing perceptual selectivity.

In the introduction to this chapter we asked, how could infants, with no prior knowledge of the world around them, select, learn, and remember information that is relevant, meaningful, and coherent, and ignore the vast amount of stimulation that is not? The model just elaborated provides an answer. Selective tuning to amodal relations at first serves as an efficient and economical substitute for the knowledge that guides adult perception. Once sufficient knowledge about multimodal events is acquired, this knowledge can in part guide further exploration, and infants may then become more attuned to other aspects of stimulation.

It appears that research on intermodal perception has made an important shift: from that of cataloguing and mapping out intermodal abilities possessed by young infants, to addressing questions regarding the mechanism for and nature of development. Although different theoretical views will continue to drive this research, important questions have emerged and new, more promising approaches have evolved for answering them. We are asking questions about the basis and nature of intermodal learning in infancy; about the conditions under which infants respond to meaningful, qualitative properties of events; about which intermodal relations are differentiated first, and drive development, and which are detected later. Two especially promising approaches for addressing these questions are training and transfer studies such as the intermodal learning method used by Bahrick (1988), and Kluver's approach for establishing the nature of the stimulus information to which infants respond. In combination with developmental studies comparing performance across age, these approaches promise to reveal much more about the nature and basis of intermodal perception in years to come.

REFERENCES

Allen, T. W., Walker, K., Symonds, L., & Marcell, M. (1977). Intrasensory and intersensory perception of temporal sequences during infancy. *Developmental Psychology, 13*, 225–229.

Bahrick, L. E. (1983). Infants' perception of substance and temporal synchrony in multimodal events. *Infant Behavior and Development, 6*, 429–451.

Bahrick, L. E. (1987). Infants' intermodal perception of two levels of temporal structure in natural events. *Infant Behavior and Development, 10*, 387–416.

Bahrick, L. E. (1988). Intermodal learning in infancy: Learning on the basis of two kinds of invariant relations in audible and visible events. *Child Development, 59*, 197–209.

Bahrick, L. E. (1992). Infants' perceptual differentiation of amodal and modality-specific audio-visual relations. *Journal of Experimental Child Psychology, 53*, 180–199.

Bahrick, L. E. (in press). The development of infants' sensitivity to arbitrary intermodal relations. *Ecological Psychology.*

Bahrick, L. E., Walker, A. S., & Neisser, U. (1981). Selective looking by infants. *Cognitive Psychology, 13*, 377–390.

Bartlett, F. C. (1932). *Remembering.* Cambridge, England: University Press.

Birch, H. G., & Lefford, A. (1963). Intersensory development in children. *Monographs of the Society for Research in Child Development, 28* (5, Serial No. 89) 1–47.

Birch, H., & Lefford, A. (1967). Visual differentiation, intersensory integration, and voluntary motor control. *Monographs of the Society for Research in Child Development, 32* (1–2, Serial No. 110).

Blank, M., & Bridger, W. H. (1964). Crossmodal transfer in nursery school children. *Journal of Comparative and Physiological Psychology, 58*, 277–282.

Bower, T. G. R. (1974). *Development in infancy.* San Francisco: Freeman.

Bower, G. H. (1976). Experiments on story understanding and recall. *Quarterly Journal of Experimental Psychology, 28*, 511–534.

Bryant, P. (1974). *Perception and understanding in young children: An experimental approach.* London: Methuen.

Bushnell, E. W. (1986). The basis of infant visual-tactual functioning: Amodal dimensions or multimodal compounds? In L. P. Lipsitt & C. K. Rovee-Collier (Eds.), *Advances in infancy research* (Vol. 4, pp. 182–194). Norwood, NJ: Ablex.

Chase, W. G., & Simon, H. A. (1973). Perception in chess. *Cognitive Psychology, 4*, 55–81.

Dodd, B. (1979). Lip reading in infants: Attention to speech presented in-and-out-of synchrony. *Cognitive Psychology, 11*, 478–484.

Fernandez, M., & Bahrick, L. E. (in press). Infants' sensitivity to arbitrary object-odor pairings. *Infant Behavior and Development.*

Field, T., Woodson, R., Greenberg, R., & Cohen, D. (1982). Discrimination and imitation of facial expressions by neonates. *Science, 218*, 179–181.

Gardner, J. M., Lewkowicz, D. J., Rose, S. A., & Karmel, B. Z. (1986). Effects of visual and auditory stimulation on subsequent visual preferences in neonates. *International Journal of Behavioural Development, 9*, 251–263.

Gibson, J. J. (1966). *The senses considered as perceptual systems.* Boston: Houghton Mifflin.

Gibson, E. J. (1969). *Principles of perceptual learning and development.* New York: Appleton-Century-Crofts.

Gibson, E. J., & Walker, A. S. (1984). Development of knowledge of visual and tactual affordances of substance. *Child Development, 55,* 453–460.

Horowitz, F., Paden, L., Bhana, K., & Self, P. (1972). An infant-control procedure for studying infant visual fixations. *Developmental Psychology, 7,* 90.

Humphrey, K., & Tees, R. (1980). Auditory-visual coordination in infancy: Some limitations of the preference methodology. *Bulletin of the Psychonomic Society, 16,* 213–216.

Kluver, H. (1933). *Behavior mechanisms in monkeys.* Chicago: University of Chicago Press.

Kuhl, P. K., & Meltzoff, A. N. (1982). The bimodal perception of speech in infancy. *Science, 218,* 1138–1141.

Kuhl, P. K., & Meltzoff, A. N. (1984). The intermodal representation of speech in infants. *Infant Behavior and Development, 7,* 361–381.

Lawson, K. R., Ruff, H. A., McCarton-Daum, C., Kurtzberg, D., & Vaughan, H. G. (1984). Auditory-visual responsiveness in full-term and preterm infants. *Developmental Psychology, 20,* 120–127.

Lewkowicz, D. J. (1985). Bisensory response to temporal frequency in 4-month-old infants. *Developmental Psychology, 21,* 306–317.

Lewkowicz, D. J. (1986). Developmental changes in infants' bisensory response to synchronous durations. *Infant Behavior and Development, 9,* 335–353.

Lewkowicz, D. J. (1991). Development of intersensory functions in human infancy: Auditory/visual interactions. In M. J. Weiss & P. R. Zelazo (Eds.), *Newborn attention: Biological constraints and the influence of experience* (pp. 308–338). Norwood, NJ: Ablex.

Lewkowicz, D. J. (1992a). The development of temporally-based intersensory perception in human infants. In F. Macan, V. Pouthas, & W. Friedman (Eds.), *Time, action, and cognition: Towards bridging the gap.* Dordrecht: Kluwer.

Lewkowicz, D. J. (1992b). Infants; response to temporally based intersensory equivalence: The effect of synchronous sounds on visual preferences for moving stimuli. *Infant Behavior and Development, 5,* 297–324.

Lewkowicz, D. J., & Turkewitz, G. (1980). Cross-modal equivalence in early infancy: Auditory-visual intensity matching. *Developmental Psychology, 16,* 597–607.

Lewkowicz, D. J., & Turkewitz, G. (1981). Intersensory interaction in newborns: Modification of visual preferences following exposure to sound. *Child Development, 52,* 827–832.

Meltzoff, A. N., & Borton, R. W. (1979). Intermodal matching by human neonates. *Nature (London), 282,* 403–404.

Meltzoff, A. N., & Moore, M. K. (1977). Imitation of facial and manual gestures by human neonates, *Science, 198,* 75–78.

Mendelson, M. J., & Ferland, M. B. (1982). Auditory-visual transfer in four-month-old infants. *Child Development, 53,* 1022–1027.

Morrongiello, B. A., & Fenwick, K. D. (1991). Developmental changes in infants' coordination of auditory-visual depth information. *Journal of Experimental Child Psychology, 52,* 277–296.

Neisser, U. (1976). *Cognition and reality.* San Francisco: Freeman.

Piaget, J. (1952). *The origins of intelligence in children.* New York: International Universities Press.

Piaget, J. (1954). *The construction of reality in the child.* New York: Basic Books.

Piaget, J., & Inhelder, B. (1969). *The psychology of the child.* New York: Basic Books.

Pickens, J. (in press). Perception of auditory-visual distance relations by 5-month-old infants. *Developmental Psychology.*

Pickens, J. N., Field, T., Nawrocki, T., Martinez, A., Soutullo, D., & Gonzalez, J. (in press). Fullterm and preterm infants' perception of face-voice synchrony. *Infant Behavior and Development.*

Reardon, P., & Bushnell, E. W. (1988). Infants' sensitivity to arbitrary pairings of color and taste. *Infant Behavior and Development, 11,* 245–250.

Rose, S. A., Gottfried, A. W., & Bridger, W. H. (1978). Cross-modal transfer in infants: Relationship to prematurity and socioeconomic background. *Developmental Psychology, 14,* 643–652.

Rose, S. A., & Ruff, H. A. (1987). Cross-modal abilities in human infants. In J. D. Osofsky (Ed.), *Handbook of infant development* (pp. 318–362). New York: Wiley.

Schank, R., & Abelson, R. (1977). *Scripts, plans, goals, and understanding.* Hillsdale, NJ: Lawrence Erlbaum Associates.

Schiff, W., Benasich, A. A., & Bornstein, M. H. (1989). Infant sensitivity to audiovisually coherent events. *Psychological Research, 51,* 102–106.

Schnierla, T. C. (1959). An evolutionary and developmental theory of biphasic processes underlying approach and withdrawal. In M. Jones (Ed.), *Nebraska Symposium on Motivation* (Vol. 7, pp. 1–42). Lincoln: University of Nebraska Press.

Schnierla, T. C. (1965). Aspects of stimulation and organization in approach/withdrawal processes underlying vertebrate behavioral development. In D. S. Lehrman, R. A. Hinde, E. Shaw (Eds.), *Advances in the study of behavior* (Vol. 1, pp. 2–74). New York: Academic Press.

Soloman, R. T., May, J. G., & Schwartz, B. D. (1981). The word superiority effect: A study using parts of letters. *Journal of Experimental Psychology: Human Perception and Performance, 7,* 552–559.

Soutullo, D., Hernandez, M., & Bahrick, L. E. (1992, May). *Infants' bimodal perception of adult and child faces and voices.* Presented at the International Conference on Infant Studies, Miami Beach, FL.

Spelke, E. J. (1976). Infants' intermodal perception of events. *Cognitive Psychology, 8,* 533–560.

Spelke, E. S. (1979). Perceiving bimodally specified events in infancy. *Developmental Psychology, 15,* 626–636.

Spelke, E. S. (1981). The infant's acquisition of knowledge of bimodally specified events. *Journal of Experimental Child Psychology, 31,* 279–299.

Spelke, E. S., Born, W. S., & Chu, F. (1983). Perception of moving, sounding objects by 4-month-old infants. *Perception, 12,* 719–732.

Spelke, E. S., & Cortelyou, A. (1980). Perceptual aspects of social knowing: Looking and listening in infancy. In M. E. Lamb & L. R. Sherrod (Eds.), *Infant social cognition* (pp. 61–84). Hillsdale, NJ: Lawrence Erlbaum Associates.

Spelke, E. S., & Owsley, C. (1979). Intermodal exploration and knowledge in infancy. *Infant Behavior and Development, 2,* 13–17.

Turkewitz, G., Lewkowicz, D. J., & Gardner, J. (1983). Determinants of infant perception. In J. Rosenblatt, C. Beer, R. Hinde, & M. Bushnel (Eds.), *Advances in the study of behavior.* New York: Academic Press.

Walker, A. S. (1982). Intermodal perception of expressive behaviors by human infants. *Journal of Experimental Child Psychology, 33,* 514–535.

Walker-Andrews, A. S. (1986). Intermodal perception of expressive behaviors: Relation of eye and voice? *Developmental Psychology, 22,* 373–377.

Walker-Andrews, A. S. (1988). Infants' perception of the affordances of expressive behaviors. In C. Rovee-Collier & L. P. Lipsitt (Eds.), *Advances in infancy research* (Vol. 5, pp. 173–221). Norwood, NJ: Ablex.

Walker-Andrews, A. S., Bahrick, L. E., Raglioni, S. S., & Diaz, I. (1991). Infants' bimodal perception of gender. *Ecological Psychology, 3*(2), 55–75.

Walker-Andrews, A. S., & Lennon, E. (1985). Auditory-visual perception of changing distance by human infants. *Child Development, 22,* 373–377.

Wertheimer, M. (1961). Psychomotor coordination of auditory-visual space at birth. *Science, 134,* 1692.

CHAPTER TEN

Effects of Colocation on Auditory–Visual Interactions and Cross-Modal Perception in Infants

Barbara A. Morrongiello
University of Guelph

Interest in the ontogeny of intermodal functioning has a very long history dating back even to Aristotle (see Boring, 1942). In the seventeenth century Molyneux posed a now classic question to Locke on the origins and development of cross-modal functioning. He asked: What perceptual abilities would be present in a blind man restored to sight? Would the sensory systems be integrated and result in a unitary percept of an object, such as when the man first looked at an object he was manipulating in his hand? Would auditory stimulation result in specific expectations about the visible properties of the sounding object? Or, would visual-based information be distinct and separate from that provided to the other senses, with coordination of intersensory knowledge only accomplished following specific cross-modal experiences? As the literature reviewed in this chapter will reveal, these fundamental questions about the origins and developmental course of cross-modal relations are still largely unresolved. Despite years of research on infants' perception of auditory-visual relations (for extensive reviews see Rose & Ruff, 1987; Spelke, 1987; Walk & Pick, 1981), theoretical advances have been slow in coming for a variety of reasons.

First, the majority of research on auditory–visual perception has focused on 4-month-olds. Although it is not apparent why this is the case, this state of affairs may reflect the methodology that has become normative for research in this area, namely, a matching paradigm in which two visual events are presented simultaneously with a sound track that matches one of them in some way and is not precisely colocated with either (cf. Spelke,

1976). This procedure runs very smoothly with 4-month-olds, resulting in low attrition rates.

Second, and related to the first point, in few studies has more than one age group been tested. Consequently, we know relatively little about the developmental course of this important aspect of perceptual functioning. Investigators have been far more interested in determining *if* infants demonstrate cross-modal matching than in understanding the conditions under which they do or do not demonstrate these competencies, and why.

Third, in most work, investigators have failed to consider how constraints in intramodal functioning might impact on infants' performance on tasks tapping cross-modal perception. For example, because accuracy in localization of sound changes with age (see Morrongiello & Gotowiec, 1990, for review), one would expect that the role of spatial colocation in infants' learning sight–sound correspondences might also vary with age. In general, neither in the design of studies nor in the discussion of results have investigators considered how such "sensory primitives" (cf. Aslin & Smith, 1988) might relate to higher order cross-modal processes.

Finally, few studies have been aimed at determining what information about cross-modal relations infants actually encode. Although such efforts would go far to extend our understanding of the basis for infants' performance patterns, there are few studies one can point to in order to demonstrate this approach. For all of these reasons our understanding of the developmental course of auditory–visual cross-modal perception in infants is relatively limited.

The aim in this chapter is to review research relevant to this topic, with an emphasis on colocation as a factor affecting cross-modal perception of sights and sounds in infants; temporal synchrony is a factor that has received considerably more attention, but to minimize redundancy with other chapters in this volume (Bahrick & Pickens, chap. 9, and Lewkowicz, chap. 8) we consider literature on this topic only as it relates to research on colocation. Because the literature review is selective, I apologize in advance to those whose work I fail to mention. I begin with discussion of research demonstrating cross-modality interactions involving orientation behaviors (e.g., eye and head orientation), because such behaviors are likely to serve an exploratory function and to aid learning about sight-sound correspondences. As is evident, this research reveals links between modalities even in the newborn period. Next I proceed with discussion of research that more directly assesses cross-modal learning and perception. Finally, I conclude with some recommendations for future research in this area and discussion of pertinent neurophysiological data on coding of multimodal information, including some speculations as to the possible implications of these data for the development of cross-modal functioning in human infants.

CROSS-MODALITY INTERACTIONS: PROVIDING
A CONTEXT FOR AUDITORY–VISUAL LEARNING

Regardless of whether infants have the capacity for cross-modal perception at birth, it seems likely that their perceptual–motor systems would have evolved to provide for experiences to promote learning about auditory–visual correspondences. Opportunities for learning become especially important when one considers that many cross-modal correspondences are arbitrary ones. For example, the visible image of a clock and the concomitant ticking sound produced by the clock are united logically only on the basis of colocation. They lack the provision of other amodal features, such as temporal synchrony. The prevalence of such arbitrary auditory–visual relations in the environment suggests that perceptual learning probably plays an important role in the early acquisition of cross-modal knowledge. Exploratory behaviors, such as head and eye orientation, therefore likely function to promote learning about auditory-visual correspondences. Research examining the impact of sound on eye and head orientation in infants is relevant to this point. In discussing this literature, I begin by considering research in which the sound and/or visual stimulus is presented from a fixed location. Subsequently, I discuss research involving sound and/or visual sources that move through space.

Fixed-Location Effects

In very young infants, the introduction of a sound results in increased visual activity and attention (Hainline, 1978; Haith, 1973; Haith, Bergman, & Moore, 1977; Horowitz, 1974), suggesting early links between auditory and visual processing. Furthermore, properties of the sound have differential effects on visual orienting behaviors (Butterworth & Castillo, 1976; Crassini & Broerse, 1980; Wertheimer, 1961). A soft sound has been shown to elicit an eye movement in the direction of the sound, whereas a loud sound is more likely to result in orienting away from the sound (Hammer & Turkewitz, 1975; Turkewitz, Birch, Moreau, Levy, & Cornwell, 1966).

Location of the sound also influences properties of eye movements. When presented a sound at midline, newborns centralize fixations near midline. In contrast, when presented a lateralized sound they execute horizontal scanning patterns, first toward and then away from the source (Mendelson & Haith, 1976); these differential scanning patterns may reflect greater difficulty in pinpointing the location of the sound off midline as compared to near midline (see Morrongiello & Rocca, 1990, for further discussion).

Lateralized sound also influences head orientation behavior. With sufficiently long presentation of a lateralized sound, newborns orient their head in the direction of the sound (Clifton, Morrongiello, Kulig, & Dowd, 1981a; Muir & Field, 1979), and also show evidence of differentiating the location of sounds within a hemifield (see Morrongiello & Rocca, 1987, for discussion of the importance of distinguishing localization from lateralization). For example, when presented with a 20-sec recording of a rattle sound at either 36, 54, 72, or 90 degrees from midline, the extent of head rotation shown by neonates relates systematically to the locus of the sound (Morrongiello, Fenwick, Hillier, & Chance, 1994, in press). As can be seen in Fig. 10.1, as the sound was displaced further from midline, the extent of head rotation increased in a linear fashion. Thus, newborn infants just a few hours old have some capacity for localization of a sound along the horizontal axis. Although the accuracy with which they do so is much poorer than at older ages (Morrongiello, Fenwick, & Chance, 1990), if looking behavior was well coordinated with head orientation, then this integrated orientation system would support learning about cross-modal correspondences. Head orientation to sound would facilitate bringing the sounding object into foveal view, thereby maximizing extraction of visual information about the sounding object or event.

The newborn's ability to constrain the location of a sounding object in space, in conjunction with the operation of an integrated eye-head orientation

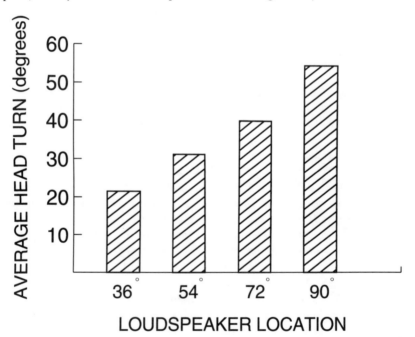

FIG. 10.1. Extent of newborn head rotation (in degrees) as a function of sound displacement from midline (0 degrees). The data are taken from Morrongiello, Fenwick, Hillier, and Chance (in press).

system, would both be minimal prerequisites to early learning of sight–sound correspondences. It is noteworthy that recent research with adults also reveals links between the auditory spatial channel and the oculomotor system, with audition serving specifically to bring the target into foveal view and enhance speed of visual processing and identification (Perrott, Saberi, Brown, & Strybel, 1990). In fact, visual search and event identification in adults are superior when guided by auditory spatial information, as compared to when only visual information is available. Taken together, these studies involving infants and adults indicate that links between auditory and visual spatial processing may be present from birth and function similarly throughout the life cycle. In the neonate such links would optimize opportunity for learning sight–sound correspondences by increasing the likelihood that the source of the sound would be brought into foveal view.

Bower (1974) argued that links between auditory and visual functioning in neonates indicate cross-modal perception. According to his view, neonates expect to see something when they hear a sound, and orienting behaviors indicate active visual search for something corresponding to the auditory stimulus. The results of numerous other studies, however, refute these conclusions and suggest that orienting behaviors may be largely reflexive in the newborn period and need not indicate intentional search for a visible object (Clifton, Morrongiello, Kulig, & Dowd, 1981b; McGurk, Turnure, & Creighton, 1977). It is worth emphasizing that these perspectives do not necessarily differ in the importance ascribed to orientation behaviors in neonates; saying that the behavior is reflexive does not deny the critical function it could serve for the newborn, such as supporting cross-modal learning by enhancing foveal inspection of sounding objects. Rather, the issue is with the degree of intentionality evidenced by such behaviors.

In support of conceptualizing head orientation to sound as a neonatal reflex, Clifton et al. (1981b) noted that head orientation to sound does not habituate over trials in newborns, even if there is nothing to observe. By contrast, after 5 months of age, the behavior quickly habituates unless there is something to observe. This observation, in conjunction with other changes in head orientation to sound over the first few months, led Clifton et al. (1981b) to conclude that orientation to sound in newborns is reflexive, whereas in infants 4 months and older it is volitional, with the intention in older infants being to search for the sounding object. Consistent with this view, newborns turn their head and eyes toward sound even when in a dark environment that precludes visual inspection (Mendelson & Haith, 1976), and they show such behaviors even when their eyes are closed (Turkewitz et al., 1966). For newborns the spatial coordination between auditory and oculomotor systems does not depend on a stimulus being present in the visual field.

In summary, although infants demonstrate behaviors that indicate links between auditory and visual functioning at birth, and these behaviors could certainly provide for learning about auditory–visual correspondences, such behaviors need not imply cross-modal perception. Rather, they are likely to function to provide a context for acquiring knowledge about auditory–visual relations.

One interesting developmental progression during the first few months after birth that may have implications for the idea that visual orienting to sound plays an important role in learning auditory–visual correspondences is the finding that head orientation toward sound actually drops out at about 2–3 months and does not reemerge until 4 months of age (Field, Muir, Pilon, Sinclair, & Dodwell, 1980). Is the decline in head orientation to sound between 2 and 4 months likely to limit learning about auditory–visual correspondences during this age range? I think not. In fact, it seems likely that *if* head orientation to sound is linked with visual functioning, then one might predict such changes in the behavior at 2–3 months, because this is the age at which several investigators hypothesize reorganization at the neurophysiological level of the visual system (Bronson, 1974; Johnson, 1992; Maurer, 1975), and substantial changes in visual response patterns have been noted (e.g., Milewski, 1976). Furthermore, a decline in head orientation to lateralized sound at 2–3 months does not preclude the possibility that infants have ample opportunities to learn about auditory–visual events during this age range. Not only does accuracy in sound localization improve throughout this age range (Morrongiello et al., 1990), but after 6 weeks of age the effective visual field expands, thereby increasing the spatial range from midline within which a visible target can serve to elicit an infant's gaze (Tronick, 1972). Moreover, directional looking toward lateralized sound has been noted to occur at 2–3 months even in the absence of head orientation, and estimates of this behavior are as high as 70% of sound trials for meaningful stimuli, such as speech (Field et al., 1980). Hainline (1978) also provided evidence that the addition of a sound can serve an organizing effect on visual scanning behavior between 1 and 3 months of age. For these reasons, the impact on cross-modal learning of a decline in head orientation toward sound for a short time in early infancy is probably minimal.

Although sound affects the occurrence and directionality of orienting behaviors in newborn and young infants, very few studies have addressed the important question of whether sound presentation actually influences visual processing, as it does in adults (Perrott et al., 1990). A study by Castillo and Butterworth (1981) is relevant to this point. They evaluated eye movements in newborns under three visual conditions:

1. The location of the sound (22 degrees from midline) was marked by a pair of red circles.
2. The location of the circles was in the hemifield opposite to the location of the sound.
3. The sound occurred without any visual stimulus present.

The sound was a 450-Hz tone of 1 sec duration. Infants made a significant number of eye movements in the direction of the sound only when a visual stimulus was colocated with the sound; they did not do so when the sound was presented in a blank visual field. However, they looked toward the visual stimulus even if the sound was not colocated with it but was presented in the contralateral hemifield. One important difference emerged between responses for the different trial types, however. As discussed in Butterworth (1981), infants showed response habituation over trials for the colocation condition but did not do so for the condition in which the sound and visual stimulus were not colocated. Although Butterworth discussed these results in terms of visual dominance, it is equally plausible that the colocated sound may have facilitated visual processing, perhaps because the stimulus complex was experienced as a unitary event. According to this notion, infants may have shown habituation due to the more rapid processing of the stimulus event with correlated auditory–visual properties. To address this hypothesis directly, what is needed, and what we are undertaking, are studies that more directly measure infants' processing of information when sight–sound correspondences are and are not present. For example, does the occurrence of sound with a visual stimulus promote processing of distinctive visual features or memory for these? Without such knowledge we can only speculate as to what functions these early auditory–visual behavioral interactions might serve.

Effects of Motion

McGurk and his colleagues examined oculomotor behavior in newborns under a variety of visual- and sound-presentation conditions (McGurk et al., 1977). They reported that tracking of a moving visible stimulus was unaffected by the addition of a sound, whether moving with the stimulus or stationary. This result is surprising because previously discussed research seems consistently to indicate that sound serves to enhance attention to visual stimuli (e.g., Hainline, 1978; Mendelson & Haith, 1976). In addition, McGurk et al. (1977) were unable to recruit visual tracking to their moving sound stimulus alone, although this is a common enough occurence that it appears on the Neonatal Behavioral Assessment Scale by Brazelton (1973). The fact that the auditory stimulus, a "cricket" type sound, did not elicit directionally appropriate eye orientation when presented laterally and without a visual stimulus makes it hardly surprising that the infants performed as they did under the other conditions.

Examining the impact of sound on visual tracking in 1- and 2-month-olds, Lawson and Ruff (1984) found that by 2 months infants reliably followed objects more when sound accompanied their presentation as compared to when they were presented in silence. However, tracking behavior did not vary depending on whether the sound was colocated or displaced (4 ft) relative to the moving target's location. These findings suggest that colocation is not especially critical at young ages. Rather, sound may influence tracking and processing of visual events by promoting arousal and attention to these, rather than by facilitating localization per se.

In a series of studies, Bull (1978, 1979) examined the impact of moving sound on visual tracking in 4-month-old infants. Infants were presented two visual conditions: *nonocclusion* trials, in which a visual stimulus moved along a track and was continuously in view, and *occlusion* trials, in which a screen blocked viewing of the center area of the track. On *moving* sound trials the sound moved along with the visual stimulus, and on *stationary* trials the sound was not colocated with the moving visual stimulus but was presented at a fixed location. Results indicated that sound did not affect tracking before occlusion or on nonocclusion trials. This result is not surprising, because the auditory stimulus would have provided completely redundant information about object location when the visual stimulus was available. Consequently, one might not expect it to influence infants' visual tracking. However, on occlusion trials, a sound moving with the visual stimulus in a colocated fashion promoted attention to the screen following occlusion, and anticipation of the target's reappearance. Thus, by 4 months, infants' visual tracking of a moving object's location in space was influenced by colocated sound. Infants apparently interpreted the sound as specifying the continued existence of the object, and they used auditory-based information to guide visual tracking in the absence of visual cues to object location.

In a study recently completed in our lab it would appear that other systematic relations between visual behaviors and head orientation in response to sound are also evident in young infants. We tested 6-, 12-, and 18-month-old infants in the dark and presented them with a sound that started at midline and then moved continuously to various points along the horizontal axis (experimental trial) or remained at midline (control trial); to manipulate task difficulty we varied speed of movement. Using an observer-based procedure (cf. Morrongiello et al., 1990; Olsho, Koch, Halpin, & Carter, 1987), if the experimenter judged correctly that infants tracked the moving sound, then a light display was presented to reinforce the infant's behavioral responses. We monitored visual and head orientation behaviors to examine the integration of these and their relation to localization acuity when the sound moved. One aspect of these data is considered in the context of this chapter, namely, the integration of visual and head orientation behaviors during sound movement.

Frame-by-frame scoring of the videorecords of several subjects at each age revealed several interesting patterns of performance; the remaining videorecords are still being scored. First, all initial eye and head movements were in the direction of the moving sound source and there were few secondary movements in the opposite direction. Thus, when localizing this moving sound source infants did not oscillate their heads in an effort to maximize binaural cues for sound localization as they have been shown to do for stationary sound sources presented in the dark (Clifton, Perris, & Bullinger, 1991). Rather, they generally held their heads stationary while the sound moved, and they determined the hemifield (and possibly the location) of the sound before they initiated any orientation responses. Furthermore, on about 50% of correct experimental trials, infants initiated an eye movement well in advance of a head movement; on the remaining trials these orientation responses were initiated simultaneously. These performance patterns suggest that the mechanisms controlling the directionality of these two responses are tightly coupled in young infants, and we see no evidence of age changes between 6 and 18 months in this aspect of functioning of the auditory–oculomotor system. Because the superior olivary complex plays an integral role in the control of both eye and head movements (Stein, 1984), our findings suggest it is sufficiently developed to provide for an integrated eye–head orientation system by at least 6 months of age, and possibly earlier (see previous literature review).

Second, surprisingly, infants blinked on about two-thirds of the trials. Is this blinking integrated in some specific way with eye and head orientation behaviors? To determine this we considered only those trials on which infants executed a blink, eye, and head movement, and used a video-frame counter to determine the relative temporal ordering of these events. At all ages, the predominant ordering of events was blink before onset of an eye and/or head movement, which is a pattern that adults display when orienting to lateralized sound (Perrott et al., 1990). The data also suggest, however, an age-related increase in blinking before the onset of an eye and/or head movement. In fact, by 18 months, this performance pattern was evident on nearly every trial, whereas 6-month-olds showed this much less frequently, with 12-month-olds' performance falling at an intermediate level between that of the 6- and 18-month-olds. This age trend suggests that the auditory–oculomotor system does undergo important changes in some aspects of functioning throughout infancy.

Because spontaneous eye blinks have been shown to reflect the influence of higher nervous system processes (Ponder & Kennedy, 1927), it is perhaps not surprising that we see a transition from less blinking at 6 months to more blinking at 18 months; we know that there are significant changes in brain functioning and neurological development during this age range. However, what is interesting is the question of why infants at any age systematically blink on this sound localization task, because no visual-based information was provided or made relevant to the task, in contrast to the work with adults by Perrott and his colleagues (1990) in which they noted the occurrences of blinking. Furthermore, because we see an increase in blinking with age before the initiation of a directional orientation response and there is a concomitant increase in localization acuity for moving (Morrongiello, in preparation) and stationary (see Morrongiello & Gotowiec, 1990) sound sources during this age range, the question naturally arises as to whether these two age trends are in some way related. Specifically, does the increase in blinking with age somehow promote greater accuracy in sound localization?

Blinks have been shown to relate to aspects of visual information processing in adults, and there is evidence that they function largely to allow the subject time to abstract and process visual information without interference from new incoming information (Fogarty & Stern, 1989). Thus, blinking promotes accurate identification of visible events in adults. By this logic, possibly, on sound localization tasks, blinks function to eliminate any cross-modal (i.e., visual) based distraction and promote attention to auditory-based information relevant for enhancing infants' performance on this sound localization task. With age, as infants have increasing experience with the spatial correspondences of auditory–visual events they may become increasingly facile at using this attentional strategy to minimize distraction and therefore maximize accuracy when the task is to localize sounds only, as opposed to localize and identify auditory–visual events. If the blinks we are observing are voluntary ones and reflect an attentional strategy to maximize performance, then one might expect the incidence and/or duration of these to vary at an age depending on the difficulty level of the localization task. By comparing the incidence of blinks across experimental and control trials and correct and incorrect trials we hope to gain greater insights into the functional significance of this behavior for infants' performance on sound localization tasks. Suffice it to say, our preliminary findings suggest developmental changes in infancy in some aspects of the auditory–oculomotor system (i.e., functioning relevant for information extraction and processing of location and event identification) and little or no change in other aspects of the system (i.e., the directionality function of the system).

In summary, sound serves to recruit attention and guide the direction of orienting behavior, and it does so from birth. The literature strongly suggests that orientation to sound is reflexively, as opposed to intentionally, mediated in neonates. Nonetheless, assuming this to be true does not diminish the potential importance of this primitive perceptual–motor system. Such an organization could provide for observation of auditory–visual correlations and promote cross-modal learning. Furthermore, developmental improvements in the acuity with which infants localize sound, coupled with concomitant increases in the infant's effective visual field, could provide for increasing refinements in the detection of auditory–visual correspondences and tracking of moving sounding–visible objects. Direct tests of cross-modal perception in neonates and very young infants certainly are needed. Nonetheless, the findings reviewed indicate that infants are well prepared to acquire auditory–visual knowledge at young ages.

DIRECT TESTS OF AUDITORY–VISUAL CROSS-MODAL PERCEPTION IN INFANTS

One of the first studies that attempted to assess cross-modal knowledge directly in young infants was an investigation with 1-month-olds that used a violation-of-expectancy paradigm to examine infants' understanding of the importance of colocation for the bimodally specified event of a person talking (Aronson & Rosenbloom, 1971). In this study, 2-month-old infants were presented a visual stimulus at one location (i.e., mother making mouthing movements of speech) and a sound corresponding to this stimulus in another location (i.e., mother's voice from a loudspeaker). The authors hypothesized that infants would become distressed with this arrangement if they had cross-modal perception, because they would expect the mother's voice to be co-located with her visible image. The infants responded as hypothesized and the authors concluded that cross-modal perception was innate and there was a common mapping of auditory–visual spatial location, supporting theoretical arguments that perceptual unity is evident from birth (Bower, 1974). Although intriguing, unfortunately, these results have not been replicated when more rigorous methodological constraints have been imposed (Condry, Haltom, & Neisser, 1977; McGurk & Lewis, 1974; Turkewitz et al., 1966). Consequently, we do not yet know what the youngest age is at which infants demonstrate cross-modal perception for colocated auditory–visual events, and what specific role colocation plays in the acquisition of this knowledge.

A number of studies involving older infants indicate perception of auditory–visual correspondences at 4 months (see Rose & Ruff, 1987, for extensive review). A few of these investigations are relevant to our interest in colocation as a factor influencing cross-modal learning. Lyons-Ruth (1977) examined 4-month-olds' abilities to learn arbitrary auditory–visual associations. She familiarized infants with toys (rattle, bell, squeak toys) that were presented at midline and colocated with a sound. Although not discussed at length by the author, it is noteworthy that each toy produced sound when a rocking hand motion was executed. Thus, not only was colocation evident, but there was an additional feature that may have contributed to performance, namely, temporal synchrony of the sight and sound. Following familiarization, she measured infants' responses to the same sound in another location (90 degrees from midline) but paired either with a novel or familiar toy. She found that infants looked away most often when a novel toy accompanied the familiar sound, a result she interpreted as indicating distress at the violation of expectancy that the sound would be paired with the familiar toy. Thus, the findings suggest that by 4 months infants can learn sight–sound correspondences when colocation and temporal synchrony are both present.

Lawson (1980) assessed more directly the necessity of colocation and how this interacts with temporal synchrony to influence infants' learning about sight–sound correspondences in 6-month-olds. She presented infants with a variety of conditions, including a condition under which sights and sounds occurred in temporal synchrony but were not colocated, and a condition under which the reverse occurred—that is, sights and sounds were colocated but not temporally synchronous. When infants were presented with a sight and sound that was temporally synchronous but not colocated, they did not learn to associate the two events. Obviously, temporal synchrony was not sufficient for learning about auditory–visual correspondences if colocation was not evident. However, colocation alone did not guarantee that infants would learn any auditory–visual association. Colocation was sufficient for cross-modal learning when some types of temporal asynchrony were present (when object moved toward and then away from the infant and sound was intermittent) but not when other types of temporal asynchrony occurred (object moved intermittently, either up and down or side to side, and sound was continuous).

Lawson's data suggest that neither temporal synchrony nor colocation in isolation will necessarily result in cross-modal learning at 6 months. Rather, it would seem that both are properties of auditory–visual events that are evaluated by 6-month-olds and that influence their determination of correspondences to learn. Quite possibly, a prerequisite for 6-month-olds to learn an auditory–visual correspondence is that they must be able to integrate and make sense of the information about the object that is indicated by both of these properties. Stated another way, at the least, a prerequisite for learning by 6 months may be that information about colocation and temporal synchrony does not blatantly conflict. Applying this logic, it is interesting to note that although Lawson conceptualizes movement of the toy toward and then away from the infant as "continuous," one could also consider this "discontinuous" in terms of path of movement. By this interpretation, pairing with an intermittent sound might be likely to support learning because of similarity in auditory–visual properties (i.e., both specify discontinuity), even though precise temporal synchrony of changes in direction with sound were not evident. By contrast, the reverse condition that Lawson presented, of a discontinuous path of movement visually (object moving up and down or side to side) coupled with a continuous sound, would pose greater challenges to integration of auditory and visual sources of information about the object and, consequently, would be less likely to support auditory–visual learning. Lawson's results are consistent with this reinterpretation of her test conditions.

Although I suggest that blatant violations of colocation and temporal synchrony are likely to result in a failure of 6-month-old infants to learn arbitrary sight–sound correspondences, it is important to emphasize that this does not mean that such violations will necessarily preclude infants from recognizing the unity of auditory–visual correspondences and responding to these based on a single factor, either colocation or synchrony. What matters is the degree of discrepancy between colocation and temporal synchrony, and the infant's sensitivity to these sources of information and their expectations about how these should relate. For example, in Spelke's procedure (1976) the sound is presented between two visual displays, as opposed to being precisely colocated with either. Despite this imprecision in colocation, 4-month-olds detect temporal synchrony if it is present and look to the film that matches the sound (Spelke, 1979). This pattern of looking presumably results because they weigh the factors of colocation and synchrony differently than do older infants. Spelke's (1979) results may also reflect 4-months-olds' poor precision in sound localization, which could serve to minimize their perception of conflicting information between co-location and temporal synchrony. Related to these points, it seems likely that infants' learning of sight–sound correspondences is driven selectively by factors like colocation and temporal synchrony. For example, infants at 4 months learn to associate a sound with a synchronously moving object even if another asynchronized object is present and they spend time looking at the latter (Spelke, 1981). Thus, infants do not arbitrarily associate sights and sounds that occur simultaneously. Rather, factors of colocation and temporal synchrony selectively direct this learning process, with synchrony being especially critical at younger ages when sound localization skills are poorer, and colocation information gaining in prominence as localization skills improve.

A study recently completed in my lab nicely illustrates these points. In this study we (Morrongiello, Fenwick, & Nutley, in preparation) tested 4- and 8-month-olds using a procedure that incorporated aspects of Bahrick's intermodal-learning procedure (1988) and Lawson's (1980) procedure. Similar to Bahrick, infants were first familiarized with a specific sight–sound pair and then given a paired preference test to assess their learning to associate the two events. However, during familiarization, two objects were always presented, with one sound. During four familiarization conditions, toys and sounds varied with respect to spatial colocation and temporal synchrony; sometimes these cues were presented in isolation (i.e., two toys accompanied by a pulsing sound that was colocated with one toy, thereby providing colocation information only), and other times they supported learning the same sound–sight pairing (i.e., colocated and synchronous toy and sound) or conflicted and supported learning different sight sound pairings (i.e., stationary toy colocated with a pulsing sound, with a second toy moving in synchrony to the sound but not colocated). Similar to Lawson, during the test phase infants received two trials: the two familiar objects presented with the familiar sound, and also with a novel sound. Preferential looking to one toy more than another was used to determine whether the infants learned an association of the sound with either of the toys presented during familiarization.

Measures of total duration of looking time revealed changes between 4 and 8 months in infants' relative weighting of colocation and temporal synchrony, although infants at both ages were sensitive to both sources of information. At 4 months, if synchrony was absent infants could use colocation alone as a basis for associating a toy and sound. However, temporal synchrony was primary as evidenced by the finding that colocation was not necessary if synchrony was present, and also that infants associated the synchronous non-colocated toy and sound instead of the colocated but nonsynchronous toy and sound in the conflicting-cues condition. In contrast, 8-month-olds apparently expected colocation and synchrony information to act in concert. Consequently, they did not learn sight–sound pairings when these cues conflicted, but had no difficulty when they were presented in isolation or were together and supported learning the same toy–sound pairing. In all cases, infants demonstrated knowledge of specific sight–sound pairings and did not look preferentially to either familiar toy when an unfamiliar sound was presented.

In summary, the evidence reviewed suggests that colocation and temporal synchrony are factors that *interact* to influence cross-modal learning and that infants are likely to attend to both sources of information in learning about auditory–visual events, although the relative weighting of these cues might vary with age depending on infants' skills in perceiving location and/or temporal information in the auditory and visual modalities. This organization would be highly adaptive, because it would provide for selective learning of sight-sound correspondences, which is essential given the arbitrary nature of many correspondences. Moreover, it is consistent with the behavioral evidence, and also with findings on neurophysiological coding of bimodal information (this is discussed further in the Conclusion section). Certainly, infants do not associate all sounds and sights that they perceive simultaneously. Rather, they utilize colocation and temporal synchrony information in concert to determine sight–sound associations. Surprisingly, as revealed by the preceding literature review, there are very few studies that have incorporated both colocation and temporal synchrony factors into their design. Additional research in progress in our laboratory is aimed at examining systematically how these factors interact further to affect infants' learning arbitrary auditory–visual relations at different ages. For example, how spatially separated can sights and sounds be and still provide for infants' learning to relate these? Because accuracy in localizing sound is poor in very young infants and improves with age, I predict that colocation would increasingly become a more important factor with age, and therefore older infants might not learn sight–sound pairings that younger infants do, if there is sufficient discrepancy in the spatial location of these visible and audible events.

Because infants are responsive to changes in sound amplitude at birth (e.g., Bartoshuk, 1964), and by 2 months are sensitive to dynamic cues that signal visual depth changes (see Yonas & Owsley, 1987, for review), one might expect that they also would learn about auditory–visual depth correspondences at a young age. In the natural environment, visual and auditory-based cues for depth are correlated. For example, an approaching-sounding object can be indicated by optical expansion coupled with increases in sound amplitude. Conversely, a receding object can be specified by optical contraction and amplitude decreases. Several studies have assessed infants' abilities to recognize auditory–visual depth correspondences.

Walker-Andrews and Lennon (1985) were the first to investigate 5-month-olds' abilities to recognize a correspondence between auditory and visual depth information. Using the Spelke (1976) procedure, infants were shown films of a Volkswagen automobile travelling forward or backward in depth accompanied by a sound increasing or decreasing in amplitude. When two films were shown side by side, infants looked preferentially to the approaching automobile when the soundtrack was increasing in amplitude but showed no preference for either the approaching or receding automobile when sound amplitude was decreasing.

More recently, Pickens (1990) replicated Walker-Andrews and Lennon's study using a toy train. He found that 5-month-olds integrated auditory and visual depth information for both the approaching and receding conditions when the train moved against a naturalistic landscape, and even when the background was untextured so that optical expansion and contraction were the only available visual depth cues. These findings suggest that by 5 months infants have some appreciation of how sights and sounds concomitantly change with depth. However, the discrepancy in results across these two studies for the receding condition raises some questions regarding the robustness of infants' detection of auditory–visual correspondences specifying depth at 5 months.

To understand more fully how infants respond to auditory and visual depth cues at different ages, we (Morrongiello & Fenwick, 1991) tested 5-, 7-, and 9-month-olds using the preferential-looking technique (cf. Spelke, 1976). Infants were shown two video images side by side on separate video monitors accompanied by a soundtrack, and their looking behavior was monitored. The video images were of a panda, Santa, or clown; each toy was beating on a drum. The study addressed three questions:

1. Do infants recognize that changes in amplitude can specify that an object is moving in depth? To answer this question, a stationary toy was paired with a toy approaching and receding in depth. On half of these trials

the sound was constant in amplitude and on the other trials the sound increased and decreased in amplitude. This condition also provided a test of whether infants simply prefer visual movement in depth regardless of the accompanying sound.

2. Do infants recognize that changes in amplitude specify movement in a particular dimension (i.e., depth)? To answer this question, a toy moving horizontally was paired with a toy approaching and receding in depth. The accompanying soundtrack was either nearly constant in amplitude or systematically increasing and decreasing.

3. Do infants recognize that increasing amplitude corresponds to approaching objects and that decreasing amplitude corresponds to receding objects? To answer this question, a toy that first approached and then receded (approach/recede video image) was paired with a toy that first receded and then approached (recede/approach video image), accompanied by a soundtrack with amplitude changes synchronized with the movement of one of the toys. It was reasoned that if infants recognized the appropriate auditory–visual correspondences they would look preferentially to the video display that corresponded to the particular sound presented during each trial.

The answer to the first question was that all three age groups looked preferentially to the stationary toy when it was correct, but only the 7- and 9-month-olds looked preferentially to the moving toy when it was correct. The average proportion of time spent looking to the correct video image at each age is shown in Fig. 10.2.

The answer to the second question can be seen in Fig. 10.3. The 5-month-olds did not look preferentially to the horizontally moving toy when it was correct. Nor did they look to the toy moving in depth when it was correct. In contrast, both the 7- and 9-month-olds looked preferentially to these video images when their corresponding auditory tracks were presented.

The answer to the final question was that neither the 5- nor the 7-month-olds recognized the precise synchronization between a sound increasing in amplitude and an approaching object and a sound decreasing in amplitude and a receding object (see Fig. 10.4). In contrast, the 9-month-olds did.

To examine the possibility that the performance of the 5-month-olds was constrained by conflicting depth information between the two-dimensional video display and the three-dimensional depiction of depth in the video images, we tested a separate group of 16 5-month-olds in exactly the same manner as the original subjects except that the infants wore an eye patch. Results provided no evidence that wearing an eye patch enhanced performance to the depth condition. In fact, the same pattern of results emerged for the eye-patch control group as for the original 5-month-olds. These results would indicate that the 5-month-olds' limitations in perform-

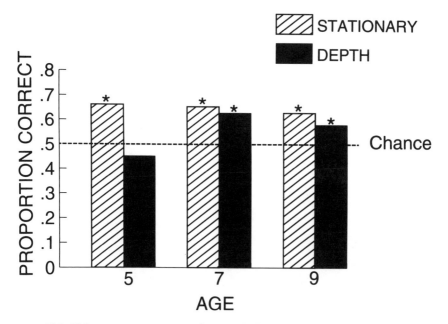

FIG. 10.2. Average proportion of correct looking to the stationary versus depth video image as a function of age in months. Asterisk indicates significantly above chance level (.50). The data are taken from Morrongiello and Fenwick (1991).

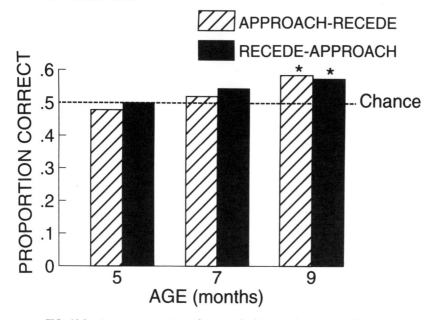

FIG. 10.3. Average proportion of correct looking to the horizontal versus depth video image as a function of age in months. Asterisk indicates significantly above chance level (.50). The data are taken from Morrongiello and Fenwick (1991).

MORRONGIELLO

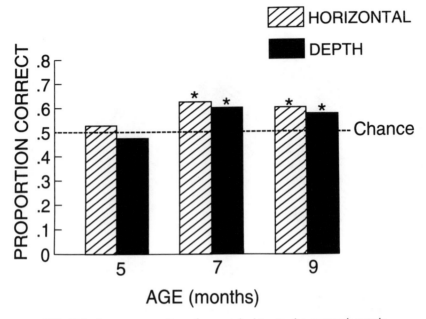

FIG. 10.4. Average proportion of correct looking to the approach–recede versus recede–approach video image as a function of age in months. Asterisk indicates significantly above chance level. The data are taken from Morrongiello and Fenwick (1991).

ance were not a result of disturbances in visual depth perception resulting from mode of stimulus presentation.

The results described above indicate age-related changes between 5 and 9 months in infants' coordination of auditory–visual depth information. Five-month-olds looked preferentially to the stationary video image when the sound was constant in amplitude but failed to look preferentially to the correct video image for all other conditions. Note, however, that the 5-month-olds did not look preferentially to the stationary video image when the sound was changing in amplitude. Thus, their performance did not reflect a simple visual preference for the stationary video image but must have been driven by detection of an auditory–visual correspondence between a constant-amplitude sound and a stationary object. To state this another way, although they did not recognize that changing amplitude specifies movement of an object in space, they did recognize that changing amplitude is not a property of stationary objects.

At 7 months, infants not only recognized that a stationary object and a constant-amplitude sound were correlated but also that changing amplitude corresponds to an object that is moving in space. Furthermore, 7-month-olds recognized that increasing and decreasing amplitude corresponds to movement in depth and not to horizontal movement. However, limitations in 7-month-olds' recognition of auditory–visual depth correspondences were observed. Specifically, 7-month-olds did not match increases in amplitude with an approaching object and decreases in amplitude with a receding object. Thus, although 7-month-olds demonstrated recognition that matches of amplitude change with object movement are restricted to a particular spatial dimension, their coordination of specific directions of movement and amplitude change was somewhat imprecise.

By 9 months, infants precisely coordinated auditory–visual depth information. They matched increasing amplitude with an approaching object and decreasing amplitude with a receding object even when the two were presented simultaneously. Thus, by 9 months, infants recognized that amplitude changes specify a particular type of movement in depth.

To account for the obtained developmental trends in performance, two broad areas of perceptual development need to be addressed: intramodal competency and intermodal integration. Regarding intramodal competency, it is possible that age-related changes within the auditory modality and/or visual modality were responsible for the observed developmental trends independent of auditory–visual integration abilities. For example, if auditory depth perception improves between 5 and 9 months, then perhaps the 9-month-olds' superior performance was due to their increased ability to recognize the changing amplitude cue as specifying changes in object distance. Similarly, if the younger infants were insensitive to the available visual depth cues, then it is possible that improvements in performance for the older infants were due to their increased ability to differentiate approaching and receding movements of the toy.

Research on auditory depth perception in infancy renders unlikely the possibility that the younger infants' performance was limited by their ability to use amplitude cues to discriminate changes in sound distance. Morrongiello, Hewitt, and Gotowiec (1991) found that 6-month-olds had no difficulty, relative to 12-month-olds, in discriminating changes in sound distance based on amplitude cues. Furthermore, research from our lab has yielded no evidence of developmental changes in auditory depth perception between 6 and 12 months, using a conditioned discrimination procedure (Morrongiello et al., 1991), or between 4 and 9 months, using reaching to sound in the dark as a measure (Morrongiello, Hillier, & Armstrong, in preparation). Finally, evidence that 5-month-olds can coordinate amplitude changes with visual depth changes under some conditions (Pickens, 1990; Walker-Andrews & Lennon, 1985) suggests that they recognize that sound amplitude can provide information about changing depth.

The possibility that the observed developmental trends are attributable to the younger infants' insensitivity to the visual depth cues in the video images is also unlikely. First, the 5-month-olds looked preferentially to the stationary video image and not to the video image displaying movement in depth when the sound was of constant amplitude. Thus, the infants must have perceived a difference between the two video images. Second, the 5-month-olds tested with an eye patch did not perform differently from those tested without the eye patch. Finally, previous research indicates that infants at very young ages are responsive to optical expansion as a cue for depth (e.g., Nanez, 1988), which is a primary cue provided in our stimuli. Thus, it seems unlikely that visual depth perception was the limiting factor responsible for the 5-month-olds' performance.

An alternative explanation for the observed developmental changes is that improvements in infants' abilities to integrate auditory and visual depth information occurs between 5 and 9 months. One line of evidence that suggests that intermodal integration accounted for age-related improvements in performance concerns performance by individual infants on trials in which the toy approaching and receding in depth was the correct video image (i.e., the sound was changing in amplitude). Considering all of these trials, only 33–50% of the 5-month-olds looked preferentially to the correct video image. Furthermore, the 5-month-olds' performance on these trials showed little consistency. As can be seen in Table 10.1, only 22% of the sample (4/18) looked preferentially to the approach/recede video image on all of the trials where it was the correct video image. By 7 months, half the sample (8/18) consistently looked preferentially to the approach/recede video image when it was correct. By 9 months, 78% of infants (14/18) did so. Thus, visual inspection of individual performance patterns indicates that only a very small sample of 5-month-olds successfully coordinated auditory and visual cues to depth, whereas most 9-month-olds had no difficulty with this task, and 7-month-olds performed at an intermediate level. Considered together with the results based on analysis of the group data, these findings strongly suggest that there are age-related changes in infants' intermodal coordination of auditory-visual depth information between 5 and 9 months. Furthermore, the evidence just reviewed would suggest that these intermodal develop-

TABLE 10.1
Number of Infants (Maximum = 18) for Whom the Proportion of Total
Looking Time to the Sound-Matched Video for the
Approach–Recede Film Was Above Chance Level (.50) as a
Function of Video Image Pairing and Age (in Months)

	Video Image Pairing			
Age	ST-AR and HO-AR	HO-AR and AR-RA	ST-AR and AR-RA	All Three Pairs
5	5	4	5	4
7	13	10	9	8
9	15	14	16	14

Note. ST, object is stationary; HO, object moves along the horizontal plane; AR, object approaches then recedes in depth; RA, object recedes then approaches in depth.

ments are relatively independent of intramodal changes in perceptual abilities.

SUMMARY AND CONCLUSIONS

At any one moment in time a multitude of stimuli impinge on the senses. One critical task facing the developing infant is to determine how sensory streams relate to one another. Although our senses separately code information about properties of a stimulus, most events in the environment provide for multi-modal stimulation. Detection of cross-modal correspondences is essential to the experience of a unified world and to our ability to draw inferences about environmental events and act efficiently toward these events.

The literature reviewed in this chapter does not provide strong support for any one theoretical viewpoint on the origins of cross-modal perception. Bower (1982) argued that there is a "primitive unity" of the senses at birth, including a common mapping of auditory and visual space, and that development proceeds with increasing differentiation of the sensory systems. Although evidence of links between the auditory and oculomotor/head orientation systems is present at birth, the reflexive nature of these behaviors makes it untenable to interpret these results as providing evidence of cross-modal perception per se at birth. What is needed is further research examining responses to conflicting information about location of sights and sounds by neonates and very young infants. If infants come into the world with a unity of the senses and a common auditory–visual map of space, then displacements of sights and sounds, particularly those that are temporally synchronous, might be especially distressing or attention-getting. Research examining the effects of auditory stimulation on visual processing would also provide information relevant to this theoretical position. Auditory stimulation should not only result in reflexive orientation responses, but these should vary depending on the visual stimulus and its properties, specifically, the extent to which these visual properties are consonant with information specified by the auditory stimulus.

Unlike Bower, Piaget (1952) argued that the senses provided distinct and separate information at birth, and these sources of information became increasingly integrated with accumulated sensory-motor experiences that gave rise to the knowledge that stimulus information coded in one modality was predictably correlated with that coded in another modality. Obviously, one limitation of Piaget's view is that he failed to give adequate consideration to the role that early-appearing perceptual-motor links of a primitive nature might play in this developmental process. Links between the auditory and oculomotor/head orientation systems in newborns do not support the view that the senses are completely unrelated at birth. Nonetheless, evidence of intermodal interactions does not imply cross-modal perception, and there is at least limited evidence that cross-modal learning proceeds during the first several months and cross-modal perception changes with age (see Bahrick & Pickens, chap. 9, and Lewkowicz, chap. 8, this volume). The issue that remains to be addressed, however, is whether such changes reflect increasing integration and coordination of the senses that follows from motor and cognitive advances, as Piaget proposed, or increasing stimulus differentiation that does not relate to cognition but is tied to perceptual-learning processes, as Gibson (1969) suggested.

According to Gibson (1969), infants are innately driven to detect "amodal" information available in the ambient array, and to use this information to guide exploration of multimodal events, thereby promoting the acquisition of cross-modal knowledge. Perceptual learning is reflected in increasing differentiation of amodal invariant information, not in the creation of such information. Thus, infants might discern which visible object corresponds to an audible event on the basis of recognizing the amodal property of synchrony or colocation; amodal properties provide redundant information to more than one sense modality. Detection of amodal properties presumably is innate and requires no perceptual learning. In fact, detection of amodal properties provides a foundation for perceptual learning. Infants presumably use amodal relations they have detected to guide exploration of the unified event, thereby promoting cross-modal knowledge and increasing differentiation of amodal relations.

The majority of research on auditory-visual perception in infants has been conducted from a Gibsonian viewpoint (e.g., see Bahrick & Pickens, chap. 9, this volume; Spelke, 1987; Walker, 1982). The results of these studies are consistent with the notion that infants detect amodal properties of auditory–visual events. Some recent research by Bahrick even suggests a hierarchy of infants' learning arbitrary auditory–visual relations, consistent with the notion of increasing specificity of amodal relations over age (Bahrick, 1992). Nonetheless, many aspects of this theory remain to be tested. In particular, research with infants under 3–4 months is needed to evaluate if detection of amodal properties is innate, and the extent to which there is a predictable progression in infants' learning auditory–visual relations that derive from amodal properties.

What do I conclude about the ontogeny of auditory–visual functioning and the role of colocation in cross-modal learning? Based on the current data, I think there is little basis for ascribing auditory–visual perception to neonates. Although a few studies have attempted to document distress in neonates and 1-month-olds when typical cross-modal experiences are violated artificially (e.g., Aronson & Rosenbloom, 1971), others have failed to replicate such distress reactions (e.g., McGurk & Lewis, 1974). The variety of reflexive behaviors the newborn possesses serves to guarantee experiences that may be critical to promote perceptual learning and development. The rooting reflex, for example, provides infants the opportunity for learning about tactual and visual relations. Head orientation to sound provides the young infant with countless instances in which auditory and visual stimulation is coincident in time and space. Such perceptual-motor response patterns may serve to promote coding of location relative to the self and an appreciation for how auditory and visual information in the ambient array is correlated with information arising from motor output. I suggest that infants learn about equivalences between auditory and visual space based on these very early experiences. Indeed, the failure to learn about such equivalences may explain the difficulties encountered in teaching some congenitally blind infants to orient toward sound, such as noted by Schwartz (1984).

Once audition and vision are integrated with respect to location, then it would make sense that infants have expectations to see a visible object at the judged location of a sound, because they should have abstracted the rule or invariant that sights and sounds that specify the same object should be colocated. Presumably, appreciation of the common mapping of auditory–visual space is evident when head orientation to sound reemerges as a volitional behavior at about 4 months. It is at this time, for example, that head orientation to sound rapidly habituates unless there is something interesting to observe (Clifton et al., 1981b). Other lines of evidence are consistent with this view. For example, infants by 4 months realize that sound specifies the availability of an object in space, and they reach in the dark and successfully retrieve objects on the basis of sound cues alone (e.g., Hillier, Hewett, & Morrongiello, 1992). In the absence of visual localization cues, they use auditory cues to draw inferences about the movement path of an occluded object (Bull, 1978, 1979). Furthermore, by 4 months, infants relate knowledge obtained in the auditory modality to that obtained in the visual one and perceive sound as an attribute of a specific object (Lyons-Ruth, 1977).

Because temporal synchrony between a sight and sound typically results from movement of the object in space (e.g., bouncing a ball, shaking a rattle), one might predict very early sensitivity to this amodal auditory–visual relation, because even newborns are especially responsive to visual movement (see Nelson & Horowitz, 1987). In fact, there is speculation that detection of movement in the visual field is subcortically mediated by the superior colliculus and therefore well developed at very young ages (e.g., Morton & Johnson, 1991). For example, although infants at 1 month were reported to show no preference for face patterns, Johnson and his colleagues found a visual preference, even for schematic diagrams of faces, when movement was involved (Johnson, Dziurawiec, Ellis, & Morton, 1991, Experiment 3). Certainly, visual tracking of visible as well as auditory stimuli is elicited readily enough in normal newborns that it is an item on neonatal assessment scales (e.g., Brazelton, 1973). Possibly, expectations about colocation of sights and sounds develop, in part, because of infants' early experiences with synchronous auditory–visual events (e.g., caregiver talking and lips moving, rattle shaking and making noise), coupled with increasing refinements in sound localization skills, an expanding effective visual field, and improvements in visual and auditory acuity. Infants must learn, for example, to differentiate auditory–visual events that occur concurrently by chance from those that occur concurrently because they specify the same event. Knowledge that temporally synchronous events should also covary spatially could serve infants' distinguishing between bimodal information that specifies a single event and that which occurs concurrently by chance. One obvious implication of these speculations is that one should observe interactions between colocation and temporal synchrony in infants' learning auditory–visual relations. Lawson (1980) noted the presence of such interactions in cross-modal learning at 6 months of age, and we (Morrongiello et al., in preparation) noted similar interactions at 4 months. Nonetheless, research at younger ages is needed if we are to understand how these factors interact to promote the acquisition of cross-modal knowledge and ontogeny of cross-modal perception.

Information on the neural basis of multimodal perception would also suggest that temporal synchrony and colocation should show interactive effects in cross-modal perception, and that the nature of these effects might change with age. The superior colliculus, a subcortical structure that controls orientation of the eyes, head, and pinna to external stimuli, has been strongly implicated as a site for integration of multimodal information in lower order species, such as cats and guinea pigs. In an elegant series of studies, Stein and Meredith and their colleagues (see review in Stein & Meredith, 1990, and Stein, Meredith, & Wallace, chap. 5, this volume) documented the convergence of auditory, visual, and somatosensory inputs and the representation of these inputs in maplike fashions in the deep layers of the colliculus. In fact, different modalities tend to overlap, with the most common multisensory cell being one that responds both to auditory and visual information. These multisensory cells have sensory receptive fields that are topographically aligned with one another. Such alignment ensures, for example, that colocation of a visual and auditory stimulus evokes neural activity in the same region of the colliculus. Furthermore, incoming sensory information is precisely matched to outgoing motor control centers so that orientation responses are synchronized to stimulus location in the environment. This organization allows different sensory inputs (e.g., visual, auditory) to interface with the same motor circuits and the organism to produce the same orientation responses to stimuli arising from different modalities. Most pertinent to our discussion, temporal synchrony of an auditory and visual event (spatially colocated) results in an overlap in neural discharge in response to these modality-specific sources of stimulation, which maximizes neural stimulation and orientation to the bimodal event; the level of stimulation reflects an interactive process, as opposed to simply an additive one. However, when the sight and sound are temporally synchronous but the sound is outside the receptive field of the visual stimulus (i.e., not colocated), then there is a marked inhibition of neural responses to the visual stimulus. These findings suggest that colocation may be a particularly salient property of bimodally specified events, directly influencing neural responsiveness to these events and possibly even minimizing responsiveness to temporal synchrony when sights and sounds are synchronous but not colocated.

Given the topographic organization of these visual and auditory maps in the superior colliculus, however, one might not expect such interactions before a common mapping of auditory-visual space is accomplished. Consistent with this hypothesis, Stein and Meredith (1990, p. 69) noted that multimodal cells in the cat are not present at birth or even at 8 days of age when visual functioning is present. Rather, integration of multimodal information at the neural level occurs some time after the sensory systems are functional and the organism presumably has experienced multimodally specified events and produced orientation responses to these events. Obviously, there is much research to be done if we are to understand fully how factors such as temporal synchrony and colocation direct learning about auditory–visual correspondences and the ontogeny of cross-modal functioning during early infancy. Nonetheless, I think that results to date on neural coding of bimodal events reinforce the value of examining how temporal synchrony and colocation interact to influence infants' learning of auditory–visual correspondences at very young ages.

In summary, despite the fairly large body of literature on the perception of auditory–visual relations in infancy, relatively little is known about the actual developmental course of this important perceptual ability. Knowledge of changes in cross-modal learning and functioning with age is needed to address important theoretical issues, such as whether the sensory modalities are unified at birth and later become differentiated, or whether they are distinct at birth and progress toward increasing differentiation. Furthermore, if infants are innately responsive to amodal properties of auditory–visual events, then we need to know what properties they are responsive to at what ages, and how these change with development and lead to expansions in cross-modal knowledge. To address these issues, assessment of auditory–visual integration in the newborn and early infancy period is sorely needed. Auditory–visual interactions in neonates can provide a rich context for learning about bimodally specified events, particularly if orientation responses are evident and infants have some capacity to localize and track moving multimodal events. Studies examining the interactive effects of colocation and temporal synchrony on auditory–visual learning and cross-modal matching in young infants are underway in our lab and should provide an empirical context to promote theoretical advances in this area.

ACKNOWLEDGMENTS

Preparation of this chapter and the research by the author that was reported herein were supported by grants from the Natural Sciences and Engineering Research Council of Canada. The author extends her thanks to Tanya Nutley for library assistance and Kim Fenwick for comments on a previous draft of this chapter.

REFERENCES

Aronson, E., & Rosenblum, S. (1971). Space perception in early infancy: Perception within a common auditory-visual space. *Science, 172*, 1161–1163.

Aslin, R. N., & Smith, L. B. (1988). Perceptual development. *American Review of Psychology, 39*, 435–473.

Bahrick, L. (1988). Intermodal learning in infancy: Learning on the basis of two kinds of amodal invariant relations in audible and visible events. *Child Development, 59*, 197–209.

Bahrick, L. (1992). Infants' perceptual differentiation of amodal and modality-specific audio-visual relations. *Journal of Experimental Child Psychology, 53*, 180–199.

Bartoshuk, A. K. (1964). Human neonatal cardiac responses to sound: A power function. *Psychonomic Science, 1*, 151–152.

Boring, E. (1942). *Sensation and perception in the history of experimental psychology.* New York: Irvington.

Bower, T. G. R. (1974). The evolution of sensory systems. In R. B. MacLeod & H. L. Pick, Jr. (Eds.), *Perception: Essays in honour of James J. Gibson* (pp. 141–165). Ithaca, NY: Cornell University Press.

Bower, T. G. R. (1982). *Development in infancy* (2nd ed.). San Francisco: Freeman.

Brazelton, T. B. (1973). *Neonatal behavioral assessment scale.* London: Heineman Medical Books.

Bronson, G. (1974). The postnatal growth of visual capacity. *Child Development, 45*, 873–890.

Bull, D. (1978, April). *Auditory-visual coordination in infancy: The perception of moving sights and sounds.* Paper presented at International Conference on Infant Studies, Providence, RI.

Bull, D. (1979, April). *Infants' tracking of auditory-visual events.* Paper presented at the Society for Research in Child Development, San Francisco.

Butterworth, G. (1981). The origins of auditory-visual perception and visual proprioception in human development. In R. Walk & H. Pick (Eds.), *Intersensory perception and sensory integration* (pp. 37–70). New York: Plenum.

Butterworth, G., & Castillo, M. (1976). Coordination of auditory and visual space in newborn human infants. *Perception, 5*, 155–160.

Castillo, M., & Butterworth, G. (1981). Neonatal localisation of a sound in visual space. *Perception, 10*, 331–338.

Clifton, R. K., Morrongiello, B. A., Kulig, W., & Dowd, J. M. (1981a). Newborns' orientation toward sound: Possible implications for cortical development. *Child Development, 52*, 833–841.

Clifton, R. K., Morrongiello, B. A., Kulig, J. W., & Dowd, J. M. (1981b). Developmental changes in auditory localization in infancy. In R. Aslin, J. Alberts, & M. Petersen (Eds.), *Development of perception: Psychobiological perspectives* (Vol. 1, pp. 141–160). New York: Academic Press.

Clifton, R., Perris, E., & Bullinger, A. (1991). Infants' perception of auditory space. *Developmental Psychology, 27,* 187–197.

Condry, S. M., Haltom, M., & Neisser, U. (1977). Infant sensitivity to audio-visual discrepancy: A failure to replicate. *Bulletin of the Psychonomic Society, 9,* 431–432.

Crassini, B., & Broerse, J. (1980). Auditory-visual integration in neonates: A signal detection analysis. *Journal of Experimental Child Psychology, 29,* 144–155.

Field, J., Muir, D., Pilon, R., Sinclair, M., & Dodwell, P. (1980). Infants' orientation to lateral sounds from birth to three months. *Child Development, 51,* 295–298.

Fogarty, C., & Stern, J. (1989). Eye movements and blinks: Their relationship to higher cognitive processes. *International Journal of Psychophysiology, 8,* 35–42.

Gibson, E. J. (1969). *Principles of perceptual learning and development.* New York: Appleton-Century-Crofts.

Hainline, L. (1978). Developmental changes in visual scanning of face and nonface patterns by infants. *Journal of Experimental Child Psychology, 25,* 90–115.

Haith, M. M. (1973). Visual scanning in infants. In L. J. Stone, H. T. Smith & J. B. Murphy (Eds.), *The competent infant* (pp. 33–59). New York: Basic Books.

Haith, M., Bergman, T., & Moore, M. (1977). Eye contact and face scanning in early infancy. *Science, 198,* 853–855.

Hammer, M., & Turkewitz, G. (1975). Relationship between effective intensity of auditory stimulation and directional eye turns in the human newborn. *Animal Behaviour, 23,* 287–290.

Horowitz, F. D. (1974). Visual attention, auditory stimulation and language discrimination in young infants. *Monographs of the Society for Research in Child Development, 38* (5–6, Serial No. 158).

Hillier, L., Hewitt, K. L., & Morrongiello, B. A. (1992). Infants' perception of illusions in sound localization: A reaching paradigm. *Journal of Experimental Child Psychology, 52,* 277–296.

Johnson, M. H., Dziurawiec, S., Ellis, H., & Morton, J. (1991). Newborns' preferential tracking of face-like stimuli and its subsequent decline. *Cognition, 40,* 1–19.

Lawson, K. R. (1980). Spatial and temporal contiguity and auditory-visual integration in infants. *Developmental Psychology, 16,* 185–192.

Lawson, K. R., & Ruff, H. (1984). Infants' visual following: Effects of size and sound. *Developmental Psychology, 20,* 427–434.

Lyons-Ruth, K. (1977). Bimodal perception in infancy: Response to auditory-visual incongruity. *Child Development, 48,* 820–827.

Maurer, D. (1975). Infant visual perception. In L. Cohen & P. Salapatek (Eds.), *Infant perception: From sensation to cognition* (Vol. 1, pp. 1–76). New York: Academic.

McGurk, H., & Lewis, M. (1974). Space perception in early infancy: Perception within a common auditory-visual space? *Science, 186,* 649–650.

McGurk, H., Turnure, C., & Creighton, S. J. (1977). Auditory-visual coordination in neonates. *Child Development, 48,* 138–143.

Mendelson, M. J., & Haith, M. M. (1976). The relation between audition and vision in the human newborn. *Monographs of the Society for Research in Child Development, 41* (Serial No. 167).

Milewski, A. (1976). Infants' discrimination of internal and external pattern elements. *Journal of Experimental Child Psychology, 22,* 229–246.

Morrongiello, B. A. (in preparation). *Infants' localization of moving sound sources.*

Morrongiello, B. A., & Fenwick, K. D. (1991). Infant's coordination of auditory and visual depth information. *Journal of Experimental Child Psychology, 52,* 277–296.

Morrongiello, B. A., Fenwick, K., & Chance, G. (1990). Sound localization acuity in very young infants: Estimates of minimum audible angle. *Developmental Psychology, 26,* 75–84.

Morrongiello, B. A., Fenwick, K., Hillier, L., & Chance, G. (in press). Newborn infants' localization of sounds. *Developmental Psychobiology.*

Morrongiello, B. A., Fenwick, K., & Nutley, T. (in preparation). *Developmental changes in the role that co-location and temporal synchrony play in infants' learning auditory-visual associations.*

Morrongiello, B. A., & Gotowiec, A. (1990). Recent advances in the behavioral study of infant audition: Sound localization. *Journal of Speech Language Pathology and Audiology, 14*, 187–208.

Morrongiello, B. A., Hewitt, K., & Gotowiec, A. (1991). Infants' discrimination of changes in auditory depth: Approaching vs. receding sounds. *Infant Behavior and Development, 14*, 187–208.

Morrongiello, B., Hillier, L., & Armstrong, K. (in preparation). *Infants' reaching to sounds in the dark.*

Morrongiello, B. A., & Rocca, P. (1987). Infants' localization of sounds in the horizontal plane: Effects of auditory and visual cues. *Child Development, 58*, 918–927.

Morrongiello, B. A., & Rocca, P. T. (1990). Infants' acuity in localizing sounds along the horizontal plane: Within hemifield localization. *Child Development, 61*, 1258–1270.

Morton, J., & Johnson, M. H. (1991). CONSPEC and CONLERN: A two-process theory of infant face recognition. *Psychological Review, 98*, 164–181.

Muir, D., & Field, J. (1979). Newborn infants orient to sounds. *Child Development, 50*, 431–436.

Nanez, J. (1988). Perception of impending collision in 3- to 6-week-old human infants. *Infant Behavior and Development, 11*, 447–463.

Nelson, C., & Horowitz, F. (1987). Visual motion perception in infancy: A review and synthesis. In P. Salapatek & L. Cohen (Eds.), *Handbook of infant perception: From sensation to cognition* (Vol. 1, pp. 123–154). New York: Academic Press.

Olsho, L., Koch, E., Halpin, C., & Carter, E. (1987). An observer-based psychoacoustic procedure for use with young infants. *Developmental Psychology, 23*, 627–640.

Perrott, D. R., Saberi, K., Brown, K., & Strybel, T. Z. (1990). Auditory psychomotor coordination and visual search performance. *Perception & Psychophysics, 48*(3), 214–226.

Piaget, J. (1952). *The origins of intelligence in children.* New York: International Universities Press.

Pickens, J. (1990). Perception of bimodal distance relations by 5-month-old human infants (Doctoral dissertation, Florida International University, 1990). *Dissertation Abstracts International, 51*(4).

Ponder, E., & Kennedy, W. (1927). On the act of blinking. *Quarterly Journal of Experimental Psychology, 18*, 89–110.

Rose, S. A., & Ruff, H. A. (1987). Cross-modal abilities in human infants. In J. Osofsky (Ed.), *Handbook of infant development* (2nd ed., pp. 318–362). New York: Wiley.

Schwartz, M. (1984). The role of sound for space and object perception in the congenitally blind infant. In L. Lipsitt & C. Rovee-Collier (Eds.), *Advances in infancy research* (Vol. 3, pp. 23–57). Norwood, NJ: Ablex.

Spelke, E. S. (1976). Infants' intermodal perception of events. *Cognitive Psychology, 8*, 553–560.

Spelke, E. S. (1979). Perceiving bimodally specified events in infancy. *Developmental Psychology, 15*, 626–636.

Spelke, E. S. (1981). The infant's acquisition of bimodally specified events. *Journal of Experimental Child Psychology, 31*, 279–299.

Spelke, E. S. (1987). The development of intermodal perception. In P. Salapatek & L. Cohen (Eds.), *Handbook of infant perception: From sensation to cognition* (Vol. 2, pp. 233–274). New York: Academic Press.

Stein, B. (1984). Development of the superior colliculus. *Annual Review of Neuroscience, 7*, 95–125.

Stein, B., & Meredith, A. (1990). Multisensory Integration. In A. Diamond (Ed.), The development and neural bases of higher cognitive functions. *Annals of the New York Academy of Sciences, 608*, 51–65.

Tronick, E. (1972). Stimulus control and the growth of the infant's effective visual field. *Perception and Psychophysics, 11*(5), 373–376.

Turkewitz, G., Birch, H. G., Moreau, T., Levy, L., & Cornwell, A. C. (1966). Effects of intensity of auditory stimulation on directional eye movements in the human neonate. *Animal Behavior, 14*, 93–101.

Walk, R. D., & Pick, H. L. (Eds.). (1981). *Intersensory perception and sensory integration.* New York: Plenum.

Walker, A. S. (1982). Intermodal perception of expressive behaviors by human infants. *Journal of Experimental Child Psychology, 33*, 514–535.

Walker-Andrews, A. S., & Lennon, E. M. (1985). Auditory-visual perception of changing distance by human infants. *Child Development, 56*, 544–548.

Wertheimer, M. (1961). Psycho-motor coordination of auditory-visual space at birth. *Science, 134*, 1692.

Yonas, A., & Owsley, C. (1987). Development of visual space perception. In P. Salapatek & L. B. Cohen (Eds.), *Handbook of infant perception* (Vol. 2, pp. 80–122). Orlando, FL: Academic Press.

CHAPTER ELEVEN

From Hand to Eye: Findings and Issues in Infant Cross-Modal Transfer

Susan A. Rose
Albert Einstein College of Medicine

Our research in cross-modal perception has dealt primarily with infants' recognition of an object in the face of a change in sensory modality. More specifically, we have studied infants' recognition by sight of an object previously only felt or recognition by touch of an object previously only seen. The recognition of identity or similarity between the impressions gained in different modalities has been referred to as cross-modal (or intersensory) matching, cross-modal transfer, or sensory equivalence.

Cross-modal abilities represent an intriguing type of equivalence problem. What are the laws that govern such correspondences? What underlies the ability to recognize visually an object we have previously felt but not seen? How complete is the perceived correspondence? What are its limits? Do cross-modal equivalences develop over time or are they present from birth? These issues have a long history in both philosophy and psychology, figuring prominently in major philosophical treatises since the time of Aristotle, who postulated the existence of a common sense to appreciate the "common sensibles" (see Marks, 1978).

Interest in how the different sensory modalities communicate information to one another continues to occupy a central place in modern philosophy and psychology. One notable aspect of this issue lies in the problematic nature of the relationship between phenomena that, on at least one level, are so ostensibly unrelated. For example, although the different sensory patterns produced by hand and eye can leave us with the perception of similarity or even identity between what is touched and what is seen, the sensory patterns produced by touch and vision are themselves entirely different. Grasping, handling, or feeling an object produces a set of deformations on the skin. The exact pattern of these deformations is a function not only of various properties of the object itself (such as its size, thickness, and texture) but also of the patterning of the hand and finger movements used to explore it. Viewing an object produces something quite different—namely, a pattern of light energies on the retina (see Bower, Broughton, & Moore, 1970). Despite these different sense impressions, and the different modalities in which the object is experienced, it is represented in memory in a unified way.

Until quite recently, examination of cross-modal abilities has focused almost exclusively on the study of school-aged children and adults. It was widely believed that these abilities serve as a critical underpinning to human cognitive functioning (e.g., Birch & Lefford, 1967; Ettlinger, 1967; Geschwind, 1965). It was also widely believed that such abilities were not present in animals, nor in human infants. Differences between the human brain and the brains of other primates were such that many believed that even apes would be unable to form intermodal associations. Repeated difficulties encountered in experimental attempts to obtain cross-modal transfer in animals during the 1960s gave added weight to scepticism about the existence of such capabilities in non-humans.

These views about cross-modal transfer have been dramatically altered in recent years. First, and largely as a result of changing research paradigms, the old view that cross-modal transfer is uniquely human has proved untenable. Various forms of cross-modal transfer have now been documented in other species, for example, transfer between vision and touch has been found in apes (e.g., Davenport, Rogers, & Russell, 1975) as well as monkeys (e.g., Murray, & Mishkin, 1985; Gunderson, Rose, & Grant-Webster, 1990). Second, the view that cross-modal linkages are achieved by language (Ettlinger, 1967) is clearly no longer tenable. Not only do animals show cross-modal abilities, but our own work, and that of others, has shown that even young, prelinguistic infants are capable of various forms of cross-modal transfer.

In our work on cross-modal transfer, the infant is called on to recognize an object from experience in two different modalities—vision and touch. To do so, the infant must have some capacity to associate the two kinds of information. Such intermodal association makes abstract representation possible because a single object or common event is perceived despite the different modalities in which it is encountered. This sort of cross-modal transfer should be distinguished from those simple associations that do not require mapping, but simply the arbitrary linkage of stimuli from different modalities (e.g., a blue disk with a warbler's trill). As Smith (1987) noted, these two types of cross-modal transfer undoubtedly involve different mechanisms.

In this chapter, I first describe some of our own work on infants' tactual–visual cross-modal transfer of shape. This work has dealt with several aspects of the phenomenon, including (a) the role of development and risk, (b) the nature and equivalence of information picked up in different modalities, (c) asymmetries in transfer, and (d) similarities between human and monkey infants. Next, I highlight two factors that need to be considered in specifying the basis of cross-modal perception of shape, namely, the nature of the stimulus properties involved and the way different exploratory strategies are used to gather information. Finally, I attempt to identify what I think have been muddled distinctions regarding the nature and origin of cross-modal correspondences.

TACTUAL–VISUAL CROSS-MODAL TRANSFER

To evaluate tactual–visual (T-V) cross-modal functioning in infants, we modified the standard visual paired comparison technique used for assessing recognition memory (Fagan, 1974). First, when assessing visual recognition, such tests begin with a brief period of familiarization, during which the infant is allowed to look at a stimulus. Next, the infant is shown the familiar object paired with a new one. Typically, infants demonstrate a visual preference for the new stimulus. This differential visual fixation is taken as evidence for visual discrimination and recognition memory. Although our cross-modal experiments follow the same logic and general experimental procedure, our infants are not allowed to look at the initial stimulus. Instead, they are given an object to explore tactually (by mouth or by hand) rather than visually during the familiarization period. The tactual object is then removed and the infant is given the paired-comparison visual test.

For oral familiarization, the object was attached to a thin transparent filament and then placed in the infant's mouth. The experimenter held the end of the filament in one hand and cupped her other hand over the infant's upper lip, thereby shielding the object from the infant's view and touch. Infants tended to explore the object actively with their lips and tongue. For tactual (manual) presentation, the object was placed in one of the infant's hands (right and left counterbalanced). The experimenter shielded the object from the infant's view by cupping both her hands around his. Most infants tended to actively explore the object; however, if they did not spontaneously palpate it, the experimenter moved the object a half or quarter turn every 10–15 sec. (Because we have used the term *tactual* in much of our published work, we continue its use here, although the infant's palpation of the object is more aptly characterized as haptic, given its active nature and the attendant kinesthetic and proprioceptive feedback.)

Six-Month-Olds

Three experiments were conducted using 6-month-olds (Rose, Gottfried, & Bridger, 1981b). In each, there were three tasks, one of oral–visual transfer, in which the shapes used were a small sphere and cube, and two of tactual–visual transfer: One used a red cross and tapered ellipsoid, the other used two pink cylinders, one of which was incised with curved indentations. Each task began with a 30-sec familiarization period, during which the infant orally or manually explored one object. The object was then carefully removed, without the infant seeing it, and the infant was given the paired-comparison visual test. In the test, both members of the pair were presented, one matching the original stimulus and one novel. Presentation consisted of two 10-sec test trials, with the left–right position of the novel and familiar reversed for the second test trial.

In the first experiment, the 6-month-olds failed to show differential fixation on any of the three tasks: The mean percent of total fixation time to the novel shape was 49.8% for the oral–visual task, and 52.2% and 48.9% for the two tactual–visual tasks. None of these values differed significantly from the chance level of 50%. This failure was surprising, because all three tasks were identical to those that had evoked a differential preference for the novel stimulus in 1-year-olds (Gottfried, Rose, & Bridger, 1977).

Before concluding that this type of cross-modal functioning was nonexistent at the earlier age, we considered the possibility that developmental differences in the speed of processing information may be important, and that the younger infants were hampered because they processed information more slowly than did older infants.

Assuming that 30 sec was not sufficient for adequate tactual and oral exploration, we doubled these times—allowing 60 sec familiarization for each problem. This increase was sufficient for 6-month-olds to show the cross-modal effect on both tactual–visual problems, with the mean percent of total fixation to the novel stimulus being 55.2% and 57.3% (p values < .05). Thus, it appears that the younger infants were able to discriminate the stimuli visually and tactually, to store and retrieve from storage the initial tactual information, and to associate the information from the two modalities. They were, however, slower than 1-year-olds in acquiring information, and this had hampered their performance in the first experiment.

Even with the increased familiarization time in Experiment 2 there was still no evidence of oral–visual transfer (mean percent of total fixation time to the novel was 49.1%). Failure in this oral–visual task cannot be attributed to the object's small size. When these same objects were used in a task of visual recognition memory, where infants simply looked at one member of the pair for 30 sec before the test phase, they showed a significant novelty response on test, spending an average of 56.3% of the time looking at the novel test object ($p < .05$). Although it is unclear why the cross-modal effect was not found in the oral–visual task, cross-modal effects were clearly shown on both tasks involving manual exploration. (It should be kept in mind that, because the stimuli used in the oral and tactual tasks differed, these findings are not relevant to any consideration of the relative superiority of tactual over oral transfer.)

Overall then, a major difference between 6-month-olds and 1-year-olds seems to be the slower processing of younger infants. Using the same stimuli the younger infants required longer familiarization to achieve success on both tactual–visual tasks, and failed to achieve it at all on the oral–visual task. Thus, we concluded that cross-modal transfer is less robust at 6 months. This slower rate of information processing, as reflected in the need for longer familiarization time, seems to be a basic characteristic of development, one which we have repeatedly observed in our studies of visual recognition memory and multimodal processing (Rose, 1983; Rose, Gottfried, & Bridger, 1979; Rose, Gottfried, Melloy-Carminar, & Bridger, 1982).

One-Year-Olds

In the parallel cross-modal study with 1-year-olds (Gottfried et al., 1977), infants were given the same three T-V tasks. Each task consisted of a 30-sec familiarization period, during which the infant mouthed or handled one member of a pair, followed by a visual test in which both members of the pair were presented together for two 10-sec test trials. Here, each trial concluded with a reaching test, during which the infant was permitted to pick up one member of the pair. At this older age, the infants spent a greater proportion of time looking at the novel object in all three tasks: They had a mean novelty response of 62.7% after exploring the object orally, and novelty scores of 56.0% and 57.4% after tactual exploration. The percentages of reaches to the novel were similarly high in all tasks: 76.9%, 68.0%, and 66.6%, respectively. By 1 year, then, infants evidenced cross-modal transfer by looking significantly more at the novel on all three problems and by reaching significantly more often for it as well.

Risk

There is a large body of literature showing that cross-modal skills are related to school performance (e.g., Birch & Belmont, 1964) and social class (Connors, Schuette, & Goldman, 1967), and that they are deficient in various clinical populations of older children and adults, including those with mental retardation, brain-damage, and learning disability (see Friedes, 1974, for a review). Cross-modal difficulties, when they occur, have generally been attributed to cortical damage or to a delay in the development of the requisite mediating mechanisms.

Using the same three tasks used in the two studies discussed above, we assessed cross-modal transfer in a group of infants thought to be at risk because of biological and/or social factors (Rose, Gottfried, & Bridger, 1978). The sample included a group of 1-year-olds who had been born prematurely (at birth, their gestational age averaged 32.6 weeks, their weight 1650 g), and another who, although born at term, were being raised in disadvantaged backgrounds. These two target populations were selected because there is ample evidence showing that both are at risk for lags or deficits in cognitive development during the preschool and school (e.g., Klein, Hack, & Breslau, 1989). All tasks commenced with a 30-sec familiarization, after which the oral or tactual object was removed and the infant was presented with the paired visual stimuli.

Both groups showed cross-modal deficits. In fact, neither showed any differential looking in the test phase of either of the three tasks—that is, mean percent fixations to the novel did not depart significantly from chance (50%). Also, unlike the middle-class infants, who consistently reached for the novel in all three tasks, the reaching response of both risk groups was inconsistent.

These results showed that, whereas middle-class 1-year-old infants gain knowledge about the shape of an object by feeling it and mouthing it and can make this information available to the visual sense, at-risk infants have difficulty doing so. The findings suggest that infant cross-modal transfer may be a particularly sensitive index of cognitive impairment, and knowledge of its development may be important in characterizing the nature and ontogeny of cognition.

Infant Monkeys

We recently replicated two of our findings with infant monkeys (Gunderson et al., 1990). First, using the same paradigm for tactual–visual transfer we had used in human infancy research, we found evidence of this ability in monkeys whose level of biologic maturation was considered comparable to that of 1-year-old human infants. Second, we showed that these abilities in infant monkeys, like that of the human infant, were impaired in those at biologic risk. These results emerged in examining the cross-modal effect in 27 infant pigtail macaque monkeys, 12 of whom were at low risk for future cognitive deficits, and 15 of whom were at high risk, due to either low birthweight ($n = 5$), failure-to-thrive ($n = 1$), birth trauma ($n = 4$), or prenatal ethanol exposure ($n = 5$).

The infant monkeys were tested on three tactual–visual problems, using the same familiarization and test times we used with 1-year-olds (30 and 20 sec, respectively) as well as similar stimuli. The mean postnatal age of the low-risk monkeys was 13.5 weeks. Because the ratio between pigtail macaques and human infants in perceptual development appears to be approximately 4 : 1 it was anticipated that the monkeys' performance would be similar to that of the 1-year-old human infants.

The low-risk group of monkeys showed a significant novelty response (58.2%) whereas the high-risk group did not. The performance of both groups closely paralleled that of their human counterparts: As noted earlier, the magnitude of the novelty score exhibited by low risk human infants was 58.7% whereas that of the high-risk human infants did not differ from chance. Additionally, as in human infants, monkeys' transfer was based on the discriminability of the outer contour of the test objects.

The similarities in human and monkey performance suggest (a) that the ontogeny of these abilities may be similar in both species and (b) that the processes underlying normal and aberrant development also share cross-species similarity. Such similarities may allow for the development of a primate model of mental retardation.

Cross-Modal (T-V) and Visual Intramodal (V-V)
Comparisons: Recognizing Abstraction

The age difference we found had suggested that infants find cross-modal tasks more difficult than intramodal visual tasks. In the next study, we directly assessed whether this was the case and also sought to learn more about the nature of the information picked up visually and tactually. We assumed that difference in the outer contour of the shapes was the key distinguishing feature between members of a pair, but we were not certain how abstract this representation of object structure could be and the object still be recognized.

In this study (Rose, Gottfried, & Bridger, 1983), 1-year-old infants were allowed to look at or feel an object and then were presented with visual choices that consisted of the objects themselves, silhouette pictures of them, or line drawings of them. One choice matched the original stimulus in shape, and the other was novel. These test stimuli were selected to reflect different degrees of pictorial abstractness, with the outline drawings considered more abstract than the pictures.

In the first experiment, one group of infants was given 30 sec of visual familiarization with an object before the visual test (V-V), whereas a second group was given 30 sec of tactual familiarization before the visual test (T-V). Infants showed V-V transfer to all three types of test displays (objects, picures, and line drawings) with average novelty scores ranging from 57.2% to 63.1%, but showed T-V transfer only when the test stimuli were objects (55.7%). When the visual test choices were pictures or line drawings of the objects, T-V transfer was chance (47.7%).

A second experiment suggested that infants need to feel the object longer before they could recognize its contour in a pictorial display. Here, where the tactual familiarization time was increased from 30 to 45 sec, T-V transfer was successful in all three conditions (novelty scores for visual tests with objects, pictures, and line drawings averaged 58.2%, 55.9%, and 57.5%, respectively).

The results of a third experiment lent support to the idea that recognition on the basis of pictorial contour alone is relatively difficult, even visually. When visual familiarization was reduced to 15 sec, V-V transfer was successful when the test stimuli were objects (56.2%) but not when the test stimuli were pictures or line drawings (51.5% and 47.5%, respectively).

These results support the ideas that:

1. Lengthier inspection is needed to pick up information tactually than visually.

2. Lengthier inspection is needed in both modalities to recognize pictures and line drawings than to recognize objects.

3. Given sufficient inspection time, quite abstract representations of structure can be detected (see also Rose, 1986).

It should be pointed out that infants of this age are not confusing the object with its representations. Quite the contrary, they recognize the relation between the two while at the same time appreciating their differences (Rose, 1977). The evidence clearly indicates that the infants are using the object's contour to judge cross-modal equivalences in structure.

VISUAL–TACTUAL CROSS-MODAL TRANSFER

Tactual Recognition Memory

In order to assess cross-modal transfer in the reverse direction, from vision to touch, we had to be able to assess tactual recognition memory. We developed a technique to do this, videotaping 1-year-olds' manipulation of novel and familiar objects in total darkness, under infrared light. In the first study using this procedure (Gottfried & Rose, 1980), we assessed tactual recognition after bimodal exploration in which the infant gained tactual and visual information simultaneously. First, the infant was given five identical objects to manipulate and visually inspect for 60 sec. Then, the room lights were extinguished and the five original objects were presented again, along with five replicas of a novel object, for a 2-min tactual test. Some infants were tested with star- and disc-shaped objects, others with hexagonal and hourglass shapes. With both sets, infants spent more of the time in the darkened room engaged in activity with the novel than with the familiar objects: more manipulation (64.1%), mouthing (61.1%), and hand-to-hand transfers. Their differential responsiveness to the novel stimuli indicated that they could discriminate the objects tactually, and recognize the original stimuli by touch alone.

Cross-Modal (V-T) and Tactual Intramodal (T-T) Comparisons

We next used this measure of tactual recognition to compare tactual (T-T) intramodal performance with visual–tactual (V-T) cross-modal performance in 1-year-olds (Rose, Gottfried, & Bridger, 1981a). The initial familiarization, which was tactual in one case and visual in the other, lasted for either 30 or 60 sec; the test phase, which was always tactual, lasted for 2 min. This time, all tactual exploration, whether during familiarization or test, was carried out in total darkness and videotaped, using infrared light.

With 60 sec of familiarization, infants differentiated the novel from familiar objects in both conditions, V-T and T-T. In both cases, they spent significantly more time manipulating novel shapes on the tactual test, and this difference was even more pronounced in T-T than V-T (65.7% vs. 57.9%, respectively). With less exploration (30 sec familiarization) performance did not exceed chance in either condition. The finding of successful T-T transfer with 60 sec of familiarization was confirmed in a second experiment using different stimuli and a modified procedure that more closely approximated the paired-comparison design we had used in visual work. In this second experiment, V-T transfer was chance.

These results show that infants are able to recognize shape exclusively on the basis of tactual cues after having previously viewed them (V-T) or felt them (T-T), although performance was better in the tactual intramodal condition.

ASYMMETRIES IN CROSS-MODAL TRANSFER

In order to further explore the relationship of cross-modal to intramodal functioning, we recently carried out a study that included the entire set of four conditions necessary for a "complete" design, namely, the two cross-modal conditions (T-V, V-T) and their two intramodal controls (V-V, T-T). In juxtaposing results from several earlier studies, there had been indications of cross-modal asymmetries, with T-V easier than V-T, but because these conditions were investigated in different studies, and often with somewhat different stimuli and procedures, no firm conclusions could be drawn.

In the present study (Rose & Orlian, 1991), each 1-year-old received four problems: two with visual familiarization, two with tactual familiarization. After visual familiarization, they were tested either for visual recognition (V-V) or V-T cross-modal transfer; after tactual familiarization they were tested either for tactual recognition (T-T) or T-V cross-modal transfer. There were three groups of children, with groups differing in terms of whether they received 15, 30, or 60 sec of familiarization.

The results indicated that the V-V condition was easiest. Infants showed visual recognition after all three familiarization times, even the shortest used (15 sec). The T-T and T-V conditions were of intermediate difficulty, with infants showing recognition memory in both after 30 and 60 sec of familiarization. For the most part, infants failed to show any evidence of V-T transfer at all. The difficulty of the four conditions was as follows (with > indicating easier than): V-V > T-T = T-V > V-T. The superiority of T-T over V-T was also reflected in the differential use of exploratory behaviors, with more grasping and fingering of the novel object in the T-T condition, but not in the V-T condition.

This ordering has several implications for the basis and limits of transfer. First, differences between the two intramodal conditions appear to be primarily due to rate-related factors (Rose et al., 1983), with the eye processing information faster than the hand (a well-established finding with older children). Second, the greater difficulty of V-T transfer, compared to either type of intramodal transfer, suggests that this cross-modal failure is due to difficulty in recognizing equivalences across modalities, and not, as is sometimes the case, to difficulties in intramodal processing. Third, the asymmetry in cross-modal transfer (T-V > V-T) suggests that the eye and hand may pick up different object characteristics, rather than directly pick up the same invariants or amodal properties (but see Rose & Orlian, 1991, for a discussion of methodological factors that could have been implicated in this asymmetry).

TOWARD SPECIFYING THE BASIS OF CROSS-MODAL PERCEPTION OF SHAPE

Stimulus Properties

Relatively little attention has been given to identifying the actual stimulus properties and contrasts that can be perceived cross-modally—or to tracing developmental changes in such perception. Two characteristics of studies stand out in this regard. First, many studies use but one or two pairs of objects and are thus of limited generalizability. For example, Ruff and Kohler (1978) used a cube and sphere; Meltzoff and Borton (1979), a sphere and a sphere-with-nubs; Bryant, Jones, Claxton, and Perkins (1972), a sphere and a sphere-with-indentations for one group and a cube and a cube-with-indentations for another group. Although some studies have, like many of ours, used greater numbers of pairs (Brown & Gottfried, 1986; Wagner & Sakovits, 1986), pairings have generally not been selected with a view toward systematically searching for the basis for the infant's response.

Second, if one examines the pairings that are used in various studies, it becomes clear that they usually differ in global ways—rounded versus angled, smooth versus notched. Although investigators have generally not assessed which of such global features are most easily differentiated, Bushnell and Weinberger's (1987) study of 11-month-old infants' detection of visual–tactual discrepancies is a notable exception. Unlike the studies discussed so far, where information must first be gathered in one modality and then used in another, in Bushnell's paradigm, objects are presented simultaneously to vision and touch and discrepancies are created with a mirror arrangement. In such discrepancies, the infants see one object but feel another, and their behavioral reactions on such trials are compared with their reactions on matched control trials, where the same object is both seen and felt. The results indicate that infants more readily discriminate a rectilinear from a curved shape (cube vs. sphere) than they discriminate two rectilinear forms from one another (cube vs. cross), although the relative difficulty of the latter depends on which is seen and which is felt. Rectilinear forms were relatively difficult to differentiate cross-modally even when they differed in texture (smooth vs. furry cube), although here again, the relative ease was affected by which object was seen and which was felt.

These findings indicate that infants are sensitive to differences involving curves, angles, and edges, but apparently have more difficulty if the test objects consist of all straight edges. Data from two other studies support these findings. First, Bryant et al. (1972) found cross-modal matching in 8-month-olds when the test consisted of a sphere and a sphere with angled indentations, but not when it consisted of a cube and a cube with angled indentations. Second, in the study of Gunderson et al. (1990) discussed earlier, the low-risk monkeys exhibited T-V transfer for only two of the three pairs of stimuli used. When adults were asked to rank order the pairs in terms of the discriminability of their members, they overwhelmingly ranked as most difficult the pair the monkeys failed. Whereas the outer contours of objects in the other two pairs differed quite obviously from one another, adults described the more difficult pair as being "all edges."

Further studies are needed to determine whether the infants extract information specifying a configural whole from their tactual exploration, or simply glean some rather general information as to the rectilinearity or curvilinearity of an object's contour. There is evidence to suggest that visually presented information about contour can be used to specify the object's complete shape. Rose (1988) found that 1-year-olds recognized shapes after having seen their contour traced out by a moving point source of light. They had to integrate the information over space and time to do so. Infants recognized the shape even when it took up to 10 sec to complete a single tracing, a time frame that rules out purely retinal mechanisms and implicates central ones. Thus, by 1 year of age, we find evidence, at least visually, that infants can store successive bits of information about contour, and integrate that information into some sort of perceptual schema or figural whole. Whether they can do the same tactually is not yet known.

In order to understand better the asymmetries in cross-modal matching noted earlier, it will be necessary to determine:

1. The limits and extent to which the information gleaned tactually and visually is processed and stored in a similar manner (e.g., as a configuration or simply as a collection of local features).
2. The dimensions along which discriminations can be made in both modalities.
3. The extent to which the accuracy of matching is affected by the modality in which the standard is presented.

Exploratory Strategies

To understand the basis for cross-modal transfer, as well as asymmetries and failures in transfer, it would also seem important to examine the infant's tactual exploration of objects. To my knowledge, there are only three studies that have looked at this factor in any detail.

In one, our study of cross-modal asymmetries (Rose & Orlian, 1991), we videotaped infants' manipulatory behavior of novel and familiar objects during tactual test periods. Three broad categories of manipulation were analyzed: fingering, grasping, and touching. (Several fine-grained variants of these behaviors were distinguished, but because they occurred rarely, they were grouped with the three major variants.)

The specific manipulatory behaviors engaged in with objects changed with increasing familiarity. After 15 sec of tactual familiarization, there was no differential manipulation whatsoever on test; after 30 sec, infants engaged in significantly more grasping of the novel than the familiar stimuli, and after 60 sec, they engaged in more fingering as well as more grasping of the novel stimuli. Thus, infants' increasing recognition of objects in T-T conditions was reflected in their differential use of specific tactual exploratory strategies with novel and familiar stimuli. There was no evidence of differential use of these particular manipulatory strategies in the test phase of V-T conditions, although there was some evidence of differential use of a strategy we dubbed "exclusive touch." This is a measure of the duration of touching one object while not touching the other, a mode of exploration we thought captured particularly focused attention. With this measure, we uncovered differential effects that were otherwise obscured.

Bushnell and Weinberger (1987) distinguished several other types of manual behavior. For those trials where one object was seen yet a different one was available to touch (discrepancy trials), visually distinctive features were found to be more compelling than tactually distinctive ones. So, for example, when infants saw a furry cube but felt a smooth wooden one, they exhibited greater poking, gripping, digging, etc. than when they (a) saw and felt the same object or (b) saw the smooth wooden cube but felt the distinctive furry one. Finally, Gibson and Walker (1984) found evidence for differential use of exploratory strategies by 1-month-olds in their cross-modal perception of rigid versus flexible substances—rigid shapes were stroked, flexible ones poked.

MUDDLED DISTINCTIONS

On the Nature of Cross-Modal Correspondences

As the reader of this volume has no doubt observed, the types of studies referred to under the rubric *cross-modal* cut a wide swath. Although our own work has dealt with aspects of object identity, in which the different senses inform about the *same* referent, this type of cross-modal transfer can and should be distinguished from at least two other broad types—those where the cross-modal matches detected are based on common (or similar) properties shared by different objects or events, and those where they are based on arbitrary properties, whether from the same or different referents. Such distinctions are important not only because they will lead to better typologies, and hence to clearer distinctions about the nature of the phenomena involved, but also because the underlying mechanisms are no doubt quite different.

Arbitrary Associations. The most extensive work in this area has been done with animals, particularly by Spear and his colleagues (for summary, see Spear & Molina, 1987, and Spear & McKenzie, chap. 7, this volume). In their studies with preweanling rats they found that transfer of conditioning between modalities occurs quite readily in the very young. These findings are important because this sort of transfer is not characteristic of adulthood. Their results come from experiments in which the animals are first conditioned within one sensory modality by, for example, pairing an odorant (the conditioned stimulus, or CS) with footshock (the unconditioned stimulus, or US). A few such pairings are sufficient to condition a moderate level of aversion. Next, the animals are given a subthreshold level of conditioning using a different CS, so, for example, a black compartment is now paired with the footshock, but only for a single trial. This latter conditioning is termed subthreshold because ordinarily no aversion to the black compartment would be expressed to such a pairing, either by infant or adult rats. However, when the olfactory conditioning precedes the subthreshold visual conditioning, infant rats (but not adult ones) now show a strong aversion to the black compartment—"transferring" between modalities. Similar results were found for olfactory–tactual, visual–gustatory, and tactual–gustatory pairings.

Because of the developmental shifts found between infancy and adulthood, these results raise the possibility that the young organisms who show "cross-modal transfer" may do so because they actually fail to differentiate input from different modalities and not because they recognize some similarity or equivalence in the face of successful differentiation (see also Turkewitz, Gardner, & Lewkowicz, 1984, and Lewkowicz, 1991, who express a similar view about the human infant).

However, two things must be kept in mind about these intriguing findings. First, it is not clear that young organisms really do fail to make the modality distinctions involved. Although their responses may be governed by other factors, such as overall amount of stimulation, they may nonetheless make the modality-specific distinctions perfectly well. Second, whether cross-modal transfer did or did not occur, it must be kept in mind that these cross-modal pairings are arbitrary. As such, they may be more important in understanding issues central to early learning than to understanding the development of those correspondences that have traditionally been the domain of concern to cross-modal transfer, namely, those based on nonarbitrary commonalities.

Common Properties. Here the concern is with those similarities or commonalities that are perceived among certain features *common to different referents*. The properties often selected for study are quantitative ones—such as intensity, duration, extent (size)—dimensions that seem to possess a unitary and well-ordered psychophysics and where the intermodal instantiations may share a common psychophysiology (Stevens, 1957). Such quantitative properties are sometimes spoken of as *amodal* or *supramodal* because they cut across, transcend, or are separable from the specific modality of sensory input. Thus, for example, when asked to match pitch to brightness, adults generally line up low-pitched sounds with dim lights and high-pitched sounds with bright lights (see Marks, Hammeal, & Bornstein, 1987). The clearest correspondences are those where the dimensions represent a continuum marked by a polar structure: One pole is positive, with movement toward it representing the direction of increase, and the other pole is negative, with movement toward that pole representing the direction of decrease (Smith & Sera, 1992).

In a recent study, Marks et al. (1987) included children as young as 4 years in an assessment of the understanding of three polar correspondences: pitch–brightness, loudness–brightness, and pitch–size. Children of all ages, like adults, spontaneously matched soft or low-pitched sounds with dim or dark colors, and loud or high-pitched sounds with bright or light colors, but pitch–size relations were not appreciated until about age 11. These results led the authors to suggest that whereas some relations may be based on common sensory codes, others (such as pitch–size) may depend on the linguistic structure of the words used to talk about them.

Smith and Sera (1992), in a study that used different correspondences, and children aged 2–5 years, also found results that could not be explained entirely by positing a common sensory structure. These investigators looked at size–loudness, size–darkness, and darkness–loudness correspondences. Although size–loudness relations showed an invariant and unidirectional development that was virtually complete by age 4 (big-loud/little-quiet), these particular correspondences were not appreciated in children as young as 2 years, and others actually reversed polarity over this age range. To the extent these cross-modal correspondences are thought to rest entirely on a common perceptual code, it is puzzling that such structures are not yet in place by 2 years.

Although the cross-modal appreciation of polar correspondences has rarely been studied in infancy (see Wagner, Winner, Cicchetti, & Gardner, 1981, for a notable exception), infants have achieved other cross-modal matches that appear to be based on common perceptual or sensory codes. For example, infants have shown cross-modal matching of auditory and visual information specifying intensity, rhythm, tempo and the structure common to speech production and facial patterns of movement (for a review, see Rose & Ruff, 1987). Such matches are revealed through nonverbal techniques, using habituation/dishabituation or preference designs. It remains unclear whether polar correspondences are inherently more difficult to appreciate cross-modally, or whether assessment of such competence is hampered because of young children's difficulty in understanding or complying with the verbal instructions used to convey the task requirements.

Identity. This type of cross-modal correspondence, the one with which our own work has been concerned, is where the input received in different modalities specifies a single referent—a single object or event. It is that sort of transfer that allows us to identify a puppy as such by either seeing, feeling, or hearing it. It is that sort of transfer that also allows for the realization that the touch, sight, or bouncing sound identifies a ball. In such cases, the information, whether perceived visually, tactually, or auditorially, allows for recognition of a single, unique object. This level of cross-modal coordination may be the highest, because experience in one modality leads directly to expectations about what will be experienced through other modalities, and because the integration of such experiences is central to the appreciation of object identity and undergirds the very perception of a unified object.

One way the senses identify an object is to extract common information. In our own work, we found that information about contour is extracted from objects seen and felt (Gunderson et al., 1990; Rose et al., 1983). Bushnell and Weinberger's (1987) work showed that vision sometimes plays a directive role in exactly what features are attended to. Streri and Spelke (1988, 1989) argued that cross-modal detection of the common motion of surfaces is used to specify object unity: Whether seen or felt, these patterns of motion share common properties that specify a single, unique object. Further work is needed both to identify more fully the types of information extracted, the means by which such extraction precedes, and the developmental course infants follow in coming to perceive object unity from information presented to different modalities.

On the Origins of Cross-Modal Correspondences

Three major views have been put forward to explain the origin of cross-modal correspondence. They suggest that such correspondences are achieved (a) by default, because of an actual lack of differentiation among the senses, (b) through direct perception, or (c) through intermodal mappings built up by experience or achieved by language.

Lack of Differentiation. The idea that cross-modal matching results from a failure to differentiate—or through an initial unity of the senses—was expressed by Bower (1974). He suggested that the newborn infant is born with systems undifferentiated so that the infant does not "know" whether he is seeing or hearing, or feeling something: He simply responds to the object or event. The same phenomenal aspects of stimulation are initially perceived regardless of modality, not because invariants are extracted but rather because the modalities themselves are not differentiated. Turkewitz et al. (1984) and Spear and Molina (1987) proposed variants of this view.

Direct Perception. The view that identity is directly perceived is perhaps best associated with James Gibson (1966) and Eleanor Gibson (1969). They contended that the same information is directly picked up by the different senses without any prior coordinated experience, matching, or transfer being required. Because the invariants are revealed through movements of the object and/or observer, the modality detecting them is irrelevant. Development basically consists of the progressive differentiation of distinctive features; these features are then available to different modalities without any prior coordinated experience. In other words, *identical* properties are picked up by different sense systems and, despite the enormous difference in the nature of the sensory inputs, are perceived in some unified fashion. Whereas many other investigators have suggested that some quantitative dimensions are directly picked up cross-modally, unlike the Gibson's, they do not contend that such direct pick-up is characteristic of all cross-modal correspondences. So, for example, Turkewitz and Mellon (1989) proposed that whereas quantitative amodal properties are likely to be mediated directly by low-level, common neural processes, equivalences of form and rhythm are dependent on more elaborate psychological processes. Stevens (1957) also believed that the direct perception of cross-modal correspondences was restricted to quantitative dimensions, which he thought might possess a common sensory physiology.

Intermodal Mappings. The supposition that the senses become connected through experience is strongly associated with the legacy of the British empiricists. According to this view, equivalences must be achieved by the imposition of a mediating process, which is attached to the sensations in both modalities and which serves to bridge the gap that exists between modalities. Such mediation could be in the form of a common physiological bedrock that is shared by modalities, a cortical area that is the common way station for input from different modalities, a perceptual link or code that may develop either through experience with cross-modal relations in the world, or through experiences common in the language. The major issue confronting this view is how a unique pattern of stimulation in one modality comes to be regarded as equivalent to a unique pattern in a second modality. This is especially problematic because of the ways the modalities differ in what is perceived and how information is stored, and because the nature of the mapping may differ for different types of cross-modal linkages.

Toward a Synthesis. Issues about the origins of cross-modal correspondences have often been of greater concern to philosophers than to psychologists. To move ahead in this field, the range and variety of cross-modal relations must first be identified, their development better understood, and their underlying mechanisms explored. Smith and Sera (1992) suggested that cross-modal appreciation probably involves the interaction of many factors. To explain their own findings on polar structure, they called on the structure of sensory systems, cross-dimension relations in languages, and cross-dimension relations in the world. They urged investigators to take a dynamic systems approach to these issues. This is a useful suggestion, because converging forces probably shape the appreciation of most cross-modal correspondences.

REFERENCES

Birch, H. G., & Belmont, L. (1964). Auditory-visual integration in normal and retarded readers. *American Journal of Orthopsychiatry, 34*, 852–861.

Birch, H. G., & Lefford, A. (1967). Visual differentiation, intersensory integration and voluntary motor control. *Monographs of the Society for Research in Child Development, 32* (2, Serial No. 110).

Bower, T. G. R. (1974). The evolution of sensory systems. In R. B. MacLeod & H. L. Pick, Jr. (Eds.), *Perception: Essays in honor of James J. Gibson* (pp. 141–165). Ithaca, NY: Cornell University Press.

Bower, T. G. R., Broughton, J. M., & Moore, M. K. (1970). The coordination of visual and tactual inputs in infants. *Perception and Psychophics, 8*, 51–53.

Brown, K. W., & Gottfried, A. W. (1986). Cross-modal transfer of shape in early infancy: Is there reliable evidence? In L. P. Lipsitt & C. Rovee-Collier (Eds.). *Advances in infancy research* (Vol. 4, pp. 163–170). Norwood, NJ: Ablex.

Bryant, P. E., Jones, P., Claxton, V., & Perkins, G. M. (1972). Recognition of shapes across modalities by infants. *Nature, 240*, 303–304.

Bushnell, E. W., & Weinberger, N. (1987). Infants' detection of visual-tactual discrepancies: Asymmetries that indicate a directive role of visual information. *Journal of Experimental Psychology: Human Perception and Performance, 13*, 601–608.

Connors, C. K., Schuette, C., & Goldman, A. (1967). Informational analyses of intersensory communication in children of different social class. *Child Development, 38*, 251–266.

Davenport, R. K., Rogers, C. M., & Russell, I. S. (1975). Cross-modal perception in apes: Altered visual cues and delay. *Neuropsychologia, 13*, 229–235.

Ettlinger, G. (1967). Analysis of cross-modal effects and their relationship to language. In F. L. Darley & C. H. Millikan (Eds.), *Brain mechanisms underlying speech and language* (pp. 53–60). New York: Grune & Stratton.

Fagan, J. F. (1974). Infant recognition memory: The effects of length of familiarization and type of discrimination task. *Child Development, 45*, 351–356.

Friedes, D. (1974). Human information processing and sensory modality: Cross-modal functions, information complexity, memory and deficit. *Psychological Bulletin, 81*, 284–310.

Geschwind, N. (1965). Disconnexion syndromes in animals and man. *Brain, 88*, 237–294.

Gibson, E. J. (1969). *Principles of perceptual learning and development.* New York: Appleton-Century Crofts.

Gibson, E. J., & Walker, A. S. (1984). Development of knowledge of visual-tactual affordances of substance. *Child Development, 55*, 453–460.

Gibson, J. J. (1966). *The senses considered as perceptual systems.* Boston: Houghton-Mifflin.

Gottfried, A. W., & Rose, S. A. (1980). Tactual recognition memory in infants. *Child Development, 51*, 69–74.

Gottfried, A. W., Rose, S. A., & Bridger, W. H. (1977). Cross-modal transfer in human infants. *Child Development, 48*, 118–123.

Gunderson, V. M., Rose, S. A., & Grant-Webster, K. S. (1990). Cross-modal transfer in high- and low-risk infant pigtailed macaque monkeys. *Developmental Psychology, 26*, 576–581.

Klein, N. K., Hack, M., & Breslau, N. (1989). Children who were very low birth weight: Developmental and academic achievement at nine years of age. *Journal of Developmental and Behavioral Pediatrics, 10*, 32–37.

Lewkowicz, D. J. (1991). Development of intersensory functions in human infancy: Auditory/visual interactions. In M. J. Weiss & P. R. Zelazo (Eds.), *Newborn attention: Biological constraints and the influence of experience* (pp. 308–338). Norwood, NJ: Ablex.

Marks, L. E. (1978). *The unity of the senses: Interrelations among the modalities.* New York: Academic Press.

Marks, L. E., Hammeal, R. J., & Bornstein, M. H. (1987). Perceiving similarity and comprehending metaphor. *Monographs of the Society for Research in Child Development, 52,* 1 (Serial No. 215).

Meltzoff, A. N., & Borton, R. W. (1979). Intermodal matching by human neonates. *Nature, 282,* 403–404.

Murray, A., & Mishkin, M. (1985). Amygdalectomy impairs cross-modal association in monkeys. *Science, 228,* 604–606.

Rose, S. A. (1977). Infants' transfer of response between two dimensional and three dimensional stimuli. *Child Development, 48,* 1086–1091.

Rose, S. A. (1983). Differential rates of visual information processing in full-term and preterm infants. *Child Development, 54,* 1189–1198.

Rose, S. A. (1986). Abstraction in infancy: Evidence from cross-modal and cross-dimension transfer. In L. P. Lipsitt & C. Rovee-Collier (Eds.), *Advances in infancy research* (Vol. 4, pp. 218–229). Norwood, NJ: Ablex.

Rose, S. A. (1988). Shape recognition in infancy: Visual integration of sequential information. *Child Development, 59,* 1161–1176.

Rose, S. A., Gottfried, A. W., & Bridger, W. H. (1978). Cross-modal transfer in infants: Relationship to prematurity and socio-economic background. *Developmental Psychology, 14,* 643–652.

Rose, S. A., Gottfried, A. W., & Bridger, W. H. (1979). Effects of haptic cues on visual recognition memory in fullterms and preterms. *Infant Behavior and Development, 2,* 55–67.

Rose, S. A., Gottfried, A. W., & Bridger, W. H. (1981a). Cross-modal transfer and information processing by the sense of touch in infancy. *Developmental Psychology, 17,* 90–98.

Rose, S. A., Gottfried, A. W., & Bridger, W. H. (1981b). Cross-modal transfer in 6-month-old infants. *Developmental Psychology, 17,* 661–669.

Rose, S. A., Gottfried, A. W., & Bridger, W. H. (1983). Infant's cross-modal transfer from solid objects to their graphic representations. *Child Development, 54,* 686–694.

Rose, S. A., Gottfried, A. W., Melloy-Carminar, P., & Bridger, W. H. (1982). Familiarity and novelty preferences in infant recognition memory: Implications for information processing. *Developmental Psychology, 18,* 704–713.

Rose, S. A., & Orlian, E. K. (1991). Asymmetries in infant cross-modal transfer. *Child Development, 62,* 706–718.

Rose, S. A., & Ruff, H. A. (1987). Cross-modal abilities in human infants. In J. Osofsky (Ed.), *Handbook of infant development* (2nd ed., pp. 318–362). New York: Wiley.

Ruff, H. A., & Kohler, C. J. (1978). Tactual-visual transfer in six-month-old infants. *Infant Behavior & Development, 1,* 259–264.

Smith, L. B. (1987). Perceptual relations and perceptual language. Commentary. In L. E. Marks, R. J. Hammeal, & M. H. Bornstein, Perceiving similarity and comprehending metaphor. *Monographs of the Society for Research in Child Development, 52,* 1, Serial No. 215.

Smith, L. B., & Sera, M. D. (1992). A developmental analysis of the polar structure of dimensions. *Cognitive Psychology, 24,* 99–142.

Spear, N. E., & Molina, J. C. (1987). The role of sensory modality in the ontogeny of stimulus selection. In N. A. Krasegnor, E. M. Blass, M. A. Hofer, & W. P. Smotherman (Eds.), *Perinatal development: A psychobiological perspective* (pp. 83–109). Orlando, FL: Academic Press.

Streri, A., & Spelke, E. S. (1988). Haptic perception of objects in infancy. *Cognitive Psychology, 20,* 1–23.

Streri, A., & Spelke, E. S. (1989). Effects of motion and figural goodness on haptic object perception in infancy. *Child Development, 60,* 1111–1125.

Stevens, S. S. (1957). On the psychophysical law. *Psychological Review, 64,* 153–181.

Turkewitz, G., & Mellon, R. C. (1989). Dynamic organization of intersensory function. *Canadian Journal of Psychology, 43.*

Turkewitz, G., Gardner, J., & Lewkowicz, D. J. (1984). Sensory/Perceptual functioning during early infancy: The implications of a quantitative basis for responding. In G. Greenberg &

E. Tobach (Eds.), *Behavioral evolution and integrative levels*. Hillsdale, NJ: Lawrence Erlbaum Associates.

Wagner, S. H., & Sakovits, L. J. (1986). A process analysis of infant visual and cross-modal recognition memory: Implications for an amodal code. In L. P. Lipsitt & C. Rovee-Collier (Eds.), *Advances in infancy research* (Vol. 4, pp. 196–217). Norwood, NJ: Ablex.

Wagner, S., Winner, E., Cicchetti, D., & Gardner, H. (1981). "Metaphorical" mapping in human infants. *Child Development, 52,* 728–731.

CHAPTER TWELVE

Constraints on Intermodal Transfer Between Touch and Vision in Infancy

Arlette Streri
Michèle Molina
Université René Descartes–C.N.R.S.

The multimodal perception of an object is the ability to perceive different pieces of information extracted by the sensory modalities in a unified way. This makes it possible for us to perceive objects as unitary and stable entities in time and space. This ability is remarkable because the amodal properties of objects such as shape and texture are specified in strikingly different ways in the tactual and visual modalities. What are the developmental origins of the capacity to perceive amodal properties of objects through touch and vision?

Research with infants has typically used an intermodal transfer matching technique with a paired comparison method. Generally, the experiment consists of two phases, an initial familiarization phase where infants are allowed limited exploration of an object in the first modality, followed by a test phase in the second modality. This method is a complex one, and infants are called on to process information in several steps. In step 1, information is extracted and processed in the first modality. In step 2, this information is stored and a representation is created. Then, in step 3, new information is processed in the second modality and compared against the information from the first modality. Recognition results from the comparison of the two forms of information or the two forms of representation.

Intermodal transfer from touch to vision has been reported in infants from the age of 6 months on (Rose, Gottfried, & Bridger, 1981a; Ruff & Kohler, 1978; see Rose & Ruff, 1987, and Streri, 1991/1993, for a review). These findings suggest that there may be a central processing mechanism in infants of this age that is independent of the sensory modalities involved in the capture of information. However, these studies do not fully address the time-honored philosophical issue of the unity or separation of the sensory modalities at birth. Coordination between vision and prehension is well established in 6-month-old infants. By this age, infants reach for seen objects and transport handled objects to view. By 6 months, then, intermodal transfer might result from the infant's newly acquired ability to explore an object bimodally.

Other studies (Meltzoff & Borton, 1979; E. J. Gibson & Walker, 1984) have shown that 1-month-old infants recognize visually an object they have previously explored orally based on its texture (smooth vs. not smooth) and substance (hard or soft). Within the haptic modality, however, it is likely that the oral and the prehensile modalities present different mechanisms for the exploration of object space, despite their structural and physiological similarities. This is because the hand, aside from its perceptual function, also serves to transport objects: a property that enlarges its field of applicability (Hatwell, 1986). Thus, coordination between oral and visual exploration may be meaningful for a study of intermodal perception in very young infants but is not a functional reality for the young child. For example, Rose, Gottfried, and Bridger (1981b) did not obtain oral–visual transfer at 6 months of age but did obtain visual recognition of the shape of a felt object.

In general, young infants appear to be capable of extracting and remembering information obtained in the haptic modality (manually or orally) and then recognizing that information in the visual modality. In contrast, only a few studies have been able to demonstrate the reverse: tactual recognition of visually acquired information. Rose, Gottfried, and Bridger (1981a) reported intermodal transfer from vision to touch in a single study with 12-month-old infants. In a later study, however, Rose and Koenigsberg (1991) failed to find vision–touch transfer at the same age and using identical objects. All these studies suggest that amodal perception is possible (E. J. Gibson, 1969). However, if an amodal central processor actually exists, then transfer in either direction should be equally possible.

Our own research was designed to further investigate the proposal that a single, amodal process underlies object perception. Specifically, we wanted to examine the development of transfer both from touch to vision and from vision to touch before the emergence of eye–hand coordination. Two specific age groups were tested, 2- and 5-month-old infants. At 5 months, visually guided prehension is developing rapidly. We wanted to know whether intermodal perception of objects was possible during the onset of visually guided reaching. Our reason for testing 2-month-old infants was to determine whether intermodal perception of objects was possible prior to the onset of visually guided reaching. The neonatal reaching reflex to a visual target extinguishes at around 2 months of age, and infants at this age generally exhibit low levels of manual activity (von Hofsten, 1984). To test visual–

tactual and tactual–visual transfer, first each infant was habituated either visually or haptically with an object and then was given an intermodal test followed by an intramodal test. Discrimination in the intramodal test would indicate that a lack of intermodal transfer could not be explained by infants' inability to make intramodal discriminations.

Infants were seated in a semireclining canvas seat in a large white experimental box. During the tactual familiarization period and the tactual test, a white cloth was tied to both sides of the seat to separate the infant's tactual space from his or her visual space and to block his or her view of his or her body. The cloth left the arms free to move. Infants were familiarized with the object in either the visual or the haptic modality, and then two tests were conducted using either the same or a different object. If the infants recognized the object in the new modality, we expected the exploration time for the familiar object presented in the new modality to be shorter than that for the new object. In addition, we expected the infants to recognize the familiar object when it was presented in the first familiar modality.

Stimuli were red wooden shapes, 45 mm in diameter and 7 mm thick. For the 5-month-olds, one pair of stimuli consisted of a square and a square with a hole in the center, and the other pair consisted of a star and a flower (Streri & Pêcheux, 1986a). For the 2-month-old infants a single stimulus pair consisting of a ring and a disc was used (Streri, 1987). In the visual habituation and visual test phases, the objects were suspended on an invisible string and were in constant rotation. In the tactual habituation and test phases, the experimenter placed the object into the infant's right hand. The findings from the 2-month-olds indicated visual recognition of the shape of the felt object but no tactual recognition of the seen objects (Streri, 1987, Experiment 2). The reverse was observed for the 5-month-olds; results indicated transfer of object shape from vision to touch but not from touch to vision (Streri & Pêcheux, 1986a, Experiment 1). In both cases when recognition was evidenced, infants preferred the novel object.

This transfer asymmetry cannot be accounted for by a lack of discrimination of the objects in either of the modalities. In both modalities, infants differentiated the shapes of the two objects intramodally (Streri, 1987, Experiment 1; Streri & Pêcheux, 1986b). After either visual or tactual habituation to an object, both 2- and 5-month-olds held or looked longer at a new object than the one with which they had been familiarized. The observed intermodal transfer asymmetry, then, raises questions about the nature of the information that is being transferred from one modality to the other at 2 and 5 months and the nature of the optimal conditions for two-way transfer.

One possibility is that beyond the functional analogies of these two systems, the specialization of each modality constrains information transfer. Studies (Hatwell, 1986) have pointed clearly to two major differences between the haptic and visual systems. The first concerns the way in which information about objects is gathered (Revesz, 1933/1950). Haptic perception is fragmentary and successive. To obtain a coherent representation of the whole, pieces of information need to be assembled synthetically. Second, the haptic and the visual systems are composed of a sensory component and a motor component, which are tightly linked when the sensory organs are called into play to perceive objects. The basic difference between the systems lies in the motor component. The visual system relies on several motor mechanisms, which serve to enhance the quality of visual information available to the retina (binocular convergence, adjustment of the lens, changes in the pupil size, etc.) (Aslin, 1987). The motor component of the manual system calls for more degrees of freedom. Manual exploration consists of moving the hand on the surface of an object, which produces a deformation of the skin (tactual perception) that involves, if exploration is dynamic, the underlying muscular and articulatory layers of the hand (haptic perception) (Lederman & Klatsky, 1987, 1990).

For adults, the manual system performs two distinct functions. The first is related to the haptic perception of manually explored objects. The second is specific to the motor system and concerns the manipulation and displacement of objects in the environment. Lederman and Klatzky (1987) analyzed the perceptual function of the manual system thoroughly in adults. They found a relation between specific perceptual properties of objects and the exploratory procedures used by adults in extracting information about these properties. Blindfolded adult subjects use different procedures to perceive substance properties such as texture and weight than structure properties such as volume and shape. For example, while it is possible to perceive the texture and consistency of an object through simple contact or lateral movement of the object in the hand, adults extract information about the exact shape of an object through "contour following" (i.e., dynamic exploration along edges). Lederman and Klatzky pointed out that although perception of exact shape requires fine manipulation, a variety of low-level information such as gross shape, weight, and texture can be extracted through simple enclosure of the object in the hand, a movement of which even very young infants are capable. The second function of the manual system, that of operation on and manipulation of objects in the environment, requires, in contrast, quite different types of behavior. Movement of an object toward a goal, displacement, or transformation of an object (i.e., destruction or deformation) involves broad movements of the upper limbs as a whole (Hatwell, 1986) rather than fine manual exploration. This latter function begins to develop at around 5 months of age, with the onset of eye–hand coordination. How does the development of these different functions of the manual system affect infants' ability to perceive objects and their properties?

Research on haptic sensitivity has shown that even in-utero, the fetus responds to touching of the palm of the hand as early as 10.5 weeks (Humphrey, 1964). By birth, the grasping reflex is one of the organism's basic responses. Twitchell (1970) provided an excellent description of this reflex: From 8 to 20 weeks, the reflex can be divided into two phases. Adequate stimulation produces rapid and sudden flexing of the fingers and thumb (grasping). Flexing is maintained by traction of the fingers (holding). By the age of 2 months, infants are able to hold objects, but they need to overcome the grasping and avoidance reflexes to be able to perform fine manual exploration. At roughly 4–5 months, a new function appears that involves more global motor behaviors: transport of objects for purposes of visuo-prehensile coordination. This evolution in tactual exploration of objects has been described in detail in 2- to 5-month-old infants (Rochat, 1989). Global motor behaviors, which make multimodal exploration of objects possible, emerge at about 4 months, whereas monomanual exploration with strong grasping is dominant at 2 months. We found similar changes in motor control in our study of intramodal haptic exploration at 2 and 5 months of age (Streri, 1987, Experiment 1; Streri & Pêcheux, 1986b). At 2 months, during tactual habituation, first the infants held the objects tightly and then sometimes slid a finger, often the thumb, along the surface of the object. They did not, however, perform movements that would enable them to move the object in their hand to obtain a more accurate perception of the form of the whole object. This type of manual behavior is called enclosure by Lederman and Klatsky (1990); it demands little motor output but serves to extract low-level information simultaneously about several dimensions such as temperature, texture, or vague form. In contrast, 5-month-old infants in our study were highly active. Although we observed finer manual control, these infants often performed broad arm movements while holding tightly onto the object. They also tried to see the object or bring it to their mouth through the screen or to change hands. For 5-month-olds, the greatest difficulties apparently involved an inability to master fine distal exploration. Thus, in the first months after birth, the haptic system is apparently primarily dependent first on its ability to hold objects and then on the infant's general tendency to move the upper limbs.

Our hypothesis was that the asymmetries of transfer observed at 2 and 5 months of age were highly dependent on the development of the haptic system. We designed experiments to determine what conditions were necessary for reversible transfer to take place. The assumption was that grasping in 2-month-olds inhibits full exploration of objects, and that this might account for the lack of recognition of seen objects. At 5 months, although finer manipulation of held objects is possible, bringing them to the mouth, to the field of vision, or to the other hand is carried out so dynamically that it may interfere with a fine exploration and prevent the identification of object structure needed for visual recognition.

INTERMODAL TRANSFER AT 2 MONTHS:
THE WEAKNESS OF THE PERCEPTUAL FUNCTION
OF THE HAND

In the first experiment (Streri, 1987, Experiment 2), tactual recognition of seen objects was tested in a single-trial design. It is possible that infants failed to exhibit transfer from vision to touch because a single trial was insufficient for them to handle and explore the object thoroughly. Moreover, it may have been difficult for 2-month-old infants to compare a representation stored in memory with their immediate perception of an object in a different modality. We concluded that a procedure that was simpler for the infant might reveal both touch–vision and vision–touch transfer. Therefore, we devised an intermodal matching procedure that allowed the infant to extract and compare information about the objects in both modalities simultaneously across a number of trials (Streri & Milhet, 1988). This procedure greatly reduced the memory load, because the infant could make a direct comparison and did not need to rely on a stored representation. The infant's tactual field and the visual field were separated by a screen. The infant could explore an object visually, and at the same time feel another object that had either the same shape or a different shape. Six different objects were used that were identical to those used in the previous studies (Streri, 1987; Streri & Pêcheux, 1986a, 1986b). Intermodal matching was tested in four trials. In two of these trials infants were presented with the object first in the haptic modality for 10 sec prior to the matching task (Tv condition), and in the two other trials they were presented with the object visually before the matching task (Vt condition). In each trial, both tactual and visual information were available during 50 sec. Twenty-four infants were tested in an intermodal matching condition and 12 infants were tested in a visual or a tactual unimodal condition (control group).

When the visual and the tactual objects were the same shape, the 2-month-olds exhibited avoidance reactions (dropping objects or looking away). These avoidance reactions were more frequent than in the condition where the two objects had different shapes, and as frequent as in the unimodal condition. These results provide evidence that babies are able to compare tactual and visual objects simultaneously and that they react more often when information is redundant than when it is not. Nevertheless, avoidance reactions were more frequent from touch to vision (condition Tv) than from vision to touch (condition Vt). Thus, when infants begin by exploring the shape tactually, they seem to recognize it visually when it is presented in the matching task and exhibit numerous avoidance reactions. In contrast, when infants begin by exploring visually, the findings are much less clear. In this case, no difference was observed in reactions when the objects had the same shape and when they had different shapes. Thus, even with a procedure that provides much longer object recognition time than in the Streri (1987) experiment, the vision–touch intermodal relationship was not observed.

One possible explanation for the absence of vision-touch transfer at 2 months of age focuses on the difference in the information that is available to the infants through the movements of the objects in the two modalities. For infants to have sufficient knowledge of an object in the visual modality, the object must move continually; single or multiple static positions are not sufficient for accurate visual perception of three-dimensional form (Kellman, 1984; Owsley, 1983). In the experiments we conducted, the seen objects rotated and hence the conditions for satisfactory information capture were fulfilled. The babies had an overall and full view of the objects presented to them. When the object was presented in the haptic modality, the experimenter placed an object in the infant's hand and let her explore freely. However, because 2-month-old infants cannot turn an object in their hand (although at times they may slide a finger gently along the surface of the object or press it), they may be unable to extract sufficient information to construct a complete haptic representation of the object. The highly infrequent attempts at changing hands or bringing the object to the mouth or into the field of vision fail most of the time. Thus the conditions in which exploration takes place in the two modalities are not comparable.

A second possible explanation for the asymmetry in transfer is the complexity and elaborate nature of the percept that young infants construct when they explore objects with their hands and when they look at objects. Visually derived representations of objects may be more holistic than tactually derived representations. Studies of 4-month-old infants' visual perception provide evidence that the mechanisms of object perception take as input a representation of the three-dimensional surface layout; they do not operate on lower level representations of retinal elements and relations (Kellman, Gleitman, & Spelke, 1987; Kellman, Spelke, & Short, 1986). Moreover, studies on newborns have shown that even at birth, infants are capable of visually discriminating between a real three-dimensional object and its drawing (Fantz, 1961; Slater, Morrison, & Rose, 1984). In contrast, at 2 months, the motor control skill of the hand appears to be less efficient at processing information because of the predominant grasping reflex (Twitchell, 1970). According to Revesz (1933/1950), young infants' hands can extract partial information about objects that they cannot yet integrate into a coherent and synthetic representation of the whole. The young infant is sensitive to individual features such as curves, straight lines, angles, and the presence or absence of a hole, but cannot form an overall, structured representation of the object.

A final possible explanation for this asymmetry of transfer focuses on the different levels of representation in the two modalities. As mentioned earlier, infants are able to form integrated, holistic visual representations of objects, whereas they cannot do so in the haptic modality. This difference in representations may dramatically influence infants' ability to compare representations across modalities. In the touch–vision transfer situation, the infant holds an object, a star, for example, in her hand. The infant feels the points of the star and that something is pricking. She then sees the star, a shape with points that resemble the ones that she has already felt, and recognition is based on this part of the object. In the vision–touch transfer situation, the infant is presented with the rotating star visually. It is likely that the infant has full and overall perception of the object. The object is then placed in her hand, and she only captures partial, fragmented information that is not comparable with the information she has seen. Thus, when young infants are familiarized tactually with an object, they construct a representation of its parts, but do not form a fully integrated representation of its whole structure. When infants are subsequently presented visually with an object, they are able to recognize the object they have felt by moving from a partial level to a higher level representation. Transfer takes place in this way. In contrast, when infants are familiarized visually with objects, they construct a complete representation. When they are subsequently presented with the objects in the tactual modality, they may fail to recognize them because recognition requires that they move down from a holistic representation to a partial representation. Moreover, it may be more difficult to recognize the lower level components of a high-level representation than it is to recognize the high level structure implicit in a lower level representation, because it is likely that normal perceptual processing proceeds from lower to higher levels (see Marr, 1982; Pinker, 1984).

All three of the preceding accounts for the asymmetry of transfer across modalities in 2-month-old infants emphasize the inadequacy of the haptic system both in perceiving information and forming an adequate representation of objects in comparison with the visual system. To test this possibility we conducted an experiment (Streri & Molina, in press) using the preferential looking time procedure (see Spelke, 1985). The amount of information presented in the visual modality was simplified and reduced, without degrading the information. It was hoped that this simplification of the visual information would make it more comparable to that obtained in the haptic modality, thus facilitating intermodal transfer. Infants were tactually presented with solid objects, and they were visually presented with two-dimensional silhouettes of these same objects. The tactually presented objects were a cross and a cotton reel (see Fig. 12.1). The visual displays were silhouette pictures where only object contours and surfaces were specified. A visual display was created for each tactual object, using a procedure developed by Rose, Gottfried, and Bridger (1983). These displays were made by tracing the object and then painting the tracing red. They were glued on small white cards and were presented on a board, which was shaken at the beginning of

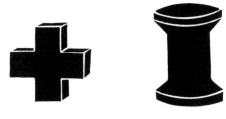

FIG. 12.1. Tactual objects (top) and their silhouette pictures (bottom) for experiments on visual–tactual and tactual–visual transfer tasks between objects and pictures. From Streri and Molina (in press). Reprinted by permission.

each trial, causing the display to undergo a rigid, jiggling motion. We expected that substituting two-dimensional silhouettes for solid objects would enhance young infants' performance on visual to haptic transfer tasks.

The method of these experiments was the same as that of Streri and Spelke (1988, 1989) and Streri (1987). To investigate intermodal transfer from touch to vision, infants were habituated to a solid object in the tactual modality and then were tested visually with the two-dimensional silhouette of the felt object and the two-dimensional silhouette of another object for six trials in alternation. The infants in the baseline condition received the same visual test but no prior habituation sequence. Infants in the experimental condition were expected to look longer at the picture corresponding to the new object than at the picture corresponding to the felt object, relative to the baseline condition. Results in the first experiment indicated strong evidence of intermodal transfer from haptically explored solid objects to their visually presented silhouettes. In this study, recognition was evidenced by a familiarity preference; infants looked longer at the picture corresponding to the familiar object. This finding confirms previous results on intermodal transfer of object shapes from touch to vision in 2-month-olds using habituation and matching procedures (Streri, 1987; Streri & Milhet, 1988) and shows that similar results can be obtained with a preferential looking time procedure. Transfer from touch to vision in young infants has thus been obtained using three different procedures and with a variety of displays, objects, and pictures. All these findings suggest that contour information can be detected and used to assess invariance across modalities, as proposed by J. J. Gibson's (1966, 1979) theory. However in previous reports, infants exhibited a preference for the novel object, while in this experiment a preference for the silhouette corresponding to the familiar object was evidenced. The shift of preference may be due to the difference between the visual displays across studies (i.e., picture or object). Further, older infants (12 months of age) exhibit similar abilities only after 45 sec of manipulation (Rose et al., 1983). In our experiments, intermodal transfer was found after about 150 sec of holding time. This difference most likely reflects developmental changes in the efficiency of manipulation.

To investigate intermodal transfer from vision to touch, infants were habituated to a silhouette picture of an object in the visual modality and were then tested haptically with the solid object corresponding to that picture and with a different solid object. In this case, infants in the baseline condition received the same tactual test but no prior visual habituation. In contrast to our previous studies (Streri, 1987; Streri & Milhet, 1988), we found evidence of intermodal transfer from the visually presented silhouette of an object to the object itself. Infants held the object that they had previously seen in a two dimensional silhouette reliably longer than a novel object. This finding is the first demonstration of visual to tactual transfer in 2-month-old infants. It is possible that surface and contour information provided by the two-dimensional visual display comes closer to paralleling the information extracted through haptic manipulation and may thus facilitate object recognition. The data also suggest that the visual modality is more mature than the tactual modality at 2 months of age and that infants can extract a full representation of object information from vision but not from touch.

Although these experiments indicate that visual–tactual transfer is possible in 2-month-olds, they do not explain directly why vision-to-touch transfer of object properties is more difficult when the visual information is represented in three dimensions. Is haptic perceptual organization different from visual perceptual organization? We addressed this issue in a series of studies with three conditions (Molina & Streri, 1992). The displays were identical to those described in Streri and Molina (1992), that is, a solid cross and a solid cotton reel versus their two-dimensional silhouette pictures (see Fig. 12.1). The method of this experiment was the same as of that the previous studies except that in all conditions the test was presented in the visual modality. In the first (intermodal) condition, the infant explored an object tactually and was then presented visually with the familiar object and its two-dimensional silhouette picture for six trials in alternation. In the second (intramodal visual) condition, the infant was visually habituated to an object and in the test phase was presented visually with the previously seen object and its silhouette picture. During the familiarization period, an infant-controlled procedure was used. In the third, control condition, infants received the same visual test without any prior familiarization. Comparison on the visual test of performance across all three conditions thus permitted an assessment of a difference or lack of difference in object recognition between modalities.

The infants in the control group showed no preference for the object or its picture. After visual habituation to the object, all the infants looked longer at the two-dimensional picture than at the object, providing evidence that they could discriminate between the two-dimensional and three-dimensional representations of the stimuli. This latter finding accords completely with studies (Slater, Rose, & Morison, 1984) that reported that at birth, infants can detect similarities and differences between three dimensional stimuli and their two dimensional representations. In contrast, in the intermodal condition the infants looked longer at the solid object across all pairs of test trials when it was presented first, and looked longer at its two-dimensional silhouette across all pairs of test trials when it was presented first. No order effects were observed in either the control or the visual intramodal group. These findings may be interpreted in several ways. It could be that the tactual percept is weak and thus no visual recognition of the felt object takes place. In that case, however, infants should look for an equal amount of time at the two displays without systematic order effect. It is possible that this order effect may be a result of the change in modality; similar order effects did not appear, however, in the previous experiments (Streri & Molina, in press) when infants were presented with two different pictures following haptic habituation. It is also possible that after tactual exploration of an object, babies form an ambiguous representation of the object and that both the object and the silhouette support transfer. In this experiment, the information on contour and surface was similar in the two visual displays (object and picture) and the order effect might have been due to this similarity, the first trial determining the preference for one of the stimuli. In order to distinguish between these interpretations, we ran a second series of experiments.

A major difference between the object and the two-dimensional silhouette was the fact that the object had volume and the silhouette was flat. Was this information relevant, or did infants disregard it during transfer? To determine the answer to this question, we conducted further experiments with 2-month-olds (Molina & Streri, 1992) using the same preferential looking method described earlier. In these studies, the visual displays were both drawings and where only the contour was specified so as to make the object appear in perspective or flat. The haptically presented objects were a cube and a ring. We produced two drawings of these objects that specified their contour. In one of the drawings, the three dimensions of the objects were specified and the overall structure of the object was preserved. In the other drawing, the dimensions of the objects were flattened and the representation ceased to denote the object (see Fig. 12.2). In both drawings, the information on the contour and the total surface area was held constant.

We tested visual recognition of the two drawings after tactual exploration of the solid cube or ring (intermodal condition) and after visual exploration

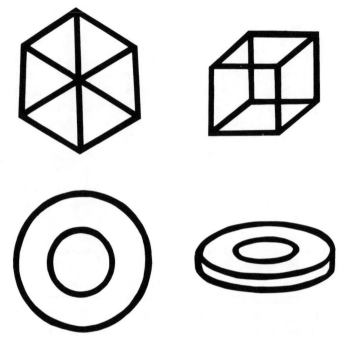

FIG. 12.2. Drawings of a cube and a ring for experiments on haptic and visual representation of object shape presented in the visual test. From Molina and Streri (1992). Reprinted by permission.

(intramodal condition) of the same solid object. For the ring, the perspective display was presented vertically or horizontally. The control group received the same visual test without prior familiarization. If infants construct a three-dimensional representation of the object during tactual exploration, they should look differently at the three dimensional and the flat representations of them on the visual test. If, during tactual exploration, the infants only extract contour information (the corners or curves) and not the structure and the volume of the object, they should look for an equal amount of time at both drawings on the visual test. After visual habituation, a clear preference for one of the two displays was predicted, either for the perspective or the flat drawing.

In the habituation period, the accumulated holding time through criterion was about 75 sec and the accumulated visual time was about 132 sec. For the test period, the results are presented in Table 12.1. As in the previous experiment, we obtained an order effect after tactual exploration of the cube or of the ring. The infants looked longer at the drawing that was presented first, regardless of what it was. No such order effect was observed in the babies in either the control or the visual intramodal groups. After visual habituation to the cube, the infants looked longer at the Necker cube, and after visual habituation to the ring, the infants looked longer at the flat drawing.

TABLE 12.1
Visual Preferences Observed in a Control Group
with No Habituation Familiarization or After Tactual and
Visual Habituation with a Cube or a Ring
in 2- and 4-Month-Old Infants

		Directions of Visual Preference After		
Ages	Objects	Haptic Habituation	Visual Habituation	No Habituation
2 Months	Cube	Order effect	3D+	NO
	Horizontal ring	Order effect	2D+	NO
	Vertical ring		2D+	NO
4 Months	Cube	3D+	2D+	NO
	Horizontal ring	3D+	3D+	NO
	Vertical ring		3D+	NO

These experiments show that at 2 months of age, haptic perceptual organization differs from visual perceptual organization. Apparently during intermodal transfer, the volume of the object is not considered to be relevant and contour information alone is transferred, because the infant recognizes the felt object in both perspective and the flattened versions. This finding appears to be specific to the intermodal transfer situation because in the visual modality, the babies detected differences between the representation of volume and the flattened version. Experiments on visual–haptic and haptic–visual transfer between objects and pictures also indicate that 2-month-old infants detect a difference between the same object presented in a flat or rounded shape (Streri & Molina, in press).

At what age do the perceptual representations of an object become similar in the visual and haptic modalities? To answer this question, we replicated the experiment with the cube and ring objects in 4-month-old infants. The experimental conditions and the tactual and visual displays were identical to those used for the 2-month-olds. The results are presented in Table 12.1. The findings showed that after visual habituation to the cube, infants preferred to look at the flattened drawing of the object over the drawing that specifies the three dimensions of the cube. After visual habituation to the ring, infants preferred to look at the perspective drawing over the flattened drawing. These data contrast with the results from the 2-month-olds, as the younger infants preferred the drawing of the Necker cube and the flattened drawing of the ring. Hence there is a shift in visual perceptual organization. After tactual habituation to the cube, the 4-month-old babies preferred to look at the perspective drawing of both the cube and the ring than the flattened drawing. No order effect was observed. The control group showed no preference for either of the displays. Hence it seems that haptic perceptual organization also undergoes change and appears to be more clear-cut at 4 months of age. With regard to intermodal transfer, the volume of the object apparently becomes a salient dimension. However, this experiment is uninformative as to whether 4-month-olds can organize their representation of a held object into a single, unitary entity. An infant may be sensitive to a contour or a volume and not be able to form a clear representation of the object.

These data need further confirmation by other experiments using other objects. Nonetheless, they suggest that constraints in object manipulation in 2-month-olds reduce the efficiency of the infants' overall structured information capture. Babies need to have overcome the grasping reflex to be able to carry out fine exploration of the object and hence obtain a clear representation. Similar constraints are apparently not present in the visual modality.

INTERMODAL TRANSFER IN 5-MONTH-OLD INFANTS: THE IMPORTANCE OF MOTION IN HAPTIC EXPLORATION OF OBJECTS

Studies have shown that 5-month-old infants do not visually recognize the shape of objects they have previously held monomanually (Streri & Pêcheux, 1986a, Experiment 1). This result is not due to an inability of the visual modality to recognize a felt object since 2-month-old infants do recognize the felt objects. Indeed, this hypothesis would fly in the face of all the data on the development of visual perceptual abilities in the infant (e.g., Banks & Salapatek, 1983; Dodwell, Humphrey, & Muir, 1987). It is equally problematical to account for this finding by proposing an inability of the haptic system to process information during habituation, because 5-month-olds are capable of discriminating objects intramodally in the haptic modality (Streri & Pêcheux, 1986b). It is possible, however, that a complex procedure may not allow infants, in one trial, to compare visual and tactual information adequately. To eliminate this difficulty, a second experiment using the usual matching method was performed (Streri & Pêcheux, 1986b, Experiment 2). After 80 sec of tactual familiarization with an object (a square and a square with hole, a flower, and a star), the familiar object and a novel object were presented visually simultaneously for 20 sec each. Again the findings showed no transfer of the shape of objects from touch to vision. Pineau and Streri (1990), however, succeeded in showing visual recognition of held objects. Five-month-olds felt a complex object containing a novel feature (a diamond) between two identical objects (two rings) (see Fig. 12.3). The diamond was placed at the left, at the right end, or in the center of the rings.

The findings showed that the infants were able to locate the central or eccentric position of the diamond during tactual habituation and to transfer this information to vision. Infants looked longer at the new display than at

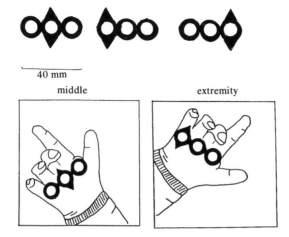

FIG. 12.3. Tactual and visual objects for experiments on intermodal transfer of spatial arrangement of the components parts of an object. From Pineau and Streri (1990). Reprinted by permission.

the display already felt. This finding does not run counter to the data from Streri and Pêcheux (1986a); rather, it suggests is that it is easier to detect a strange element in an object than to represent a shape as a unitary entity.

The asymmetry of transfer observed at 5 months cannot be interpreted in the same way as asymmetry at 2 months. Two-month-old infants do not perform movements that would enable them to move the object. The infants hold the objects tightly and sometimes slide a finger along the surface of the object. In contrast, 5 months is the age of rapidly developing visuo-prehensile coordination. It is a crucial step in the life of an infant. Taking objects, bringing them to the mouth and into the field of vision are clearly more stimulating than feeling them or recognizing their shapes. An object held in a hand is an object to be looked at, sucked, and so forth, rather than to be recognized. What predominates at this age is motor activity of the arm and not the infant's manipulatory activity. We do not mean that intermodal transfer from touch to vision is difficult to observe in 5-month-old infants, but that when infants hold a small and simple object in their hands as those in Streri and Pêcheux's (1986a, 1986b) experiments, in the process of trying to transport the object to the mouth or the eyes they detect little information. Although this information is sufficient to discriminate the object intramodally, it is not sufficient to recognize it visually. Infants' attention is focused on the transport of the object, not on the manipulation of objects. It is possible that with more complex objects intermodal transfer from touch to vision would be evidenced. To test this hypothesis, we examined the ways in which the infants' movement of the object could interfere with awareness of object properties.

The study was composed of two experiments during which only haptic information was provided in both the familiarization and test phases (Streri & Pineau, 1988). The first experiment tested infants' ability to discriminate a sphere from a cube by touch. The experiment was composed of a habituation phase and a discrimination test phase. The findings showed that the sphere was clearly differentiated from the cube. Infants held the novel object longer than the familiar object. The second experiment was designed to test the effect of the infant's actions on her manual perceptual abilities. The experiment made use of a music box from which the sound had been removed and that had a turnable crank. Attached to the end of the crank was either the sphere or the cube used in Experiment 1. The infant was helped to take the end (cube or sphere) in his or her hand and turn the crank. She turned the crank in a circular fashion for eight 10-sec trials (the mean duration of the habituation phase in the previous experiment). After this familiarization period, object discrimination was tested as in the first experiment. In this experiment, however, no evidence of discrimination was found. This experiment clearly points to the interference of motion on the perceptual capacities of the hand. Infants cannot simultaneously attend to the action on the device and to the properties of the object they are holding. The constraints of movement are too great.

Nevertheless, if, as predicted, movement of the arms is both more stimulating and more informative than handling objects for 5-month-olds, activities where there is high motor activity on objects should also lead to visual recognition of information gathered during this activity. We tested this hypothesis in a series of experiments on bimanual object handling (Streri & Spelke, 1988, 1989; Streri, Spelke, & Rameix, 1993). These experiments delve once again into the issue of perception of the object boundaries that has often been investigated in the visual modality (see Spelke, 1990, for a review). In the visual modality, like adults, 4-month-old infants perceive a center-occluded object as a complete and continuous unit if the visible surfaces of the object move in depth, vertically or laterally together (Kellman & Spelke, 1983; Kellman et al., 1986). Infants do not perceive the complete object when the visible surfaces are stationary. These studies provide evidence that motion specifies object unity to infants in the visual modality and that static configurational properties, in contrast, do not.

In our studies, we wanted to investigate further the role that motion plays in haptic perception. These experiments investigated whether infants perceive the unity and boundaries of objects under the same conditions when they feel objects as when they see them (Streri & Spelke, 1988). Four- to 5-month-old infants held two rings, one in each hand, under a cloth that blocked their view of the rings and the space between them. In one condition the rings were rigidly connected and moved together, whereas in the other condition the rings could be moved independently. After exploring the rings haptically, infants received a haptic or visual test with pairs of rings that were connected or separated. Across all experiments:

1. Infants explored the rings bimanually during habituation, producing patterns of rigid or independent motion.
2. Infants haptically discriminated between the two motion patterns (Experiment 1).
3. This discrimination transferred from touch to vision (Experiment 2).

Moreover, the experiments provided evidence that infants perceived the unity and boundaries of objects by detecting the motion patterns they themselves produced. Infants who explored the independently moveable rings perceived two distinct objects, whereas those who explored the rigidly moveable rings perceived a single object (Experiments 3 and 4).

In the visual modality, infants appear to perceive object unity by analyzing motion relationships but not by analyzing figural goodness (Kellman & Spelke, 1983; Kestenbaum, Termine, & Spelke, 1987). We wanted to test whether figural goodness or motion relationships predominate in the haptic modality. Infants held two rings, one in each hand, out of view. The rings moved rigidly together and were either the same in substance, weight, texture, and shape (Experiment 1), or they differed from one another on these dimensions (Experiment 2). After haptic habituation to a ring assembly, patterns of preferential looking to visibly connected versus separated rings provided evidence that the infants perceived the rings in both experiments as parts of one connected object. This perception was no weaker when the rings differed in shape, substance, texture, and weight, even though infants had been shown to be able to detect this difference (Experiment 3). These data suggest that in the haptic modality, as in the visual modality, infants appear to perceive object unity by analyzing motion relationships but not by analyzing figural goodness.

Infants' visual perception of object boundaries has also been studied using reaching and preferential looking methods (von Hofsten & Spelke, 1985; Spelke, von Hofsten, & Kestenbaum, 1989). Five-month-old infants viewed two adjacent or separated objects that were stationary, moved together, or moved separately. Infants reached for the objects as distinct units when they moved independently or when they were separated by a visible spatial gap. When the two objects moved together or were stationary, infants reached for the objects as one unit. In order to compare infants' haptic perception of these motions with their visual perception, we adapted these experiments to the haptic modality and used an intermodal transfer method (Streri, Spelke, & Rameix, 1993). In five experiments, 4- to 5-month-old infants manipulated a device made up of a small and a large surface that they could hold in each hand by a handle. In one condition, these surfaces were rigidly connected. In the second condition, the handles could be moved by sliding the small surface vertically along the edge of the large surface. In the final condition, the small surface could be pulled away from the large one and pushed towards it (see Fig. 12.4). Two additional conditions were also run in which the infant held the device, but the experimenter performed the sliding and distancing motions. After habituation to one of these assemblies, infants were presented with a single, connected object and with two object parts that were separated by a gap for six trials in alternation. When infants handled the rigidly connected device, they visually perceived the display as a single unit. When infants explored the device either by sliding or by moving apart the two elements, they visually perceived it as two units. When the experimenter moved the display, the infants' responses were indeterminate.

This series of studies points to the importance of arm movements in the perceptual organization of objects as units. Manual exploration in these experiments is restricted to firm holding of rings or handles. Although grasping is sufficient for infant to detect information on texture, weight, and so forth correctly as shown by their ability to discriminate these properties intramodally (Streri & Spelke, 1989, Experiment 3), this information does

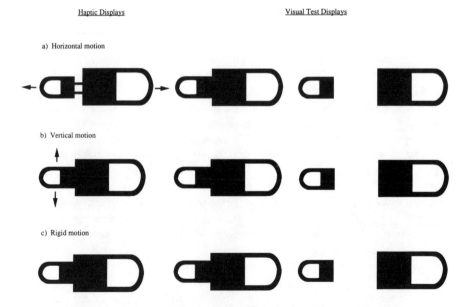

FIG. 12.4. Tactual (left) and visual (right) displays for experiments on modality-specific and amodal aspects of object perception in infancy: the case of active touch. From Streri, Spelke, and Rameix (1993). Reprinted by permission.

not influence visual transfer in a way that is analogous to our experiments on object shape (Streri & Pêcheux, 1986a).

CONCLUSION

Our prime focus of inquiry was why we were unable to observe reversible transfer of object shapes in infants under the age of 6 months, in particular in groups of subjects aged 2 and 5 months. Intermodal transfer of object form is only observed from touch to vision in 2-month-old infants and only from vision to touch in 5-month-old infants. one interpretation is that a given modality may be dominant at a specific point in development, and this dominance can shift with age. This interpretation holds for the relationships between other modalities such as vision and audition (Lewkowicz, 1988a, 1988b), where motor behavior plays a lesser role. However, this explanation does not take into account the major changes in the motor development of the haptic system, which can temporarily upset intermodal relationships. Further, although dominance relationships can be demonstrated in perceptual conflict situations (Bushnell, 1982), intermodal transfer situations are not perceptual conflict situations.

Our studies have focused on an age range where neonatal reaching is fading (von Hofsten, 1984) and at an age when reaching is developing rapidly. I have argued elsewhere that the quality of the sensory-motor relationship between eye and hand may have an impact on intermodal transfer (Streri, 1991). The basic idea is that constraints operate not so much at the perceptual level but rather at the motor level, and hence undermine capacities for transfer of information. The nature of these constraints differs as a function of whether we are looking at intermodal perception in 2- or in 5-month-olds.

A number of conclusions can be drawn from the experiments on intermodal transfer of object form at 2 months. At this age, infant unimanual grasping dominates and although it does not prevent overall information capture of the entire set of object properties, it impinges on the gathering of fine-grained information. This is compatible with J. J. Gibson's (1962) proposal that only active touching serves to extract fine information. This line of reasoning is also congruent with empirical work by Lederman and Klatsky (1987, 1990) on adult abilities to extract different object properties via the hand. They provided evidence that the motor subsystem facilitates the perceptual and cognitive functions. Sensory input can vary with hand movements and type of information. Importantly, accurate information capture of object shape is associated exclusively with exploratory procedures which consist of following a contour of an object. Two-month-olds are not capable of this type of haptic performance. Young infants cannot extract fine-grained information on object form. This weakness would explain why we failed to observe haptic recognition of a seen object.

Comparing visual and haptic representations of the same objects shows that the thickness of objects and their volume play little role in transfer for 2-month-old infants, even though this information is detected in both the haptic and visual systems. Volume only becomes important 2 months later. These findings shed light on some of the more intriguing aspects of infant behavior. In 2-month-olds there is no transfer from vision to touch when the visual display is an object (Streri, 1987; Streri & Milhet, 1988), yet transfer is observed when the display is a flat drawing of the object (Streri & Molina, in press). Second, after haptic exploration of an object, the observed transfer is ambiguous when one of the objects is two-dimensional and the other is three-dimensional, whether the comparison deals with an object versus a silhouette picture or a perspective versus a flat drawing of an object. There is no ambiguity after visual habituation to the object (Streri & Molina, 1991).

These findings suggest that the visual system constructs an object representation more efficiently and/or fully than the haptic system. overall, these results are congruent with the notion of levels of representation (Marr, 1982). They also suggest that once a holistic level representation of a stimulus has been constructed, access to the analytic level representation that the higher representation was based on can be lost. It is thus difficult to recognize analytic level properties of a stimulus once its holistic level has been perceived.

The asymmetry of transfer observed at 5 months is also linked to constraints on the infant's motor system. Fine motor activity in distal exploration of objects is less of a focal point than the infant's newly acquired ability to transport objects, to move his/her arms and to coordinate both hands. Objects are there to be taken and seen and not to be haptically recognized. This finding is compatible with observations on reaching. Bower (1974) described a highly particular type of reaching behavior, similar to neonatal ballistic movement. When 4- or 5-month-old infants miss in their reaching for objects, they tend not to correct their movement but rather start the reach over from the beginning. Thus the movement is the predominant feature, not immediate success of the action. This behavior is specific to this age and then vanishes. In a similar way, the absence of touch–vision transfer of object shape is specific to 5-month-olds. By the age of 6 months, the data show that infants visually recognize felt objects (Ruff & Kohler, 1978; Rose, Gottfried, & Bridger, 1981a). Bimanual transfer of object unity from touch to vision can be accomplished in $4\frac{1}{2}$-month-olds when exploration is bimanual and when it involves considerable movement of the device (Streri & Spelke, 1988, 1989; Streri, Spelke, & Rameix, 1993).

The constraints we have described to account for asymmetries of transfer at 2 and 5 months may be confined to this age range. Joint multimodal exploration through visuo-prehensile coordination becomes an efficient means of judging sameness of information and setting up complimentarities for a given object. This behavior clearly has an impact on the relationships between sensory modalities and intermodal transfers.

ACKNOWLEDGMENTS

We express our gratitude to Roger Lécuyer and to Gretchen Van de Walle for their helpful comments on earlier drafts and stylistic corrections of the paper.

REFERENCES

Aslin, R. N. (1987). Motor aspects of visual development in infancy. In P. Salapatek & L. Cohen (Eds.) *Handbook of infant perception: from sensation to perception* (Vol. 1, pp. 43–113). London: Academic Press.

Banks, M. S., & Salapatek, P. (1983). Infant visual perception. In M. M. Haith & J. J. Campos (Eds.), *Infancy and developmental psychobiology* (Vol. 2, pp. 435–571). In P. Mussen (Gen. Ed.), *Handbook of Child Psychology.* New York: Wiley.

Bower, T. G. R. (1974). *Development in infancy.* San Francisco: Freeman.

Bushnell, E. N. (1982). Visual-tactual knowledge in 8-, $9\frac{1}{2}$- and 11-month-old infants. *Infant behavior and Development 5,* 63–75.

Dodwell, P. C., Humphrey, G. K., & Muir D. W. (1987). Shape and Pattern perception. In P. Salapatek & L. Cohen (Eds.), *Handbook of infant perception: from perception to cognition* (Vol. 2, pp. 1–77). London: Academic Press.

Fantz, R. L. (1961). The origin of form perception. *Scientific American, 204,* 66–72.

Gibson, E. J. (1969). *Principles of perceptual learning and development.* New York: Appleton-Century-Crofts.

Gibson, E. J., & Walker, A. (1984). Development of knowledge of visual-tactual affordances of substance. *Child Development, 55,* 453–460.

Gibson, J. J. (1962). Observations on active touch. *Psychological Review, 69,* 477–491.

Gibson, J. J. (1966). *The senses considered as perceptual systems.* Boston: Houghton Mifflin.

Gibson, J. J. (1979). *The ecological approach to visual perception.* Boston: Houghton Mifflin.

Hatwell, Y. (1986). *Toucher l'espace* [Touching space]. Lille: Presses Universitaires de France.

Humphrey, T. (1964). Some correlations between the appearance of human fetal reflexes and the development of the nervous system. *Progress in Brain Research, 4,* 93–135.

Kellman, P. J. (1984). Perception of three-dimensional form by human infants. *Perception & Psychophysics, 36 (4),* 353–358.

Kellman, P. J., Gleitman, H., & Spelke, E. S. (1987). Object and observer motion in the perception of objects by infants. *Journal of Experimental Psychology: Human Perception and Performance, 13,* 586–593.

Kellman, P. J. & Spelke, E. S. (1983). Perception of partly occluded objects in infancy, *Cognitive Psychology, 15,* 483–254.

Kellman, P. J., Spelke, E. S., & Short, K. (1986). Infant perception of object unity from translatory motion in depth and vertical translation. *Child Development, 57,* 72–86.

Kestenbaum, R., Termine, N., & Spelke, E. S. (1987). Perception of objects and object boundaries by three-month-old infants. *British Journal of Developmental Psychology, 5,* 367–383.

Lederman, S. J., & Klatzky, R. L. (1987). Hand movements: A window into haptic object recognition. *Cognitive Psychology, 19,* 342–368.

Lederman, S. J., & Klatzky, R. L. (1990). Haptic classification of common objects: Knowledge-driven exploration. *Cognitive Psychology, 22,* 421–459.

Lewkowicz, D. J. (1988a). Sensory dominance in infants I: Six-month-old infants' response to auditory-visual compounds. *Developmental Psychology, 24,* 155–171.

Lewkowicz, D. J. (1988b). Sensory dominance in infants II: Ten-month-old infants' response to auditory-visual compounds. *Developmental Psychology, 24,* 172–182.

Marr, D. (1982). *Vision: A computational investigation into the human representation and processing of visual information.* San Francisco: Freeman.

Meltzoff, A. N., & Borton, R. W. (1979). Intermodal matching by human neonates. *Nature, 282,* 403–404.

Molina, M., & Streri, A. (1992, May). *Do infants process information about volume in touch and in vision?* Poster presented at the International Conference on Infants Studies, Miami.

Owsley C. (1983). The role of motion in infants' perception of solid shape. *Perception, 12,* 707–718.

Pineau A., & Streri, A. (1990). Intermodal transfer of spatial arrangement of the component parts of an object in infants aged 4/5 months. *Perception, 19,* 795–804.

Pinker, S. (1984). Visual cognition: An introduction, 1. *Cognition, 18,* 1–64.

Revesz, G. (1950). *Psychology and art of the blind.* New York: Longmens, Green. (Original work published 1933)

Rochat, P. (1989). Object manipulation and exploration in 2- and 5-month-old infants. *Developmental Psychology, 25,* 871–884.

Rose, S. A., & Ruff, H. A. (1987). Cross-modal abilities in human infants. In J. D. Osofsky (Ed.), *Handbook of infant Development* (pp.). New York: Wiley.

Rose, S. A., Gottfried, A. W., & Bridger, W. H. (1981a). Cross-modal transfer in 6-month-old infants. *Developmental Psychology, 17,* 661–669.

Rose, S. A., Gottfried, A. W., & Bridger, W. H. (1981b). Cross-modal transfer and information processing by the sense of touch in infancy. *Developmental Psychology, 17,* 90–98.

Rose, S. A., Gottfried, A. W., & Bridger, W. H. (1983). Infants' cross-modal transfer from solid objects to their graphic representations. *Child Development, 54,* 686–694.

Rose, S. A., & Koenigsberg, O. (1991). Asymmetries in infant cross-modal transfer. *Child Development, 62,* 706–718.

Ruff, H. A., & Kohler, C. J. (1978). Tactual-visual transfer in six-month-old infants. *Infant Behavior and Development, 1,* 259–264.

Slater, A., Rose, D., & Morison, V. (1984). Newborn infants' perception of similarities and differences between two- and three-dimensional stimuli. *British Journal of Developmental Psychology, 2,* 287–294.

Spelke, E. S. (1985). Preferential looking method as tools for the study of cognition in infancy. In G. Gottlieb & N. A. Krasnegor (Eds.), *Measurement of audition and vision in infancy* (pp. 323–363). New York: Ablex.

Spelke, E. S. (1990). Principles of object perception. *Cognitive Science, 14,* 29–56.

Spelke, E. S., von Hofsten, C., & Kestenbaum, R. (1989). Object perception in infancy: Interaction of spatial and kinetic information for object boundaries. *Developmental Psychology, 25,* 185–182.

Streri, A. (1987). Tactile discrimination of shape and intermodal transfer in 2- to 3-month-old infants. *British Journal of Developmental Psychology, 5,* 213–220.

Streri, A. (1993). *Voir Atteindre. Toucher: Les relations entre la vision et le toucher chez le bébé* [Seeing, reaching, touching: The relations between vision and touch in infancy]. London: Simon and Schuster. (Original work published 1991)

Streri, A., Milhet, S. (1988). Equivalences intermodales de la forme des objets entre la vision et le toucher chez les bébés de 2 mois [Intermodal matching of objects shape between vision and touch in 2-month-old infants]. *L'Année Psychologique, 88,* 329–341.

Streri, A., & Molina, M. (1991, July). *The ambiguity of the tactual representation in infancy.* Minneapolis, I.S.S.B.D. (International Society for the Study of Behavioral Development).

Streri, A., & Molina, M. (in press). Visual-tactual and tactual-visual transfer between objects and pictures in 2-month-old infants. *Perception.*

Streri, A., & Pêcheux, M.-G. (1986a). Vision to touch and touch to vision transfer of form in 5-month-old infants. *British Journal of Developmental Psychology, 4,* 161–167.

Streri, A., & Pêcheux, M.-G. (1986b). Tactual habituation and discrimination of form in infancy: A comparison with vision. *Child Development, 57,* 100–104.

Streri, A., & Pineau, A. (1988, April). *Motor and cognitive functions of the hand in 5-month-old infants.* Paper presented at the 6th annual International Conference on Infant Studies, Washington, DC.

Streri, A., & Spelke, E. S. (1988). Haptic perception of objects in infancy. *Cognitive Psychology, 20,* 1–23.

Streri, A., & Spelke, E. S. (1989). Effects of motion and figural goodness on haptic object perception in infancy. *Child Development, 60,* 1111–1125.

Streri, A., Spelke, E. S., & Rameix, E. (1993). Specific and amodal mechanisms of object perception and exploration in infancy: The case of active touch. *Cognition, 67,* 251–279.

Twitchell, T. E. (1970). Reflex mechanisms and the development of prehension. In K. Connoly (Ed.), *Mechanisms of motor skill development* (pp. 25–38). New York: Academic Press.

von Hofsten, C. (1984). Developmental changes in the organization of pre-reaching movements. *Developmental Psychology, 20,* 378–388.

von Hofsten, C., & Spelke, E. S. (1985). Object perception and object-directed reaching in infancy. *Journal of Experimental Psychology: General, 114,* 198–211.

CHAPTER THIRTEEN

Intermodal Participation in the Formation of Action in the Infant

Henriette Bloch
Laboratoire de PsychoBiologie du Développement

This chapter is devoted to the examination of facts and hypotheses concerning the formative processes of action, and more particularly the role of perceptions and intermodal connections in sensory motor interactions. Acting calls for the harmonization of movement and perception. In the human infant, the issue of the relationships between perceptual modalities and action cannot be approached directly. We first need to examine what *action* refers to at the early phases of life, and what criteria can be retained for the behavioral repertoires accessible to us. Similarly, we need to know what an infant can apprehend perceptually in the situations where the infant can produce observable changes. At first sight, to act calls for a linkage between exteroception and proprioception, and we should consider that intermodal relations are always implied. However, as we discuss later, proprioceptive sensitivity in early infancy is still not well understood and we do not know whether or how infants use prioprioceptive information in relation with exteroceptive information. Moreover, it may be that the possible linkage differs from one exteroceptive modality to another. So it is not easy to approach the multimodal relations in the infant's action, considering that they are parts of a common dynamic. A possible way to unpack them could be to adopt a functionalistic orientation. With such an orientation, I deliberately restrict myself here to perspectives that seek to account for fairly well-defined behaviors or clearly identified changes. This chapter focuses primarily on the organization of actions as sensory-motor combinations, rather than on their cognitive consequences as object or spatial knowledge. Most often, cognitive theories of development have considered the outcome of action rather than its mechanisms. However, understanding the mechanisms of action does not prevent any cognitive interpretation but only requires that indicators of cognition could be extracted from the observed relations between perception and movement while the individual is acting. The methods of study I stress here are experimental and owe a great deal to advances in technology since the mid 1970s. This progress has yielded a harvest of empirical data that is still insufficient and at times lacks coherence. This, at least in part, explains the clashes between various theoretical positions present in the current literature. The overview presented here is thus provisional.

Moving and Acting

It is relatively easy for an adult to define the action of a baby who points to objects in his or her environment, vocalizes to request them, moves to get them, attracts them toward him, moves closer to the person calling him, and so on. Behaviors such as these, which can be observed at about 7–8 months, provide sets of convergent criteria that enable an adult to describe the action in functional terms, by pointing out the desired or attained goal, or the intention manifested by voluntary movements: "He wanted his teddy bear, he bumped into a chair while he was creeping to get it."

In contrast, it is more problematical to define what action is or could be in younger infants. There is no longer any doubt that "mass agitation" does not characterize the newborn or the infant. We can now distinguish many diversified motor repertoires during the neonatal period. These repertoires differ in terms of the form of the movements that compose them, their frequency, velocity, periodicity, their relationship to states of vigilance, the body segments they affect, and the postures they give rise to (Cioni, Ferrari, & Prechtl, 1989; Mellier, 1990; Prechtl & Nolte, 1984).

The existence of the distinct motor repertoires leads to the question of which of these constitute actions in the strict sense (i.e., which will lead to a change in a relationship with the outside world). In this respect, and despite advances in the field, some notions are diehard: Some psychologists still subscribe to Gesell's claim that up to the age of 2 months, the infant is an "external fetus" who reproduces endogenous patterns, despite transition to the external environment. The continuity exemplified by certain movement repertoires prompted Prechtl (1984) to suggest that motility in the newborn tends to obey endogenous determinants, rather than responding to situations. A view of this type, which assesses motor behavior in terms of the absence of immediate effects, has only limited value from a developmental perspective because it ignores the possibility of long-term effects and does not raise questions about prerequisites. The assumption is that not all movements are at the source of actions, but rather that certain movements, whose purposes are not always detectable at the outset, may play a considerable role in the later formation of an action. Two examples are particularly illustrative of this. For years, the grasping reflex was seen as the source of prehensile actions, because it was presumed that it led directly to manual exploration by exercise of contact sensitivity. However, data showing that for the newborn, reaching only results in brief touching without grasping (Halverson, 1937; de Schonen & Bresson, 1984) and showing the absence of recourse to manual tact sensitivity over the first 3 months (Twitchell, 1970) both argue against this hypothesis. It has also been shown (Brown & Frederickson, 1977) that nonnutritive sucking favors grasping such that the sucking response mediates the transition from reflex grasping to voluntary holding. This suggests that the status of these two responses is different and that the sucking response is closer to action than palm grasping, that is, more open to the outside world, and more conducive to acting as an instrumental response in very young infants; the sucking response might provide information on the stimulus whereas the palm grasping did not. We come up again on this point later.

On the other hand, we have reasons to believe that rhythmicities strengthen basic motor patterns. They are initially forms of exercise "for its own sake" and they persist for a long period of time parallel to the emergence of adaptive responses (Thelen & Fisher, 1982). Later they become parts of automatic components of actions and can have the role of a regulator in the preparation for acting.

These comments suggest that movement in itself is not the synonym of action. In the remainder of this chapter, action is considered to include one or several movements in relation to a physical, distinguishable object that is external to it. I define a *physical element* as an object, an event, or a transformation. *Acting* here refers to act on something. Defining an action thus means that we must identify the element it is directed toward, and show that there is a connection between the movement(s) and this element. However, this places few restrictions on the scope of what I have termed *action*. Peristaltic contractions in the stomach that swirl the gastric pouch deserve to be included just as we would include grasping a cup, tying shoes, or reading. In all these instances, an action produces an observable change in the situation, and the resulting state of the movement(s) differs from the one which existed before.

We thus need to scrutinize the connection itself. Stomach contractions are produced each time and as soon as food enters the stomach. They are triggered by the arrival of food. In the last analysis, food is the cause of the contractions, which is the cause of their transformation. On the one hand, we are dealing with an automatic act. In the case of object-directed action, however, a behavior is produced that the object (cup or book) does not necessarily elicit in all instances. In the latter case, the connection between movement and object assigns a meaning to this reached object, whatever the modality of reaching. Thus, we can define an action as a meaningful relation established between an agent and a target-object. This leads to admit that any action is related to information processing on the target, regardless of how poor the processed information would be.

Perceiving and Acting

Is perception necessary for action from the outset, or does it become necessary over the course of time? It is always troubling to observe the apparent dissociation in 2- to 4-month-olds between their simultaneous activities: They can touch or suck an object they never look at, or propel an arm toward a region of nearby space while their attention is obviously directed to another region. This apparent dissociation between perception and action occurs against a background of awkwardness: fingers intermingled, cramping postures, the hand pushing away an object it was moving toward, and so forth. These features raise doubts as to whether perception can help the young infant to act.

The hypothesis that sensitivities first fulfill the function of a warning system, when elicitations reach a sufficient level of intensity (Turkewitz, Gardner, & Lewkowicz, 1984) and are rapidly but transiently mobilized, has nevertheless scarcely been exploited except for the visual system, where researchers have taken up the argument of anatomic differentiations and their different developmental chronologies (Bronson, 1974). Because it is clear, however, that sensory response always requires motor participation, and that each sense organ is a motor organ, the motor facet of this hypothesis consists of viewing the motor aspects that govern the optimal positions of these organs as innate and reflexive. Although complex, the orientation reflex has been cited to strengthen the picture of a perceptual capacity that is all in all "impoverished" (Banks, 1980)—too impoverished in any case to play the role of guide that perception plays later. At best, it can trigger a movement or a sequence of movements, but not intervene in their unfolding. Thus, when Regal, Ashmead, and Salapatek (1983) found that 10-week-old infants in a tracking task initiate a head movement toward a target before moving their eyes as often as the reverse, whereas adults move their eyes first, they viewed this response as the sign of a behavioral instability that is still immature and forms an obstacle to the establishment of head–eye coordination. By using other methods, Owen and Lee (1986) showed that at the same age, head movement adjusts better to the movement of a visual target than eye movement, and Owen and Lee reached a radically different interpretation than Regal et al.: They claimed that the head and not the eye can serve as a reference plane for the establishment of geographic co-ordinates that serve to maintain the ocular fixation point.

The role of perception as a trigger, although often mentioned in attempts to account for the first prereaching gestures and reaching or hand–mouth transport, gives rise to varied hypotheses regarding the role of perceptual information and the role of different modalities.What kind of perceptual information is used in action? Is spatial localization enough ("where?") or is knowledge of the object ("what") needed? In each case, neither the same pathways nor the same structures govern localization and object knowledge (Atkinson & Braddick, 1989). This explains the need to know what perceptual information, or what information is engaged first in the initiation of an action.

Two general and opposed types of theories have been proposed regarding the relationships between perception and action. The Piagetian theory claims that perceptual knowledge derives from action. This theory assumes that, initially, a localization is enough to trigger a movement toward a source of stimulation, and that the effects of this response will engender knowledge. The other theory, whose major proponent is E. Gibson, views perceptual knowledge as the sine qua non condition for action. Both take different stances in regard to the sensory modalities involved.

RELATIONSHIPS BETWEEN PERCEPTION AND ACTION IN THEORIES OF DEVELOPMENT

Piagetian Theory

Piaget was among the first to consider perception–action relationships and aim at describing and accounting for their evolution over time. Piaget described a series of stages that begin with a set of reflexes "from hereditary assembly," corresponding to the first reflex movements of the newborn, and lead to unified and unificatory action schemes such as walking by the end of the first year.

According to Piaget, what occurs first of all is the effect produced by reflex movements on the body itself, which leads to their repetition. For example, sucking repeated "for its own sake" is consolidated, through repetition, and, when applied to all objects which come into contact with the mouth, is a source of extension, "recognitory assimilation," and discrimination. Perception at this stage is reduced to discontinuous information gathering; nevertheless, perception enables the infant, by registering the effects of movement, to structure a "buccal sensory motor space." The key feature, however, is that exercise of movement is in itself constitutive of a scheme, that is, of a stable sketch, which will serve so to speak as a yardstick, a building block, for situations the infant encounters. The first sucking scheme "all of a piece, with no internal mobility" cannot, however, coordinate with others. Several months will have to elapse before movements, operating on objects in the environment in the "secondary circular reactions" stage, and teleonomic sensitivities (vision in particular) can take part in the creation of new schemes. Piaget sets the emergence of coordination, which he terms *vision prehension*, at about $4\frac{1}{2}$ months. This coordination unifies the visual and haptic fields. The infant grasps objects when he has perceived them in the same visual field as his own hand (Piaget, 1936). Various sequential gestures such as arm-hand approach, opening of the hand adjusted to the object, grasping, touching, and/or transportation of the object to the mouth are repeatedly performed and often performed with the aid of vision. Such behavioral sequences can be moreover modulated and enriched: The sight of a rattle hung above the baby's crib prompts the baby to look for the string that allows him to move it. This search behavior calls for a unified action space, including visual localization of the object, the element connected to it (the string), the gesture(s) that will be applied to it, and the effect produced. Starting from these first stages, a prolongation of systems associated in action gives rise to progressively more complex and more flexible schemes that coalesce in the generalized coordination scheme represented at the end of the first year of life by the emergence of independent walking. Locomotion unifies all the local or partial spaces built previously in a movement space and thus completes giving actions a structure whose laws of composition are already in practice those of the operatory structures which will be constructed later. This practical prefiguration makes the sensory-motor period the first step in intelligence. What has bearing for our purposes in Piagetian theory is the idea that "the ontogenesis of space, in sensory motor intelligence, is entirely dominated by the progressive organization of movements" (Piaget, 1947, p. 136). Movements, when associated with perceptions, accomplish what according to Piaget perception alone cannot do, that is, bring some order to the outside world for the individual. Hence action, in Piagetian theory, is the source of knowledge (Piaget, 1974).

Gibsonian Theory

The theories put forward by J. J. Gibson (1950, 1979) and that E. J. Gibson has continued to clarify and enhance are diametrically opposed to Piagetian positions. Gibsonian theory is centered around three key assumptions:

First, the Gibsons assume that perception provides the observer with direct knowledge of the outside world, through the functional organization of sensory organs and the active mobility of the organism. As deficient as a child may seem to be in his possibilities for "active mobility," these possibilities are far from nonexistent. Moving his eyes, turning his head, sucking his thumb (mobilities that are all present in the fetus) are sufficient for activities of other parts of the body to be integrated into the activity of the receptor sensory organs proper, such that the activity of a *perceptual system* in the Gibsonian sense groups several sorts of sensitivities. The mere fact of looking at an object combines vision, vestibular sensitivity, and proprioception. The production of a movement itself is the source of a *functional equivalence* of perception.

Second, as a logical corollary of the extension of the notion of perceptual system, the contents of perception are not specified according to their sensory input. For example, a characteristic of a visually perceived object is not initially specified as visual because the same object can be specified by equivalent information in other modalities, which make it *amodal.* This leads to the idea that perceiving does not consist of receiving stimulations and then processing them but rather extracting *invariants*—either amodal or multimodal—directly from objects or events. Thus a property that is first perceived tactually, for example, roughness, is transfered immediately, without any need for analysis, and recognized visually.

Third, the Gibsons stipulated that an individual does not perceive external physical properties, whose objectivity needs to be verified, but rather "affordances" (J. J. Gibson, 1979), that is, qualities, properties, or features related to his own action capabilities, and hence relevant to him. Nevertheless, affordances are not subjective. According to Adolf, Gibson and Eppler (1990), an affordance is an objective relationship "between physical properties of an actor, and those of the environment." When this relationship changes, the scope of possible actions changes. For instance, Warren and Whang (1987) studied how, to get through a door, a person walking needs to change his posture as a function of the width of the door. The perception of this dimension determines either maintaining an upright posture, or twisting trunk and shoulders. The same physical width values do not result in twisting in all subjects. These values vary as a function of subjects' girth.

Gibsonian theory was not initially a theory of development. However, in this framework, it is clear that development can be characterized by changes in optimal conditions for action and that the transition from one form of action to another, which occurs as the systems that underpin behavior and growth of the organism mature, are relative to perceptual information, which specifies a new affordance. According to Gibsonian theory, understanding development no longer requires describing general mechanisms of transformation and discovering their principles, because affordances are specific to age. The theory does not explain a genesis and does not need to refer to explanatory concepts, such as *filiation* or *equilibration.*

Conclusion

Does perception govern action, of which it is an integral part as of the start of life as the Gibsons claim, or rather does it come in second, to connect effect to movement—an achievement in itself—and hence enable consolidation and the extension of motor schemes, as Piaget argued?

The opposed positions of Piaget and Gibson on action in the young child should not conceal the fact that both theories view action as a sensory-motor organization, and believe that this organization is (Gibson) or becomes (Piaget) cognitive.

However, the real conflict in their positions with regard to the deep ties between perception and movement also demonstrates, first of all, our ignorance. Because our definitions are fuzzy, our criteria far from appropriate, and our methods limited, the data we obtain are sketchy or tentative. However, if we accept the fact that a theory outlines a provisional state of knowledge, and that at best it points to a promising route to follow, it is reasonable to review the facts that apparently disconfirm one theory or the other to see whether they undermine the edifice or only demolish part of it.

The following example is illustrative of this. Piaget (1936) situated the emergence of prehension–vision coordination at about $4\frac{1}{2}$ months. More recent research (Bloch, 1990; Von Hofsten, 1982, 1983) has shown that relationships are initiated between eye and hand as early as the first days following birth. A demonstration of the precocity of these relationships does not suffice. We need to raise the issue of similarity between these early relationships and those observed in the 4-month-old by Piaget. First of all, are these relationships part of an action? Comparison of movements in the presence and the absence of a target object provides a clear-cut response: Yes, it is really an action with respect to the target object in the environment. The unfolding of the action, however, differs in some respects from the one Piaget described: Visual localization of the object does not necessarily give rise to a prolonged fixation. Newborns never look at the limb moving toward the object. We only observe to-and-fro gazing when the hand has stopped near the object. Reaching rarely terminates by object grasping. However, the reaching movement, which appears to be triggered but not guided by visual input, presents stable parameters when the situation is repeated, in that the latency and the slow velocity of arm and hand transport, and the shape of the trajectory have considerable individual consistency. This suggests that we are witnessing a motor scheme that experience, through initial steps, consolidates.

To restate the question concerning the functional aspects of reaching behavior in the newborn in Gibsonian terms, can we discern an "affordance" relationship determined by the perceptual extraction of an object quality? In this respect, the absence of contact, or grasping in case of contact, and the absence of tactual exploration shed little light on a possible relationship of this type and suggest that although reaching does not have object grasping as a goal, the maintenance of the hand in the periphery near the object acts to frame the useful visual field to optimize the visual perception of the object. Hence manual motor activity is apparently served by perception. This appears to favor E. Gibson's interpretation. An analysis of fine finger movements when the newborn is presented an object or a person (Rönnqvist & Von Hofsten, 1994) reveals systematic differences in movement patterns, testifying to perceptual distinction. However, this does not necessarily imply an amodal distinction. There are several reasons to believe that assigning a visual goal is based on a type of dominance of the visual system rather than on an amodal perception (Bloch, 1989).

THE BABY'S SENSORY-MOTOR TOOLS

Functionality of the Sensory Systems

Newborns, except in special cases, are exposed to a multimodal environment, just as the adult is. The infant has already been in this type of environment before birth: noises and sounds, odors and tastes were part of the uterine world. All the sensory systems are functional when the fetus is born at term.

There is little question that more than one modality is involved in the newborn's actions, although all the sensory systems are relatively immature at birth. However, they represent a mosaic of various levels of immaturity. Thus, it may be the case that only certain sensititivies, the ones used in utero, are part of his or her immediate repertory and are more apt than others to enable the newborn to assign a meaning to the world around him. We now have a fairly good idea of the chronology of prenatal maturation of the sensory systems (see Gottlieb, 1983). We know less about what produces variations in the rhythm of development of a given system, but it is clear that the sensory systems develop at different rates. Nevertheless, there is no nullifying condition to the involvement of any of the sensory modalities in the infant's actions at birth.

Intermodal and Postural Functionality

There is no doubt that all the sensory systems in humans are complex and that they are composed of different subsystems, which carry out several functions. Although none seems as complex as the visual system, none is unidimensional either. This should prevent us from viewing intersensorality in terms of growing complexity as compared to unimodality, but rather prompt us to inquire under what conditions one or the other may have the opportunity to converge.

There is also no question that no sensory modality is completely isolated from any other. No sensory exercise is free from repercussions on other sensitivities. This is shown by shared pathways such as the thalamus, where the major sensitive inputs converge; the organization of the subcortical structures such as the colliculus in which layers of differentiated cells respond to unimodal and multimodal activations and where motor commands are issued based on the multimodal inputs and the importance of associative areas: "A surprisingly large expanse of what appeared to be 'association' cortex is actually given over to multiple representation of sensory and motor fields" (Shepherd, 1988, p. 627). At the behavioral level, we can assess to what extent certain sensitivities are intertwined: smell and taste, for example. When we have a cold or a stuffed nose, we tend to find that food has no taste.

The use of sensory organs relies on the mobility of the sensitive receptors. This mobility is governed by the mobility of the sensory organ itself—for example, the eye—or by the mobility of the transporting segment: Head mobility makes the ear mobile. Because the head carries almost all the exterioceptors, it is clear why its mobility plays a major role in perceptual capture of information from the environment. At birth, however, the head is a source of noise. The newborn cannot hold his head upright, although he can produce some righting reactions (Fiorentino, 1981).

In addition to poor head control, axial hypotonicity in the human newborn is associated with a hypertonicity of the extremities (Mackawa & Ochiai, 1975). This distribution of tone forms an obstacle to organized perceptions. For example, the fall of the head leads to a randomization of gaze positions, which prevents the baby from associating the positions of a stimulus successively perceived to his own position. This is also true for hearing. Hypertonicity of the hand hinders tactual sensitivity during grasping.

According to Grenier (1981), the perceptual inabilities of the newborn are partly due to the relative weight of the different parts of the body and the resulting mechanical constraints. These act to impede the sensory channels. When a newborn is "actively" helped to maintain back and head upright, he remains in a quiet alert state, attends to the environment, and is capable of behaviors analogous to those that he will not produce spontaneously until about 3 months. However, this active postural support is only achieved by a raising of axial tone, which is slow and costly in terms of energy for the infant. Many infants fail (only 17% of infants between the ages of 7 days and 3 weeks succeed; Grenier, 1981). The behavioral changes that accompany an upright head position, whether righting is active or maintained passively through neck support, nevertheless indicate that similar to movements, perceptions are part of a postural framework that responds to their organization.

Posture includes dynamic aspects, such as antigravitational reactions and projections of body segments into external space. This calls for geographic referents, or at least geographical correspondents of egocentric references. Directed movements such as turning the head, extending the arm, stepping, and so forth require a spatial calibration of the head, arm, or leg movement. The orientation response shows that this type of calibration is possible at birth. It allows the neonate to move in a determined direction in space, discriminated from others. The issue is whether this spatial calibration can be established on a proprioceptive basis alone or whether there is a need for exteroceptive cooperation. Because of the many and rapid changes in the size of body segments and because of their allometric relationships, it was claimed that proprioception could not be the prime candidate (Ganz, 1975). This point of view has been challenged by studies in dynamic system development (Thelen, Kelso, & Fogel, 1987; Von Hofsten, 1989) and by studies of visual proprioception (Butterworth, 1983; Jouen, 1988; Jouen & Bloch, 1981). These studies have shown that postures can change in relation to visual stimulation. Another approach consists in studying how directed movements and perception vary in relationship to postural changes used as independent variables in experiments.

To date, very few studies have focused on the relationship between posture and directed movements and their consequences for perceptual response in infants. The available data show with a remarkable degree of consistency to what extent these movements and perceptions depend on the postural framework in which they are set. Turkewitz, Moreau, and Birch (1966) were the first to point to this important role played by the position of the head in orientation reactions to a source of sound in the newborn, and later in establishing lateral differences that affect perceptual thresholds (Turkewitz, 1977). In a series of studies of visual pursuit in pre- and full-term newborns (Bloch, 1989; Bloch, Mellier, & Fuenmajor, 1984), we have shown that the upright position of the head plays a key role in the organization of visual activity. Infants were tested either in the supine position or with the head upraised on a pillow, or in the sitting position with the torso and the head well supported but free to move. These different positions had no major effect on the extent of pursuit. They did, however, lead to some significant qualitative differences in the frequency of stimulus loss, gaze centration, and vestibulo-ocular reflex. This prompted the conclusion that vision acts as an organizer of space when the visual coordinates are harmonized with the head coordinates, in reference to the median vertical axis of the head (Bloch & Carchon, 1992).

In a study using a passive displacement space to investigate anticipation of an attractive stimulus in 4- to 6-month-olds, Bloch (1977) reported that this response (a rotation of the head in the direction where the stimulus was to appear) varied systematically as a function of the position in which the baby had been placed in a mobile seat (i.e., whether his back was upright or inclined). More recently, Pieraut-Le Bonniec (1990) and Rochat (1990) showed that manual prehension gestures change as a function of stage in the sitting position. In a longitudinal study of prehension, Corbetta (1992) reported that interlimb coordination, when assessed according to criteria of synchronous tension of the same muscle groups on the left and the right, emerges as the infant acquires the sitting position, coincides with gradual mastery, and is manifest in a transient bimanuality between 5 and 8 months.

HOW DO PERCEPTIONS INTERVENE IN ACTION?

The question of how perceptions intervene in action is linked to choice of theoretical position concerning maturity. If it is assumed that action is governed by a "prestructured set of muscular commands which enable movement to unfold fully and once triggered, independently of sensory reafferences" (Keele, 1968, p. 388), that is, if a closed definition of the notion of motor program is adopted, little interest will be devoted to perceptual information capture. The criterion for assessing intervention of perception in action, regardless of modality, is the motor flexibility, which enables structural modifications, rectifications in trajectories and speed, adjustments in direction and distance, and anticipations to take place. This flexibility may, according to von Holst (1954), be governed exclusively through proprioception, thanks to the "efference copy" it produces. It enables the individual to differentiate the effect of his own movement from the effect of the movement of an object perceived in the environment.

Viewing action in terms of sensory-motor coordination lends greater weight to exteroceptive sensitivities and particular to teleonomic sensitivities which capture distal information. From this point of view, all sensory-motor coordination includes intermodal coordination (Lockman, 1990).

Sequential segmentation of action in this perspective presents several advantages for examination of the differentiated or unitary role of perceptions in action. It serves to identify the phases where perceptual intervention takes place, and to determine which modalities are involved simultaneously or successively. We can assess the effect of perceptual intervention *a contrario*, by suppressing a category of perceptual information or by momentary deprivation of sensory input (see Bloch, 1990). This calls for measurement techniques of perceptual activity and temporally complex motor activity, and fine-movement analysis techniques, which should be as noninvasive as possible when used on the newborn. This explains in part why despite the striking increase in experiments in this area, only a small body of data is currently available.

Feedback or Feedforward Effects?

This question is not only related to early perceptual mechanisms but also to positions about motor control. If perception is presumed to influence action as a feedback, no correction of movement can be expected when the act is performing, but only from trial to trial (as in a learning process).

On the other hand, the hypothesis of feedforward effects implies that perception guides the movement step by step during execution. To shed light on whether perceptions can exert a feedforward or only a feedback effect in the infant, a number of studies are reviewed.

Data reported in von Hofsten (1982, 1983) on reaching, results in Bloch (1987) and Bloch and Carchon (1992) on head–eye coordination, and data in Rochat (1987, 1989); Butterworth and Hopkins (1988), and Blass, Filion, Rochat, Hoffmeyer, and Metzger (1989) on hand–mouth coordination argue in favor of a proactive role of perception from birth, but also reveal hierarchical differences between the modalities involved in these situations. The major indicators for a feedforward role of perception are as follows:

- Hand–mouth coordination is generally considered to be the first, with lengthy preparation during fetal life by the activity of nonnutritive sucking (Humphrey, 1970) and transport of the thumb into the mouth. In the newborn, substance differentiation prompts the introduction of fingers in the mouth (Blass et al., 1989; Rochat, 1987).

- Independence of hand movement toward the mouth as compared to the rooting reflex (Butterworth & Hopkins, 1988).

- Observed direct trajectories, with anticipated mouth opening (Butterworth & Hopkins, 1988).

The fact that the ingestion of several drops of sugar water is enough to produce an increase in subsequent hand–mouth transport, whereas the same quantity of pure water does not, prompted Rochat (1990) to view taste as a primary trigger for nonnutritive sucking, encouraging the baby to seek out buccal contact with sweet substances. However, he argued that it is tactilo–buccal sensitivity that governs hand–mouth transports. They do not always give rise to a sucking response (nonnutritive) but to exploratory mouth movements, which are accompanied by adoption of a posture that favors short manual movement trajectories and accurate aiming.

A description has been put forward by Bloch (1989) with regard to the role of a direct and beneficial sensitivity of action for other behaviors such as head–eye pursuit and reaching. The main arguments derive from the following observations: Visual experience prompts the premature infant to regulations that favor the association of the head with visual pursuit. In the full-term infant, the possibilities for maintaining sustained visual contact with the target determine the emergence of an associated head movement; the first directional eye–head coupling is only maintained when the infant is fixating the target with little and slow eye displacements (i.e., exhibits continuity; Carchon & Bloch, 1993). In reaching, the visual mode plays a similar role. Hand movements gain in directional accuracy (Von Hofsten, 1986) and frequency (Bloch, 1989) as cumulative fixation times on the object increase. Reaching does not generally end in capture or manual exploration of the objec*, but rather in a placement of the hand in the visual field. This placement is not random. It situates the hand in the vicinity of the target, but a* its periphery with respect to the infant's midline. The hand is thus seen beyond the target, and forms the boundary for exploratory gaze movements. It seems to bound the midpoint of the visual field. Studies by Mellier (1990) on newborns with impaired vision show that the visual activity of these newborns, which is initially disorganized, becomes more regular and more clearly oriented when their visual field is bounded by structured screens (checkerboards).

In the earliest coordinations, it appears that one sensory modality orients actions and fixes the goal. No competition or intermodal interference has been reported and there have been few reports of cooperation: Vision plays practically no role in hand–mouth transport, and the tactile mode appears to be lacking in the rare contacts with objects in reaching situations.

These observations are not sufficient to determine whether the control of an exteroceptive modality on action resides exclusively in goal designation or the meaning it confers on this goal; that is, is it restricted to general orientation, or does it consist of step-by-step guidance of reaching movements? The scope and levels of multisensory integration presumed to be operant in the two cases differ considerably.

One specific difficulty concerning the infant is that we have little information on his abilities for proprioceptive discrimination and processing. There are good reasons to believe that the functional development of the vestibular system and its tight links to the visual system and in particular peripheral vision enable discrimination of movements perceived in the environment and retinal displacement (for a review see Jouen & Bloch, 1981; Yonas & Owsley, 1987). Neonates produce vestibular reactions to optical flow (Jouen & Lepecq, 1989) and become able during the first 3 months to use motion parallax as depth cues (Kellman, Hofsten, & Soares, 1987). However, little is known about abilities for processing proprioceptive information by nonspecific systems. We have poor information about early kinesthetic acuity and about the possible use of information provided from the neuromuscular spindles. This question remains open even for adults (Bloch, 1993; Clark, 1992). Observations on congenitally blind infants show that the orientation of their hand movements toward a source of sound is clearly impaired, and appears to be linked to head position (bent forward when the infant is held in a sitting position; Bullinger & Mellier, 1988). Only the effects of exercise in the construction of motor patterns (Maciaszczyk & Bloch, 1988; Zelazo, Cohen, & Zelazo, 1989) suggest that young infants differentiate relative positions of their limbs and code their movements in space.

On the other hand, Bahrick and Watson (1985) have shown that 3-month-old infants do not visually distinguish a film of their own leg movements from a film of the leg movements produced by a peer, whereas 5-month-olds are sensible to the proprioceptive–visual matching. It seems that vision can influence posture and movement at a time when proprioception has no reciprocal influence on vision.

Perceptual Guidance and Development

Guidance of action presupposes that the exteroceptive control modality (or modalities) processes along with propriocepive information, the successive position of the parts of the body in movement, extracts the direction in terms of the goal and the distance from the goal, and contributes if necessary to correcting these parameters. In visuomotor tasks such as reaching, two forms of guidance have been distinguished in both animals and human adults: *directional guidance*, driven by peripheral vision and referenced to egocentric coordinates (Jeannerod & Biguer, 1982), and *positional guidance*, driven by central vision with a framework that is geographic (allocentric) (Paillard & Amblard, 1985). The former is thought to intervene in the first phases of movement toward the goal-object. The latter is thought to emerge later and operate in later phases (see Von Hofsten & Lee, 1982). Although at birth vision clearly exercises control over directed movements, for example, reaching for an object (Rader & Stern, 1982), this control at best probably consists of directional guidance (Von Hofsten, 1982). It is assumed furthermore that the features of this guidance differ from features of adult directional guidance in both duration and continuity. Because this hypothesis has never been tested, we are currently testing this possibility in an experiment comparing situations where peripheral vision is restricted to entirely analog situations versus when it is not (the subjects are newborns aged 3–5 days).

What happens during the first 3 months of life does not shed much light on the problem of guidance. As of the seventh week (Von Hofsten, 1984), the baby looks much more attentively at objects, but the frequency of reaching movements decreases considerably as though visual activity exhausted capacities for movement. A number of factors, including the simultaneous activation of agonistic and antagonistic muscles (which has the effect of blocking movement; Gatev, 1972), dissociation of a prewired movement pattern linked to the postural maturation of the cephalic motor system (Mounoud & Vinter, 1981), and overly high intensity values of visual stimulation (McGuire & Turkewitz, 1978), have been cited as some of the reasons for the observed changes. An alternative interpretation is that maintaining a visual centration on the object may restrict the peripheral visual field and the infant might not assign a precise direction when initiating the arm-hand movement. This can be tested experimentally by bringing the baby's hand passively into the object zone, which serves to measure whether the frequency of "active" reaches increases or not after the experimenter lets go of the hand.

In other situations, it has been observed that the infant's visual attention increases at about 3 months. Rochat (1984) noted that infants at this age bring all objects placed in their hands to their mouths, and do so quickly. However, G. Butterworth and D. Lew (personal communication, 1992) reported considerable individual differences. Some infants look at what they have in their hands, and this gaze results in a specific organization of transport to the mouth—the mouth opens earlier, and hand aiming into the oral cavity is more accurate and the movement is slower.

Between the first and the third month, visual perception becomes more tightly coupled with the head motor system. Head displacement is more adjusted in direction and velocity, and shows efficient visual tracking or pursuit. However, the determinants and processes involved in this coupling remain somewhat unclear. Mitkin (1987) suggested that it results from a change in ocular motor functioning, that is, from both the reduced amplitude of the saccade and the reduced intersaccadic intervals. Other authors do not report a smoothing process of this type. Roucoux, Culee, and Roucoux (1983) observed a decrease in saccade amplitude. Carchon and Bloch (1993) observed that the intersaccadic intervals did not decrease but rather increased during the first month, and the amplitude of the saccade became more variable as a function of target excentricity in the second and third months. This led us to conclude that continuous perception of the target, which is a sign of visual attention, is a precondition for head–eye coordination. Nevertheless, more data are needed to check whether this condition of visual continuity indeed determines strength of coupling.

All these observations suggest that very early on, sensory-motor coordinations are endowed with considerable adaptive flexibility, a feature that is consistent with Thelen's (1992) view of the development of prehension as moving "from an individual selection of appropriate task-directed solutions."

There is a general consensus in the field that the changes that involve the hand occur at about 4–5 months. Reaching slows down at the end of the trajectory (braking). The hand opens before reaching the object. But that would not represent an anticipated shaping, because the opening is not governed by the size of the target object, according to the observations of Lockman, Ashmead, and Bushnell (1984). At this age, however, the gesture results in capture. The object captured is not only looked at but felt, turned over, explored tactually, and only later brought to the mouth, if at all (McCall, 1974; Ruff, 1990). At this age, the baby apparently simultaneously associates visual perception and tactual perception.

Opinions differ as regards the emergence between 4 and 5 months of positional guidance. Gazes to and fro between hand and object just before capture, which Piaget (1936, 1947) cited, have unfortunately not been studied systematically. Adjustment of the hand to the orientation of an object in space (e.g., when the object is a thin bar presented either horizontally or vertically) is not very accurate (Lockman et al., 1984; Von Hofsten & Fazel-Zandy, 1984). Nevertheless, at $4\frac{1}{2}$ months, babies easily catch a target with a speed reaching 30 cm/sec (Von Hofsten & Lindhagen, 1979), although this velocity is still an obstacle to visual pursuit with continuous fixations (Bloch, 1988).

The hypothesis of manual pointing with multimodal visuo-haptic guidance is also problematical. It implies a calibration of the movement such that the adjustment for distance of the outreached arm-hand takes the length of the arm into account (Ashmead, 1990). In addition, it involves a "preshaping" of the qualities of the target object such as size or volume, presence of angles, concavity, irregularities, and so forth. Calibration, as Ashmead and Hart (1989) showed, is dependent on posture. Because the baby has not mastered the sitting position, he must control a broad set of body segments, including shoulders and the torso. Results obtained by Rochat (1990) indicate that this calibration progresses as a function of mastery of the sitting position, between 4 and 6–7 months. In addition, anticipated adjustment of the hand to object features has just begun to emerge (Pieraut-Le-Bonniec, 1990).

Overall, these data suggest that at about 4 months the goal of the reaching activity changes, rather than its organization. The association of visual and tactual exploration of an object emerges as a sort of end product of the reaching act. This multimodal association has a hierarchical organization. In this respect, the observed asymmetry between visual and tactual exploration reported by Bushnell, Shaw, and Strauss (1985) in the 6-month-old, and replicated by Bushnell and Weinberger (1987) at 10 and 12 months, forms a compelling argument in favor of visual dominance. The visual perception of object characteristics conditions manual exploration, even for features described as tactual, such as texture.

After 4–5 months, grasping is mastered and researchers have generally turned to other modes of object exploration. Steele and Pederson (1977) found that manipulative exploration of an object depended on its visual characteristics in 6-month-olds. Latencies and duration of visual and manipulative responses were considered and led researchers to conclude that a stimulus selection determined the nature of responses. A change of color trained only an increase of looking. Changes of shape and texture elicited both increasing visual and manipulative exploration. Ruff (1984) showed that from 6 to 12 months, the repertoire of actions on objects enriches considerably and involves modes of explorations differentiated as a function of object characteristics. By comparing what infants do at 6, 9, and 12 months with objects that varied in rigidity, shape, texture, and weight, Palmer (1989) observed that motor acts such as shaking, banging, mouthing, and pressing were specifically related to visually perceived characteristics. The age effect is less apparent in these relationships than in the growing range of different acts. This led Palmer (1989) to confirm, after Ruff, that development in the second half of the first year of life consists in an economy of action; she argued for a confirmation of "affordances" in the relationship between perceived characteristics and action.

CONCLUSION AND A LOOK TO THE FUTURE

Overall, the data on the first year of life can be restated briefly as follows: Infants first act to know, then act because they know. The first form of sensory-motor coordination appeals to vision as a prime modality for goal specification in space. The second form of coordination testifies to multimodal perceptual knowledge, determining verifications through action.

Is this conclusion consistant with the data (i.e. with the successive organization of behaviors)? Doesn't it derive in fact from a change in focus between studies on the young infant and those that deal with later ages? Studies on exploratory behavior draw up categories of motor acts without analyzing them. Studies such as those by Diamond and Gilbert (1989) show that the organization of prehensile movements changes between the ages of 7 and 8 months in relation to the properties of the object to grasp and that obstacles related to bimanual coordination can still prevent the infant from taking objects placed in front of him a short distance away. Second, studies on younger infants have rarely varied the objects or the properties of the objects presented. It cannot be claimed that infants do not explore before the ages of 5–6 months, as they use means other than their hands. Visual anticipation and expectations studied by Haith, Hazan, and Goodman (1988), use of auditory cues for localizing a target and organizing head and eye movements (Clifton, Morrongiello, Kulig, & Dowd, 1981) and later, reaching in the dark (Butterworth, 1992) clearly indicate that perceptive information serves to divide space, or space and time, into different areas and to direct exploratory movements into areas of capture. Butterworth (1992) observed that peripherical locations of the target object are more accurately reached in the dark than central locations at every age between 3 and 12 months. Bushnell, Boudreau, Roder, and Weinberger (1992) showed that manual explorations of two very different objects vary at light and in the dark in infants from 7 to 12 months old.

The activity of the teleonomic sensory modalities deserves finer investigation, and comparison with the activities of contact modalities, to determine whether their frameworks are the same, whether they preside over similar organizations of movement, whether they intervene in action at identical points in time, or, one after the other, whether they are "interchangeable" or provide different information.

There is no doubt that action even in the newborn associates exteroception and proprioception. It is not assumed, however, that this association is
strong enough for impending groping and errors. It is not clear whether all
the exteroceptive modalities play an identical role. The study of actions in
the case of congenital sensory deprivation would provide useful information.
There are few studies of this type. It appears, however, that vision substitutes
do not consist of automatic compensations and call for specific learning
(Mellier, 1994). This suggests that vision plays a specific role in actions on
the environment. Vision has been said to be dominant. My position is that
vision plays a qualitatively different role from the other sensory modalities,
and a role of prompter: There is appeal to vision in postural activities, in
the orientation of the body in space, which conditions activities of transport
of the limbs. There are strong reasons to believe that vision has the task of
homogenizing systems of geographic and egocentric coordinates. Vision
thus intervenes before a movement is initiated, in preparatory positioning,
and hence contributes to framing action. In the case of visual privation,
auditory perception can provide a subsidiary frame of spatial reference.

In addition, the connections that are established between information
gathered through different sensory modalities are not exclusively based on
equivalences or intermodal invariants, as Katz pointed out (1989). Tactual
images (e.g., the softness of velvet) are translated into visual images, and
reciprocally the exploratory procedures for tactual properties depend on
visual cues. However, visual exploration has no such reciprocal dependency
on tactual cues (see Klatzky, Lederman, & Matula, 1991). Thus, in what
Spear and Molina (1987) termed the "selection of a stimulus" (the elements
of the stimulation that are discriminated and stored in memory), the sensory
modalities appear to play specific roles.

Nevertheless, although this issue has sparked much debate among
specialists of early childhood, I believe the controversy is due to extrapo-
lations on experiments on intermodal transfer. Total reciprocity is never
shown in transfers: neither at all ages, nor for all the properties between
the two modalities that are assumed to process them (see Lewkowicz, 1993;
Rose, chap. 11, this volume; Streri & Molina, chap. 12, this volume).

Mutimodal participation in action is, to put it one way, a principle. This
does not imply that it can incorporate any kind of modality. The difficulty
does not only arise from greater or lesser accessibility of perceptual
categories of information. Although action always represents a sensory-motor
integration, the sensory-motor relationships within the systems involved also
deserve analysis.

In the current state of the art—a sketchy one—perceptuomotor integration
seems to be partially constituted at birth; it becomes completely formed and
is reinforced during the entire first year of life through transformations of
different types—changes in mechanisms and functional changes, that is,

changes in goal. The latter appear to be the source of recurrent reorganizations, from the effects produced by action. They are also easier to recognize than internal changes whose immediate impacts escape us. In this respect, reintroducing experience, looking for what the baby learns by carrying out an action, would be of great interest. This is a perspective that the theory of dynamic systems has adopted (Thelen, 1990) by rehabilitating the notion of intent. This perspective can also be inscribed in other frameworks and other issues without necessarily having recourse to "loaded" notions such as intention, whose operational criteria need to be defined (Bloch, 1989; Willatts, 1990).

REFERENCES

Adolph, K. E., Gibson, E. J., & Eppler, M. A. (1990). Perceiving affordances of slopes : The ups and downs of toddlers' locomotion. *Emory cognition project.* (Tech. Rep. No. 16). Atlanta: Emory University.

Ashmead, D. H. (1990). Behavioral oraganization and perceptual coding in prehensile and postural development. In H. Bloch & B. I. Bertenthal (Eds.), *Sensory motor organizations and development in infancy and early childhood* (pp. 285–290). Dordrecht: Kluwer.

Ashmead, D. H., & Hart, C. (1989). Coordination of reaching and posture in human infants in prone and seated positions. *Acts of the 56th SRCD,* Kansas City, MO.

Atkinson, J., & Braddick, O. J. (1989). "Where" and "what" in visual search. *Perception, 18,* 181–189.

Bahrick, L. E., & Watson, J. S. (1985). Detection of intermodal proprioceptive contingency as a potential basis of self-perception in infancy. *Developmental Psychology, 21,* 963–973.

Banks, M. S. (1980). The development of visual accomodation during early infancy. *Child Development, 51,* 646–666.

Blass, E. M. (1990). Suckling : Determinants, changes, mechanisms and lasting impressions. *Developmental Psychology, 26,* 520–533.

Blass, E. M., Filion, T. J., Rochat, P., Hoffmeyer, L. B., & Metzger, M. A. (1989). Sensorymotor and motivational determinants of hand-mouth coordination in 1-3-day old human infants. *Developmental Psychology, 25,* 963–975.

Bloch, H. (1977). Quelques données sur les possibilités de structuration spatiale chez le bébé. (Some evidences on infant's spatial structuration). In *Psychologie expérimentale et comparée* (pp. 353–362). Paris: Presses Universitaires de.France.

Bloch, H. (1988, April). Early coordinations and visual anticipation. *Infant Behavior and Development* (Special ICIS Issue, 365–368).

Bloch, H. (1989). On early coordinations and their future, In A. De Ribaupierre (Ed.). *Transition mechanisms in child development* (pp. 259–282). New York: Cambridge University Press.

Bloch, H. (1990). Status and function of early sensory-motor coordination. In H. Bloch & B. I. Bertenthal (Eds.), *Sensory-motor organizations and development in infancy and early childhood* (pp. 163–178). Dordrecht: Kluwer.

Bloch, H. (in press). Proprioception et gestion de la motricité chez bébé: Peut-on répondre à Claparéde? (Proprioception and motor control in infancy: Can we respond to Claparede ?). *Année Psychologique.*

Bloch, H., & Carchon, I. (1992). On the onset of eye-head coordination in infants. *Behavioral Brain Research, 49,* 85–90.

Bloch, H., Mellier, D., & Fuenmajor, G. (1984, April). Organization of visual pursuit in pre-term infants. *Infant Behavior and Development, 7,* (Special ICIS Issue), 38.

Bronson, G. (1974). The postural growth of visual capacity. *Child Development, 45*, 873–890.

Brown, J. V., & Frederickson, W. T. (1977). The relationship between sucking and grasping in the human newborn: A precursor of hand mouth coordination? *Developmental Psychobiology, 10*, 489–498.

Bullinger, A., & Mellier, D. (1988). Influence de la cécité congénitale sur les conduites sensorimotrices chez l'enfant (Sensory-motor behaviors of blind-born infants). *European Bulletin of Cognitive Psychology, 8*, 191–203.

Bushnell, E. W., & Weinberger, N. (1987). Infants' detection of visual tactual discrepancies : Asymmetries that indicate a directive role of visual information. *Journal of Experimental Psychology, 13*, 601–608.

Bushnell, E. W., Shaw, L., & Strauss, D. (1985). Relationship between visual and tactual exploration by 6-month old. *Developmental Psychology, 21*, 591–600.

Bushnell, E. W., Boudreau, J. P., Roder, B., & Weinberger, N. (1992, May). Grasping in the dark: infants' haptic exploration with and without vision. *Infant Behavior and Development, 15* (Special ICIS Issue), 328.

Butterworth, G. (1983). Visual proprioception in infant. In S. de Schonen (Ed.), *Le Développement dans la première année* (pp. 107–128). Paris: Presses Universitaires de France.

Butterworth, G. (1992, May). Common spatial characteristics of infant's auditory and visual reaching space. *Infant Behavior and Development, 15*, (Special ICIS Issue), 330.

Butterworth, G., & Hopkins, B. (1988). Hand mouth coordination in the newborn baby. *British Journal of Developmental Psychology, 6*, 363–414.

Carchon, I., & Bloch, H. (1993). Fonctionnement oculaire et coordination oculo-céphalique (Oculo-motor functioning and oculo-cephalic coordination). *Psychologie Française, 38*, 19–32.

Cioni, G., Ferrari, F., & Prechtl, H. F. R. (1989). Posture and spontaneous motility in fullterm infants. *Early Human Development, 18*(4), 237–309.

Clark, F. J. (1992). How accurately can we perceive the positions of our limbs ? *Behavioral Brain Sciences, 15*, 725–726.

Clifton, R. K., Morrogiello, B. A., Kulig, J. W., & Dowd, J. M. (1981). Newborns' orientation toward sound: Possible implications for cortical development. *Child Development, 52*, 833–838.

Corbetta, D. (1992, May). Interlimb coordination during the first year of life. *Infant Behavior and Development, 15* (Special ICIS Issue), 234.

De Schonen, S., & Bresson, F. (1984). Développement de l'atteinte manuelle d'un objet chez l'enfant. (Development of manual reaching of an object in infant). In J. Paillard (Ed.), *La lecture de l'expérience sensorimotrice et cognitive de l'expérience spatiale* (pp. 99–114). Paris: Edit. du CNRS.

Diamond, A. (1991). Inhibition, planning and coordination in reaching. *Journal of Experimental Psychology, 13*, 601–608.

Diamond, A., & Gilbert, J. (1989). Development as progressive inhibitory control of action: Retrieval of a contiguous object. *Cognitive Development, 4*, 234–249.

Fiorentino, M. R. (1981). *A basis for sensorimotor development, normal and abnormal : the influence of primitive, postural reflexes on the development and distribution of tone.* Springfield, IL: Thomas.

Ganz, L. (1975). Orientation in visual space by neonates and its modification by visual deprivation. In A. H. Riesen (Ed.), *The developmental neuropsychology of sensory deprivation* (pp. 169–210). New York: Academic Press.

Gatev, V. (1972). Role of inhibition in the development of motor-coordination in early childhood. *Developmental Medicine and Child Neurology, 14*, 336–341.

Gibson, E. J. (1969). *Principles of perceptual learning and development.* New York: Appleton-Century-Crofts.

Gibson, E. J. (1987). Introductory essay: What does infant perception tell us about theory of perception. *Journal of Experimental Psychology, 13*, 515–523.

Gibson, J. J. (1950). *The perception of the visual world.* Cambridge, MA: Houghton-Mifflin.

Gibson, J. J. (1979). *The ecological approach to visual perception.* Boston: Houghton-Mifflin.

Gottlieb, G. (1983). The psychobiological approach to developmental issues. In M. M. Haith & J. J. Campos (Eds.), *Handbook of child psychology* (Vol. 2, pp. 1–26). New York: Wiley.

Grenier, A. (1981). Motricité libre par fixation manuelle de la nuque au cours des premières semaines de la vie (Free movements in relation with nuqual-hand-holding of the head in early infancy). *Archives Françaises de Pédiatrie, 38*, 557–562.

Haith, M. M., Hazan, C., & Goodman, G. S. (1988). Expectation and anticipation of dynamic visual events by 3-5 month old babies. *Child Development, 59*, 467–479.

Halverson, H. M. (1937). Studies of the grasping response of early infancy. *Journal of Genetic Psychology, 51*, 371–447.

Humphrey, T. (1970). The development of human fetal activity and its relation to postnatal behavior. In H. W. Reese & L. P. Lipsitt (Eds.), *Advances in child development and behavior* (Vol. 5, pp. 1–57). New York: Academic Press.

Jeannerod, M., & Biguer, B. (1982). Visuomotor mechanisms in reaching within extrapersonnal space. In D. Ingle, M. Goodale & R. Mansfield (Eds.), *Advances in the analysis of visual behavior* (pp. 387–409). Boston: MIT Press.

Jouen, F. (1988). Visual proprioceptive control of posture in newborn infants. In B. Amblard, A. Berthoz, & F. Clarac (Eds.), *Positive and gait: Development, adaptation and modulation* (pp. 13–22). Amsterdam: Elsevier.

Jouen, F., & Bloch, H. (1981). Le rôle des informations visuelles dans les premiers contrôles posturaux (The role of visual information in the earliest postural adjustments). *L'Année Psychologique, 81*, 197–221.

Jouen, F., & Lepecq, J. C. (1989). La sensibilité au flux optique chez le nouveauné (Sensitivity to optical flow in the neonate). *Psychologie Française, 34*, 13–18.

Katz, D. (1989). *The world of touch.* Hillsdale, NJ: Lawrence Erlbaum Associates.

Keele, S. W. (1968). Movement control in skilled motor performance. *Psychological Bulletin, 70*, 387–403.

Kellman, P. J., Von Hofsten, C., & Soares, J. (1987). Concurrent motion in infant's visual perception. *Perception & Psychophysics, 36*, 353–358.

Klatzky, R. L., Lederman, S. J., & Matula, D. E. (1991). Imagined haptic exploration in judgments of objects properties. *Journal of Experimental Psychology, 17*, 314–322.

Lewkowicz, D. J. (1993). Le rôle des indices spécifiques de modalité dans la perception des équivalences intermodales chez les bébés. (Modality specific cues in infant's intermodal perception of equivalences). *Psychologie française, 36*, 194–201.

Lockman, J. J. (1990). Perceptuo-motor coordination in infancy. In C. A. Hauert (Ed.), *Developmental psychology, cognitive, perceptuomotor and neuropsychological perspectives* (pp. 85–111). Amsterdam: Elsevier.

Lockman, J. J., Ashmead, D. H., & Bushnell, E. W. (1984). The development of anticipatory hand orientation during infancy. *Journal of Experimental Child Psychology, 37*, 176–186.

McCall, R. B. (1974). Exploratory manipulation and play in the human infant. *Monographs of the SRCD, 39*, (No. 155).

Mackawa, K., & Ochiai, Y. (1975). EMG studies on flexor hypertonia of the extremities of newborn infants. *Developmental Medicine and Child Neurology, 17*, 440–446.

Maciaszczyk, S., & Bloch, H. (1988). Effects of training in automatic walking on posture and movement organizations. *Infant Behavior and Development, 11* (Special ICIS Issue) 198.

Mc Guire, I., & Turkewitz, G. (1978). Visually elicited finger movements in infants. *Child Development, 48*, 362–370.

Mellier, D. (1990). Categorization and analysis of preterm and full term newborn movment. In H. Bloch & B. I. Bertenthal (Eds.), *Sensory motor organizations and development in infancy and early childhood* (pp. 123–134). Dordrecht: Kluwer.

Mellier, D. (in press). Les compositions sensori-motrices en développement chez le bébé normal et bébé handicapé (How sensory-motor organizations develop in normal and handicapped infants). Paris: Presses Universitaires de France.

Mitkin, A. (1987). Eye movements and visual function in infancy. The problem of interdependence. *Abstracts of the IXth Biennial Meeting of ISSBD*, Tokyo, 80–90.

Mounoud, P., & Vinter, A. (1981). Representation and sensory-motor development. In G. Butterworth (Ed.), *Infancy and epistemology: An evaluation of Piaget's theory* (pp. 200–235). Brighton: Harvester.

Owen, B. M., & Lee, D. N. (1986). Establishing a frame of reference for action. In M. G. Wade & H. T. A. Whiting (Eds.), *Motor development in children: Aspects of coordination and control* (pp. 287–305). Dordrecht: Martinus. Nijhoff.

Paillard, J., & Amblard, B. (1985). Static versus kinetic visual cues for the processing of spatial relationships. In D. J. Ingle, M. Jeannerod & D. M. Lee (Eds.), *Brain mechanisms of spatial vision* (pp. 299–330). Dordrecht: Martinus Nijhoff.

Palmer, C. F. (1989). The discriminative nature of infants' exploratory actions. *Developmental Psychology, 25*, 685–693.

Perris, E., & Clifton, R. (1988). Reaching in the dark toward sound as a measure of auditory localization in infants. *Infant Behavior and Development, 11*, 473–491.

Piaget, J. (1936). *La naissance de l'intelligence* (The origins of intelligence). Paris: Delachaux et Niestlé.

Piaget, J. (1947). *La psychologie de l'intelligence* (Psychology of intelligence). Paris: A. Colin.

Piaget, J. (1953). *The origins of intelligence in children.* London: Routledge and Kegan Paul.

Piaget, J. (1974). *Réussir et comprendre* (Succeeding and understanding). Paris: Presses Universitaires de France.

Pieraut-Le-Bonniec, G. (1990). Reaching and hand adjusting to target properties. In H. Bloch & B. I. Bertenthal (Eds.), *Sensory-motor organizations and development in infancy and early childhood* (pp. 301–314). Dordrecht: Kluwer.

Prechtl, H. F. R. (1984). Continuity and change in early neural development. In H. T. R. Prechtl (Ed.), *Continuity in neural functions from prenatal to postnatal life* (pp. 1–15). Philadelphia: J.B. Lippincott.

Prechtl, H. F. R., & Nolte, R. (1984). Motor Behaviour of preterm infants. In H. F. R. Prechtl (Ed.), *Continuity of neural functions from prenatal to postnatal life* (pp. 79–92). Oxford: SIMP.

Rader, N., & Stern, J. D. (1982). Visually elicited reaching in neonates. *Child Development, 53*, 1004–1007.

Regal, D. M., Ashmead, D. H., & Salapatek, P. (1983). The coordination of eye and head movements during early infancy: A selective review. *Behavioral Brain Research, 10*, 125–132.

Rochat, P. (1984). Oral activity by young infants: Development of two differentiated patterns of response. *Infant Behavior and Development, 7* (Special ICIS Issue), 305.

Rochat, P. (1987). Mouthing and grasping in neonates: Evidence for the early detection of what hard or soft substances afford for action. *Infant Behaviour and Development, 10*, 435–449.

Rochat, P. (1989). Object manipulation and exploration by 2 to 5 month old infants. *Developmental Psychology, 25*, 871–884.

Rochat, P. (1990). Sitting and reaching in infancy. *Infant Behavior and Development, 13* (Special ICIS issue), 183.

Ronnqvist, L., & Von Hofsten, C. (in press). Varieties and determinants of fingers movements in neonates. *Early Development and Parenting.*

Ruff, H. A. (1984). Infants manipulative exploration of objects: Effects of age and object characteristics. *Developmental Psychology, 20*, 9–20.

Ruff, H. A. (1990). The infant's use of visual and haptic information in the perception and recognition of objects. *Canadian Journal of Psychology, 43,* 302–319.

Shepherd, N. (1988). *Neurobiology.* New York: Oxford University Press.

Spear, N. E., & Molina, J. C. (1987). The role of sensory modality in the ontogeny of stimulus selection. In N. A. Krasnegor, E. Blass, M. A. Hofer, & W. P. Smotherman (Eds.), *Perinatal development: A psychobiological perspective* (pp. 83–108). New York: Academic Press.

Spelke, E. S., Von Hofsten, C., & Kestenbaum, R. (1989). Object perception and object directed reaching in infancy: Interaction of spatial and kinetic information for object boundaries, *Developmental Psychology, 25,* 185–196.

Steele, D., & Pederson, D. R. (1977). Stimulus variables which affect the concordance of visual and manipulative exploration in 6-month-old infants. *Child Development, 48,* 104–111.

Thelen, E. (1990). Coupling perception and action in the development of skill: A dynamic approach. In H. Bloch & B. I. Bertenthal (Eds.), *Sensory motor organizations and development in infancy and early childhood* (pp. 39–56). Dordrecht: Kluwer.

Thelen, E. (1992, April). Nathan learns to reach: Report of longitudinal multidimensional study. *Infant Behavior and Development, 15* (Special ICIS Issue), 232.

Thelen, E., & Fisher, D. M. (1982). The organization of spontaneous leg movements in newborn infants. *Journal of Motor Behavior, 15,* 353–382.

Thelen, E., Kelso, J. A. S., & Fogel, A. (1987). Self organizing systems and infant motor development. *Developmental Review, 7,* 39–65.

Turkewitz, G. (1977). The development of lateral preferences in the human infant. In S. Harnad & R. Dorry (Eds.), *Lateralization in the nervous system* (pp. 251–259). San Diego: Academic Press.

Turkewitz, G., Gardner, J. M., & Lewkowicz, D. J. (1984). Sensory/perceptual functioning during early infancy: The implication for a quantitative basis of responding. In G. Greenberg & E. Tobach (Eds.), *Behavioral evolution and integration levels* (pp. 167–195). Hillsdale, NJ: Lawrence Erlbaum Associates.

Turkewitz, G., Moreau, T., & Birch, H. G. (1966). Head position and receptor organization in the human neonate. *Journal of Experimental Psychology, 4,* 169–177.

Twitchell, T. E. (1970). Reflex mechanisms and the development of prehension. In K. Connolly (Ed.), *Mechanisms of motor skill development* (pp. 25–59). New York: Academic Press.

Von Hofsten, C. (1982). Eye-hand coordination in the newborn. *Developmental Psychology, 18,* 450–461.

Von Hofsten, C. (1983). Catching skills in infancy. *Journal of Experimental psychology: Human, Perception and Performance, 9,* 75–85.

Von Hofsten, C. (1984). Developmental changes in the organization of heredity movements. *Developmental Psychology, 20,* 378–388.

Von Hofsten, C. (1986). The emergence of manual skills. In M. G. Wade & H. T. A. Whiting (Eds.), *Motor development in children: Aspects of coordination and control* (pp. 197–206). Dordrecht: Martinus Nijhoff.

Von Hofsten, C. (1989). Motor development as the development of systems. *Developmental Psychology, 25,* 950–953.

Von Hofsten, C., & Fazel Zandy, S. (1984). Development of visually guided hand orientation in reaching. *Journal of Experimental Child Psychology, 38,* 208–219.

Von Hofsten, C., & Lee, D. N. (1982). Dialogue on perception and action. *Human Movement Science, 1,* 125–138.

Von Hofsten, C., & Lindhagen, K. (1979). Observations on the development of reaching for moving objects. *Journal of Experimental Psychology, 28,* 158–173.

Von Holst, E. (1954). Relations between the central nervous system and the peripheral organs. *British Journal of American Behavior, 2,* 89–94.

Warren, W. H., & Whang, G. S. (1987). Visual guidance of walking through apertures: Body scaled information for affordances. *Journal of Experimental Psychology: Human Perception and Performance, 13,* 371–383.

Williatts, P. (1990). The goal directed nature of early sensorymotor coordinations. In H. Bloch & B. I. Bertenthal (Eds.), *Sensorymotor organizations and development in infancy and early childhood* (pp. 179–186). Dordrecht: Kluwer.

Yonas, A., & Owsley, C. (1987). Development of visual space perception. In P. Salapatek & L. B. Cohen (Eds.), *Handbook of infant perception* (Vol. 2, pp. 79–122). New York: Academic Press.

Zelazo, N. A., Cohen, K. M., & Zelazo, P. D. (1988, April). Specificity of practice on elementary neuromotor patterns, *Infant Behavior and Development, 11* (Special ICIS issue), 353.

CHAPTER FOURTEEN

Faces and Speech: Intermodal Processing of Biologically Relevant Signals in Infants and Adults

Andrew N. Meltzoff
Patricia K. Kuhl
University of Washington

The human face stands out as the single most important stimulus that we must recognize in the visual domain. In the auditory domain the human voice is the most important biological signal. Our faces and voices specify us as uniquely human, and a challenge in neuro- and cognitive science has been to understand how we recognize and process these two biologically relevant signals.

In both domains the conventional view is that the signals are at first recognized through unimodal mechanisms. Faces are thought to be visual objects and voices to be the province of audition. We intend to show that these stimuli are analyzed and represented through more than a single modality in both infancy and adulthood. Speech information can be perceived through the visual modality, and faces through proprioception. Indeed, visual information about speech is such a fundamental part of the speech code that it cannot be ignored by a listener. What listeners report "hearing" is not solely auditory, but a unified percept that is derived from auditory and visual sources. Faces and voices are thoroughly intermodal objects of perception.

Recent experiments have discovered that infants code faces and speech as intermodal objects of perception very early in life. We focus on these intermodal mappings, and explore the mechanism by which intermodal information is linked. Faces and speech can be used to examine central issues in theories of intermodal perception. How does information from two different sensory modalities mix? Is the input from separate modalities translated into a "common code?" If so, what is the nature of the code?

One phenomenon we discuss is infants' imitation of facial gestures. Infants can see the other person's facial movements but they cannot see their own movements. If they are young enough, they have never seen their own face in a mirror. How do infants link up the gestures they can see but not feel with those that they can feel but not see? We show how this phenomenon illuminates models of intermodal development. New data indicate that infants correct their behavior so as to converge on the visual target through a series of approximations. Correction suggests that infants are guiding their unseen motor behavior to bring it into register with the seen target. In this sense, early imitation provides a key example of intermodal guidance in the execution of skilled action. Other new data reveal an ability to imitate from memory and imitation of novel gestures. Memory-based facial imitation is informative because infants are using information picked up from one modality (vision) to control nonvisual actions at a later point in time, after the visual target has been withdrawn. This suggests that infant intermodal functioning can be mediated by stored supramodal representations of absent events, a concept that is developed in some detail.

Intermodal speech perception involves auditory–visual mappings between the sound of speech and its visual instantiation on the lips of the talker. During typical conversations we see the talker's face, and watch the facial movements that are concomitant by-products of the speech event. As a stimulus in the real world, speech is both auditory and visual. But is speech truly an intermodal event for the listener/observer? To what extent are the visual events that accompany the auditory signal taken into account in determining the identity of the unit?

Adults benefit from watching a talker's mouth movements, especially in noise. People commonly look at the mouth of a talker during a noisy cocktail party because it feels like vision helps us to "hear" the talker. The second author of this chapter has been known to say to the first: "Hold on, let me get my glasses so I can hear you better." These are not examples of superstitious behavior. Research shows that watching the oral movements of a talker is equivalent to about a 20-dB boost in the auditory signal (Sumby & Pollack, 1954). A gain of 20-dB is substantial. It is equivalent to the difference in level between normal conversational speech (65 dB SPL) and shouting (85 dB SPL).

Here we also discuss new research on auditory–visual "illusions" showing that visual information about speech virtually cannot be ignored by the listener/observer. The development of the multimodal speech code and the necessary and sufficient stimulus that allows adults and infants to detect intermodal speech matches are explored. Finally, we hypothesize that infant babbling contributes to the intermodal organization of speech by consolidating auditory–articulatory links, yielding a kind of intermodal map for speech. Understanding the multimodal nature of the speech code is a new and complex issue. The mapping between physical cues and phonetic percepts goes beyond the realm of the single modality, audition, typically associated with it. This chapter reveals the rather surprising extent to which speech, both its perception and its production, is a thoroughly intermodal event both for young infants and for adults.

INFANT FACIAL IMITATION AS AN INSTANCE OF INTERMODAL FUNCTIONING

There is broad consensus among developmentalists that young infants are highly imitative. However, all imitation is not created equal: Some is more relevant to intermodal theory than others. For example, infants can see the hand movements of others, and can also see their own hands. In principle, infants could imitate by visually matching their own hands to those of another. This would require visually guided responses and visual categorization (the infant's hand is smaller and seen from a different orientation than the adult's), but it would not put much demand on the intermodal system per se.

What is intriguing for students of intermodal functioning is that facial imitation cannot, even in principle, rely on such *intra*modal matching. Infants can see the facial movements of others, but not their own faces. They can feel their own movements, but not the movements of others. How can the infant relate the seen but unfelt other to the felt but unseen self? What bridges the gap between the visible and the invisible? The answer proposed by Meltzoff and Moore (1977, 1983, 1992, 1993; Meltzoff, 1993) is intermodal perception.

It has been known for 50 years that 1-year-old infants imitate facial gestures (e.g., Piaget, 1945/1962). It came as rather more of a surprise to developmentalists when Meltzoff and Moore (1977) reported facial imitation in 2- to 3-week-old infants and later showed that newborns as young as 42 min old could imitate (Meltzoff & Moore, 1983, 1989). The reason for this surprise is instructive. It is not because imitation demands a sensory-motor connection from young infants: There are many infant reflexes that exhibit such a connection. The surprise was engendered by Meltzoff and Moore's hypothesis that early facial imitation was a manifestation of active intermodal mapping (the AIM hypothesis), in which infants used the visual stimulus as a target against which they actively compared their motor output.

At the raw behavioral level, the basic phenomenon of early imitation has now been replicated and extended by many independent investigators. Findings of early imitation have been reported from infants across multiple cultures and ethnic backgrounds: United States (Abravanel & DeYong, 1991; Abravanel & Sigafoos, 1984; Field et al., 1983; Field, Goldstein, Vaga-Lahr, & Porter, 1986; Field, Woodson, Greenberg, & Cohen, 1982; Jacobson, 1979), Sweden (Heimann, Nelson, & Schaller, 1989; Heimann, & Schaller, 1985), Israel (Kaitz, Meschulach-Sarfaty, Auerbach, & Eidelman, 1988), Canada (Legerstee, 1991), Switzerland (Vinter, 1986), Greece (Kugiumutzakis, 1985),

France (Fontaine, 1984), and Nepal (Reissland, 1988). Collectively, these studies report imitation of a range of movements including mouths, tongues, and hands. It is safe to conclude that certain elementary gestures performed by adults elicit matching behavior by infants. The discussion in the field has now turned to the thornier question of the basis of early imitation: Does the AIM hypothesis provide the right general framework, or might there be some more primitive explanation, wholly independent of intermodal functioning? Apparently infants poke out their tongues when adults do so, but what mechanism mediates this behavior?

Imitation Versus Arousal

One hypothesis Meltzoff and Moore explored before suggesting AIM was that early matching might simply be due to a general arousal of facial movements with no processing of the intermodal correspondence. Studies were designed to test whether imitation could be distinguished from a more global arousal response by assessing the specificity of the matching (Meltzoff & Moore, 1977, 1989). It was reasoned that the sight of human faces might arouse infants. It might also be true that increased facial movements are a concomitant of arousal in babies. If so, then infants might produce more facial movements when they saw a human face than when they saw no face at all. This would not implicate an intermodal matching to target.

The specificity of the imitative behavior was demonstrated because infants responded differentially to two types of lip movements (mouth opening vs. lip protrusion) and two types of protrusion actions (lip protrusion vs. tongue protrusion). The results showed that when the body part was controlled— when lips were used to perform two different movements—infants responded differentially. Likewise, when the same general movement pattern was demonstrated (protrusion) but with two different body parts (lip vs. tongue), they also responded differentially. The response was not a global arousal reaction to a human face, because the same face at the same distance moving at the same rate was used in all of these conditions. Yet the infants responded differentially.

Memory in Imitation and Intermodal Mapping

The temporal constraints on the linkage between perception and action was also investigated. It seemed possible that infants might imitate if and only if they could respond immediately, wherein the motor system was entrained by the visual movement pattern. To use a rough analogy, it would be as if infants seeing swaying began swaying themselves, but could not reenact this act from a stored memory of the visual scene. In perceptual psychology the term *resonance* is sometimes used to describe tight perception–action couplings of this type (e.g., J. J. Gibson, 1966, 1979; or Gestalt psychology). The analogy that is popular (though perhaps a bit too mechanistic) is that of tuning forks: "Information" is directly transferred from one tuning fork to another with no mediation, memory, or processing of the signal. Of course, if one tuning fork were held immobile while the other sounded, it would not resonate at a later point in time. If early imitation were due to some kind of perceptual-motor resonance or to a simple, hard-wired reflex, it might fall to chance if a delay was inserted between stimulus and response.

Two studies were directed to assessing this point: one using a pacifier and short delays (Meltzoff & Moore, 1977) and the other using much longer delays of 24 hours (Meltzoff & Moore, 1994). In the 1977 study, a pacifier was put in 3-week-old infants' mouths as they watched the display so that they could observe the adult demonstration but not duplicate the gestures on-line. The pacifier was effective in disrupting imitation while the adult was demonstrating; the neonatal sucking reflex was activated and infants did not tend to push the pacifier out with their tongues or open their mouths and let it fall out. However, when the pacifier was removed and the adult presented only a passive face, the infants initiated imitation.

The notion that infants could match remembered targets was further explored in a recent study that lengthened the memory interval from seconds to hours (Meltzoff & Moore, 1994). In this study 6-week-old infants were shown facial acts on three days in a row. The novel part of the design was that infants on day 2 and day 3 were used to test memory of the display shown 24 hr earlier. When the infants returned to the laboratory, they were shown the adult with a passive-face pose. This constituted a test of cued-recall memory. The results showed that they succeeded on this imitation-from-memory task. Infants differentially imitated the gesture they had seen the day before. This could hardly be called resonance or a reflexive automatically triggered response, because the actual target display that the infants were imitating was not perceptually present; it was stored in the infant's mind. The passive face was a cue to producing the motor response based on memory. This case is interesting for intermodal theory because infants are matching a nonvisible target (yesterday's act) with a response that cannot be visually monitored (their own facial movements).

Novel Behaviors and Response Correction

Another question concerned whether infants were confined to imitating familiar, well-practiced acts or whether they could construct novel responses based on visual targets. Older children can use visual targets to fashion novel body actions (Meltzoff, 1988); it is not that the visual stimulus simply acts as a "releaser" of an already-formed motor packet. Response novelty was investigated by using a tongue protrusion to the side (TP_{side}) display as one of the stimuli in the 3-day experiment (Meltzoff & Moore, 1994). For this act, the adult protruded and withdrew his tongue on a slant from the corner of his mouth instead of the usual, straight-tongue protrusion from midline. The results showed that infants imitated this display, and the overall organization and topography of the response helped to illuminate the underlying mechanism. It appeared that the infants were correcting their imitative responses.

Infant tongue protrusion responses were subdivided into four different levels that bore an ordinal relationship according to their fidelity to the TP$_{side}$ display. Time sequential analyses showed that over the 3-day study there was a progression from level 1 to level 4 behavior for those infants who had seen the TP$_{side}$ display. This was not the result of a general arousal, because infants in control groups, including a group exposed only to a tongue protrusion from midline, did not show any such progression. These findings of infants homing in on the target fit with Meltzoff and Moore's AIM hypothesis. The core notion is that early imitation is a matching-to-target process. The gradual correction in the infant's response supports this idea of an active matching to target. The "target" was picked up visually by watching the adult. The infants respond with an approximation (they usually get the body part correct and activate their tongue immediately) and then use proprioceptive information from their own self-produced movements as feedback for homing in on the target.

Although this analysis highlights error detection and correction in the motor control of early imitation, Meltzoff and Moore did not rule out visual-motor mapping of basic acts on "first effort," without the need for feedback. It seems likely that there is a small set of elementary acts (midline tongue protrusion?) that can be achieved relatively directly, whereas other more complex acts involve the computation of transformations on these primitives (e.g., TP$_{side}$) and more proprioceptive monitoring about current tongue position and the nature of the "miss." Infants cannot have innately specified templates for each of the numerous transformations that different body parts may be put through. There has to be some more generative process involved in imitation. It is therefore informative that infants did not immediately produce imitations of the novel TP$_{side}$ behavior; they needed to correct their behavior to achieve it. Such correction deeply implicates intermodal functioning in imitation.

Development and the Role of Experience

It has been reported that neonatal imitation exists, but then disappears or "drops out" at approximately 2–3 months of age (Abravanel & Sigafoos, 1984; Fontaine, 1984; Maratos, 1982). The two most common interpretations are that newborn imitation is based on simple reflexes that are inhibited with a cortical take over of motor actions, or that the neonatal period entails a brief period of perceptual unity that is followed by a differentiation of the modalities, and therefore a loss of neonatal sensory-motor coordinations (including imitation), until they can be reconstituted under more intentional control (Bower, 1982, 1989). The reflexive and the modality-differentiation views emphasize an inevitable, maturationally-based drop out of facial imitation. Meltzoff and Moore (1992) recently presented a third view. They argued that learned expectations about face-to-face encounters play a more central role in the previously-reported disappearance of imitation. This may not be as exciting as the notion that a completely amodal perceptual system differentiates at 2–3 months of age, but it better accounts for the results we recently obtained.

Meltzoff and Moore (1992) conducted a multitrial, repeated-measures experiment involving 16 infants between 2 and 3 months of age, the heart of the drop-out period. The overall results yielded strong evidence for imitation at this age; however, these infants gave no sign of imitating the adult gestures in the first trials alone. The same children who did not imitate on first encounter successfully imitated when measured across the entire repeated-measures experiment. This is hardly compatible with a drop-out due to modality differentiation; it is more suggestive of motivational or performance factors that can be reversed.

Further analysis suggested that the previously reported decline in imitation is attributable to infants' growing expectations about social interactions with people. When these older infants first encountered the adult, they initiated social overtures as if to engage in a nonverbal interchange—cooing, smiling, trying out familiar games. This behavior supplanted any first-trial imitation effects. After the initial social gestures failed to elicit a response (by experimental design because our *E* did not respond contingently to the infant), infants settled down and engaged in imitation.

It thus appears that development indeed affects early imitation. Imitation is a primitive way of interacting with people that exists prior to other social responses such as cooing, smiling, and so on. Once these other responses take hold, they become the first line of action in the presence of a friendly person. Hence the *apparent* "loss" of imitation. If the typical designs are modified, however, this is reversible and there is quite robust imitation among older infants. What develops are social games that are higher on the response hierarchy than is simple imitation, but there is no fundamental drop out of competence.

Converging Evidence

Returning to the mechanism question, Meltzoff and Moore have proposed that information about facial acts is fed into the same representational code regardless of whether those body transformations are seen or felt. There is a "supramodal" network that unites body acts within a common framework.

Imitation is seen as being tied to a network of skills, particularly to speech–motor phenomena, which also involve early perception-production links involving oral-facial movements (Meltzoff, Kuhl, & Moore, 1991). The development and neural bases for such an intermodal representation of the face are a pressing issue for developmental neuroscience (Damasio, Tranel, & Damasio, 1990; de Schonen & Mathivet, 1989; Stein & Meredith, 1993).

That neonates can relate information across modalities is no longer the surprise it was in 1977. There has been an outpouring of findings that are compatible with this view, although the ages, tasks, and intermodal information have varied widely (e.g., Bahrick, 1983, 1987, 1988; Bahrick & Watson, 1985; Bower, 1982; Bushnell & Winberger, 1987; Butterworth, 1981, 1983, 1990; Dodd, 1979; Lewkowicz, 1985, 1986, 1992; Meltzoff, 1990; Rose, 1990; Rose & Ruff, 1987; Spelke, 1981, 1987; Walker, 1982; Walker-Andrews, 1986, 1988). One example from our own laboratory is particularly relevant, because it involves neonates of about the same age as in the studies of imitation and involved vision and touch. Meltzoff and Borton (1979) provided infants tactual experience by molding a small shape and fitting it on a pacifier (Fig. 14.1). The infants orally explored the shape but were not permitted to see it. The shape was withdrawn from their mouths, and they were given a choice between two shapes, one that matched the shape they had tactually explored and one that did not (tactual and visual shapes were appropriately counterbalanced). The results of two studies showed that 29-day-old infants systematically looked longer at the shape that they had tactually explored. The finding of cross-modal perception in 1-month-olds was replicated and cleverly broadened in an experiment by E. J. Gibson and Walker (1984), who used soft versus rigid visual and tactual objects (instead of shape/texture information), and by Pêcheux, Lepecq, and Salzarulo (1988), who used Meltzoff and Borton's shapes and examined the degree of tactual familiarization necessary to recognize information across modalities. More recently the oral–visual cross-

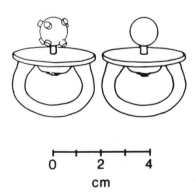

0   2   4
cm

FIG. 14.1. Shapes used to assess tactual–visual matching. The pacifiers were inserted in the infants mouths without them seeing them. After a 90-sec familiarization period the shape was withdrawn, and a visual test was administered to investigate whether the tactual exposure influenced visual preference. From Meltzoff and Borton (1979). Reprinted by permission.

modal matching effect was extended to a newborn population by Kaye (1993), who found visual recognition of differently shaped rubber nipples that were explored by mouth. Streri (1987; Streri & Milhet, 1988; Streri & Spelke, 1988) conducted tactual–visual studies in 2- to 4-month-old infants and demonstrated cross-modal matching of shapes from manual touch to vision. Finally, Gunderson (1983) used Meltzoff and Borton's shapes mounted on pacifiers and replicated the same effect in 1-month-old monkeys, indicating that cross-modal matching is not specific to neonatal humans.

We have been especially interested in pursuing infant intermodal perception of biologically relevant stimuli. Toward that end we have investigated other phenomena involving faces. In particular, we have found that young infants recognize the correspondence between facial movements and speech sounds. This line of work affords a particularly detailed look at the nature of the information that is "shared" across modalities.

SPEECH PERCEPTION AS AN INSTANCE
OF INTERMODAL FUNCTIONING

Speech perception has classically been considered an auditory process. What we perceived was thought to be based solely on the auditory information that reached our ears. This belief has been deeply shaken by data showing that speech perception is an intermodal phenomenon in which vision (and even touch) plays a role in determining what a subject reports hearing. Visual information contributes to speech perception in the absence of a hearing impairment and even when the auditory signal is perfectly intelligible. In fact, it appears that when it is available, visual information cannot be ignored by the listener; it is automatically combined with the auditory information to derive the percept.

The fact that speech can be perceived by the eye is increasingly playing a role in theories of both adult and infant speech perception (Fowler, 1986; Kuhl, 1992, 1993a; Liberman & Mattingly, 1985; Massaro, 1987a; Studdert-Kennedy, 1986, 1993; Summerfield, 1987). This change in how we think about speech results from two sets of recent findings. First, studies show that visual speech information profoundly affects the perception of speech in adults (Dodd & Campbell, 1987; Grant, Ardell, Kuhl, & Sparks, 1985; Green & Kuhl, 1989, 1991; Green, Kuhl, Meltzoff, & Stevens, 1991; Massaro, 1987a, 1987b; Massaro & Cohen, 1990; McGurk & MacDonald, 1976; Summerfield, 1979, 1987). Second, even young infants are sensitive to the correspondence between speech information presented by eye and by ear (Kuhl & Meltzoff, 1982, 1984; Kuhl, Williams, & Meltzoff, 1991; MacKain, Studdert-Kennedy, Speiker, & Stern, 1983; Walton & Bower, 1993). The work on infants and adults is discussed in turn.

Auditory–Visual Speech Perception in Infants

Our work on the auditory–visual perception of speech began with the discovery of infants' abilities to relate auditory and visual speech information (Kuhl & Meltzoff, 1982). A baby-appropriate lipreading problem was posed (Fig. 14.2). Four-month-old infants were shown two filmed images side by side of a talker articulating two different vowel sounds. The soundtrack corresponding to one of the two faces was played from a loudspeaker located midway between the two facial images, thus eliminating spatial clues concerning which of the two faces produced the sound. The auditory and visual stimuli were aligned such that the temporal synchronization was equally good for both the "matched" and "mismatched" face–voice pairs, thus eliminating any temporal clues (Kuhl & Meltzoff, 1984). The only way that infants could detect a match between auditory and visual instantiations of speech was to recognize what individual speech sounds looked like on the face of a talker.

Our hypothesis was that infants would look longer at the face that matched the sound rather than at the mismatched face. The results of the study were in accordance with the prediction. They showed that 18- to 20-week-old infants recognized that particular sound patterns emanate from mouths moving in particular ways. In effect the data suggested the possibility that infants recognized that a sound like /i/ is produced with retracted lips and a tongue-high posture, whereas an /a/ is produced using a lips-open, tongue-lowered posture. That speech was coded in a polymodal fashion at such a young age—a code that includes both its auditory and visual specifications—was quite surprising. It was neither predicted nor expected by the then existing models of speech perception.

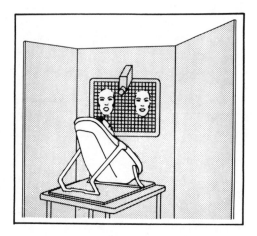

FIG. 14.2. Experimental arrangement used to test cross-modal speech perception in infants. The infants watched a film of two faces and heard speech played from a central loudspeaker. From Kuhl and Meltzoff (1982). Reprinted by permission.

Generality of Infant Auditory–Visual Matching for Speech

The generality of infants' abilities to detect auditory-visual correspondence was examined by testing a new vowel pair, /i/ and /u/ (Kuhl & Meltzoff, 1988). Using the /u/ vowel was based on speech theory because the /i/, /a/, and /u/ vowels constitute the "point" vowels. Acoustically and articulatorily, they represent the extreme points in vowel space. They are more discriminable, both auditorially and visually, than any other vowel combinations and are also linguistically universal. The results of the /i/–/u/ study confirmed infants' abilities to detect auditory–visual correspondence for this vowel pair. Two independent teams of investigators have replicated and extended the cross-modal speech results in interesting ways. MacKain et al. (1983) demonstrated that 5- to 6-month-old infants detected auditory–visual correspondences for disyllables such as /bebi/ and /zuzi/ and argued that such matching was mediated by left hemisphere functioning. More recently, Walton and Bower (1993) showed cross-modal speech matching for both native and foreign phonetic units in 4.5-month-olds.

THE BASIS OF AUDITORY–VISUAL SPEECH PERCEPTION: PARAMETRIC VARIATIONS

From a theoretical standpoint the next most important issue was to determine how infants accomplished the intermodal speech task. As in all cases of intermodal perception, a key question is the means by which the information is related across modalities. One alternative is that perceivers recode the information from each of the two modalities into a set of basic common features that allows the information from the two streams to be matched or combined. The central idea is that complex forms are decomposed into elementary features and that this aids in intermodal recognition. We conducted a set of experiments to determine whether speech was broken down into its basic features during intermodal speech perception. In these studies we presented both infants and adults with tasks using nonspeech stimuli that captured critical features of the speech stimulus. The underlying rationale of the studies was to determine whether an isolated feature of the speech unit was sufficient to allow the detection of intermodal correspondence for speech.

Speech and Distinctive Feature Theory

The goal of these studies was to "take apart" the auditory stimulus. We wanted to identify features that were necessary and sufficient for the detection of the cross-modal match between a visual phonetic gesture and its concomitant sound. Distinctive Feature Theory provides a list of the elemental features that make up speech sounds (Jakobson, Fant, & Halle, 1969). Speech events can be broken down into a set of basic features that describe the phonetic units. For example, one acoustic feature specifies the location of the main frequency components of the sound. It is called the *grave-acute* feature and distinguishes the sounds /a/ and /i/. In the vowel /a/, the main concentration of energy is low in frequency; in the vowel /i/ the main concentration of energy is high in frequency. The vowel /a/ is thus *grave* and the vowel /i/ *acute* in Distinctive Feature Theory (Jakobson et al., 1969). Features such as grave and acute can be duplicated with simple nonspeech sounds.

That speech features can be approximated with nonspeech sounds such as simple tones was recognized by Isaac Newton. His notebooks described how he created the impression of a series of vowels, beginning with low-pitched vowels like /a/ and /u/ up to high ones such as /i/, by slowly filling a deep pitcher with a constant stream of beer (see also Helmholtz, 1885/1954). When a small amount of beer was in the container, low-pitched sounds resembling /a/ were produced; when the pitcher of beer was filled, higher tones resembling /i/ were produced.

This experiment can also be conducted in a laboratory rather than a pub (although it is a bit more tedious). Psychoacoustic matching experiments have demonstrated that individual vowels are perceived to have "predominant pitches" corresponding to the grave-acute feature of Distinctive Feature Theory (Chiba & Kajiyama, 1958; Fant, 1973; Farnsworth, 1937). For example, Farnsworth (1937) presented subjects with 22 pure tones ranging from 375 to 2400 Hz. Subjects were instructed to label each of the tones as one of 12 vowels. The results showed that tones in the high frequency range tended to be labeled as vowels like /i/, while tones in the low to middle frequencies tended to be labeled as vowels like /a/ and /u/. These experiments establishing the psychological reality of features used solely unimodal tasks and all involved adults.

Is Intermodal Speech Perception Based on a Feature Analysis?

We tested whether the "predominant pitch" of the vowel (as captured in a nonspeech stimulus, a pure tone) was sufficient to produce the cross-modal matching effect observed in infants (Kuhl et al., 1991). We also examined this in adults by administering unimodal, cross-modal, and amodal tasks.

Two kinds of nonspeech stimuli were used, single isolated pure tones and three-tone complexes. The pure-tone signals varied from 750 to 4000 Hz. The three-tone complexes approximated the speech signals more closely in that they contained three tones, one located at each of the center frequencies of each of the first three formants of the vowels. (The three-tone complexes provided additional features that matched those in the original vowels, such as the relationships between individual formant frequencies.) Neither of these two nonspeech signals sounded like speech. Our question was to what extent these nonspeech signals could be related to vowel stimuli, especially in a cross-modal matching experiment.

The adult tests involved a number of conditions. For the auditory task the vowel was presented as an auditory stimulus; for the cross-modal task the vowel was presented as a face pronouncing the vowel; for the amodal task the vowel was simply "imagined" by having subjects think about the vowel (an amodal task, because the stimulus was not in any sensory modality). Infants were tested only in the cross-modal format. The question here was whether infants would detect a cross-modal match between the visually presented faces and a nonspeech stimulus that captured a prominent feature of speech. Everything was the same as in Kuhl and Meltzoff (1982), but rather than hearing one of the real vowels presented auditorially, they heard either a pure-tone stimulus or a three-tone analog. The amplitudes (loudness) of the nonspeech signals were varied to match the amplitudes of the original vowels. As the mouths opened the nonspeech signal grew louder; as the mouths closed the nonspeech signal became softer. The fact that the auditory amplitude envelope was appropriate for the stimulus being seen created a situation in which it was not trivially obvious that the mouth could not be producing the sound that was being presented. In fact, the data showed that infants fixated the faces just as long in the nonspeech conditions in this experiment as they did in the speech conditions tested in Kuhl and Meltzoff (1982). The question was whether variations in frequency of the pitch resulted in differential looking at the faces, as was the case when the real /a/ and /i/ vowels were presented.

The results revealed clear developmental differences. Adults successfully related pure tone signals to the vowels /a/ and /i/. Adults matched pure tones to vowels unimodally (when the vowels were auditorially presented), cross-modally (when the vowels were visually presented), and amodally (when the vowels were imagined). In all cases adults matched low-frequency pure tones to the vowel /a/ and high-frequency pure tones to the vowel /i/, in line with the predominant pitch idea. The results on the adult tests with the three-tone analogs of /a/ and /i/ were a bit more complicated but strongly supported the same conclusion (Kuhl et al., 1991). Once again, adults had no difficulty relating three-tone analogs to vowels presented auditorially and visually.

The infant results were quite different. Infants in both experiments— whether listening to pure tones of various frequencies or three-tone non-speech analogs derived from the vowels—showed no ability to match nonspeech auditory signals to visually presented vowels. They smiled at the faces and looked at them just as long as they had in previous experiments;

however, there was no cross-modal effect. The nonspeech analogues of /a/ versus /i/ did not differentially affect which face infants fixated.

Implications For Intermodal Theory

The results provided support for two inferences: Adults can relate speech stimuli such as the vowels /a/ and /i/ to nonspeech stimuli on the basis of a simple isolated feature, and infants do not rely on the same simple feature for intermodal speech perception under similar test conditions. These speech findings have implications for both auditory–visual and general theories of intermodal processing.

First consider the connection adults perceive between vowels and pitch, and the possible basis for this perception. Two alternatives can be put forward. The perceptual/linguistic alternative argues for a fairly direct mapping between vowels and tones of a particular frequency. On this view, spectral features that are responsible for the perceived predominant pitch of the vowel are derived during the perceptual analysis of the sound. If featural properties such as grave-acute are automatically derived in perceptual processing, then the link between vowels and pitch is based on the psychological reality of decomposing speech into featural elements. A second alternative is that the link between /a/ vowels and low sounds and between /i/ vowels and high sounds may be mediated by more metaphorical thinking (Gentner & Grudin, 1985; Ortony, 1979) as part of a larger cognitive network. Some work in our laboratory on "phonetic symbolism" and the semantic qualities associated with vowels shows that adults think of /a/ as a "strong" sound, whereas /i/ is "weaker." The attribute "strong" is typically associated with maleness, and male voices are predominantly low in pitch, which could be the network through which the association is made between /a/ vowels and low tones. If true, this would be more "cognitively mediated" than the first alternative. The current findings show that features embodied in nonspeech stimuli can be used in cross-modal and amodal speech perception, but do not decisively sort between these alternatives.

These results with adults become more interesting when considered in relation to the findings from infants. Infants did not display the same link between vowel and pitch exhibited by adults. Their visual fixations were not differentially affected by the nonspeech stimuli; however, when real speech stimuli were used, infants did make differential visual choices. Thus, 4-month-old infants detect face–voice matches when speech stimuli are presented auditorially while failing to do so when the auditory stimulus is stripped down to its simplest featural component, as in a pure tone, or when three-tone nonspeech analogs of the vowels are presented.

It appears that infants' detection of cross-modal correspondence for speech requires the whole speech stimulus. (A whole stimulus is a signal that is sufficient to allow the *identification* of the speech signal. Synthetic speech signals qualify as whole stimuli by this definition; they do not include all of the speech information present in a natural utterance, but still allow the identification of the speech stimulus.) From a developmental viewpoint, the findings suggest that the intermodal perception of speech does not progress through a developmental sequence that goes from "parts" to "wholes." Infants do not begin relating faces and voices on some simple feature, and then gradually build up a connection between the two that involves, on the auditory side, an identifiably whole speech stimulus. Perceptual developmental theorists have suggested that infants may at first be maximally responsive to wholes, especially in the form of complex natural stimuli that are later differentiated into component aspects (e.g., Bower, 1982; E. J. Gibson, 1969; J. J. Gibson, 1966). The case of intermodal speech perception provides data compatible with such a developmental model, inasmuch as older but not younger subjects detect an intermodal match when provided only a "part" of the stimulus—one that cannot be independently identified as speech.

The hypothesis just stated raises a point about the boundary conditions of intermodal perception for infants. It begins to tell us when intermodal processing breaks down. Of course, this depends on the assumption that nonspeech signals can be processed by infants in the first place. They can be. Previous unimodal tests showed that nonspeech stimuli supported many of the same phenomena as the full speech signal. The phenomenon of categorical perception has been shown in adults with nonspeech signals (e.g., Diehl & Walsh, 1989; Pisoni, Carrell, & Gans, 1983). Categorical perception of nonspeech signals has also been shown by infants for both two-tone and three-tone analogs derived from real speech syllables (Jusczyk, Pisoni, Walley, & Murray, 1980; Jusczyk, Pisoni, Reed, Fernald, & Myers, 1983). There seems to be a striking dissociation between unimodal and intermodal tasks.

This dissociation is further corroborated by other work from our laboratory in which 4- to 5-month-old infants were tested with nonspeech signals in another cross-modal task, one that involves vocal imitation. In the case of vocal imitation, infants have to relate the auditory perception of the vowels /a/ and /i/ to their own motor productions of speech. In our work on vocal imitation, infants listened either to speech stimuli (the vowels /a/ and /i/) or the nonspeech pure-tone signals used in the present studies. The results again showed that nonspeech signals were not effectively related to articulation. In response to speech signals, infants produced speechlike utterances. However, in response to the nonspeech signals infants did not produce speechlike vocalizations; they listened intently but did not produce speech (Kuhl & Meltzoff, 1988).

Taken together it can be inferred that, in cross-modal speech tasks, young infants need the whole signal, one that is identifiable as a speech sound.

Although infants need this more complete specification in order to link the perception and production of speech, they do not need it in unimodal tasks; moreover, for adults, a "part" of the stimulus is sufficient in cross-modal (and amodal) situations. The ontogenesis of this ability to use parts in a cross-modal setting and the reason for its absence in early infancy are currently being investigated in our laboratory in longitudinal studies.[1]

ADULT AUDITORY–VISUAL ILLUSIONS AND INTERMODAL SPEECH PERCEPTION

The next series of experiments utilized adult subjects to examine in more detail the nature of the code or metric that is used to combine information about speech from two modalities. To investigate this we moved from studying cross-modal matches to cross-modal illusions, in which the information from the two modalities is clearly discrepant. In this case the percept does not derive from the detection of "invariant" information; there is no invariant that can be recognized in the two modalities. Rather, the percept results from the unification of discrepant information. By systematically varying the signals one can uncover the nature and form of the information at the time that the input from the two modalities mix.

The auditory–visual "illusion" reported by McGurk and MacDonald (1976) is a robust phenomenon (Green & Kuhl, 1989, 1991; Green et al., 1991; Massaro, 1987a, 1987b; Summerfield, 1987). The illusion results when auditory information for /b/ is combined with visual information for /g/. Perceivers report the phenomenal impression of /d/ despite the fact that this information was not delivered to either sense modality. Speech scientists are now beginning to find out how the phenomenon works. Of primary

---

[1]It might be useful to clarify the "wholes" versus "parts" argument. Cross-modal tasks can be accomplished on the basis of what some might call simple attributes, such as the synchrony between simple tones and flashes of light (e.g., Lewkowicz, chap. 8, this volume). However, in cases such as tone–light synchrony it is not clear that our whole–part distinction comes into play. Synchrony is the most prominent aspect of these stimuli, the gestalt. It makes little sense to say the stimulus is "broken down" into synchrony. In the cases we are addressing, the speech signal is a whole, but it can be broken down into parts. Thus, our point about the limitations of tones in the cross-modal situation is not one about tones per se, but "parts versus wholes." In such cases the developmental question becomes whether infants first operate on the whole and then differentiate it into parts, or conversely. Our data indicate that for infants perceiving speech, the cross-modal system (but not the unimodal system) requires the whole signal to map audition to articulation, as measured by both the lip-reading and the vocal imitation studies. We do not hold that tones and other such stimuli can never support cross-modal relations in infancy, but suggest that cross-modal relations for speech (and perhaps more generally) may at first require whole stimuli; later, separate parts are sufficient. We have shown this for speech, and it would be interesting to see if a similar pattern would obtain with the wholes versus parts of visual objects (faces, geometric solids) in a cross-modal task. Although some unimodal tests have been conducted, there are few developmental cross-modal tests on this point.

interest is the nature of the interaction between the two modalities and the manner in which optic and acoustic information is mixed to yield the unified percept of /d/ when there was no /d/ presented in the stimulus.

Early accounts of the process suggested that the information in each modality was featurally categorized and then combined in some sort of additive process. The hypothesis was that the visual modality provided "place" information whereas the auditory modality provided "manner" information. The "place of articulation" feature describes the location in the mouth where the primary constriction of the airflow takes place. When producing a /b/, /p/, or /m/, for example, the primary constriction takes place at the lips, and the sound is said to have a bilabial place of articulation. In contrast, the sounds /t/, /d/, and /n/ result from a primary constriction created when the tongue tip touches the alveolar ridge behind the teeth and the sounds are said to have an alveolar place of articulation. Place of articulation features are visible on the face of the talker: You can see whether a person makes a bilabial speech sound by looking to see if the two lips close. In contrast the manner of articulation feature is nearly impossible to see on the face of the talker. The manner feature refers to the way in which a sound was produced. For example, sounds that are produced by lowering the velum and allowing air to escape from the nose are said to have a nasal manner of articulation (see Kuhl & Meltzoff, 1988, for further details). It is the manner feature that distinguishes two speech sounds with the same place of articulation, such as /b/ and /m/, which are visually identical.

Our recent data, as well as those of others, provide convincing evidence that at the point of integration the information is in a precategorical state (Grant et al., 1985; Green & Kuhl, 1989, 1991; Green et al., 1991; Green & Miller, 1985; Massaro, 1987a, 1987b). That is, the speech stream has not yet been rigidly coded as having a defined and specific place or manner of articulation before the intermodal integration takes place. The principal question now is the form of this precategorical information that makes such illusory auditory–visual blends possible.

Visually Caused Shifts in the Phonetic Boundaries Underlying Manner Features

Two studies conducted by Green and Kuhl (1989, 1991) showed that the "vision provides place information and audition provides manner information" hypothesis cannot be sustained. The data demonstrate that vision affects even the assignment of the manner feature, and this underscores the depth of communication between the visual and auditory pick up of speech information.

Green and Kuhl (1989) utilized a well-established phenomenon in auditory speech perception to study whether features were assigned prior to the integration of information in the cross-modal perception of speech. The well-established phenomenon is a change in the location of the category boundary on a voiced–voiceless continuum (a manner feature) that occurs with changes in place of articulation (Abramson & Lisker, 1970; Miller, 1977). Thus, within the auditory modality, it is known that auditory place influences decisions about auditory manner. The question posed by Green and Kuhl (1989) was whether visually specified place could also be influence (auditory) manner information; that is, whether the location of the phonetic boundary for the manner feature would shift when the place of articulation was specified by eye instead of by ear.

Observers were presented with an auditory /ibi/ and a visual /igi/. As expected, subjects perceived an illusory syllable, the syllable /idi/. The question was: Given that the perception of place information was a blend of both auditory and visual information, was the voicing information solely determined by the auditory signal, because no voicing information was available visually, or was even the perception of voicing (a classic "auditory" feature) affected by the visual information?

The results showed that the location of the voicing category boundary shifted in the auditory–visual condition. That is, when the /ibi/ and /ipi/ stimuli were presented in an auditory-alone condition, a voiced-voiceless category boundary typical for bilabial stimuli was obtained. However, when observers heard these same auditory stimuli while watching the visual /igi/, the voiced-voiceless category boundary was shifted to one that was appropriate for an alveolar place of articulation (the /d/–/t/ continuum) because through the illusion subjects now perceived a continuum ranging from /idi/ to /iti/. This was true even though the auditory information remained the same in the two conditions.

The result is interesting because it indicates that although a single modality (in this case, the auditory modality) provided the sensory input about voicing, the visual stimulus still influenced the perception of voicing. This suggests that the integration of information from the two modalities takes place prior to the time that it is categorized into phonetic features. Data and theory advanced by Massaro (1987a, 1987b) and Summerfield (1987) also support this inference.

Integral Processing of Visual and Auditory Speech Information

A second study provided converging evidence that the integration of information from the two modalities takes place prior to the time that features are assigned. A speeded classification design created by Garner (1974) was used. Garner showed that when two dimensions of a stimulus are processed "integrally," the reaction time to classifying syllables on one dimension is significantly increased by variations in information in the other dimension. When the dimensions are processed independently this increase in reaction time does not occur. Auditory experiments have shown that when classifying information along the voicing dimension, variation in the place feature results in increased reaction times (Eimas, Tartter, Miller, & Keuthen, 1978), which indicates that the two features are processed integrally rather than separately. It is well established, in both speech studies and other studies using visual objects, that when two features are processed separately, variation in an irrelevant second dimension does not cause an appreciable increase in reaction time (Eimas et al., 1978; Garner, 1974).

Green and Kuhl (1991) examined the reaction time to classify four auditory–visual syllables (/b/, /p/, /d/, /t/) that varied along two dimensions—place and voicing. In the study, subjects were asked to classify the speech syllables along the voicing dimension (classifying them as either voiced or voiceless), or along the place dimension (classifying them as either bilabial or alveolar). The voicing information in the four syllables varied only in the auditory domain, whereas the place information varied only in the visual domain. Green and Kuhl reasoned that if speech was not deeply bimodal then subjects ought to be able to selectively attend to separate modalities (auditory for voicing classification and visual for place classification), and thus process the featural information separately. The results showed that when classifying the auditory stimuli according to the voicing feature, variation in the (visual) place feature produced an increase in classification times, even though vision does not overtly contribute information regarding the voicing feature; similarly, when classifying the visual stimuli according to the place feature, irrelevant variation in the (auditory) voicing feature resulted in significant increases in classification times. This "interference effect" indicates that even when the featural information is typically carried by a specific modality (auditory-voicing and visual-place), the information from the two modalities is integrated prior to phonetic feature assignment and not treated as separate. We believe that this is due to the fact that the auditory and visual information are not initially classified featurally and then combined, but that precategorical auditory and visual information are mapped onto a stored representation at the same time (see also Massaro, 1987a, 1987b).

These studies show that at the time that the auditory–visual information is mixed, speech is not featurally classified, suggesting that it has maintained some of the detail of an analog form. If the information at the point of conflux is extremely detailed then one might be able to disrupt integration by making the information in the two modalities so noticeably different that the two streams could not mix. The next experiment addressed this point.

The Cross-Gender Speech Illusion Experiment

In cognitive psychology, cross-modal inputs that could not have derived from a common biological or physical source are said to violate the "unity" assumption (Welch & Warren, 1980). Results show that violations of the unity assumption impede intermodal perception. For example, in the ventriloquism effect, a large spatial separation between auditory and visual input (which suggests that information could not have derived from a common source) profoundly dampens the effect (Warren, Welch, & McCarthy, 1981).

The goal of the Green, Kuhl, Meltzoff, and Stevens (1991) study was to violate the unity of source for auditory–visual speech information and test whether listeners perceived a unified phonetic percept despite the fact that such a percept would have to be derived from two obviously different talkers. We created a situation in which there was an obvious discrepancy between the gender of the talker presenting the information in the two modalities. A visual male face was combined with the voice of a female talker, and vice versa. We took pains to choose our speakers such that the gender incompatibility was highly salient. A very male-looking football player's face was paired with a high and feminine-sounding female voice, and vice versa. There was no mistaking the gender mismatch for these auditory–visual stimuli.

The rationale of the study was twofold. The first was to test whether violating the unity assumption would prevent multimodal combination at the phonetic level of speech. We thought that intermodal relations for phonetic units might involve a mandatory process wherein visual phonetic information cannot be ignored by the listener, and that the two inputs might be combined despite the clear violation of the unity assumption. Second, we were interested in the detail versus abstractness of the information at the point of integration. The specific talker producing a speech sound greatly alters the acoustic detail (absolute frequencies) of the phonetic unit. If the information at the point of integration preserves that detail then it might be difficult to integrate phonetic information across talkers of different gender. However, if the information about the identity of the phonetic unit is more abstract ("talker neutral"), then the fusion of a male face and a female voice into one unified phonetic percept might still occur.

The results showed that the gender discrepancy was readily apparent. Subjects readily reported the mismatch and judged it "peculiar" and "funny" to hear a high-pitched voice come out of a whiskered, large male face. Nonetheless, the data revealed that the integration of auditory and visual information was as pervasive in the gender-discrepant situation as in the gender-congruent case. The number of auditory–visual illusions was not significantly different in the two situations. An interesting finding was the strong dissociation between the judgments of gender identity versus those of phonetic identity. There was no blending in the gender judgments: The stimuli simply looked like males and sounded like females (or vice versa) with no blending. Conversely, there was blending at the level of the phonetics: The perceivers were not able to report what they saw or what they heard, because they perceived something else, something that was not presented to either modality, a phonetic unit that was a blending of the two modality streams.

Evidently, violations in the unity assumption indicating that the input could not have derived from a common biological source do not disrupt phonetic perception. They suggest that at the time of auditory–visual integration, the phonetic information from the two modalities is in a somewhat abstract form that neutralizes differences across talkers. When available, both auditory and visual speech information, even though noticeably discrepant, are used to derive a unified phonetic interpretation of the speech signal. It is as if integrating the auditory and visual information is mandatory.

Intermodal Visual and Tactual Speech Studies: The Whole Is Greater Than the Sum of Its Parts

Further studies have shown that the information fed into the two separate modalities is not simply additive. The speech that is perceived is more than the sum of its unimodal parts. This suggests that multimodal input maps onto stored representations of linguistic information that go beyond the raw input from either modality alone.

In one study, a speaker sat at a window in a soundproof booth and read aloud from a novel (Grant et al., 1985). An observer sat outside the booth and could not see or hear the speaker. The observer listened to a pure-tone signal that followed the fundamental frequency and the amplitude of the speaker's voice. When presented by itself, the pure tone was unintelligible. No words, syllables, or phrases of the novel could be heard. Then the observer was instructed to turn and face the window, thereby bringing the speaker into view. Under these conditions the observer could obtain visual information about the speech that was produced. The results were quite dramatic. Speech perception jumped from the 37% that could be perceived with visual cues alone (pure lipreading) to nearly 80% intelligibility. Subjects reported that turning toward the speaker and allowing them to see the speaker's mouth movements while listening to the pure tone produced an astounding change in what they "heard." It is striking that the intelligibility of the information from each of the two modalities was more than additive. Considered separately, the two signals provided "37% intelligibility" (0% from audition alone + 37% from lipreading). However, when the two were combined, intelligibility was 80%.

An even more startling finding concerns speech information perceived through the skin. Research tested whether the pure-tone information following the fundamental frequency of the voice of the speaker could be presented tactually rather than auditorially (Grant, Kuhl, Ardell, & Sparks, 1986). Subjects viewed the talker reading a novel but there was no auditory information delivered. Instead, the pure-tone information was delivered through an electrocutaneous device that could be worn on the forearm. It consisted of eight electrodes, each of which covered a limited range of frequencies, that were arranged spatially in a line from wrist to elbow. The receiver was exposed to the face of the talker and tested both with and without the electrocutaneous information. (The electrocutaneous information by itself was 0% intelligible.) The results demonstrated that the tactually delivered information significantly increased speech perception over that obtained by lipreading alone. When "feeling" and seeing the speech, intelligibility increased 20% over lipreading alone.

These two experiments demonstrate that the information fed into the two separate modalities is not simply added. This is similar to the auditory–visual findings reported at the neurophysiological level by Stein and Meredith (1990, 1993) using nonspeech stimuli.

Further experiments investigated what kinds of speech information could be delivered through the skin. In these studies, electrocutaneous stimulation occurred via a matrix of 144 electrodes that presented the entire spectrum of speech in a frequency × amplitude array. The device displayed the information spatially and was worn as a belt circling the abdomen. The studies demonstrated that manner information delivered through the skin could be combined with place information delivered visually, resulting in the correct perception of individual syllables (Sparks, Kuhl, Edmonds, & Gray, 1978) and excellent perception of connected discourse (Sparks, Ardell, Bourgeois, Wiedmer, & Kuhl, 1979).

Speech information can be delivered to the skin and integrated with that perceived by eye or by ear. The important theoretical point is the penetrability of the speech-processing mechanism by the information picked up by touch (or vision). Speech is not solely the province of audition, nor even of audition plus vision. Information delivered tactually also appears to have access to the speech-processing mechanism. The speech code is thoroughly intermodal in nature.

IMPLICATIONS FOR THEORY: VIEWING FACES AND SPEECH THROUGH AN "INTERMODAL LENS"

A variety of phenomena concerning intermodal functioning have been discussed both in infants and adults. We here intend to draw out the theoretical implications of these findings. Discussed are the developmental aspects of intermodal perception, its bases, and functional utility.

Infant Babbling as Viewed Through an Intermodal Lens

It has been discussed how speech is perceived through different sensory modalities—auditory, visual, and even the tactile sense. We now turn to speech production for clues about the developmental history of the inter-modal organization of speech.

There is ample evidence to suggest that by adulthood we have a set of rules specifying the relation between sounds and speech movements. The mapping is not restricted to the production of articulatory acts that are overlearned. We can reach an auditory target if we hold a foreign object in our mouths (a pencil, food, or even a novel object). This has been demonstrated experimentally in studies in which an adult, instructed to produce a vowel such as /i/, is suddenly prevented from doing so by the introduction of a weight or load imposed on the lip or jaw. Under these conditions, the speaker produces a perfectly adequate /i/ vowel, but uses a different set of muscles than those typically used in the production of that sound. Detailed measurements of the muscle movements show that in this situation compensation is virtually immediate, prior to the time that auditory feedback could have led to the compensation (Perkell, Matthies, Svirsky, & Jordan, 1993). Such rapid motor adjustments suggest a flexible set of rules; we call it an auditory-articulatory "map," relating articulatory movements to sound.

How does this auditory-articulatory map develop? It can be suggested that one important developmental contributor is the practice infants gain from their own self-produced sound. Normal infants the world over produce speech milestones on a fairly predictable schedule. At 3 months infants will "coo," producing vowel-like utterances; by 7 months, infants will "babble," producing reduplicative consonant-vowel syllables like *bababab* (e.g., Ferguson, Menn, & Stoel-Gammon, 1992; Locke, 1993). The classical, now outdated view, was that these speech-production milestones were matura-tionally driven, perhaps due to the unfolding of an internal motor program (Lenneberg, 1967). However, data derived from a comparison of speech production in normal children, deaf children, and blind children shows how deeply early speech production is affected by environmental input.

It has been shown, for example, that deaf infants do not babble in the way that is universal among hearing infants. They do not babble on the same time schedule that hearing infants do, and the durations of their babbled utterances do not match those of normal infants (Oller & Eilers, 1988; Oller & Lynch, 1992). Moreover, the phonetic content of the babbled utterances of hearing-impaired infants is different than that of normal infants (Stoel-Gammon, 1988; Stoel-Gammon & Otomo, 1986). Hearing-impaired infants babble using a disproportionally high level of bilabial sounds—/b/, /m/, and /d/—sounds that are easily seen. Normally hearing infants include a higher proportion of sounds such as /g/ that cannot be readily seen and require audition to perceive in detail. Thus, speech production does not mature independent of experience, but is modified by the auditory environment. Perhaps more surprising, it appears that the lack of visual information during development can have an effect on infant vocal productions. Blind children learn sounds that have visible articulation more slowly than sighted children and manifest a different pattern of articulatory errors (Mills, 1987). These alterations in the typical pattern of speech development may occur because blind infants cannot see how other speakers move their articulators to achieve particular targets. This interpretation is in line with results from facial imitation, which directly demonstrated that seeing others' mouth movements influences the oral movements of infants. The natural experiment of blindness shows that the absence of such visual input alters early speech production.

Infant speech production is thus influenced by experience and is a thoroughly intermodal affair—what babies produce with their own articulators is profoundly influenced both by what they see and hear. Infants who are engaged in cooing and babbling in their bassinets are engaged in serious business: They are mastering quite general rules about the auditory consequences of their own vocal tract manipulations. They are solidifying an auditory-articulatory intermodal map of speech. In developing this map they use auditory and proprioceptive information from the self and visual information from others to learn what to do with their own vocal tracts when producing speech. They learn, for example, that raising versus lowering the tongue blade has a particular kind of impact on the sound that is emitted.

Two kinds of studies serve as metrics for infants' acquisition of auditory-articulatory rules, studies of vocal imitation and studies of auditory–visual speech perception. Both assess infants' connections between audition and articulation, and both can be used to chart developmental progress (Kuhl & Meltzoff, 1984, 1988; Studdert-Kennedy, 1986).

Studies of vocal imitation show that as young as 12 weeks of life infants alter their vocalizations to match the vocalizations they hear another produce (e.g., Kuhl & Meltzoff, 1988, 1994; Legerstee, 1991). In our recent study, infants saw a video presentation of a woman articulating one of three vowels, /a/, /i/, or /u/. The infants' vocalizations were analyzed by a phonetically trained listener who transcribed the vocalizations of the infants (while remaining uninformed about the actual stimulus).

The results provided evidence of vocal imitation in 12-week-old infants. The analysis showed that infants produced more /a/-like vocalizations in response to hearing the model say /a/ then in response to hearing the model say either /i/ or /u/. Similarly, they produced more /u/-like vocalizations in response to the model's /u/ than in response to either her /a/ or /i/. Spectrographic analyses of infants' /a/-, /i/-, and /u/-like vowels indicated that the formant patterns of the infants' vocalizations resembled those characteristic of the adult model's vowels (Kuhl & Meltzoff, 1994). These data indicate that by 12 weeks of age infants have learned something about what to do with their articulators to produce a sound that matches one they hear. They have begun to bring their articulatory and auditory systems into register with one another.

A second measure of infants' relating auditory and articulatory instantiations of speech is infants' ability to detect a match between an auditory presentation of a sound and the sight of a person producing that sound, such as we presented in the lipreading experiments (Kuhl & Meltzoff, 1982, 1984). In this situation the speaker is someone other than themselves. The task demands that infants recognize articulatory movements by eye and relate them to the concomitant auditory information. The fact that 18-week-old infants recognize the correspondence between the sound of the vowel /a/ and the sight of a person with a wide open mouth, and between the sound of the vowel /i/ and the sight of a person with retracted lips, provides converging evidence of infants' acquisition of auditory-articulatory maps.

We are thus emphasizing intermodal connections between the sound, sight, and movements involved in speech, and the role that experience plays in that development. Infants have auditory–motor as well as auditory–visual linkages, and the two may feed on one another during development.

Could real-world cooing and babbling experience contribute to the laboratory effect of infant lipreading? There might be such a developmental effect. It would require that infants relate the articulations they see in our experiment to the auditory-articulatory events they themselves produced when cooing. There is research demonstrating that infants can relate mouth movements they see to their own self-produced mouth movements. Infants can imitate oral gestures. There is thus an underlying ability to map the seen articulatory movements to their own articulations (Meltzoff, 1993). On the auditory side, Kuhl's (1979, 1983, 1985) speech categorization work demonstrates that young infants can recognize the equivalence between the vowels uttered across talkers, including those produced by children and adults. Thus there is also an underlying ability to recognize an equivalence between the heard adult vowels and their own self-produced sounds.

In short, infants have the requisite tools, as manifest by facial imitation and the cross-talker categorization of vowels, to use self-produced speech movements to help solve the intermodal speech task involved in lipreading. The auditory-articulatory mappings experienced during their own cooing and babbling may contribute to infants' ability to recognize cross-modal equivalences for speech when they see those same relations posed on the face of others. The emerging developmental picture is that intermodal abilities support one another, underscoring the web that connects them in ontogenesis.

Stored Targets and Representations and Their Role in Intermodal Theory

The intermodal phenomena we discussed can be organized within three broad classes. The first is a situation in which infants (or adults) detect *perceptual–perceptual matches* between information picked up from two separate perceptual modalities. This encompasses both infant auditory–visual speech perception and the tactual–visual perception of objects. The second involves *perceptual–motor matches*. The visual–motor examples was gestural imitation; the auditory–motor examples were vocal imitation and babbling. Here the infant perceives information in one modality (vision or audition) and this drives a matching event using their own motor systems. The third involves the *blending of discrepant multimodal information into a new and unified percept*. The examples were the auditory–visual blend illusion and the tactual–vision perception of speech. In these cases the information in the two modalities is not equivalent. What unites the two modalities is not "invariant" information picked up by the perceiver. Rather, we suggest that in the case of speech the discrepant information is united by a higher order phonetic representation of speech that acts as a mediator between nonidentical information in the two modalities.

The notion that stored representations link intermodal information provides leverage in discussing several seemingly diverse phenomena. We first apply it to the speech cases and next to the understanding of faces and gestural imitation.

Early exposure to a particular linguistic environment has long-term effects on both speech perception and production. Indeed, the linguistic environment begins to have an effect very early in life. Kuhl and her colleagues showed that exposure to a particular language alters infants' perception of speech by 6 months of age (Kuhl, Williams, Lacerda, Stevens, & Lindblom, 1992). Six-month-old infants in two countries, the United States and Sweden, were tested with English and Swedish vowel "prototypes," vowels that were particularly good instances of the category. The results showed that infants in both cultures treated the native-language sounds in a special way: They generalized further around the native-language prototype than around the foreign-language prototype even though psychophysical distance was strictly equated. In explaining these results, Kuhl (1992, 1993a) argued that infants develop stored representations of the native-language sounds that they previously heard and that these affect the processing of current inputs.

We believe that these stored representations for speech in turn serve as targets that guide the motor system. This can be seen in two types of recent studies. First, the results of our studies on vocal imitation in 12-week-old infants show that auditory input is sufficient to drive infant production (Kuhl & Meltzoff, 1982, 1988). Second, it has also been discovered that infants from different cultures babble in different ways at least by 10 months (de Boysson-Bardies, 1993; de Boysson-Bardies, Halle, Sagart, & Durand, 1989; de Boysson-Bardies, Sagart, & Durand, 1984), suggesting that exposure to native-language speech shapes the particulars of infant production. The inference is that at an early age, speech is represented in a way that unites information from multiple modalities, linking auditory, visual, and motor instantiations of speech. Experience clearly plays a major role in elaborating this representation, inasmuch as infants' representations seem to vary as a function of being reared in different linguistic environments (due to the different auditory and visual input), and also as a function of abnormalities in which the sensory filters or cognitive machinery are atypical (Kuhl, 1993b). Moreover, early exposure seems to have virtually permanent effects on both perception and production, suggesting a "sensitive period" in development. It is difficult to hear speech distinctions that are not used phonemically in one's native language (perception), and it is nearly impossible to lose a foreign accent (production).

Thus, in the case of speech, information originally derived from one modality (audition) has long-term effects for later motor behavior, implicating memory. A parallel case can be made for the visual modality. In the case of gestural imitation it is the visually derived information that drives motor production. Facial imitation is doubly interesting because the motor output cannot be monitored using the same sense modality with which the incoming target was perceived. Meltzoff and Moore suggested that early imitation is mediated by a supramodal representation of the adult's act. The newer findings of imitation after a delay (which indicates memory storage) as well as imitation of novel motor patterns and response correction lend support to the theory that a supramodal representation of the adult's behavior serves as the "internal target" that infants use to generate and correct their behavior.

The ability to act on the basis of supramodal representations is postulated to be an aspect of the human perceptual-cognitive system that is present at birth (Meltzoff, 1990); it allows infants to profit from and organize multimodal experience such that the representations of faces and voices become ever more richly specified (as in the arguments regarding babbling). It would be of great value to investigate the neural basis of such a supramodal representational capacity as it develops in the infant. Highly instructive in this regard are the discoveries by Stein and Meredith (1990, 1993; Stein, Meredith, & Wallace, chap. 5, this volume) about multisensory convergence in the brains of nonhuman animals, as well as recent work on brain growth and plasticity by Greenough (Greenough & Alcantara, 1993; Greenough & Black, 1989) and Edelman (1987, 1989). The extrapolation that can be made on the basis of this neural data is that the brain is ready to accept multimodal input and indeed that the input from both self-generated experience (e.g., babbling) and other-generated experience may help to consolidate the multimodal links, to "grease the skids," as it were, for later perception.

SUMMARY

Faces and speech are among the most important signals that our perceptual systems have evolved to perceive. These biologically important events provide ideal stimuli for exploring the origins, development, and mechanisms of intermodal functioning in humans.

Research shows that newborn infants can relate the facial movements they see to their own unseen facial movements. It was proposed that facial imitation is mediated by active intermodal mapping (the AIM hypothesis). On this view, facial imitation is among the earliest, most complex, and socially significant manifestations of intermodal functioning in the newborn.

Facial imitation involves a mapping from vision to the motor/proprioception domain. Other research indicated that infants can relate objects they feel to those that they see, suggesting a mapping between touch and vision in the first month of life. Further research in our laboratory and others has focused on the generality of these early intermodal connections. We investigated auditory–visual relations by presenting infants with moving faces (vision) and speech sounds (audition). The results showed that 4-month-old infants could recognize what particular facial movements corresponded to what particular speech sound.

The basis and development of such lipreading was investigated by decomposing the auditory speech stimulus into its elementary "features." Nonspeech sounds that were synchronous with the visible movements they saw were presented to infants. The results showed that adults matched these speech "parts" to faces. Infants did not. We concluded that there is a development in the intermodal perception of speech; infants need to hear the whole speech signal, one that is identified as speech, to make the connection to articulation. This may be related to the fact that when they babble they hear and feel whole speech units.

Adult subjects were also used to investigate further the intermodal organization of speech. Here the principal phenomena were an auditory–visual "illusion" and the finding that speech can be perceived by touch as well as by eye and ear. This work underscored the fact that the cross-modal integration of speech information is so powerful that illusory blends are sometimes mandatory, and are obtained even in cases in which the adult "knows" that the visual and auditory sources cannot go together (the cross-gender experiment). This work differs from ordinary cross-modal studies because here there is no match between the information fed into the separate modalities, but rather the formation of a unified percept that combines discrepant information. Other research shows that the percept is more than the simple sum of the information fed into the two separate modalities. In our view, a stored supramodal representation of speech is the basis for the unitary perception and multiplicative effect.

The role of development, and especially the role of self-produced experience, was highlighted. Infant cooing and babbling was viewed as consolidating an auditory-articulatory map. Such a map could then be used when infants relate a speech sound to a seen articulation, as in lipreading. This would occur because infants have the underlying ability to connect the articulations they feel themselves make to those they see on the face of others (as manifest and practiced in facial imitation). As infants elaborate their knowledge of faces and speech, they are building a network that interconnects a variety of intermodal phenomena, including facial imitation, babbling, and lipreading, using information from one domain to bootstrap their understanding in another.

Faces and speech are intermodal sources of information. Stimulation from the external world coupled with the infant's own self-produced stimulation provides input about the human body, its movement transformations, and auditory concomitants that may affect neural development (Edelman, 1987, 1989; Greenough, Black, & Wallace, 1987; Stein & Meredith, 1993). Our thesis, which is at root an interactive-developmental one, is that many biologically important signals are not only intermodal in the real physical world—things that can be seen, heard, and touched—but also intermodally organized in the infant's mind. Experience both with others' and with their own bodies plays a role in the ontogenesis of this intermodal organization.

ACKNOWLEDGMENTS

Preparation of this manuscript was supported by grants from NIH (HD-22514 and HD-18286). We gratefully acknowledge the long-term collaboration of M. Keith Moore and Kerry P. Green and on aspects of the research reported here. We are indebted to Craig Harris and Erica Stevens for their assistance on all aspects of the research.

REFERENCES

Abramson, A. S., & Lisker, L. (1970). Discriminability along the voicing continuum: Cross-language tests. In *Proceedings of the Sixth International Congress of Phonetic Sciences Prague 1967* (pp. 569–573). Prague: Academia.

Abravanel, E., & DeYong, N. G. (1991). Does object modeling elicit imitative-like gestures from young infants? *Journal of Experimental Child Psychology, 52,* 22–40.

Abravanel, E., & Sigafoos, A. D. (1984). Exploring the presence of imitation during early infancy. *Child Development, 55,* 381–392.

Bahrick, L. E. (1983). Infants' perception of substance and temporal synchrony in multimodal events. *Infant Behavior and Development, 6,* 429–451.

Bahrick, L. E. (1987). Infants' intermodal perception of two levels of temporal structure in natural events. *Infant Behavior and Development, 10,* 387–416.

Bahrick, L. E. (1988). Intermodal learning in infancy: Learning on the basis of two kinds of invariant relations in audible and visible events. *Child Development, 59,* 197–209.

Bahrick, L. E., & Watson, J. S. (1985). Detection of intermodal proprioceptive-visual contingency as a potential basis of self-perception in infancy. *Developmental Psychology, 21,* 963–973.

Bower, T. G. R. (1982). *Development in infancy* (2nd ed.). San Francisco: Freeman.

Bower, T. G. R. (1989). *The rational infant.* New York: Freeman.

Bushnell, E. W., & Weinberger, N. (1987). Infants' detection of visual-tactual discrepancies: Asymmetries that indicate a directive role of visual information. *Journal of Experimental Psychology: Human Perception and Performance, 13,* 601–608.

Butterworth, G. (1981). The origins of auditory-visual perception and visual proprioception in human development. In R. D. Walk & H. L. Pick (Eds.), *Intersensory perception and sensory integration* (pp. 37–70). New York: Plenum.

Butterworth, G. (1983). Structure of the mind in human infancy. In L. Lipsitt (Ed.), *Advances in infancy research* (Vol. 2, pp. 1–29). Norwood, NJ: Ablex.

Butterworth, G. (1990). On reconceptualizing sensori-motor development in dynamic systems terms. In H. Bloch & B. I. Bertenthal (Eds.), *Sensory-motor organizations and development in infancy and early childhood* (pp. 57–73). Dordrecht, Netherlands: Kluwer.

Chiba, T., & Kajiyama, M. (1958). *The vowel—Its nature and structure.* Tokyo: Phonetic Society of Japan.

Damasio, A. R., Tranel, D., & Damasio, H. (1990). Face agnosia and the neural substrates of memory. *Annual Review of Neuroscience, 13,* 89–109.

de Boysson-Bardies, B. (1993). Ontogeny of language-specific phonetic and lexical productions. In B. de Boysson-Bardies, S. de Schonen, P. Jusczyk, P. MacNeilage, & J. Morton (Eds.), *Developmental neurocognition: Speech and face processing in the first year of life* (pp. 353–363). Boston: Kluwer.

de Boysson-Bardies, B., Halle, P., Sagart, L., & Durand, C. (1989). A crosslinguistic investigation of vowel formants in babbling. *Journal of Child Language, 16,* 1–17.

de Boysson-Bardies, B., Sagart, L., & Durand, C. (1984). Discernible differences in the babbling of infants according to target language. *Journal of Child Language, 11,* 1–15.

de Schonen, S., & Mathivet, E. (1989). First come, first served: A scenario about the development of hemispheric specialization in face recognition during infancy. *Cahiers de Psychologie Cognitive, 9,* 3–44.

Diehl, R. L., & Walsh, M. A. (1989). An auditory basis for the stimulus-length effect in the perception of stops and glides. *Journal of the Acoustical Society of America, 85,* 2154–2164.

Dodd, B. (1979). Lip reading in infants: Attention to speech presented in- and out-of-synchrony. *Cognitive Psychology, 11,* 478–484.

Dodd, B., & Campbell, R. (1987). *Hearing by eye: The psychology of lip-reading.* Hillsdale, NJ: Lawrence Erlbaum Associates.

Edelman, G. M. (1987). *Neural Darwinism: The theory of neuronal group selection.* New York: Basic Books.

Edelman, G. M. (1989). *The remembered present.* New York: Basic Books.

Eimas, P. D., Tartter, V. C., Miller, J. L., & Keuthen, N. J. (1978). Asymmetric dependencies in processing phonetic features. *Perception & Psychophysics, 23,* 12–20.

Fant, G. (1973). *Speech sounds and features.* Cambridge, MA: MIT Press.

Farnsworth, P. R. (1937). An approach to the study of vocal resonance. *Journal of the Acoustical Society of America, 9,* 152–155.

Ferguson, C. A., Menn, L., & Stoel-Gammon, C. (Eds.). (1992). *Phonological development: Models, research, implications.* Timonium, MD: York Press.

Field, T., Goldstein, S., Vaga-Lahr, N., & Porter, K. (1986). Changes in imitative behavior during early infancy. *Infant Behavior and Development, 9,* 415–421.

Field, T. M., Woodson, R., Cohen, D., Greenberg, R., Garcia, R., & Collins, E. (1983). Discrimination and imitation of facial expressions by term and preterm neonates. *Infant Behavior and Development, 6,* 485–489.

Field, T. M., Woodson, R., Greenberg, R., & Cohen, D. (1982). Discrimination and imitation of facial expressions by neonates. *Science, 218,* 179–181.

Fontaine, R. (1984). Imitative skills between birth and six months. *Infant Behavior and Development, 7,* 323–333.

Fowler, C. A. (1986). An event approach to the study of speech perception from a direct-realist perspective. *Journal of Phonetics, 14,* 3–28.

Garner, W. R. (1974). *The processing of information and structure.* Potomac, MD: Lawrence Erlbaum Associates.

Gentner, D., & Grudin, J. (1985). The evolution of mental metaphors in psychology: A 90-year retrospective. *American Psychologist, 40,* 181–192.

Gibson, E. J. (1969). *Principles of perceptual learning and development.* New York: Appleton-Century-Crofts.

Gibson, E. J., & Walker, A. S. (1984). Development of knowledge of visual-tactual affordances of substance. *Child Development, 55,* 453–460.

Gibson, J. J. (1966). *The senses considered as perceptual systems.* Boston: Houghton Mifflin.

Gibson, J. J. (1979). *The ecological approach to visual perception.* Boston: Houghton Mifflin.

Grant, K. W., Ardell, L. A. H., Kuhl, P. K., & Sparks, D. W. (1985). The contribution of fundamental frequency, amplitude envelope, and voicing duration cues to speechreading in normal-hearing subjects. *Journal of the Acoustical Society of America, 77,* 671–677.

Grant, K. W., Ardell, L. A. H., Kuhl, P. K., & Sparks, D. W. (1986). The transmission of prosodic information via an electrotactile speechreading aid. *Ear and Hearing, 7,* 328–335.

Green, K. P., & Kuhl, P. K. (1989). The role of visual information in the processing of place and manner features in speech perception. *Perception and Psychophysics, 45,* 34–42.

Green, K. P., & Kuhl, P. K. (1991). Integral processing of visual place and auditory voicing information during phonetic perception. *Journal of Experimental Psychology: Human Perception and Performance, 17,* 278–288.

Green, K. P., Kuhl, P. K., Meltzoff, A. N., & Stevens, E. B. (1991). Integrating speech information across talkers, gender, and sensory modality: Female faces and male voices in the McGurk effect. *Perception & Psychophysics, 50,* 524–536.

Green, K. P., & Miller, J. L. (1985). On the role of visual rate information in phonetic perception. *Perception & Psychophysics, 38,* 269–276.

Greenough, W. T., & Alcantara, A. A. (1993). The roles of experience in different developmental information storage processes. In B. de Boysson-Bardies, S. de Schonen, P. Juscyck, P. MacNeilage, & J. Morton (Eds.), *Developmental neurocognition: Speech and face processing in the first year of life* (pp. 3–16). Boston: Kluwer.

Greenough, W. T., & Black, J. E. (1989). Induction of brain structure by experience: Substrates for cognitive development. In M. Gunnar & C. Nelson (Eds.), *Developmental behavioral neuroscience: Minnesota Symposia on Child Development* (Vol. 24, pp. 155–200). Hillsdale, NJ: Lawrence Erlbaum Associates.

Greenough, W. T., Black, J. E., & Wallace, C. S. (1987). Experience and brain development. *Child Development, 58,* 539–559.

Gunderson, V. M. (1983). Development of cross-modal recognition in infant pigtail monkeys (*Macaca nemestrina*). *Developmental Psychology, 19,* 398–404.

Heimann, M., Nelson, K. E., & Schaller, J. (1989). Neonatal imitation of tongue protrusion and mouth opening: Methodological aspects and evidence of early individual differences. *Scandinavian Journal of Psychology, 30,* 90–101.

Heimann, M., & Schaller, J. (1985). Imitative reactions among 14–21 day old infants. *Infant Mental Health Journal, 6,* 31–39.

Helmholtz, H. (1954). *On the sensations of tone as a physiological basis for the theory of music.* New York: Dover. (Original work published 1885)

Jacobson, S. W. (1979). Matching behavior in the young infant. *Child Development, 50,* 425–430.

Jakobson, R., Fant, C. G. M., & Halle, M. (1969). *Preliminaries to speech analysis: The distinctive features and their correlates.* Cambridge, MA: MIT Press.

Jusczyk, P. W., Pisoni, D. B., Reed, M. A., Fernald, A., & Meyers, M. (1983). Infants' discrimination of the duration of a rapid spectrum change in nonspeech signals. *Science, 222,* 175–177.

Jusczyk, P. W., Pisoni, D. B., Walley, A., & Murray, J. (1980). Discrimination of relative onset time of two-component tones by infants. *Journal of the Acoustical Society of America, 67,* 262–270.

Kaitz, M., Meschulach-Sarfaty, O., Auerbach, J., & Eidelman, A. (1988). A reexamination of newborn's ability to imitate facial expressions. *Developmental Psychology, 24,* 3–7.

Kaye, K. L. (1993, March). *Cross-modal matching in human newborns.* Presented at the meeting of the Society for Research on Child Development, New Orleans, LA.

Kugiumutzakis, J. (1985). *Development of imitation during the first six months of life* (Uppsala Psychological Reports No. 377). Uppsala, Sweden: Uppsala University.

Kuhl, P. K. (1979). Speech perception in early infancy: Perceptual constancy for spectrally dissimilar vowel categories. *Journal of the Acoustical Society of America, 66,* 1668–1679.

Kuhl, P. K. (1983). Perception of auditory equivalence classes for speech in early infancy. *Infant Behavior and Development, 6,* 263–285.

Kuhl, P. K. (1985). Categorization of speech by infants. In J. Mehler & R. Fox (Eds.), *Neonate cognition: Beyond the blooming, buzzing confusion* (pp. 231–262). Hillsdale, NJ: Lawrence Erlbaum Associates.

Kuhl, P. K. (1992). Infants' perception and representation of speech: Development of a new theory. In J. Ohala, T. Nearey, B. Derwing, M. Hodge, & G. Wiebe (Eds.), *The Proceedings of the International Conference on Spoken Language Processing* (pp. 449–456). Edmonton, Alberta: University of Alberta Press.

Kuhl, P. K. (1993a). Innate predispositions and the effects of experience in speech perception: The Native Language Magnet theory. In B. de Boysson-Bardies, S. de Schonen, P. Jusczyk, P. MacNeilage, & J. Morton (Eds.), *Developmental neurocognition: Speech and face processing in the first year of life* (pp. 259–274). Boston: Kluwer.

Kuhl, P. K. (1993b). Developmental speech perception: Implications for models of language impairment. In P. Tallal, A. M. Galaburda, R. R. Llinás, & C. von Euler (Eds.), *Temporal information processing in the nervous system* (Vol. 682, pp. 248–263). New York: New York Academy of Sciences

Kuhl, P. K., & Meltzoff, A. N. (1982). The bimodal perception of speech in infancy. *Science, 218,* 1138–1141.

Kuhl, P. K., & Meltzoff, A. N. (1984). The intermodal representation of speech in infants. *Infant Behavior and Development, 7,* 361–381.

Kuhl, P. K., & Meltzoff, A. N. (1988). Speech as an intermodal object of perception. In A. Yonas (Ed.), *Perceptual development in infancy: The Minnesota Symposia on Child Psychology* (Vol. 20, pp. 235–266). Hillsdale, NJ: Lawrence Erlbaum Associates.

Kuhl, P. K., & Meltzoff, A. N. (1994). Infant vocalizations in response to speech: Vocal imitation and developmental change. *Journal of the Acoustical Society of America,* under revision.

Kuhl, P. K., Williams, K. A., Lacerda, F., Stevens, K. N., & Lindblom, B. (1992). Linguistic experience alters phonetic perception in infants by 6 months of age. *Science, 255,* 606–608.

Kuhl, P. K., Williams, K. M., & Meltzoff, A. N. (1991). Cross-modal speech perception in adults and infants using nonspeech auditory stimuli. *Journal of Experimental Psychology: Human Perception and Performance, 17,* 829–840.

Legerstee, M. (1991). The role of person and object in eliciting early imitation. *Journal of Experimental Child Psychology, 51*, 423–433.

Lenneberg, E. H. (1967). *Biological foundations of language.* New York: Wiley.

Lewkowicz, D. J. (1985). Bisensory response to temporal frequency in 4-month-old infants. *Developmental Psychology, 21*, 306–317.

Lewkowicz, D. J. (1986). Developmental changes in infants' bisensory response to synchronous durations. *Infant Behavior and Development, 9*, 335–353.

Lewkowicz, D. J. (1992). Infants' response to temporally based intersensory equivalence: The effect of synchronous sounds on visual preferences for moving stimuli. *Infant Behavior and Development, 15*, 297–324.

Liberman, A. M., & Mattingly, I. G. (1985). The motor theory of speech perception revised. *Cognition, 21*, 1–36.

Locke, J. L. (1993). *The child's path to spoken language.* Cambridge, MA: Harvard University Press.

MacKain, K., Studdert-Kennedy, M., Spieker, S., & Stern, D. (1983). Infant intermodal speech perception is a left-hemisphere function. *Science, 219*, 1347–1349.

Maratos, O. (1982). Trends in the development of imitation in early infancy. In T. G. Bever (Ed.), *Regressions in mental development: Basic phenomena and theories* (pp. 81–101). Hillsdale, NJ: Lawrence Erlbaum Associates.

Massaro, D. W. (1987a). Speech perception by ear and eye. In B. Dodd & R. Campbell (Eds.), *Hearing by eye: The psychology of lip-reading* (pp. 53–83). Hillsdale, NJ: Lawrence Erlbaum Associates.

Massaro, D. W. (1987b). *Speech perception by ear and eye: A paradigm for psychological inquiry.* Hillsdale, NJ: Lawrence Erlbaum Associates.

Massaro, D. W., & Cohen, M. M. (1990). Perception of synthesized audible and visible speech. *Psychological Science, 1*, 55–63.

McGurk, H., & MacDonald, J. (1976). Hearing lips and seeing voices. *Nature, 264*, 746–748.

Meltzoff, A. N. (1988). Infant imitation after a 1-week delay: Long-term memory for novel acts and multiple stimuli. *Developmental Psychology, 24*, 470–476.

Meltzoff, A. N. (1990). Towards a developmental cognitive science: The implications of cross-modal matching and imitation for the development of representation and memory in infancy. In A. Diamond (Ed.), *The development and neural bases of higher cognitive functions. Annals of the New York Academy of Sciences, 608*, 1–31.

Meltzoff, A. N. (1993). The centrality of motor coordination and proprioception in social and cognitive development: From shared actions to shared minds. In G. J. P. Savelsbergh (Ed.), *Advances in Psychology Series: The development of coordination in infancy* (pp. 463–496). Amsterdam: Elsevier.

Meltzoff, A. N., & Borton, R. W. (1979). Intermodal matching by human neonates. *Nature, 282*, 403–404.

Meltzoff, A. N., Kuhl, P. K., & Moore, M. K. (1991). Perception, representation, and the control of action in newborns and young infants: Toward a new synthesis. In M. J. S. Weiss & P. R. Zelazo (Eds.), *Newborn attention: Biological constraints and the influence of experience* (pp. 377–411). Norwood, NJ: Ablex.

Meltzoff, A. N., & Moore, M. K. (1977). Imitation of facial and manual gestures by human neonates. *Science, 198*, 75–78.

Meltzoff, A. N., & Moore, M. K. (1983). Newborn infants imitate adult facial gestures. *Child Development, 54*, 702–709.

Meltzoff, A. N., & Moore, M. K. (1989). Imitation in newborn infants: Exploring the range of gestures imitated and the underlying mechanisms. *Developmental Psychology, 25*, 954–962.

Meltzoff, A. N., & Moore, M. K. (1992). Early imitation within a functional framework: The importance of person identity, movement, and development. *Infant Behavior and Development, 15*, 479–505.

Meltzoff, A. N., & Moore, M. K. (1993). Why faces are special to infants—On connecting the attraction of faces and infants' ability for imitation and cross-modal processing. In B. de Boysson-Bardies, S. de Schonen, P. Jusczyk, P. MacNeilage, & J. Morton (Eds.), *Developmental neurocognition: Speech and face processing in the first year of life* (pp. 211–225). Boston: Kluwer.

Meltzoff, A. N., & Moore, M. K. (1994). Imitation, memory, and the representation of persons. *Infant Behavior and Development, 17,* 83–99.

Miller, J. L. (1977). Properties of feature detectors for VOT: The voiceless channel of analysis. *Journal of the Acoustical Society of America, 62,* 641–648.

Mills, A. E. (1987). The development of phonology in the blind child. In B. Dodd & R. Campbell (Eds.), *Hearing by eye: The psychology of lip-reading* (pp. 145–161). Hillsdale, NJ: Lawrence Erlbaum Associates.

Oller, D. K., & Eilers, R. E. (1988). The role of audition in infant babbling. *Child Development, 59,* 441–449.

Oller, D. K., & Lynch, M. P. (1992). Infant vocalizations and innovations in infraphonology: Toward a broader theory of development and disorders. In C. A. Ferguson, L. Menn, & C. Stoel-Gammon (Eds.), *Phonological development: Models, research, implications* (pp. 509–536). Timonium, MD: York.

Ortony, A. (1979). *Metaphor and thought.* Cambridge: Cambridge University Press.

Pêcheux, M.-G., Lepecq, J.-C., & Salzarulo, P. (1988). Oral activity and exploration in 1–2-month-old infants. *British Journal of Developmental Psychology, 6,* 245–256.

Perkell, J. S., Matthies, M. L., Svirsky, M. A., & Jordan, M. L. (1993). Trading relations between tongue-body raising and lip rounding in production of the vowel /a/: A pilot "motor equivalence" study. *Journal of the Acoustical Society of America, 93,* 2948–2961.

Piaget, J. (1962). *Play, dreams and imitation in childhood.* New York: Norton. (Original work published 1945)

Pisoni, D. B., Carrell, T. D., & Gans, S. J. (1983). Perception of the duration of rapid spectrum changes in speech and nonspeech signals. *Perception and Psychophysics, 34,* 314–322.

Reissland, N. (1988). Neonatal imitation in the first hour of life: Observations in rural Nepal. *Developmental Psychology, 24,* 464–469.

Rose, S. A. (1990). Cross-modal transfer in human infants: What is being transferred? *Annals of the New York Academy of Sciences, 608,* 38–50.

Rose, S. A., & Ruff, H. A. (1987). Cross-modal abilities in human infants. In J. D. Osofsky (Ed.), *Handbook of infant development* (pp. 318–362). New York: Wiley.

Sparks, D. W., Ardell, L. A., Bourgeois, M., Wiedmer, B., & Kuhl, P. K. (1979). Investigating the MESA (Multipoint Electrotactile Speech Aid): The transmission of connected discourse. *Journal of the Acoustical Society of America, 65,* 810–815.

Sparks, D. W., Kuhl, P. K., Edmonds, A. E., & Gray, G. P. (1978). Investigating the MESA (Multipoint Electrotactile Speech Aid): The transmission of segmental features of speech. *Journal of the Acoustical Society of America, 63,* 246–257.

Spelke, E. S. (1981). The infants' acquisition of knowledge of bimodally specified events. *Journal of Experimental Child Psychology, 31,* 279–299.

Spelke, E. S. (1987). The development of intermodal perception. In P. Salapatek & L. Cohen (Eds.), *Handbook of infant perception: Vol. 2. From perception to cognition* (pp. 233–273). New York: Academic Press.

Stein, B. E., & Meredith, M. A. (1990). Multisensory integration: Neural and behavioral solutions for dealing with stimuli from different sensory modalities. In A. Diamond (Ed.), *The development and neural bases of higher cognitive functions. Annals of the New York Academy of Sciences, 608,* 51–70.

Stein, B. E., & Meredith, M. A. (1993). *The merging of the senses.* Cambridge, MA: MIT Press.

Stoel-Gammon, C. (1988). Prelinguistic vocalizations of hearing-impaired and normally hearing subjects: A comparison of consonantal inventories. *Journal of Speech and Hearing Disorders, 53,* 302–315.

Stoel-Gammon, C., & Otomo, K. (1986). Babbling development of hearing-impaired and normally hearing subjects. *Journal of Speech and Hearing Disorders, 51*, 33–41.

Streri, A. (1987). Tactile discrimination of shape and intermodal transfer in 2- to 3-month-old infants. *British Journal of Developmental Psychology, 5*, 213–220.

Streri, A., & Milhet, S. (1988). Équivalences intermodales de la forme des objects enter la vision et le toucher chez les bébés de 2 mois [Intermodal equivalences between vision and touch for the form of objects in 2-month-old infants]. *L'Anneé Psychologique, 88*, 329–341.

Streri, A., & Spelke, E. S. (1988). Haptic perception of objects in infancy. *Cognitive Psychology, 20*, 1–23.

Studdert-Kennedy, M. (1986). Development of the speech perceptuomotor system. In B. Lindblom & R. Zetterström (Eds.), *Precursors of early speech* (pp. 205–217). New York: Stockton Press.

Studdert-Kennedy, M. (1993). Some theoretical implications of cross-modal research in speech perception. In B. de Boysson-Bardies, S. de Schonen, P. Jusczyk, P. MacNeilage, & J. Morton (Eds.), *Developmental neurocognition: Speech and face processing in the first year of life* (pp. 461–466). Boston, MA: Kluwer.

Sumby, W. H., & Pollack, I. (1954). Visual contribution to speech intelligibility in noise. *Journal of the Acoustical Society of America, 26*, 212–215.

Summerfield, Q. (1979). Use of visual information for phonetic perception. *Phonetica, 36*, 314–331.

Summerfield, Q. (1987). Some preliminaries to a comprehensive account of audio-visual speech perception. In B. Dodd & R. Campbell (Eds.), *Hearing by eye: The psychology of lip-reading* (pp. 3–51). Hillsdale, NJ: Lawrence Erlbaum Associates.

Vinter, A. (1986). The role of movement in eliciting early imitations. *Child Development, 57*, 66–71.

Walker, A. S. (1982). Intermodal perception of expressive behaviors by human infants. *Journal of Experimental Child Psychology, 33*, 514–535.

Walker-Andrews, A. S. (1986). Intermodal perception of expressive behaviors: Relationship of eye and voice? *Developmental Psychology, 22*, 373–377.

Walker-Andrews, A. S. (1988). Infants' perception of the affordances of expressive behaviors. In C. K. Rovee-Collier (Ed.), *Advances in infancy research* (Vol. 5, pp. 173–221). Norwood, NJ: Ablex.

Walton, G. E., & Bower, T. G. R. (1993). Amodal representation of speech in infants. *Infant Behavior and Development, 16*, 233–243.

Warren, D. H., Welch, R. B., & McCarthy, T. J. (1981). The role of visual-auditory "compellingness" in the ventriloquism effect: Implications for transitivity among the spatial senses. *Perception & Psychophysics, 30*, 557–564.

Welch, R. B., & Warren, D. H. (1980). Immediate perceptual response to intersensory discrepancy. *Psychological Bulletin, 88*, 638–667.

CHAPTER FIFTEEN

Bimodal Speech Perception Across the Life Span

Dominic W. Massaro
University of California, Santa Cruz

The theme of this book involves the development of intersensory perception and how it occurs across different species. The present chapter is concerned with the understanding of spoken language, a skill so far unique to humans. Although spoken language is usually thought of as unimodal, there is now good evidence for its multimodal nature. Hence many speech scientists are turning from the study of auditory speech perception to spoken language understanding. Within the domain of spoken language, the scientist views understanding as being influenced by many sources of information. In addition to auditory information and situational context, two important sources in face-to-face communication are gestures and facial movements of the lips and tongue.

The multimodal nature of speech perception should come as no surprise once it is acknowledged that speech perception is simply a form of pattern recognition. More generally, pattern recognition consists of evaluating and integrating several sources of influence or sources of information. Consider the recognition of the word *performance* in the sentence "The actress was praised for her outstanding performance." The recognition of the critical word is achieved by integrating a variety of sources of information. In information-processing terms, bottom-up sources include the auditory and visual stimulus properties. The evidence for multiple auditory sources of information in speech perception comes from the discovery of many different cues or features that contribute to the discriminable contrasts found in speech. The phonetic difference between voiced and voiceless stop consonants in medial position appears to have up to 18 acoustic characteristics that could function as acoustic features. For example, the perceived distinction between /aga/ and /aka/ can be influenced by the preceding vowel duration, the silent closure interval, the voice-onset time, and the onset frequency of the fundamental.

In addition to these bottom-up sources, phonological, lexical, and sentential constraints function as top-down sources of information. Massaro and Cohen (1983) asked subjects to identify a liquid consonant in different phonological contexts (Massaro, 1989b). Each speech sound was a consonant cluster syllable beginning with one of the four consonants /p/, /t/, /s/, or /v/ followed by a liquid consonant ranging from /l/ to /r/, followed by the vowel /i/. Both the bottom-up source (the acoustic properties of the liquid consonant) and the top-down source (the initial consonant) had a strong influence on performance. The probability of an /r/ response increased systematically as the test phoneme varied from /l/ and /r/. Subjects responded /r/ more often given the context /t/ than given the context /p/. Similarly, there were fewer /r/ responses given the context /s/ than given the context /p/. An important result was that the phonological context effect was greatest when the information about the liquid was ambiguous. More generally, given multiple sensory sources of information, we can expect the least ambiguous source to have the greatest influence.

Recent research has also found that visible speech also contributes to perception. One is more likely to visually attend to a person speaking if the environment is noisy and distracting or if one has a hearing loss. There is evidence that the deaf gain phonological information primarily from a code based on how words look when they are said. Similar phonological information is obtained by both deaf and hearing children, suggesting that information can be derived from visual as well as auditory speech (O'Connor & Hermelin, 1981). Although these demonstrations of a significant contribution of visible speech involve the case in which the auditory signal is either absent or degraded by white noise, or is presented to hearing-impaired listeners, there seems to be a positive influence even when the auditory speech is perfectly intelligible. Perhaps the most convincing demonstration of the intersensory property of speech is the McGurk effect (McGurk & MacDonald, 1976). Viewing a videotape of a speaker uttering the syllable /ga/, which has been dubbed with the auditory syllable /ba/, the viewer reports "perceiving" or "hearing" the syllable /va/, /da/, or /ða/. This demonstration and subsequent sophisticated experimental studies have shown that the perception of face-to-face spoken language is truly intersensory—it is influenced by both sight and sound.

The availability of auditory and visual information in face-to-face speech perception illustrates the multiplicity of cues in a natural situation. One might expect the validity and reliability of the cues to be perfectly correlated. However, variation and noise in the environment and in the sensory systems involved could alter these two sources of information differentially because they are somewhat independent. For example, the perceiver might have a varying view of the speaker's face, and extraneous background noise might vary randomly over time. Thus, for any particular speech event, its auditory quality is not necessarily correlated with its visual quality. In experiments, one can accordingly manipulate the auditory and visual sources independently of one another. Given that the two cues are not perfectly correlated in the natural situation, the factorial manipulation of the cues will not be completely new to the perceiver. Central to our experimental inquiry are expanded factorial designs that independently manipulate multiple aspects of speech input jointly and in isolation.

Our research follows the logic of falsification and strong inference. We formulate a set of alternative hypotheses about speech perception by eye and ear. To pursue this goal, we build on the developments in information-integration theory (Anderson, 1981, 1982) and mathematical model testing (Townsend & Ashby, 1983). The alternative hypotheses—called binary oppositions—are considered to be central to a complete description of the phenomenon. A hierarchical set of binary oppositions concerning speech processing is illustrated in Fig. 15.1.

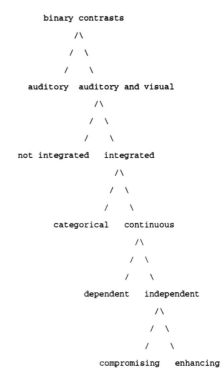

FIG. 15.1. Tree of wisdom illustrating binary contrasts central to the domain of speech perception by eye and ear.

The top contrast addresses the question of whether speech is unimodal or bimodal. As noted in the preceding paragraph, there is good evidence that perceivers can be influenced by visible speech. The next contrast asks the important question of whether the two modalities are actually combined (integrated) in speech perception. It is possible that only a given modality has an influence at any given time. Our research has shown, however, that perceivers naturally integrate the two modalities when presented with bimodal speech (Massaro, 1987, 1989a). The next question has a long history in the study of speech perception and asks whether perceivers are limited to categorical information. Although categorical perception has been the accepted dogma for several decades, there is now overwhelming evidence that perceivers of speech have continuous information (Massaro, 1992). The fourth contrast addresses the degree to which the auditory and visual sources of information are evaluated independently of one another. Our research has shown that the two sources are evaluated independently of one another, and then integrated. The last contrast concerns the nature of the integration process. The tests of mathematical models of performance has supported the idea of an enhancing integration process in which several ambiguous sources of information can create a less ambiguous event for the perceiver (what we call an enhancing integration; Massaro, 1987, 1989a).

In some cases, the contrast at one level is dependent on the answers to the contrasts at higher levels. As an example, the issue of whether or not multiple sources of information are integrated (combined) in perception requires that multiple sources, rather than just a single source, be available to the perceiver. Similarly, questions about the nature of integration are meaningful only if integration occurs. On the other hand, whether sources of data provide continuous or categorical information can be assessed regardless of whether or not they are processed independently.

As illustrated in Fig. 15.1, a falsification and strong-inference strategy of inquiry guides the present research. Results are informative only to the degree that they distinguish among alternative theories. Thus, the experimental task, data analysis, and model testing are devised specifically to reject some theoretical alternatives. Following the research strategy of strong inference (Platt, 1964), a fuzzy logical model of perception (FLMP), an auditory dominance model (ADM), and a categorical model of speech perception (CMP) are formalized and tested against the results. Our experience has convinced us of the superiority of the FLMP, and we begin with the description of this model.

FUZZY LOGICAL MODEL OF PERCEPTION

We believe that human recognition of speech is robust because there are usually multiple sources of information that the perceiver evaluates and integrates to achieve perceptual recognition. The results from a wide variety of experiments can be described within a framework of a fuzzy logical model of perception (FLMP). The assumptions central to the model are:

1. Each source of information is evaluated to give the degree to which that source specifies various alternatives.
2. The sources of information are evaluated independently of one another.
3. The sources are integrated to provide an overall degree of support for each alternative.
4. Perceptual identification follows the relative degree of support among the alternatives.

Support for these assumptions can be found in Massaro (1987, 1989a, 1989b, 1990).

According to the FLMP, well-learned patterns are recognized in accordance with a general algorithm, regardless of the modality or particular nature of the patterns. Three operations assumed by the model are illustrated in Fig. 15.2. The three stages are drawn as overlapping in Fig. 15.2 in order to illustrate that the stages can be overlapping in time. In the first operation, continuously valued features are evaluated to give some degree of support for each of the relevant alternatives. The relevant alternatives consist of the

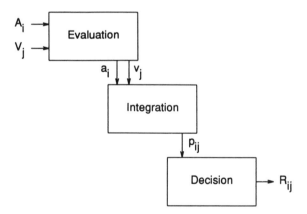

FIG. 15.2. Schematic representation of the three stages involved in perceptual recognition. The three stages are drawn as overlapping in order to illustrate that the stages can be overlapping in time. The evaluation of the auditory source of information A_i produces a truth value a_i, indicating the degree of support for alternative R. An analogous evaluation occurs for the visual source V_j. Integration of the truth values gives an overall goodness of match p_{ij}. The response R_{ij} is equal to the value p_{ij} relative to the goodness of match of all response alternatives.

fundamental speech categories in the perceiver's language. We use syllables as test alternatives because of the important role of syllables in language perception (Massaro, 1975). There is evidence that the evaluation of the auditory sources occurs independently of the evaluation of the visual source. The next operation combines or integrates these degrees of support made available by the evaluation process. The outcome of integration provides an overall goodness-of-match with each of the relevant alternatives. The decision operation uses the outputs of the integration operation to make a discrete decision about which alternative was presented. The choice of a given alternative is based on the relative goodness-of-match with the relevant alternatives.

In a typical experiment, synthetic auditory and visual speech are manipulated in an expanded factorial design. This design is shown in Fig. 15.3. Given an expanded factorial design, we must describe how the identification of each bimodal syllable occurs as a function of the processing of the unimodal syllables that compose it. This design is more powerful than simple factorial in differentiating among different models of categorization behavior (Massaro & Friedman, 1990). The onsets of the second and third formants were varied to give an auditory continuum between the syllables /ba/ and /da/. In analogous fashion, we systematically varied parameters of an animated face to give a continuum between visual /ba/ and /da/. Five levels of audible speech varying between /ba/ and /da/ were crossed with five levels of visible speech varying between the same alternatives.

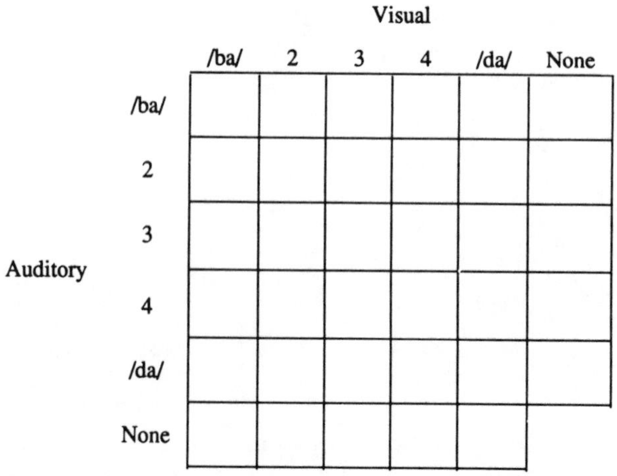

Visual

	/ba/	2	3	4	/da/	None
/ba/						
2						
3						
4						
/da/						
None						

Auditory

FIG. 15.3. Expansion of a typical factorial design to include auditory and visual conditions presented alone. The five levels along the auditory and visible continua represent auditory and visible speech syllables varying in equal physical steps between /ba/ and /da/.

Applying the FLMP to this task, both sources are assumed to provide continuous and independent evidence for each of the response alternatives. Response alternatives simply correspond to alternatives in the perceiver's language that match the auditory and visual sources of information. Defining the onsets of the second (F2) and third (F3) formants as the important auditory feature and the degree of initial opening of the lips as the important visual feature, the prototype for /da/ might be something like:

/da/: Slightly falling F2-F3 & Open lips.

The prototype for /ba/ would be defined in an analogous fashion,

/ba/: Rising F2-F3 & Closed lips.

A prototype would exist for each of the potential response alternatives.

Given a prototype's independent specifications for the auditory and visual sources, the value of one source cannot change the value of the other source. The integration of the features defining each prototype is evaluated according to the product of the feature values. If a_{Di} represents the degree to which the auditory stimulus A_i supports the alternative /da/, that is, has Slightly falling F2-F3; and v_{Dj} represents the degree to which the visual stimulus V_j supports the alternative /da/, that is, has Open lips, then the outcome of prototype matching for /da/ would be:

/da/: $a_{Di} v_{Dj}$

where the subscripts i and j index the levels of the auditory and visual modalities, respectively. Analogously, if a_{Bi} represents the degree to which the auditory stimulus A_i has Rising F2-F3 and v_{Bj} represents the degree to which the visual stimulus V_j has Closed lips, the outcome of prototype matching for /ba/ would be:

/ba/: $a_{Bi} v_{Bj}$

In general, the support for a given syllable alternative is equal to the auditory support for that alternative times the visual support for that alternative.

The decision operation computes the support for one alternative relative to the sum of the support for all possible response alternatives. This is called a relative goodness rule (RGR) by Massaro and Friedman (1990). With only a single source of information, such as the auditory one A_i, the probability of a /da/ response, $P(/da/)$, is predicted to be the auditory support for /da/ divided by the sum of the auditory support for all alternatives:

$$P(/\text{da}/ \mid A_i) = \frac{a_{Di}}{\sum_k a_{ki}} \tag{1}$$

In Equation 1, the numerator is the support for the alternative /da/ and the denominator is the sum of the merits of all k response alternatives.

Given two sources of information A_i and V_j, P(/da/) is predicted to be the auditory support for /da/ times the visual support for /da/, divided by the sum of the combined auditory/visual support for all alternatives:

$$P(/\text{da}/ \mid A_i \text{ and } V_j) = \frac{a_{Di} \times v_{Dj}}{\sum_{k} a_{ki} \times v_{kj}} \tag{2}$$

In Equation 2, the numerator is the bimodal support for the alternative /da/ and the denominator is the sum of the bimodal merits of all k response alternatives.

In general, the probability of response r, P(r), is predicted to be:

$$P(r \mid A_i \text{ and } V_j) = \frac{a_{ri} \times v_{rj}}{\sum_{k} a_{ki} \times v_{kj}} \tag{3}$$

One important assumption of the FLMP is that the auditory source supports each alternative to some degree and analogously for the visual source. Each alternative is defined by ideal values of the auditory and visual information. Each level of a source supports each alternative to a differing degree represented by feature values. Because we cannot predict the degree to which a particular auditory or visible syllable supports a response alternative, a free parameter is necessary for each unique syllable and each unique response. An auditory parameter is forced to remain invariant across variation in the different visual conditions, and analogously for a visual parameter.

In our previous research, it has been important to distinguish between information and information processing. *Information* refers to just the output of the evaluation operation in the FLMP (see Fig. 15.2). *Information processing* refers to how this information is processed. That is, information processing corresponds to the nature of the evaluation, integration, and decision operations. Our latest work primarily addresses differences in information processing across aging. We did not attempt to control for either hearing impairment or visual impairment across the two age groups for several reasons. First, it is well known that hearing impairment does not predict everyday communication difficulties (Working Group on Speech Understanding and Aging, 1988). Thus, controlling for hearing impairment would not have necessarily equated the two groups in communication difficulty. Second, we accept the fact that aging will be correlated with decreases in information because of hearing loss (presbycusis) and visual loss. Our goal is to determine whether aging is correlated with changes in information processing—the mental operations in integrating the auditory and visual speech and making a categorization decision. Our experimental task enables us to make this assessment without having an exact control over the amount of information in the two groups. The expanded factorial design presents unimodal stimuli that provide a direct index of the information available from the auditory and visual speech, respectively. The FLMP and the other models of speech perception being tested have free parameters that index the amount of available information. The experiment provides a test of the nature of the information processing, without a confounding of potential differences in information.

Although perceivers of different ages might process bimodal speech in the same manner, a given level of auditory or visual information will not necessarily have equivalent effects across different ages. In fact, given the sensory changes across aging, it is unlikely that a given speech stimulus will be identified equivalently by two different subjects or by two subjects of different ages. For example, some hearing loss occurs with aging (Corso, 1959, 1963; van Rooij, Plomp, & Orlebeke, 1989; Working Group on Speech Understanding and Aging, 1988). There is also some evidence that the hearing loss occurs earlier for men than for women (Corso, 1963). There is also some evidence for aging differences in the use of visual information. Van Rooij et al. (1989) found that elderly adults were slower than young adults in simple and choice reaction time tasks. This result may be of particular interest given the fact that the visual evoked response is positively correlated with lipreading skill (Samar & Sims, 1983; Shepard, 1982). Farrimond (1959) found changes in lipreading skill across aging, with a decline after middle age. The hypothesis of no differences in information processing only predicts that the two sources of information will be processed in the same manner across different ages. The alternative hypothesis predicts that the FLMP will fail and will not give a good description of the results for different age groups. For example, because of experience with a hearing loss, senior citizens might be overly influenced by visible speech in bimodal speech perception. If this hypothesis is correct, then the FLMP should fail. Both young adults and senior citizens should be as good in identifying visible speech when presented alone, but senior citizens should be more influenced by this information in the identification of bimodal speech.

AUDITORY DOMINANCE MODEL

A second potential explanation is that an effect of visible speech occurs only when the auditory speech is not completely intelligible (Sekiyama & Tohkura, 1991). Sekiyama and Tohkura tested four labial and six nonlabial consonants in the context /a/, under auditory and auditory–visual conditions. The auditory speech was presented either in quiet or in noise. As expected, identification of the auditory speech was very good in quiet and poor in noise. The influence of visible speech in the bimodal condition depended on the quality of the auditory speech. There was very little influence with good-quality auditory stimuli and substantial visible influence with poor-quality auditory speech. In many cases, visible speech had an influence for only those auditory stimuli that were not perfectly identified in the auditory condition. However, there were exceptions to this general trend. The auditory syllable /ma/ was perfectly identified in the auditory condition, but was identified as nonlabial about 6% of the time when it was paired with a nonlabial visible articulation. The hypothesis that auditory intelligibility determines whether or not visible speech will have an effect is difficult to test, primarily because intelligibility is not easily defined. Furthermore, the hypothesis rests, at least implicitly, on the assumption that intelligibility is an all-or-none property rather than a continuous property. However, any reasonable definition of intelligibility requires some continuous measure. Intelligibility cannot be equated with 100% correct identification, because 100% in one condition might not give 100% in another.

Even given these limitations in the measure of intelligibility, we can formulate a testable model, called the *auditory dominance model* (ADM), that can predict the influence of visible speech solely as a function of whether or not the auditory speech is identified correctly. This model is related to a single-channel model (Thompson & Massaro, 1989) in which only a single source of information is used on each trial.

On auditory alone trials, the predicted probability of a /da/ response is predicted to be the likelihood of identifying the auditory stimulus as /da/ plus those trials on which the auditory source is not identified as any given alternative, times the bias of identifying the auditory source as /da/ when the auditory source has not been identified.

$$P(/\text{da}/|A_i) = a_{Di} + N \times w_D \qquad (4)$$

In Equation 4, a_{Di} is the probability of identifying the ith level of the auditory source as /da/, N is the probability of not identifying the auditory source as any specific alternative, and w_D is the bias of identifying the auditory source as /da/ when the auditory source has not been identified.

For visual alone trials, the visual speech is identified as /da/ or some other alternative. Therefore, the predicted probability of a /da/ response on visual alone trials is equal to

$$P(/\text{da}/|V_j) = v_{Dj} \qquad (5)$$

where v_{Dj} is the probability of identifying the jth level of the visual source as response /da/.

On bimodal trials, the auditory speech is identified or it is not. When the subject identifies the auditory stimulus as /da/, she responds with that alternative. In the case that no identification is made the subject responds according to the visual information as described earlier. Therefore, the predicted probability of a /da/ response on bimodal trials is equal to

$$P(/\text{da}/|A \text{ and } V) = a_{Di} + Nv_{Dj} \tag{6}$$

Equation 4 states that either the auditory stimulus is identified or else the subject bases his or her decision on the visual information. In Equation 6, a_{Di} is the probability of identifying the ith level of the auditory source as /da/, N is the probability of not identifying the auditory source as any specific alternative, and v_{Dj} is the probability of identifying the visual source as /da/.

The predictions for the other response alternatives are exactly analogous to those given in Equation 4–6.

CATEGORICAL MODEL OF PERCEPTION

The central assumption of the categorical model of perception (CMP) is that only categorical information is available from the auditory source and from the visual source. The $i$the level of the auditory source elicits a /da/ categorization with the probability a_{Di}, and so on for all possible categorizations of the visual source. Similarly, the jth level of the visual source elicits a /da/ categorization with probability v_{Dj}, and so on for all possible categorizations of the visual source.

For unimodal trials, the probability of response /da/ is simply equal to a_{Di} for the auditory trials and v_{Dj} for the visual trials. For the bimodal trials, the identification judgment is based on the separate categorizations of the auditory and visual sources. If the two categorizations to a given speech event agree, the identification response can follow either source. When the two categorizations disagree, it is assumed that the subject will respond with the categorization to the auditory source on some proportion p of the trials, and with the categorization to the visual source on the remainder $(1-p)$ of the trials. The weight p reflects the bias to follow the auditory source rather than the visual.

Given these assumptions, the probability of a /da/ identification response, $P(/\text{da}/)$, given a particular bimodal speech event is predicted to be

$$P(/\text{da}/ \mid A_i \text{ and } V_j) = (p)(a_{Di}) + (1-p)(1-v_{Dj}) \tag{7}$$

where i and j index the levels of the auditory and visual modalities, respectively. The a_{Di} value represents the probability of a /da/ categorization given the auditory level i, and v_{Dj} is the probability of a /da/ categorization given the visual level j. The predictions for the other alternatives are exactly analogous to those given in Equation 7 (see Massaro, 1987, chap. 5).

TESTS OF THE MODELS ACROSS THE LIFE SPAN

There is now a good body of evidence supporting the FLMP over the ADM and CMP (Massaro, 1987, 1992). The bulk of this research has been carried out with young adults of college age. However, any theory of language processing must eventually consider the acquisition and maintenance of the processes involved in this skill. It is surprising how little research on speech perception across development has been carried out relative to the large number of studies of infants and young adults. The focus of this chapter is to evaluate these models across the life span. To illustrate the value of the falsification and strong inference framework in the study of developmental changes, consider a subset of an experimental study reported in Massaro (1987). An expanded factorial design was used: Preschool and college subjects identified auditory, visual, and bimodal speech. The three tasks taken in combination assessed the role of auditory and visual information in speech perception. One question addressed how bimodal speech perception results from some combination of the auditory and visual sources of information.

Three experimental conditions were tested between blocks of trials: bimodal, visual, and auditory. During each trial of the bimodal condition, one of the five auditory stimuli on the continuum from /ba/ to /da/ was paired with one of the two visual stimuli, a /ba/ or a /da/ articulation. Trials in the visual condition used the same videotape but without the speech sounds. In the auditory condition, the TV screen was covered so that only the auditory information was presented. In the bimodal condition, subjects were instructed to watch and to listen to the "man on the TV" and to tell the experimenter whether the man said /ba/ or /da/. Before the visual condition, each child watched the experimenter's mouth as she demonstrated silent articulations of the two alternatives. In this condition, children were instructed to report whether the speaker's mouth made /ba/ or /da/. The college students were told simply to lip-read. In the auditory condition, the subjects were instructed to listen to each test sound to indicate whether the man said /ba/ or /da/. Because the task required a two-alternative forced-choice judgment, a single dependent variable, the proportion of /da/ responses, provides all the information about choice performance. Figure 15.4 shows the results from this experiment. For both groups, the auditory and visual variables produced significant differences, as did the interaction between these two variables in the bimodal condition.

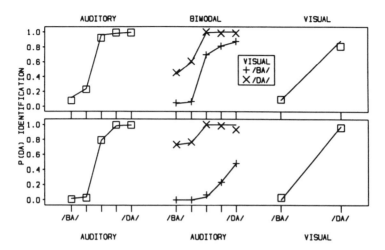

FIG. 15.4. Observed (points) and predicted (lines) proportion of /da/ identifications for auditory (left panel), bimodal (center panel), and visual (right panel) trials as a function of the auditory and visual levels of the speech event for experienced preschool children (top panel) and college students (bottom panel). The predictions are for the FLMP.

The results were tested against the FLMP and CMP. The FLMP gave a much better description of performance than did the CMP for both groups of subjects. This advantage of the FLMP held both for the results of individual subjects and for the results of the average subject. The fit of the FLMP to the average subject was about three or four times better than was the description given by the CMP. The much better description given by the FLMP is especially impressive given that this model required one fewer free parameter than did the CMP. The good fit of the FLMP suggests that preschool children integrate independent and continuous sources of information in the same manner as adults. Using the FLMP, we ask whether the information values for the auditory and visual sources change with age and whether the processes involved in the perceptual recognition of speech differ with age.

A reasonable measure of information value is the degree to which a subject discriminated the different levels of the speech dimensions. An index of discrimination can be determined by taking the difference in response probabilities given two different levels of a speech dimension. In this case, visual discrimination is given by the degree of /da/-ness of a visual /da/ minus the degree of /da/-ness of a visual /ba/. Visual discrimination for the preschoolers was .885 minus .087 or .792. The auditory discrimination is given by the degree of /da/-ness of the most /da/-like auditory syllable minus the degree of /da/-ness of the most /ba/-like auditory syllable (that is, the two endpoints along the auditory continuum). This auditory discrimination value was .992 minus .114 or .878 for the preschoolers.

Corresponding values for the college students were .962 for visual discrimination and .975 for auditory discrimination. Thus, the significantly larger discrimination values for the college students indicate that they had significantly more information about both auditory and visual speech than did the preschool children. This result is consistent with McGurk and MacDonald's (1976) original finding of a larger influence of visible speech on adults than on young children (age 3–8).

In summary, these results, and the good description by the FLMP of both groups, suggest that the developmental differences are due only to information differences. The better fit of the FLMP than the CMP for both age groups argues against a developmental change from one type of process to another in perceptual recognition of speech. At every age, performance is more appropriately described as following the operations of the FLMP, which accordingly provides a framework for assessing life-span differences in information value. The processing of the information appears to follow the operations of the FLMP for both groups.

This developmental study of speech perception by ear and eye revealed some remarkable similarities and differences. With respect to the binary oppositions described in Fig. 15.1, the outcomes of the tests did not change across development. The fundamental processes involved in pattern recognition appear to be the same for preschool children and adults. Even though the processes underlying speech perception were the same, there were significant differences in performance. A distinction between information and information processing is central to understanding these differences. There were significant differences in the informational value of audible and visible speech as a function of age. These differences are easily seen in the unimodal conditions of Fig. 15.4. The adults gave better discrimination of the /ba/ and /da/ alternatives than did the preschool children. These changes are readily explained in terms of increasing experience with development. Preschool children are still acquiring speech-perception skills. They do not lip-read as well as adults and are less able to discriminate changes along an auditory speech continuum. The differences in performance are accurately described in terms of the feature evaluation stage of the FLMP. A given source of information is less informative for preschool children than for adults. This is not surprising given that it is experience with speech that permits speech data to be treated as information. We can expect that the prototype descriptions of the distinguishing characteristics of speech will increase in resolution with experience.

One question for the present chapter is whether bimodal speech is processed in the same manner across the life span. The study of bimodal speech perception has been primarily limited to the study of young adults (Massaro & Cohen, 1990; Summerfield, 1979, 1983). Bimodal speech perception offers a valuable domain for the study of aging differences and similarities. It is important to know to what extent the results to date are dependent on the subject population being used. In addition, aging differences offer a powerful paradigm for broadening the domain for inquiry (Massaro, 1992). Our empirical findings, theories, and models tend to be limited to highly specific situations. Developmental and aging studies allow us to assess the degree to which we can generalize our conclusions.

It might be expected that a loss of hearing with aging might lead to an enhanced ability to perceive the lip and facial movements of the speaker, called *speechreading*. It has been found that visual information from the speaker's face contributes more to speech perception with decreases in the auditory signal-to-noise ratio (Sumby & Pollack, 1954). If perceivers somehow attend more to the visual information in situations with less auditory information, then the aging person with some hearing impairment might develop increased speechreading ability. However, Farrimond (1959) found a decrease of about 8% per decade for the speechreading of men after age 30–39. Similarly, Shoop and Binnie (1979) found a decline of the visual perception of speech across the adult life span. Finally, Ewertsen and Nielsen (1971) found a decline from 20 to 50 to 70 years of age in auditory, visual, and auditory–visual speech perception. It appears that there is a slight decline in speechreading ability with increases in age.

To assess these contrasting models across the life span, we tested two populations of subjects. In the first group, 13 subjects in the age range of 53–81 with a median age of 69 participated. The other population of subjects consisted of students with an age range of 17–46 and a median age of 19.

As in our previous work, the stimuli consisted of synthetic auditory and visible speech. Using an auditory speech synthesizer, we created a continuum of sounds that varied between a good /ba/ and a good /da/. The first sound was a good /ba/. The last sound was a good /da/. The middle sound was halfway between /ba/ and /da/. The second sound was somewhat more /ba/-like and the fourth sound was somewhat more /da/-like. In an exactly analogous manner using computer animation, we synthesized a face saying /ba/ and /da/ and also saying three syllables intermediate between them. Thus, a five-step continuum going from /ba/ to /da/ was created. An expanded factorial design was used, as illustrated in Fig. 15.3. There were 5 auditory and 5 visual syllables, and 25 auditory–visual syllables created by crossing the two continua.

In order to create the synthetic auditory speech, tokens of the first author's /ba/ and /da/ were analyzed using linear prediction to derive a set of parameters for driving a software formant serial resonator speech synthesizer (Klatt, 1980). By altering the parametric information specifying the first 80 msec of the consonant-vowel syllable, a set of five 400-msec syllables covering the range from /ba/ to /da/ was created. The center and lower panels of Fig. 15.5 show how some of the acoustic synthesis parameters

386   MASSARO

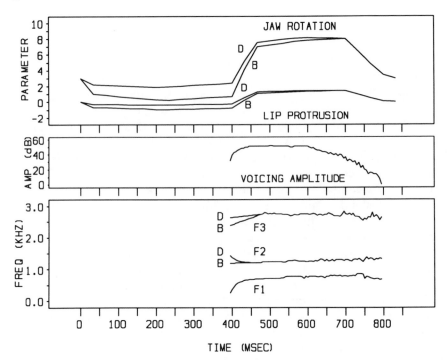

FIG. 15.5. Visual and auditory parameter values over time for visual /ba/ and /da/ stimuli and auditory /ba/ and /da/ stimuli. Bottom panel shows formants F1, F2, and F3, middle panel shows voicing amplitude, and top panel shows jaw rotation and lip protrusion. See text for details.

changed over time for the most /ba/-like and /da/-like of the 5 auditory syllables. During the first 80 msec, the first formant (F1) went from 250 to 700 Hz following a negatively accelerated path. The F2 followed a negatively accelerated path to 1199 Hz, beginning with one of five values equally spaced between 1187 and 1437 Hz from most /ba/-like to most /da/-like, respectively. The F3 followed a linear transition to 2729 Hz from one of five values equally spaced between 2387 and 2637 Hz. All other stimulus characteristics were identical for the 5 auditory syllables.

To create the synthetic visible speech, we used a parametrically controlled polygon topology to generate a fairly realistic animation facial display (Cohen & Massaro, 1990; Parke, 1974). The animation display was created by modeling the facial surface as a polyhedral object composed of about 900 small surfaces arranged in three dimensions, joined together at the edges (Parke, 1974, 1975, 1982). The left panel of Fig. 15.6 shows a framework rendering of this model. To achieve a natural appearance, the surface was smooth shaded using Gouraud's (1971) method (shown in the right panel of Fig. 15.6). The face was animated by altering the location of various

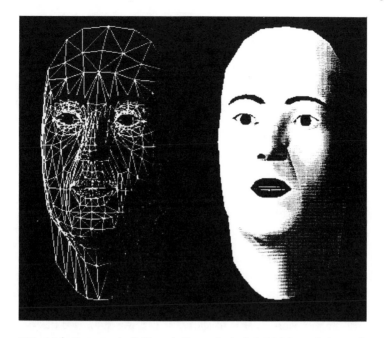

FIG. 15.6. Framework (left) and Gouraud shaded (right) renderings of polygon facial model.

points in the grid under the control of 50 parameters, 11 of which were used for speech animation. Control parameters used for several demonstration sentences were selected and refined by the investigator by studying his own articulation frame by frame and estimating the control parameter values (Parke, 1974). Recently, this software and facial topology has been translated from the original JOVIAL language to C and given new speech- and expression-control routines (Pearce, Wyvill, Wyvill, & Hill, 1986). In this system, a user can type a string of phonemes, which are then converted to control parameters, which are changed over time to produce the desired animation sequence. Each phoneme is defined in a table according to target values for segment duration, segment type (stop, vowel, liquid, etc.), and 11 control parameters. The parameters that are used are jaw rotation, mouth x scale, mouth z offset, lip corner x width, mouth corner z offset, mouth corner x offset, mouth corner y offset, lower lip "f" tuck, upper lip raise, and x and z teeth offset.

The revised software of Pearce et al. (1986) was implemented by us on a Silicon Graphics Inc. IRIS 3030 computer. We adapted the software to allow new intermediate test phonemes and wrote several output processors (pipes) for rendering the ploygonal image information in different ways. One pipe produces wireframe images, a second produces Gouraud shaded images with a diffuse illumination model, a third also includes specular illumination (white highlights), and a fourth pipe uses tesselation (recursive polygon subdivision) for improved skin texture appearance as well as randomly determined hair. The diffuse pipe used in the present experiment now takes about 1 min to render and record each frame, whereas the diffuse plus specular rendering takes 3 min. To create an animation sequence, each frame was recorded using a broadcast quality BETACAM video recorder under control of the IRIS.

Figure 15.7 gives pictures of the facial model at the time of maximum stop closure for each of the five levels between /ba/ and /da/. The top panel of Fig. 15.5 shows how the visual synthesis parameters changed over time for the first (/ba/) and last (/da/) visual levels. For clarity, only two of the visual parameters are shown—jaw rotation (larger parameter means more open), and lip protrusion (smaller number means more protrusion). Not shown in the figure, the face with the default parameter values was recorded for 2,000 msec preceding and 2,000 msec following the time shown for a total visual stimulus of 4,866 msec. A dark screen of the same total duration was presented for the auditory alone trials.

Following the synthesis a BETACAM tape was dubbed to $\frac{3}{4}$-in. U-MATIC tape for editing. Only the final 4,766 msec of each video sequence was used for each trial. A tone marker was dubbed onto the audio channel of the tape at the start of each syllable to allow the playing of the 400-msec auditory speech stimulus just following consonant release of the visual stimulus. The marker tone on the video tape was sensed by a Schmidt trigger on a PDP-11/34A computer, which presented the auditory stimuli from digitized representations on the computer's disk. Figure 15.5 shows the temporal relationship between the auditory and visual parts of the stimulus. As can be seen in the figure, the parameter transitions specifying the consonantal release occurred at about the same time for both modalities.

In this experiment, synthetic auditory and visual speech were manipulated in an expanded factorial design previously illustrated in Fig. 15.3. The onsets of the second and third formants were varied to give an auditory continuum between the syllables /ba/ and /da/. In analogous fashion, we systematically varied parameters of the facial model to give a continuum between visual /ba/ and /da/. Five levels of audible speech varying between /ba/ and /da/ were crossed with five levels of visible speech varying between the same alternatives. In addition, the audible and visible speech also were presented alone for a total of 25 + 5 + 5 = 35 independent stimulus conditions. Six random sequences were determined by sampling the 35 conditions without replacement, giving six different blocks of 35 trials. These trials were recorded on videotape for use in the experiments. Six random sequences were determined by sampling the 35 conditions without replacement.

Subjects were instructed to listen and to watch the speaker, and to identify the syllable as /ba/, /da/, /bda/, /dba/, /ða/, /va/, /ga/, or "other." These response alternatives were determined from pilot studies in which the

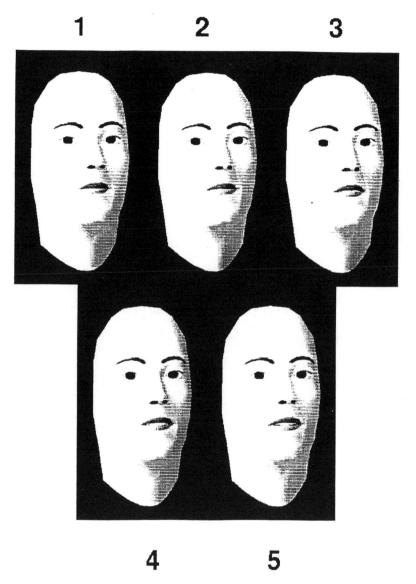

FIG. 15.7. The facial model at the time of maximum stop closure for each of the five levels of visible speech between /ba/ and /da/.

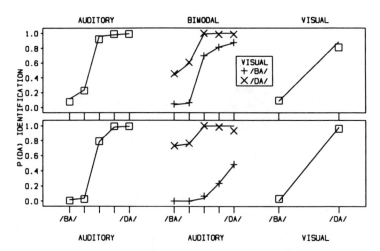

FIG. 15.8. Observed (points) and predicted (lines) proportion of /da/ identifications for auditory (left panel), bimodal (center panel), and visual (right panel) trials as a function of the auditory and visual levels of the speech event for experienced preschool children (top panel) and college students (bottom panel). The predictions are for the FLMP.

responses were not constrained. Each of the 35 possible stimuli were presented a total of 12 times during two sessions and the subject identified each stimulus during a 3-sec response interval. Prior to the experimental stimuli, subjects were given 15 practice trials to familiarize them with the task. Subjects were given a short break, approximately 5 min, after completing the tape of 210 trials. Unknown to the subjects, the tape was rewound and played again, repeating the 210 trials.

The mean observation proportion of identifications was computed for each subject for each of the unimodal and bimodal conditions. Separate analyses of variance were carried out on the auditory, visual, and bimodal conditions. The factors in the design were auditory speech, visible speech, and response. In all cases, there were significant effects (at $p < .001$). Both the auditory and the visual sources of information had a strong impact on the identification judgments. As illustrated in Fig. 15.9 and 15.10, the proportion of responses changed systematically across the visual continuum, both for the unimodal and the bimodal conditions. Similarly, the pattern of responses changed in an orderly fashion across the auditory continuum, for both the unimodal and bimodal conditions. Finally, the auditory and visual effects were not additive, as demonstrated by the significant auditory–visual interaction on response probability in the bimodal condition.

The two groups did not show any difference with respect to identification of the syllables as a function of the auditory continuum alone, the visual continuum alone, or either the auditory or visual levels in the bimodal

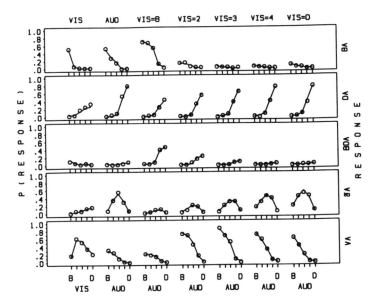

FIG. 15.9. Observed (points) and predicted (lines) proportion of /ba/, /da/, /bda/, /ðra/, and /va/ identifications for the visual alone (left panel), auditory alone (second panel) and bimodal (remaining panels) conditions as a function of the five levels of the synthetic auditory (AUD) and visual (VIS) speech varying between /ba/ (B) and /da/ (D). The observations are from 13 college students. The lines give the predictions for the FLMP.

condition. There was, however, a significant complex interaction of the visual and auditory levels by group for the bimodal stimuli. This interaction reflected the greater number of /bda/ judgments for the college students when visual /ba/ is paired with an auditory /da/ (see Fig. 15.9 and 15.10).

RELATIVE INFLUENCE OF VISIBLE
AND AUDIBLE SPEECH

One question of interest is the relative contribution of visible and audible speech in the bimodal condition. An index of the magnitude of the effect of one modality can be described by the difference in response probabilities to the two endpoint stimuli from that modality. This difference was computed for each subject for both audible and visible sources of information. As an example, an overall .90 probability of /da/ given the /da/ endpoint stimulus and an overall .2 probability of /da/ given the /ba/ endpoint stimulus would give an effect of .7 Analyses of variance were carried out on these scores. The magnitude of the visual effect did not differ across the two groups, and

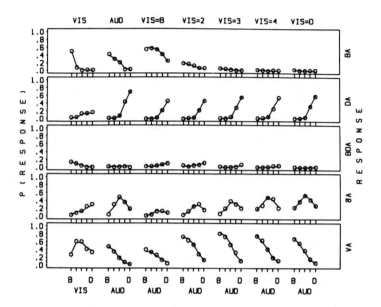

FIG. 15.10. Observed (points) and predicted (lines) proportion of /ba/, /da/, /bda/, /ða/, and /va/ identifications for the visual alone (left panel), auditory alone (second panel) and bimodal (remaining panels) conditions as a function of the five levels of the synthetic auditory (AUD) and visual (VIS) speech varying between /ba/ (B) and /da/ (D). The observations are from 13 senior citizens. The lines give the predictions for the FLMP.

the average effect was .101. The magnitude of the auditory effect was marginally significant across the two groups. The average effect was .144 for the college students and .123 for the senior citizens, consistent with the general finding of a decrease in auditory sensitivity with aging (van Rooij et al., 1989; Working Group on Speech Understanding and Aging, 1988).

TESTS OF THE MODELS

The FLMP, ADM, and CMP were fit to the individual results of each of the 26 subjects in the two groups. The quantitative predictions of the model are determined by using the program STEPIT (Chandler, 1969). A model is represented to the program in terms of a set of prediction equations and a set of unknown parameters. By iteratively adjusting the parameters of the model, the program minimizes the squared deviations between the observed and predicted points. The outcome of the program STEPIT is a set of parameter values that, when put into the model, come closest to predicting the observed results. Thus, STEPIT maximizes the accuracy of the description of a given model. Of greatest interest here is the goodness-of-fit of a model indexed by the root mean square deviation (RMSD)—the square root of the average squared deviation between the predicted and observed values.

Figures 15.9 and 15.10 show that the FLMP provided a good description of the identifications of both the unimodal and bimodal syllables for both age groups. The average RMSD was .0525 and .0468 for the college students and senior citizens, respectively. These averages were computed from the fits of the 13 individual subjects in each group.

Figures 15.11 and 15.12 give the average observed results and the average predicted results of the ADM. The RMSD was .0958 and .0732 for the young and old adults, respectively. An analysis of variance on the RMSD values showed that the FLMP gave a significantly better description of the results than did the ADM.

Figures 15.13 and 15.14 give the average observed results and the average predicted results of the CMP. As can be seen in the figures, the CMP gave a poor description of the observed results. The RMSD was .1113 for the college students and .0878 for the senior citizens. An analysis of variance on the RMSD values showed that the FLMP gave a significantly better description of the results than did the CMP.

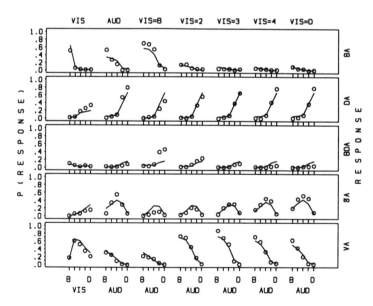

FIG. 15.11. Observed (points) and predicted (lines) proportion of /ba/, /da/, /bda/, /ða/, and /va/ identifications for the visual alone (left panel), auditory alone (second panel) and bimodal (remaining panels) conditions as a function of the five levels of the synthetic auditory (AUD) and visual (VIS) speech varying between /ba/ (B) and /da/ (D). The observations are from 13 college students. The lines give the predictions for the ADM.

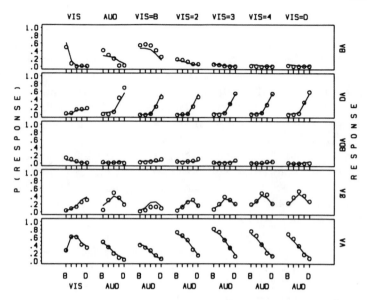

FIG. 15.12. Observed (points) and predicted (lines) proportion of /ba/, /da/, /bda/, /ða/, and /va/ identifications for the visual alone (left panel), auditory alone (second panel) and bimodal (remaining panels) conditions as a function of the five levels of the synthetic auditory (AUD) and visual (VIS) speech varying between /ba/ (B) and /da/ (D). The observations are from 13 senior citizens. The lines give the predictions for the ADM.

The CMP is mathematically identical to weighted adding or a weighted averaging model (Massaro, 1987). Thus, a test of the CMP also allows a test of whether the inputs are added or combined in a nonadditive manner. The good fit of the FLMP relative to the CMP is evidence against additive integration. The integration of the multiple sources appears to result in the least ambiguous sources having the most impact on processing. Given that the FLMP is mathematically equivalent to Bayes' theorem—an optimal algorithm for integrating multiple sources of information—the good fit of the model to the present results is evidence for optimal integration of auditory and visual information in speech perception.

NUMBER OF /bda/ JUDGMENTS

A frequent response is the consonant cluster /bda/ when the stimulus is an auditory /da/ paired with a visible /ba/. This perceptual judgment is reasonable because visible /bda/ is almost identical to visible /ba/, and audible /da/ is very similar to audible /bda/. The alternative /dba/ is not reasonable because of the huge mismatch of visible /dba/ with visible /ba/. The /bda/

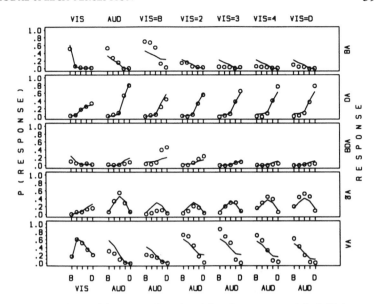

FIG. 15.13. Observed (points) and predicted (lines) proportion of /ba/, /da/, /bda/, /ða/, and /va/ identifications for the visual alone (left panel), auditory alone (second panel) and bimodal (remaining panels) conditions as a function of the five levels of the synthetic auditory (AUD) and visual (VIS) speech varying between /ba/ (B) and /da/ (D). The observations are from 13 college students. The lines give the predictions for the CMP.

cluster is also a reasonable response alternative in English because this cluster occurs in compound words and across word boundaries. In English, we can have compound words like crabdish and word boundaries separating /b/ and /d/, as in curb dog or tab down or lab dirt, and so on. Similarly, one can have rap time or nap time or crap time. It is of interest whether older adults give as many cluster responses as younger adults.

As can be seen in Fig. 15.9 and 15.10, senior citizens give fewer /bda/ judgments than college students. It turns out that a given subject either did or did not give predominantly /bda/ responses. Only 3 of the 13 old adults gave /bda/ responses, but they gave them about as frequently as the typical young adult. In like fashion, 4 of the 13 college students did not respond /bda/. Thus, in terms of whether /bda/ judgments occur, there were a few college students that resembled senior citizens and a few senior citizens that resembled college students. Most importantly, however, the FLMP gave a good description of the individual subjects independently of whether they tended to give /bda/ responses.

There are probably various tenable explanations of aging effects on the number of /bda/ judgments. Generally, there may be age differences in the

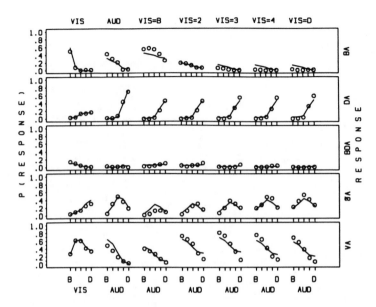

FIG. 15.14. Observed (points) and predicted (lines) proportion of /ba/, /da/, /bda/, /ða/, and /va/ identifications for the visual alone (left panel), auditory alone (second panel) and bimodal (remaining panels) conditions as a function of the five levels of the synthetic auditory (AUD) and visual (VIS) speech varying between /ba/ (B) and /da/ (D). The observations are from 13 senior citizens. The lines give the predictions for the CMP.

quality of the memory trace for the consonant cluster /bda/. On the other hand, older adults may have simply been less willing to give cluster responses in the task. There is also some literature supporting the distinction between fluid and crystallized processing. Older adults tend to be more crystallized than younger adults, and this might account for fewer adults giving /bda/ judgments.

One question of interest is whether the fundamental processes underlying performance differ as a function of the occurrence of /bda/ responses. One way to test this question is to determine if the accuracy of the FLMP description differs for the different response protocols. In all cases, the FLMP gave a good description of the results. Although we are not sure why a young adult relative to an elderly adult is more likely to respond with /bda/ given a visible /ba/ and an auditory /da/, the fundamental processes seem to work equivalently across these different response patterns.

There is a body of research supporting the idea of a mental slowing for the elderly. We take this slowing as representative of a loss in information derived from the senses and memory. In our view, mental slowing does not reflect differences in information processing—by which we mean differences in the mental processes supporting speech perception.

SUMMARY

We have been concerned with the development and maintenance of intersensory speech perception. Understanding spoken language is a form of pattern recognition involving the evaluation and integration of multiple sources of information. Although the perception of spoken language is usually thought of as unimodal, we observed good evidence for its multimodal nature. Our experimental studies using expanded factorial designs and tests of quantitative models have shown that the perception of face-to-face spoken language is truly intersensory—it is influenced by both sight and sound.

A new experiment was successful in comparing bimodal speech perception across aging. The results indicated that the processes engaged by bimodal speech are fundamentally equivalent across the life span. The only observed difference indicated that a smaller percentage of older adults gave /bda/ judgments relative to the percentage of younger adults. Although one could conceive of a variety of explanations for this finding, we give little significance to the finding itself. We distinguish between information and information processing. Information refers to just the output of the evaluation operation in the FLMP (see Fig. 15.2). Information processing refers to how this information is processed. That is, information processing corresponds to the nature of the evaluation, integration, and decision operations. The tests among the three quantitative models address the issue of differences in information processing across aging. The outcome of these tests revealed that the FLMP gave a significantly better description of performance for both young and older adults. Thus, the process assumed by the FLMP account for both groups and we can conclude that the processing of bimodal speech appears to be constant across aging.

ACKNOWLEDGMENTS

The research reported in this paper and the writing of the paper were supported, in part, by grants from the Public Health Service (PHS R01 NS 20314), the National Science Foundation (BNS 8812728), the graduate division of the University of California, Santa Cruz. The author thanks Michael M. Cohen for help in all aspects and the research and Antoinette Gesi for testing subjects.

REFERENCES

Anderson, N. H. (1981). *Foundations of information integration theory.* New York: Academic Press.
Anderson, N. H. (1982). *Methods of information integration theory.* New York: Academic Press.
Chandler, J. P. (1969). Subroutine STEPIT—Finds local minima of a smooth function of several parameters. *Behavioral Science, 14,* 81–82.

Cohen, M. M., & Massaro, D. W. (1990). Synthesis of visible speech. *Behavioral Research Methods and Instrumentation, 22,* 260–263.

Corso, J. (1959). Age and sex differences in pure-tone thresholds. *Journal of the Acoustical Society of America, 31,* 498–507.

Corso, J. (1963). Age and sex differences in pure-tone thresholds. *Archives in Otolaryngology, 77,* 385–405.

Ewertsen, H. W., & Nielsen, H. B. (1971). A comparative analysis of the audiovisual, auditive and visual perception of speech. *Acta Otolaryngologica, 72,* 201–205.

Farrimond, T. (1959). Age differences in the ability to use visual cues in auditory communication. *Language and Speech, 2,* 179–192.

Gouraud, H. (1971). Continuous shading of curved surfaces. *IEEE Transactions on Computers,* C-20(6), 623–628.

Klatt, D. H. (1980). Software for a cascade/parallel formant synthesizer. *Journal of the Acoustical Society of America, 67,* 971–995.

Massaro, D. W. (Ed.). (1975). *Understanding language: An information processing analysis of speech perception, reading, and psycholinguistics.* New York: Academic Press.

Massaro, D. W. (1987). *Speech perception by ear and eye: A paradigm for psychological inquiry.* Hillsdale, NJ: Lawrence Erlbaum Associates.

Massaro, D. W. (1989a). Multiple book review of *Speech Perception by Ear and Eye: A Paradigm for Psychological Inquiry. Behavioral and Brain Sciences, 12,* 741–794.

Massaro, D. W. (1989b). Testing between the TRACE model and the Fuzzy Logical Model of Perception. *Cognitive Psychology, 21,* 398–421.

Massaro, D. W. (1990). A fuzzy logical model of speech perception. Proceedings of the XXIV International Congress of Psychology. In D. Vickers & P. L. Smith (Eds.), *Human information processing: Measures, mechanisms, and models* (pp. 367–379). Amsterdam: North Holland.

Massaro, D. W. (1992). Broadening the domain of the fuzzy logical model of perception. In H. L. Pick, Jr., P. Van den Broek, & D. C. Knill (Eds.), *Cognition, conceptual, and methodological issues* (pp. 51–84). Washington, DC: American Psychological Association.

Massaro, D. W., & Cohen, M. M. (1983). Phonological context in speech perception. *Perception & Psychophysics, 34,* 338–348.

Massaro, D. W., & Cohen, M. M. (1990). Perception of synthesized audible and visible speech. *Psychological Science, 1,* 55–63.

Massaro, D. W., & Friedman, D. (1990). Models of integration given multiple sources of information. *Psychological Review, 97,* 225–252.

McGurk, H., & MacDonald, J. (1976). Hearing lips and seeing voices. *Nature, 264,* 746–748.

O'Connor, N., & Hermelin, B. (1981). Coding strategies of normal and handicapped children. In R. D. Walk & H. L. Pick (Eds.), *Intersensory perception and sensory integration* (pp. 315–343). New York: Plenum.

Parke, F. (1974). *A parametric model for human faces* (Tech. Rep. UTEC-CSc-75-047). Salt Lake City: University of Utah.

Parke, F. (1975). A model for human faces that allows speech synchronized animation. *Computers and Graphics Journal, 1*(1), 1–4.

Parke, F. (1982). Parameterized models for facial animation, *IEEE Computer Graphics, 2*(9), 61–68.

Pearce, A., Wyvill, B., Wyvill, G., & Hill, D. (1986). Speech and expression: A computer solution to face animation. *Graphics Interface '86.*

Platt, J. R. (1964). Strong inference. *Science, 146,* 347–353.

Samar, V. J., & Sims, D. G. (1983). Visual evoked-response correlates of speechreading performance in normal-hearing adults: A replication and factor analytic extension. *Journal of Speech and Hearing Research, 26,* 2–9.

Sekiyama, K., & Tohkura, Y. (1991). McGurk effect in non-English listeners: Few visual effects for Japanese subjects hearing Japanese syllables of high auditory intelligibility. *Journal of the Acoustical Society of America, 90,* 1797–1805.

Shepherd, D. C. (1982). Visual-neural correlate of speechreading ability in normal-hearing adults. *Journal of Speech and Hearing Research, 25,* 521–527.

Shoop, C., & Binnie, C. A. (1979). The effect of age upon the visual perception of speech. *Scandinavian Audiology, 8,* 3–8.

Sumby, W. H., & Pollack, I. (1954). Visual contribution to speech intelligibility in noise. *Journal of the Acoustical Society of America, 26,* 212–215.

Summerfield, A. Q. (1979). Use of visual information in phonetic perception. *Phonetica, 36,* 314–331.

Summerfield, A. Q. (1983). Audio-visual speech perception. In M. E. Lutman & M. P. Haggard (Eds.), *Hearing science and hearing disorders.* London: Academic.

Thompson, L. A., & Massaro, D. W. (1989). Before you see it, you see its parts: Evidence for feature encoding and integration in preschool children and adults. *Cognitive Psychology, 21,* 334–362.

Townsend, J. T., & Ashby, F. G. (1983). *Stochastic modeling of elementary psychological processes.* London: Cambridge University Press.

van Rooij, J. C. G. M., Plomp, R., & Orlebeke, J. F. (1989). Auditive and cognitive factors in speech perception by elderly listeners. I: Development of test battery. *Journal of the Acoustical Society of America, 86,* 1294–1309.

Working Group on Speech Understanding and Aging. (1988). Speech understanding and aging. *Journal of the Acoustical Society of America, 83,* 859–893.

PART FOUR

FUTURE DIRECTIONS

Insights into Mechanisms of Intersensory Development: The Value of a Comparative, Convergent-Operations Approach

David J. Lewkowicz
New York State Institute for Basic Research

Robert Lickliter
Virginia Polytechnic Institute and State University

A fundamental question that motivates most research on intersensory integration is how developing organisms come to parse the multimodal world into unitary, discrete, and functionally meaningful objects and events. As the chapters in this volume illustrate, investigators have used a variety of techniques and have relied on a variety of theoretical approaches to answer this question. The principal purpose of this concluding chapter is to briefly outline our view of the current state of affairs in research on the development of intersensory integration and to suggest one way of conceptually and methodologically grappling with the variety of issues and problems discussed in the various chapters in this volume. Our basic message is simple and straightforward: As researchers we need to shift away from demonstration studies and direct our experimental efforts to the discovery of the specific processes and mechanisms that underlie the development of intersensory perception. This shift in focus will most likely require a reassessment and reformulation of some traditional conceptual and methodological approaches to the study of early intersensory organization, a point made by several of the contributors to this volume.

A survey of the preceding chapters demonstrates the variety of methods and techniques that have been successfully applied to the study of intersensory development across different species in recent years. For example, Stein, Meredith, and Wallace have utilized the single-cell recording technique in their investigations of the neural mechanisms underlying multimodal integration in the colliculi of the cat. Lickliter and Banker have used the early exposure method to ask how perinatal sensory experience might influence the development of intersensory functioning in precocial birds, whereas Tees has used the deprivation method to ask similar questions with neonatal rats. Spear and McKinzie have applied classical conditioning techniques to determine what classes of multimodal stimulation neonatal rats can successfully associate. A number of other contributors (Bahrick & Pickens; Bloch; Bushnell; Lewkowicz; Meltzoff & Kuhl; Morrongiello; Rose; Streri & Molina; Walker-Andrews) have used measures of visual attention to determine whether human infants' visual preferences can be modified either by preceding experience in another sensory modality or by concurrent input to another modality. Finally, Massaro has utilized psychophysical techniques to explore patterns of intersensory integration across the life span.

Although a number of the investigators represented in this volume have employed similar methods and techniques in their work, in many cases they have approached the study of intersensory perception from rather different theoretical perspectives. For example, those investigators advocating the Gibsonian approach to perception propose that the environment contains a great deal of structured information that specifies intermodal invariance. Furthermore, they assume that the infant comes into the world prepared to respond to much of this structure (see Bahrick & Pickens or Walker-Andrews for excellent expositions of this theoretical perspective). On the other hand, several investigators (Lewkowicz; Lickliter & Banker; Turkewitz) argue that some intersensory functions are present early in development whereas others emerge later in development and that all intersensory functions, regardless of their time of emergence, are the product of a complex epigenetic process. This latter approach makes no a priori assumptions about infants' preparedness to respond to intermodal relationships, and its principal aim is to discover the salient characteristics of both the organism and its developmental context that make intersensory integration possible.

NEED FOR A SHIFT IN FOCUS: MECHANISMS

The various methodological and conceptual approaches represented in this volume illustrate the diversity of analytical perspectives currently applied to the study of early intersensory organization. Although these various approaches have generated a great deal of empirical evidence in recent years, a review of the chapters in this volume makes it clear that a good deal of this work is descriptive in nature. The specific processes and mechanisms that contribute to the emergence of intersensory integration in early development still remain largely unknown and unexplored for most species, including humans.

Although there are a number of pragmatic reasons for this state of affairs, we believe that the time has come to advance beyond descriptive studies and shift our focus toward experimental examinations of the various sensory and nonsensory factors that allow humans and other animals to exhibit early intersensory functioning. This shift in focus will require a reconsideration and perhaps even revamping of several of the traditional methodological and conceptual approaches usually employed in the study of early perceptual organization. We believe that such a change in focus will require an approach that is explicitly interdisciplinary in nature and that places a strong emphasis on comparative developmental studies. In other words, an empirical concern with mechanisms underlying intersensory integration will require information about the development of intersensory functions from a variety of analytical levels and from a variety of animal species. For purposes of convenience, we term this type of approach the *convergent operations* approach. It explicitly acknowledges that a developmental analysis of early perceptual organization must include both a descriptive or normative assessment stage and an experimental manipulation stage to uncover the conditions, experiences, and events necessary and sufficient for normal development to occur.

One way in which the experimental analysis of early intersensory organization will move forward and provide fresh insights into underlying mechanisms will be through the identification of appropriate animal models. The use of different animal models, at different phyletic levels, will provide the needed comparative perspective that will inform us about the similarities and differences in the mechanisms that have developed during evolution in order to solve the problem of intersensory integration. Such a comparative approach has largely been neglected in much of contemporary developmental psychology. Given that the development of a specific behavioral function is the product of an interaction between multiple, hierarchically organized, levels (Edelman, 1992; Gottlieb, 1991), we believe that the incorporation of a comparative approach is critical to discovering the various regulatory factors underlying the emergence of intersensory function. For example, the sensory deprivation method and the early exposure method employed in studies of animal infants have yielded important information regarding the experiential conditions necessary for the normative development of intersensory organization in both altricial and precocial neonates (Banker & Lickliter, 1993; Gottlieb, Tomlinson, & Radell, 1989; Kenny & Turkewitz, 1986; Lickliter & Banker, chap 4., this volume; Radell & Gottlieb, 1992; Tees, chap 6., this volume; Tees & Symons, 1987).

Of course, in nearly all cases, the sensory deprivation method and the early exposure method only can be successfully utilized with infrahuman species. What is sorely needed to make significant progress in our understanding of the processes and mechanisms underlying the development of human intersensory organization are comparable methods and techniques that can be employed appropriately with human subjects. Given that systematic manipulations of early experience are typically precluded in humans (except in some cases of prematurity or developmental anomalies), we need to identify and delineate other experimental means for asking critical developmental questions regarding the influence of early experience on subsequent perceptual capacity.

TYPES OF INFLUENCES AND THEIR RELATIONSHIPS

In our view, significant progress in our understanding of the effects of early experience on the development of intersensory organization will depend on a greater understanding of three sets of nested influences:

1. The nature and structure of the infant's developmental context.
2. The nature and structure of the neural and sensory substrates governing sensitivity and responsiveness to that context.
3. The nature of the dynamic interaction over the course of development between features of the developmental context and features of the neural and sensory substrates.

Although all three influences are obviously critical, we believe that an empirical concern with the dynamic relationship between the structure of the organism and the structure of its developmental context remains the unexplored frontier in studies of intersensory development (for similar views see Gottlieb, 1991; Turkewitz & Mellon, 1989).

Developmental Context

As far as the nature and structure of the infant's developmental context are concerned, a continuing focus on the effects of a limited collection of stimulus properties and attributes will not suffice. In our view, fresh insights into the mechanisms underlying early intersensory integration will come from an examination of responsiveness to a broad spectrum of sensory stimulation, ranging from the familiar and naturalistic to the unfamiliar and synthetic. By varying the nature and structure of stimulation across a wide spectrum or continuum, it will be possible to make systematic progress in determining what role specific stimulation histories play in the development of various forms of intersensory functioning in human infants.

At first glance, our suggestion that we broaden the range of stimulation presented in our studies and that this range span a continuum from the naturalistic to the synthetic appears to differ from some investigators' concern with ecological validity. For example, Johnston (1985) and Gottlieb (1985) argued that the most effective approach in studies of perceptual development is an ecological one. In their view, an analysis of a given perceptual function should start with a study of the organism's response to those aspects of its environment that are normally present and relevant to its everyday functioning. The results of such a study then can be used to constrain the design of further experiments to probe the specific mechanisms underlying infant responsiveness. This is typically done by systematically manipulating the dimensions of stimulation identified in the initial naturalistic studies.

Although we agree that a focus on the naturalistic aspects of the infant's developmental context is necessary and important, we believe that such a naturalistic approach is not in itself sufficient. As noted earlier, by broadening our investigations to the examination of the young organism's responsiveness to unfamiliar or atypical stimuli, we are in a position to assess the role of early experience in the development of intersensory integration. In addition, by testing infants' responsiveness to unfamiliar or atypical stimuli, we are in a position to determine the limits of integrative capacity and thus of the necessary and sufficient conditions for integration to occur. Broadening the range of stimulation that we employ in our investigations is particularly valuable in studies of human infants, where systematic manipulations of sensory experience are usually not possible. Given that fact, presentation of carefully chosen stimuli, even if they are synthetic, can illuminate the mechanisms underlying a particular function. For example, one can systematically manipulate the degree to which a set of auditory and visual stimuli resemble the infant's naturalistic circumstances at a particular stage of development and ask how the response to some specific relationship between such stimuli is affected by the "familiarity" level of the stimuli. This type of manipulation is tantamount to asking how developmental experience affects responsiveness.

The value of testing responsiveness to a broad range of stimulation in humans is illustrated by comparing and contrasting the work of Lewkowicz (in press) and Bahrick (1987, 1988). These two investigators have reported what appear to be contradictory findings on intersensory matching. Bahrick (1988) familiarized infants with two different auditory/visual events during two separate blocks of trials. During one block of trials the infants viewed a large marble ball moving inside a transparent tube and heard it make an impact sound when it hit one end of the tube. During the other block of trials, the infants viewed a set of small marble balls moving inside the tube and heard them making impact sounds when they hit one end of the tube. As soon as this familiarization phase was completed, the infants were given an intersensory paired-preference test in which they viewed the two types of visual events side-by-side and listened alternately to the sound produced by the single marble and the sound produced by the collection of small marbles. Thus, the two auditory/visual events were highly distinctive in terms of their visual characteristics; they differed in terms of the size of the individual elements making up each event, the overall number of elements comprising each event, and the color of the individual elements comprising each event. Also, the events were highly distinctive in terms of their auditory characteristics; one event was a single, discrete impact sound and the other was a more prolonged ensemble of sounds produced by the many small marbles coming into contact with the end of the tube. Finally, the two events differed in their temporal characteristics. The results obtained by Bahrick indicated that the infants directed a significantly greater proportion of their attention toward the visual event that corresponded to the appropriate sound.

Lewkowicz (in press) conducted a series of studies whose purpose was to find out whether an initial familiarization procedure might help infants overcome an apparent inability to make rate-based intersensory matches found by Lewkowicz in a set of earlier studies (Lewkowicz, 1985, 1992). To this end, 4-, 6-, and 8-month-old infants first were familiarized with a single auditory/visual event until they reached a predetermined criterion of familiarity. The familiarization stimulus was the same auditory/visual compound stimulus presented in the earlier studies yielding negative evidence of rate-based intersensory matching (Lewkowicz, 1992); the visual object, which was a small, round disk, moved up and down on the screen and a sound occurred each time it bounced. Following familiarization, the infants were given the same intersensory paired- preference test that they received in the prior (Lewkowicz, 1992) study— namely, infants saw a slowly moving stimulus on one side of a screen and a rapidly moving stimulus on the other side and heard the slowly pulsing sound on one trial and the rapidly pulsing sound on the other trial. Despite the initial opportunity to become familiar with the compound stimulus, no evidence of intersensory matching was found. Because the infants in Bahrick's studies (1988) were familiarized with both kinds of intermodal relations before they were tested for response to temporal correspondence, a second study was conducted where infants were familiarized with both intermodal relations prior to the intersensory paired-preference test. Once again, no evidence of intersensory matching was obtained.

By casting the results from these two studies into the "continuum of familiarity/experience" perspective advocated earlier in this chapter, these results can actually be viewed as providing complimentary, rather than contradictory, information about intersensory processes in early development. For example, the successful intersensory matching reported by Bahrick can be best explained by the fact that the stimulus features in that study were ones that infants of that age had already had considerable experience with even prior to the experiment (i.e., color, shape, size, density of sounds over time) and that by 3½ months of age infants are sensitive to these various stimulus features (Banks & Salapatek, 1983; Demany, 1982; Demany, McKenzie, & Vurpillot, 1977). Given the availability of various familiar, modality-specific cues in Bahrick's study, it is likely that the infants formed an association between the various modality-specific cues and that such associations permitted them to recognize the intersensory correspondence. Thus, they could associate the large blue and yellow ball with the single impact sound and the many small, yellow or blue balls with the ensemble of sounds. In other words, the relative familiarity of the stimulus features in Bahrick's study and the additional short-term experience with these already familiar features made it possible for the infants to integrate the information from the two modalities. According to this interpretation, the infants were not responding to the amodal invariance (which in this case would be the temporal equivalence of the auditory and visual information), but were matching the auditory and visual stimuli on the basis of a previously learned set of associations.

Following our continuum of familiarity/experience logic further, the results obtained by Lewkowicz show that short-term experience with stimulus features that are not already familiar, in concert with the absence of multiple modality-specific cues, makes it more difficult for infants to integrate auditory and visual information. Close examination of the visual stimuli used by Lewkowicz (in press) shows that they were identical and that the only feature that differentiated them was the rate at which they moved. Close examination of the auditory stimuli also shows that they were identical and that the only feature that differentiated them was the rate at which they were pulsed on and off. The minimal discriminative cues and the relatively unfamiliar nature of the stimuli made it much more difficult for the infants in Lewkowicz's studies to respond to the intersensory equivalence. Therefore, the only way left for the infants to recognize the equivalence was by detecting the temporal correspondence; this they did not appear to be able to do. In sum, these two sets of studies together provide clues to the mechanisms underlying intersensory integration in early infancy that each alone does not.

Neural and Sensory Substrates

With regard to the nature and structure of the neural and sensory substrates underlying early perceptual organization, a reading of the various chapters in this volume makes it clear that neural structures at many levels of the neural axis, ranging from the sub-cortical to the cortical, are involved in intersensory functioning. The work of Stein and Meredith (1993, this volume) demonstrates how basic motor responses such as spatial orientation and attention are guided and modulated by the integration of multimodal inputs to the superior colliculi. The work of Tees and his colleagues (this volume) demonstrates how the integration of multimodal inputs is mediated by cortical structures. In our view, a synthesis of the findings from these types of studies provides the necessary comparative perspective that is essential to achieving an appreciation and understanding of the similarities and differences in the underlying neural mechanisms associated with human development.

Interaction of Developmental Context and Neural Substrates

There is no doubt that a clear understanding of how the developmental context and the neural and sensory substrates each contribute to the development of intersensory organization is essential to a successful developmental analysis of intersensory integration. The ultimate and critical goal of a developmental analysis, however, is to explicate how the interaction of contextual and neural factors shapes outcome (Gottlieb, 1991). A good example of an approach that focuses on the interaction between developmental context and neural structure in the development of intersensory functioning is the work of Knudsen and colleagues.

Knudsen and Knudsen (1985) showed that the development of behaviors associated with the auditory localization map in the barn owl is dependent on both auditory and visual experience. If the owl's auditory experience is altered by inserting an ear plug into one ear, the auditory localization map is realigned in a manner consistent with the altered auditory cues. When the ear plug is removed the owl makes systematic auditory localization errors initially, but over the next few weeks comes to correct the errors. Knudsen and Knudsen (1985) showed that the correction of the errors induced by the altered auditory experience is critically dependent on the visual spatial cues that are available to the animal at the same time.

Knudsen (1985) further showed that the behavioral effects of altered sensory experience during early development are reflected in the auditory and visual spatial maps of the bimodal neurons in the optic tectum. Thus, under normal conditions the spatial tuning of the auditory and visual maps of bimodal tectal units overlap. Following removal of the earplug the maps become misaligned, but as the animal's behavioral localization errors diminish the neural maps become aligned again.

Knudsen's results demonstrate how altered sensory experience has a direct effect on the functional properties of the neural structures underlying behavior. Of course, this is only one side of the bidirectional relationship between developmental context (sensory experience) and neural structure (tectal maps). The other and less obvious side of the relationship is the fact that it is the existence of the bimodal cells in the tectum that makes it possible for the owl to respond to both auditory and visual inputs simultaneously and thus calibrate its auditory map by reference to concurrent visual information. In other words, sensory input can drive neural change and neural change can drive behavioral change; these two processes work in a reciprocal, interdependent fashion, and thus illustrate the importance of focusing on the interaction of developmental context and neural structure.

A NEW NEUROBIOLOGIAL VIEW

Recently, Gerald Edelman (1992) proposed a general theory of the development of brain function. This theory is firmly rooted in the types of epigenetic processes that we have discussed and views intersensory integration as the cornerstone of the development of behavioral functions. According to Edelman, the principal driving force behind the development of novel neural circuits is an epigenetic, selective process that operates in concert with perceptual categorization processes. The result of this process is the development of the fundamental unit of neural function, called the neuronal group, whose principal characteristic is that it responds as a unit to some specific unimodal property of the external sensory world. Novel functions emerge as the result of reentrant (back-and-forth) interactions between neuronal groups; these interactions ultimately give rise to what Edelman calls global mappings, which mediate whole integrated behavior patterns. New patterns of behavior are assembled during development through the creation of novel global mappings. What is of greatest significance to the topic of this volume is that it is the reentrant interactions between multiple neuronal groups receiving multimodal inputs that makes it possible for the brain to create novel global mappings.

Edelman is the first theorist to our knowledge to explicitly assign such a fundamental role to intersensory interactions as a basis for neurobehavioral development. In her foreword to this volume, Smith recognizes the importance of this aspect of Edelman's theory and goes so far as to suggest that intersensory interactions are not the product of development but that they are a cause that propels development forward. We, like Smith, recognize the importance of Edelman's theory and its emphasis on intersensory interactions. We also believe that the critical empirical evidence to support Edelman's theory will come from the comparative, convergent operations approach that we have been advocating, for it is only by combining the data on the interactions of neural and experiential factors during the development of different species that we will be able to fully understand the development of intersensory integration.

We fully agree with Edelman about the fundamental importance of intersensory interactions for the development of function, and, in principle, with Smith's assertion that intersensory interactions are not the product of development but that they are a cause that propels development forward.

Nonetheless, we are somewhat troubled by the possible implications of Smith's assertion. Some might argue that Smith's assertion that intersensory interactions are a cause that propels development forward implies that mature forms of intersensory interactions are present very early in development and that, as a result, the organism can organize its world into a unified and meaningful whole based on relatively mature intersensory capacities. Were that the case, the organism would be capable of responding to a variety of intersensory relations right from the beginning. As the work of many of the authors in this volume has demonstrated, however, this is not the case, and many intersensory abilities are quite rudimentary and undergo major changes during development. In addition, Edelman insists that the nervous system comes with no a priori instructions regarding its response to the world and that only through selective categorization processes does the brain become capable of responding to relations among inputs into various systems and modalities. Put differently, as far as Edelman's theoretical framework is concerned, the organism does not come into the world with ready-made response systems; they emerge through an extraordinarily complex developmental process. The developmental scientists' task is to gain insights into this very process. It is our hope that an emphasis on the kind of comparative, convergent operations approach advocated here will provide new insights into the development of intersensory integration.

REFERENCES

Bahrick, L. E. (1987). Infants' intermodal perception of two levels of temporal structure in natural events. *Infant Behavior and Development, 10*, 387–416.

Bahrick, L. E. (1988). Intermodal learning in infancy: Learning on the basis of two kinds of invariant relations in audible and visible events, *Child Development, 59*, 197–209.

Banker, H., & Lickliter, R. (1993). Effects of early and delayed visual experience on intersensory development in bobwhite quail chicks. *Developmental Psychobiology, 26*, 155–170.

Banks, M. S., & Salapatek, P. (1983). Infant visual perception. In M. M. Haith & J. J. Campos (Eds.), *Handbook of child psychology* (pp. 435–571). New York: Wiley.

Demany, L. (1982). Auditory stream segregation in infancy. *Infant Behavior and Development, 5*, 261–276.

Demany, L., McKenzie, B., & Vurpillot, E. (1977). Rhythm perception in early infancy. *Nature, 266*, 718–719.

Edelman, G. M. (1992). *Bright air, brilliant fire: On the matter of the mind.* New York: Basic Books.

Gottlieb, G. (1985). On discovering significant acoustic dimensions of auditory stimulation for infants. In G. Gottlieb & N. A. Krasnegor (Eds.), *Measurement of audition and vision in the first year of postnatal life* (pp. 3–29). Norwood, NJ: Ablex.

Gottlieb, G. (1991). Experiential canalization of behavioral development: Theory. *Developmental Psychology, 27*, 35–39.

Gottlieb, G., Tomlinson, W. T., & Radell, P. L. (1989). Developmental intersensory interference: Premature visual experience suppresses auditory learning in ducklings. *Infant Behavior and Development, 12*, 1–12.

Johnston, T. D. (1985). Environmental constraints and the natural context of behavior: Grounds for an ecological approach to the study of infant perception. In G. Gottlieb & N. A. Krasnegor (Eds.), *Measurement of audition and vision in the first year of postnatal life* (pp. 91–108). Norwood, NJ: Ablex.

Kenny, P. A., & Turkewitz, G. (1986). Effects of unusually early visual stimulation on the development of homing behavior in the rat pup. *Developmental Psychobiology, 19*, 57–66.

Knudsen, E. I. (1985). Experience alters the spatial tuning of auditory units in the optic tectum during a sensitive period in the barn owl. *Journal of Neuroscience, 5*, 3094–3109.

Knudsen, E. I., & Knudsen, P. F. (1985). Vision guides the adjustment of auditory localization in young barn owls. *Science, 230*, 545–548.

Lewkowicz, D. J. (1985). Bisensory response to temporal frequency in 4-month-old infants. *Developmental Psychology, 21*, 306–317.

Lewkowicz, D. J. (1992). Infants' response to temporally based intersensory equivalence: The effect of synchronous sounds on visual preferences for moving stimuli. *Infant Behavior and Development, 15*, 297–323.

Lewkowicz, D. J. (in press). Limitations on infants' response to rate-based auditory-visual relations. *Development Psychology*.

Radell, P., & Gottlieb, G. (1992). Developmental intersensory interference: Augmented prenatal sensory experience interferes with auditory learning in duck embryos. *Developmental Psychology, 28*, 795–803.

Stein, B. E., & Meredith, M. A. (1993). *The merging of the senses*. Cambridge, MA: MIT Press.

Tees, R. C., & Symons, L. A. (1987). Intersensory coordination and the effect of early sensory deprivation. *Developmental Psychobiology, 23*, 497–507.

Turkewitz, G., & Mellon, R. C. (1989). Dynamic organization of intersensory function. *Canadian Journal of Psychology, 43*, 286–307.

Author Index

Subject Index

A

Action, 309–328
  definition, 311
  mechanisms, 310
  motion and, 310–312
  object-directed, 311
  perception and, 312–317
    feedback, 320
    feedforward, 321
    guidance, 323
  perceptual information and, 313, 326
  sensory-motor coordination, 309, 316,
    320, 324–326
  vision perception, 324–327
Active intermodal mapping, 82, 337–340, 362
ADM, see Auditory dominance model
ADT, see Adult directed talk
Adult directed talk, 196–198
AES, see Anterior ectosylvian sulcus
Affordances, 315
Aging
  hearing loss, 378–379, 385
  information processing, 378, 396
  lipreading, 378–379
  speech perception, 383, 385–391, 395–397
AIM hypothesis, 337–340, 362
Amodal attributes, 108–110, 165–166, 198

Amodal correspondence, 110
  location attribute, 117
Amodal properties, 108–110
Amodal relations, 205–231
  auditory–visual, 208–229
  detection
    age-related, 210–215
    audiovisual, 215–221
    differentiation view, 209, 214, 226
    infants, preterm versus full-term,
      213–214
    integration view, 214, 225, 229
    intersensory perception development,
      209, 229
Amodal specification, 43–45
Animal counting, 123–124
Anterior ectosylvian sulcus, 98
  multisensory integration, 100
Arbitrary intermodal relations, 224–229
  infants, 225–226, 229
Auditory discrimination, 383
Auditory dominance model, 374, 379–381,
  392–393
Auditory sensory map, 85, 90–92
  barn owls, 120
  ferrets, 120
  guinea pigs, 120